ARMY HISTORICAL SERIES

THE U.S. ARMY IN THE OCCUPATION OF GERMANY

1944–1946

by

Earl F. Ziemke

MILITARY INSTRVCTION

CENTER OF MILITARY HISTORY

UNITED STATES ARMY

WASHINGTON, D.C., 1975

Library of Congress Catalog Card Number: 75–619027

First Printing

For sale by the Superintendent of Documents, U.S. Government Printing Office
Washington, D.C. 20402 - Price $9
Stock Number 0829–00090

iii

Foreword

Long before the dust settled on European battlefields in World War II, the U.S. Army had to face the difficult tasks of occupying and governing war-torn Germany. Its leaders and troops were called upon to deal with a series of complex challenges in political, economic, financial, social, and cultural affairs, tasks beyond the traditional combat roles of soldiers.

This volume provides an authoritative account of the role of the U.S. Army in military government and occupation of Germany from the inception of planning until the relative separation of military government and tactical troops in 1946. In the process it offers an in-depth study of the first year, the formative period of the occupation, a most eventful phase in the shaping of post-war Europe. The story ranges from Washington and theater headquarters down to military government detachments in the field, and covers the varied national and international civilian and military apparatus that evolved. Illustrating the diverse approaches of the Americans, British, and Russians, it analyzes efforts to combat hunger, disease, and crime, preserve cultural artifacts, re-establish industry and utilities, and resolve thorny problems involving currency, housing, education, newspapers, elections, and displaced persons. The account shows the pitfalls and difficulties in planning, organizing, and executing such a complex undertaking.

While this volume is part of the Army Historical Series, it continues in effect the history begun in the largely documentary volume of the U.S. Army in World War II series, *Civil Affairs: Soldiers become Governors,* as well as in the narrative volumes on the European conflict in the same series. Besides being of particular interest to that large number of men, still surviving, who participated in the events depicted here, Dr. Ziemke's volume will constitute for the Army an important source for lessons learned in planning, training, and organization for civil affairs and military government. For the scholar this book should provide a most valuable addition to the literature of the occupation, and for the general reader an enlightening and interesting account of a remarkable episode in the history of the U.S. Army and of Germany.

Washington, D.C.
30 June 1974

JAMES L. COLLINS, JR.
Brigadier General, USA
Chief of Military History

v

The Author

Earl F. Ziemke received an M.A. and Ph.D. in History from the University of Wisconsin, where he did his undergraduate work. He served in World War II with the U.S. Marine Corps in the Pacific theater. In 1951 he became a member of the staff of the Bureau of Applied Social Research, Columbia University. In 1955 he joined the staff of the Center of Military History, U.S. Army, where he became Deputy Chief of the General History Branch. Since 1967 he has been Professor of History at the University of Georgia.

Dr. Ziemke is author of *The German Northern Theater of Operations, 1940–1945*, and of *Stalingrad to Berlin: The German Defeat in the East* (Washington, 1968). He is a contributor to *Command Decisions* (New York: Harcourt, Brace and Company, 1959), to *A Concise History of World War II* (New York: Frederick A. Praeger, Inc., 1964) and to *Soviet Partisans in World War II* (Madison: University of Wisconsin Press, 1965).

Preface

The post-World War II occupation of Germany was a huge and diverse undertaking spanning almost eleven years, conducted in conjunction with three other members of the wartime alliance and involving in various degrees a number of U.S. governmental departments and agencies. The occupation was, moreover, a major event in German history and in the history of the postwar world; and for the Army it was a mission second only in scope and significance to the war itself. The subject of the present volume is that Army mission, its origin, the manner in which it was defined, and its execution to June 1946 in the period of primary Army responsibility.

The narrative begins in the 1930s, before the outbreak of war in Europe, and concludes in mid-1946, a little more than a year after the victory. Although the likelihood of U.S. military forces occupying Germany appeared infinitesmal in the late 1930s and only slightly greater in the first two years of the 1940s, the actions taken in those years were in some ways more significant than the subsequent mission-oriented plans and preparations. It was, of course, most important that the Army, albeit somewhat reluctantly, had recognized the need for civil affairs–military government doctrine and training before the requirement to administer occupied territory was placed upon it. This recognition was a true innovation in the conduct of military affairs.

To conclude the account in the middle of 1946 may appear less defensible. The occupation went on, with the Army as the executive agency for military government until 1949, and the Army continued to provide the occupation force until 1955. A good reason for stopping short of either of those two years, certainly, is space. The whole story could simply not be told in a single volume with anything like the treatment it deserves. A better reason, the author believes, is that, being a part of the Army Historical Series, the volume should concern itself with the Army experience. While military government is not the sole subject of the volume, it is one of the main subjects, and after March 1946 control of military government passed to the Office of Military Government in Berlin, which, although it was headed by an Army general, regarded itself as predominantly a civilian agency. In the field, by the end of June 1946, the military government detachments were divorced from the tactical commands, much reduced in strength, partially civilianized, and limited to observing and advising German governmental agencies. Military government as it was conceived during the war and installed in Germany in 1944 and 1945 had ended. The occupation forces had also changed. The troops that had fought the war and occupied Germany after the victory had gone home. They had been replaced by another army of occupation, and military government continued for three more years; but that is another story better told elsewhere since much of it lies outside the area of direct Army concern.

In the text, references occur in several places to Department of the Army Field Manual 27–5, *Military Government,* first published in July 1940. Over the years, FM 27–5 was revised several times and eventually superseded by other volumes, the most recent of those being FM 41–10, *Civil Affairs Operation,* published in October 1969. The purpose of those publications was and is to provide a procedural and doctrinal framework within which the Army could conduct civil affairs and military government should the need arise. FM 27–10, *The Rules of Land Warfare,* issued in October 1939 and also subsequently revised, provided guidance concerning the rights and obligations of occupation forces. Without attempting in any way to shape history to fit the field manuals, the author has assumed that the most useful purpose his work could serve would be to present a true description in one instance of the manner in which the Army actually carried out an occupation.

Although the discussion of plans has been limited to those that determined or influenced what was done, or in some instances not done, in the occupation, plans along with policy development and other preparations still figure heavily in the narrative. The chief reason why so much of the planning, more specifically the Army's involvement in it, is included is that it has not been covered elsewhere. To make the account comprehensible it has been necessary to treat matters that in combat operational histories would be left to be dealt with separately in volumes on strategy, organization, or procurement and training. The range, therefore, has had to be broad and include, in particular, plans developed over a relatively long period of time at several levels in Washington, in London, and in Germany.

At the risk of, perhaps, belaboring the obvious, it should be pointed out that geographically as well as chronologically, the volume does not purport to be a history of the whole occupation. It is concerned with those parts of Germany U.S. forces held prior to July 1945, with the considerably less than one third of the country that became the U.S. zone in July 1945, and with aspects of quadripartite control pertinent to an understanding of the Army's mission in Germany. The British share in the occupation has been dealt with in two volumes of the British official World War II history: F. S. V. Donnison, *Civil Affairs and Military Government Central Organization and Planning* (London: H. M. Stationery Office, 1966) and F. S. V. Donnison, *Civil Affairs and Military Government North-West Europe, 1944–1946* (London: H. M. Stationery Office, 1961). Official or, for that matter, any other kind of systematic histories of the occupation have been published neither in France nor in the Soviet Union. The reader interested in events in the French zone and the Soviet zone will need to consult two works, one American and one British: F. Roy Willis, *The French in Germany, 1945–1949* (Stanford: Stanford University Press, 1962) and J. P. Nettl, *The Eastern Zone and Soviet Policy in Germany, 1945–1950* (London:

Oxford University Press, 1951). Although somewhat dated, the best comparative treatment of the early occupation period in all four zones is W. Friedmann, *The Allied Military Government of Germany* (London: Stevenson and Sons Ltd., 1947).

The author is indebted to General Lucius D. Clay and Professor Oron J. Hale who read the manuscript and contributed insights from their personal knowledge of the occupation. He is likewise grateful to his former colleagues at the Center of Military History, Dr. Stetson Conn, Dr. Maurice Matloff, Col. John E. Jessup, Jr., Dr. Robert W. Coakley, Mr. Charles B. MacDonald, Mr. David Jaffé and Mrs. Christine O. Grubbs, who gave the benefit of their expertise in writing American World War II military history. The author also wishes to express his appreciation to the staff of the former National Archives World War II Records Branch in Alexandria, Virginia, who made the months spent there both pleasant and profitable.

Athens, Georgia   EARL F. ZIEMKE
30 June 1974

Contents

Charts

Maps

Illustrations

Illustrations are from Department of Defense files, with the exception of photographs on pages 199 and 229 which are reproduced by courtesy of the National Archives.

THE U. S. ARMY IN THE
OCCUPATION OF GERMANY

1944–1946

560-002 O - 75 - 2

CHAPTER I

A Difficult Birth

A School of Military Government Is Established

"The American army of occupation lacked both training and organization to guide the destinies of the nearly one million civilians whom the fortunes of war had placed under its temporary sovereignty." So stated Col. Irwin L. Hunt, Officer in Charge of Civil Affairs, Third Army, in his report on U.S. military government in Germany after World War I.[1] Military government, the administration by military officers of civil government in occupied enemy territory, is a virtually inevitable concomitant of modern warfare. The U.S. Army conducted military government in Mexico in 1847 and 1848; in the Confederate states during and after the Civil War; in the Philippines, Porto (Puerto) Rico, and Cuba after the Spanish American War; and in the German Rhineland after World War I. In each instance, neither the Army nor the government accepted it as a legitimate military function. Consequently, its imposition invariably came as a somewhat disquieting experience for both, and the means devised for accomplishing it ranged from inadequate to near disastrous. The Hunt Report, as it affectionately came to be known by the World War II generation of military government officers, for the first time in the Army's ex-

perience looked on administration of occupied territory as something more than a minor incidental of war. Colonel Hunt realized that to exercise governmental authority, even over a defeated enemy, required preparation. The Army, he urged, should not again wait until the responsibility was thrust upon it but should develop competence in civil administration among its officers during peacetime.

In the aftermath of World War I, when almost nothing appeared more remote than the possibility of the Army's again occupying foreign territory, The Hunt Report nearly—but not quite—disappeared. Because it was the only substantial document on the subject, War College committees working in civil affairs periodically brought it out of the files. But the tendency of the War College in the 1920s was to look at civil affairs and military government entirely as they related to military law, the assumption being that they were not much more than the functions of observing and enforcing law.[2] A broader interpretation began to emerge only after the 1934–1935

_____

[1] Col. Irwin L. Hunt, American Military Government of Occupied Germany, 1918–1920, 4 Mar 20, p. 88.

[2] In the interwar period and especially during World War II much thought was expended on attempts to establish a clear distinction between military government and civil affairs. Military government appeared to imply more complete control than might be assumed in all instances and was thought to ring rather too harshly on civilian ears; on the other hand, civil affairs sounded too bland for use in enemy territory. As good a definition as any would probably be that civil affairs was military government conducted on one's own or friendly territory, and military government was civil affairs conducted in enemy territory.

GENERAL GULLION

G–1 (personnel) committee at the War College prepared a draft military government manual, and a committee in the 1939–1940 class produced a manuscript on administration of occupied territory.[3]

Over the years, War College committees had also recommended several times that the Army prepare a field manual on military government. Because of the presumed close relationship between this function and military law, the job seemed to fall logically to the Judge Advocate General (JAG). In October 1939, the Judge Advocate General, Maj. Gen. Allen W. Gullion, turned down one such recommendation on the ground that his office had recently published FM 27–10, *The Rules of Land Warfare,* which contained a substantial section

on civil administration. By then, however, war had broken out in Europe, and the work of the recent War College committees had put military government in a new light. Early the next year, at the urging of G–3 (operations and training) and G–1 and with the War College materials and The Hunt Report to work from, Gullion's office began writing a manual.[4] The result, published on 30 July 1940, was FM 27–5, *Military Government,* a statement of purposes, policies, and procedures. The two field manuals, *The Rules of Land Warfare* and *Military Government,* would eventually be regarded as the Old and New Testaments of American military government; but in the summer of 1940 the country was not at war, and of everything it then lacked, the Army undoubtedly missed a military government manual least.

Another year passed, and the Axis Powers had occupied all of Europe except Sweden, Spain, Portugal, and Switzerland and were driving deep into the Soviet Union and across North Africa toward Egypt. In World War I, military government had not been needed until after the armistice, because the war had been fought mainly in France, and the French authorities had handled civil affairs for all the armies. World War II was clearly going to be different; governments had disappeared, gone into exile, or become collaborating puppets. Whenever the anti-Axis forces challenged the Germans on land, they would almost certainly have to deal with civilian populations from the outset. The British had already had some experience in late 1940 in the Italian African colonies, Eritrea, Cyrenaica, and Italian Somaliland.

In early 1941 the Intelligence Training

---

[3] History of the Civil Affairs Division, War Department Special Staff, World War II to March 1946, pt. I, p. 4. MS in CMH files.

[4] *Ibid.,* pp. 66–68.

Centre of the British War Office inaugurated politico-military courses at St. John's College, Cambridge. Their purpose was "to train officers in postwar reconstruction and other missions incident to military operations in foreign countries."[5] Two U.S. Army officers, Maj. Henry H. Cumming and Lt. Charles A. H. Thomson, attended the third course, which began in October 1941, and thereby became the first American officers to receive military government training. The politico-military courses dealt with history, geography, economics, and politics and aimed at giving the officer-students background knowledge rather than specific instruction in military government.

Later, it became customary—and even fashionable during the period of combined operations in Europe—to trace the origins of Army military government training through Cumming's and Thomson's reports—submitted on their return in January 1942—to the Cambridge courses. The British program, along with deepening U.S. involvement in the war in the late summer of 1941, did in fact probably give the first impetus to proposals for instruction in the Army; but beyond this connection the American development was collateral, not derivative. The foundation had actually been laid earlier in FM 27–5. Army field manuals, even those in as little demand as FM 27–5 was in 1940 and 1941, have stature, for unless superseded, declared obsolete, or rescinded they represent the Army's intent to do something in a specified way. FM 27–5, harking back to Colonel Hunt's plea for military government training, established in paragraphs 7 and 8 requirements for timely procurement and training of military government personnel. On 5 September 1941, General Gullion, as Judge Advocate General, had called these paragraphs to G–1's attention and recommended that the training be given.[6]

FM 27–5 had accomplished something else as well; namely, it had assigned responsibility for military government personnel, training, and planning to G–1. G–1, the personnel division of the General Staff, seemed at the time a logical choice. The work on military government in the interwar years had been done by the G–1 committees in the War College, and the primary General Staff concern with military government appeared to be the procurement of specialized personnel. On 15 September, G–1 proposed to begin training officers for assignment to task force staffs and to create a nucleus of officers for military government and reconstruction.[7] G–2 (military intelligence), G–3, and the War Plans Division objected. Any possible missions seemed to them too remote and too vague to justify diverting officers who were needed to train the expanding Army. When G–1 refused to accept the nonconcurrences and the Chief of Staff referred the proposal back for further study, G–3 conceded that the proposal was appropriate but wanted nothing more done than some planning for courses which could be given on short notice when a need arose.[8] Enthusiasm outside the JAG office and G–1 was obviously slight.

In the fall of 1941, General Gullion briefly acquired an additional assignment;

[5] G–3 Brief, 18 Sep 41, in PMG, MG Div, classified decimal files 008.

[6] Memo, OPMG for Gullion, sub: School of Military Government, 10 Jan 42, in PMG, MG Div, decimal file 314.7.

[7] Memo, G–1 for ACofS G–3, sub: Politico-Military Courses, 15 Sep 41, in PMG, MG Div, classified decimal file 008.

[8] G–3 Brief, 18 Sep 41, in PMG, MG Div, classified decimal file 008.

GENERAL WICKERSHAM

besides being the Judge Advocate General, he became Provost Marshal General (PMG), which was shortly to become his sole assignment. One of his first tasks as Provost Marshal General was to create a military police branch. The Army had never before had a military police corps. In the past, military police, like military government, had been organized in the field when needed. For the new branch, General Gullion was organizing a military police school, and on 19 November 1941, he offered to include military government instruction. G–1, strictly a staff agency, was pleased to have a place to put the training function; but G–3 objected, insisting that military government, according to FM 27–5, was so different from military police that no advantage could result from combining the two types of instruction. Maj.

Gen. Myron C. Cramer, who had succeeded Gullion as Judge Advocate General, agreed that, strictly speaking, military government did not belong in a school for military police but argued that strong objections could be found as well against assigning it to any other existing Army agency. Gullion, Cramer argued, was willing to do the job; moreover, as a law school graduate, former National Recovery Act administrator in Hawaii, and Judge Advocate General when FM 27–10 and FM 27–5 were written, he was as qualified to supervise the training as any officer in the Army.[9] On 3 December, over the G–3 objection, Brig. Gen. Wade H. Haislip, G–1, asked the Chief of Staff, General George C. Marshall, to authorize military government training in a school to be operated "for other purposes" by the Provost Marshal General.[10] General Marshall concurred on 6 January 1942.[11]

After Pearl Harbor, as the Japanese overran the Pacific islands, military government seemed less essential than ever to the Army at large. On the other hand, the internment of enemy aliens, the declaration of martial law in Hawaii, and the projected resettlement of the west coast Japanese imposed significant civil affairs responsibilities on the Army, particularly on the Provost Marshal General's Office. In January 1942, having by then decided that military government training ought to be given separately, Gullion made Jesse I. Miller his adviser on the subject and asked him to

[9] Memo, JAG for ACofS G–1, sub: Training of Personnel for Military Government, 23 Dec 41, in PMG, MG Div, decimal file 314.7.
[10] Memo, G–1 for CofS, sub: Training of Personnel in Military Government and Liaison, 3 Dec 41, in PMG, MG Div, decimal file 314.7.
[11] Memo, OPMG for Gullion, sub: School of Military Government, 10 Jan 42, in PMG, MG Div, decimal file 314.7.

determine what ends such training should serve.[12] Miller, later (November 1942) placed on active duty as a colonel, was working at the time without pay as an adviser on the internment of enemy aliens. He had served in World War I in the JAG branch and had practiced law in Washington, D.C., in the years between the wars.[13] Nobody had given thought to the content of military government courses, and all Miller had available to him were FM 27–5 and the Cumming and Thomson reports which, originally submitted to G–2, had found their way to G–1 and finally to the PMG's office. Although Miller acquired from the Cambridge courses the concept of broad area orientation, he added the idea of a program directed at developing skills in handling practical problems of civil government. The American program, therefore, although to a lesser degree than some later thought it should have, undertook to train officers in technique and practice, as well as to give them a certain area expertise.

In early February, General Gullion was authorized to set up a separate school.[14] The Cambridge courses had given military government instruction an academic aspect, and a university seemed the natural site for the Army school. Hardy C. Dillard (later a colonel), who like Miller was working at the time for the PMG as a civilian, suggested the University of Virginia in Charlottesville, Virginia, little more than two hours from Washington by car or train.[15] Gullion accepted Charlottesville as the site after the university offered to furnish all the necessary facilities at a rent of $75 per month. It had many advantages, he said, including economy.[16] Economy was to be a strong feature of the school. The largest item of expense, professional personnel, was $11,000 in 1942, and the total budget for 1943 was $98,680,[17] increased somewhat by expansion during the year.

An order of the Secretary of War, on 2 April 1942, established the school "to be known as the School of Military Government" at the University of Virginia, and Brig. Gen. Cornelius W. Wickersham was appointed its commandant and director.[18] General Wickersham, chosen for his experience as a lawyer, had been G–2, First Army. Miller had done much of the work in organizing the school, and when he accepted a civil service appointment in May, Gullion named him associate director. Col. Frank H. Hastings, former executive officer of the Army Industrial College, became assistant commandant. By April, Wickersham had visited various universities looking for faculty and had canvassed other government departments for lecturers. He had hired three civilian experts, one each for Germany (Arnold Wolfers, Yale), Italy (Henry Powell, Johns Hopkins), and Japan

---

[12] Conf, Col Dillard with Lt Col Mason, 9 Mar 44, sub: Beginnings of the School of Military Government, Charlottesville, Va., in SHAEF G–5, 22.01.
[13] Memo, PMG for CG, ASF, sub: Recommendation for Distinguished Service Medal, 1 May 44, in PMG, MG Div, classified decimal file 200.6.
[14] Memo, AG for PMG, sub: Training of Personnel for Military Government, 9 Feb 42, in PMG, MG Div, decimal file 008.

[15] Conf, Col Dillard with Lt Col Mason, 9 Mar 44, sub: Beginnings of the School of Military Government, Charlottesville, Va., in SHAEF G–5, 22.01.
[16] Memo, Atg Asst CofS for CofS, sub: Training of Personnel for Military Government and Liaison, 5 Mar 42, in PMG, MG Div, decimal file 008.
[17] Memo, AG for PMG, sub: Establishment of School of Military Government, 13 Mar 42, in PMG, MG Div, decimal file 008.
[18] ASF, OPMG, Order No. 47, 2 Apr 42, in PMG, MG Div, decimal file 008.

(Hugh Borton, Harvard). Col. Cuthbert P. Stearns headed the four-officer military part of the faculty.[19] All told, the staff numbered twelve officer and civilian instructors, twenty-five other civilians, and one enlisted man.[20]

With so modest a structure, the school could not hope to handle more than a hundred students at a time and, in fact, intended to enroll only about half that number. The courses were scheduled to run four months. Because some students were commissioned directly from civilian life, Army organization and regulations also had to be taught. The specialized instruction was given in three forms: by lectures and seminars, by the War College committee-syndicate system of working on broad problems, and by the Command and General Staff School (Leavenworth) system under which the students worked out specific assigned problems. Since many of the students were senior field-grade officers and others possessed pertinent civilian skills, the War College system in particular enabled the school to research and solve problems, as well as to instruct. The first course, with fifty officers attending, opened on 11 May 1942.

The Army Takes the Lead

The School of Military Government had been conceived before Pearl Harbor to remedy a potential deficiency by providing the Army with a nucleus of trained military government officers. However, the country was then plunged into a global war, and long before the first class assembled at Charlottesville, the Army's eventual engagement in military government was inevitable. What had been a contingency was soon to become a reality and a vital one. How large, though far from certain, was fast becoming awesomely apparent. The reports on the Cambridge courses had added another dimension by raising a question of posthostilities reconstruction, the likelihood that the Army would have to assume worldwide relief obligations as well as govern occupied enemy territory. Such a situation could mean that at some time all the forces in the field would have substantial civil affairs or military government responsibilities. One of the first studies made at Charlottesville tried to determine how many officers the Army might need. The Rhineland occupation after World War I, which only involved a population of about one million, required 213 military government officers, or .1 percent of the occupation force. On this basis, the study showed, an Army of four million men, without any allowance for the larger civilian population to be governed, would need 4,000 officers, as many as the School of Military Government could produce in ten years.[21]

Gullion's venture into military government training had only exposed the Army's problem, not solved it. Charlottesville could not train the requisite number of officers, and even if it could, enough candidates with the desired skills and talents could not be found within the Army. On the other hand, the Army had either to find and train the officers and assert its predominance, at least as long as hostilities lasted, or let some other agency do so. If another agency assumed the responsibility, theater commanders would find themselves having to

[19] Conf, Col Dillard with Lt Col Mason, 9 Mar 44, sub: Beginnings of the School of Military Government, Charlottesville, Va., in SHAEF G–5, 22.01.

[20] Memo, AG for PMG, sub: Establishment of School of Military Government, 13 Mar 43, in PMG, MG Div, decimal file 008.

[21] Memo, Jesse I. Miller for Gen Wickersham, sub: Conference with Representatives of the Board of Economic Warfare, 21 May 42, in PMG, MG Div, decimal file O14.13.

contend not only with the enemy but also with highly placed American civilians in a separate chain of command. In any case, the Army would have to maneuver carefully among several important and numerous lesser governmental agencies already entitled to a voice in the administration of occupied or liberated territory.

The most powerful of these agencies, and for the incipient Army program probably the most important, was the Board of Economic Warfare. It operated directly under the President, advising him on all economic affairs related to the war or to the postwar period, particularly in the international sphere. All departments, including the War Department, were required to comply with the board's policies and to secure the board's approval for any activities with economic effects or implications. No Army activity fell more completely under the board's aegis than military government. Consequently, Miller reported with considerable satisfaction, after three Board of Economic Warfare representatives visited Charlottesville on 20 May 1942, that they had seemed to agree that the War Department should control planning, administration, and training in military government. The board representatives had talked about finding areas of co-operation, and Miller had proposed that they might help the Army find specialists who could be trained to make up a personnel reservoir.[22]

The time when military government might be needed still appeared very remote in the early half of 1942. The Army first had the war to fight and win; this priority was the very reason that Gullion and his associates were becoming uneasy. Civilian agencies, such as the Board of Economic Warfare, with mandates to look ahead to

the end of hostilities and with plenty of time to do so, could in the meantime develop plans that would infringe on Army control. In June, Gullion declared his intention to set up a division in his office to assert Army leadership in military government and to enlist the services of other governmental agencies. Since the primary responsibility for military government rested with the Army, he stated, it should logically take the initiative in preparing policies and plans.[23]

On 28 June, Gullion made the first move toward securing clear-cut Army predominance. He requested authority to enlarge the training program and to reconcile any conflicting views between the military and civilian establishments. The latter authority, he stated, would be used to establish the Army's right to absolute control over occupied areas during the period of military necessity and to make certain that adequate preparations were made to fulfill occupation missions.[24]

Shortly thereafter, Gullion received an unexpected, and not entirely welcome, assist from another quarter. On 17 July, President Franklin D. Roosevelt forwarded to Under Secretary of War Robert P. Patterson a memorandum submitted by Arthur C. Ringland of the War Relief Control Board, another civilian agency with a built-in concern with occupational questions. Ringland had heard about the Charlottesville school and about a school that the Navy was opening in the summer at Co-

---

[22] Ibid.

[23] Memo, Gullion for CG, SOS, 23 Jun 42, in PMG, MG Div, decimal file 321.19. Partial text in Harry L. Coles and Albert K. Weinberg, Civil Affairs: Soldiers Become Governors, United States Army in World War II (Washington, D.C., 1964), p. 14.
[24] Memo, Gullion for CofS, sub: Training of Civil Affairs Officers, 13 Sep 43, in PMG, MG Div, decimal file 353.

lumbia University, but he did not believe the two together could turn out enough trained men. Private groups and other interested government agencies, he suggested, could help, and he proposed that the President appoint a committee to explore the personnel problem and make suggestions on administration.[25] The Ringland memorandum immediately accomplished what Gullion, working through several staff levels, might have needed months to do; it made civilian involvement a War Department concern. It secured, moreover, potent support for Gullion from Secretary Patterson. In his reply Patterson agreed with Ringland on most points, including the need for studies on personnel and administration, but proposed they be carried "informally and with no publicity whatsoever," in other words, without a committee and at least without calling on private groups.[26]

While Patterson did not attempt to exclude Ringland's and other government agencies, his backing made such interference easier to avert than might have been expected. On the night of 29 July, Wickersham, apparently at Patterson's behest, met informally with five U.S. senators and several Board of Economic Warfare representatives. He outlined the Army program, including the projected War Department leadership of all interested agencies, and reported that all present were "highly pleased." The next morning the President's office called Patterson's office to request the return of the Ringland memorandum. The caller implied that the President was satisfied with the War Department program.[27]

Two weeks later, on 14 August, Gullion received authority to set up a military government division in the Provost Marshal General's Office "to engage in broad planning."[28] Miller organized the division and became its director when he was restored to active duty in November. The PMG proposals had also recommended giving the division the supervision of operations in the field when they materialized; but to have done so would have abridged the theater commanders' authority to conduct all operations in their theaters, including military government, as they saw fit.[29] In fact, the term "broad planning" was meant to be restrictive, excluding planning for specific operations.

In the meantime the G–1 section, without being specifically relieved of the responsibilities assigned under FM 27–5, had all but disappeared from the scene. G–1 had considered military government a somewhat incongruous assignment from the first and found it an impossible one after the General Staff reorganization of March 1942. In the reorganization G–1 had shrunk from seventy-three officers to thirteen and from one hundred civilians to twenty. Military government had passed to the "Miscellaneous Branch," where it was lumped together with six other vaguely related activities.[30]

The Military Government Division, PMG, received its first and, in the end, most portentous mission before it officially

[25] Coles and Weinberg, *Soldiers Become Governors*, p. 14.

[26] *Ibid.*, p. 15.

[27] Memo, PMG for Chief, Administrative Services, 31 Jul 42, in PMG, MG Div, decimal file 014.13.

[28] Memo, OPMG, MG Div, for Control Div, sub: Monthly Progress Report for MG Div, 10 Oct 42, in PMG, MG Div, decimal file 310.1.

[29] Memo, Miller for Gullion, sub: Initial Organization of a Military Government Division, 25 Jul 42, in PMG, MG Div, decimal file 310.1.

[30] Edgar L. Erickson, An Introduction to Military Government and Civil Affairs in World War II, pt. I, pp. 8–10. MS in CMH files.

opened for business.[31] On the morning of
4 September, Secretary Patterson met with
Secretary of the Treasury Henry J. Morgenthau, Jr., Secretary of the Navy Frank
Knox, and several State Department and
the Board of Economic Warfare officials.
Patterson had thought the subject was to
be currency for use in North Africa. He
was surprised to learn that Morgenthau
had included the entire question of occupation planning on the agenda, that he knew
about what had been done so far, and that
he was apparently having some work done
in his own department. Patterson was also
somewhat startled when Knox reported
having talked about the subject with the
President, who had told him that he
thought military government ought to be
put under the Joint Chiefs of Staff (JCS).
After the meeting, Patterson told Gullion
that the time had come to get the War Department views set down on paper and to
head off for good freewheeling discussions
like the one Morgenthau had engineered
that morning. Gullion summoned Wickersham and Miller from Charlottesville, and
before the day's end they had drafted a
document entitled "Synopsis of the War
Department Program for Military
Government."

The Synopsis projected a national program within a framework of War Department doctrine. The first paragraph asserted
initial Army predominance. Any occupation of hostile or Axis-held territory, it
stated, could be divided into two phases:
a period of military necessity and a later
period when military necessity would no
longer exist. During the first phase the
armed forces would be obligated to set up
and maintain military government. In the

second phase a civilian authority would
probably supplant the military, but until
the second phase began, the government
of any occupied territory would be in Army
hands. The subsequent paragraphs outlined
the program. Basic policies to be administered by the Army in occupied territory
would be developed, when needed, by the
appropriate government agencies, the State
Department, the Board of Economic Warfare, the Treasury Department, and others.
The Army, meanwhile, would recruit and
train specialists to execute its mission. For
the present the Army particularly needed
the co-operation of other agencies in finding specialists. It also proposed to call on
certain agencies for special studies and for
materials and lecturers for the School of
Military Government.[32] Later, the Military
Government Division gave the gist of the
Synopsis as being "to assert and maintain
War Department leadership in military
government and at the same time invite
and employ a wide co-operation with
other departments and agencies of the
government."[33]

The Military Government Division sent
out thirty-four copies of the Synopsis, nine
to the members of the cabinet, with an accompanying letter signed by Secretary of
War Henry L. Stimson, and twenty-five to
a variety of other government agencies and
semipublic organizations ranging from the
Office of Strategic Services (OSS) and the
Office of Price Administration (OPA) to
the Rockefeller Foundation and the American Library Association.[34] The recipients

---

[31] The division went into operation on 15 September 1942.

[32] Coles and Weinberg, *Soldiers Become Governors,* pp. 18–20.
[33] Memo, OPMG, MG Div, for Control Div,
sub: Monthly Progress Report for MG Div, 10
Oct 42, in PMG, MG Div, decimal file 310.1.
[34] Memo, Acting Chief, MG Div, sub: Treasury
Department, in PMG, MG Div, decimal file
014.13.

SECRETARY STIMSON

were asked "to designate some person . . . to establish and maintain liaison . . . with Maj. Gen. Allen W. Gullion,
the Provost Marshal General, who is
directly in charge of the military government program."[35]

The Program Under Attack

In World War II the Army assumed
many new and unusual responsibilities.
Among these duties, military government
was distinguished above all others by its
capacity for generating early and durable
controversy. The term alone sounded
vaguely unconstitutional and seemed to imply a sternness that probably ought not to
be visited even on U.S. enemies. Although
the United States had conducted military

government in nearly all of its past wars, it
had always done so as a kind of reluctant
afterthought. Deliberate planning seemed
to suggest coldbloodedness, disregard for
the traditional civil-military relationship,
and disdain for the presumed natural superiority of civilians in the art of government. The Army learned this lesson early
and painfully. The opening of the school in
Charlottesville in May 1942 brought a rash
of newspaper stories describing the Army's
"school for Gauleiters." When the War Department clamped a tight prohibition on
news from Charlottesville, the volume of
press discussion subsided, but the school
became a more attractive target for speculation and sensational journalism. Born
with a bad public image, which it would
never quite overcome, the program was
soon fighting for its life against a flood of
official criticism and suspicion.

The tide began to roll on 29 October,
when the Synopsis was brought before a
full cabinet meeting. Several members, who
apparently would have liked larger roles
for themselves and their departments,
voiced suspicions; and Secretary of the Interior Harold L. Ickes expressed outright
alarm at what he saw as a germ of imperi-
alism. The President seemed to think the
school was a good idea but had doubts
about the quality of the faculty. After the
meeting, Secretary Stimson concluded that
the composite picture his fellow cabinet
members had drawn was one of incipient
grandiose War Department plans on the
one hand and mediocre Army effort on the
other.[36]

Later in the day, the President's opinion
changed. In a memo to Stimson he said
he understood that the Provost Marshal

[35] Coles and Weinberg, *Soldiers Become Governors,* p. 20.

[36] Draft memo, Secretary of War for the President [no date, not sent], in PMG, MG Div, classified decimal file 333.

General was training officers "to assume the duties of Military Governor or civilian advisors to Military Governors." He asked for a complete explanation and lists of all the personnel, military and civilian, undergoing such training. The matter, he said, was something which should have been taken up with him in the first instance. Governing civilian territory was predominantly a civilian task and required "absolutely first class men."[37]

In a few sentences the President's memo converted an interdepartmental squabble into a monumental misunderstanding and a dire threat to the principle of unity of command. Obviously he had assumed that the Army was attempting to train a species of proconsuls at Charlottesville and he was convinced that such posts should go to high-powered civilians and not to the military at all. The Army doctrine that made the theater commander the military governor at least until hostilities ended not only was apparently unknown to him but could not even be fitted into his concept of military government. The President, like the public, was thinking in terms of domestic government; he considered civil administration, no matter where it was conducted, a civilian responsibility and was totally unimpressed by the argument of military necessity.

Stimson dictated two letters explaining the War Department concept, particularly the need to have military operations and civil administration under a single authority in the war zone. Neither letter was sent. Most likely Stimson wanted to avoid, if he could, precipitating a decision that could in one stroke force the Army out of military government and create in-

calculable command problems for the future. Instead, he made an oral report at the cabinet meeting of 6 November, in which he described the objectives of the school at Charlottesville and disclaimed any Army desire to control occupied areas after the war ended. He let this report stand as the answer to the President's question.[38]

In November, attacks came from all directions. Within the War Department the questions raised a year earlier were brought forth again. Was the training worthwhile when the times and places of future occupations were unknown? Should the Army create a large pool of officers for whom it had no assignments?[39] Early in the month the criticisms from outside centered on the alleged second-rate quality of the faculty at Charlottesville and on the content of the courses.[40] Later the charges became more diversified, and Gullion surmised that several civilian departments were becoming jealous of each other, although they were still somewhat united in their attack on the Army. The new attacks concentrated mostly on Gullion's supposed personal ambition, on the political composition of the Charlottesville faculty and students, and on the caliber of the students. Gullion, a Democrat, was accused of having packed the school with anti-New Dealers and Republicans. Toward the end of the month, the President sent Ambassador William C. Bullitt and Jonathan Daniels to Charlottesville to investigate separately the quality of the students, the courses, and the plans

---

[37] Memo, President for the Secretary of War, 29 Oct 42, in PMG, MG Div, classified decimal file 333.

[38] Coles and Weinberg, *Soldiers Become Governors*, p. 24.

[39] Memo, Gullion for CofS, sub: Training of Civil Affairs Officers, 13 Sep 43, in PMG, MG Div, decimal file 353.

[40] Memo, PMG for Sec War, sub: School of Military Government, 9 Nov 42, in PMG, MG Div, classified decimal file 333.

being made there.[41] The dismal month ended with some cheer when Bullitt advised the President to "cease worrying about the school" and reported that the charges against it were without foundation.[42]

The most ominous charge leveled against the program, because it was the most valid, was the one alleging the low quality of students at Charlottesville. No one knew this better than Gullion, who in November grimly predicted that unless the student body improved materially and rapidly in quality, there was a real danger that the commanding general in each theater would have a "commissar" by his side, or a civil governor with power deriving directly from the President and authority to act independently of the commanding general.[43]

The school might be capable of raising storms in high places, but within the Army the priority of its claim on officer talent was low. In November, Gullion secured authority to commission 2,500 specialists from civilian life, but these people would have to be found first.[44] In the meantime all the students would have to be officers already in the Army, and in the long run they would still make up the majority of the trainees. The trouble was that the students had to be selected from lists submitted by the armies and service commands, and they were not likely to volunteer to relinquish their best officers. Wickersham complained that of some two hundred and fifty officers on the lists for the third course at Charlottesville only thirty-eight would

make suitable students, and these were "nothing to brag about."[45] The service commands, in Wickersham's opinion, were largely composed of culls anyway, and Charlottesville was thus getting the culls of the culls. Gullion tried to get approval for direct application by individual officers, only to have his proposal sidetracked and then buried in G–1.[46]

The Civil Affairs Division

While the War Department was engaged in defending its fledgling program against attacks from the cabinet and White House, it began to discover that, far from having fallen victim to an inordinate ambition, it had in fact sorely underestimated the potential role of civil affairs and military government in the war. On 8 November 1942 U.S. and British forces landed in Algiers and Morocco. French North Africa was assumed, in spite of some doubts, to be friendly territory in which civil administration could be left entirely to local authorities; the President assigned policy formulation and execution to the State Department and the provision of relief supplies to the Lend-Lease Administration. He saw in North Africa the beginning of an eventually worldwide program to fulfill the promises of the Atlantic Charter and the United Nations Declaration.

The War Department acceded to the delegation of control over civil matters in North Africa to the State Department, except when such matters directly affected

[41] Memo, Gullion for CofS, 27 Nov 42, in PMG, MG Div, decimal file 210.63.

[42] Coles and Weinberg, *Soldiers Become Governors*, p. 25.

[43] Memo, Guillion for CofS, 27 Nov 42, in PMG, MG Div, decimal file 210.63.

[44] Memo, ACofS G–1 to PMG, sub: Appointment of Persons Skilled in Military Government, 23 Nov 42, in PMG, MG Div, decimal file 008.

[45] Memo, Director, MG Div, for Gen Gullion, sub: Gen Wickersham's Tentative Estimate of Lists of Students for Third Course, 23 Nov 42, in PMG, MG Div, decimal file 210.63.

[46] Memo, Director, MG Div, for Gen Gullion, sub: Directive to Service Commands and Armies for Fourth Course, 13 Feb 43, in PMG, MG Div, decimal file 210.63.

or were affected by military operations.[47] The solution was logical enough except that it, like the President's decision from which it derived, ignored the main issue, namely, that for the time being at least the Americans had only one reason for being in North Africa—to fight the war. The theater commander, Lt. Gen. Dwight D. Eisenhower, protested that until North Africa including Tunisia, then still in Axis hands, was secure, everything done there directly affected the military situation. His chief civil administrator, Minister Robert D. Murphy, Eisenhower added, could not be a member of the theater staff and at the same time be independently responsible to the State Department. The Chief of Staff, General Marshall, agreed and on 28 November informed Eisenhower that Murphy would not function independently and the State Department would not assume control of civil matters until the military situation permitted. The Secretary of State, Marshall said, was in complete agreement, though he had proposed an earlier transition period in which Eisenhower would be able to divest himself of some civil authority.[48]

Although Marshall had rescued the principle of military necessity, the North African campaign, in its first weeks, had set a pattern for civil affairs and military government that would persist throughout the war. The two concepts were established as civilian functions in the thinking of the highest civilian circles of government. The Army might and in fact would throughout the war actually control both, but it would do so always as a stand-in. The role itself was a proper enough one and was essentially what had been proposed in the Synopsis; but what the Army had claimed in the Synopsis as a matter of right, it received after North Africa only on sufferance.

While civilian boards and committees proliferated in Washington, operations on the scene in North Africa limped ahead. In early December, Eisenhower called attention to the adverse political effects that would result from a failure to meet civilian needs after public assurances had been given in the United States. Thirty thousand tons of civilian supplies were needed every month, but the Lend-Lease Administration was hard put to get them together in time to meet the convoys leaving for North Africa. On arrival in the theater the supplies had to be unloaded and moved by the Army, since the North African Economic Board did not have the staff even to supervise the work; and both the military and the civilian agencies agreed that on the drive into Tunisia the Army would have to assume complete responsibility for civilian relief.

Simply stated, the United States could not simultaneously fight the war and launch into essentially postwar relief and rehabilitation programs. On the other hand, the War Department realized that it had taken too narrow a view and in January expanded its policy on planning for future operations to include preparations for food, health, housing, and security of civilian populations. It proposed in the initial period to handle all aspects of civil affairs as part of the military operation and to include civilian supplies with the military stores.[49] Colonel Jesse I. Miller had pointed out a month earlier that the long-view

---

[47] Coles and Weinberg, *Soldiers Become Governors,* p. 38.
[48] *Ibid.,* p. 43.

[49] War Dept, Statement of Policy of War Dept, sub: Provision for Care of Civilians in Territory Recovered by Invasion, 20 Jan 43, in PMG, MG Div, decimal file 014.13.

GENERAL HILLDRING

same area.[51] Mayor Fiorello La Guardia, who had been considered a possible co-ordinator of all civilian activities in North Africa, had already proposed that, in the future, civil affairs be handled entirely by the military commands. But the President had remarked that he would delay any such decision "for a *long* time."[52]

Although the President's decision would in fact be a long time coming and never be entirely definitive, the Army was engaged in North Africa in civil affairs on a scale it had not contemplated. Decisions had to be made, problems solved, and liaison maintained with the civilian agencies; the War Department discovered that it had no organization capable of doing all three. Technically, responsibility for civil affairs was still vested in G–1, which had never exercised it. The Military Government Division of the PMG office stood far down in the chain of command; in the 1942 reorganization the PMG had dropped out of the General Staff and become a subordinate office in the Services of Supply. Besides, the Military Government Division had no operational authority, only a planning mission, and only eight officers, mostly junior, and fourteen civilians. Owing to the inferior position of the Military Government Division, most civil affairs matters were being routed through the Operations Division of the General Staff and being decided in offices scattered all over the Pentagon.

policy ought to be left to the civilian departments but implementation in the period of military necessity should be in the hands of the military command.[50] Some indirect support for the War Department was also coming from civilians. In early February, James Webb, Director of the Bureau of the Budget, warned the President that U.S. global operations were approaching a breakdown on their first trial, in North Africa. The Board of Economic Warfare, he stated, was planning, hoped to direct, and might engage in development; the Lend-Lease Administration was planning, purchasing, financing, and distributing; the State Department planned and attempted to direct; and the Army planned, administered, and directed—all with respect to the

Eisenhower added a further complication when, on 9 February 1943, he asked for guidance on policy relating to Operation HUSKY, the projected invasion of Sicily. It would be the first United States occupation of enemy territory and would set the pattern for subsequent operations

---

[50] Coles and Weinberg, *Soldiers Become Governors,* p. 56.

[51] *Ibid.,* p. 60.
[52] *Ibid.,* p. 56.

in Europe. What concerned him most were the relationships between civil and military authorities, the handling of the civilian population, and the arrangements with respect to both which would have to be made with the British.[53]

By mid-February 1943 it was clear that if the War Department proposed to control civil affairs operations in the future or even if it desired no more than to manage the problems that inevitably would come its way, it would have to establish an appropriate organization at a high level. The absence of such an organization was already being acutely felt in the department. Gullion pointed out that Gov. Herbert H. Lehman, director of the State Department's Office of Foreign Relief and Rehabilitation, had remarked on the lack of any single War Department agency to deal with all phases of civil affairs. Marshall discussed the problem with the ranking officers in the Services of Supply and the Operations Division and with the Secretary of War. Before the end of the month, the conferences resulted in a verbal directive to Lt. Gen. John E. Hull, Chief of the Theater Group, Operations Division, to set up a civil affairs division in the General Staff.[54]

The Civil Affairs Division (CAD) was established on 1 March 1943, and Maj. Gen. John H. Hilldring became its director a month later. In assigning the division's mission, the War Department reasserted its claim to leadership in civil affairs and military government. The division was to report directly to the Secretary of War on "all matters except those of a military nature" and to represent the Secretary of War to outside agencies. On matters relating to military operations it would act for the Chief of Staff, and it would co-ordinate for the War Department all actions of civilian agencies in theaters of operations. For the future, War Department officials contemplated placing full responsibility for civil affairs in the staff of the theater commander "until such time as the military situation will allow other arrangements," and the Civil Affairs Division was charged with making certain that all plans to occupy enemy or enemy-controlled territory included detailed planning for civil affairs.[55] On 10 April, the Joint Chiefs of Staff confirmed the Civil Affairs Division as "the logical staff to handle civil affairs in nearly all occupied territory."[56]

Military Government Training Expands

Not the least of the problems besetting the military government program in its infancy were the need to develop a pool of officers to fill a demand that did not yet exist and the requirement to give these officers highly specialized training in duties which they might have no opportunity to perform for years. The Military Government Division, revising the Charlottesville estimates upward, concluded in September 1942 that 6,000 trained officers would be needed worldwide, another 6,000 being recruited from tactical units as areas were occupied.[57] Since Charlottesville could not then graduate more than 450 per year, the

---

[53] Hqs, ETOUSA, Incoming Msg from Algiers, Eisenhower to Marshall, 9 Feb 43, in USFET, AG, 311.22.

[54] Edgar L. Erickson, An Introduction to Military Government and Civil Affairs in World War II, pt. I, p. 11. MS in CMH files.

[55] Memo, War Dept, AG, for Col J. H. T. Haskell, sub: Organization of CAD, 1 Mar 43, in SHAEF G–5, 26.

[56] Ltr, CofS to the Commander in Chief of the Army and Navy to Sec War, 10 Apr 43, in CCS 014 (3–22–43).

[57] Draft, Final Report of the Present Director, MG Div, PMGO, Mar 45, in PMG, MG Div, decimal file 314.7.

Military Government Division proposed to establish a second school at Fort Oglethorpe, Georgia, to train another 1,200 junior officers annually.[58]

Although hit by the storm of criticism in October and November, Gullion and the Military Government Division remained convinced that their estimates were valid. Thereafter, however, they knew that the program would be under persistent, powerful, and by no means benign scrutiny. Henceforth, until, as Gullion put it, "the need had become more apparent to those concerned," seeing the program through would require determination, circumspection, and a touch of guile as well.[59] In January 1943 the need was not apparent anywhere. Gullion had eighty-five Charlottesville graduates but no assignments for them. Sixty graduates had been scheduled to go to North Africa, but the requisitions were canceled after the decision to leave civil affairs there to civilian agencies.[60]

The program, as Gullion and Wickersham knew better than their critics, was most vulnerable on the score of the quality of the officers nominated for training. The authority to commission 2,500 specialists from civilian life received in November seemed to be the most practical way to improve the quality, and in early January 1943 on Gullion's advice Stimson requested Assistant Secretary of the Interior Oscar Chapman to head a committee, composed mainly of non–War Department civilians, to select candidates for commissions in military government.[61] The committee was a useful device for forestalling criticism from the civilian agencies, but through no fault of its own, it was less than an immediate success at locating talent. The recruitment authority restricted the commissions to be granted to captains and lieutenants only and set the minimum age at thirty-five. Practically all good candidates over age thirty-five were well established in civilian jobs and carrying more prestige and authority than captains in the Army.[62]

While awaiting the flow of high quality trainees, which in the winter of 1942–1943 seemed all but unattainable from among either the military or civilians, the Military Government Division revised the school plan. Another exclusively Army-run school of the kind projected at Fort Oglethorpe might have drawn the same fire to which the Charlottesville school had been subjected. Furthermore, the uncertainties of recruitment and of the Army's future in military government combined with the certainty, as Gullion and his officers saw it, that before the war ended the Army would need trained officers by the thousands, necessitated a training system for the time being that was unobtrusive but capable of rapid expansion. The result was the Civil Affairs Training Program (CATP).

The training program, which was expected to draw its students mostly from civilian life, was divided into two phases. The first consisted of a month's military and basic military government training at the Provost Marshal General's School at Fort Custer, Michigan. In the second phase the students would receive three months' training at one of a number of universi-

---

[58] Memo, OPMG, MG Div, for Control Div, sub: Monthly Progress Report for MG Div, 10 Oct 42, in PMG, MG Div, decimal file 310.1.

[59] Memo, Gullion for CofS, sub: Training of Civil Affairs Officers, 13 Sep 43, in PMG, MG Div, decimal file 353.

[60] Memo, Gullion for Director of Training, SOS, 22 Jan 43, in PMG, MG Div, classified decimal file 353.

[61] Untitled, undated memo in PMG, MG Div, decimal file 000.7.

[62] Ltr, Oscar Chapman to Gen Gullion, 10 Feb 43, in PMG, MG Div, decimal file 210.63.

ties.[63] The universities provided the means for rapid expansion. Their faculties could provide courses in many fields on short notice, and when training demands increased, additional universities could be brought into the program.

The CATP schools offered substantially different training from the kind given at Charlottesville. Although the students eventually ranged in rank from second lieutenant to lieutenant colonel, most held junior grades and all were expected to be given assignments as specialists and technicians in the field instead of staff assignments for which Charlottesville provided training. Consequently, in the training program the emphasis was on information, not on problem-solving as at Charlottesville. The student spent half his time studying a foreign language and most of the other half in foreign area studies. The CATP graduate was expected to deal directly with the people in occupied areas, the Charlottesville graduate primarily with his own and allied staffs.[64]

At its inception, CATP's most attractive aspect was its ultimate expandability, since for the time being military government officers seemed to be both unwanted and unobtainable. Charlottesville, meanwhile, had completed its second course at the end of December 1942, having graduated a total of 130 officers in the two courses.[65] The school's enrollment capacity had been raised to 150 officers, but the prospects of securing that many qualified candidates were slight. Consequently, Wickersham recommended also commissioning at least half the Charlottesville students from civilian life.[66]

In March 1943 the recruitment problem eased somewhat when the War Department authorized commissioning some civilians in the field grades. In April, Gullion again requested permission also to accept individual applications from officers already commissioned.[67] The first 100 CATP trainees entered Fort Custer at the beginning of June. By then the military government training program was a year old but had produced fewer than three hundred trained officers.

The invasion of Sicily in July 1943 and the consequent flow of requisitions for military government officers finally broke the recruiting jam. In June, Hilldring had ordered the training program to draw on already commissioned officers to the maximum and only fill the deficit with civilians. In July, he withdrew the order and instructed the Military Government Division to accelerate its civilian recruitment to the originally authorized limit, 300 per month.[68] In July, too, Gullion received permission to select students within the Army both from unit lists and through individual applications at a rate as high as 400 officers per month.[69]

[63] The first universities to conduct courses were Yale, Harvard, Pittsburgh, Chicago, Michigan, and Stanford.

[64] (1) War Dept, Bureau of Public Relations, "Civil Affairs Training Program," 13 Feb 44, in PMG, MG Div, decimal file 000.7. (2) Memo, Gullion for CofS, sub: Training of Civil Affairs Officers, 13 Sep 43, in PMG, MG Div, decimal file 353.

[65] Memo, Wickersham for PMG, sub: Increase in Strength for the School of Military Government, 4 Jan 43, in PMG, MG Div, classified decimal file 352.01.

[66] *Ibid.*

[67] Memo, Guillion for CofS, sub: Training of Civil Affairs Officers, 13 Sep 43, in PMG, MG Div, decimal file 353.

[68] (1) Memo, PMG, MG Div, for ACofS G–1, sub: Securing AUS Officers for Military Government Training, 1 Jul 43, in PMG, MG Div, decimal file 210.63. (2) Memo, MG Div for Col Gray, 30 Jul 43, in PMG, MG Div, decimal file 310.1.

[69] Memo, Gullion for CofS, sub: Training of Civil Affairs Officers, 13 Sep 43, in PMG, MG Div, decimal file 353.

The value of the readily expandable program was proved sooner than anyone expected. In August, the impending Italian surrender brought more requisitions, and by September the planning for the invasion of France plus the possibility that the German defeat might come sooner than previously anticipated raised the prospect of vastly increased demands in the near future. At Charlottesville the classes were increased to 175 students and the course reduced to twelve weeks. The CATP took in 450 students per month, and the number of participating universities was increased to ten.[70] In the last four months of 1943, Charlottesville and the CATP schools together turned out more than two thousand graduates, thereby nearly filling the estimated wartime European requirements. Recruitment for the European training program ended in December, and the last European courses at the schools were completed in April 1944.

One problem, the accumulation of thousands of unassigned military government officers in the United States, never materialized. The demand from overseas always more than kept pace with the output from the schools, the largest shipments going to England in January and February 1944. The Military Government Division could also claim at least to have made a monumental effort to overcome the early deficiency in student quality. The 2,000 officers selected for training in the last quarter of 1943 were drawn from 25,000 nominees. Selectivity was even more stringent in the civilian recruitment with only 960 having been accepted out of 50,000 applicants up

to the time civilian procurement stopped in October 1943.[71]

The Army Is Given Control

In creating the Civil Affairs Division, the War Department had given itself the means for directing and co-ordinating U.S. military government operations. Whether it would be able to carry out this mission still remained to be seen. North Africa, while it had hardly demonstrated the superiority of civilian control, had brought powerful civilian agencies onto the scene. In March 1943, the President gave Governor Lehman's Office of Foreign Relief and Rehabilitation the mission of planning and administering U.S. relief for victims of war in liberated areas.[72] At the same time, an interdepartmental committee of civilian representatives under State Department chairmanship undertook to secure personnel for overseas service and provide for training. The President had directed the committee also to determine the relationship between the civilian administration and military government, which it would supersede as soon as civil government could be restored.[73]

The big question was how much time, if any, would be allotted to the military commander before he was required to relinquish his supremacy. On the basis of the President's directive, Governor Lehman attempted to set ninety days as the limit of

---

[70] Memo, PMG, Director, MG Div, for Director, Control Div, sub: Annual Rpt, ASF–MG Div, 13 Jul 44, in PMG, MG Div, decimal file 319.1. The universities added were Northwestern, Boston University, Wisconsin, and Western Reserve.

[71] Draft, Final Report of the Present Director, MG Div, PMGO, Mar 45, in PMG, MG Div, decimal file 314.7.

[72] Ltr, President to Gov Lehman, 19 Mar 43, in PMG, MG Div, decimal file 014.13.

[73] Memo, Acting Director, CAD, for Assistant Secretary of War, sub: Meeting of Interdepartmental Committee, 17 Mar 43, in PMG, MG Div, decimal file 014.13.

military control.[74] The dictum that there should not be two independent commanders on the same battlefield had never carried much weight in civilian circles, and in 1943 the prevailing view, both civilian and military, of civil affairs operations hardly seemed to necessitate an extended period of tight military control. Civil affairs still seemed almost entirely separable from military operations. Civilian populations, friendly or enemy, were regarded as victims of the war, not participants in it, and their administration was seen as a humanitarian, not a punitive or even precautionary, obligation. In Army doctrine as well as U.S. civilian thinking, the war ended for civilians almost as soon as they passed under American occupation. FM 27–5 prescribed a military government that was "just, humane, and as mild as practicable," the object being to obtain an enduring peace and convert former enemies into friends.[75] The directive for Operation Husky, issued in early 1943, established "benevolence," to the extent consistent with strict military requirements, as the watchword in civil affairs for the invasion of Sicily.[76] Hence, the welfare of the civilian populations appeared to be the predominant purpose of civil affairs whether administered by civilians or by the military. The one point at issue between them was—aside from the military concern over a divided command—who could do the better job.

The President remained convinced that the job was a civilian one, and in June 1943 he undertook to put policy-making and direction clearly in civilian hands. He proposed to establish an interdepartmental policy committee, chaired by an assistant secretary of state, to give central direction to all U.S. economic operations in liberated areas. For each area, a director would be appointed who would occupy a similar central position in his own area. He would be subordinate to the military commander; but he would also receive orders directly from the assistant secretary of state, would have wide latitude and authority to act on his own responsibility, and would function as the major channel of contact for civilian agencies with the U.S. military and with the allies.[77] Civil affairs seemed, after all, to have slipped out of the War Department's hands in the worst imaginable manner, namely, with the establishment of a second separate and complete command channel. Secretary Stimson protested the danger and "the real unwisdom" of moving too quickly from military to civilian authority in occupied areas; but the most the War Department managed to achieve was a redefinition that placed the area director nominally in the theater command channel.[78]

By the summer of 1943, however, political preferences, even those of the President, could not long resist the course of the war. Military governments would have to be established. They would require men and resources and the means to deploy them when and where they were needed. The Army had this ability. The civilian agencies did not, and as the summer progressed they became increasingly doubtful of their own ability to meet the needs. Moreover, in September, when the President created the Foreign Economic Administration to con-

[74] History of the CAD, War Department Special Staff, World War II to March 1946, bk. II, ch. I, p. 5. MS in CMH files.
[75] FM 27–5 (1940), par. 9.
[76] Memo, Military Government Branch, CAD, no date, in 26. CAD–War Dept.

[77] Ltr, President to Secretary of State, 3 Jun 43, in PMG, MG Div, decimal file 014.13.
[78] Ltr, Stimson to the President, 11 Jun 43, and Ltr, McCloy to Director of the Budget, 15 Jun 43, in PMG, MG Div, decimal file 014.13.

solidate the civilian effort, these agencies objected as much to a unified civilian direction as they had to War Department leadership.[79] In the interval, the Army had instituted military government in Sicily and parts of Italy.

It had not been proved that in the long run civilians would not perform better, but at the moment they could not perform at all. On 10 November the President acknowledged this state of affairs in a letter to Stimson in which he stated, "Although other agencies are preparing themselves for the work that must be done in connection with relief and rehabilitation of liberated areas, it is quite apparent that if prompt results are to be obtained the Army will have to assume the initial burden." Continuing, he assigned to the Army the planning and execution of civil relief and rehabilitation "until civilian agencies are prepared to carry out the longer range program."[80] After nearly a year of uncertainty, the Army at last had a clear, if temporary, mandate.

---

[79] History of the CAD, War Department Special Staff, World War II to March 1946, bk. II, ch. I, p. 32. MS in CMH files.

[80] Ltr, President to the Secretary of War, 10 Nov 43, in SHAEF G-5, 10.04.

CHAPTER II

Overseas Beginnings

A Mission Emerges

At Casablanca in January 1943, President Roosevelt, somewhat to the surprise of his conference partner, Prime Minister Winston S. Churchill, pronounced unconditional surrender to be the goal of American and British military operations against the Axis Powers. Although the announcement itself was apparently made, as he said later, on the spur of the moment, Roosevelt had discussed the idea of unconditional surrender with the Joint Chiefs of Staff early in January. At the time, he had conceived it as being primarily a way to reassure Soviet Marshal Joseph V. Stalin about the Western Powers' determination to carry the war against Germany through to the finish. Not thinking yet of a public announcement Roosevelt had proposed sending General Marshall to Moscow to inform Stalin that "the United Nations will continue until they reach Berlin and that their only terms are unconditional surrender."[1] Quite obviously, although he later included Italy and Japan in the formula, Germany was from the first uppermost in the President's mind. For the moment, his

chief concern was probably maintaining the East-West coalition through the fighting still ahead; but he had also, whether intentionally or not, laid the groundwork for the eventual Allied occupation of Germany. Very likely, since the failure to bring home to the Germans the full extent of their defeat was considered a major mistake of World War I, some kind of supervision would have been imposed on Germany in any case. The demand for unconditional surrender made this likelihood a certainty; moreover, given the character of Hitler's government, the demand meant that the war and, in its wake, Allied military government would be carried into the heart of Germany.

When the President and Prime Minister met at Casablanca, however, the Nazi *Wehrmacht* was deep in the Soviet Union, and neither the Russians nor the Western Allies were in a position to threaten Germany directly in the near future. The Americans and the British had agreed in principle in April 1942 on Operation ROUNDUP, a cross-Channel invasion to be executed in the spring of 1943; but ROUNDUP had given way to the North African invasion. At Casablanca the Mediterranean strategy won out again, at least as far as Sicily was concerned. The march on Germany would not begin in 1943. The staffs, however, became all the more determined that it should then start in 1944, and the conference agreed to establish in England a combined planning staff for a

---

[1] OPD, Executive File, Item 10, Min of Meeting at the White House on Thursday, January 7, 1943, at 1500, in OPD, ABC 387, sec. 1A. On the unconditional surrender announcement see also Michael Howard, *Grand Strategy*, vol. IV (London: H. M. Stationery Office, 1972), pp. 281–85, and Maurice Matloff, *Strategic Planning for Coalition Warfare, 1943–1944*, United States Army in World War II (Washington, 1959), p. 37f.

cross-Channel attack in 1944. The chief of staff would be British; the supreme commander would be selected later.[2] The decision to revive the planning for a cross-Channel attack had the growing American influence and power behind it, and before the year was out it would come to dominate the planning for the war in western Europe. Germany would become the target of military operations and, inevitably, also of military government.

Theater Planning Begins

In previous wars U.S. military government had always been a field operation carried out with minimum direction from Army headquarters. In World War II, War Department and General Staff interest assured central control; nevertheless, in this war too the field organizations emerged and to a substantial extent evolved independently of the Washington headquarters. The Army's first tactical civil affairs section in fact antedated all but the vaguest glimmerings of concern for military government in the Army Staff. On 31 December 1941, V Corps (Reinforced) under Maj. Gen. Edmund L. Daley, then stationed at Camp Beauregard, Louisiana, received orders to prepare for shipment overseas. FM 27–5 specified the creation of a civil affairs section in corps and higher staffs operating outside the United States, and on 4 February 1942, Col. Arthur B. Wade was named Civil Affairs Officer, V Corps. No similar staff section existed or had existed since the early 1920s in the Army. Working from FM 27–5 and The Hunt Report, Colonel

Wade developed a V Corps civil affairs plan which established the section's main function as being to foster and maintain harmonious relations between the military force and civilian populations in either friendly or occupied enemy territory. V Corps shipped out from Fort Dix, New Jersey, on 29 April 1942 and arrived in Belfast, Northern Ireland, on 12 May.[3] The Army thus had a civil affairs section in being in an overseas theater one day after the first class assembled at Charlottesville.

On 8 June, Headquarters, European Theater of Operations, U.S. Army (ETOUSA), assumed command of all U.S. Army forces in Europe. ETOUSA had two commanders in its first month: initially Maj. Gen. James E. Chaney, then General Dwight D. Eisenhower.

ETOUSA was slower to recognize the need for a civil affairs section than V Corps had been. V Corps had been formed in the United States to perform an indefinite mission; ETOUSA came into being in London, and if its mission was considerably less than precise, it knew that it would be engaged primarily in assembling American forces in the British Isles. This mission did not seem to establish a compelling requirement for a civil affairs section.

When a British group, the Administration of Territories (Europe) Committee— began meeting in July to deal with civil affairs subjects relating to the planning for Roundup, ETOUSA sent the theater's judge advocate general, Col. Edward C. Betts, as U.S. observer. Colonel Betts was impressed by the serious interest the British civilians and military on the AT(E) Committee showed in occupation problems, and at the end of the month he recommended appointment of a civil affairs officer for

---

[2] Matloff, *Strategic Planning*, p. 26. See also Michael Howard, *Grand Strategy*, vol. IV (London: H. M. Stationery Office, 1972), pp. 252–55, and Forrest C. Pogue, *The Supreme Command* (Washington, 1954), pp. 98–103.

[3] V Army Corps, Plan for CA Sec, SHAEF G–5, 31.01.

ETOUSA. On 5 August, Colonel Wade was transferred from V Corps to act as the temporary civil affairs officer for ETOUSA and to become, a few days later, the first and, for the moment, only member of a newly created ETOUSA civil affairs section. By then the AT(E) Committee had progressed to the appointment of a Deputy Chief Civil Affairs Officer (DCCAO) to take charge of the military planning for civil affairs, and on 10 August in a letter to Washington, Eisenhower asked for a qualified colonel whom he could appoint as a counterpart to the British DCCAO.[4]

By August, however, ROUNDUP had given way to TORCH, the North African invasion, and ETOUSA's future mission, if any, was becoming more nebulous. Colonels Betts and Wade continued to sit as observers on the AT(E) Committee, but a DCCAO was not appointed. As trained civil affairs officers from the first course at Charlottesville began to arrive in the theater, they were assigned to the British civil defense regions, where they maintained liaison between the regional commissioners and the U.S. troops. Scattered across England, the Civil Affairs Section, ETOUSA, could not begin to perform any staff functions at all until after mid-January 1943 when seven officers, four of them recent Charlottesville graduates, were finally assembled at headquarters. This group, however, after working out a study for a military government operation in an indeterminate area of northwestern Europe, found it had exhausted its resources and the staff's interest as well and subsided into collecting library materials. In early 1943 the Civil Affairs Section had no coherent organiza-

tion and no mission other than general instructions to follow the principles of FM 27–5.[5]

In the spring of 1943, after the Casablanca Conference, civil affairs at ETOUSA began to show signs of renewed life and purpose. The emergence of the Civil Affairs Division in Washington lent an inevitable prestige to civil affairs Army-wide that it had not had before; and the beginning of British War Office negotiations with the Dutch and Belgian exile governments and the Free French on the administration of liberated territory increased the possibility of ETOUSA's opening negotiations too. In the third week of March, civil affairs finally emerged, on paper at least, as a full-fledged staff section with a chief civil affairs officer and more branches in its table of organization than it had qualified officers to fill.[6] Lt. Gen. Frank M. Andrews, then commanding ETOUSA, asked for more officers and for a chief who had "substance," preferably General Wickersham, the commandant at Charlottesville, and declared that ETOUSA needed the strongest possible civil affairs section since in the long run all theaters would be secondary to the European Theater of Operations (ETO).[7] ETOUSA would get more and more officers but never the grand mission it was beginning to see in the making.

In April a new staff appeared. Lt. Gen. Frederick E. Morgan, as Chief of Staff to the Supreme Allied Commander (COSSAC), began forming a combined British-American staff to start the cross-

---

[4] (1) Historical Record, CA Sec, ETOUSA, in SHAEF G–5, 10.03. (2) M. A. Staniforth, "The Administration of Territories (Europe) Committee, op. 6," in SHAEF G–5, 60, Jacket 9.

[5] Historical Record, CA Sec, ETOUSA, in SHAEF G–5, 10.03.
[6] Ibid.
[7] Cable, USFOR, London to WAR, No. 7992, 18 Mar 43, in PMG, MG Div, classified decimal file 312.1.

Channel invasion planning provided for at Casablanca. General Morgan was assumed to be serving as the stand-in for a supreme commander yet to be appointed, who would be British. Maj. Gen. Ray W. Barker, as the first in a stream of officers from ETOUSA, moved over to the COSSAC staff to become Morgan's deputy.

Although General Morgan appeared at first to be building primary a British staff with an interlarding of American officers on detached duty from their main head-quarters, ETOUSA, his appointment marked the true beginning of operational civil affairs–military government prepara-tions, American as well as British. Until then civil affairs–military government had possessed only a nebulous staff function and practically no definable mission; COSSAC was able to supply both. While he was not actually told so, Morgan could and did as-sume that his was not just a planning staff but was also the nucleus for the staff that would eventually direct the assault on Ger-many. His chief mission was to draft the plan, first named ROUNDHAMMER and later OVERLORD, for the projected 1944 in-vasion of the Continent. His responsibility did not end there, however; he was also to plan for a possible German collapse or partial collapse at any time before the spring of 1944.[8] The latter contingency made not only the planning but also the execution of civil affairs and military gov-ernment major concerns of COSSAC.

While the terms of Morgan's mission suggested the need for military government, one of his early conclusions as COSSAC was that no such capability existed. At the end of May, uncertain even where the ulti-mate responsibility lay, he reported an urgent requirement for a civil affairs head-quarters and an operating organization equipped with a coherent body of policy procedure.[9] The TRIDENT Conference, held in Washington earlier in the month, had given COSSAC a target date, 1 May 1944, and some specific figures on forces. Morgan apparently assumed the civil affairs organization would be formed sepa-rately from the military command, which seemed to be in keeping with American and British thinking, but, as was to happen re-peatedly in the future, his request foun-dered in turmoil and uncertainty at the higher command levels. On the American side the argument over civilian versus mili-tary control was still so far from settled that the War Department could not have ven-tured a decision. Consequently, what was decided emerged piecemeal in the wake of events, the product of necessity more than of policy.

In July, with no decision yet on a sepa-rate organization or on a branch within COSSAC—which General Morgan pro-posed in June—civil affairs suddenly moved into the foreground of COSSAC's planning. Within days of each other, came the landing in Sicily and the failure of the German offensive against the Kursk salient in Russia. Henceforth the Axis would be on the defensive in the East and the West. Germany's condition appeared strikingly like that of July 1918 when Ludendorff's *Friedenssturm* halted and Germany went from near victory to complete defeat in less than four months.

Before the end of July, COSSAC had orders to give first priority to the planning for a return to the Continent in the event of a partial or complete German collapse. Since he was to anticipate such a contin-gency any time after 1 August, his staff

---

[8] Historical Subsec, SGS, SHAEF, History of COSSAC, May 44, in USFET SGS 314.8.

[9] Memo, COSSAC for SAC, sub: COSSAC 7th Weekly Report, 31 May 43, in SHAEF G–5, 11.01.

would also have to be prepared to act as the executive agency for any operation that might ensue. Morgan now found himself with an urgent task and still no civil affairs staff. Meetings in June and July between COSSAC and ETOUSA representatives had produced agreement that he ought to have some such staff to procure uniformity in U.S. and British dealings with civilian populations; but the final authority, to the extent that it existed, remained vested in and divided between the Civil Affairs Section, ETOUSA, and the Civil Affairs Directorate of the British War Office.[10]

On 28 July, in letters to the Under Secretary of State, War Office, and Headquarters, ETOUSA, Morgan proposed a combined civil affairs section within the COSSAC staff and urged its early establishment. His mission, he explained, required him to enter and take control on short notice in any of a halfdozen countries, including Germany. Whether he might have to assume such control next month or next year he could not tell, but at the moment he could not do it at all. He asked for U.S. and British section chiefs to be appointed immediately. They would head a central executive, to be concerned with high policy, and a co-ordinating section, which would supervise groups charged with planning for specific countries.[11]

The COSSAC staff, meanwhile, worked on the various possibilities of a return to the Continent before the appointed date for OVERLORD. The staff took its guidance from a high-level British intelligence estimate which described the German situation at the end of July as "verging on the desperate" and predicted that in the coming winter Germany could suffer "an over-whelming defeat and irretrievable disaster on the Russian front."[12] Whoever was then in control in Germany, the estimate continued, would have to decide between unconditional surrender or abandonment of the occupied territories in western and southern Europe in order to concentrate forces against the Russian advance, postpone the hour of final defeat, and ensure the ultimate occupation of Germany by Anglo-American rather than by Russian forces.[13]

From this rather blatantly optimistic estimate, the COSSAC planners deduced three so-called cases to which they assigned the collective code name RANKIN. Cases A and B were concerned with the prospect of an invasion before 1 May 1944, the target date for OVERLORD, to exploit a drastic German weakening in France and the Low Countries or a voluntary German withdrawal. Morgan especially remembered how unprepared the Allies had been in early 1917 for the German withdrawal to the Hindenburg Line. Case C dealt with the possibility of an unconditional German surrender.[14]

Were it not for case C, the whole RANKIN plan could be dismissed as only one more of the waves of wishful thinking that had periodically swept over the Western Allies since the beginning of the war. Case C, however, marked a new high in optimism and therewith added another aspect to the planning. While the first two cases could be handled as variations of OVERLORD, RANKIN C was concerned with the end of the war, the beginning of

---

[10] Earl Crum, "Civil Affairs Section, ETOUSA," in SHAEF G–5, 60, Jacket 1.

[11] COSSAC History, in SHAEF G–5, 11.04.

[12] COSSAC (43) 40, Operation RANKIN, in SHAEF G–5, 115.25.

[13] *Ibid.*

[14] (1) Sir Frederick E. Morgan, *Overture to OVERLORD* (London: Hodder, 1950), p. 118. (2) Ltr, COSSAC to Chiefs of Staff Committee, War Office, 13 Aug 43, in SHAEF G–5, 11.02.

the occupation, and the reorientation of effort into directions which so far had not even been defined, much less explored. Moreover, even if such a situation did not become a reality in the near future, it was likely to arise sometime and perhaps suddenly. When it did, COSSAC pointed out, combat forces might well be less useful than the ability to control and direct civil affairs. Morgan therefore requested that the British and United States governments, "as a matter of urgency," lay down policy on military government in enemy territory and civil affairs in liberated territory and provide resources with which to execute such policy. As of August 1943, he pointed out, he had nothing from which even to improvise a civil affairs organization.[15]

A Civil Affairs Section, COSSAC

In RANKIN C, General Morgan had proposed an operation for which he had no staff to do the detailed planning, no organization to execute any plans that might be made, and no policy direction on which to base plans in the first place. The first two and a reasonable substitute for the last would be found because they had to be found, but not without their appropriate measures of administrative agony. Without waiting for action elsewhere, Morgan, in August, took in hand the organizing of a civil affairs section for COSSAC. Where once the European theater had no civil affairs planning staff, it would soon have two, which would prove to be one too many.

On 23 August, COSSAC established a civil affairs section under Maj. Gen. Sir Roger Lumley. The COSSAC section consisted of a central organization which would be concerned with operational planning for OVERLORD and the RANKIN operations and a planning board to direct the work of four "country houses," one each for France, Belgium, the Netherlands, and Norway. The country houses would provide the nucleus civil affairs staffs for their assigned areas. No staff was created for Germany because COSSAC assumed that the United States and Britain would handle the occupation of Germany separately.[16] ETOUSA assigned twenty officers to the Civil Affairs Section, COSSAC, leaving twenty-three officers in its own civil affairs section.[17]

In August, Lt. Gen. Jacob L. Devers, commanding ETOUSA, named Col. Cornelius E. Ryan the acting chief of the U.S. Civil Affairs Staff, COSSAC.[18] Ryan was at the same time chief of the ETOUSA Civil Affairs Section, having replaced Wade a month earlier. In July, after nearly a year in limbo, the Civil Affairs Section, ETOUSA, had finally found a firm billet in the special staff. At the end of the month it had established a table of organization consisting of four planning branches—civilian relief, military government, economics, and personnel and training—and a fifth branch—area research—which was conceived as having an operating as well as a planning function since it would be concerned with areas to be occupied, including Germany.[19] The section's directive gave it

---

[15] (1) COSSAC (43) 40, Operation RANKIN, in SHAEF G–5, 115.25. (2) COSSAC to Sec, Chiefs of Staff Committee, Office of the War Cabinet, 17th Report by the CofS to SAC (Designate), 9 Aug 43, in SHAEF G–5, 11.06.

[16] Hqs, COSSAC, CA War Diary, in SHAEF G–5, 11.01.

[17] Historical Record, CA Sec, ETOUSA, in SHAEF G–5, 10.03.

[18] Ltr, CG, ETOUSA, to Lt Gen F. E. Morgan, 3 Aug 43, in SHAEF G–5, 11.01.

[19] ETOUSA, CAS, Memo No. 1, sub: Directive to Branch Chiefs, 24 Jul 43, in SHAEF G–5, 10.04.

responsibility for planning military government in all enemy and enemy-occupied areas in the European theater, authority to recommend general and specific policies for military government, and control of civilian supplies and civil affairs personnel.[20]

The question then was on which of the two sections would the mantle of responsibility eventually fall. The Civil Affairs Section, ETOUSA, assumed that COSSAC, when it became an active command, would be predominantly British with a British commander and Americans in the minority on the staff. ETOUSA would then still have to represent the War Department in the European theater and at least control the supplies, training, and transportation of American forces in the theater. The ETOUSA section was particularly emphatic on the score of representing the U.S. interest in the combined planning. The British side of COSSAC, the Civil Affairs Section maintained, was already seeking to dominate the planning by drawing on the resources of British governmental agencies, which it had close at hand, and by presenting the Americans with *faits accompli* in the form of papers on important and complicated subjects on which British experts outside the COSSAC staff had obviously worked for months. The Americans were expected either to come forward on short notice with something better or to accept the British position. ETOUSA, the Civil Affairs Section urged, should therefore be invited by the British to observe all preliminary conferences and negotiations; should be the channel of communication from the Civil Affairs Division, War Department, to the U.S. element in COSSAC; and should

review all plans, directives, and agreements put out by COSSAC.

The position of the Civil Affairs Section, ETOUSA, however, seemed bound to become completely precarious if COSSAC became a full-fledged combined command. As Maj. E. R. Baltzell, who had been ETOUSA's civil affairs liaison officer with COSSAC, predicted, once the Supreme Commander was appointed he would have full authority in planning as well as operations; consequently, the Civil Affairs Section, ETOUSA, would not have any functions left to perform, except possibly minor ones in connection with the United Kingdom and Iceland.[21] Since the decision on the Supreme Commander had not yet been announced, Headquarters, ETOUSA, on 13 September, tentatively confirmed the Civil Affairs Section as the final channel of civil affairs authority in the theater with responsibility for all phases of planning for civil affairs in combined operations.[22]

The whole question was reopened in October when COSSAC revised its approach to civil affairs. The country house organization had been modeled on the Allied Military Government of Occupied Territory (AMGOT) created for Italy, under which the military governor was subordinate to the Supreme Commander, but AMGOT itself was otherwise completely separate from the combat forces. Under the AMGOT concept the country houses would each have evolved into civil affairs headquarters, practically national military administrations for their assigned countries;

---

[20] CG, ETOUSA, Draft Directive for CAS, 16 Jul 43, in SHAEF G–5, 10.04.

[21] Memo, ETOUSA, CAS, MG Br, for Chief, CAS, sub: Relationship Between CAS ETOUSA and CAS COSSAC, 7 Sep 43, in SHAEF G–5, 10.02.

[22] Ltr, Hqs, ETOUSA, to Chief, CAS, 13 Sep 43, sub: Combined Planning for CA, in SHAEF G–5, 10.02.

but, except for Germany, the countries of western Europe would be liberated, not occupied, and according to a decision of the Quebec Conference in August, were to be returned to their native governments as soon as possible. AMGOT, moreover, after it went into action in Italy in September, rapidly began to look like a prize example of the fallacy of permitting two independent commands in the same theater. Additionally, COSSAC soon realized that the country houses would impose a tremendous drain on personnel. Each would have a full staff of experts in all civil affairs fields, virtual shadow governments for a half dozen or more countries.[23]

Although its demise would not be as complete as was then intended, the country house era in COSSAC came to an end in late October. On the 13th, Col. Karl R. Bendetsen became Chief Staff Officer (U.S.) for Civil Affairs, COSSAC. With this assignment, the American side of the Civil Affairs Section, COSSAC, and the Civil Affairs Section, ETOUSA, were separated. Until then Colonel Ryan had headed both. En route to London, Bendetsen had spent five days in Washington. He said later, he had spent the time reading reports, and no particular form of civil affairs organization had been recommended to him.[24] But it could hardly have been unknown to him that the Civil Affairs Division, War Department, was not happy with the dual command channels AMGOT had created, and within days after his arrival in the theater, Bendetsen began dismantling the country houses. He gave as his reason the Supreme Commander's need for a single compact staff that could deal in broad principles. He was also concerned,

he reported, about ETOUSA's place in civil affairs. If ETOUSA received a civil affairs mission, he maintained, part of COSSAC's area planning would obviously be useless.[25]

The projected abolition of the country houses brought with it the first truly significant development in civil affairs doctrine of the war. Civil affairs and military government finally achieved integration into the operating military forces. Within COSSAC, the change was described as being from a static, regional approach to a mobile plan. In other words, civil affairs would move with the combat troops and be part of the continuing operation, not just a substitute for native government in liberated and occupied areas.[26] Until then, considered in both civilian and military circles as primarily a rear area and postwar activity, civil affairs would find a place in the war itself.

The revised COSSAC concept of civil affairs for a few days seemed also to breathe new life into ETOUSA's prospect of acquiring an operational civil affairs mission. At the end of the month General Devers proposed that COSSAC assume responsibility for all combined planning and ETOUSA take responsibility for planning and the conduct of civil affairs by U.S. forces.[27] What was not yet known in the theater was that at Quebec in August the President and the Prime Minister had decided that the Supreme Commander should be an American. By early November, with the Tehran Conference in the offing, the naming of the Supreme Commander was becoming urgent, and his ap-

---

[23] COSSAC History, in SHAEF G–5, 11.04.

[24] Interv, SHAEF G–5, Historical Sec, with Col Karl R. Bendetsen, in SHAEF G–5, 10.

[25] Ltr, Bendetsen to Hilldring, 27 Oct 43, in SHAEF G–5, 10.02.

[26] Ltr, Maj Gen R. W. Barker to Lt Gen Devers, 28 Oct 43, in SHAEF G–5, 10.02.

[27] Memo, Devers for Dep COSSAC, 31 Oct 43, in SHAEF G–5, 10.03.

pointment would automatically finish off ETOUSA as an operational command.[28] On 12 November the Civil Affairs Division (CAD) advised Devers that COSSAC henceforth would speak with final authority on all civil affairs matters, and the U.S. side of COSSAC would be the War Department's channel of communication. The Civil Affairs Section, ETOUSA, would be absorbed into the 1st (later 12th) U.S. Army Group.[29]

Toward a Plan

Although COSSAC achieved a civil affairs planning capability late and a clear mandate to do such planning even later, it had, nevertheless, by the end of the year 1943 laid the foundations for civil affairs in northwest Europe and for military government in Germany. One major step was the decision already mentioned for a mobile civil affairs organization. Another was the projected division of the German territory to be occupied by the Western Allies into a northwestern (British) zone and a southwestern (American) zone, which aroused such prolonged controversy at so high a level that it will have to be left for discussion elsewhere. The rest of COSSAC's work for the most part took the form of single, often random-seeming decisions, but ones necessary to the construction of a coherent organization and plan. In each instance the COSSAC staff was literally striking out into unexplored territory.

In the last quarter of 1943 RANKIN C continued to be COSSAC's main concern. Its object was conceived as being to occupy areas on the Continent, particularly in Germany, from which the British and American forces could enforce the terms of surrender. Of the probable civil affairs tasks, the foremost seemed to be to maintain law and order. A German surrender was scarcely conceivable without also either a collapse or overthrow of the Nazi regime; consequently, the country might be found to have very little in the way of a functioning government or none at all. Additionally the defeat could be expected to set off a massive movement of people as the German troops still scattered across Europe from the North Cape to Crete attempted to make their way home, as millions of prisoners of war and displaced persons took to the roads out of Germany, and possibly as the Germans themselves fled in panic from their most feared enemy, the Russians. The economy, on the other hand, having survived four years of war, was expected to be able to provide adequately for the country after the surrender.[30]

Having postulated the conditions under which military government in Germany might expect to operate, the COSSAC staff also undertook to define its purpose. FM 27–5 had recommended benevolence toward both friendly and enemy populations. In the COSSAC thinking a sterner line emerged and with it the germ of what was to become a fundamental assumption in all later planning for the occupation, namely, that for the Germans hostilities would not necessarily end when the shooting stopped. The purpose of military government in Germany would be to assist the

[28] Ltr, Sec of War to President's Special Assistant, 10 Nov 43, in Department of State, *The Conferences at Cairo and Tehran, 1943,* in "Foreign Relations of the United States" (Washington, D.C., 1961).

[29] Memo, Hqs, ETOUSA, CofS for Maj Gen G. W. Barker, Dep COSSAC, 12 Nov 43, in SHAEF G–5, 11.01.

[30] COSSAC, CA, Plan 26/4, Outline of Operations for Civil Affairs Planning—RANKIN Case C, 15 Nov 43, in SHAEF G–5, 115.25c.

military commander to impose his will on the enemy, and the first concern would be to help maintain the striking power of the military forces by controlling movements of people and by preventing disease and disorder. Relief, an important function in liberated Allied territory, would be restricted in Germany "to those measures which the Supreme Allied Commander may specifically direct to prevent a general breakdown of civil life and the spread of disease."[31]

The most difficult practical question RANKIN C raised was one of means. A German surrender could create a sudden need for a full-blown civil affairs organization to administer all of western Europe. The first proposal, in October 1943, was to form a combined U.S.–British civil affairs military government force totaling 5,000 officers and enlisted men. A month later, as the RANKIN plan began to take shape, the number was increased to 2,400 U.S. officers, 5,000 U.S. enlisted men, 2,500 British officers, and 4,500 British of other ranks.[32] The choice General Morgan then faced seemed to be either to call into being so large a force and risk there being no assignments for it for months, possibly even years, or to go ahead and draft plans which he knew he could not execute. Fortunately, the choice was not quite as stark as it appeared. The British contingent could be assembled at fairly short notice if RANKIN C were to materialize suddenly. A British civil affairs school at Wimbledon had been training officers since February 1943 and returning them to their original units or to civilian life. They could be

quickly recalled.[33] The Americans were a different case. They and all their equipment would have to be assembled in the United States and brought across the Atlantic. Morgan saw no alternative but to accept the risk that they might have to be "kept hanging about" for a long time as the price for having them at hand if they were suddenly needed.[34]

On 5 October, General Devers alerted General Hilldring to the impending requirement to ship the entire projected U.S. civil affairs contingent to England.[35] The first arrivals could not be expected before January 1944, just barely in time if a disastrous winter in Russia forced a German surrender. If not, the U.S. civil affairs personnel would have to wait and go back to school in England. ETOUSA would make space available in the American Schools Center at Shrivenham, sixty miles due west of London, which already housed a variety of other ETOUSA schools ranging from cooking and baking to military intelligence. On 1 December, Col. Cuthbert P. Stearns, as commandant, activated the Civil Affairs Center at Shrivenham. The Civil Affairs Center would be responsible not only for training but for the entire U.S. field organization for civil affairs in the European theater.[36] The first group of trainees, forty

[31] Memo, Chief, CAD, COSSAC, for Branches, sub: CA Administrative Appreciation, Nov 43, in SHAEF G–5, 11.02.

[32] Memo, COSSAC, CA, for COSSAC, 18 Nov 43, SHAEF G–5, 11.03.

[33] Note on British School of Military Government [no date], in PMG, MG Div, classified decimal file 350.1.

[34] Memo, COSSAC, CA, for COSSAC, 18 Nov 43, in SHAEF G–5, 11.03.

[35] F. Van Wyck Mason, ed., "The Education and Training of Allied Officers for Duty with Civil Affairs, Military Government, European Theater of Operations," in SHAEF G–5, 60, Jacket 7.

[36] (1) Memo, CA Center, American School Center, for Ch, Hist Subsec, COSSAC, 31 Dec 43, in SHAEF G–5, 17.02. (2) Memo, COSSAC for CG, ETOUSA, sub: Assignment of U.S. Personnel to CA Duty Under RANKIN C, 29 Dec 43, in SHAEF G–5, 11.03.

officers, arrived at Shrivenham on 13 January 1944.[37]

In December 1943, with the announcement of General Eisenhower's appointment as Supreme Commander, the COSSAC phase of combined planning drew to a close. On the 13th COSSAC published what was to be the most important document on civil affairs produced during its tenure, the Standard Policy and Procedure for Combined Civil Affairs Operations in Northwest Europe. Divided into three parts, one dealing with nomenclature and organization and two with operations in the field (on Allied and on enemy territory), the Standard Policy and Procedure was designed to reconcile American and British practices and policies as far as they were then known. As such, it was mostly a routine compilation distinguishable only by its subject matter from dozens of similar staff manuals. What made it a civil affairs milestone was that it assigned full control of and responsibility for civil affairs and military government to the military commanders, from the Supreme Commander on down. In the European theater, civil affairs was to have no existence separate from the combat commands. In occupied enemy territory the Supreme Commander would be the military governor and would delegate appropriate authority to his subordinate commanders, who would then bear the responsibility in their own areas. The chief object would be to maintain conditions among the civilian population which would at least not hinder military operations and if possible assist them; and the task of the civil affairs staffs and detachments would be to relieve the combat troops of civil commitments.[38]

---

[37] Hist Sec, G–5, SHAEF Rear, Chronology of Civil Affairs–Military Government, ETO, May 41–6 Jun 44, 24 Dec 44, in SHAEF G–5, 60, Jacket 1.

[38] (1) SHAEF, Standard Policy and Procedure for Combined Civil Affairs Operations in Northwest Europe, 13 Dec 43, in SHAEF, SGS, 014.1. (2) Report on Standard Policy and Procedure [no date], in SHAEF G–5, 32.

CHAPTER III

Washington Versus London

The AT(E) Committee and CCAC

What strategy is to military operations, policy is to civil affairs and military government. Policy lends form and purpose to the government of occupied and liberated territory and is ultimately as much concerned with winning wars as the military strategy itself. Washington and London both were aware of this fact, and neither questioned the extension of the partnership developed in the war to the formulation of civil affairs and military government policy. The partnership was not one without differences, however, and the partners were not without independent ambitions; civil affairs and military government gave ample scope to both.

The first organization, either British or American, to be concerned specifically with defining civil affairs policy was the Administration of Territories (Europe) Committee. The AT(E) Committee traced its origins back to the early planning for ROUNDUP in the spring of 1942. As a committee of the British War Office, it held its first meeting on 2 July 1942 under the chairmanship of the Permanent Under Secretary for War, Sir Frederick E. Bovenschen. By then ROUNDUP, after a brief period of combined planning, was reverting to the British while the Americans took up the planning for the North Africa operation. Although the AT(E) Committee was entirely British, under its terms of reference it assumed broad authority to devise policy that would "ensure efficient civil adminis-

tration of the territories liberated in Europe as the result of operations by forces of the United Nations" and to maintain contact for this purpose with the Allied exile governments and with ETOUSA.

ROUNDUP, never much in favor with the British Chiefs of Staff, quickly fell into abeyance, but the AT(E) Committee met regularly after July 1942, concerning itself chiefly with relief and with the negotiation of civil affairs agreements with the exile governments. The occupation of Germany as yet seemed too remote to be pertinent. At its first meeting the committee agreed to arrange for an ETOUSA representative to sit in on future meetings; therefore, from the third meeting on, at least one liaison officer from ETOUSA attended—first Colonel Betts, later Colonel Wade, and for a time both. Their instructions were to attend the meetings "without accepting the responsibility of making final decisions which have not already received the approval of this headquarters."[1] The Americans' status was uncertain from the beginning. The British apparently wanted to regard the men as full-fledged members. ETOUSA seems at first to have intended to negotiate with the committee through them but, as the American concern with ROUNDUP declined in the summer of 1942, came to regard them merely as observers.[2]

---

[1] Staniforth, "The Administration of Territories (Europe) Committee," p. 5.

[2] Memo, Theater Judge Advocate for CofS, ETOUSA, sub: Administration of Territories (Europe) Committee (Br), 31 Jul 42, in SHAEF G–5, 10.04.

The revival of the cross-Channel attack in early 1943 raised, more urgently than the 1942 approach to ROUNDUP had, the question of combined civil affairs planning for northwestern Europe. In April, the representatives of the British Chiefs of Staff on the Combined Chiefs of Staff (CCS) proposed that civil affairs policy-planning during the period of military control be delegated to the AT(E) Committee and that special War Department representatives be assigned to sit on the committee. For the subsequent period of civilian control they proposed the creation of a committee in Washington under State Department leadership composed of interested British and U.S. civilian agencies including War Department and CCS representatives.[3] The U.S. Joint Chiefs objected that the British proposals would create a dual chain of command and jeopardize the hard-fought principle of military necessity. They proposed, instead, the creation of a combined civil affairs committee to function under the Combined Chiefs of Staff with authority both to formulate directives to commanders in the field and to co-ordinate the activities of U.S. and British civilian agencies.[4]

Although the Joint Chiefs of Staff (JCS) did not comment specifically on the AT(E) Committee, the Americans clearly indicated that they did not regard it as a suitable vehicle for combined civil affairs planning. On 13 April, at a meeting in the U.S. Embassy in London, the Commanding General, ETOUSA, at the time General Andrews, expressed the American view

that COSSAC would handle all plans for cross-Channel operations and, thus, would supersede the AT(E) Committee. Two weeks later, Colonel Wade reported that the committee had completed the estimates for the military phase in cross-Channel operations and was moving on to long-range planning which did not concern ETOUSA; he recommended, therefore, that active ETOUSA participation on the committee be withdrawn.[5]

The Americans had, in fact, come to regard civil affairs as a unilateral concern and the AT(E) Committee as a British committee with which they might exchange opinion but could not negotiate, since neither ETOUSA nor the War Department itself had anybody authorized to do so at the time. Consequently, while in the British view the AT(E) Committee performed a valuable and needed service for the alliance, the Americans saw in it an attempt to pre-empt the civil affairs planning in the British interest, particularly after the committee and its most active offshoot, the Shipping and Supply Sub-Committee, began to concentrate on relief and seemed about to assign the furnishing of relief supplies to the United States and their distribution to British agencies. The overt American objections to the AT(E) Committee were that it renewed the danger of civilian interference in the military phase and that civil affairs ought to be in exactly the same command channel as the tactical troops, namely, under the Combined Chiefs of Staff.[6]

Toward the end of May, the British War Office agreed with two provisos, to accept a combined civil affairs committee in Washington under the CCS. In the first

---

[3] Memo, Representatives of Br, CofS (CCS 190/1), 11 Apr 43, in CAD 092 (3-22-43), sec. 1. See Coles and Weinberg, *Soldiers Become Governors*, p. 119.

[4] JCS 250/4, 19 Apr 43, in CAD 092 (3-22-43), sec. 1. See Coles and Weinberg, *Soldiers Become Governors*, p. 120.

[5] Staniforth, "The Administration of Territories (Europe) Committee," p. 31.

[6] History of the CAD, bk. II, ch. IV, pp. 5-8.

proviso the War Office required exemption from combined control for recovered territories which had originally been possessions of the United Kingdom, the Dominions, or the United States. In the second it insisted on expanding the AT(E) Committee into a fully combined committee "with strong U.S. representation which must be fully authorized to speak for the U.S. Government."[7] Within less than a week, the Civil Affairs Division of the U.S. War Department had recast the JCS proposal to incorporate the British provisos, but the agreement in principle thus easily reached was to meet far rougher going when it came to writing a charter for a combined civil affairs committee. In a foretaste of similar arguments to come, the British and Americans fell to debating hypothetical aspects of the first British proviso, meanwhile ignoring the immediate and practical implications of the second.

On 3 July, after nearly a month's intensive discussion, the Combined Chiefs of Staff approved a tentative charter for the Combined Civil Affairs Committee (CCAC). Paragraph 6, concerned with CCAC authority in areas in which one or the other of the partners claimed sovereignty, was still undergoing revision; but since the CCAC would not have to deal with any such problems for awhile, it could function adequately without the paragraph.[8] On 7 July, General Marshall authorized General Devers to appoint an officer from the ETOUSA staff to serve as U.S. member of the AT(E) Commit-

tee.[9] In Washington, the CCAC held its first formal meeting on the 15th under the chairmanship of Assistant Secretary of War John J. McCloy, but by then the CCAC was already quickly lapsing into a state of paralysis.

Some weeks before, the AT(E) Committee had sent to Washington a draft civil affairs agreement with Norway. According to their understanding of the CCAC charter, the British expected the U.S. Joint Chiefs to review the document and return it to London, where the combined negotiations would be completed by the U.S. representation on the AT(E) Committee. The Americans insisted on prior submission to the CCAC, which they maintained constituted the final authority in civil affairs decisions.[10] Until then neither side had fully enlightened the other as to its interpretation of the charter. The British now revealed that they considered the AT(E) Committee to be the principal combined planning agency for all civil affairs operations based in the United Kingdom, hence for all of northwestern Europe.[11] The Americans, on the other hand, had never intended to recognize the AT(E) Committee as a combined agency. In recommending approval of U.S. membership on the committee General Hilldring had stated, "it does not appear to be desirable to have the War Department recognize and be a part of any agreements which are made by the War Office Committee [AT(E)]."[12]

Subsequently, through the summer, the

---

[7] Msg, War Office to British Joint Staff Mission, 28 May 43, in CAD 092 (3–22–43), sec. 1. See Coles and Weinberg, *Soldiers Become Governors*, p. 121.

[8] CCS 190/6/D, Charter of the CCAC, 3 Jul 43, in CCS 334 (6–5–43), sec. 1. See Coles and Weinberg, *Soldiers Become Governors*, p. 123f.

[9] Cable, AGWAR to ETOUSA, 7 Jul 43, in SHAEF G–5, 11.01.

[10] Memo, Representatives of Br, CofS, 10 Jul 43, in CAD 014 (5–13–43). See Coles and Weinberg, *Soldiers Become Governors*, p. 125.

[11] History of the CAD, bk. II, ch. IV, p. 27.

[12] Memo, Hilldring for CofS, 1 Jun 43, in CAD 092 (3–22–43), sec. 1. See Coles and Weinberg, *Soldiers Become Governors*, p. 122.

combined planning degenerated into a tug of war over the Norwegian agreement, with the Americans insisting that one way or another, no matter how fleetingly, the paper had to pass through the CCAC and with the British staunchly refusing to have the CCAC lay so much as a finger on it. By mid-September the frustration reached such intensity that General Hilldring contemplated a direct assault on the AT(E) Committee. To General Barker, chief of the U.S. element in COSSAC, he expressed the opinion that the AT(E) Committee no longer had "any real function to perform" (because primary responsibility for combined planning was vested in the CCS and CCAC) and, therefore, if Barker considered it politically expedient, the U.S. representative on the committee ought to be withdrawn.[13] The suggestion was not acted upon, though it almost certainly would eventually have been had the committee not resolved on its own accord in October to suspend its meetings while the War Office and Foreign Office reassessed its relationship to the CCAC.[14]

The EAC and CCAC(L)

In Moscow the Tripartite Conference of Foreign Ministers, under a secret protocol signed on 1 November 1943, created the European Advisory Commission (EAC) and charged it with tripartite planning on questions pertaining to the occupation. At the conference, Secretary of State Cordell Hull, British Secretary of State for Foreign Affairs Sir Anthony Eden, and Soviet People's Commissar for Foreign Affairs Vyacheslav M. Molotov had been mostly concerned with the agenda for the forthcoming Big Three conference at Tehran. Hull and Eden, however, had also hoped to begin establishing, for the last stage of the war against Germany, something like the collaboration that had existed between the Western Allies since 1941 but had so far not been attained with the Soviet Union. Since OVERLORD would meet the long-standing Soviet demand for a full-scale second front, the development of common approaches and objectives not only for the war but also for the period after the victory seemed both possible and necessary. The British and American thinking on the RANKIN plan, since it presupposed a German surrender before Western forces were on the Continent, even lent a degree of urgency to tripartite agreement on occupation policy.

The Americans and British were pleased, and a trifle surprised, to find the Russians willing to discuss postwar questions, but the Americans were much less pleasantly surprised when Eden proposed that the European Advisory Commission have its seat in London and be the vehicle for tripartite decisions. The Americans saw in this proposal an attempt to replace the faltering AT(E) Committee with a more powerful body and capture for London the entire field of postwar planning. The Russians, for their part, were quite willing to participate in broad decision-making for areas of primary concern to the Western Allies but gave no indication that they would reciprocate where areas of direct interest to them were concerned. As finally drafted, the terms of reference of the EAC were left sufficiently indefinite to accommodate both the British expectations and the American and Soviet reservations. "The Commission," the Moscow protocol stated, "will

[13] Memo, War Dept, Ch, CAD, for Gen Barker, sub: AT(E) Committee, 13 Sep 43, in SHAEF G–5, 11.01.
[14] Staniforth, "The Administration of Territories (Europe) Committee," p. 33.

study and make joint recommendations to the three Governments upon European questions connected with the termination of hostilities which the three Governments may consider appropriate to refer to it."[15]

The European Advisory Commission was to meet in London. Eden, on his return from Moscow, named as United Kingdom delegate Assistant Under Secretary of State in the Foreign Office Sir William Strang, who was already thoroughly familiar with the British thinking on postwar plans. As the seat for the commission, the British government renovated and redecorated the palatial Lancaster House to make it "a building where medium-sized international conferences could be held in conditions worthy of a great capital."[16] Strang's was a full-time appointment and the British were somewhat chagrined when the United States and the Soviet Union appointed as their delegates their ambassadors in London, John G. Winant and Fedor T. Gousev, who would both continue to perform their ambassadorial duties.[17]

In the War Department, the creation of the EAC aroused severe misgivings, particularly after reports from London described the preparations to house it as being made on a scale extensive enough to accommodate "a major interallied organization."[18] Moreover, no matter what the eventual scope of the EAC, it would inevitably lend a political aspect to civil affairs and military government. The Supreme Commander, when he was appointed, would from the beginning not be guided solely by military considerations and international law but would be saddled with and constantly have to adjust his plans to any developments in national or international policy conveyed to him either by the governments or through the EAC. The War Department, in turn, would have to accept increased State Department influence in civil affairs and military government planning.[19]

In November, the tug of war between Washington and London brought civil affairs planning outside of COSSAC to a standstill. After General Barker reported that the AT(E) Committee "unhappily," he said, was not as defunct as the Americans had thought, ETOUSA acted to hasten the committee's demise by withdrawing the U.S. representative.[20] The British, on the other hand, now wanted the CCAC transferred to London and, to emphasize their desire, ordered their representatives on the committee to refuse to talk about anything having to do with Europe. For several weeks the CCAC ceased meeting altogether. Caught between the withdrawal of U.S. recognition and its own government's pursuit of more important prizes, the AT(E) Committee finally became a causalty of the struggle. It held its last meeting on 2 December.

After Hull returned from Moscow, Stimson undertook to impress on the President before his departure for Tehran the War Department's antipathy toward a strong EAC.[21] Later in the month, Assistant Secretary of War McCloy went along as a

---

[15] Department of State, *General*, in "Foreign Relations of the United States, 1943," vol. I (Washington, D.C., 1963), p. 756.
[16] William Strang, *Home and Abroad* (London: Andre Deutsch, 1956), p. 203.
[17] *Ibid.*
[18] Rudolph A. Winnacker, The Office of the Secretary of War Under Henry L. Stimson, pt. I, p. 299. MS in CMH files.

[19] Memo, School of Military Government, Asst Dir of Instr, for Acting Comdt, sub: State Department Liaison, 24 Nov 43, in PMG, MG Div, decimal file 014.13.
[20] (1) Staniforth, "The Administration of Territories (Europe) Committee," p. 33. (2) Coles and Weinberg, *Soldiers Become Governors*, p. 128.
[21] Winnacker, The Office of the Secretary of War Under Henry L. Stimson, p. 300.

member of the United States delegation to preliminary talks with the British in Cairo to argue the case for the Washington CCAC. On the British side, the Prime Minister had been briefed to urge the CCAC's transfer to London.[22]

The President and the Prime Minister did not take up the matters either of the EAC or the CCAC, but McCloy found Eden eager to talk about both and, in the end, came away believing he had gotten what he needed. When McCloy complained about the British CCAC representatives' tongues being tied, Eden replied that if the United States agreed to treat the EAC seriously he would see to it that the tongues were loosened. In return for support of the EAC, Eden proposed to have the commission's recommendations submitted to the CCAC for comment, give up the attempt to have the CCAC shifted to London, and allow the British representatives in the CCAC to participate fully in decisions related to operations based in the United Kingdom.[23]

In subsequent talks both with Eden and with the War Office Director of Civil Affairs, Maj. Gen. S. W. Kirby, McCloy explained the War Department's desire to keep the civil affairs control in Washington as a necessity of U.S. domestic policy. He asked Eden to avoid playing up the EAC as the "great decider" of all postwar questions, and he told General Kirby that isolationism and anti-British feelings were far from dead in the United States and would increase if the decisions were being made in London. He indicated to both that the

War Department was not as much interested in where the decisions were actually made as it was in preserving the appearance of having them emanate from Washington. Hence, the CCAC would have to stay in Washington, even if most of the decisions were made in London and only funneled through Washington.[24]

The spirit of Cairo, such as it was, did not outlast the meeting. On 14 December, the War Department, apparently not aware that the AT(E) Committee was defunct, directed ETOUSA to make certain that any U.S. personnel who might attend meetings of the committee did not take an active part in the discussions; a week later the U.S. civil affairs officers in COSSAC received orders not to attend AT(E) Committee meetings at all.[25] On 5 January 1944, anticipating the first formal session of the EAC early in the new year, Adm. William D. Leahy sent the JCS guidelines for the U.S. delegation of the EAC to Secretary Hull. "The EAC," Leahy wrote, "from the U.S. point of view is an important body, whose functioning and development should be guided and maintained in accordance with the U.S. concept as to the scope of its activities and the manner of its operation." The scope, from the JCS point of view, was to be narrow, with a tight rein kept on the manner of operation. "The EAC," Leahy continued, "should keep strictly within the letter and spirit of its directive and in so doing in particular avoid problems relating to the conduct of military operations and concerning civil affairs of liberated or enemy territory prior to the end of hostilities." The JCS strictures further required that Ambassador Winant

[22] F. S. V. Donnison. *Civil Affairs and Military Government, Central Organization and Planning* (London: H. M. Stationery Office, 1966), p. 74.
[23] Department of State, *The Conferences at Cairo and Tehran, 1943,* in Foreign Relations of the United States (Washington, D.C., 1961), p. 352.

[24] (1) *Ibid.* (2) Donnison, *CA–MG, Central Organization and Planning,* p. 74.
[25] Staniforth, "The Administration of Territories (Europe) Committee," p. 34.

submit "all studies and proposed recommendations of the EAC" for approval by appropriate U.S. agencies before making commitments on them and that all questions involving military matters "either directly or indirectly" be passed on by the JCS, the theater commander, or the War or Navy Departments as appropriate.[26] The State Department had, in fact, in its instructions to Winant already excluded the period of hostilities from the EAC's area of discussion, and the President had earlier, according to Hull, warned against allowing the EAC to arrogate to itself the general field of postwar organization. Consequently, in the U.S. concept as transmitted to Winant, the EAC could have at the outset only two functions: to draft the surrender documents for Germany and her allies and to devise the Allied control machinery to be imposed after the surrender.[27]

On his return to London, General Kirby found understanding for the American attitude as expressed by Assistant Secretary McCloy but no inclination to abandon the struggle for control of civil affairs. The most the War Office would concede was the formation of a second CCAC in London possessing the authority formerly claimed for the AT(E) Committee, namely, control of civil affairs and military government in operations based in the United Kingdom. In January, Sir Frederick Bovenschen went to Washington to try to secure agreement on these terms.[28] Sir

Frederick's mission was, as the British official historian stated, "on paper, entirely successful."[29] On 29 January, the CCS approved a new CCAC charter. Under it the Washington committee was to recommend general civil affairs policies to the Combined Chiefs of Staff and be responsible for broad civil affairs planning. A London committee—CCAC(L)—was created which was to give guidance and make recommendations to the European and Mediterranean theater commanders ("within the framework of CCS directives"), resolve questions raised by the theater commanders ("not requiring submission to the CCS"), and make recommendations to the CCS.[30] The new charter, like the old, skirted the main question: Where did the ultimate authority really lie?

The first EAC meeting, on 14 January, and the approval of the CCAC(L) charter two weeks later completed the formative period of the Allied and combined planning agencies for the occupation of Germany. In neither instance was there or would there ever be a full consensus on the role of the two bodies. In the EAC, the Soviet interpretation of the commission's terms of reference soon proved to be more restrictive even than that of the United States. The CCAC(L), excluded from broad planning by the Washington committee and from decisions in the theater by SHAEF (Supreme Headquarters, Allied Expeditionary Force), held only seven formal meetings, and these with its American members under orders to see that the committee accomplished as little as possible.[31] The Washington CCAC emerged as the

---

[26] Ltr, Leahy to Hull, sub: Procedure for Instructing the American Representative on the European Advisory Commission, 5 Jan 44, in CAD 334 (12–8–43).

[27] Department of State, *General*, in "Foreign Relations of the United States, 1944." vol. I (Washington, D.C., 1966), pp. 6–14.

[28] (1) AT(E) Committee, Minutes of Conferences, 27th–39th, 2 Dec 43, in SHAEF G–5, 4. (2) Donnison, *CA–MG, Central Organization and Planning*, p. 75f.

[29] Donnison, CA–MG, *Central Organization Planning*, p. 76.

[30] CCS 190/10/D, Charter of the CCAC, 24 Jan 44, in CCS 334 (6–5–43), sec. 1.

[31] History of the CAD, bk. II, ch. IV.

principal combined civil affairs and military government planning agency; but the authority to decide major issues, the subject of the struggle between Washington and London, for the most part remained outside its grasp. The Norwegian agreement never was submitted to the CCAC nor were the civil affairs agreements with other occupied countries. After the British failed to have the agreements adopted in the EAC, the United States, the United Kingdom, and (for Norway) the Soviet Union negotiated identically worded but separate agreements with the countries concerned.[32] For the military government of Germany the CCAC would provide the appearance but little substance of combined policy.

---

[32] Department of State, *Foreign Relations, 1944,* vol. I, p. 38.

CHAPTER IV

The Supreme Command

SHAEF Concentrates on OVERLORD

General Eisenhower arrived in London on 15 January 1944 to begin converting the COSSAC staff into the Supreme Headquarters, Allied Expeditionary Force (SHAEF). Planning would continue for months yet, but now with troops and a solid purpose. OVERLORD was coming to the fore. The hope of an early German collapse, strong in the fall, had dwindled with the arrival of winter. At the turn of the year COSSAC had put aside RANKIN C, and shifted to RANKIN B, a projected lodgment on the Continent in the event of a German withdrawal from France. COSSAC completed a directive for RANKIN B on 14 January. By then, however, the Germans were reinforcing France, and a voluntary withdrawal to the West Wall was becoming very unlikely. SHAEF's concern would be with OVERLORD, the invasion and drive into Germany, although the RANKIN conditions, a sudden partial or complete German collapse, could not be put entirely out of mind.[1]

In the RANKIN operations, civil affairs and military government would have been paramount from the first. Under OVERLORD they would be subsidiary until the issue had been decided in the field, but ultimately no less essential. RANKIN would have resulted in an improvised occupation with limited forces probably not capable of reaching into Germany beyond the coastal cities and the line of the Rhine River. Even such a limited occupation, however, presupposed control with token forces and, hence, would have required a complete absence of German resistance and Soviet interference, especially the latter, since the Russians would probably have the overwhelming preponderance of strength on the scene. OVERLORD, on the other hand, would array fully operational U.S. and British forces on the Continent and, whether opposed or under so-called RANKIN conditions, would very likely culminate in a deep sweep into Germany. SHAEF would command the assault on Hitler's "Fortress Europe" and be the executive organ for establishing the occupation. Therefore, OVERLORD would require a military government able to operate in the wake of battle almost side by side with the frontline troops as well as to govern a defeated Germany from top to bottom. Either was a massive enough undertaking in its own right. Doing both required answers to questions that had so far barely been raised.

Civil Affairs Becomes G–5

Under COSSAC, civil affairs had found solid acceptance in principle but had remained an anomaly in the staff structure. COSSAC had used the American "G" system but had not assigned a G number to civil affairs. In October 1943, the country

---

[1] Memo, Combined Planners (SHAEF), sub: Operation RANKIN B, 14 Mar 44, in SHAEF G–5, 501.

houses had given way to the Civil Affairs
Division, COSSAC, which consisted of a
small planning staff to work on the
RANKIN plans and six advisory branches.
The branches, made up of the former country house personnel, were designated by
function: legal, fiscal, supply, governmental
affairs, economic affairs, and information.
Their assignment had been to produce instructions for subordinate commands and
to reconcile U.S. and British civil affairs-
military government policies, that is, to
write a combined manual—the Standard
Policy and Procedure.[2]

In November, the War Department had
authorized two general officers, ninety
other officers, five warrant officers, and sixteen enlisted men for the Civil Affairs Division, COSSAC; but in the third week of
the month only fifteen officers and one warrant officer had been assigned.[3] In the
branches, which numbered nearly two
hundred officers, the Americans were only
sparsely represented. Late in November,
Brig. Gen. Frank J. McSherry, who had
served in military government in Sicily and
Italy, became the ranking U.S. civil affairs
officer in COSSAC and coequal chief of
the Civil Affairs Division with General
Lumley.

Although COSSAC had, in the Standard Policy and Procedure, stipulated a
complete fusion of civil affairs-military
government with the military command,
it had in the Civil Affairs Division in fact
maintained what amounted to a separate
staff too diverse in its functions to be integrated with the military command. Eisenhower's chief of staff, Maj. Gen. Walter

GENERAL SMITH. (*Photograph taken
in 1946.*)

Bedell Smith, on his arrival in London
early in January immediately recognized
the latent similarity to AMGOT, toward
which he had not developed the antipathy
that prevailed in COSSAC and to some
extent in the Washington Civil Affairs
Division. Already thoroughly convinced by
his Mediterranean experience of the value
of civil affairs and in good part responsible
himself for the AMGOT organization,
Smith objected only to the "ponderous and
unwieldy" dual British-American headship
of the COSSAC Civil Affairs Division. He
proposed to appoint a single head and,
going even a step beyond the AMGOT
analogy, asked for a civilian of subcabinet
rank to fill the post, naming Assistant Secretary of War McCloy as his choice. General
Hilldring, while replying that Secretary
of War Stimson would not part with

---

[2] COSSAC, Civil Affairs War Diary, in SHAEF
G–5, 11.01.
[3] Opns Br, Hist Sec, G–5 SHAEF Rear, Chronology of Civil Affairs-Military Government, European Theater of Operations, May 41–6 Jun 44,
in SHAEF G–5, 60, Jacket 1.

McCloy, attempted to divert Smith from the idea of a civilian head by suggesting that he use the War Department Civil Affairs Division, which had a military chief, as his model. Anxious, however, to avoid seeming to interfere with a theater commander's right to organize his own staff, Hilldring assured Smith that he (Smith) and Eisenhower had a completely free hand in organizing civil affairs for SHAEF. He had asked for a high-powered civilian, Smith then explained, in order not only to have an expert administrator but to acquire a kind of lightning conductor as well. The idea of civil affairs entirely in professional military hands obviously made him somewhat uneasy. The Civil Affairs Division, he agreed, was military, but it had the Secretary of War behind it.[4] No doubt, Smith was aware that the simplest solution for him and for Eisenhower would have been to turn civil affairs over to McCloy or to Hilldring, whom he also invited to assume the job, and thus draw the War Department into a kind of partnership within the theater.

By the end of the month, when Hilldring also declined the position, citing Chief of Staff Marshall's "forcible" opposition to his trying to "break out" of the Pentagon, Smith had become immersed in fundamental civil affairs problems that could not wait until a chief was found.[5] Obviously the whole COSSAC Civil Affairs Division, a conglomerate of the former COSSAC civil affairs planning staff and the country house personnel to which a number of American officers were being added, could not be taken into the SHAEF staff. General McSherry advocated a virtually outright return to AMGOT, then beginning to be referred to more loftily as the Mediterranean system, with civil affairs subordinate to the Supreme Commander but otherwise practically autonomous.[6] Smith also was still thinking in terms of the Mediterranean approach. Colonel Bendetsen as a proponent of integrating civil affairs into the military command stood alone among the Americans and would shortly be transferred out of SHAEF.

On 5 February, General Lumley, as the senior of the COSSAC Civil Affairs Division's dual heads, sent Smith an organization plan. Since SHAEF would be drawn together at one location in London within the next few weeks, Lumley believed it was time to fit civil affairs directly into the staff. To do this he proposed creating a G–5 division at SHAEF, initially with thirty-five or forty officers, later to be brought up to a strength of about sixty. G–5 would formulate policy and co-ordinate the work of a rear echelon to be composed of the existing Civil Affairs Division branches plus a German planning unit. The only completely separate function then would be training, which would be carried out at the American center in Shrivenham and at a British center in Eastbourne.[7]

In his plan, Lumley had solved the problem of dual heads and that of civil affairs' place in the command structure, neither, however, to Smith's satisfaction. The next day Smith told Hilldring that he had secured Eisenhower's approval for a plan of his own. SHAEF would retain a small civil affairs section, "possibly to be designated G–5." Lumley would head it but would have to be supported "by a deputy . . . in whom both the Commander in Chief and

---

[4] Coles and Weinberg, *Soldiers Become Governors*, p. 675.
[5] *Ibid.*, p. 674.

[6] Pogue, *The Supreme Command*, p. 81.
[7] Memo, SHAEF CAD for CofS, sub: Organization of CA at SHAEF, 5 Feb 44, in SHAEF G–5, 35.08.

myself have complete confidence." For this assignment, Smith asked for Brig. Gen. Julius C. Holmes, who was then in Italy. Civil affairs training, organization, and detailed planning would be done under McSherry outside the general staff.[8] In his reply to Lumley on the 7th, Smith commented acidly that the general staff division would not need sixty officers. It should be a small, policy-making body. Lumley would be G–5, but McSherry would have to be "considerably more than a superintendent of training."[9]

A conference in the Civil Affairs Division three days later predictably culminated in a victory for the advocates of the Mediterranean system. Lumley and McSherry agreed that Lumley would become Assistant Chief of Staff, G–5, with Holmes as his deputy, but G–5 would have no more than thirty-five officers and would be limited to policy-making, advisory, and review functions. McSherry would be appointed Deputy Chief Civil Affairs Officer (DCCAO) and head a civil affairs special staff removed organizationally and physically from SHAEF G–5, its seat being at Shrivenham. The DCCAO would direct training and prepare detailed plans and instructions. To accomplish the latter function, country missions, a revival of the old country houses including a German section, would be established. After the invasion, the country missions would "sit alongside" restored governments in liberated countries, with the German section eventually becoming the U.S. element in the Allied control organization for Germany. SHAEF G–5 would review the DCCAO's plans and "exercise general supervision over their execution," but only one of the G–5's six sections would be concerned directly with civil affairs operations. The rest would handle fiscal, supply, legal, economic, and staff duties within SHAEF.[10]

In Staff Memorandum No. 2, 15 February 1944, Smith established SHAEF G–5 and the Special Staff, effective on this date, and confirmed Lumley and McSherry in their appointments.[11] Ironically, on this day the members of the Civil Affairs Division were drawn together in one place for the first time. The division had begun moving the day before from scattered locations in London, at Cadogan Square and Norfolk House, to Prince's Gardens. By the 16th, when the move was completed, the reorganization had also been accomplished and the staffs, though in physical proximity, were organizationally separate. Even this condition would not last long. The Special Staff was to move to Shrivenham before the end of the month and the G–5 section would go in early March to the SHAEF headquarters compound, WIDEWING, in Bushy Park on the outskirts of London.[12]

No AMGOT

In the conversion of Civil Affairs Division, COSSAC, into G–5 and the Special Staff, SHAEF, the Mediterranean concept seemed to have won out. G–5 had been practically shorn of operational control, the means for exercising it being concentrated

[8] Coles and Weinberg, *Soldiers Become Governors,* p. 674.

[9] Memo, CofS, SHAEF, for Gen Lumley, sub: Organization of CA at SHAEF, 7 Feb 44, in SHAEF G–5, 35.08.

[10] (1) Analysis Sheet, SHAEF G–5, Hist Sec, Summary of Conference held at 1000, 10 Feb 44, presided over by Maj Gen Lumley, in SHAEF G–5, 16.02. (2) Memo, SHAEF CAD for CofS, sub: Organization of CA SHAEF, 11 Feb 44, in SHAEF G–5, 35.08.

[11] SHAEF, Staff Memo No. 2, 15 Feb 44, in SHAEF G–5, 15.02.

[12] Note in SHAEF G–5, 15.01.

in the Special Staff. The proponents of the Mediterranean system, however, had not yet scored a complete victory. Staff Memorandum No. 2 had in no way rescinded the Standard Policy and Procedure, which had been the fundamental guidance for the army groups and armies since December 1943. In fact, on 12 February Eisenhower had approved 21 Army Group's first joint air and ground force plan for the invasion, and General Sir Bernard L. Montgomery's staff, following the Standard Policy and Procedure, had assumed civil affairs to be an integral function of the tactical commands from the army group on down.[13] On 19 February, General Smith revealed that he had in fact not made a definitive choice between the proposed COSSAC and the Mediterranean systems; he approved a G–5 directive to McSherry, confirming the missions assigned to the DCCAO four days earlier but only during the planning and preparation for OVERLORD. The real issue, how civil affairs in northwestern Europe (military government in Germany) would be conducted during and after the invasion, then, remained undecided.[14]

After Holmes arrived in London, his and Lumley's views proved so divergent as to impel them, on 10 March, to appeal jointly to Smith for a decision.[15] On the surface, Lumley appeared to have entered an unequal contest; he had been a reluctant choice for G–5. Smith had asked for Holmes. Holmes had two proposals to make: the first, to cancel the Standard Policy and Procedure; the second, to issue a new directive to McSherry expanding his authority and extending it into the period following the invasion. Standard Policy and Procedure, Holmes argued, was inconsistent with Staff Memorandum No. 2. The memorandum placed civil affairs planning and operations on a countrywide basis, while the Standard Policy and Procedure put all the authority in the hands of the individual military commanders. Furthermore, the Standard Policy and Procedure made no provision for the so-called hiatus areas, parts of a liberated country which might not actually be occupied by SHAEF troops. This omission and the statements suggesting that SHAEF and its subordinate commands might not set up military governments everywhere they went were, Holmes insisted, in violation of both international law and declared United Nations objectives. Moreover, Holmes said, to claim, as some were doing, that the Standard Policy and Procedure had to be continued in force because it constituted the only guide for planning by subordinate echelons was fallacious. FM 27–5 and the British War Manual provided adequate general policy statements.[16]

As his second proposal, Holmes wanted to delegate the Supreme Commander's legal authority to conduct military government to McSherry as DCCAO, making him the commander of all civil affairs organizations in northwest Europe. He would appoint chiefs for each country, and the staffs at Army group and lower formations would be special staffs receiving their orders through civil affairs channels, not from the military commands. McSherry would control all of the civil affairs detachments working directly under SHAEF,

---

[13] Analysis Sheet, SHAEF G–5, Hist Sec, sub: ANXF, GOC 21 AGp, CINC, AEAF, to SCAEF, 1 Feb 44, in SHAEF G–5, 15.01.

[14] SHAEF G–5, Directive to DCCAO, Special Staff, SHAEF, 19 Feb 44, in SHAEF G–5, 16.01.

[15] Memo, SHAEF C–5 for CofS, sub: Organization of Civil Affairs, 10 Mar 44, in SHAEF G–5, 322.

[16] Memo, Brig Gen Holmes for CofS, sub: Standard Policy and Procedure, Brig Gen Holmes' Views, 9 Mar 44, in SHAEF G–5, 322.

issue technical instructions to any other detachments, and dispatch orders to the army group and lesser commands through the appropriate G sections of SHAEF.[17]

Lumley defended the Standard Policy and Procedure, not in its details but in what he called its basic conception, namely, that the first purpose of civil affairs was to further military operations. Full-scale military government, he therefore maintained, ought to be confined to the areas where military necessity was paramount, the zones of operations and communications. In hiatus areas of liberated countries the indigenous governments should be responsible, under just enough surveillance by SHAEF missions to make certain that they did not prejudice military operations by their actions or through failure to establish their authority. In the agreements with the exile governments, Lumley pointed out, promises had been given not to interfere in civil matters any more than was essential to military operations and to restore authority to the national governments as soon as the military situation permitted. Germany, he conceded, was a somewhat special case since the whole country would be placed under military government, and a country headquarters would be required because SHAEF would not relinquish control to a German government but rather to an Allied agency of some kind. To these arguments Lumley added one other: canceling the Standard Policy and Procedure would reverse and reject COSSAC's policy after it had been in effect for several months. "The British Army particularly" would not be happy, and much good will built up for civil affairs in the military staffs might be lost by so complete a turn-

about. The best course, he suggested, would be to keep the Standard Policy and Procedure in force as a general guide, supplementing it as needed with additional plans and directives while holding to the basic premise of civil affairs integration into the staffs at all levels.[18] The Supreme Commander, Lumley insisted, should delegate his military government authority not to a DCCAO but to the army group commanders, who could redelegate it as needed to their subordinate commanders. Plans drafted in the Special Staff would then be approved by G–5 and issued to the army groups for them to convert into operational directives.

Smith's reply read like a death sentence for the Mediterranean system. He admonished Lumley and Holmes, though Lumley scarcely needed it, to bear two points in mind: first, that the Mediterranean organization, although it did a good job, had many defects; and second, that conditions in northwest Europe were different from those in the Mediterranean. Therefore, he continued, civil affairs staffs would be closely integrated with normal staffs throughout the chain of command; civil affairs headquarters would not be established unrelated to military headquarters; and the AMGOT approach would be avoided. That AMGOT would not be duplicated in northwest Europe, he stated, had been directed in "the latest paper from the U.S. Chiefs of Staff."[19] Continuing, he described the Standard Policy and Procedure as a sound document in which revisions could be made as long as they did

[17] Memo, Brig Gen Holmes for CofS, sub: Organization of Civil Affairs, 9 Mar 44, in SHAEF G–5, 322.

[18] Memo, SHAEF G–5 for CofS, sub: Organization of Civil Affairs, Tab A, 10 Mar 44, in SHAEF G–5, 322.

[19] Smith was apparently referring to JCS 723, Administration of Germany in the Occupation Period, 22 Feb 44 (in CCS 383.21 [2–22–44], sec. 1).

not end in scrapping the basic principles. He rejected Holmes's proposals on organization completely except for a civil affairs technical communications channel, but even it would run through G–5 SHAEF to the appropriate sections in lower headquarters, not through the Special Staff. Although he had put operating personnel in the Special Staff, Smith insisted, he had not meant thereby to enhance the DCCAO's role. The command and staff channel would run from SHAEF and G–5. G–5 should add one or two officers to its Operations Branch for each of the national areas. In the operations zone, SHAEF would relieve the army groups of civil affairs duties outside combat areas as soon as it could, and would assume the responsibility itself.[20]

In the reply to Lumley and Holmes, Smith made the fundamental decision on civil affairs organization for the SHAEF period. He now accepted Standard Policy and Procedure, which he had undercut in Staff Memorandum No. 2, almost intact along with Lumley's defense of it. Lumley's success, however, unfortunately for him, was going to shorten his tenure as G–5 rather than prolong it.

If Smith had not changed his mind during the month after G–5 and the Special Staff were created, he had certainly developed a much firmer attitude toward the two systems than could have been deduced from Staff Memorandum No. 2. The reasons are not hard to find. He had no doubt concluded, as Lumley also suggested, that the Standard Policy and Procedure, even though it was sired by Colonel Bendetsen, an American, had been an agreed document, one which could not be discarded simply because Americans coming

from the Mediterranean liked the system they had used there better. Moreover, he had had time to become aware, if he had not been before, of the Quebec decision in August 1943 not to establish national military governments in liberated countries.[21] Most importantly, in the document to which Smith had referred in his reply to Lumley and Holmes, the JCS, while recognizing as Lumley had in his memorandum the probable need for some kind of co-ordinated military government, had described a fully combined U.S.–British military government on the pattern used in Italy as apparently not feasible for Germany.[22]

After Smith made his decision, although the controversy by no means ended, the case for the Standard Policy and Procedure rapidly became stronger. On 13 March Smith had asked how G–5 could be reorganized to permit it to supervise detailed planning and later on to co-ordinate operations on the Continent without country headquarters. In its answer, G–5 undertook to delineate the respective advantages of a functional organization (for example, supply, public health, labor, and law, without regard to national boundaries) and a regional organization. The functional organization as recommended in the Standard Policy and Procedure, G–5 maintained, would permit the Supreme Commander to govern with an even hand throughout northwest Europe and not have to contend with national staffs each devising its own policy. In any event most civil affairs problems would not fall within specific national boundaries. A regional organization, on the other hand, would ease the way for restora-

---

[20] Memo, CofS for Gen Lumley, Gen Holmes, sub: Organization of Civil Affairs, 14 Mar 44, in SHAEF G–5, 322.

[21] SHAEF G–5, Opns Br, Hist Sec, Chronology of Civil Affairs–Military Government, May 41–6 Jun 44, 2 Dec 44, p. 7, in SHAEF G–5, 60, Jacket 1.

[22] See fn. 19, above.

tion of national governments and would take account of differences in laws, languages, and customs. In general, the advantages of the one were the disadvantages of the other. Nevertheless, the weight of advantage lay on the functional side because Eisenhower's responsibility would be for the whole continent and many problems could be dealt with functionally without reference to boundaries, but few could be handled on a purely national basis. In its proposal, then, G–5 attempted to give predominance to the functional organization without entirely excluding the regional. G–5 would revise its functional branches to enable them also to cope with problems which required a national approach, and it would set up nuclei of a few officers around which national staffs could be built if they were required after operations began.[23]

Subsequently, the weight of advantage shifted even more decisively to the functional organization when Smith showed himself to be receptive. The Mediterranean system's advocates lost ground when they could not prove that because the system had been tested in action in Sicily and Italy it would succeed under different conditions in northwestern Europe. The proponents of the Standard Policy and Procedure, on the other hand, who had argued, while they were on the defensive, mainly for the basic concept, could also cite practical military advantages: the elimination of a separate civil affairs command channel, the direct tailoring of the civil affairs plan to the military plan, and the integration of civil affairs and military supplies. This last point was particularly telling. A frequent complaint of the civil affairs operation in

the Mediterranean had been that it had last call on shipping space for relief supplies and even when it was able to obtain ships could not get them loaded and unloaded. Under the Standard Policy and Procedure the military commanders, being responsible for civil affairs, would have to combine civil affairs supplies with their military supplies. One balance sheet drafted in G–5, probably in late March or early April, enumerated eleven points in favor of the functional organization as opposed to four for the Mediterranean system.[24]

Before the end of March the functional system clearly predominated. On the 24th, G–5 announced a forthcoming reorganization designed to eliminate the last serious doubts on this score and at the same time strike enough of a compromise to avoid an absolute rejection of the Mediterranean approach. G–5 would be divided into two parts, Policy and Operations. Policy, subdivided into functional branches, would come directly under the Assistant Chief of Staff, G–5. McSherry would head Operations, bringing enough officers with him from Shrivenham to establish country branches. He would retain the functions he had as DCCAO without the title, which in civil affairs usage implied direct subordination to the Supreme Commander who was also the Chief Civil Affairs Officer. He would gain one function, policy supervision of army group plans and their execution, but without direct command authority. He would also continue to control, through a deputy, the Special Staff which, made up of the country sections less the officers drawn into the Operations side of G–5, would stay at Shrivenham. Although McSherry if anything seemed to have gained

---

[23] Memo, SHAEF G–5 for Opns Br, sub: Reorganization of G–5 Div, 13 Mar 44, in SHAEF G–5, 15.01.

[24] Memo for record [no source], sub: Points of Policy at Issue [undated], in SHAEF G–5, 15.01.

somewhat, his and the Special Staff's loss of autonomy was a crippling blow for the Mediterranean system, and it was underscored by a provision that hard-and-fast lines would not be drawn to separate the competences of Operations and Policy.[25]

The watchword for SHAEF reorganizations in those early days was "no sooner said than done," but this one took over a month to accomplish. In part the delay can probably be attributed to the Mediterranean forces fighting a rear guard action, the rest, no doubt, to Smith's determination not to have Lumley as chief of the reorganized G–5. Smith had not been happy with Lumley in January and did not want him at all as Assistant Chief of Staff of a much enlarged G–5. Even though civil affairs would not have a separate role, he still wanted an officer with more rank and military stature than Lumley possessed. Lumley, like some other ranking British civil affairs officers, was not a professional soldier but a former colonial administrator, most recently governor of Bombay.[26] Smith, who by no means objected in principle to a uniformed civilian, did not see the same potentials in one from the upper reaches of the British civil service that he saw in a deft Pentagon and Washington hand like McCloy. Whether the G–5 chief was a civilian in uniform or career military, Smith's apprehension of the inherent touchiness of civil affairs made him prefer an American. But the position in the end fell to British Lt. Gen. Sir A. E. Grasett, until then chief of SHAEF's European Allied Contact Section. Although Smith proposed several American officers, Eisenhower preferred to leave the post to the British to avoid friction in an area where England had strong traditional interests.[27] Grasett took over as Assistant Chief of Staff, G–5, in mid-April, receiving his official appointment on the 22d. Lumley was relieved, and Holmes remained as deputy.

Among Grasett's first actions as G–5 was an attempt to lay to rest the Standard Policy and Procedure–Mediterranean system controversy still smoldering in the background. On 19 April he issued a policy statement for general distribution to serve "as a guide to all future planning and preparations." In the introductory paragraph he stated: "It has become apparent to me that some confusion of thought exists on the method by which civil affairs will be conducted once operations start. Time is short and cannot be wasted on fruitless discussion." SHAEF, he said, would control civil affairs operations directly, as would the subordinate commands. There would be no intermediate staffs between SHAEF and the forces in the field. How the country sections would be employed, if at all, had not been determined; but no matter what the decision, they would work under SHAEF, not independently of it, in the liberated countries and in Germany as well.[28]

The fight took its toll. Lt. Col. James H. Shoemaker, of the Provost Marshal General's Civil Affairs Division, in England at the time on a two-week tour of duty, found morale sagging. Most civil affairs officers, as far as he could discover, tended to favor the Standard Policy and Procedure system. General Holmes, however, still wanted a substantial role for the country sections, and many officers not familiar

[25] Memo, SHAEF G–5 for all Branches, sub: Reorganization of G–5, 24 Mar 44, in SHAEF G–5, 35.08.
[26] Pogue, *The Supreme Command*, p. 80.

[27] *Ibid.*, p. 82.
[28] Memo, SHAEF G–5 (Grasett) for Distribution, sub: CA Organization in the Field, 19 Apr 44, in OMGUS 3/35, dec. 322 CA.

with the whole picture saw only serious disorganization.[29]

On the 28th, Grasett announced the final form of the reorganization, to be effective on 1 May. G–5, Policy, would form six branches: legal, fiscal, supply, public health, displaced persons, and economics. Operations was to have a plans branch and six country sections. Through the Special Staff, it would supervise the old country sections at Shrivenham as units and the training sections at Eastbourne and Shrivenham.[30] Though this was not by any means to be the last reorganization, it did establish an important principle: as long as SHAEF existed, civil affairs and military government were to be a direct responsibility of the military commanders. The principle was underscored on 1 May in the publication of a revised Standard Policy and Procedure in which all of COSSAC Civil Affairs Division's basic assumptions were retained. Two concessions to the Mediterranean concept were added in the form of a provision for a direct civil affairs channel of communications and an authorization to establish civil affairs in and undertake rehabilitation of a whole country even though SHAEF forces occupied only a part of it.[31] The second point was in part also a response to the President's transfer of relief operations in Europe to the Army in November 1943.

The principle was established but the uncertainty did not diminish. Three weeks later, on 25 May, Brig. E. A. L. Gueterbock, McSherry's deputy in charge of the Special Staff, attempted to explain the status of the German Country Unit to its members. It was curious, he said. They were definitely not part of SHAEF. They were a planning unit but not a control mission in embryo, though they might someday in some fashion become one. He was sorry that it all sounded somewhat "woolly," but the decisions at the highest level had not yet been made.[32]

---

[29] Memo, PMG, MG Div, Liaison and Studies Br, Lt Col James H. Shoemaker, for Dir, MG Div, sub: Report on Two Weeks' Tour of Duty in ETO, 27 Apr 44, in PMG, MG Div, classified decimal file 300.7.

[30] (1) Memo, SHAEF G–5 for all Branches, sub: Reorganization of G–5 Div, 28 Apr 44, in SHAEF G–5, 35.08. (2) Memo, SHAEF G–5 for all Branches, sub: Reorganization of G–5 Div, 28 Apr 44, in SHAEF G–5 15.01.

[31] (1) Pogue, *The Supreme Command*, p. 83. (2) SHAEF, Standard Policy and Procedure for Combined Civil Affairs Operations in Northwest Europe, 1 May 44, in Admin Hist Collection, ETOUSA, Nr. 146, G–5 CA.

[32] Analysis Sheet, SHAEF G–5, Hist Sec, Ltr, Col C. E. D. Bridge, British Officer in German Unit, to Brig. E. A. L. Gueterbock, sub: War Establishment, 23 May 44, in SHAEF G–5, 15.02.

CHAPTER V

SHAEF's New Missions

Displaced Persons

One of the familiar human products of war is the refugee, the resident of a combat zone set adrift either by anticipated or actual destruction of his home and means of livelihood. An object of pity as an individual, in the mass he becomes a menace, clogs roads, imposes potentially ruinous burdens on already strained civilian services, and spreads panic. The British and French had some experience with refugees in the 1940 campaign, and it had become accepted Allied doctrine that the Germans were exceptionally adept at exploiting these unfortunates for tactical and even strategic advantage.

To the traditional picture of the refugee, the war had by 1944 added another figure, the displaced person (DP). A refugee was almost always a citizen of the country in which he was encountered and usually no great distance from home. If he was a potential threat, he was at least a transitory one. In liberated territory the local authorities could be expected to take care of him, and in enemy territory they would be compelled to do so. The DP was a different and more complex species altogether. He and his fellows had only two characteristics in common: they would all be citizens of one of the United Nations (by definition, enemy aliens no matter where they were found could not qualify), and they would all be outside their national boundaries at the time of liberation. They were certain

in large numbers to be Russians and Poles with some Yugoslavs and Greeks, and inside Germany would be French, Belgians, and Dutch. They were the result of the vast transfer of population that Germany had begun in early 1942 to provide labor for its war industry, farms, and military construction. An Allied agency had estimated that as of October 1943 there were 21 million displaced persons in Europe, mainly in Germany or in territory annexed by the Reich.[1] To the DPs could be added an indeterminate but large number of what would later come to be called RAMPs (recovered Allied military personnel): prisoners of war of all nationalities, many of whom had been held in Germany since the early campaigns of the war and, if they were soldiers of defeated nations, used as common labor.

Even at a distance and in the abstract, the DPs constituted a towering problem for SHAEF. Allied propaganda had played heavily on the plight of the so-called slave laborers, making their liberation and rehabilitation major United Nations war aims. Persuaded by their own propaganda, which in fact proved all too true, the military planners assumed that the DPs' first desire at the moment they realized they were free would be to get away from their German masters and, if possible, get out of Germany. The human flood thus unloosed would vastly overshadow the refugee

[1] Donnison, *CA–MG, Central Organization and Planning,* p. 192.

problems of the British and French in 1940. Furthermore, the DPs could not be left for the Germans to control. As victims of nazism and as United Nations citizens, they would become SHAEF's responsibility. Initially, they would have to be prevented from hopelessly clogging the armies' routes of advance and communications; secondly, they would have to be cared for with some solicitude; finally, they would have to be returned to their homes. The interval between the first and the last stage might be a long one since it would be determined by the state of the war, the condition of the European transportation systems, and in some instances by the people themselves, not all of whom would be able or willing to return to their home countries.

The DPs, moreover, could not be ignored even briefly or in the heat of battle, for they might harbor among them a danger to human life, both military and civilian, that was potentially greater than the war itself—the virus-like micro-organism *Rickettsia*. A benign parasite of the body louse, *Rickettsia*, when it passes from the feces of a louse into a human body through a bite or opening in the skin, causes typhus, the most feared epidemic disease in Europe since the bubonic plague. Napoleon's army in Russia reportedly suffered more losses from typhus than from combat. During and after World War I, an estimated three million persons died from the disease in the Balkans and the Ukraine. In World War II, a thousand cases had been registered in Naples by early 1944. Always serious and frequently fatal, typhus is endemic in parts of eastern Europe. When war breaks out it begins to spread; humans carrying the louse, host of the disease, provide its transportation. The Germans encountered it in their eastern campaigns, and it was known to have come into Germany with forced laborers and transports to concentration camps.[2]

The U.S. government had established the U.S. Typhus Commission in December 1942 to study the disease and devise methods of control.[3] By early 1944, DDT had been proven highly effective against the louse, hence indirectly also against the disease; however, it had to be applied individually and more than once, since it killed the insect but did not affect the eggs. In a reasonably static population, DDT could in a short time practically wipe out the disease; in a mass eruption and uncontrolled migration of people, carriers might still spread it from one end of Europe to the other in a few weeks.

"Displaced Persons" appeared for the first time as a separate branch of the G-5 in the reorganization of 1 May 1944. (In the Standard Policy and Procedure the designation "DP" was still regarded as a synonym for refugee, and pertinent duties were divided among the civil affairs detachments in the field, the provost marshal, and the local police.)[4] Although nobody then knew what the DPs' full impact on military government would be, the branch from the beginning was one of two reserved for a senior U.S. officer (Supply being the other). On 13 May, General Gullion became branch chief.[5]

Monuments, Fine Arts, and Archives

Next to simple ignorance and neglect, war has always been the greatest destroyer

---

[2] Hqs, U.S. First Army, Office of Civil Affairs, sub: Control of Typhus Fever, 12 May 44, in SHAEF G-5, 17.16.

[3] EO 9285, 24 Dec 42.

[4] SHAEF, Standard Policy and Procedure, par. 115.

[5] SHAEF G-5, Opns Br, Hist Sec, Chronology of Civil Affairs–Military Government, May 41–6 Jun 44, 2 Dec 44, p. 26, in SHAEF G-5, 60, Jacket 1.

of man's noblest relic of his past, and what fire and pillage once had done, the bombers and artillery of World War II could do a thousand times more completely. In its conception alone, Operation OVERLORD—a massive armed sweep, with tactical and strategic air support, across northern France and the Low Countries and into Germany as deep as might be necessary to bring down nazism—made a strong bid to break all previous records for destructiveness. The war thus far had not been quite as devastating as anticipated. The art, particularly the architecture, of Italy was in great danger, but the war there was on nowhere near the scale contemplated for northwest Europe. In their early campaigns, the Germans had won rather easily; consequently, they had been careful to spare valuable art and buildings even in the East. After all, among their topmost leaders were several admirers and collectors of art. To the Americans and the British the protection of art and historical monuments had been an entirely peripheral consideration until they landed in Sicily and Italy in the summer of 1943.

The Italian campaign, however, had revealed the military commanders to be distinctly unwilling to risk tactical advantage or the lives or welfare of their troops to protect cultural intangibles. Neither could civilians, in the midst of a life-or-death ideological struggle, easily urge soldiers in battle to respect the shrines. Nevertheless, knowledgeable individuals and groups both inside and outside the government were deeply concerned with at least preventing needless destruction. In early 1943, the American Defense–Harvard Group and the Committee on Protection of Cultural Treasures in War Areas of the American Council of Learned Societies (ACLS) had begun preparing inventories of European cultural monuments, museums, and private collections. They received valuable assistance from the Frick Art Reference Library, where the staff was already engaged in producing cultural maps and atlases. By spring 1944, the ACLS committee was able to furnish for Army publication detailed maps showing the locations of cultural monuments in continental Europe, information on looted art objects, and instructions for salvage and protection of art work to be included in civil affairs handbooks.[6]

Inside the government, Justice Harlan F. Stone of the U.S. Supreme Court had asked the President, on 8 December 1942, to create an organization for the protection and conservation of works of art, monuments, and records in Europe; and in the spring of 1943 the U.S. government had proposed establishing an Allied agency for such purposes to the British and the Russians. In August 1943 the President had appointed Supreme Court Justice Owen J. Roberts chairman of an interdepartmental committee to be known as the American Commission for the Protection and Salvage of Artistic and Historic Monuments in Europe. The Roberts Commission, as it quickly came to be known, took in hand the vast job of assessing in detail the extent of German and other Axis appropriation of cultural property and acted as the Army's channel to museums and universities for information and for personnel.[7]

By early 1943 the War Department, too, had recognized the desirability of protecting European art and monuments from war damage. On 1 April General Wickersham, Director of the School of Military

---

[6] USFET, General Board, Study No. 36, Civil Affairs and Military Government Activities in Connection with Monuments, Fine Arts, and Archives, 11 May 46, in Hist Div, Hqs, ETO, 97–USF 5–03.0.

[7] *Ibid.*

Government, writing to the Acting Director, Civil Affairs Division, recommended commissioning several art experts and, after they had taken the course at Charlottesville, attaching one or two as advisers to each theater commander's staff. In July, Hilldring had reported to McCloy that the directive for the Sicilian landing contained a reference to the preservation of historic monuments and that Eisenhower had been given two experts as staff advisers and had been supplied with all the material the ACLS Committee on Protection of Cultural Treasures in War Areas had so far completed. By the fall of 1943, the protection of art treasures "to the fullest extent consistent with military operations" had become established War Department policy; and in April 1944, Col. Henry C. Newton, an architect in civilian life, was brought into the Civil Affairs Division to set up procedures for putting the War Department policy and the work for the civilian groups into effect.[8]

Overseas, the Monuments, Fine Arts, and Archives Subcommission (MFA&A) had readily found a place in civil affairs, first in AMGOT and later, on the COSSAC staff. Determining its functions, however, was a more difficult matter, one which would never be completely settled. Within civil affairs, MFA&A was an anomaly in that it was basically less concerned with the affairs of civilians than with the actions of its own troops.

In Sicily and Italy and as projected in COSSAC's Standard Policy and Procedure, the MFA&A mission was to protect historic buildings and art work against wanton damage and looting but to do so without encroaching on the troop commander's overriding concerns where the outcome of a battle or his troops' lives and welfare in or out of combat were at stake. A line between avoidable and unavoidable damage was impossible to draw since each case could ultimately be judged only by one man, the commander on the spot. Consequently, beyond what could be accomplished by advice and persuasion, MFA&A on its own authority could do little in the way of active protection. Most often it could not begin to function until after the most crucial time had passed. Although even then, no doubt, much could often still be done to prevent further damage, the MFA&A role tended to become less that of a guardian than of an insurance adjustor assessing the loss, looking for what was salvageable, and attempting to forestall unwarranted claims. Late in December 1943, shortly before he left the Mediterranean, Eisenhower had undertaken to strengthen the preventive and protective aspect of MFA&A by directing higher commanders to determine the locations of historic monuments ahead of and behind their lines and to keep in mind and impress on their subordinates that the term "military necessity" did not embrace military or personal convenience.[9] Although he required only compliance with the spirit of the directive, Eisenhower ordered separately on the same day that no building listed as a work of art in the zone handbooks on Italy was to be used for military purposes without his or the 15 Army Group commander's permission in each case.[10]

MFA&A in SHAEF, after a somewhat uncertain start in COSSAC (the first American art expert to arrive was sent down to Shrivenham to be a librarian because he did not possess enough military rank), began its existence with two modest

---

[8] *Ibid.*

[9] Coles and Weinberg, *Soldiers Become Governors*, p. 417.
[10] USFET, General Board, Study No. 36.

advantages: it was better situated within the military chain of command, at least theoretically, than it had been in the Mediterranean where, with the rest of civil affairs, it was completely separate; and it could assume from the outset that the tenor of Eisenhower's December directive for Italy would also apply in northern Europe. In January, Professor Geoffrey Webb, Slade Professor of Fine Arts at Cambridge University, became the semiofficial MFA&A adviser to the Supreme Commander pending his confirmation as civilian adviser and subsequent appointment as lieutenant colonel and section chief. The MFA&A functions that he proposed were to protect monuments and art work from avoidable loss or damage, prevent their deterioration after combat, and collect evidence on German looting or desecration. The civil affairs instructions for OVERLORD, issued in February, confirmed these duties and added requirements for protecting Allied governments from false claims and Allied troops from slanderous accusations. To execute its missions, MFA&A was to have four officers attached to each army, one at army headquarters and three with the frontline troops. The chief would further maintain a pool of eight officers at SHAEF. Since experience had demonstrated that without some weight of rank MFA&A officers were helpless, the chief was to be a lieutenant colonel and the other officers majors. To avoid immobility, which had long beset MFA&A in the Mediterranean, the section would have three jeeps and a truck of its own.[11]

Compared with the setup in the Mediterranean, the MFA&A organization proposed for SHAEF appeared almost ideal.

As such, unfortunately, it was also to prove unattainable even within the elaborate SHAEF structure. Military organizations do not easily assimilate highly specialized, autonomous functions; consequently, for MFA&A within the military chain the question was still not what was desirable but rather what was feasible. This situation was true both in personnel and in organization. The argument that MFA&A officers needed the prestige of rank could not prevail against the Army's reluctance to grant field grade commissions to art specialists with no military experience; therefore, what MFA&A received were captains and lieutenants. While Professor Webb awaited his own confirmation as civilian adviser, which did not come until 1 April, MFA&A led a shadow existence within G–5, SHAEF; and the German and French country units in the Special Staff at Shrivenham set up their own MFA&A subsections which, as Webb at one point complained, scarcely seemed aware that a policy-making section existed in G–5.[12] In the 1 May 1944 G–5 reorganization, MFA&A suffered the ultimate indignity: it did not appear in the organization chart at all. The omission was not remedied until nearly a month later when a place was made for it in the Operations Branch.

For a time in April, MFA&A in northwest Europe even seemed about to be reduced to the impotence it had experienced during the early months in Italy. When the Governmental Affairs Branch, Special Staff, recommended issuing a letter and a general order similar to those Eisenhower had put out in Italy in December 1943, G–5 Operations objected on the ground that existing civil affairs instructions pro-

---

[11] *Ibid.*

[12] Coles and Weinberg, *Soldiers Become Governors,* p. 864.

vided ample protection for art and monuments.[13]

Although, as the end of the planning period approached, MFA&A had still not found a secure position in the command structure, it did at the last minute find strong support at least for its purpose. Over all objections, Webb had insisted that an order on art and monuments from the Supreme Commander, not merely instructions to civil affairs officers, was necessary in northwestern Europe where initially the British and American troops would be fighting on friendly territory. In May, Colonel Newton of the Civil Affairs Division, at the time the War Department's candidate ultimately to become military chief of SHAEF's MFA&A, visited the theater. Although Newton did not get the appointment, he took a strong and somewhat influential interest in assuring MFA&A's effectiveness and supported Webb's stand. Moreover, on 15 February, U.S. bombers in Italy had unloaded six hundred tons of bombs on the monastery at Monte Cassino, one of the oldest and most venerated historical structures in Europe. The Allied command considered military necessity proven beyond question, but the prospect of more such instances in the future pointed up the need for a firm policy. On 26 May, Eisenhower addressed a letter to the army group, naval, and air commanders for OVERLORD. In it he made every commander responsible for protecting and respecting the historical monuments and cultural centers "which symbolize to the world all we are fighting for." Where success of the military operation would be prejudiced, as at Cassino, military necessity would prevail even if it meant the

destruction of some honored site. But in the many instances where damage and destruction could not be justified, commanders would be responsible for preserving objects of historical and cultural signficance.[14] In the second week of June, SHAEF dispatched official lists of monuments together with atlases to the army groups for distribution down to the divisions.

A Directive for Germany

Although planning for Germany was excluded from the COSSAC's range of civil affairs competence, Morgan's staff had been aware that a sharp division between the end of the military phase of OVERLORD-RANKIN and the beginning of the occupation proper would not be possible. In December 1943, Lumley had detailed Lt. Col. Sir T. St. Vincent Troubridge to study the German administrative system and determine how it could be adapted to the initiation of military government in Germany. Completed in January 1944 and thereafter referred to as Slash 100, taken from its file number, the Troubridge study looked at the transition from war to occupation as a process rather than as a single event conditional on the German surrender.[15] From Slash 100, SHAEF derived both the requirement for and the limits of its participation in the occupation of Germany. These aspects were expressed in terms of three phases: a military phase of complete military government either set up before

---

[13] USFET, General Board, Study No. 36.

[14] AG (SHAEF G–5, 751) to GOC 21st AGp, CG U.S. 1st AGp, Allied Naval Commander, Exped Force, Air CinC, Allied Exped Forces, sub: Preservation of Historical Monuments, 26 May 44, in SHAEF G–5, 10.

[15] SHAEF G–5, Hist Div, Historical Statement of the German Country Unit, Aug 44, in SHAEF G–5, 60, Jacket 10.

the German final collapse or necessitated by chaotic conditions in Germany after the surrender; a transitional middle phase in which the military command would pass its authority to a control commission; and a final phase in which the occupation would assume permanent form.[16] On this basis the Supreme Commander could assume that he would have a military government mission in Germany before the surrender and for an indeterminate period thereafter.

The Supreme Commander could assume that he had a mission but not much more. Responsibility for launching the occupation would probably be his, but its nature and purposes were almost totally unknown. The second and third phases, as Slash 100 pointed out, depended on political decisions which had not yet been made. This deficiency loomed large as soon as G–5 moved into the planning for the first phase. On 10 February, Smith laid the problem before the CCAC (Combined Civil Affairs Committee). SHAEF, he said, was beginning to plan for military government in Germany, recognizing that its direct concern was only with the first phase, but such SHAEF decisions could affect the whole occupation machinery. Therefore, the first phase policies ought to be attuned from the start to those of the other two phases. To accomplish this, SHAEF needed political and economic guidelines.[17]

Smith did not know it, but he had asked the impossible. There was no agency that could give him what he wanted nor would there be one for the duration of SHAEF's

existence. The first impulse in the CCAC was to put Smith off with an assurance that the major policy decisions could be expected from the European Advisory Commission (EAC) in due time.[18] To do so, however, would have amounted to CCAC's abdicating its function as the source of combined civil affairs policy as far as Germany was concerned. Furthermore, the U.S. Joint Chiefs of Staff had independently arrived at an estimate of the way the occupation would be imposed on Germany that coincided with the SHAEF view derived from Slash 100; consequently, as far as the U.S. staff was concerned, Smith's request was highly pertinent.[19] The JCS, therefore, agreed that SHAEF would most likely have to establish military government in Germany and maintain it for what "could be considerable length of time" after the capitulation. Hilldring sent this information to Smith on 22 February.[20]

However, as Supreme Commander, Eisenhower was under the CCS not the JCS, and his instructions would have to come through the CCS in order to be valid. In the CCAC, the British members proposed, not unexpectedly but nevertheless disquietingly for the Americans, that the questions Smith had raised be referred to the CCAC(L), which could secure opinions directly from the EAC.[21] Thereafter, for both the British and the Americans the issue became one of supplying an adequate answer to Smith without prejudicing either Washington's or London's claim to be the fountainhead of occupation policy. In a meeting on 9 March, Hilldring advanced

---

[16] Memo, CCAC, Director to Civil Affairs Division, sub: Problems of Occupation of Germany, 27 Feb 44, in ASW 370.8.

[17] Cable, SHAEF to CCAC, sub: The Administrative System of Germany and Some Problems of Occupation, 10 Feb 44, in OPD, ABC 387, sec. 7–A.

[18] CCAC 69, Proposed Cable, CCS to SCAEF [no date], in OPD, ABC 387, sec. 7–A.

[19] Ltr, JCS to Sec of State, JCS 623, Appendix B, 18 Dec 43, in OPD, ABC 387, sec. 1–A.

[20] JCS 723, Administration of MG in Germany–Occupation Period, 22 Feb 44, in SHAEF G–5, 30.

[21] History of the CAD, bk. VI, p. 18.

the thought that the EAC, as a negotiating body for the governments, would not be much help as a source for informal judgments and advice; he stated that the Civil Affairs Division (CAD) was already well along in drafting basic directives for Germany which ought soon to be expanded into detailed directives. Four days later the British representatives suggested issuing an interim directive to take effect before the EAC completed its work, the details being left to the CCAC(L).[22]

In a meeting on 19 March, McCloy asserted that the military could not wait for the EAC to act. A military directive would have to be prepared beforehand and the necessity for it would have to be made clear to the British and Soviet governments. Hilldring added that, as a matter of fact, the CAD had completed a draft of a basic directive which it would submit for British approval and for expansion in detail by the CCAC(L). Alarmed at the broad hint in McCloy's remarks that the Americans were ready to ignore the EAC entirely, the British conceded that since the Russians probably had their own prepared directives for fringe areas such as Estonia and East Prussia, the Americans and British could probably do the same, "having in mind the recommendations being put forward by the U.S. and U.K. representatives on the EAC."[23] Having reached an agreement, which as usual was open to disparate interpretation, the CCAC finally sent a reply to Smith telling him a directive for Germany was being prepared.[24]

Another six weeks passed before the directive reached Eisenhower by special air courier on 28 April as "CCS 551," because it first had to be transmitted to London for British review and approval. At British insistence the scope was limited specifically to the period before the German defeat or surrender to avoid infringing on the competence of the London-based EAC. In the meantime, working parties in the CCAC had prepared supplementary political, financial, and economic and relief guides.

The basic directive was Eisenhower's charter to establish military government in whatever parts of Germany his forces occupied. As Supreme Commander he would have the supreme executive, legislative, and judicial authority which he could delegate as necessary to his subordinate commanders. Military government administration, however, would be identical throughout the occupied parts of Germany.[25]

A political guide, sent with the directive, stated that military government was to be "firm . . . at the same time just and humane with regard to the civilian population as far as consistent with strict military requirements." The purposes were to be to assist continuing military operations, to destroy nazism and fascism, to maintain law and order, and to restore normal conditions in the population as soon as possible.[26]

Financial and economic and relief guides reached SHAEF on 31 May. The first provided for tight control of German banking and currency and for the introduction of Allied military marks as occupation currency. The Allied military marks were to be used in Germany by the U.S., British, and Soviet forces, each country redeeming

---

[22] *Ibid.*, p. 19.

[23] Min, CCAC 26th Meeting, 16 Mar 44, in SHAEF G–5, 3–A.

[24] Cable, Gov 15 (CCAC 69/2), 19 Mar 44, in OPD, ABC 387, sec. 7–A.

[25] Analysis Sheet, SHAEF G–5, Hist Sec, sub: Directive for MG in Germany Prior to Defeat or Surrender, 6 May 44, in SHAEF G–5, 1–A.

[26] CCAC 69/5 [CCS 551], Directive for Military Government in Germany Prior to Defeat or Surrender, 28 Apr 44, in CCS 383.21 (2–22–44), sec. 1.

them in its national currency for its own troops. The Germans would continue to use the Reichsmark and would only be able to exchange Allied military marks for Reichsmarks.

The U.S. Bureau of Engraving and Printing in Washington had made plates for the Allied military marks earlier in the year and had begun printing for all three governments when the Soviet Union demanded it be given duplicate plates from which to do its own printing. The Soviet government had explained, with almost disarming candor, that it wanted to do its own printing to be sure of having a constant supply of marks available. Neither the Americans nor the British had openly raised the obvious objection to putting duplicate plates in Soviet hands, namely, the lack of control over the amounts printed; but the British had argued against relinquishing the plates on the ground that the whole issue might be discredited because of the unlikelihood of the Russians' being able to produce identical notes even from duplicate plates, which in fact proved fortunately true. For both the British and the Americans, however, the real dilemma was whether or not they wanted to see a separate Soviet occupation currency introduced into Germany, a move which the Russians threatened to make if they were not given the plates. To avoid such a development and its implications for projected Allied unity in the occupation, the duplicate plates had been made and sent.[27]

The economic and relief guide combined two marginally related subjects in one paper. The economic part gave Eisenhower full control over German industrial produc-

tion which he was instructed to use to orient German industry toward helping the war against Japan, to convert industry not needed against Japan to peacetime production, to make goods available for restitution and reparations, and to integrate the German economy into the European and world economies. With regard to relief, the guide specified that critical German shortages were to be alleviated only to the minimum extent necessary to prevent disease and unrest. Excess German food and other commodities were to be used for relief in liberated countries.[28] After he received the guide, Eisenhower pointed out that it assumed a surplus in Germany but made no provision in the event the assumption proved wrong. The CCAC then revised the guide and empowered him to plan for relief in Germany on the same scale as in liberated countries, except that if supplies proved inadequate, Germany as the enemy country would receive the lesser share.[29]

Although the directive and the guides categorically disclaimed any purpose beyond providing Eisenhower with a basis for conducting military government in areas he might occupy before the surrender, they were obviously conceived as being readily convertible to final policy statements. They were firm, even severe, on specifics but on the whole remarkably moderate. Although the elimination of nazism and of the German ability to make war were assumed, the mission would be to restore normal conditions and to recreate a peaceable Germany. The authors had learned Colonel Hunt's lessons well, but The Hunt Report

---

[27] Min, CCAC, 27th Meeting (1 Apr 44) and 28th Meeting (13 Apr 44), 1 and 15 Apr 44, in SHAEF G–5, 3–A.

[28] CCAC 69/8, Directive for Military Government in Germany Prior to Defeat or Surrender, 31 May 44, in CCS 383.21 (2–22–44), sec. 1.

[29] (1) Memo, Dir, CAD, sub: Civilian Relief in Germany, 19 Jul 44, in SHAEF G–5, 3–A. (2) Cable, CCS to SHAEF, 19 Aug 44, in CCS 383.21 (2–22–44), sec. 2.

had been absorbed only into Army doctrine, not into United States high policy.
Elsewhere, specifically in the White House,
other lessons were being drawn from the
two world wars.

Eisenhower and Smith had been troubled since the inception of SHAEF by the
unconditional surrender formula. In April,
when Under Secretary of State Edward R.
Stettinius, Jr., visited London, they asked
for a clarification, an announcement of
principles on which the treatment of defeated Germany would be based, in order
to "create a mood of acceptance of unconditional surrender in the German Army."
They proposed a political directive similar
in tenor to CCS 551 then being drafted
in the CCAC, one that would differentiate
between the crimes of nazism and militarism and the German people's desire for
a tolerable future.[30] Stettinius took the request to the President who declared himself open-minded but inquired how Eisenhower imagined he could back up any
promise to the Germans that they would
be treated humanely when he would have
to be speaking also for the Russians, the

Norwegians, and all the other peoples who
had suffered in the war and would not be
inclined "to be soft."[31] Actually, the President had a month before flatly rejected a
similar proposal from the JCS.[32] He had
said then: "The trouble is that the reasoning . . . presupposes reconstituting a German state which would give active co-operation apparently at once to peace in
Europe. A somewhat long study and personal experience in and out of Germany
leads me to believe that the Germany philosophy cannot be changed by decree, law,
or military order. The change in German
philosophy must be evolutionary and may
take two generations. To assume otherwise
is to assume, of necessity, a period of quiet
followed by a third world war."[33]

---

[30] Cable, Stettinius to Sec of State, 13 Apr 44,
in USFET SGS 091.412.

[31] Ltr, E. R. Stettinius to Hon Wm. Phillips,
11 May 44, in USFET SGS 371.
[32] The JCS had urged that because the Nazi
propaganda interpretation of unconditional surrender was bolstering the German will to resist,
Allied propaganda should "stress that ordinary
Germans will be given a chance to live normal
lives." (1) JCS 718, Effect of "Unconditional
Surrender" Policy on German People, 19 Feb 44,
in CCS 387 (12–17–43), sec. 2. (2) Memo, JCS
for the President, 25 Mar 44, in OPD, ABC 387,
sec. 3.
[33] Memo, F. D. R. for the Joint Chiefs of Staff,
1 Apr 44, in OPD, ABC 387, sec. 3.

CHAPTER VI

Shrivenham and Manchester

The Civil Affairs Center

Shrivenham, situated a few miles north of the railroad from London to Bath and Bristol, is not found on every map; and gazetteers, when they do so at all, give its location in relation to Swindon, which lies six miles to the southeast and bears the distinction of actually being on the railroad. A thoroughly unremarkable Berkshire village of somewhat less than six hundred inhabitants, Shrivenham was, nevertheless, long to remain in the memories of the World War II generation of American civil affairs officers—excepting possibly the minority who experienced the elegance (mostly architectural) of the British center in the Grand Hotel at Eastbourne.

On the grounds of what had been a private school for girls at Shrivenham, ETOUSA had established the American School Center in the summer of 1942 to train officer candidates and various categories of supply specialists. When Colonel Stearns visited there in October 1943 looking for space to billet the American civil affairs contingent, he found room for 1,000 men. Upon activating the Civil Affairs Center in December, he planned to receive the shipments of civil affairs officers and enlisted men at Shrivenham and there assign them to detachments and give them additional training.[1] The program, as it de-

veloped, envisioned a regulated, synchronized flow of officers and men and a course of training and instruction that would produce fully organized and equipped detachments, each thoroughly acquainted with its pinpoint assignment—the actual locality for which it would be responsible in the occupation.[2] The detachments which had completed their training would be sent to Manchester, where Stearns had located 8,000 billets, to await their move to the Continent.

The program looked good, but some early signs were ominous. On close inspection, Shrivenham proved to be sorely wanting in the amenities expected by officers, particularly field grade officers, of whom there would be a substantial number. All officers, lieutenant colonels and below, would have to be billeted sixteen to a room. They would do their own cleaning and sweeping, and some rooms would have to double as classrooms in the daytime. The officers would be required to carry knives, forks, and cups to the dining hall where they would eat off compartmented·metal trays which they would have to wash themselves.[3]

---

[1] SHAEF G–5, Hist Sec, The Education and Training of Allied Officers for Duty with Civil Affairs, Military Government, European Theater of Operations, Sep 41–July 45 [no date], in SHAEF G–5, 60, Jacket 7.

[2] Rpt, ECAD Training Div, Admin Sec, to Director of Training Div, sub: Organization and Activities Through 27 May 44, in SHAEF G–5, 604.

[3] Memo, SHAEF CAD for ACofS G–5, sub: Accommodations at Joint CA Center, 19 Feb 44, in SHAEF G–5, 17.03.

On the other side of the Atlantic, the Provost Marshal General's Office had found the morale of the officers who were slated for shipment to Shrivenham already sagging. One of its inspectors who observed the graduates of the Civil Affairs Training Program (CATP) assembled at Camp Reynolds, Pennsylvania, reported that they were "feeling pretty well kicked around." Many had graduated from the course in one university and then been sent to another to take the same course a second time. All they would accomplish at Camp Reynolds would be to acquire enough familiarity with the .45-caliber pistol to fire for record. They would then go to the staging area at Camp Kilmer, New Jersey, where they would wait for an undetermined time before being shipped out.[4]

In December, when Stearns set up the Civil Affairs Center there, Shrivenham, in addition to being the reception and training depot, became the administrative headquarters for civil affairs–military government in the field. The Civil Affairs Center proposed to continue as parent organization for the detachments after they were formed and when they went into action on the Continent. For the time being, however, two functions, assignment and training, overshadowed everything else.

For the incoming officer, his encounter with the assignment division of the Civil Affairs Center could easily be the most important event in his military career. Its four boards would determine where he was to serve, and this placement in most instances proved permanent. The numerical designation of each board, as new officers quickly learned, reflected the level and, hence, desirability of the assignments it controlled.

The first board selected men for army group, army, corps, and division staffs, the second for civil affairs detachments, and the third for service with the British. The fourth board, really the first in the order in which incoming officers encountered them, screened all officers and sent them on to the others for final assignment. The vast majority of the officers would go to the detachments. The early assumption was that British and U.S. personnel would be mixed about fifty-fifty, but, in fact, only 250 U.S. officers were sent to Eastbourne, and they later returned to serve with American detachments.

The detachment board additionally selected officers for specific types of detachments.[5] There were four types: A (17 officers, 2 warrant officers, and 24 enlisted men), B (9 officers, 2 warrant officers, and 16 enlisted men), C (5 officers and 9 enlisted men), and D (4 officers and 6 enlisted men).[6] The A detachments were designed for employment in major cities, including national capitals such as Berlin and Paris, and were regarded as elite detachments. The others would be stationed in smaller cities or rural communities. The A and B detachments offered the most desirable berths in terms of probable location and opportunity to specialize, not to mention rank and prospects for advancement. But the C and D detachments, although individually smaller and destined most likely to operate in unglamorous and out-of-the-way places, would be needed in far greater numbers and would absorb the larger number of officers.

The training division had the mission of

---

[4] Memo, Col Harley L. Swift for Col George G. Berry, sub: Camp Reynolds Inspection, 7 Jan 44, in PMG, MG Div, classified decimal file 333.

[5] Hqs, CA Center, American School Center, to Chief, Hist Subsec, COSSAC, 31 Dec 44, in SHAEF G–5, 17.02.

[6] Memo, Liaison Officer at FUSAG for Col H. McE. Pendleton, sub: G–5, Its Evolution and Functions, 17 May 44, in USFET CAD 314.7.

turning out essentially finished detachments, an estimated 70 of them for France and 273 for Germany.[7] As originally planned, each class would be given two months of general civil affairs instruction and military training which would be followed by an indefinite period of regional study and planning for pinpointed areas. In the later part of the second stage the enlisted men would join the teams. Col. Hardy C. Dillard, who had been associated with civil affairs training since its early days in the Provost Marshal General's Office and at Charlottesville, was transferred from the United States to head the division. On his arrival in December along with the 48-officer faculty and staff, most of them also from the United States, the division opened at Shrivenham with no students. When the first forty students came in mid-January, they were outnumbered by the faculty.

The regulated flow of officers that had been planned was not going to materialize. At noon on 27 January the first large shipment, 416 officers, arrived at Shrivenham with full field packs after a twenty-hour trip by train from port. The center mustered enough trucks to transport the lieutenant colonels and majors; all the others marched the two miles from the station in rain carrying their packs. Two days later, while the boards were immersed in interviews with the first group, another 308 officers arrived.

At the end of the month the Civil Affairs Center, with none two weeks before, now had 770 officer trainees aboard and, if nothing else, a statistical sample of the men who would make up the civil affairs organization in the field. About 40 percent of the officers were commissioned directly from civilian life. The rest had received their

commissions in other branches of the Army or in the National Guard. The youngest was 22 years old, the oldest 60. The average age was a few months short of 40; and the largest single increments were from ages 38 to 46, which together constituted about 40 percent of the total.[8] (Subsequent shipments brought the proportion of commissioned civilians down to near 30 percent, but the average age remained constant.)[9] Youth was going to be in somewhat short supply, which was no surprise since few officers below the draft age limit, 38 years, and in first-rate physical condition had been accepted for civil affairs duty.

Maturity was considered to be an asset in a civil affairs officer. It did not prove to be so for many, however, in their initial confrontation with the English climate. On 14 February, out of a thousand officers then at Shrivenham, 46 percent went on sick call, most with colds which had already put 10 percent in the hospital.[10]

On 7 February, after the assignment boards had processed the January arrivals and detailed at least an officer or two as a cadre to each of the 343 detachments, the training division started its first course. By then the center was on notice to expect another thousand officers at the end of the month and large shipments of enlisted men in March. With these additions, the civil affairs force for northwest Europe would be practically complete, and something would have to be found for it to do, since RANKIN was dimming and OVERLORD not expected until late spring. In both opera-

---

[7] SHAEF G–5, Hist Sec, Education and Training, in SHAEF G–5, 60, Jacket 7.

[8] Hist Rpt, Hqs, CAC, ASC, to Chief, Hist Subsec, SHAEF, sub: Activities of CAC, 18 Jan–1 Feb 44, in SHAEF G–5, 17.12.

[9] Hist Rpt, Hqs, CAC, ASC, to Chief, Hist Sec, SHAEF G–5, sub: Activities at CAC, 15 Feb–1 Mar 44, in SHAEF G–5, 17.02.

[10] Hist Rpt, CAC, ASC, to Chief, Hist Sec, SHAEF G–5, sub: Activities of CAC, 1 Feb–15 Feb 44, in SHAEF G–5, 17.12.

tions, civil affairs–military government had the same two, though not mutually complementary, missions: to be ready and to wait. Waiting would be the more difficult.

Before the first course began, the training division had revised its program. The first course ran for nine weeks. The second began in late February for the officers arriving then and lasted six weeks. In the first week of April the two classes were merged and given a composite course. To handle the whole student load in two increments instead of four or five as had been planned at first, the faculty had to be doubled. Since there was no other source, the additional faculty were recruited from among the incoming officers even though doing so increased the risk of the whole program being looked upon as busy work by students and faculty alike.

Since the first segments of both courses would be given before planning at SHAEF had progressed far enough to provide more pertinent subject matter, they contained little that the students had not heard before at least once. To compensate, the training division decided to concentrate on the known weaknesses of the trainees, languages and military training—the latter embracing both formal military drill and physical conditioning. Intensive courses were offered in French, German, and Russian; and the training schedule included two to four hours per day of military training in the form of calisthenics, games, and, specifically, two or three road marches of four to twelve miles each week—this last activity being less than universally popular with the students.[11]

The composite course started on 6 April

and ran for eight rather than six weeks, ending on 27 May. During this time, the students, their theoretical training complete and pinpoint assignments in hand, were to have studied the towns and cities in which they would be posted. By April, a pinpoint location had been determined for each detachment, but by then, too, SHAEF had imposed severe security restrictions on any information that might compromise OVERLORD. Consequently, the locations could not be revealed to the detachments. The disappointment was enormous, but the actual loss was probably not much since the assignments all had to be changed later anyway. As a substitute for the pinpoint training, all students took part in a four-week exercise, an elaborate but obviously contrived military government war game vaguely laid out in the German *Land* (state) Hesse. When the war game ended, the course reverted to lectures and conferences sporadically enlivened by guest lectures on Germany, France, and the Low Countries; language and military training also continued. Toward the end, in near desperation, the faculty resorted to demonstrations and dramatizations—a detachment in action in a mythical German town, a military government court, bomb disposal—some useful, some not, and all undisguisable time-killers.[12] Word that SHAEF would stock the British Stella water purifier for use on the Continent set off a search across southern England for a specimen around which, hopefully, more hours of instruction could be devised. One was found, but then SHAEF announced that it would retain the already familiar U.S. equipment after all.

To the student officers the courses at Shrivenham seemed most of the time to be an elaborate effort to generate mass bore-

---

[11] Rpt, ECAD Training Div, Admin Sec, to Director of Training Div, sub: Organization and Activities Through 27 May 44, in SHAEF G–5, 604.

[12] *Ibid.*

dom while at the same time assaulting individual self-esteem and possibly physical well-being as well. Hastily devised courses led by instructors with no more knowledge than the students, and sometimes less, resulted in disgruntlement that no amount of ingenuity in devising lectures, recitations, demonstrations, and similar activities could dispel.[13] The living conditions of recruits, unheated classrooms, drills, and cross-country hikes during midwinter and a cold, damp spring smacked almost of sadism to middle-aged men who assumed, not illogically, that if the Army needed them at all it ought to be for something better. They had come expecting to be given important work but instead found themselves trudging across the English countryside or taking canned courses and solving stereotype problems. Worst of all was the feeling of being excluded from what appeared to be very worthwhile and important activity going on around them. The SHAEF Special Staff and the country sections, which had moved to Shrivenham in March, seemed to be immersed in vital projects. From occasional appearances as lecturers by members of these groups, the student officers gathered that the really important work was going on behind a curtain of security and that they were only marking time. A morale study in the Civil Affairs Center in April reported the commonest complaint to be the feeling of working in a vacuum without knowing what was really going on.[14]

The truth was that most of the more than two thousand civil affairs officers in training at Shrivenham, barring a sudden development of so-called RANKIN conditions, were only getting a taste of the frustration they would experience before finding their place in the war. Sooner or later they would have to be so informed, hopefully in a manner that would raise their morale, or at least not destroy it completely. Consequently, 9 May 1944 was later remembered as the first day of spring in Shrivenham by the students and as something akin to Resurrection Day by the Civil Affairs Center staff. In the morning, Eisenhower arrived to inspect the school. Toward the end of the ceremony, which had included a more or less well-executed and enthusiastic parade, he invited the students to break ranks and gather around him, saying they reminded him too much of a firing squad "standing out there." Having implied that he too saw the incongruity of field grade officers doing close-order drill, he went on to assure them that they were not forgotten. They were as modern, he said, as radar, and just as important to the command. Although humanitarian in its results, their job was to help win the war. If they failed, the armies would fail; the fighting front of the modern army was "only the fringe of a tremendous organization." What Eisenhower said was less important than that he said it, particularly his closing remarks:

Now a word about what you are doing here. No commander can ever accumulate the supplies, the organization, the men that he needs in exact timing with the existence of that need. In other words, he piles up reserves. For some time you have been in reserve. You're probably getting bored, some of you. You are a little tired of idleness, particularly when some of you were extraordinarily busy men in civilian life, and you gave up many things—made many sacrifices—and you are getting damned tired of not being used usefully in view of your sacrifices. Your time is coming, so don't worry.[15]

---

[13] SHAEF G–5, Hist Sec, Education and Training, in SHAEF G–5, 60, Jacket 7.

[14] Memo for Brig Gen McSherry, 19 Apr 44, in SHAEF G–5, 17.02.

[15] Coles and Weinberg, *Soldiers Become Governors*, p. 679.

MILITARY GOVERNMENT TRAINING AT SHRIVENHAM

Nothing substantive had changed, but the Supreme Commander had shown that he was aware of the students. They were at least not the victims of wanton mismanagement. To enhance the mood, the Civil Affairs Center sponsored an all-day press conference at Shrivenham on the 10th. Fifty correspondents attended. It gave the newsmen something to write about at a time when the security on all other SHAEF activities was at its tightest, and the ensuing publicity made the continued waiting in the wings a little less onerous for the student officers.

Although it continued in nominal existence until the last week of June, the Civil Affairs Center completed its essential work in May. By the end of the month, the whole anticipated U.S. civil affairs officer contingent for northwest Europe had been assigned—and sometimes, as plans changed, which they often did, reassigned.[16] After the training division completed the composite course at the end of May, there remained only a small course for warrant officers and officers with no previous civil affairs training. Ever since the first full de-

_____
[16] Hqs, ECAD, Extract from Hist Rpt, May 44, 17 Jun 44, in USFET CAD 314.7.

tachment, a D detachment, was formed and sent to U.S. First Army on 15 March, the student officers had been moving out, gradually in April and in large numbers in May, to join their detachments.[17] On its closing in June, the Civil Affairs Center left behind in St. Andrews Parish Church in Shrivenham a plaque and two bells to complete the church's octave of chimes.

ECAD

One of the first lessons learned from AMGOT in Sicily and Italy was that military government in the field ought to be able to take care of itself. The line troops there had frequently been too busy and almost always too preoccupied with what they regarded as more important affairs to provide support and services for members of an organization whose acronym they were inclined to read as "Aged Military Gentlemen on Tour."[18] More often than not the AMGOT officers had gone into action with no more than their personal gear, flags, proclamations, some stationery, and some money. They had counted themselves lucky when they had a jeep, a trailer, some spare gasoline, a tent, and a typewriter. Their priority was so abysmally low that before the Sicily landing some tactical units had even refused to embark the civil affairs officers themselves.[19]

Civil affairs plans for northwestern Europe recognized early the need for a housekeeping organization. The detachment concept, developed under COSSAC, provided a basic unit; but the detachments, although they would be attached to the tac-

tical commands, would not be part of them. Neither would they be self-sustaining. They would, as AMGOT had, exist in a kind of administrative void. To correct this shortcoming, Civil Affairs, ETOUSA, had begun thinking in the fall of 1943 of creating a separate administrative organization for the detachments and in November had asked Washington to furnish seven skeletonized military police (MP) battalions, that is, headquarters and medical personnel only.[20] The detachments would be attached to the battalions which would go into the field with them providing continuous administrative services and support and thereby integrating civil affairs solidly into the Army. The Civil Affairs Center would do the same at the top.[21]

Apparently because seven military police battalion headquarters were not to be had in the United States, General Hilldring was obliged to invent the European Civil Affairs Division (ECAD). At the end of December he proposed that in place of the MP battalions, ETOUSA set up a division with a normal division headquarters, twenty-eight companies (the equivalent of seven battalions), and seven medical detachments. The division, he suggested, ought to provide administration for all U.S. civil affairs personnel in the European theater except those assigned to SHAEF and Headquarters, 1st U.S. Army Group.[22] Two weeks later the Civil Affairs Division approved a strength of 2,528 officers, 124 warrant officers, and 5,147 enlisted men (total 7,799) for the division. Of these numbers, 2,280 officers, 120 warrant officers, and 3,600 enlisted men would be

---

[17] Rpt, Hqs, ECAD, G–2, Historian, sub: The Manchester Phase of the ECAD, 20 Jan 45, in USFET CAD 314.7.

[18] C. R. S. Harris, *Allied Military Administration of Italy* (London: H. M. Stationery Office, 1957), p. 82.

[19] *Ibid.*, p. 28.

[20] ECAD G–3, ECAD Organization and Development 1944 [no date], USFET CAD 322.

[21] Rpt, Hqs, CAC, ASC, to Chief, Hist Subsec, COSSAC, 31 Dec 43, in SHAEF G–5, 17.02.

[22] ECAD G–3, ECAD Organization and Development 1944, USFET CAD 322.

detachment personnel and the rest administrative, except for forty-eight instructors and several dozen enlisted men assigned to the Civil Affairs Center.[23]

On 7 February 1944, by General Order No. 13, Headquarters, ETOUSA, established the European Civil Affairs Division (U.S. Contingent, SHAEF Provisional).[24] A letter accompanying the order named Colonel Stearns as division commander and gave him a free hand in organizing the division within the War Department personnel allotment. On the 12th, Stearns, in the first ECAD general order, activated the division at Shrivenham and formally assumed command. At the same time he attached the Civil Affairs Center to the division, thereby giving civil affairs outside the higher staffs a single and separate administration.[25]

From the first, one thing everyone associated with the division was aware of was that ECAD was an unusual military organization, unique in some respects, curious in others. No unit like it had ever existed before in American history. Perhaps somewhat overestimating the importance of the distinction, the division's historians extended it also to world history.[26] Among other firsts, the division was the first known to have been organized entirely outside the continental boundaries of the United States, and it claimed the record in World War II for achieving combat readiness— ten weeks, as opposed to thirteen months for the average infantry division.[27] On the

curious side, the division had the overt characteristics of a tactical organization without being one. In the field it would have no command function. Its operating personnel would receive their orders exclusively through the tactical units to which they would be attached. ECAD would in fact cease to be a unit in the usual sense once it left England. Some part of it would go wherever SHAEF troops went. The sole function of the division headquarters would be to act as parent organization for the civil affairs personnel, "keeping their records, promoting them as they deserve, disciplining them if necessary, paying them, getting their mail to them, relieving them, taking care of them if they are ill, burying them if they die, and getting them help if they need it."[28]

The division was formed into three regiments, the 6901st, 6902d, and 6903d (all provisional) European Civil Affairs Regiments. The 6901st Regiment, with eight companies, was earmarked for France and the Low Countries but was to be trained also for Germany. The 6902d and 6903d Regiments, ten companies each, were to be trained exclusively for Germany.[29] Each company would have 80 civil affairs officers and 113 civil affairs enlisted men, plus an organic component of officers and enlisted men not specializing in civil affairs, who would provide services and administration.[30] The detachments were designated

[23] *Ibid.*

[24] GO 13, Hqs, ETOUSA, 7 Feb 44, in USFET CAD 314.7.

[25] Hist Rpt, Hqs, CAC, ASC, to Chief, Hist Sec, SHAEF G–5, sub: Activities at CAC, 15 Feb–1 Mar 44, in SHAEF G–5, 17.02.

[26] Draft ECAD History, Sep 45, in USFET CAD, Hist Doc file.

[27] Hqs, ECAD, Extract from Hist Rpt, May 44, 17 Jun 44, in USFET CAD 314.7.

[28] Hist Rpt, Hqs, CAC, ASC, to Chief, Hist Sec, SHAEF G–5, sub: Activities at CAC, 15 Feb–1 Mar 44, in SHAEF G–5, 17.02.

[29] A fourth regiment, brought into being briefly in the spring of 1944, was to have had responsibility for officers serving with British detachments, as was also a fifth regiment, which was planned but not activated.

[30] Hist Rpt, Hqs, CAC, ASC, to Chief, Hist Subsec, SHAEF, sub: Activities of CAC, 18 Jan–1 Feb 44, in SHAEF G–5, 17.12, Jacket 1.

by type, company, and regiment, hence D5B1 was the fifth D detachment of B Company, 6901st Regiment. In action, the companies would move with the tactical commands to which their detachments were attached, and the regiments would station themselves as close as possible to their companies, though they—and to an even greater degree the division headquarters—could scarcely avoid becoming remote entities for most of the detachments.

The outstanding peculiarity of ECAD was that only its smallest components, the detachments, had an operating civil affairs–military government role. Independently of the division, they would be the instruments through which the combat troops would be relieved of civil commitments and the primary SHAEF civil affairs objective would be attained, namely, "to ensure that conditions exist among the civilian population which will not interfere with operations, but will promote these operations."[31] They would be small, self-contained and partially self-sufficient headquarters, which, although not designed to govern, would have sufficient authority and possess enough technical knowhow to revive, instruct, and supervise local governments. In doing so they would accomplish the second SHAEF civil affairs objective, which was to achieve the first with maximum economy of military manpower.

In liberated areas, the degree of military control would depend on how well the indigenous authorities functioned without assistance. In enemy territory, however, military government, though indirect, would be firm and comprehensive, and each detachment in its own locality would be concerned with the whole spectrum of governmental affairs. In the first stage of the occupation every detachment would carry out the following essential actions:

Governmental Affairs

1. Hold a conference of local officials. Announce the military government proclamations and ordinances and make the necessary plans for enforcing them.
2. Post the proclamations and ordinances, noting time and date.
3. Reconnoiter the area.
4. Make arrangements for billeting military personnel in the area.

Public Safety

1. Hold a conference of local public safety officials.
2. Secure guards for supplies, important installations, and municipal records.
3. Control circulation of the local population (especially displaced persons and refugees).
4. Impound all weapons, explosives, narcotics, and radio transmitters in civilian hands.
5. Inspect local prisons and detention camps.
6. Investigate unexploded bombs, mine fields, booby-trapped areas, and ammunition dumps.

Public Health

1. Re-establish local public health organizations.
2. Secure care for civilian sick and wounded.
3. Report incidence of communicable diseases.
4. Correct serious hazards in environmental sanitation, particularly in water supply and sewage disposal systems.
5. Establish strict control over medical supplies.

Public Welfare

1. Re-establish local agencies for handling relief.
2. Provide adequate food distribution facilities.
3. Establish information and lost and found bureaus.

---

[31] Hqs, First U.S. Army, Office of CA Officer, sub: Guide to Initial Functions of CA Detachments Operating with Combat Units, 27 May 44, in SHAEF G–5, 17.16.

Utilities and Communications

1. Establish military control over all means of communications and all utilities.

2. Restore civilian services, including water, sewage, power and gas, telephone and telegraph, and postal service as well as streets and roads.

Labor, Transportation, and Salvage

1. Co-ordinate local labor exchanges.

2. Establish control over all means of transportation.

3. Set up a system of salvage collection.

Resources, Industry, Commerce, and Agriculture

1. Procure and provide materials and services for the military and food for civilians.

2. Restore price and rationing controls; supress black markets; institute first aid for restoration of normal civilian requirements.

Legal

1. Set up military government courts as necessary.

2. See that proper proclamations, ordinances, regulations, and orders are posted and published.

3. Co-operate with the public safety contingent and Counterintelligence Corps on release of political prisoners.

4. Make recommendations on local legislation to be suspended.

Fiscal

1. Guard banks and other depositories of funds.

2. Require continuance of local tax collection.

3. Assure proper custody of all enemy, abandoned, or absentee-owned property.

Supply

1. Contact local government officials in charge of food and clothing supplies and find location of storage points and available stocks.[32]

At SHAEF and in the higher staffs the main functions would have specialists assigned to them. In the detachments an officer could be judge or prosecutor in a military government court one day, sewage

and waterworks inspector the next, and financial, transportation, rationing, or police expert as the situation might require.

Since ECAD existed almost entirely to enable the civil affairs–military government detachments to work, subsist, and move independently of the tactical units that they would serve, the division's table of equipment was its outstanding—officers who served with ECAD might even say sole—asset. In the early planning, before exact civil affairs needs could be known, Colonel Stearns had prepared a special list of equipment (SLOE) based on the standard table of equipment of a military police battalion multiplied by seven. To the result he added for good measure enough jeeps and weapons carriers to bring the total number of vehicles to just a few short of two thousand.[33] In December 1943, General McSherry took the special list of equipment to Washington. At this time the possible imminence of RANKIN assured its fast approval and secured for it an A–2 priority with SHAEF, an astoundingly high priority for civil affairs, which would never again hold any higher than A–6. Outfitted with a gilt-edge hunting license, ECAD was embarrassed by a lack of drivers until February, when Stearns recruited volunteers from among the student officers to begin driving the vehicles to Shrivenham from depots all over England.[34] Later, when what was needed to make the detachments self-sufficient was better known, a revised special list of equipment added trailers, tents, field desks, safes, drafting instruments, and electric and gasoline lanterns. ETOUSA's approval for this revision came

---

[32] *Ibid.*

[33] Rpt, Hqs, ECAD, G–2, Historian, sub: The Manchester Phase of the ECAD, 20 Jan 45, in USFET CAD 314.7.

[34] Hist Rpt, Hqs, CAC, ASC, to Chief, Hist Sec, SHAEF G–5, sub: Activities at CAC, 15 Feb–1 Mar 44, in SHAEF G–5, 17.02.

much more slowly, and the division's G-4 section spent most of May, June, and July on the road scouring the depots for the new items.

Although it was well outfitted—by AMGOT standards even lavishly—ECAD had an early and persistent weakness; it was not a table of organization unit. The grades of its personnel, from private to colonel, were allotted to it, not determined by the organizational structure and needs of the division. This arrangement meant that throughout the division, but particularly in the detachments, the grades of officers and enlisted men were those they brought with them and not those appropriate to the positions to which they were assigned, which were in fact usually higher. After ETOUSA made the allocation, the number of officers in the ranks of major and above was about half what the division thought it needed, and eight times as many lieutenants were allotted as the division wanted.[35] Since the imbalance originated largely in the War Department policy that virtually restricted direct commissions for civilians to the company grades, the real experts in civil administration as often as not were bracketed in the lower ranks. ECAD requests for upgrading were uniformly turned down in ETOUSA, where the reasoning prevailed that by the time a full-scale civil affairs organization was needed, the fighting would be over and an ample selection of higher ranks would be avilable from the combat branches. Consequently, the prospects for promotion in ECAD were, and would remain, dismal.

In comparison with the rest of the European civil affairs organization, ECAD was remarkably stable, a condition that some of its members interpreted—with some rea-son—as a symptom of stagnation. The upheavals in SHAEF in the winter and spring of 1944 only barely reached down to the division. As a result of the G-5 reorganization in April, the country sections which had been in the Special Staff were attached to ECAD for administration and assigned unit designations, the U.S. element of the German country section becoming the 6911th European Civil Affairs (ECA) Unit.[36] In May after wrestling for two months with the organizational peculiarities necessitated by the grade allotments, ECAD solved part of the problem by eliminating one company each from the second and third regiments. Also in May, when ETOUSA reacquired an operating civil affairs mission (in the Communications Zone), Colonel Stearns became Assistant Chief of Staff, G-5, ETOUSA, and Colonel Henry McE. Pendleton assumed command of ECAD. On 6 June ECAD applied a final organizational touch by converting from provisional to permanent (though still not table of organization) status. The 6901st, 6902d, and 6903d ECA Regiments (Provisional) became the 1st, 2d, and 3d ECA Regiments, and the 6911th ECA Unit (Provisional) became the 6th Civil Affairs (CA) Unit.[37]

The Manchester Phase, ECAD

In late February, 12 ECAD officers and 19 enlisted men went to Manchester, where at the end of March they received and billeted 661 enlisted men and 29 company officers from the United States, the first large civil affairs–military government en-

---

[35] ECAD G-3, ECAD Organization and Development 1944, USFET CAD 322.

[36] *Ibid.*

[37] SHAEF G-5, Opns Br, Hist Sec, Chronology of Civil Affairs–Military Government, ETO, May 41–6 Jun 44, 24 Dec 44, in SHAEF G-5, 60, Jacket 1.

listed contingent. A day later, in a morning fog so thick that the rear ranks could not see him standing fifty feet away, Stearns greeted the new arrivals. He told them they would be specialists, but for the time being their muscles were needed to set up a reception center for the several thousand men who would be coming after them.

Manchester was almost the only large city in England not already saturated with American or British troops. The British Army had requisitioned some buildings and had established a system for billeting in private homes through the local police but had not used them, except briefly for the Dunkirk survivors in 1940. In March, ECAD took over as its local headquarters the Nicholls Hospital, a former orphanage built in the late nineteenth century, and as enlisted billets the Denton hat factory plus thirty-two large dwellings in Heaton Moor.[38] The buildings, vacant for several years, were dirty; messing equipment and plumbing needed cleaning and repairs; and beds had to be set up and mattresses stuffed. The three main locations were about four miles from each other and they did not have all the space needed for offices, storerooms, classrooms, and the like. These facilities had to be situated elsewhere in the city wherever a vacant store, garage, meeting hall, or large dwelling could be found.

By early April, when nearly three thousand enlisted men arrived within four days, they could be taken off the trains on which they came, assigned quarters, given a hot meal, have their papers processed and be classified during the night while they slept, and the next morning be given their company and detachment assignments. When the second and third shipments arrived, some men had to be billeted in private homes. At the beginning there was a flurry of medical certificates presented by householders seeking exemptions, but soon more space was being offered than was needed.

While Manchester, with its persistent smoke, rain, and fog, was hardly a place American soldiers would have chosen to be stationed, particularly in a gloomy wartime winter, the ECAD troops and Manchester civilians struck it off from the start. Recreation was plentiful in every form from motion pictures and plays to dancing, boxing, and wrestling and motorcycle and greyhound racing at the Belle Vue Zoological Gardens, the largest amusement park in the British Isles. The ECAD soldiers met the people in the pubs and in their homes, and, inevitably, before long some Manchester girls were becoming American wives. In June a former lord mayor of Manchester publicly praised the deportment of the ECAD troops in a newspaper article, and later Eisenhower commented that military-civilian relations in Manchester were the best of any place in the United Kingdom.[39]

The enlisted men detailed to ECAD were not specialists in the sense of having been given previous civil affairs training, and about a third were former limited-service men. These two circumstances gave rise early to a rumor which was never entirely laid to rest, even within ECAD itself, that the civil affairs enlisted personnel were mostly mental misfits. A few of the limited-service men had previous records of functional mental disturbances—later some were transferred in who had broken down in combat—but the most common defect was impaired vision. The enlisted classifica-

---

[38] Hist Rpt, Hqs, ECAD, to Chief, Hist Subsec, SHAEF, sub: Activities of ECAD, 1–31 Mar 44, in SHAEF G–5, 17.12.

[39] Hist Rpt, Hqs, ECAD, to Chief, Hist Sec, SHAEF G–5, sub: Activities of ECAD, 1–30 Jun 44, in USFET CAD 314.7.

tion section found the median ECAD enlisted man to have an AGCT (Army General Classification Test) score in group II (110 or higher). He was between the ages of twenty-three and twenty-nine, had at least a high school education, and in civilian life had been either a student or a skilled white-collar worker. Of the total ECAD enlisted personnel, 68 percent were in AGCT groups I and II as compared with 37 percent of the Army as a whole, and 61 percent were high school graduates (Army average 41 percent). About 20 percent had at least one year of college. The enlisted men were generally younger than the officers under whom they would serve, only 2 percent being over thirty-eight years of age, but they had a substantial leavening of maturity. Forty-six percent were between ages twenty-three and twenty-nine, and 23 percent were over thirty. Although they did not have Army civil affairs training, many had background experience superior to that of some civil affairs officers. Over fifty were graduate engineers or architects. Four were former museum directors. Others had been lawyers, college instructors, teachers, policemen, and social investigators. About 30 percent were ASTP (Army Specialist Training Program) trainees, who in one sense constituted a potential core of disgruntlement since they had expected to get commissions. On the other hand, their nine months of college training in foreign languages and other areas put them well ahead in this respect of many of the officers under whom they would serve.[40]

On 20 March, Maj. D. I. Glossbrenner, the division's executive officer, took charge of the advance echelon headquarters at Nicholls Hospital and began the work of bringing ECAD into existence. The officers were at Shrivenham, and the enlisted men were coming into Manchester. The task was to bring the two together within the next ten weeks, equip them, and have the three regiments ready to go into action any time they might be called after 1 June. Aside from seeing to details even down to road maps and stationery, the advance echelon had to make certain that each officer and enlisted man had enough weapons training to be able to "shoot his way in and out" and that each knew how to operate and maintain the vehicles he might be expected to use.[41]

The first complete company, Company B, 1st European Civil Affairs Regiment (ECAR), moved out on 14 April to join First Army. The whole 1st ECAR was put together by 1 May and moved to Shrivenham to await its call to join tactical units. The 2d and 3d ECARs, with some vacant personnel spaces, were ready at the end of the month. On 8 June, two days after the invasion, two detachments, D5B1 and D3B1, landed on OMAHA Beach; and three days later, D3B1 was in operation at Trévière and D5B1 at Isigny, the first sizable towns liberated.[42] At the end of the month four companies were on the Continent, and the division headquarters had closed at Shrivenham and moved to the Kenilworth Hotel in Manchester to join the undeployed elements.[43]

But the waiting was not over. Germany did not break under the invasion, and the

---

[40] Hqs, ECAD, Classification Sec, AG, to SHAEF G–5, sub: Classification of Enlisted Personnel for ECAD, 10 Aug 44, in SHAEF G–5, 17.12, Jacket 4.

[41] Hist Rpt, Hqs, ECAD, to Chief, Hist Sec, SHAEF G–5, sub: Activities of ECAD, 1–31 May 44, in USFET CAD 314.7.

[42] Draft ECAD History, Sep 45, in USFET CAD, Hist Doc file.

[43] Hqs, ECAD, Historian, to Chief, Hist Subsec, SHAEF G–5, sub: Activities of ECAD, 1–30 Jun 44, in SHAEF G–5, 17.12.

MILITARY GOVERNMENT OFFICERS PRACTICE RIVER CROSSING

French showed themselves surprisingly capable of running their own governmental affairs. The whole 1st ECAR shipped out early in the second week of July, and the Headquarters, 2d ECAR, with five of its companies followed late in the month.[44]

In Manchester in July, the division headquarters, which after D-day had seemed not to have much left to do except to continue training and wait for its call, suddenly found itself plunged into a round of replanning. Decisions being made out-side SHAEF, in Washington and London and in the European Advisory Commission, added a new and important dimension to ECAD's role in Germany; besides providing civil affairs support for the armies in combat, it would be required to establish territorial military government for a U.S. zone in Germany. The detachments, thus far organized specifically to assist military operations, would also have to become the executive instruments of U.S. purposes and policies in the occupation.[45]

The new role could not be accommo-

---

[44] Hist Rpt, Hqs, ECAD, to SHAEF, sub: Activities of ECAD, 1–30 Jul 44, in SHAEF G–5, 17.12, Jacket 4.

[45] See also below, p. 77.

dated without revamping the detachments. Organized under the anti-AMGOT principles of the Standard Policy and Procedure, they were not capable of administering territory beyond the span of control of a single detachment. Such ability as existed was vested in the tactical G–5s, ETOUSA, and SHAEF and, except for SHAEF, was to be exercised within unit boundaries, not political boundaries. Although they varied somewhat in size, hence also in potential span of control, the detachments formed only a compartmentalized horizontal structure. For Germany they would have to be given a vertical dimension as well.

Zonal military government under the new scheme, as far as it concerned the ECAD detachments, would cover all governmental levels in Germany except the national level. Common sense required that it should also conform to existing German administrative boundaries, which raised two problems. In the first place, the German internal subdivisions varied widely in area and population. For instance, one *Land* (state), Prussia, comprised close to two-thirds of the total prewar area and population of the Reich. However, except for Bavaria, which was substantially less than half the size of Prussia, the remaining *Laender* (states) were much smaller, some no larger than counties in the United States, and some—Hamburg and Bremen—were single cities. Several Prussian provinces, such as Hanover and the Rhine Province, were larger than any of the other *Laender* except Bavaria. In fact the smaller *Laender* were more nearly comparable to the Prussian *Regierungsbezirke* (provincial districts). At the *Kreis* level the disparities, though still there, were less pronounced. The *Landkreise* (rural districts, roughly similar to small U.S. counties in size and function) provided an element of unifor-

mity. The *Stadtkreise* (equivalent to U.S. incorporated municipalities) again varied depending on population, since every city, whether large or small, constituted a single *Stadtkreis*. Secondly, while the division into three zones could be assumed, which of the two western zones would go to the United States was not yet decided. The British and the Americans both wanted the northwestern zone. Trying to keep abreast of shifting arguments between the two governments, ECAD drafted various plans: the "1700 North Plan" in mid-July, the "1500 North Plan" in early August, the "900 South" and "1100 South" plans also in August, and the "1186 South Plan" and "1737 North Plan" at the end of August. (The numbers all referred to the number of officers to be assigned.) The "1186 South Plan," as amended in mid-September, was the one finally adopted, but by that time the revamping of the detachments was completed, having been based mostly on the "North" plans.[46]

First estimates for twenty-four new detachment types boiled down finally to five types given the letter designations E to I. E detachments (26 officers and 35 enlisted men) were originally conceived of as regional detachments capable of administering *Laender* and Prussian provinces. They would supervise German authorities at these levels and the military government detachments assigned to subordinate levels. F detachments were designed to fit in at the level of the *Regierungsbezirke* and smaller *Laender*. When the southwestern zone became the American zone, E detachments were assigned to the *Land* and *Regierungsbezirk* governments and F detachments to the larger municipalities. The G (9 officers and 15 enlisted

---

[46] ECAD G–3, ECAD Organization and Development 1944, USFET CAD 322.

men), H (5 officers and 10 enlisted men), and I (4 officers and 6 enlisted men) detachments were designed for *Stadtkreise* and *Landkreise*. The H and I detachments were always the most numerous, and in the initial distribution constituted about four-fifths of the planned 250 detachments.[47] The system of designation continued to be by detachment type, number in company, and regiment, for example, E1B3 and F2H3. The A- to D-type detachments would not be used in Germany with one notable exception, Detachment A1A1, the Berlin detachment.

Since regional detachments had not been contemplated in the original scheme for ECAD, their inclusion at this time added some functions that in Germany were administered primarily through regional agencies, such as, transportation (particularly railroads); postal, telegraph, and telephone services; public utilities, education; and religion. Furthermore, in all functions the German regional agencies concerned themselves less with the public than with management of the lower governmental levels, so functional specialization became important. Whereas at the *Kreis* level public health might be concerned mainly with communicable diseases and sanitation, on the regional scale it would involve administering health insurance programs and licensing medical practitioners. In the *Landkreise,* transportation meant finding enough conveyances to move food supplies and products; at the regional level it could mean running a major segment of the national railroads. In July, ECAD began an eight-week regional program to train officers in twelve functional specialties: finance; economics and public utilities;

property control; transportation; labor; postal, telephone, and telegraph; food and agriculture; legal; education and religion; interior; public safety and public health.[48] The approximately 150 E detachment officers so trained were expected later to instruct the *Regierungsbezirk* and lower level detachment officers whom they would advise and supervise in the occupation.

The regional program began on 3 July, and the detachments were recast and ready to begin training for Germany by the end of the month. Since security restrictions no longer prevented pinpoint training, the plan was to familiarize each detachment so thoroughly with the area in which it would operate that the members would feel at home there from the day they arrived, even down to knowing by name the persons with whom they might have to do business.[49] Eventually the detachments would get such training, but in August the war suddenly seemed to be moving too swiftly for it to be accomplished in Manchester.

The beachhead phase of the invasion ended in July. On 1 August, 12th Army Group became operational. With First and Third Armies, it would make the drive northeastward into Germany. The Germans were in trouble in France and at home, where dissident General Staff officers had attempted to assassinate Hitler on 20 July. At mid-August, Montgomery trapped the German Seventh Army in the Mortain-Falaise pocket, and the Germans began a retreat that they would have practically no chance of stopping short of their own western border, if there.

On 18 August, Pendleton received orders

---

[47] ECAD, Regional Staff Program, Memorandum No. 1, 1 Jul 44, in SHAEF G–5, 17.12, Jacket 4.

[48] Hist Rpt, Hqs, ECAD, to SHAEF, sub: Activities of ECAD, 1–31 Jul 44, in SHAEF G–5, 17.12, Jacket 4.

[49] ECAD CA Trng Div, to CO, ECAD, sub: Training Program Progress Report (No. 21), 2 Aug 44, in SHAEF G–5, 17.12, Jacket 4.

to move ECAD to France in the first two weeks of September and complete its reorganization and training there while standing by for duty in Germany. The decision had been talked over in SHAEF G–5 a week and a half earlier, the conclusion then being that, if nothing else, the detachments would benefit from living under field conditions.[50] During the interval the war had moved fast, and by the time the orders reached ECAD, SHAEF had instructed 12th Army Group to concentrate on preparing for military government in Germany, "starving" France to free the maximum number of detachments for training for Germany and being prepared if necessary to dismantle the whole civil affairs structure then in France and dispatch it to Germany.[51]

The division had packed and weighed, determined the cubage of its equipment, and held a practice loading in July; a forward headquarters echelon had gone to France late in the month to take in charge the undeployed companies of the 1st and 2d ECARs and begin reorganizing and retraining them for Germany. When the call came for the whole division to move, the forward echelon had its headquarters in the Chateau du Mont Epinque near Cherbourg. By then the front was moving fast and 12th Army Group wanted the division to set up farther east. In the first week of September, the forward echelon and the units under it moved to Rochfort-en-

Yvelines, thirty miles southwest of Paris. Until two weeks earlier the chateau had housed German troops, and some were still there as prisoners of war put to work cleaning up for ECAD's arrival.

On 1 September the division moved to Dunham Park a few miles outside Manchester. Simultaneously with this short move, the division assumed a new character, painting out the "CA" markings on its truck and jeep bumpers and substituting "MG." Detachment commanders, previously called CAOs (civil affairs officers) became MGOs (military government officers). The tone of the term "military government," considered too harsh for friendly ears, seemed just right for the Germans; hence civil affairs ceased to exist except in the designations of the division and the regiments, where the CA was retained apparently for the sake of euphony.

During the several days spent at Dunham Park, the division completed gas mask and personal equipment inspections, and the officers and men drew ammunition, insect powder, and K rations. On the 7th the division began the first serious test of its mobility as serials of about sixty vehicles each, carrying men and equipment, started moving out of Dunham Park to Hursley Camp outside Southampton. From here, as quickly as space became available, the division moved onto the Southern Railway docks at Southampton to board ships. Nearly everyone spent several nights bivouacked on the docks waiting to go aboard the Liberty ships on the cross-Channel run. By this time, the ships were all thoroughly dirty and rat-infested from two months of such trips.

While the division was aboard ship, off UTAH Beach waiting to land its vehicles, word came through on 15 September that the U.S. zone in Germany would be in the

---

[50] Memo, SHAEF G–5, for Chief, Opns Br, G–5, sub: Admin and Deployment of MG Personnel in Germany, 9 Aug 44, in SHAEF G–5, 803.

[51] The one exception was Paris which, not yet liberated, was to be "given enough detachments to do the job . . . [its] importance . . . in the eyes of the world warrants." Memo, Hqs, 12th AGp, ACofS G–5, Opns and Personnel Br, for ACofS G–5, sub: Opns and Personnel Meeting, 17 Aug 44, in SHAEF G–5, 17.16.

southwest. Every detachment had to be re-assigned and fast; the first American troops had already crossed the German border south of Aachen on the 11th. In another four days 12th Army Group was calling for four military government companies to move up to Verviers (Belgium) and Verdun behind First and Third Armies and be ready to enter Germany as more terri-tory was taken. Because the detachments organized for Germany were still either bringing their vehicles ashore in landing craft or making their way inland along side roads (to leave the main arteries open for priority traffic), the forward echelon had to put together the companies from the 2d ECAR detachments that it had at Rochfort and send them off to the armies.[52] The last ECAD convoy pulled into Rochfort on 24 September. Five days before, on the 19th, the first detachment to operate in Ger-many, D8B1, had gone into action at Roetgen.[53]

---

[52] Hist Rpt, Hqs, ECAD, to SHAEF, sub: Activi-ties of ECAD, 1–30 Sep 44, in USFET CAD 314.7.

[53] Draft ECAD History, Sep 45, in USFET CAD, Hist Doc file.

CHAPTER VII

Staffs for Germany

The German Country Unit

Although the COSSAC approach rejected the idea of national military government headquarters separate from the combat commands, the COSSAC planners themselves, before they were finished, found that they could not be entirely consistent in applying the Standard Policy and Procedure to Germany. The Moscow and Tehran Conferences had made the Allied administration of Germany after the war a certainty. Furthermore, of the three phases Colonel Troubridge identified in his report known as Slash 100, the second phase, coming between the end of hostilities and the assumption of control by an Allied commission, entailed a period of central administration by SHAEF in the western zones. How long the period would last could not be determined exactly, but the first SHAEF estimate, according to Troubridge, was six months. Consequently, the Supreme Commander would have to be prepared to conduct military government in Germany through the normal military command channels specified in the Standard Policy and Procedure until the fighting stopped, and through military government technical channels for some time thereafter.[1] In his first proposal concerning the SHAEF civil affairs organization, Lumley included a German country unit which would prepare plans and eventually form the agency through which the Supreme Commander would control the British and American zones until the control commission took over.[2]

The SHAEF reorganization of February 1944, however, influenced by the AMGOT philosophy, disregarded the COSSAC separation of the two phases of military government and gave the German Country Unit responsibility for exercising control in Germany "from the time Allied military forces enter Germany until such control passes to an Allied High Commission," that is, during both the first and the second phases.[3] Under the reorganization, the German Country Unit moved into the Special Staff under the DCCAO, McSherry, and on 16 February, Col. C. E. D. Bridge (British) and Colonel Troubridge, assisted later by one other British officer and three U.S. officers, Lt. Col. Bernard Bernstein and Majors Galen Snow and L. J. Chawner, began laying out the missions and structure of the unit.[4] They identified its tasks as being to plan for and later constitute the main military government headquarters for Germany, to write a handbook which would be a comprehensive military govern-

---

[1] Interv Sheet, SHAEF G–5, Hist Sec, sub: Interview with Sir T. St. V. Troubridge on Achievements and Policy of British CC, 23 Aug 44, in SHAEF G–5, 30.

[2] Memo, SHAEF CAD for CofS SHAEF, sub: Organization of CA at SHAEF, 5 Feb 44, in SHAEF G–5, 35.08.

[3] German Country Unit, Hist Div, Historical Statement of the German Country Unit, Aug 44, p. I–3, in SHAEF G–5, 60, Jacket 1.

[4] *Ibid.*, p. I–2.

ment manual for Germany, and to provide advice and direction to the military commands and to the other civil affairs echelons. Lumley, trying to prevent the unit and its ambitions from expanding too rapidly, proposed limiting it at first to a 20- or 30-officer complement. The planning committee rejected his idea, however, and set the minimum initial strength at 102 officers with an anticipated progressive expansion of 400 to 600 officers.[5] At conferences in late February, General McSherry approved the committee's action, and on 2 March the thirty-three officers then assigned to the unit began assembling for work in the Watson West building at Shrivenham. On the 5th, Col. Edgar Lewis was named Chief Planner and Head of the German Section with Colonel Bridge as his deputy.

Colonel Lewis's appointment brought into the unit one of the few American officers who had previously done work on military government organization for Germany. He was also apparently not an advocate of the AMGOT philosophy prevalent in the unit when he arrived. As chairman of a student committee at Charlottesville in the spring of 1943, he had directed the drafting of a plan for Germany that prefigured some later COSSAC and SHAEF concepts. Lewis's committee had envisioned a tactical military government to be used as long as hostilities continued; some months later COSSAC planning included this same idea. Looking farther ahead than COSSAC did, however, the committee had also proposed retaining territorial military government, which would be installed after resistance ended, under the commanding generals of the field armies as military dis-

trict commanders. Such an arrangement would limit the scope of the national control authority in Berlin to matters such as communications, transportation, and money and banking, which absolutely required central direction. The committee's report had further projected a pool of trained military government teams similar to ECAD.[6]

The bent of Lewis's previous thinking was probably somewhat related to his assignment to the German Country Unit, since the AMGOT-Mediterranean approach to the planning for Germany had run into trouble at higher levels even while it seemed to be having a triumphant inception in the SHAEF Special Staff. In February the British War Office had begun pressing for the early creation of a separate Allied control authority to take all posthostilities planning away from SHAEF. The Director of Civil Affairs, War Office, pointedly asked to have explained the purpose of the German Country Unit as well as the "necessity for the institution" of such a group.[7] General Morgan, the SHAEF Deputy Chief of Staff, found reasons to justify the existence of a German unit in SHAEF, but not one with as wide ranging a mission as the planners had set for themselves. Morgan emphasized the need for a handbook on Germany; he furthermore stressed both SHAEF's responsibility to provide advanced training for civil affairs officers and the belief that the "minor machinery" of SHAEF and the Allied control authority should be the same in order to avoid duplication.[8] Morgan's explanations were not enough, however, to get prompt

---

[5] Memo, SHAEF CAD, Actg Chief, German Unit, for DCCAO and Executive, sub: Formation of the German Unit, 22 Feb 44, in SHAEF G–5, 16.01.

[6] German Country Unit, Historical Statement, p. I–7f.
[7] SHAEF SGS, Summary of Decisions, vol. I, in SHAEF SGS 016.1.
[8] Ibid.

War Office approval concerning British officer assignments to the German Country Unit, and as of mid-April, only eighteen officers out of the British quota of fifty-one were at work. By then, all the U.S. officers were present plus twenty-four additional men temporarily filling spaces allotted to the British. The shortage on the British side persisted throughout the unit's existence.[9]

In the SHAEF G–5 reorganization in April the German Country Unit figured primarily as an embarrassment. The revised SHAEF thinking excluded it from military government before the German surrender, and because of the British opposition, its role after the end of hostilities was in doubt. The handbook was all that remained of the unit's original mission. As the planning papers delicately stated, it was "not possible to foresee the exact requirements" for the unit.[10] Morale hit a phenomenal low in May when for nearly the whole month nothing was announced concerning the unit's place in the SHAEF scheme other than that the U.S. personnel would henceforth constitute the 6911th ECA Unit in ECAD. When Brigadier Gueterbock on the 5th described the situation as "curious," he was giving voice to a sentiment already widely held in the unit. He did manage to decrease the curiousness somewhat by implying that, as SHAEF's organization for governing Germany after the surrender, the unit existed for an eventuality that was no longer expected to materialize.[11] Morale in the unit again im-

proved slightly after G–5, on the 29th, finally announced its designation as the German Country Unit, SHAEF, and its retention under the Operations Branch, G–5, for matters of policy, operations, and planning.[12]

On 7 June 1944, the day after the Normandy landing, the German Country Unit, having never really fitted into ECAD, began moving from Shrivenham to Prince's Gardens, London. Its arrival in the city coincided with the start of the German V-bomb campaign against England, and in early July, the unit's offices on Exhibition Row were wrecked by a near miss. The bomb hit early in the morning before anyone was in the offices, but five enlisted men were injured on the same day by a bomb that struck the enlisted billets some distance away. Nevertheless in June and July, working in partially demolished rooms without panes in the windows or plaster on the walls and ceilings, the German Country Unit seemed at last to have found its purpose in the war. The handbook had to be finished, not as an exercise but because within weeks detachments might be in Germany and would need it. The unit also became involved in the ECAD reorganization, the regional training program, the assignment of detachment pinpoint locations, and the various "north" and "south" plans for the British and U.S. zones.[13]

At the same time, once the troops had landed in France and begun moving, no one really expected SHAEF's German Country Unit to last out the summer. The British government had never accepted the estimated six-month period of SHAEF control after the surrender and only very reluc-

[9] German Country Unit, Historical Statement, p. I–9.

[10] Memo, SHAEF G–5 for Distribution, sub: CA Organization in the Field, 19 Apr 44, in SHAEF G–5, 35.08.

[11] Analysis Sheet, SHAEF G–5, Hist Sec, Ltr, C. E. D. Bridge, British Officer in German Unit, to Brig E. A. L. Gueterbock, sub: War Establishment, 23 May 44, in SHAEF G–5, 15.02.

[12] German Country Unit, Historical Statement, p. I–14.

[13] Ibid., pp. I–15–19.

tantly contemplated any SHAEF period at all. No doubt, in considerable part the British attitude stemmed from an unwillingness to see policy-making authority vested in an agency of SHAEF, which in turn took its direction from the Combined Civil Affairs Committee (CCAC) in Washington. By late spring, however, both the British and the Americans realized that getting the Soviet Union to participate in tripartite control in Germany would be more difficult if the United Kingdom and the United States pursued a combined policy in their zones. Brigadier Gueterbock had already strongly suggested to the officers of the German Country Unit in May that they might have a future as members of separate British and U.S. country missions but very likely did not have one as part of SHAEF. For the U.S. contingent in the unit, the denouement began on 17 August when G–5 reassigned some officers to the training cadre of ECAD and some to Headquarters, ECAD, leaving only slightly more than a third under Colonel Lewis to await transfer to the U.S. Group Control Council soon to be formed.[14]

The Handbook Controversy

The one task the German Country Unit had throughout its existence was the writing of a military government handbook for Germany. The job, though a large one, was essentially routine, and the German handbook would have passed into obscurity along with its linear ancestor, the AMGOT "Bible" for Sicily and Italy, and the handbooks for the liberated countries of northwestern Europe had it gone as intended to the military government detachments and not made an unscheduled detour through the White House. Theoretically,

the handbook was to be the only document a working military government officer would need in the field, compact enough to fit into a pocket but comprehensive enough to incorporate "all that . . . (he) requires in order to carry out his duty, and no more."[15] During March, April, and May, regardless of its organizational ups and downs, the German Country Unit worked on the handbook. It had completed the third draft by 15 June when an editorial board took over to co-ordinate the work on what was assumed to be the final draft. Several hundred copies of the third draft were mimeographed and distributed within SHAEF and to civil agencies in Washington and London.

The handbook differed from the related compilations, FM 27–5 and Standard Policy and Procedure, in that, while they were broad procedural guides used mainly by staffs in planning, the handbook dealt with concrete military government problems anticipated in Germany. Its outstanding virtue was that it would save the field officer the work and protect him from the pitfalls of having to adapt general procedures and policies to German conditions. This adaptation would be done for him on every foreseeable question in one or another of the three sections of the handbook. In the first section he would find descriptions of the probable conditions in Germany and of the organization and workings of military government. The second section, considered to be the heart of the handbook, contained a chapter each on the twelve primary civil affairs–military government functions, such as food, finance, and education and religion. For the functional specialists each chapter was expanded and issued separately as a manual. The third section contained sample report forms and

---

[14] *Ibid.*, p. I–23.

[15] *Ibid.*, p. II–1.

other basic information and the Supreme Commander's proclamation, ordinances, and laws.[16]

The proclamation, ordinances, and laws—also printed separately in large format for posting—would constitute the legal bond between the Germans and military government. Although not strictly required in international law, the proclamation was assumed to be accepted United States practice.[17] Addressed to the people of Germany in the name of General Eisenhower as Supreme Commander, Allied Expeditionary Forces, it declared his assumption of "supreme legislative, judicial, and executive power within the occupied territory"; suspended German courts and educational institutions; and required all officials and public employees to remain at their posts until further notice. The first of the three ordinances defined nineteen crimes against the Allied forces punishable by death. The second ordinance established military government courts, and the third made English the official language of military government. The laws, with gaps left in the numbering system to accommodate future legislation, fell into two classes: those necessary to establish and maintain military government control and those dealing with national socialism. Law No. 1 abrogated nine fundamental Nazi laws together with their subsidiary decrees and regulations and prohibited any interpretation of German law in accordance with Nazi doctrine. Other laws abolished the National Socialist Party, its auxiliary organization, and the use of its emblems.[18]

On 15 August the German Country Unit had a fourth draft of the handbook ready for final approval and publication. The foreward defined the scope as embracing "the objectives and policies to be pursued by commands and staffs in planning for an operating military government in Germany whether in the mobile, transitional, or static phase [that is, both before and after the surrender]."[19] At the time, CCS 551, restricted to the presurrender period, was still the only directive SHAEF had received, hence the handbook overstepped SHAEF's authority in some degree; but SHAEF had directed the country units to keep the handbook under constant examination and up to date with new policy if any came from the CCS.[20] Until the Normandy landing and for some time thereafter, a German collapse or surrender before Allied troops had entered the Reich itself seemed likely; consequently, to develop elaborate plans and exclude this contingency from them would not have made sense.

Even though the CCAC had trouble composing agreed policy papers, there had been no fundamental philosophical disagreement over the treatment of the Germans in either CCAC, in SHAEF, or in the other British and American agencies directly concerned. The American officers, considering the newness of their specialty, had a remarkably homogeneous outlook fostered by The Hunt Report, the military government manual (FM 27–5), and the schools, Charlottesville in particular. They all had read The Hunt Report, at least in its abridged wartime edition; many had

[16] Ibid., p. II–2.

[17] Department of the Army, FM 27–10, The Law of Land Warfare, p. 140, par. 357.

[18] USFET, General Board, Study No. 85, Legal Phases of Civil Affairs and Military Government, 15 May 46, in Hist Div, Hqs, ETO, 97–USF 5–03.0.

[19] US Gp CC, Hist Sec, sub: Handbook for MG in Germany, Comparison of Drafts 15 Aug 44 and 1 Sep 44, in SHAEF G–5, 17.05.

[20] Memo, SHAEF G–5 for all Branches, sub: Role and Responsibilities of Country Units, 5 Jun 44, in SHAEF G–5, 16.03.

listened to lectures by World War I veterans; and the belief that the U.S. administration in the Rhineland had been better than those of the British and French because it was the most benevolent and enlightened had become practically an article of faith. FM 27–5 as revised in December 1943 no longer stated the conversion of enemies into friends as an object of military government, but it predicted that properly conducted military government could "minimize belligerency, obtain co-operation, and achieve favorable influence on the present and future attitude toward the U.S and its allies."[21] On 15 August 1944 the Civil Affairs Division had a proposed postsurrender directive ready in which it instructed Eisenhower to maintain a "firm, just, and humane" administration. Under this directive, he would be required to destroy nazism and fascism but also to preserve law and order and "restore normal conditions among the population as soon as possible." The economic guide would have instructed him to prevent inflation, control prices, reduce unemployment, and provide emergency relief and housing.[22]

While the German Country Unit was strongly conscious of the dearth of combined guidance for the handbook, the basic lines of British and U.S. policy appeared to be clear enough. The COSSAC planners had used both FM 27–5 and the Military Manual of Civil Affairs (British) in writing the Standard Policy and Procedure and had not found any glaring conflicts. At the very highest level the President and Prime Minister had made what appeared to be a clear and public statement of combined policy in the Atlantic Charter (14 August 1941) in which they promised the "final destruction of Nazi tyranny" but did not exclude the German people from the better world to be built after the war. CCS 551, the presurrender directive and the only concrete piece of agreed policy guidance that the German Country Unit had, except for its detailed instructions on dealing with nazism, read much like a version of FM 27–5 adapted specifically to Germany. In fact, except concerning nazism, militarism, reparations, and war crimes, the German Country Unit assumed that the policy toward Germany would differ in some degree from that for the other western European countries but would have essentially the same tendency, namely, to provide as much supervision as necessary and as little as possible. Toward midsummer 1944, postwar planning papers then beginning to circulate in the EAC took up the idea of German collective responsibility; however, this concept did not seem to require changes in

---

[21] War Department, *Army-Navy Manual of Military Government and Civil Affairs*, FM 27–5, 22 Dec 43. Later critics have sometimes attributed a deliberate hardening of policy to the revised FM 27–5. (See Carl J. Friedrich, ed., *American Experiences in Military Government in World War II* [New York: Rinehart and Company, Inc., 1948], pp. 31–37.) The manual does seem to have struck a more severe tone by its emphasis on employment of civil affairs to aid and promote military operations and its consequent apparent abandonment of the overt humanitarianism of the 1940 edition. But by 1943 the tone was bound to have changed somewhat. In the interval between the two editions the United States had become involved in a war in which humane considerations were more than usually disregarded on both sides. Still, for its time, the 1943 FM 27–5 was a remarkably mild document. The shift in approach was mostly toward recognizing civil affairs and military government as having a place in the active conduct of the war, hence the concern with using them to promote combat operations—if necessary at some expense to the welfare or comfort of civilian populations. Otherwise, the manual continued to insist on "just and reasonable" treatment of civilians and prompt rehabilitation of economies.

[22] CCAC 119, Directive for Military Government in Germany (Post-Surrender), 15 Aug 44, in CCS 383.21 (2–22–44), sec. 2.

SHAEF's plans beyond the substitution of the term "military government" for all references in the handbook to "civil affairs," which was done by order on 28 July.[23] FM 27–5 had already prescribed the term "military government" for use as the over-all designation for civil affairs in enemy territory but had not insisted on its being used exclusively.

In early August 1944, Secretary of the Treasury Morgenthau, whose overt involvement in occupation planning had for two years been limited to financial matters and the nomination of occasional Treasury officials for civil affairs appointments, made a trip to Europe. He went to observe the effects of the Treasury's financial arrangements for liberated France; but, as he later said, on the flight over he chanced to read a State Department paper dealing with postwar policy for Germany, and he was filled with misgivings.[24] In London he talked with the U.S. representatives in the EAC and discussed the SHAEF plans for Germany with Colonel Bernstein, who had gone from the Treasury Department into civil affairs and had been associated with the German Country Unit from its inception. When Morgenthau returned to Washington he brought with him a copy of the German handbook which, with an accompanying list of his criticisms, he passed on to the President and thus, not unwittingly, precipitated the opening thunderclap of a storm in U.S. policy that would be long in passing.

The errant handbook arrived in Stimson's office on the 26th accompanied by a presidential memorandum which began, "This so-called Handbook is pretty bad. I should like to know how it came to be written and who approved it down the line. If it has not been sent out as approved, all copies should be withdrawn and held until you get a chance to go over it." There followed passages from the handbook pertaining to economic rehabilitation that Morgenthau had singled out as particularly objectionable. "It gives the impression," the memorandum continued, "that Germany is to be restored as much as the Netherlands or Belgium, and the people of Germany brought back as quickly to their prewar estate." The President said he had no such intention. It was of "the utmost importance" that every person in Germany should recognize that "this time" Germany was a defeated nation. He did not want them to starve. If they needed food "to keep body and soul together," they could be fed "a bowl of soup" three times a day from Army soup kitchens. (The first version reportedly read, "a bowl of soup per day.") He saw no reason, however, for starting "a WPA, PWA, or CCC for Germany." The German people had to have it driven home to them that "the whole nation has been engaged in a lawless conspiracy against the decencies of modern civilization."[25]

The President's idea of what the coming defeat would mean for Germany was not very clear. A year hence most Germans

---

[23] See "Draft Directive to the Three Allied Commanders-in-Chief, General Directive for Germany" by the Planning Committee, U.S. advisers to Ambassador Winant, in Department of State, Foreign Relations, 1944, vol. I, pp. 244–46. See also German Country Unit, Historical Statement, p. I–17.

[24] John Morton Blum, From the Morgenthau Diaries, vol. III (Boston: Houghton Mifflin Company, 1967), p. 334.

[25] (1) U.S. Senate, Committee on the Judiciary, Subcommittee to Investigate the Administration of the Internal Security Act and Other Internal Security Laws, Morgenthau Diary (Germany), 20 Nov 67, vol. I, pp. 440–45. (2) Cordell Hull, Memoirs, vol. II (New York: The Macmillan Company, 1948), p. 1602. (3) Notes on Conference in Col Gunn's Office, 1130–1145, 14 Nov 44, in SHAEF G–5, 17.11, Jacket 3.

would have been happy to have three meals a day from Army soup kitchens, had the Army been able to provide them. In fact, his concept of the German postwar condition was probably no more austere than the authors of the handbook had assumed it would be and vastly brighter than it actually was. Nevertheless, Roosevelt set the whole U.S. occupation policy off on a course that would be difficult to steer and for too long impossible to abandon.

On the afternoon of the 28th, General Hilldring telephoned Smith, Eisenhower's chief of staff, and told him to "get to work right away" suspending and withdrawing the handbook and recalling all copies of several draft postsurrender directives SHAEF had recently sent out for review. He said that "very strenuous" objections had been raised "at the very highest level on the U.S. side." Since neither the War Department nor the Combined Chiefs of Staff had issued any postsurrender instructions, he added, it would be well "to bear in mind in General Eisenhower's own interest" that any instructions SHAEF issued could only apply to the presurrender period. "It appears to us," Hilldring concluded, "that there may be some considerable difference in what we do during the active operational period in the treatment of those who come under control of SHAEF and those measures which we will adopt which come through the defeat of the German Army. Is that philosophy clear to you?"[26] To Smith it was not at all clear, and he said so. The philosophy bothered him less than two practical matters which he bluntly called to Hilldring's attention: first, the troops were approaching Germany and might be there in a few days, and

SHAEF could scarcely afford at this point to scrap the handbook; second, "on matters of such importance" SHAEF as a combined command had to receive its orders through the Combined Chiefs of Staff (CCS).[27]

A day later by urgent cable the CCS told SHAEF to defer further action on the German handbook pending instructions which would be issued "in the near future."[28] The agreement of the British members in the CCAC to hold up the handbook had been easily obtained. They were not bound to follow the President's wishes even if the memorandum had been shown to them, which it probably had not; but in the meantime, the War Office had expressed its own strong dislike for the handbook which it documented with a list of specific criticisms almost as long as the handbook itself. While the British reaction saved the CAD the trouble of having to engineer unilaterally an about-face on a combined project, the relief was mixed with dismay. The British comments, on close reading, proved to be chiefly concerned with demonstrating that the handbook should not have been assigned to the German Country Unit in the first place and now ought to be done over by the CCAC(L).[29]

The job of reworking the handbook, however, did not go to the CCAC(L) but to G-5, SHAEF, the German Country Unit having ceased to exist. SHAEF's compelling interest at the moment was to get the handbook cleared in some form and issued before the troops made their way into Germany. G-5 put out a hasty revision dated 1 September in which it attempted

---

[26] Telecon, Maj Gen J. H. Hilldring, Col J. B. Sherman, 28 Aug 44, in USFET SGS 337/2, vol. II.

[27] Cable, Smith to Hilldring, 30 Aug 44, in SHAEF G-5, 25.31.
[28] Cable, Gov 100, CCS–CCAC, to SHAEF, 31 Aug 44, in SHAEF G-5, 25.31.
[29] History of the CAD, bk. VI, ch. I, p. 62.

to disarm further criticism by emphasizing the work's inconclusiveness with a statement in the preface that "portions should become inapplicable with changing circumstances" and by inserting a section of blank pages as a token of changes to come.[30] Although the CCAC, after examining the handbook closely, found it to be far from a bad job and recognized SHAEF's urgent need for something to give to military government officers about to enter Germany, the U.S. membership could not put its imprimatur on a document that did not show some clear and serious effort to incorporate the President's thinking. The solution settled upon was to allow Eisenhower to publish the handbook provided he affixed to the front of each copy a warning, like those on patent medicines, consisting of three principles composed by the CCAC, and had a number of specified revisions made in the text.[31]

In the list of required revisions, the CCAC tried to tailor the language of the handbook to the spirit of the President's memorandum and to the British criticisms, which in many instances were not compatible. At the same time, the CCAC tried to retain almost the entire substance of the original because it came closer to the current British and American views than another effort from scratch ever could. Since the handbook had no chance of being recognized as definitive of either British or United States policy, most of the revisions had no actual significance; whatever national policy they embodied would be stated more authoritatively elsewhere. Only a few, therefore, are of even moderate historical interest. Among these few, one

stands out because it seemed at the time to get at the very heart of the problem with the handbook and because it still illustrates the semantic pitfalls to be encountered in this kind of writing.

In the original handbook version the first paragraph of the Supreme Commander's proclamation had referred to Germany as a "liberated" country and did not mention militarism among the evils that the occupation forces proposed to eradicate in Germany. This omission was easily corrected by inserting a sentence condemning militarism between one concerned with the Nazi party and its institutions and another pertaining to war crimes and atrocities. The use of the word "liberated" in addressing the German people, however, raised problems. The U.S. and British planners were long accustomed to differentiating between "liberated" friendly and "occupied" enemy territory, but the Atlantic Charter promised the Germans, too, a kind of liberation, and the word "occupiers" was ruled out because it had come to be synonymous with "exploiters." Furthermore, the military commands, already feeling trapped by their governments' rhetoric in the unconditional surrender formula, wanted to avoid additional psychological handicaps. The answer found was the sentence, "We come as conquerors, but not as oppressors"—in English at once martial and pacific, forceful and vague. It had the kind of lofty ambivalence the Americans and British appreciated, but not so much the Germans. In German there is no way of muting the connotations of plunder and annexation of territory in the word *Eroberer* (conqueror), which the Psychological Warfare Division, SHAEF, hurried to point out when the first copies of the proclamation came out in print.[32]

[30] US Gp CC, Hist Sec, sub: Handbook for MG in Germany, Comparison of Drafts 15 Aug 44 and 1 Sep 44, in SHAEF G–5, 17.05.

[31] Ltr, Brig John Foster to Charles Peake, 8 Sep 44, in SHAEF G–5, 25.31.

[32] Cable, PWD, SHAEF, to SHAEF Forward, 17 Sep 45, in USFET SGS 388.5/1.

The search for a better word eventually went all the way to the Pentagon's top German translator who substituted *ein siegreiches Heer* (a victorious army), which to the Germans only emphasized the obvious.[33] In English, "We come as conquerors" quickly found a place among the durable quotes of the war.

The three principles, as drafted in the Civil Affairs Division, were ready to be sent to SHAEF along with the revisions in the first week of September, but reconciling them with British views took almost another month. Point One in the CAD version read, "No steps looking toward the economic rehabilitation of Germany are to be undertaken except such as may be immediately necessary in support of military operations." Obviously meant to give effect to the President's strictures against any involvement by military government in restoring the German economy, it was also, in a more stringent form, something Eisenhower had asked for earlier in another context (see below, p. 100). On British insistence a second sentence was added in the final version which read, "In accordance with this policy, the maintenance of existing German economic controls and anti-inflationary measures should be mandatory upon the German authorities and not permissive as in the present edition of the handbook." One of the strongest British objections to the handbook had been to the use of the words "will be permitted to continue" with reference to rationing and price and marketing controls. Moreover, the British had not supported Eisenhower's request to be relieved of economic responsibility and had argued that as much of the German economy should be saved as possible.[34] As a result, the first sentence of Point One ordered military government to do nothing to support the German economy and the second ordered it to require the German authorities to continue the controls that had sustained the economy through the war.

Point Two went as it was written by the CAD. It read, "No relief supplies are to be imported or distributed beyond the minimum necessary to prevent disease and such disorder as might endanger or impede military operations." Although the disease and disorder (more often unrest) formula was later frequently cited as the most inhumane feature of the occupation policy, no objection to it was voiced in the CCAC because it had long ago been accepted by both the British and the Americans. In its earliest relief planning the CAD had assumed, as the AT(E) Committee also had, that the Army would hold its relief activity to the minimum in liberated as well as enemy territory, not out of insensitivity or inhumanity but because winning the war had to come first.[35] The COSSAC planners had proposed not to import relief supplies into enemy territory, "except where military operations or the health of our forces would otherwise be jeopardized."[36] Standard Policy and Procedure established the criteria for relief as "a general breakdown of civil life and spread of disease" for enemy

---

[33] Military Government-Germany, Supreme Commander's Area of Control, Proclamation No. 1, in SHAEF G–5, 17.09.

[34] (1) CCAC 122/5, Occupation and Control of Germany, Handbook, 21 Sep 44, in CCS 383.21 (2–22–44), sec. 3. (2) F. S. V. Donnison, *Civil Affairs and Military Government, Northwest Europe* (London: H. M. Stationery Office, 1961), p. 201.
[35] Memo, War Dept, AG, for CG, ETOUSA, sub: Organization and Plans for Conduct of Civil Affairs, 29 Jul 43, in Admin Hist Collection, ETOUSA No. 146.
[36] Memo, COSSAC, Chief, CA Div, for Branches, sub: CA Administrative Appreciation, Nov 43, in SHAEF G–5, 11.02.

territory and "the development of conditions which might interfere with military operations" for liberated populations. CCS 551 used the disease and unrest formula in its text, but in the economic and relief guide, it made the standard of relief for Germany the same as for liberated countries.[37]

The first sentence of Point Three, written in the CAD, read, "Under no circumstances shall active Nazis or ardent sympathizers be retained in office for purposes of administrative convenience or expediency." The handbook had contemplated, as had anyone who had given thought to the subject, the necessary use of some Germans with unique technical skills even though they were Nazis. Point Three closed the door on "active Nazis and ardent sympathizers" without defining either one. The two concluding sentences, both British in origin, added: "The Nazi Party and all subsidiary organizations shall be dissolved. The administrative machinery of certain dissolved Nazi organizations may be used when necessary to provide certain essential functions as relief, health, and sanitation."[38] Point Three is notable as the first outright plunge into the semantic jungle of denazification. This point rejected expediency where individuals were concerned but appeared to condone it at least in the case of some organizations. (An attempt was made later to correct this apparent contradiction by establishing the second part as a separate fourth point.) The third principle also assumed that the categories "active Nazi" and "ardent sympathizer"

would be as self-evident on the ground in Germany as they were across the Atlantic in Washington.

When the CCS transmitted the three principles to SHAEF on 6 October, it pronounced the first SHAEF revision of the handbook "greatly improved but not yet satisfactory" and authorized a minimum distribution provided the principles were prominently attached at the front.[39] A second revision was completed in mid-October, just in time to be put out of date by EAC decisions on the zones and control machinery which made another revision necessary in December.[40] Once it had been printed and distributed in December, the handbook promptly faded from the higher echelons' view. As an officer in SHAEF stated during the controversy, ". . . nobody ever reads handbooks anyhow, except very junior officers whose subsequent actions can have very little effect."[41] The three principles, on the other hand, had a life of their own. They constituted, presumably, an expression of War Department policy based on the President's desires, and as a CCS document they became agreed combined policy, of which there was and would be very little. As such they had the force of a basic directive in all matters to which they applied. Viewed in this light, they appear severe, even harsh. Studied individually, however, they reveal an ambivalence almost too striking to be accidental; even aside from the British contributions, the severity was at least as much rhetorical as real.

---

[37] (1) SHAEF, Standard Policy and Procedure, pp. 20 and 35. (2) CCAC 69/6, Memo by Dir, CAD, sub: Civilian Relief in Germany, 19 Jul 44, in SHAEF G–5, 3.a.
[38] Cable, CCS to SHAEF Main, 6 Oct 44, in ASW 370.8.

[39] *Ibid.*
[40] Analysis Sheet, SHAEF G–5, Hist Sec, 3 Dec 44, in SHAEF G–5, 25.31.
[41] Ltr, L. F. Field, SHAEF G–5, Economics and Supply Branch, to F. Hollis, British Element, Control Council for Germany, 2 Oct 44, in SHAEF G–5, 25.31.

The U.S. Group Control Council

With the invasion imminent in the late spring of 1944, no decision had yet been reached in the EAC on the mechanics of tripartite control in Germany after the surrender. Independently, the JCS in Washington and the British authorities in London had concluded early in the year that, initially at least, the three commanding generals would head a central authority to which the JCS gave the name "Control Council" and the British, "Control Commission."[42] Both had accepted the three phases used by SHAEF—a military phase during active hostilities, a transitional phase after the surrender, and a phase of permanent Allied control—but they tended to disagree on the duration and form of control appropriate to each phase. The JCS saw the first two phases as essentially military and possibly extensive; the British wanted them to be brief, even fleeting, and wished to move into permanent direct control by the governments almost immediately. The words "council" and "commission" became symbolic embodiments of these divergent views and adherence to them became, hence, almost a point of national honor.

As D-day approached and passed, Eisenhower had a problem. As Supreme Commander he had a military government organization that considered itself fully capable of governing as much of Germany as might fall to the British and American combined forces; however, as Commanding General, ETOUSA, he had not even an embryo organization to head military government in a U.S. zone or to form the U.S. element of a control authority. His own preference was for a permanent combined administration in the western zones, but in this opinion he was out of tune with both Washington and London.[43] The JCS and the President were convinced of the necessity of separate zones to protect the national interest. The British had already begun planning their element of the Control Council/Commission in late 1943 and by early 1944 had set up one segment of it, the Control Commission (Military Section) (CCMS).[44] In the EAC, the British delegation proposed on 2 May 1944 that the Control Commission be prepared to take over in the "middle" (second) period "at the earliest possible date" and that a British-American-Soviet team for the purpose be formed in London soon.[45]

The U.S. delegation in the EAC began work in May on its own proposals for control machinery and presented a plan on 8 June in which it called for the early establishment of Control Council cadres.[46] The planning committee of the U.S. delegation also drafted principles relating to the nature and functions of a control council. On 19 June these principles began the process of clearance through the delegation's military advisers, submission to Washington, and eventual presentation in the EAC.[47]

---

[42] (1) JCS 1060/1, Administration of Military Government in Germany—Occupation Period, 22 Feb 44, in SHAEF G–5, 30. (2) EAC (44) 3, Memorandum by the United Kingdom Representative to the European Advisory Commission (Strang), 15 Jan 44, in State Department, *Foreign Relations, 1944,* vol. I, pp. 154–57.

[43] Ltr, E. R. Stettinius to Hon Wm. Phillips, 11 May 44, and Ltr, Eisenhower to Marshall, 27 May 44, in USFET SGS 371.

[44] Donnison, *CA–MG, Northwest Europe,* p. 250.

[45] EAC (44) 17, Memorandum by the United Kingdom Representative to the European Advisory Commission (Strang), 2 May 44, in State Department, *Foreign Relations, 1944,* vol. I, pp. 211–16.

[46] OMGUS, Hist Div, History, Office of Military Government for Germany (U.S.) (U.S. Group Control Council), to Nov 45, in OMGUS 12–1/5, p. 2.

[47] (1) *Ibid.* (2) No. 16858, Ambassador in the United Kingdom to the Secretary of State, 11 Jul 44, in Department of State, *Foreign Relations, 1944,* vol. I, pp. 246–48.

SHAEF always followed what went on in the EAC closely and especially so beginning in May when the British showed themselves determined to set up their Control Commission as the principal posthostilities planning agency for Germany. In May, Eisenhower brought General Wickersham into SHAEF to assume the role of deputy chief of the European Allied Contact Section in addition to his duties as War Department adviser to Ambassador Winant in the EAC. (Wickersham had been transferred to Winant's staff in January.) The Control Council/Commission plans, especially in the British version, could easily result in another AMGOT, which by then was an anathema in SHAEF policy, though not necessarily to all of the individuals in G–5. As a practical matter, however, Eisenhower had also to consider that once the invasion had succeeded, the end for Germany might come fast; furthermore, as of June, his own authority to plan for the time after surrender as commander of the British and U.S. forces was at best doubtful. Worse, as the prospective chief U.S. representative in a tripartite administration, he had no resources for planning and none existed anywhere else other than in the EAC, which so far had produced very little.[48]

General McSherry, chief of the newly created Operations Branch, G–5, SHAEF, advocated immediate creation of a tripartite control organization, arguing that time was short. McSherry, who had earlier defended the AMGOT system, also believed that the military commanders ought to be relieved of all military government responsibilities as soon as the tripartite body could be established in Berlin.[49] As Commanding General, ETOUSA, however, Eisenhower was less concerned with the need for a tripartite planning agency than with the possibility that the EAC might bring one into being before he had anything to contribute to it. The Russians were unpredictable. Their element might never appear—as in fact it did not—on the other hand, it might show up one day fully organized and ready for work. The British had the Control Commission (Military Section) (CCMS) and half a dozen groups in the Foreign Office and Cabinet Office waiting to be converted into control sections. ETOUSA had nothing.[50]

On 20 June, Wickersham left by plane on a special mission to Washington carrying with him a memorandum from Eisenhower to the JCS. The mission was a delicate one. More was involved than just creating another planning staff. SHAEF as yet had no authority to plan for the period after surrender. The EAC had such authority, but the surrender might very well come before the EAC completed its work; consequently, SHAEF was the logical and only body capable of instituting and conducting military government in Germany during the initial postsurrender period. To fulfill this potential, SHAEF would have to have a hand in the postsurrender planning and be the EAC's executive agency then, as it already was the CCS agency for the presurrender period. The trick was to find a place for the Control Council, which would be both a necessity and an inconvenience and which would have to be both fostered and restrained. How such a task would be accomplished was, no doubt, what Wickersham went along to explain. Eisenhower

---

[48] SHAEF G–5, Min of 1st Weekly Opns Br, G–5, Mtg, 7 Jun 44, in SHAEF G–5, 15.05.

[49] Draft, from Brig Gen McSherry to . . , sub: Formation of Tripartite Control Commission for Germany, 13 Jun 44, in SHAEF G–5, 5.

[50] Ltr, Brig Heyman to Gen McSherry, 2 Jun 44, in SHAEF G–5, 5.

implied that it would be done through controlled development. He asked to have appointed under him as Commanding General, ETOUSA, a deputy chief for the Control Council and a nucleus group to consist mostly of a counterpart of the British Control Council element, the CCMS. Except for a token military government staff the U.S. element of the Control Council would concern itself exclusively for the time being with planning for German demobilization and disarmament.[51]

In Washington, Wickersham successfully shepherded Eisenhower's memorandum, which in the process acquired a JCS number (923/1), through twenty-five offices including those of the President and General Marshall.[52] After he returned to London in mid-July, Wickersham turned over his duties in the EAC to Brig. Gen. Vincent Meyer and worked full time on organizing a military section for the projected Control Council, modeled on the British CCMS. When Brig. Gen. John E. Lewis arrived at the end of the month, a cadre of U.S. Army, Navy, and Air Force officers assembled in Norfolk House, London, which also housed the British CCMS.[53] The two groups, though expecting to be merged, maintained a scrupulous separateness while awaiting a Soviet contingent. Later, however, when, on Wickersham's urging, the Soviet delegate to the EAC, Ambassador Gousev, sent a description of the organization and its personnel requirements to Mos-

cow, the reply stated curtly that the Soviet Union could not spare officers from combat.[54]

Formal JCS approval arrived on 5 August. It authorized Eisenhower to set up a nucleus planning staff to be known as the U.S. Group Control Council (Germany) and named Wickersham as the acting deputy to the chief U.S. representative on the Control Council (not yet appointed). The U.S. Group's mission would be to plan for posthostilities control in Germany in accordance with EAC directives or, in the absence of such directives, in accordance with U.S. views on subjects pending before the EAC. The U.S. Group would belong to ETOUSA not to SHAEF, but in Germany, until the combined command terminated, it would be subordinate to SHAEF "in implementing on behalf of the U.S. and U.K. governments policies agreed upon by the three governments."[55]

The JCS gave Eisenhower more than he had asked for, in effect a directive to begin setting up a full Control Council element, not just a counterpart CCMS. Group Memorandum No. 1 of 10 August took this authorization restrainedly into account in creating three divisions within the U.S. Group Control Council: the Armed Forces Division, charged with planning for German disarmament, disposition of the German armed forces, demilitarization, care and repatriation of Allied prisoners of war, and intelligence with respect to German research and inventions; Military Government Division A, to deal with economics

[51] Memo, Hqs, ETOUSA, for JCS, sub: Post-Hostilities Planning, 20 Jun 44, in SHAEF G–5, 115.05A.

[52] JCS 923/1, Post-Hostility Planning, 26 Jun 44, in CCS 334 (6–20–44), sec. 1.

[53] (1) Memo, Wickersham for Smith, sub: Report of Visit to Washington, 17 Jul 44, in USFET SGS 319.1/4. (2) Hqs, US Gp CC, Hist Unit, Draft Historical Statement, 31 Oct 44, in SHAEF G–5, 30.

[54] OMGUS History, p. 6.

[55] (1) Cable, AGWAR–JCS to SHAEF, sub: Post-Hostilities Planning, 5 Aug 55, in SHAEF G–5, 31. (2) Hqs, ETOUSA, GO 80, Establishment of U.S. Group Control Council, 9 Aug 44, in SHAEF G–5, 5.

"in a broad general sense"; and Military Government Division B, to handle political matters in the same fashion.[56] The nucleus of the Armed Forces Division already existed at Norfolk House under General Lewis. The military government divisions did not come into being until later in the month when officers from the disbanded German Country Unit were assigned and chiefs were appointed, Brig. Gen Eric F. Wood for Division A and Brig. Gen. Bryan L. Milburn for Division B.[57]

From the moment of its inception the U.S. Group Control Council constituted the wave of the future for military government in Germany. The United States accepted the principle of tripartite policy-making, and the JCS had assigned to the U.S. Group, along with the British and the supposed Soviet groups, the mission of converting general policies drafted in the EAC into operational plans. Presumably, once the EAC began to produce and the Soviet element of the Control Council put in an appearance, there would not be much scope left for SHAEF. Already in mid-August the British Chiefs of Staff proposed that the U.S. and British groups begin working together at once with what guidance was available and refer questions they could not resolve to the CCAC(L).[58] The British proposal would in one sweep have taken postsurrender planning—and probably presurrender planning as well, since the two had to conform to each other— away from both the CCAC in Washington and SHAEF. Had the Russians come, some such development could hardly have been avoided. The actual events, however,

prompted McCloy to move quickly in the CCAC to get an interim postsurrender directive for Eisenhower and thus affirm his and the CCAC's mandate for the duration of the combined command. (See below, p. 101).[59]

Henceforth the going would not be easy either for the CCAC or for SHAEF; but SHAEF had, no doubt, known from the start the risks associated with calling the Control Council even into shadow existence. Furthermore, SHAEF was itself a potent organization. It was the actor on the stage and the Control Council the understudy in the wings. Both were powers but not yet equal powers. In an agreement on 23 August, later nicknamed "the Treaty of Portsmouth" by the Control Council staffs, SHAEF established its relationship with the Control Council Staffs. Before the German surrender the British Control Commission Staff would be responsible to its own government and the U.S. Group Control Council to Eisenhower as Commanding General, ETOUSA. After the surrender, until the combined command was terminated, both would function under Eisenhower as Supreme Commander, Allied Expeditionary Force. Before the surrender the control staffs would have no executive authority. SHAEF, however, would adjust its policies to conform with the long-term plans made by the Control Council/Commission in accordance with EAC directives.[60]

In September, when for a while the occupation of most of Germany, including Berlin, seemed likely, SHAEF also undertook to regulate the posthostilities relation-

---

[56] OMGUS History, p. 7.

[57] Hqs, US Gp CC, Hist Unit, Draft Historical Statement, 31 Oct 44, in SHAEF G–5, 30.

[58] History of the CAD, bk. VI, ch. XIII, p. 9.

[59] *Ibid.*, p. 11.

[60] Staff Memo No. 104, SHAEF, sub: Relationship between SHAEF and the British and U.S. Elems. of the Control Council/Commission, in SHAEF G–5, 30.

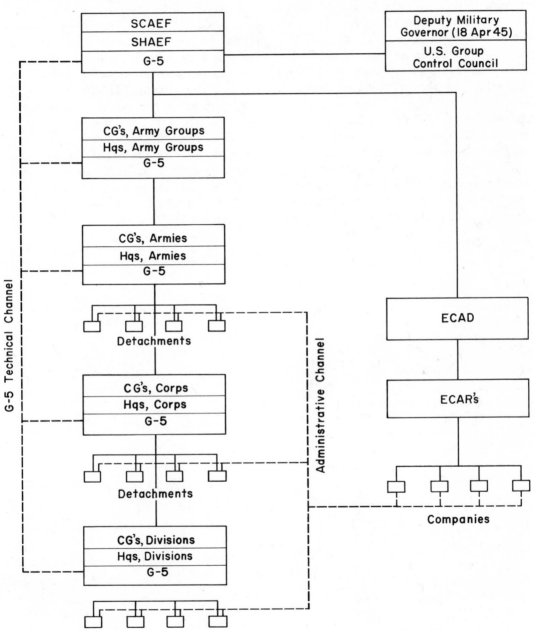

CHART 1—U.S. MILITARY GOVERNMENT RELATIONSHIPS (MOBILE PHASE, SEPTEMBER 1944–JULY 1945)

ship. (*Chart 1*) The British were known to want to turn over the administration to the control bodies immediately. "The U.S. Group Control Council," as SHAEF blandly stated, "it is believed . . , considers that both the military government of Berlin and the provision of necessary machinery at ministerial level are the responsibility of SCAEF during the initial period." SHAEF announced itself as sharing this opinion and added that the control staffs "must be integrated [including the Soviet element if British and U.S. troops reached Berlin first], must be at SCAEF's disposal, and must be under his command. . . . At no time," SHAEF added, "during the SCAEF period will any Control Council or other committee be in Berlin that is not under his command."[61]

British protests, if any, concerning the Americans' blithe assumption of authority over a separate British staff have not been found. Perhaps there were none; September was a tumultuous month in Washington and London. Nevertheless, toward the end of the month SHAEF relaxed its earlier stand to the extent of agreeing to permit a small ministerial control team of Control Council/Commission officers to enter Berlin with the SHAEF forces, provided it remained under Eisenhower's command during his period of responsibility and its channel of communications passed through SHAEF.[62]

---

[61] Memo, SHAEF G-5 for Chief, Control Commission for Germany (British Elem), Chief, U.S. Group Control Council, sub: Supreme Commander's Requirements for Military Government in the City of Berlin, 12 Sep 44, in SHAEF G-5, 115.05.

[62] SHAEF G-5, Ops/Fwd/803, sub: Agreements Reached at Meeting on Military Government of Berlin, 28 Sep 44, in SHAEF G-5, 31.

CHAPTER VIII

U.S. Policy Emergent

Fraternization

Fraternization between one's own troops and enemy civilians has been a command problem and a soldier's pastime as long as armies have existed. Odysseus knew it; the Chinese reputedly frustrated successive invasions by diligently practicing it; U.S. General Headquarters in the German Rhineland after World War I forbade it but quartered troops on civilians—with predictable results. It was bound to be a problem again in World War II, if only because the Army regarded itself as the guardian of the health and morals of the young men placed in its hands. That fraternization, or rather the prohibition of it, might become the bane of the occupation soldier's life and the figurative hairshirt of the command, however, first became apparent in the spring and summer of 1944.

In the political guide accompanying CCS 551, the Combined Chiefs of Staff directed Eisenhower to "strongly discourage fraternization between Allied troops and German officials and the population." Exactly what such discouragement might entail had not been thought out. At the time, it seemed that close contacts between troops and civilians both in liberated and in occupied territory for reasons of health and military security also needed discouragement. Later, the Civil Affairs Division mulled over the question of troop behavior in Germany, at the same time considering it sufficiently significant to become one of

the few matters submitted from the U.S. side in the CCAC (L).

In June, General Hilldring sent the gist of the CAD thinking to General Holmes. In Hilldring's opinion, and that of the CAD, an order prohibiting fraternization would be difficult if not impossible to enforce; nevertheless, the Germans needed to be made conscious of their guilt and of the contempt in which they were held by the people of the world. They needed to see the "error of their ways" and were to be "held at arm's length" until they had done so. The most practicable means, he thought, was to restrict public contacts. The troops ought not to be billeted in German households, eat in the same restaurants as the Germans, or attend their religious services.[1]

Since the statement in CCS 551 also logically implied a limit on private contacts, the CAD had a booklet printed for U.S. troops entitled "Pocket Guide to Germany." It took a rigid stand ("There must be no fraternization! This is absolute!") as well as a flexible one ("This warning against fraternization does not mean you are to act like a sourpuss or military automaton."). As if dubious of success either way, the booklet also included the regulations pertaining to marriages with foreigners and a section on venereal disease.[2]

---

[1] Ltr, Dir, CAD, Hilldring, to DACofS G–5, SHAEF, 23 Jun 44, in SHAEF G–1, 250.1–3.
[2] Memo 31, CCAC, Behavior of Allied Troops in Germany, 13 Jul 44, in OPD, ABC 387, sec. 7–A.

For SHAEF, in the summer of 1944, fraternization seemed to be among the least urgent questions of the war, one which could wait until the fighting was finished. In the second week of August, SHAEF G–1 drafted a recommendation for a nonfraternization policy along the lines Hilldring had suggested and pointed out that extensive training, education, and recreation programs would have to be devised to occupy the troops' time.[3] Two weeks later, when he got around to it, the Deputy Chief of Staff, General Morgan, called attention to a lack of realism in the G–1 proposal, namely, with regard to women. "I consider it essential," he added, "that, if we are really to follow through with the business of nonfraternization, we should import into Germany at the earliest possible moment our own women in as large numbers as may be."[4]

There the matter rested for another month, until 22 September when two cables arrived, one from Washington, the other from Moscow. American troops had begun occupying a small corner of western Germany southwest of Aachen eleven days before, and the press photographers had filed pictures showing German civilians, generally women and small children, greeting U.S. soldiers. The Washington cable, addressed to Eisenhower, came from General Marshall. "The President desired that I transmit the following message to you," he wrote:

There have appeared in the press photographs of American soldiers fraternizing with Germans in Germany. These photographs are considered objectionable by a number of our people.

It is desired that steps be taken to discourage fraternization by our troops with the inhabitants of Germany and that publication of such photos be effectively prohibited.[5]

From Moscow, Maj. Gen. John R. Deane, chief of the Military Mission, reported that *Pravda, Izvestia,* and *Red Star* had carried *Tass* quotes on 20 September from the *Sunday Express,* London, regarding American troops fraternizing with Germans.[6] The Russians were as yet nowhere on German soil.

Eisenhower replied to Marshall on the same day asking him to assure the President "that upon first appearance of the pictures of American troops fraternizing with Germans, I repeated prior orders against this practice." He had issued personal orders, he added, to all commanders "insisting that fraternization be suppressed completely."[7] Therewith began what for the next ten months the staffs strove manfully to depict as a righteous, even noble, enterprise—the SHAEF nonfraternization policy—about which the troops, unconcerned with presidential or public opinion, preferred to develop various and mostly scurrilous ideas of their own.

JCS 1067

Although the JCS and SHAEF from the beginning had contemplated a period of military administration in Germany after the surrender and before a permanent, civilian-directed occupation took shape, planning for this so-called middle period

---

[3] Memo, SHAEF G–1, sub: Conduct of Allied Troops and German Characteristics in Defeat, [8] Aug 44, in SHAEF G–1, 250.7.

[4] Memo, Dep CofS for ACofS G–1, sub: Conduct of Allied Troops and German Characteristics in Defeat, 24 Aug 44, in SHAEF G–1, 250.7.

[5] Cable, ACofS, OPD, to SHAEF, 21 Sep 44, in OPD 336, sec. II (cases 16–   ).

[6] Cable, Military Mission, Moscow, Deane to SHAEF for Eisenhower, 22 Sep 44, in SHAEF G–1, 250.1–1.

[7] Cable, Eisenhower to Marshall, 22 Sep 44, in SHAEF G–1, 250.1–1.

U.S. Troops and German Civilians *(September 1944). This and a few other pictures like it provoked the President's order against fraternization.*

had become practically impossible by D-day. Discouraged in their struggle to have London become the seat of combined post-hostilities policy-making, the British were pushing for conversion to tripartite planning and the virtual exclusion of SHAEF—hence also the CCAC in Washington—from any role in the government of Germany after the surrender. Since at the time it then still seemed likely that the Allied entry into Germany would follow a surrender negotiated before the troops had crossed the German border, the JCS

and the CAD saw the British attempt to eliminate SHAEF from the postsurrender period as a grave potential threat to Eisenhower's unity of command at what might turn out to be a confused and dangerous time. On the other hand, there did not seem to be any way to give Eisenhower guidance as combined commander, even for the middle period, except through some form of tripartite agreement. Hilldring confided his frustration on this score in a letter to Smith in which he pointed out that two recently submitted SHAEF papers on posthostilities subjects reflected careful planning but could not be regarded as authoritative because no higher level policy had yet been formulated. He thought that the Joint Post-War Committee, a JCS committee created in June 1944 to work on postwar military plans, might provide the machinery for establishing U.S. views which, when transmitted to the EAC and approved, would become guidance for the combined command. Otherwise, he could only hope that the CAD and the Joint Post-War Committee working closely together might somehow reduce the handicap imposed on SHAEF by the lack of instructions.[8]

Even though the success of the invasion increased the chance of an early German collapse, the only agreed instruction the CCS could produce was a three-stage updating of the old RANKIN concept, which it forwarded to Eisenhower on 19 June. In the first stage he was to deploy tactical air forces in the Low Countries and France, in the second to set up a barrier manned by ground forces to prevent the German troops from returning home, and in the third to occupy strategic areas in Germany for the purpose of enforcing the surrender terms.[9] On the object of the occupation the CCS was mute. When nothing more came by the first week of August and time appeared to be growing short, SHAEF finally converted the three CCS stages in a somewhat expanded form into a plan code-named TALISMAN.[10] The TALISMAN directive then became the only approved post-surrender guidance for the combined forces.

SHAEF, however, regarded TALISMAN as utopian. The plan assumed a defeated Germany that was economically and administratively intact and it assumed a German government capable of acknowledging defeat. But in August a German government capable of doing so would already have surrendered: Europe was invaded in the west; France was bound to be lost soon and probably the Low Countries as well; the Soviet forces in the east were closing to the Vistula; and Hitler had only narrowly escaped death at the hands of his own officers.

The presurrender directive CCS 551, and earlier some JCS papers, had envisioned SHAEF forces fighting their way into Germany; but they, too, had assumed an intact surrender at some point of the bulk of the German territory. In August, SHAEF was beginning to anticipate an altogether different ending to the war, one which might leave Germany a totally burned-out wreck, fought across by the armies, and with no national authority, either civilian or military, to sign a surrender or prevent complete internal chaos. Worse yet, the country, economically and politically prostrate, might well become the stage for diehard-Nazi guerrilla warfare.[11] On the 23d, Eisenhower sent these views to Washington, pointing out that if they proved correct his resources would be barely enough to get the German armed forces under control, care for displaced persons, and establish military government. To keep the economy from collapsing as well would be "utterly impossible," and he asked to be relieved of the economic re-

---

[8] Ltr, Hilldring to Smith, 1 Jul 44, in SHAEF SGS 014.1.

[9] Memo, SHAEF G–3, Chief, PHP Subsec, for ACofS G–3, sub: Post-Hostilities Planning, 26 Jun 44, in SHAEF G–3, 2.542.

[10] SHAEF G–3 to all Staff Divisions, sub: Operation TALISMAN, 6 Aug 44, in SHAEF G–5, 115.25c, Jacket 1.

[11] Memo, SHAEF G–5 for CofS, sub: Directive for Military Government in Germany, 21 Aug 44, in SHAEF G–5, 25, Jacket 2.

sponsibilities assigned to him under CCS 551.[12]

Eisenhower's cable arrived in the Pentagon on 24 August, just two days before the handbook storm broke and on the same day the British offered their proposal in the CCS to shift postsurrender planning to the Control Council groups and the CCAC(L). The three events together were bound to raise a spectacular turmoil. Eisenhower had in effect proposed a revision of CCS 551 that would convert it into a posthostilities directive, since, in his view, there probably would be no surrender. In doing so he threatened the long-standing British policy of restricting combined planning conducted in Washington to the period before the surrender, and he collided head-on with the new British effort to shear him of almost all postsurrender authority as combined commander. The British proposal, on the other hand, struck not only at SHAEF but at the hegemony in military government planning that the War Department claimed for the CCAC in Washington.

McCloy offered a compromise. The CAD would draft an interim postsurrender directive which would give Eisenhower what he asked for. When the two governments approved it, the directive would be sent to SHAEF through the CCS; thereafter the spelling-out of either CCS 551 or the postsurrender directive would be left to the Control Council elements with the CCAC(L) resolving any differences.[13] The arrangement was not exactly an equal split. That SHAEF and the CAD would leave much for the Control Council and CCAC(L) to decide was doubtful from

the outset; but the British members of the CCAC agreed on 29 August to submit the idea to London along with a draft cable to Eisenhower telling him he could plan along the lines he had described and would be given a postsurrender directive later.[14]

The reply from London came on 11 September and rejected Eisenhower's estimate and McCloy's compromise. The British government did not agree that the German economic structure would collapse and insisted that even in apparent chaos Eisenhower should count on finding stable elements through which to restore an orderly economic life.[15] The British members in the CCAC thereupon proposed to tell Eisenhower that he should do his best to carry out CCS 551 in its existing form.[16] Since the CAD was by then working to get appended to the handbook an even more radical statement on economics than Eisenhower had requested, Hilldring asked the U.S. Deputy G–5, General Holmes, to get the 24 August request withdrawn, which was done on 18 September.[17] In the meantime, however, the War Department had become convinced that a postsurrender directive was imperative because of Eisenhower's need for one, because of the British drive to capture the postsurrender planning for the London-based agencies, and, above all, because of the handbook controversy, which had raised the most serious challenge yet to the military role in the occupation.

The internal struggle over occupation policy among U.S. agencies, which for the rest of the war would overshadow anything that had gone on between the Americans

---

[12] Cable, SCAEF 68, SHAEF Forward, to War Department, 23 Aug 44, in OPD, ABC 387, sec. 7–A.

[13] History of the CAD, bk. VI, ch. I, pp. 52–55.

[14] Cable draft, CCS to SHAEF, no date, in OPD, ABC 387, sec. 7–A.

[15] *Ibid.*, p. 56.

[16] CCAC 122/2, draft, 11 Sep 44, in OPD, ABC 387, sec. 7–A.

[17] History of the CAD, bk. VI, ch. I, p. 57.

and the British, began, at least for the War Department, as a completely unanticipated collision. On 1 September the President's special assistant, Harry Hopkins, announced the formation of the Cabinet Committee on Germany to be composed of the Secretaries of State, War, and Treasury. The next day, in a preliminary meeting at which McCloy and Hilldring were present along with officials of the State and Treasury Departments, the Treasury representatives presented the Morgenthau Plan for Germany, and McCloy raised what to him and Hopkins was the more germane business of an interim postsurrender directive for Eisenhower.[18] The Treasury representatives apparently assumed, not without some reason in the light of recent events, that the Cabinet Committee existed primarily to give Morgenthau a voice in the deliberations on policy for Germany. Deputy Secretary of War McCloy, however, had a considerably different opinion since it was Secretary of War Stimson who had asked the President a week before to organize such a committee for the purpose of developing a German policy. Stimson had done so knowing Morgenthau was interested in the German question but not knowing how much.[19] At this time, the handbook controversy was still in the future—though only by one day—and Stimson had been concerned over the seeming imminence of the German defeat and the complete lack of U.S. policy or even of a decision as to which zone the American forces would occupy.

Later the interim directive for Germany, which became known as JCS 1067, would generally be taken as only a slightly anemic offspring of the Morgenthau Plan. If this assumption is true, then the birth must have occurred at the 2 September meeting; but there the War Department and the Treasury were talking about essentially two different things. The Morgenthau Plan purported to be a permanent solution to the German problem. The War Department, except for Stimson in his capacity as a cabinet member, did not then or later claim a voice in deciding what would ultimately be done with Germany. What it did insist on—without prejudice to any subsequent decisions—was a technically workable policy for the period of military responsibility. In this regard, McCloy objected at the meeting to the chief features of the Morgenthau Plan, namely, the provisions for pastoralizing and partitioning the country. All other considerations aside, he argued, the provisions would simply have spawned more troubles than the military commander could have handled in the immediate aftermath of the war.

Nevertheless at the meeting—and later in JCS 1067—there was a greater similarity between the general tenor of War Department and Treasury views than would have been likely even a week before. The views of the one, however, did not descend from those of the other, but both came from the same source, namely, the President's expressed determination to punish Germany. The reaction to the handbook had emboldened the Treasury to submit a comprehensive plan for Germany. This reaction had at the same time alerted the War Department to the danger of being made to seem to have adopted an untenable "soft" position by the simplistic arguments of people "who were utterly innocent

[18] Reproduced in full in Henry Morgenthau, Jr., *Germany Is Our Problem* (New York: Harper and Brothers, 1945), pp. 1–4.

[19] (1) Henry L. Stimson and McGeorge Bundy, *On Active Service in Peace and War* (New York: Harper and Brothers, 1948), p. 569. (2) *Morgenthau Diary (Germany)*, vol. I, p. 447.

of any realization of the extent and complexity of the problem."[20]

For McCloy especially, as the senior War Department official most deeply involved in occupation planning, the issue was not primarily one of "hard" or "soft" schools but of feasibility, and he went into the 2 September meeting prepared to opt for a feasible "hard" policy. Above all he was determined to preserve the War Department's predominance in the planning in Washington as well as the theater commander's in the field during the military period. With this goal accomplished he could afford to accommodate the tone of the Morgenthau Plan and ignore the substance, the tone having been already imposed by the President's statements in any case.

The Morgenthau Plan was in the long run only incidental to the revision of the War Department's thinking. Had the plan's influence been greater, the ultimate result might in fact have been less unsatisfactory; but the necessary compromise was much more fundamental. The emphasis until August 1944 had consistently, perhaps even somewhat blindly in the light of opinion developing elsewhere, been on making the Army an instrument of enlightened administration when it occupied enemy territory. After August 1944, as far as Germany was concerned, enlightenment in the Army's thinking gave way to justice as the President conceived it, hard and cold, but at least not to the black retribution of the Treasury plan. The shift was a retreat to a politically, if not morally, more defensible position but no surrender.

In the Cabinet Committee meetings, beginning on 5 September, and in memoran-

dums to the President, Stimson made himself a leading opponent of the Morgenthau Plan within the government. After the meeting on the 5th, at which he had stood alone against Morgenthau's proposal to destroy the Ruhr and possibly also the Saar, he wrote:

I cannot conceive of such a proposition being either possible or effective, and I can see enormous general evils coming from it.
I can conceive of endeavoring to meet the misuse which Germany has recently made of this production by wise systems of control or trusteeship or even transfers to other nations. But I cannot conceive of turning such a gift of nature into a dustheap.[21]

On the 6th, to Morgenthau's chagrin, Stimson appeared to be making headway in convincing the President.[22] On the 17th, although Morgenthau had by then apparently prevailed with the President and the Prime Minister at the OCTAGON Conference in Quebec, Stimson decided, nevertheless, to submit a memorandum he had written two days earlier. In it he condemned the philosophy of the plan. "We cannot," he wrote to the President, "reduce a nation of seventy million who have been outstanding for years in the arts and sciences and highly industrialized to poverty. . . . It would be just such a crime as the Germans themselves hoped to perpetrate on their victims—it would be a crime against civilization itself."[23]

On the 22d, McCloy met in his office with his counterparts from the State and Treasury Departments. In an all-day session they worked over a CAD draft entitled

---

[20] Ltr, McCloy to Eisenhower, 24 Oct 44, in USFET SGS 334/2.

[21] Memo, HLS (Stimson), untitled, 5 Sep 44, in ASW 370.8. See also Stimson and Bundy, *On Active Service*, p. 570.
[22] Blum, *Morgenthau Diaries*, vol. III, p. 362.
[23] (1) Memo, Stimson for the President, 15 Sep 44, in ASW, 370.8. (2) Stimson and Bundy, *On Active Service*, p. 578.

"Directive to SCAEF Regarding the Military Government of Germany in the Period Immediately Following the Cessation of Organized Resistance." With their informal approval, the directive went to the JCS as JCS 1067.[24] It was the product of a tumultuous month. Allied troops were inside Germany and might soon occupy the whole country. Eisenhower had no directive, and whether or not he would have a military government mission was far from certain. At Quebec the President and Prime Minister had put their okays on the economic features of the Morgenthau Plan. Whether the leadership in occupation planning, even during the military phase, would remain with the War Department was questionable. Under pressure from the White House, U.S. official opinion on Germany had hardened to a degree that would for months to come dismay and baffle many who saw the results but not the darker alternatives.

Few documents as important as JCS 1067 have been written under such intense and diverse influences of the moment; nevertheless, if not enlightened, the document was what it was intended to be, a proper military directive giving the theater commander workable instructions on which to base detailed planning. At the same time, it was not, as its authors were no doubt well aware, an adequate program for administering a conquered nation. The directive disavowed any intention of stating policy beyond that of a "short term and military character, in order not to prejudice whatever ultimate policies may later be determined upon."[25] Its object was to establish a "stern, all-powerful military administration of a conquered country, based on its unconditional surrender, impressing the Germans with their military defeat and the futility of any further aggression."[26] In language it was redolent of the Treasury philosophy. In substance it was an expansion of five points, none originating with the Morgenthau Plan, on which the War-State-Treasury meeting of 2 September and subsequently the Cabinet Committee had agreed unanimously. They were: dissolution of the Nazi party; demilitarization; controls over communications, press, propaganda, and education; reparation for those countries wanting it; and decentralization of the German governmental structure (without a decision either way on partitioning the country). A sixth point—aimed at permanently reducing the German standard of living to the subsistence level, eliminating the German economic power position in Europe, and converting the German economy "in such a manner that it will be so dependent upon imports and exports that Germany cannot by its own devices reconvert to war production"—had been considered and dropped. It had been acceptable to Morgenthau as a lightly camouflaged entering wedge for his plan and had been vehemently rejected by Stimson for the same reason. On the matter of relief, the directive restated the disease and unrest formula and discouraged importation of relief supplies, but did not prohibit them.

The economic section of the directive prohibited "steps looking toward the

---

[24] JCS 1067, Directive to Commander in Chief of U.S. Forces of Occupation Regarding the Military Government of Germany in the Period Immediately following the Cessation of Organized Resistance (Post Defeat), 24 Sep 44, in OPD, ABC 387.

[25] Department of State, *The Conferences at Malta and Yalta, 1945,* in "Foreign Relations of the United States" (Washington, D.C., 1955), p. 143.

[26] [Unsigned paper] German Occupation Policy, Oct 44, in ASW, 370.8.

economic rehabilitation of Germany [or] designed to maintain or strengthen the German economy" and placed the responsibility for maintaining economic controls on the German people and the German authorities.[27] This section has been cited by no less an authority on the occupation than Walter L. Dorn as evidence that JCS 1067 was "largely a Treasury document."[28] The Treasury influence was, however, mostly coincidental. In response to Eisenhower's request to be relieved of responsibility for sustaining the German economy and the President's reaction to the handbook, the CAD had, at least two weeks before the meeting at which JCS 1067 was drafted, written an almost identical statement on economic policy as the first of the three principles to be attached to the flyleaf of the handbook. (See above, p. 89.) No matter what its origin and even though it was later altered somewhat (see below, p. 212), the economic policy was going to prove unfortunate. Nevertheless, in stating the policy, the War Department was not making the Army the instrument for achieving the long-range aims of the Morgenthau Plan, but merely taking from Eisenhower the responsibility during the initial occupation period for preventing an economic collapse, which Eisenhower believed was inevitable.

Apparently the directive was acceptable to Secretary Morgenthau, not because it incorporated *his* plan but because it did not prejudice the eventual implementation of the plan. At the moment, Morgenthau did not need to have the plan written into a short-term military directive. He believed that he had it established as high national policy both of the United States and of Great Britain. When his confidence on this score evaporated, as it soon did, the directive became a great deal more important to him and to the history of the occupation, not because it incorporated the plan but because it was the only approved U.S. policy statement on Germany.

The directive received JCS approval on 24 September, and several days later Hopkins carried it to the White House. He had been involved in the writing since the 2 September meeting. In the Cabinet Committee, Hopkins had seemed at the beginning to favor the Morgenthau Plan, but he had later apparently developed at least a passing ambition to become the United States High Commissioner for Germany and had then joined the War Department representatives in pushing for a less restrictive statement.[29] The President, according to Hopkins, spent forty minutes reading the directive and then said it was in accordance with his views.[30]

In the aftermath of Quebec, Roosevelt had begun to find the Morgenthau Plan an embarrassment. The 1944 election campaign was getting into full swing, and on 24 September the major Sunday newspapers had run articles on the plan, the majority of them highly critical. Three days later the President telephoned Stimson from Hyde Park to tell him that he did not really intend to make Germany an agricultural nation. When he next saw Stimson in early October, he said Morgenthau had "pulled

---

[27] (1) Department of State, *Malta and Yalta*, in "Foreign Relations," pp. 160 and 143–54. (2) Stimson and Bundy, *On Active Service*, p. 570. (3) *Morgenthau Diary (Germay)*, vol. I, pp. 519–35.

[28] Walter L. Dorn, "The Debate Over American Occupation Policy in Germany in 1944–1945," *Political Science Quarterly*, 72:4, December 1957, p. 494.

[29] *Morgenthau Diary (Germany)*, vol I, pp. 521–24 and p. 624.

[30] Unsigned memo dated 29 Sep 44, in OPD, ABC 387.

a boner," and he seemed "staggered" to learn that a passage about agriculturalization and pastoralization was in the agreement he had initialed with Churchill at Quebec.[31]

In early October, JCS 1067 suddenly became a valuable document—to the President temporarily as evidence, should he need it, that it and not the Morgenthau Plan was the approved U.S. policy for Germany—to the War Department for many months to come as the only statement on Germany it was going to get. Having denied accepting the Morgenthau Plan, the President soon also professed complete lack of interest in postwar planning for Germany. To the Secretary of State he wrote, "it is all very well for us to make all kinds of preparations for Germany but there are some matters in regard to such treatment that lead me to believe speed in such matters is not an essential. . . . I dislike making plans for a country which we do not yet occupy."[32]

A Program for Germany?

JCS 1067 was a U.S. document. As such, although it was sent to Eisenhower, SHAEF could not put it into force until it was approved and transmitted through the CCS. After the uproar over the Morgenthau Plan, the War Department more than ever wanted it approved—and without changes—because the likelihood of agreement within the government on any other document or revision was extremely slight. The hope was that the President's influence would be enough to quell British resistance to policy originating in Washing-

ton and now, in the instance of JCS 1067, exclusively made there. Hopkins, when he took the paper to the President, had asked him to "write a note . . . and ask the Prime Minister to have his nitpickers lay off the documents."[33] But in October the British put forward in the CCAC a draft directive of their own. It differed from JCS 1067 in a number of respects, most painfully for the War Department planners in that it could be taken as an expression of long-term policy—just then the most highly explosive subject in Washington.[34]

That the British directive and JCS 1067 would die in the CCS from lack of action by either side soon became clear; thus the War and State Departments attempted to salvage their one viable piece of policy guidance by submitting it for tripartite adoption in the EAC. Pending this event, which was not to be expected soon, the CAD sent JCS 1067 to the U.S. Group Control Council to be used in planning for the postsurrender period.[35] As Supreme Commander, Eisenhower would have to continue under the presurrender directive, CCS 551. Wickersham, on his return from a trip to Washington in November, reported, "The feeling at home is that SHAEF, in the pre-defeat period, should follow Document 1067 as closely as possible"; but how Eisenhower as combined commander was to impose a strictly U.S. policy on the British contingent in SHAEF was not explained.[36]

---

[31] (1) Stimson and Bundy, On Active Service, p. 580. (2) Department of State, Malta and Yalta, in "Foreign Relations," p. 155.

[32] Department of State, Foreign Relations, 1944, vol. I, p. 358.

[33] Unsigned memo dated 29 Sep 44, in OPD, ABC 387, sec. 4–B.

[34] Memo [no source], sub: The British Draft Directive for Germany, 1 Nov 44, in ASW, 370.8.

[35] Memo for Record, H. L. S. [Stimson], 19 Dec 44, and Memo for Record, H. L. S., sub: Financial Directive, JCS 1067 [no date], in OPD, ABC 387, sec. 4–B.

[36] US Gp CC, Min of Meeting of Staff Conference Held 20 Nov 44, in SHAEF G–5, 31.04.

October was the kind of month in SHAEF that September had been in Washington. Some troops were in Germany and many more might soon join them; but the handbook was hanging fire, and all previous policy assumptions had obviously been superseded by the developments concerning the handbook and JCS 1067. The Morgenthau Plan, meanwhile, had been a godsend for the German Propaganda Ministry. Even the fertile mind of Propaganda Minister Joseph Goebbels would have been hard pressed to devise any better means to stiffen the spines of a population and army reeling under a disastrous summer's defeats.

Although SHAEF did not yet hold enough German territory to make the confusion over policy obvious, it had arrived at the point where an announced military government program could have enormous potential influence on the war. All that the German people knew so far was what their government told them about unconditional surrender and the Morgenthau Plan. In the second week of October the Psychological Warfare Division (PWD), SHAEF, circulated for comment a projected set of guidelines on military government propaganda for the Germans, in which it proposed to offer them opportunities to rebuild for a peaceful, prosperous, and democratic future. Col. T. R. Henn, the deputy chief, answered for the Operations Branch, G–5. Although he was a British officer he apparently spoke for the whole branch. The PWD paper, he said, expressed views on which the U.S. and British civil affairs officers "always have been in complete agreement," namely, "that we must plan beyond the short term view; that, in practice, neither of our nations will allow civilians in Central Europe to starve; [and] that it is essential to avoid repeating the mistakes of 1918–19 (when the blockade of

Central Europe was not lifted for two months). . . ." However, he declared, the doctrine of the professionals was no longer what mattered. The publicity given to the Morgenthau controversy had confirmed "to the last detail every statement of enemy propaganda for the past five years." A restatement of policy could only be effective if Eisenhower was willing to formulate policy independently of the CCS.[37]

The Operations Branch was coming close to talking mutiny, and the next day the G–5, General Grasett, called the first of several meetings in his office to devise propaganda themes that the Psychological Warfare Division could use without putting SHAEF in rebellion. The result was austere: the objective was to be limited to forestalling a scorched earth policy by impressing on the Germans that they would have to fend for themselves economically after the war. Glimmers of hope were to be given them in the form of promises to eradicate Nazi and *Gestapo* rule, purge the school system, restore religious freedom, and permit free labor unions. Material assistance in any form would not be mentioned, but the Germans could be told that the Allied armies would import their own food.[38]

A little later in the month SHAEF propaganda received a small and equivocal boost from Washington. In a speech on 18 October the Republican candidate for president, Gov. Thomas E. Dewey, had accused the Roosevelt administration of stiffening the German resistance by its policy towards Germany. The President replied

---

[37] Memo, SHAEF G–5, Dep Chief, Opns Br, for Exec G–5, sub: Policy to German Civilians, 12 Oct 44, in SHAEF G–5, 807.1, Jacket 1.
[38] Memo, SHAEF CofS for PWD, sub: Propaganda Treatment of Military Government, 20 Oct 44, and Analysis Sheet, SHAEF G–5, Hist Sec, 30 Dec 44, in SHAEF G–5, 117.05.

three days later,[39] promising stern retribution for "all those in Germany directly responsible for this agony of mankind"; but he did not specifically endorse, or reject, the Morgenthau Plan. He said he did not believe "that God eternally condemned any race of humanity," and offered the German people a chance "to earn their way back into the fellowship of peace-loving and law-abiding nations."[40]

Taking the speech as a guide, McCloy told Smith that some propaganda reassurance to the German people was in order. It should not, however, go beyond letting the "average German" feel he "can work in peace if he abides by the regulations." McCloy believed that this aim could be accomplished, on the one hand, by promising "punishment of war criminals and recalcitrant Germans generally" and, on the other, by "factual and colorful news of orderly life in Allied-occupied territory, things like babies being born and women hanging out wash."[41]

SHAEF waited through October and into November before issuing its own military government directive. What it then put forward was an astringent précis of CCS 551 plus the four principles the CCS had ordered affixed to the flyleaf of the handbook. The directive gave the army group commanders the following seven missions only:

1.   Imposition of the will of the Allies upon occupied Germany.
2.   Care, control, and repatriation of displaced United Nations nationals and minimum care necessary to control enemy refugees and displaced persons.
3.   Apprehension of war criminals.

4.   Elimination of nazism-fascism, German militarism, the Nazi hierarchy, and their collaborators.
5.   Restoration and maintenance of law and order, as far as the military situation permits.
6.   Protection of United Nations property, control of certain properties, and conservation of German foreign exchange assets.
7.   Preservation and establishment of suitable administration to the extent required to accomplish the above directives.

The four handbook principles, recapitulated verbatim, were given as restrictions on the missions.[42]

The directive could hardly be regarded as an achievement by those who had worked and trained for many months to make military government a purposeful instrument of national policy. Colonel Henn expressed the dilemma of military government when he wrote:

It will take a quarter century to eliminate the theories on which Nazism came to power. This can only be done by education of the next generation for which we have made no preparations and have no plan. We are proposing to cast out Nazism-militarism, but we have nothing to put in its place. We offer no hope, no ideals of democracy or world citizenship, and no prospect of an economic future.[43]

The future of military government in Germany was indeed for too long going to be officially as bleak as Colonel Henn saw it. On the other hand, armies must rely more on men than on paper schemes. The voice of Colonel Hunt was not dead, nor was the common body of doctrine acquired at Charlottesville and Wimbledon.

---

[39] John L. Snell, *Dilemma Over Germany* (New Orleans: Hauser Press, 1959), p. 101f.
[40] Cable, AGWAR, from McCloy to ETOUSA for Smith, 7 Nov 44, in SHAEF G–5, 117.05.
[41] *Ibid.*

[42] SHAEF, Office of the CofS, to Hqs, A Gps 21, 12, 6, sub: Directive for Military Government of Germany Prior to Defeat or Surrender, 9 Nov 44, in AFHQ G–5, Directives, Military Government of Germany.
[43] Analysis Sheet, SHAEF G–5, Hist Sec, 30 Oct 44, in SHAEF G–5, 25, Jacket 2.

CHAPTER IX

Tripartite Agreements

The Surrender Instrument

Putting a surrender into writing would not seem to require the intensive effort of an intergovernmental commission more than a year before the event. In World War I, the United States and the Allies had left the armistice to the generals in the field, who, when the time came, had produced a document effective enough to end the conflict. But the years between the wars had revealed, from the World War II viewpoint, a catastrophic defect in the 1918 armistice, namely, the Germans had not been convinced of their defeat. At the last minute on 6 November 1918, the German Army had refused to send a military representative to negotiate with the Allies. Mathias Erzberger, a civilian and a defeatist in the eyes of some Germans, had negotiated and signed the armistice. The military leadership, aided by right-wing politicians and press, had for two decades thereafter claimed to have been stabbed in the back. In the United States, many believed that Hitler had been successful at maneuvering his country into war because the German people and soldiers had been hoodwinked into believing they had not really been defeated in 1918. Both the form and the language of the surrender consequently seemed to be crucial in preventing a third world war.

Therefore, in agreeing at Moscow in November 1943 to make the writing of a surrender instrument the first task for the European Advisory Commission, the Allied foreign ministers had not selected an innocuous assignment for a body they viewed with mixed emotions. The Americans in particular, as little as their enthusiasm was for the London-situated EAC, attached great significance to the manner in which the surrender was accomplished, probably more than either the British or the Russians. The British saw the task as a major milestone in modern diplomacy, though neither an absolute end nor a beginning. The Russians wanted to document the fact of victory; the legal aspects concerned them less. The Americans tended to see the surrender as an end in itself, an end not only to German stab-in-the-back theories but also to the need for U.S. intervention in European wars.

When Ambassador Winant, chairing the first formal EAC session on 14 January 1944, suggested that the commission make the surrender instrument the first item on its agenda, the British representative, Sir William Strang, immediately submitted a seventy-paragraph Draft German Armistice. The document, filling thirteen legal-size pages, was formally drawn up and in effect ready for signing. The Soviet delegate, Ambassador Gousev, had nothing to submit. Neither had Winant. His instructions were awaiting JCS approval in Washington, and his military adviser-to-be, General Wickersham, was also still in Washington.

The State, War, and Navy Departments

had set up the Working Security Committee (WSC) in December, composed of members of each of the departments and charged with preparing agreed instructions and information for Winant; the WSC had not attempted to do as the British had, however, and write a specimen document. It had, instead, listed twenty-seven provisions deemed essential in a surrender document for Germany.[1]

More important than the WSC list were the concepts developed at higher levels—in the State Department and in the JCS— that the surrender document ought to be brief, attesting mainly to the fact of unconditional military surrender, and that specific provisions to be imposed on Germany should be relegated to orders, proclamations, and ordinances. These latter documents would be issued under the authority acquired through the unconditional surrender and would in no way constitute a contract with the Germans, thus avoiding from the outset any argument over terms; there would simply be none. By January, the JCS had concluded that all it wanted the Germans to sign was an admission of complete defeat. Such a document, the Joint Chiefs believed, would leave no room for quibbling and would not imply any commitments to the Germans.[2]

Winant circulated the WSC/JCS proposals in the EAC at its second meeting on 25 January. The Russians still had received no instructions of their own, and the British and American concepts were too far apart to be readily usable as the basis for negotiation. In fact, as matters stood, both concepts were being presented not for discussion but for adoption more or less *in toto*. Wickersham, who had brought the WSC/JCS papers to London, regarded them as orders to be observed to the letter, which was probably exactly how the War Department wanted him to interpret his mission.[3]

The British draft proposal, on the other hand, had been found completely unacceptable in Washington, beginning with the word "armistice" in the title. The word could be taken to imply a temporary cessation of hostilities, not a surrender; furthermore, one of the German complaints about the 1918 armistice had been that they had been tricked into signing what amounted to an unconditional surrender under the guise of an armistice. The length of the document also seemed to reduce its potential force as an unconditional surrender instrument, since by enumerating specific requirements it left room for the insinuation that the victors' powers were only those specifically claimed in the document.[4] In Washington, too, the British delegation's full-fledged surrender document, obviously designed to be a finished product and not a starting point for negotiations, had rekindled the long-standing irritation at British attempts to seize the leadership in postwar questions. The WSC's instructions to Winant had at least left the writing to the European Advisory Commission.

Probably the fundamental issue both for

---

[1] WS 10A, Provisions for Imposition on Germany at the Time of Surrender, 6 Jan 44, and JCS 623/2, Provisions for Imposition Upon Germany at the Time of Surrender, 18 Jan 44, in CCS 387 (12–17–43), sec. 1.

[2] (1) Ltr, JCS to Sec of State, 18 Dec 43, in OPD, ABC 387, sec. 1–A. (2) JCS 623/3, Instrument and Acknowledgement of Unconditional Surrender of Germany, 29 Jan 44, in CCS 387 (12–17–43), sec. 1. (3) Ltr, Adm William D. Leahy, Chm, JCS, to Sec of State, sub: Support of U.S. Views [on Unconditional Surrender Instrument], 5 Feb 44, in OPD, ABC 336, sec. 1, cases 1–5.

[3] History of the CAD, bk. III, ch. I, p. 60.

[4] JCS 623/3, sub: Instrument and Acknowledgment of Unconditional Surrender, 29 Jan 44, in OPD, ABC 387, sec. I–A.

Washington and London was the meaning of unconditional surrender. The British had written what they said was an unconditional surrender, but they called it an armistice, and to Washington it looked suspiciously conditional. This suspicion was strengthened when a British high-level intelligence estimate described fear of the consequences of unconditional surrender as the second of two forces preventing a complete breakdown in German morale. The other was fear of the *Gestapo*.[5] As a matter of fact, British and American intelligence opinions were in considerable agreement on the effect of the unconditional surrender policy, and the JCS would before long appeal to the President—unsuccessfully—to modify it, by doing at least what the British were attempting in their draft surrender, namely, stating their meaning specifically.[6] No one in the War Department, however, seems to have considered it either proper or expedient to try to spell out the meaning of unconditional surrender in the EAC document, probably because nobody was willing to give up the legal fact of unconditional surrender—as the British were proposing to do—for the sake of making the idea more palatable to the Germans. The War Department did not want the policy abandoned, only clarified enough to lay to rest what seemed to Americans the baseless, propaganda-inspired fears of the Germans.

The review of the lengthy British terms had also evoked a reassessment of the WSC proposal which would have produced a substantial document if its twenty-seven points were all included. Consequently, the War Department undertook to write its own draft, which would embody as far as possible the concentrated essence of unconditional surrender and offer a clear alternative to the British version. Hilldring had the draft as written in the Civil Affairs Division in hand the day before Winant presented the first U.S. proposal in the EAC. Compressed to thirteen paragraphs and typed double-space, it filled only two and one-half sheets of legal-size paper.[7]

Approved by the JCS, the CAD draft went to the EAC in the first week of February along with arguments for its adoption and, inferentially, against adoption of the British version. The CAD draft required the German signatories to make three acknowledgments: that their military forces were totally defeated and incapable of further resistance; that their resources and people were exhausted to the point where further resistance was futile; and that the country was ready to submit without question to any military, political, economic, or territorial terms which the victors might impose.[8] Contrary to the British draft, which had not specified who would do the signing, the U.S. draft required the signature of the "highest German Military Authority" and relegated the German civilian signatory to second place. The original instructions to Winant had already insisted on making the German High Command acknowledge the defeat whether or not a civilian government existed that was capable of doing so.[9]

A week later the U.S. stand received some moderately disquieting reinforcement from the Russians. Gousev presented a twenty-paragraph Soviet draft which almost equaled the U.S. version in brevity.

---

[5] JIC M/133, sub: Effect of Unconditional Surrender Policy on German Morale, 31 Jan 44, in OPD, ABC 387, sec. I–A.

[6] Memo, JCS for the President, 25 Mar 44, and Memo, FDR for the Joint Chiefs of Staff, 1 Apr 44, in OPD, ABC 387, sec. 3.

[7] *History of the CAD,* bk. VI, ch. II, p. 40.

[8] Department of State, *Foreign Relations, 1944,* vol. I, pp. 167–72.

[9] *Ibid.,* p. 101.

The cause for disquiet could be deduced from the title, "Terms of Surrender for Germany." The U.S. version was entitled "Instrument and Acknowledgment of Unconditional Surrender of Germany." The Russians used the term "unconditional surrender" twice in their preamble but in the text concentrated overwhelmingly on military matters, suggesting other consequences only in an article dealing with occupation zones and in a brief reference to additional "political, economic, and military" requirements.[10] In the EAC, the Russians did not conceal that they wanted to make the act of surrender as painless as possible for the Germans and leave the most unpleasant aspects to be revealed later.

In mid-February, the EAC had three complete drafts before it, had made no progress toward adopting any one or writing anything of its own, and had found moving on to any other subject impossible because the Russians insisted on settling each item completely before going to the next. The Americans and British, as had happened before, were locked in a conflict as much concerned with whose view was accepted as with what was accepted. Winant complained that he really could not see "a great practical difference" between the three documents, but in Washington the advantages of the short U.S. draft were regarded as great enough to require a letter from Roosevelt to Churchill supporting it.[11] To keep Wickersham from wavering, Hilldring forwarded part of the President's letter to him.[12] At the same time, having adopted the practice of meeting formally, the EAC could not even tentatively search out areas of agreement. Each delegation talked for

[10] *Ibid.*, pp. 173–79.
[11] *Ibid.*, pp. 188 and 190.
[12] *History of the CAD,* bk. VI, ch. II, p. 77.

the record and defended its own draft in every detail.

At the end of the first week in March, the deadlock loosened somewhat when, on Winant's suggestion, he, Strang, and Gousev met informally in Gousev's private office. Speaking unofficially, Strang said he thought his government might agree to a short document, since it was what both the Americans and the Russians wanted, provided all points covered in the British draft were included in the supplementary proclamations and orders. Winant thought the U.S. government would accept this provision. Gousev agreed to short terms and seemed to find the U.S. draft acceptable except for paragraph VII which required the German authorities and people to cooperate in apprehending war criminals and making them available for trial. The Soviet government, he said, did not want a reference to war criminals in the document because the men who came to sign might themselves fall into this category and might, therefore, refuse to do business at all. He also indicated that his government would not want the proposed proclamations and orders shown to the Germans before they had signed the surrender. What his government wanted, he said, was to get an unconditional military surrender as quickly as possible and thereafter get the Germans disarmed and demobilized. The rest, he implied, would follow naturally, and Winant rather chillingly became aware that when the Russians said "unconditional surrender" they meant it. Neither the Americans nor the British had ever really contemplated a fully unconditional surrender. Under the U.S. proposal, the proclamations and orders would have restricted the powers of the victors about as much as if the same provisions had been included in the surrender instrument as the British desired. Although not a contract with the Germans, these proclamations and orders would have constituted a contract among the Allies. The Soviet Union, Winant now began to suspect—as the British possibly had earlier when they wrote their long terms—might not be interested in either form of such a contract. The questions were whether the Russians would be willing to go on to the proclamations and orders after the surrender instrument was written and whether they would observe them after the surrender was signed. Gousev said that they would, provided the surrender instrument was completed first.[13]

Winant, Strang, and Gousev had after two futile months found a means by which they could negotiate, and after two scheduled meetings in March they never met formally again except to sign documents ready for submission to their governments. Getting the authority to negotiate took longer, certainly for Winant and probably for the other two as well. In the second week of March, Adm. Harold R. Stark, Commander, United States Naval Forces in Europe, and Winant's chief naval adviser, told Adm. Ernest J. King that progress in the EAC was being held up because Winant felt bound by the U.S. draft surrender instrument. In response, the JCS relaxed its stand slightly, saying it wanted "every effort" made to get the U.S. document adopted but did not "preclude negotiation with a view to formulating recommendations to the three governments."[14] This concession was not enough, and two weeks later Wickersham went to Washington to explain why Winant needed more latitude.

The JCS then revised its views, which were sent to Winant on 10 April. The JCS still required a short document limited to the three main features of the U.S. draft but was willing to accept different wording and "adjustments of points of view" made in the EAC.[15]

Since Washington had already agreed to include the points to be omitted from the British draft in proclamations, orders, and other policies to be written later in the EAC, full agreement with the British became relatively easy as long as the surrender instrument was not exclusively an American product. Agreement with the Russians was a different matter. The Soviet draft terms specified in three separate places that the German armed forces, including the S.A. (a paramilitary organization of the Nazi party) and the *Gestapo,* at the front, inside Germany, and outside German territory, were to be declared prisoners of war upon the signing of the surrender and "be stationed at such places and in such manner as may be determined by each Allied Commander-In-Chief on his own front."[16] Although the Americans and the British in the spring of 1944 were not disposed to be too moved by the future plight of German troops they did not propose to use Germans for forced labor, which was the only cogent reason for declaring them prisoners of war after the war was over. Furthermore, since they were committed to observe the Hague and Geneva Conventions, they recoiled from the thought of having to give millions of defeated Germans rations and billets approxi-

---

[13] Department of State, *Foreign Relations, 1944,* vol. I, pp. 197–99.

[14] JCS 623/6, Instrument and Acknowledgement of Unconditional Surrender by Germany, 20 Mar 44, in OPD, ABC 387, sec. 1–A.

[15] (1) JCS 623/7, Instrument and Acknowledgement of Unconditional Surrender by Germany, 4 Apr 44, in OPD, ABC 387, sec. 1–A. (2) Department of State, *Foreign Relations, 1944,* vol. I p. 210.

[16] Department of State, *Foreign Relations, 1944,* vol. I, pp. 174 and 176.

mately equivalent to what they provided for their own troops. Gousev, to allay the Western delegates' qualms, said the Soviet Union would abide by the conventions even though it did not regard itself as bound by them, which carried little conviction since neither the Soviet Union nor Germany had observed the conventions thus far in the war between them. Later Gousev offered to add an article providing for treatment of the prisoners of war "in a manner to be prescribed by the representatives of the Allies."[17] Whether such an article would relieve the Western Allies of their obligations under the conventions was doubtful at best. What was certain was that it would make the surrender instrument a most dangerous document if the Germans learned its contents before they surrendered and while they still held American and British prisoners.

In May the EAC subsided again into semiparalysis. The Soviet delegates refused to talk about anything but the surrender terms and refused to compromise on the prisoner of war issue. The Americans and British were ready early in the month to let the Soviet Union have the prisoners of war as long as they were not required to do the same with the German troops who fell to them and as long as token tripartite control such as the Russians had already suggested was established regarding their treatment. But as the weeks passed, it began to appear that the prisoners of war were not the real hitch. As long as the Russians and the Germans were alone on the mainland of Europe, the Russians did not seem to want to commit themselves at all to a multilateral unconditional surrender.[18]

In June the atmosphere changed. At the end of the first week Eisenhower's forces were in Normandy and thus closer to the heart of Germany than the Soviet armies. The need for agreement was acquiring some urgency in Moscow as well as in Washington and London. On 10 June Acting Secretary of State Edward R. Stettinius, Jr., asked Winant to hurry up the surrender terms because the War Department was, "with the invasion now in progress," pressing for headway on plans for the occupation. Within the hour that Stettinius' cable left the department, one from London arrived in which Winant reported that, on the day before, the three delegates had reached agreement on the surrender terms, except for details, and Gousev had agreed to begin taking up other questions.[19] Gousev had accepted a statement that all members of the German armed forces were subject to being declared prisoners of war "at the discretion of the Commander-in-Chief of the Armed Forces of the Allied State concerned . . . pending further decisions and . . . subject to such conditions and directions as may be prescribed by the Allied Representatives."[20] If the Soviet Union wanted manpower, the new terms gave them a sizable bonus by also defining as members of the German armed forces auxiliaries equipped with weapons, which could eventually have included every halfway able-bodied German male between sixteen and sixty.

The text of the draft entitled "Unconditional Surrender of Germany," as signed in the EAC on 25 July 1944 and submitted to the governments for approval, consisted of fourteen articles.[21] It was divided into

[17] History of the CAD, bk. VI, ch. II, pp. 100–102.

[18] Memo, Lt Col Henry Carter for Col Lewis, sub: Trip to London 10–12 May, 13 May 44, in OMGUS 3/35, 319.1.

[19] Department of State, *Foreign Relations, 1944,* vol. I, p. 233.

[20] *Ibid.,* p. 257.

[21] *Ibid.,* pp. 256–61.

three parts. In the first part Germany acknowledged complete military defeat on land, at sea, and in the air. The second part was a series of military articles providing for the end to hostilities and giving the Allies the power to demobilize and disarm the German forces. In the third part the Germans would be required to bind themselves to carry out unconditionally other political, administrative, economic, financial, and military requirements which the Allies would subsequently present.[22] The proclamations, orders, ordinances, and instructions yet to be written, which the Germans would not see before the signing, would convey the full meaning of this last part to the Germans.

The CAD regarded the surrender instrument as a successful compromise from the U.S. point of view. Its chief weaknesses seemed to be that it provided for an unconditional surrender without explicitly defining the term and that it anticipated a lapse of some hours between the signing and the cease-fire. But it met the U.S. requirements for brevity and broad language. The U.S. compromises had been ones of form, while those of the British and the Russians had been substantive. The British had sacrificed their long terms. The Russians had relaxed their stand on the prisoner of war question and had given up the attempt to sugarcoat the document to induce the Germans to sign.[23]

The Zones

Among the various reasons for the German military resurgence after World War I, one frequently cited was the failure of

the Rhineland occupation—because it affected only a small part of Germany—to bring home to the Germans the meaning of defeat. Maintained by the French and British until 1930, the Rhineland occupation had given the Germans an object on which to focus their resentments without giving the Allies any worthwhile leverage, either political or military. Consequently, the World War II planners always considered a total occupation to be necessary to guarantee success in preventing a future German outburst. Neither was there any serious doubt that the country should be divided into zones, one for each of the major victorious powers. The logistics of such an arrangement were infinitely simpler than would be the case in a combined occupation, and the risk of inter-Allied friction would be reduced. In any event, neither the United Kingdom nor the United States nor the Soviet Union would have been willing to relinquish control over its own forces and its independent power of decision to the extent necessary to set up an integrated occupation.

A zonal division in embryo appeared in the first COSSAC report on RANKIN presented to the Combined Chiefs of Staff at the QUADRANT Conference (Quebec) in August 1943. The COSSAC staff, then mostly British, assigned northwest Germany including the Ruhr to the British and the Rhine valley from the Swiss border to Duesseldorf to the Americans. COSSAC did not attempt to determine an eastern boundary for either zone since it did not know how much of Germany the Soviet forces might occupy and would not itself have enough troops before 1944 to deploy them deeper into Germany. The assignment of the zones, the COSSAC planners pointed out, was adjusted to the plan for OVERLORD, which in positioning the British forces on the left

---

[22] *Ibid.*, pp. 254–55.
[23] Memo, Lt Col Edgar P. Allen for Director, CAD, sub: Unconditional Surrender of Germany, 20 Jun 44, in CAD, 014 (7–10–42), sec. 7.

flank would take them through the Low Countries into northwestern Germany, while the Americans, landing on the right, would sweep eastward and strike into Germany along the upper Rhine valley.[24] While the logic of the zonal arrangement appeared inescapable to the British at QUADRANT— as it did to them throughout the long months of argument that followed—the Americans were unwilling to accept it out of hand, and the conference adjourned without making a decision on RANKIN.[25]

Some weeks later, in October, Morgan took to Washington another statement on RANKIN. In the interim, he had received a recently completed, high-level British report concerning occupation zones. Written in the Armistice and Post-War Committee, which had Deputy Prime Minister Clement Attlee as its chairman and included the Foreign Secretary and the Secretary for War in its membership, the report divided all of Germany into three zones. In the northwestern zone, which would be British, the report included, along with the Ruhr, the north German ports, Hamburg and Bremen, and the Kiel Canal. To the United States it assigned, as COSSAC had earlier, the southwestern zone, adding a sphere of influence in France to the area of U.S. responsibility since the American lines of supply and communications would presumably run across France.[26] Two JCS agencies, the Joint Strategic Survey Committee and the Joint Staff Planners, reviewed the new RANKIN proposals. The Joint Strategic Survey Committee called attention to the long-standing decision to withdraw U.S. forces from Europe quickly after the end of hostilities for deployment to the Pacific and asked for policy guidance on the U.S. role in the occupation in general and the acceptability of the southwestern zone in particular. The Joint Staff Planners advised taking the questions to the President, since the revised RANKIN appeared to embody British War Cabinet and Foreign Office postwar policy.[27]

The President took up the request for guidance emanating from the joint studies on 19 November in a meeting with the Joint Chiefs aboard the battleship *Iowa* en route to Cairo. Contemplating a need to maintain an occupation force of about a million U.S. troops in Germany "for one year, maybe two" after the surrender, he stated his requirements for the zones. The territorial dispositions, he said, in order to facilitate breaking up Germany into three, possibly five, separate states after the war, ought to conform to the geographic subdivisions of the country. He saw these entities as being a Roman Catholic south, a Protestant northwest extending to Berlin, and a northeastern region which he described as having "Prussianism" as its religion. To illustrate, Roosevelt drew the boundaries in pencil on a National Geographic Society map. Stalin, he thought, might okay such a division, and he believed the Joint Chiefs "would want to" make RANKIN conform to it. He did not like the idea of the United States taking the southwestern zone and therewith having to take responsibility for France. The United States, he believed, should take the northwestern zone in Germany where it would have direct access

---

[24] Historical Subsec, SGS, SHAEF, History of COSSAC, May 44, in USFET SGS 314.8.

[25] Matloff, *Strategic Planning for Coalition Warfare*, p. 226.

[26] William M. Franklin, "Zonal Boundaries and Access to Berlin," *World Politics*, 16:1, October 1963, p. 6.

[27] (1) History of the CAD, bk. VI, ch. I, pp. 6–8. (2) COSSAC/CA/Plan 26/4, Outline of Operations for Civil Affairs Planning—RANKIN Case "C", 15 Nov 43, in SHAEF G–5, 115.25c, jacket 1.

through Bremen and Hamburg. The United States, he said, should also have Berlin, and the Soviet Union could take the territory to the east.[28]

On 4 December, at Cairo, Marshall presented the President's wishes concerning the northwestern and southwestern zones to the Combined Chiefs of Staff, who then decided—unwillingly on the part of the British and somewhat reluctantly on the part of Marshall, who had wanted a firm decision—to direct COSSAC to examine the implications for OVERLORD planning of a switch in the zones.[29] But the COSSAC report, delivered later in the month, contributed nothing new. General Morgan maintained that in order to put the Americans in the northwest zone, he would either have to revise the OVERLORD deployment or be confronted after the surrender with an administrative tangle while the U.S. and British forces crossed each other's lines of communications on their way to the final zones. The JCS had conceded a certain inelegance in the necessity for trading zones but had refused to see it as the overwhelming problem it appeared to be to the British. In the meeting on the *Iowa*, the President had suggested, if need be, setting up a separate occupation army which could be brought in through the northwestern German ports while the OVERLORD troops were exiting from the southwest through France.[30] Most likely, the British did not really expect Morgan's report to accomplish anything, since the zoning question,

having become one of national policy, would eventually have to be decided between the President and the Prime Minister.

In January, at the first EAC meeting, Sir William Strang submitted the findings of the Armistice and Post-War Committee as the British proposal on zones. Well known to the JCS and the President through RANKIN and the Cairo Conference, the British thinking was still totally new to Winant and to the State Department. Furthermore, neither was yet aware of the objections raised in the military talks or of the zonal division the President had drawn on board the *Iowa*.[31]

Meanwhile, the President's concept of the zones had opened up another area of potential U.S.–British contention. To facilitate administration and possibly dismemberment, the British proposal laid the zonal boundaries along existing German internal political boundaries. In his regional concept, the President had paid little attention to established political subdivisions. His and the British proposal did agree approximately on the boundary between the northwestern and southwestern zones, which the President had drawn along the line of the Main River and the northern boundary of Bavaria, the traditional dividing line between north and south Germany. In fixing the boundary between the western zones and the eastern zone, however, the British followed the eastern borders of Hanover, Braunschweig, and Hesse-Nassau, which lay as much as 150 miles west of the line the President had drawn and left Berlin deep in the eastern zone. Berlin, in the British version, was to become a combined zone. Omitting East Prussia, as the British proposal did, the northwestern and eastern

---

[28] Department of State, *Cairo and Tehran,* in "Foreign Relations," pp. 253–55.

[29] (1) *Ibid.,* p. 688. (2) Matloff, *Strategic Planning for Coalition Warfare,* p. 378.

[30] (1) Department of State, *Cairo and Tehran,* in "Foreign Relations," pp. 254 and 699. (2) CCS Précis and Action Sheet, SHAEF, sub: RANKIN C., Spheres of Occupation on the Continent, 4 Feb 44, in SHAEF SGS 371.

[31] Franklin, "Zonal Boundaries and Access to Berlin," p. 14.

zones were, according to the British reckoning, almost exactly equal in population, although the eastern zone was about a fifth larger than the northwestern zone in area. The southwestern zone was substantially smaller than the other two, a full third smaller than the eastern zone in population and even smaller than that in area.[32] The British planners suggested that the United States might, if it wished, also take responsibility for Austria, which would give it an area slightly larger than the Soviet zone and a population about equal to either of the other zones.[33]

At the end of the first week in February, the President took on the task of securing the northwestern zone for the United States. On the 4th the British Chiefs of Staff had replied to the change in RANKIN proposed by the JCS at Cairo. To Morgan's arguments for keeping RANKIN as it was, the British Chiefs added a claim to "a peculiar" British interest in overseeing the German naval disarmament, thus declining "to agree to the U.S. counterproposals until such time as the U.S. Chiefs produce reasons of overriding importance in favor of their acceptance."[34] Three days later, Roosevelt dispatched a cable to Churchill. The qualms of the U.S. military about letting the northwest zone go to the British mostly involved a lurking suspicion that the British were maneuvering for long-term economic advantage in the Ruhr and through possession of the North Sea ports. The President's attitude, however, was determined entirely by an unwillingness to be tied down in Europe after the war, particularly in France. which he apparently expected to fall into chaos as soon as the German grip was loosened. For the President, Germany, northwest or southwest, was unimportant except for the implied association of France with the southwestern zone. To Churchill he wrote: "I am absolutely unwilling to police France and possibly Italy and the Balkans as well. After all France is your baby and it will take a lot of nursing to bring it to the point of walking alone." He suggested that since the Combined Chiefs of Staff had reached an impasse, the two of them should make the decision to change RANKIN.[35]

The answer from London recapitulated the British positions already taken and added an expression of faith in the ability of France to govern itself and possibly even help take over the U.S. zone in Germany if American troops had to be withdrawn. On the last day of the month, the President made a second appeal: "Do please don't ask me to keep any American forces in France. I just cannot do it! I would have

---

[32] The U.S. and British figures, compiled at the same time, vary somewhat as is shown by the following table:

	British		U.S.–WSC	
	Population millions	Area sq. mi.	Population millions	Area sq. mi.
Northwestern Zone	22.5	57,450	24.8	50,500
Southwestern Zone	15.7	47,100	15.6	45,600
Eastern Zone	22.3	76,600	22.2	71,000
East Prussia			2.2	14,300

[33] Department of State, *Foreign Relations, 1944,* vol. I, pp. 150–53. See also Philip E. Mosely, "The Occupation of Germany: New Light on How the Zones Were Drawn," *Foreign Affairs,* 28:4, July 1950, pp. 580–604.

[34] CCS Précis and Action Sheet, SHAEF, sub: RANKIN C., Spheres of Occupation on the Continent, 4 Feb 44, in SHAEF SGS 371.

[35] (1) War Cabinet, Chiefs of Staff Committee, Annex, Copy of a Telegram (No. 457) dated 7 Feb 1944 from President Roosevelt to the Prime Minister, 8 Feb 44, in SHAEF SGS 371. (2) Department of State, *Foreign Relations, 1944,* vol. I, p. 166.

to bring them all back home."[36] With this plea, the exchange stopped for three months; the impasse had gone as high as it could.

While the President and Prime Minister were engaged with each other, the Russians, perhaps unintentionally, brought the question closer to solution than anyone could have expected. In February, Winant had no instructions from Washington on the zones other than that the United States insisted on occupying northwestern Germany and the JCS considered a zonal system to be "the most practical solution."[37] Gousev was insisting on taking up one subject at a time in the EAC and the discussion of the zones seemed to be a long way off in any case, until Gousev presented the Soviet draft surrender terms for Germany on 16 February. The draft included a detailed description of the zonal boundaries, which proved to match almost exactly the boundaries proposed by the British.[38]

In Washington the apparent British-Soviet agreement was a surprise, and an unwelcome one, in that it threatened to move the zonal dispute between the British and the Americans out of the RANKIN-OVERLORD context and into the area of tripartite decision, which, if nothing else, would infringe on the War Department and JCS determination to exclude the EAC from military concerns. Probably, the military staffs in Washington preferred to leave the negotiations on boundaries in the President's hands along with those related to the northwestern and southwestern zones.

In any case, the staffs regarded the President's opinion on boundaries given aboard the *Iowa* as binding on them.[39] The problem was a particularly ticklish one for the State Department, which had to give instructions to Winant but had so far been excluded from the discussions between the JCS and the President and in the Combined Chiefs of Staff. On 19 February, Acting Secretary of State Stettinius sent a map to the White House showing the zonal boundaries as the British proposed them, asked as nearly point-blank as possible what decisions had already been made, and suggested that the President might want to outline his current views for transmission to Winant since a Soviet proposal similar to the British one had been made. The President replied that he did not agree with the British demarcation, but he mentioned no alternative and confined his comments to the reasons why the United States should have a northwestern zone.

A week later, Hilldring passed on to the State Department the U.S. paper on the zones presented to the British at Cairo and a redraft of the map the President had drawn aboard the *Iowa,* which had not been shown to the British. (*Maps 1 and 2*) The map, redrawn to emphasize an American northwestern zone, left Berlin entirely in the Soviet zone (the President's line had passed through the center of the city) but extended the boundary south of Berlin farther eastward than had the President to take in the Leipzig-Cottbus railroad and three connecting lines from Berlin.[40] Philip E. Mosely, then Chief of the Division of Territorial Studies in the State Department and a member of the Working

---

[36] Department of State, *Foreign Relations, 1944,* vol. I, pp. 181–82 and 189.

[37] (1) JCS 723, Administration of Germany—Occupation Period, 22 Feb 44, in OPD, ABC, 387, sec. 4–A. (2) Department of State, *Foreign Relations, 1944,* vol. I, p. 186.

[38] Department of State, *Foreign Relations, 1944,* vol. I, p. 177.

[39] See also Mosely, "New Light on How the Zones Were Drawn," pp. 580–604.

[40] Map reproduced in Department of State, *Foreign Relations, 1944,* vol. I, facing p. 196.

ZONES OF OCCUPATION
BRITISH AND SOVIET PROPOSALS

SOVIET ZONE
BRITISH ZONE
UNITED STATES ZONE
AUSTRIA AND UNITED STATES ZONE
JOINT ZONE

MAP 1

Security Committee, has described the consternation raised by the map in the State Department; in fact, almost two weeks elapsed before Stettinius forwarded it gingerly to Winant "for [his] recommendations."[41] Winant, who assumed, as apparently everyone in the State Department did, that the map had originated in the JCS, thought his recommendations important enough to warrant sending his Counselor of Delegation, George F. Kennan, to Washington to deliver them directly to the President. At the White House on 3 April, Kennan stressed Winant's concern over the suspicion that would be aroused in the Rus-

[41] (1) Mosely, "New Light on How the Zones Were Drawn," pp. 580–604. (2) Department of State, *Foreign Relations, 1944,* vol. I, pp. 179, 184, 195, and 207.

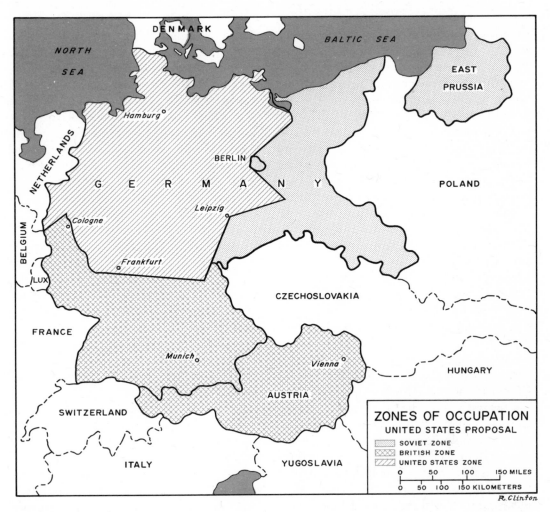

MAP 2

sians' minds by a U.S. proposal to push
the border of the Soviet zone from 50 to
150 miles farther east than the Russians
and the British had agreed upon and additionally deprive the Russians of the important railroad junction at Cottbus.

Although it took another month to get
a decision for Winant, the President seems
actually not to have attached great signifi-

cance to the zone boundaries. The instructions sent to Winant on 1 May were
worded so as to lay emphasis on the U.S.
claim to the northwestern zone. Winant
was allowed to concur in the boundaries
of the Soviet zone "as proposed by the
Soviet Delegation" and in the boundary between the northwestern and southwestern
zones "as proposed by the British Delega-

tion." With respect to the two western zones, however, he was still to insist on American possession of the northwestern zone.[42] In Washington later in May, Winant himself discussed the zones problem with the President and persuaded him not to accept a boundary between the two western zones while possession of each zone was still undecided.[43]

The border between the eastern and western zones, then, was settled in effect before the question came under formal consideration in the European Advisory Commission, which was tied up with the surrender terms through May and after. At the time, the bargain was a good one. In later years periodic rediscoveries of the Roosevelt map would cause talk of American "giveaways"—all based on the assumption that the United States could have disposed of Germany completely at its own discretion. In the spring of 1944, however, when the zones were drawn, the Western Allies still had the North Sea, the English Channel, and the Alps between them and the nearest approaches to Germany. If the German collapse had come at any time in the foreseeable future, it would have come on the front in the Soviet Union; furthermore, in this event, SHAEF did not expect to be able to do more than secure lodgements on the coast and in the Rhine valley. Laying the boundaries of the western zones farther east was slightly utopian. The Rus-

sians, no doubt, knew this too, and they were at first in no hurry to put the agreement in writing.

While the Russians, still insisting on taking one thing at a time, kept the EAC working on the surrender terms, the tug-of-war between the Americans and the British over which zone each would occupy continued behind the scenes as D-day drew closer. Needing a decision that would not at the last minute throw the whole OVER-LORD deployment into confusion Eisenhower in May reverted to a proposal he had first advanced three months earlier, namely, that the United States should refuse to accept any specific zone and agree only to accept military responsibility in Europe as long as the principle of unified command was retained. In May, Stettinius, on Eisenhower's urging, took the idea to the President, who said he was fearful that a combined command would still somehow involve the United States in responsibility for France but professed himself to be open-minded. Encouraged Eisenhower, making clear now that he was thinking only in terms of a combined administration in the two western zones, sent his proposal to the War Department once more.[44] Eisenhower believed later that his proposal was rejected because it would have seemed to establish a British and American partnership against the Soviet Union.[45] Actually two other reasons were more pertinent: the JCS and the CAD had from the beginning considered separate zones essential, and the President was by no means as open-minded as he had said. The President was not at

---

[42] Department of State, *Foreign Relations, 1944,* vol. I, pp. 207–11.

[43] The boundary between the western zones was fixed at the Quebec Conference in September 1944. At that time it was drawn farther north east of the Rhine and farther south west of the Rhine than in the original British and Soviet proposals. The shifts entailed a small increase in the area of the southwestern zone. (1) Department of State, *Foreign Relations, 1944,* vol. I, p. 231. (2) Franklin, "Zonal Boundaries and Access to Berlin," p. 19. (3) Strang, *Home and Abroad,* p. 213.

[44] Ltr, Eisenhower to Marshall, 13 Feb 44; Ltr, E. R. Stettinius to Hon Wm. Phillips, 11 May 44; and Ltr, Eisenhower to Marshall, 27 May 44, in USFET SGS 371.

[45] Dwight D. Eisenhower, *Crusade in Europe* (New York: Doubleday and Company, Inc., 1948), p. 431.

the moment in a mood to welcome suggestions, either civilian or military, that the United States occupy anything but the northwestern zone.[46] On 31 May and 2 June, Roosevelt and Churchill exchanged cables reiterating the stands they had taken in February, each implying that he assumed the other had accepted his position.[47]

In June, having completed the surrender terms, the EAC was ready to move on to the protocol on zones. By the end of the month the commission had a tentative draft ready, which accepted both the three zones defined in the earlier British and Soviet proposals and Greater Berlin as established by a German law of 1920. On 1 July the Soviet delegation created a mild stir on the American side by submitting an amendment also dividing Berlin into three zones (sectors), a northeastern Soviet sector, a northwestern sector, and a southern sector. The decision on who would occupy each of the last two was left to the Americans and the British. Until then all the proposals had presupposed an international administration in Berlin, possibly even including other members of the United Nations, and the United States instructions to its delegation had specifically opposed dividing Berlin into national sectors. A hurried inquiry to the State Department brought Winant the answer that the United States (presumably the JCS) did not like the idea of laying out sector boundaries in Berlin before the extent of destruction and availability of facilities were known, but would agree in principle to sectors within Berlin provided the running of the city remained a combined function.[48]

When the commission met on 25 July and signed its report to the governments on the surrender terms, the zones protocol seemed likely to follow quickly; but three days later Gousev suddenly announced that his government did not want to pass on a paper in which blanks appeared. The British and Americans would have to make up their minds which zones they were going to occupy before the protocol left the commission, and, he implied, the Soviet delegation would not move on to other matters until a decision was made.[49]

For the moment the EAC seemed to have lapsed into paralysis again, but the war was not going to let this happen. The decision on the western zones would be made, and the Russians would be brought around before it was made. While the State Department protested in Moscow against the assumption that the Soviet government could set time limits on negotiations between the U.S. and British governments, Eisenhower's armies rolled across France. Whether Stalin was disposed to pay attention to the protests is not known. That he watched the progress in France, however, is certain. Who might have made the best bargain on the zones became uncertain, and as it did, Soviet interest in the work of the EAC perked up remarkably. On 31 August, Gousev accepted the zones protocol with blanks in the statements on the northwestern and southwestern zones and the northwestern and southern sectors in Berlin, and on 12 September, Winant and Strang signed it for submission to the three governments with the blanks still appearing.

Meanwhile, the standoff with the British over the zones had become an exercise in futility. The War Department had never taken the affair quite as seriously as the

[46] History of the CAD, bk. VI, ch. V, p. 39.
[47] Department of State, *Foreign Relations, 1944,* vol. I, pp. 224 and 232.
[48] *Ibid.*, pp. 187, 237, and 240.

[49] *Ibid.*, p. 262.

President had, and after the invasion it wanted a definite decision either way more than it wanted a particular zone. At the end of July, Stimson told Hopkins that they had to get the President to decide; his being "hell-bent" on the northwestern zone was a mistake.[50] In a cable of 17 August, Eisenhower told the Combined Chiefs of Staff that at the speed his troops were moving they would be in Germany sooner than he had expected and in their original deployment—British 21 Army Group on the left and U.S. 12th and 6th Army Groups on the right. The British, of course, were delighted. The JCS were not so pleased at the possibility of having the U.S. forces occupying southern Germany while the President was still arguing for the northwestern zone, but they conceded that for the moment Eisenhower had no better choice.[51] A week later Stimson urged the President to take the southwestern zone and gave him five good reasons for doing so.[52] Probably the President was by then himself aware that his main reason for rejecting the southwestern zone, the supposed postliberation troubles in France, had pretty well evaporated. The French had proved remarkably willing and able to take over their own affairs, and with Roosevelt's approval Eisenhower was already transferring *de facto* administrative control to General Charles de Gaulle's Committee of National Liberation.[53]

At the opening of the OCTAGON Conference in Quebec on 12 September the Combined Chiefs of Staff referred the allocation of zones to the President and Prime Minis-

ter with a suggestion from Admiral King that the United States would be more inclined to accept the southwestern zone if it could use the north German ports. As far as the conferees knew, or were willing to say either then or afterward, the President was still adamant on having the northwestern zone. No more was heard until the morning meeting of the JCS on the 16th when Admiral William D. Leahy announced that the United States would take the southwestern zone and get access across the northwestern (British) zone to the ports.[54] Leahy said some years later that Roosevelt had told him he took the zone after Churchill in a "tedious argument" convinced him that the northwestern zone would be more valuable in the future to the British than to the United States.[55] Secretary Morgenthau said immediately after the conference that the President had told him he held up agreement on the zones until the last minute to make certain that the British, when they were in charge in the Ruhr and Saar, would have to implement the Morgenthau Plan there.[56]

On the 16th, too, the Combined Chiefs of Staff approved assignment of the ports of Bremen and Bremerhaven to the United States together with transit rights across the British zone to Bremen. Notice of the decisions went to Winant on the 20th with instructions to present them in the EAC, where amendments were then written to fill in the blanks in the protocol. A paragraph added to the description of the southwestern zone reserved for the commander of the U.S. forces the rights to "enjoy such transit facilities" and "exercise such control

---

[50] Stimson and Bundy, *On Active Service*, p. 568.

[51] History of CAD, bk. VI, ch. V, p. 45f.

[52] Stimson and Bundy, *On Active Service*, p. 569.

[53] Coles and Weinberg, *Soldiers Become Governors*, pp. 714–16.

[54] History of the CAD, bk. VI, ch. V, p. 49f.

[55] Matloff, *Strategic Planning for Coalition Warfare*, p. 511n.

[56] Department of State, *Malta and Yalta*, in "Foreign Relations," p. 136.

of the ports of Bremen and Bremerhaven . . . as may be agreed hereafter by the United Kingdom and United States military authorities to be necessary to meet his requirements."[57]

The amendment to the zones protocol, while terminating one year-long Anglo-American dispute, unveiled another that threatened for a time to be equally durable. In accepting the OCTAGON arrangement Smith and Hilldring had both interpreted the word "control," used in reference to Bremen and Bremerhaven, as meaning full control and administration, including military government. The JCS had also added a requirement for control of certain contiguous areas (several adjacent *Land* and *Stadtkreise*), which together with the cities were to become part of the U.S. zone. The reason given was the probable need for German labor and facilities in rehabilitating the ports.[58] The British interpreted control to mean control of the port facilities, not complete administrative control. Removed from the purview of the EAC by the wording of the amendment, the controversy simmered for several months in the Combined Chiefs of Staff, seeming, like the zones issue, destined to go eventually to the President and Prime Minister. The resolution, in fact, did come just before the Yalta Conference. In early January 1945, McCloy, probably trying to avoid involving the President, offered a compromise: if the British gave the Americans the degree of control they wanted, the Americans would agree to make their policies conform to those of the surrounding area in the British zone. Although the United States would

get the best of the compromise, the British Chiefs of Staff, possibly not expecting the Prime Minister to do as well against the President as he had on the original zones question, accepted.[59] An agreement signed at Yalta in early February created the Bremen enclave, which was to stand chiefly as a short-lived monument to the wartime Anglo-American contentiousness.[60]

In retrospect the effort and the energy spent on securing transit across the British zone might seem to have been more profitably expended seeking access to Berlin, and the relationships being what they were, if Berlin had been in the British zone the discussion would very likely have been more intensive. This is not to say, however, that the intramural contention with the British was allowed to obscure the need for access to Berlin. SHAEF took up the question as early as June 1944 and concluded, as the War Department would later, that free access across the Soviet zone was preferable to corridors or selected routes. SHAEF also learned that matters such as this, which the British and Americans discussed freely and as often as not heatedly, could scarcely be taken up with the Russians at all.[61] Once

---

[57] Senate Committee on Foreign Relations, *Documents on Germany, 1944–1959* (Washington, 1959), p. 3–5.

[58] Department of State, *Foreign Relations, 1944,* vol. I, pp. 354f and 369f.

[59] Summary Sheet, ACofS OPD for CofS, sub: Allocation of Zones of Occupation in Germany, 23 Jan 44, in OPD 336 (sec. III) (case 51–   ).

[60] Governing the Bremen enclave, cut off from its normal economic and administrative ties with the surrounding territory of the British zone and several hundred miles removed from the U.S. zone, later proved both unwieldy and unnecessary; and on 10 December 1945, the area outside the cities of Bremen, Wesermuende, and Bremerhaven was transferred to British control. U.S. military government teams stayed in the cities, but they operated under British supervision thereafter.

[61] Memo, SHAEF G–3 for Staff Divisions, sub: Organization and Administration of International Zone, Berlin, 1 Jun 44; Memo, SHAEF G–3, Future Plans Sub-Section, for SHAEF G–3, sub: Organization and Administration of International Zones, Berlin, 14 Jun 44; Ltr, SHAEF Political Officers to Col Grazebrook, sub: Organization and

the zones protocol was signed, the Western Allies' access to Berlin was implied; and during the discussion of the November amendments the Soviet delegate, Gousev, suggested—as was later done—that the statement on transit across the British zone be kept general, leaving the details to be worked out later. Similar arrangements, he said, would be made giving the U.S. and British forces access across the Soviet zone to Berlin.[62] Thereafter the War Department and the JCS assumed that the matter of transit across the Soviet zone would be handled by the European Advisory Commission or the Control Council, which was then still expected to begin work with the Soviet members present before the surrender. After some discussion in the U.S. delegation at Yalta, the JCS proposed an interim military agreement establishing freedom of transit across all three zones. The British accepted in early March. The Soviet General Staff did not answer.[63] Probably no one was surprised. The agreements concerning transit to Bremen were made between the U.S. and British military authorities, but in the Soviet Union such affairs were almost never left to the discretion of the military. In any event, at the time the United States was far less interested in access to any place in Germany than in the

exit from Europe, which the Bremen enclave provided.

The Control Machinery

The Moscow Conference had charged the EAC, as its next task after drafting the surrender terms, with making recommendations to the three governments on the machinery required to ensure fulfillment of the terms.[64] The protocol on zones intervened later as a preliminary, albeit a vexing one. In the British view, the EAC itself constituted—or ought to have constituted—an important part of the control machinery. This view was shared by Winant and some of his advisers but not by the other two governments and emphatically not by the War Department. The British Foreign Office had circulated to Washington and Moscow in July 1943 and again to the delegates in Moscow in November a proposal for a United Nations commission to oversee all occupations established in Europe as a result of the war and the armistices.[65]

In January 1944, along with the British papers on surrender terms and zones, Sir William Strang introduced a proposal concerning the EAC which included a projected European commission and under it a high commission for Germany. This high commission, as the British saw it, would provide a tripartite central authority having under it the German administration, including the parts of the central government that survived, and the occupation forces in the zones. While the fighting continued, the military commanders would be supreme and the essentially civilian high

---

Administration of International Zone, Berlin, 23 Jun 44; Memo, SHAEF G–3 for SHAEF Staff Divisions, sub: Organization and Administration of the International Zone, Berlin, 24 Jun 44, in SHAEF G–3, 388.3–3 GPS.

[62] Department of State, *Foreign Relations, 1944*, vol. I, p. 384.

[63] (1) Msg, JCS to U.S. Military Mission, Moscow, 27 Feb 45, in CAD 014, 7–10–42, sec. II. (2) Min US Gp CC, Staff Meeting of Division Directors, 16 Mar 45, in OMGUS 178–1/3. (3) Memo, SHAEF, Assistant Secretary of the General Staff, for CofS, sub: Freedom of Transit Across Zones of Occupation, 10 Mar 45, in USFET SGS 371. (4) History of the CAD, bk. VI, ch. VIII, pp. 1–7.

[64] Department of State, *Foreign Relations, 1943*, vol. I, p. 756.

[65] Memo, OPD, Policy Section, 19 Oct 44, in OPD, ABC 387, sec. 4–E.

commission would be advisory. When hostilities ended, the positions would be reversed. The commanders would be subordinated to the high commission and shorn of their independent authority except for the right to appeal to their governments and to declare martial law in their separate zones if necessary.[66]

In Washington, meanwhile, the CAD and the JCS had settled on several principles which they took to be fundamental to any planned control organization for Germany. One of these principles emanated from the President. In October 1943, before the Moscow Conference, and again before the Cairo Conference he had expressed a strong desire to see Germany partitioned into three or more separate states.[67] For this reason, and because it harmonized with their own thinking, decentralization became a watchword with U.S. military planners working on the control organization. Secondly, in December, War Department planning had assumed that outright military government would probably have to be maintained in Germany for a time after the surrender; therefore, the EAC ought not to devise a permanent control system, particularly not since its mandate was limited to the immediate postsurrender period.[68] Lastly, the War Department was convinced, as it always had been, of the need to preserve the theater commander's supremacy during the period of military necessity—a period which the War Department thought could possibly continue after organized resistance ended.

The U.S. proposal on control machinery transmitted to Winant in late February reflected the War Department principles. The zones would be administered separately except for Berlin, which would be under a combined authority. The combined authority, to be called the Control Council, would be composed of the ranking commanding generals of the three occupying powers. In addition to its direct responsibility for Berlin it would supervise "those governmental and economic activities which the occupation authorities may determine should continue to function on a national basis in the interest of stable and orderly life in Germany." The Control Council would co-ordinate previously approved policies and could recommend policy changes to the three governments, but it would have no command functions outside Berlin. The zone commanders would receive their instructions through their national military channels, and policy would come from the three governments.[69]

The Soviet delegation had nothing to offer of its own and, in keeping with Moscow's insistence on taking things one at a time, did not comment on the Western proposals. The British and Americans were in another deadlock. The British concept of a European high commission appeared calculated to pry policy-making away from Washington and possibly saddle the United States with responsibilities outside Germany; the idea of a German high commission raised a threat of high-powered civilian interference. On the other hand, the emphasis in the U.S. proposal on continuing military government after the surrender seemed to the British to imply also continuing the combined command and the Wash-

---

[66] Department of State, *Foreign Relations, 1944,* vol. I, pp. 155–59.

[67] (1) Department of State, *Foreign Relations, 1943,* vol. I, p. 541. (2) Department of State, *Cairo and Tehran,* in "Foreign Relations," p. 253.

[68] Ltr, JCS to Sec of State, Appendix B of JCS 623, 18 Dec 44, in OPD, ABC 387, sec. 1–A.

[69] (1) JCS 763, Administration of Germany—Occupation Period, 22 Feb 44, in OPD, ABC 387, sec. 4–A. (2) Department of State, *Foreign Relations, 1944,* vol. I, pp. 185–88.

ington-dominated Combined Civil Affairs Committee (CCAC).

With the Russians providing plenty of time to make compromises, the British and Americans cautiously moved a little closer together. In May, the British delegation conceded a period after the surrender in which the military would remain supreme. In July, Winant's advisers suggested elevating the three Allied commanders to a "Supreme Authority"—a kind of military high commission—and having the Control Council under them administer Berlin and act as a central administration for Germany to the extent needed.[70]

By summer, the British and Americans had become at least as much concerned over getting the Russians to talk about the control machinery at all as over the flaws and pitfalls in each other's proposals. Gousev stayed silent until 25 August. The Germans surrendered Paris that day at the climax of, for them, two disastrous weeks, and they were obviously soon going to lose all of France. Although the zones question was not yet settled, Gousev offered a plan for control machinery "to cover the first period of the occupation of Germany immediately following her defeat." For their own reasons, the Russians, like the Americans, did not want to make a long-term decision. Also like the Americans, they wanted the initial control to be military. The supreme authority, they proposed, would be exercised by the three commanders, "each in his own zone of occupation." Together the commanders would form the Control Council which would settle problems common to the whole of Germany and control the central organs of the German government. The Control Council would meet at least once every ten days. Under

the council, a permanent Co-ordinating Committee would conduct the day-to-day business. Also under the Control Council, a Kommandatura, consisting of the three sector commandants, would provide the city administration for Berlin.[71]

From the point of view of the U.S. occupation in Germany, the Soviet paper on control machinery was possibly the single most important document submitted in the European Advisory Commission. It coincided with the Morgenthau controversy which had raised talk in Washington about appointing a civilian high commissioner for Germany. The War Department's claim to an exclusive military period was in jeopardy again, so seriously in October in fact that Secretary Stimson and Under Secretary Patterson worked out a War Department position they hoped they would be able to maintain. Predicting chaos in Germany and a split in U.S. public opinion on Germany, they argued that "thoroughly sound" military government was the only answer for the first phase of the occupation. They concluded that therefore, in the first phase, other government agencies should not be involved and a civilian high commissioner should not be appointed.[72] Whether they could have defended their position, however, if the Russians had leaned toward the British-proposed civilian high commission is at best doubtful. The President still believed civilians could do the work better than the military.[73]

Relieved at having the Russians committed to one control system and in a hurry to get something on paper, the U.S. and

---

[70] Department of State, Foreign Relations, 1944, vol. I, pp. 185–87, 247f.

[71] Ibid., pp. 299–301.
[72] Memo, Patterson for Stimson, sub: Military Occupation of Germany, 17 Oct 44, in USFET SGS 334/2.
[73] Department of State, Foreign Relations, 1944, vol. I, p. 409.

British delegations accepted the Soviet proposal almost to the word in drafting the "Agreement on Control Machinery in Germany," which was signed and submitted to the governments on 14 November. The Russians appeared to have devised a brilliant compromise. The Americans got decentralization and an unequivocal position for the military commander; the British received a promise that the military period would be brief ("the period during which Germany will be carrying out the basic requirements of unconditional surrender") and an apparent commitment to write a second document dealing with long-term control.[74] The only reservations the War Department experts had were that too much centralization was implied in the term "Control Council"—they having lately come to prefer, because it was less specific, "Supreme Authority"—and that not enough sternness was evident in the language of the agreement.[75] One omission in the agreement, its failure to provide a name for the whole control machinery, later caused a small flurry between the British and Americans. The British objected to the term "Military Government for Germany" and the Americans opposed any use of the word "commission." Both finally accepted "Allied Control Authority for Germany."[76]

Crosscurrents

The Moscow Conference, when it created the EAC, provided for consultation with other members of the United Nations but not for admission of new members. Security—the overwhelming preponderance of the U.S., British, and Soviet contributions in the war—and questions concerning the validity of some exile governments' claims to be their countries' representatives seemed to justify the three principal allies' taking upon themselves the decisions pertaining to ending the war. In November 1943, none of Germany's continental neighbors could make a compelling claim to a major voice in inter-Allied affairs in any case. France, the largest neighbor, was represented by the Committee of National Liberation, about which the United States had recurrent severe doubts and which the Soviet Union declined to take notice of officially. In August 1944, the situation changed. Northwestern France was liberated; the Committee of National Liberation became the Provisional Government; and the country undertook to resume its place militarily in the Allied ranks. The Provisional Government at once asked for a direct voice in the EAC discussions on Germany. (Previously it had been invited, along with the exile governments, to submit its views in writing.) General Charles de Gaulle in early September expressed a desire to Eisenhower to participate in the military government of Germany.[77] The British Foreign Office promoted the French request for direct consultation until the Soviet government took the lead in late October and proposed admitting France to the EAC as a permanent member. Not wanting to be outdone by the Soviet bid for French goodwill, the United States and the British promptly agreed, and on 27 November the French ambassador at

---

[74] (1) Senate Committee, *Documents on Germany*, pp. 5–8. (2) Department of State, *Foreign Relations, 1944*, vol. I, pp. 404–06.

[75] Memo [no source] for Mr. McCloy, sub: Protocol Agreement in EAC 14 Nov 44, 23 Nov 44, in ASW 370.8.

[76] Ltr, Wickersham to Smith, 28 Dec 44, in USFET SGS 334.

[77] (1) Department of State, *Foreign Relations, 1944*, vol. I, p. 86. (2) History of CAD, bk. VI, ch. VII, p. 1.

London, René Massigli, became the fourth member of the European Advisory Commission. The commission had rushed through the zones protocol and control agreement before Massigli took his seat, hoping to avoid having to go through these matters at length again; but the tempo of the proceedings would certainly not be increased by admitting a fourth party, particularly not one under as much compulsion to reassert itself in European affairs as was France.

Between November 1944 and May 1945 the EAC made no new agreed recommendations on Germany to the governments. In the summer of 1944, draft proclamations, general orders, and directives to the occupation forces had been submitted in the commission, but none would be acted upon before the surrender. After France, in early January 1945, asked for a full partnership in the occupation, including possession of a zone, which was accorded at Yalta the next month, the documents on the surrender, zones, and control machinery had to be amended to the accompaniment of wearying negotiations. At the same time, as the war drew to a close, the Soviet willingness to engage in four-power planning progressively declined. The Soviet Control Council element, long awaited and in fact promised in the near future in the fall of 1944, never appeared; and as the months passed, the other members became doubtful that the Soviet government would even honor the agreements it had already accepted.

The likelihood of the U.S. government's exerting influence to stimulate activity in the EAC, while never very strong, evaporated completely in the fall of 1944. On the surface the trouble was in the system of communication. All instructions to Winant had to be cleared and approved

in detail by the State Department, the Joint Chiefs of Staff, the Civil Affairs Division, and the Working Security Committee. Few completed the entire process. Only five fully cleared policy papers were sent between January and October 1944. Everybody involved knew the machinery was not working and deplored it, Winant most of all. In October, summing up a lengthy recitation of complaints, he wrote: "I would like to say that I do not think any conference or commission created by governments for a serious purpose has had less support from the Governments creating it than the European Advisory Commission. At least I do not know of any like example in recorded history."[78] In Washington, Maj. Gen. George V. Strong, the senior member of the Joint Postwar Committee, wrote in a more pragmatic vein, "If adequate steps are not taken to speed up dispatch of pending questions in relation to the EAC, I am very much afraid that when the debacle in Germany comes we will be caught with our pants down."[79]

Undoubtedly, Winant's dissatisfaction stemmed in large part from the restrictive military view of the EAC's functions, which had not changed between January and October. However, even on matters where no doubts about EAC competence existed, action in Washington was painfully slow. At the time Winant wrote, for instance, he was still awaiting a response to a revision of the U.S. proposal on control machinery that his advisers had worked out in July. He did not get an answer until the end of October.[80]

---

[78] Department of State, *Foreign Affairs, 1944,* vol. I, p. 351.
[79] Memo, Maj Gen G. V. Strong for Mr James C. Dunn, sub: COMEA and EACOM Messages, 27 Sep 44, in CAD 334 (12–18–43) (1), sec. II.
[80] Department of State, *Foreign Relations, 1944,* vol. I, pp. 246 and 375.

While the War Department was not inclined to expand the EAC's area of competence, it was willing to improve the machinery for action on approved matters before the commission. A meeting of State, War, and Navy Department officials in McCloy's office on 30 September traced much of the difficulty to the anomalous position of the Working Security Committee which, while it was generally supposed to co-ordinate State Department and War Department–JCS views, actually had no specific charter and a relatively low-ranking membership—on the military side a colonel from the Joint Postwar Committee, a lieutenant colonel from the CAD, and a Navy lieutenant, junior grade. As long as the Cabinet Committee, created at the end of August and including Secretary Morgenthau, was in existence, the War Department was reluctant anyway to deal with policy at a lower level, even through the JCS.[81] In October and November, when the Cabinet Committee became inactive, the Secretaries of State, War, and the Navy held a series of meetings—calculated apparently to forestall further Treasury Department interventions in the planning for Germany—from which a new committee, the State-War-Navy Co-ordinating Committee (SWNCC), evolved. The SWNCC, organized on the assistant secretary level, took as its province "all questions of policy on politico-military matters"; its subcommittee on Europe took over the duties formerly performed by the Working Security Committee.[82] The SWNCC operated at a high enough level to be able to act for the departments and deal directly with the JCS.

Although the SWNCC eliminated, as much as was possible, the technical bottleneck in communications between Washington and the EAC delegation in London and provided an important source for policy decisions on occupation affairs, it did not solve for Winant the problem that bothered him most, namely, the narrowness of the range within which he could negotiate. He saw the EAC as the place where many questions pertaining to Germany ought to be decided. The War Department saw it as the place where only certain specified questions would be decided and in the fall of 1944 was inclined to believe that the surrender document (with the addition of the proclamation and general orders, then not completed), the zones protocol, and the control machinery agreement just about constituted an ample output for the EAC.

The controversy over the Morgenthau Plan and the President's reaction to earlier planning had made all levels in the department very chary of commitments on policy for Germany. Moreover, the direction that the EAC seemed about to take appeared likely to infringe on the theater commander's freedom of decision. The EAC had thirty-eight British draft directives before it—ranging in subject matter from the general treatment of Germany in the postsurrender period to the control of leather and footwear—that would, in War Department opinion, have bound the zone commanders to a rigid formula of administration.[83] JCS 1067, as stringent as it was in tone, at least left the zone commander latitude in its ap-

---

[81] (1) Memo, Lt Col D. C. Fahey, Jr., for Gens Tansey and Roberts, 29 Sep 44, in CAD 334 (12–18–43) (1), sec. II. (2) Memo, AACofS OPD for Gen McNarney, sub: Amb. Winant's Report on EAC Difficulties, 10 Oct 44, in OPD 336 (sec. II) (cases 16–   ). (3) History of CAD, bk. II, ch. I, p. 50.

[82] *Ibid.*, p. 53.

[83] (1) Department of State, *Foreign Relations, 1944,* vol. I, p. 361n. (2) Memo for Record [no source], sub: The British Draft Directives for Germany, 1 Nov 44, in ASW 370.8.

plication and even some leeway in interpretation. It also had the President's approval. The War Department, which had been relieved to get this approval in the first place, refused to put it in jeopardy after Lt. Col. John Boettiger, the President's son-in-law and a member of the Government Branch, CAD, reported in early November that he had "heard the President express the view that the planning for Germany should not go too deeply into detail at this time, and that major decisions, political and economic, might be deferred until we got deeper into Germany and were able to view conditions at close range."[84]

When Winant came to Washington a few days later, McCloy and Hilldring told him that the War Department would not approve detailed directives written in the

EAC since the department had a general directive, JCS 1067, which should also be used in the EAC. The reason they gave for this stand was to avoid "tying the hands of the commander in the field by directives issued at governmental level which he could not alter."[85] In London on 20 November, Wickersham, just returned from Washington, told the U.S. Group Control Council, Document 1067 is now our 'Bible.' " It had been "recommended," he said, that the EAC not prepare any directives. The War Department preferred to have the directives written by the Control Council elements "and . . . approved by the military authorities on this side."[86]

---

[84] History of CAD, bk. II, ch. IV, p. 73.

[85] (1) *Ibid.*, p. 74. (2) Memo of Conference held in Mr. McCloy's Office on 8 Dec 44 at 1030 AM, in ASW 370.8.

[86] US Gp CC, Min of Meeting of Staff Conference Held 20 Nov 44, in SHAEF G–5, 31.04.

CHAPTER X

The Rhineland Campaign, 1944

Military Government In Action

Two hours before dark on 11 September 1944 a five-man patrol from First Army's V Corps waded across the Our River into Germany. By nightfall, two other patrols had crossed and brought back souvenirs: a German cap, some currency, and a packet of soil—the soil, no doubt, very similar to that of Luxembourg on the west side of the river.[1] Behind the border opposite V Corps lay the German West Wall in the rugged, heavily wooded, sparsely populated Eifel region. Appropriately, since V Corps had been the first corps in the Army to establish a civil affairs section, a V Corps military government officer posted the first proclamations in Germany in one of the border villages on the 12th. But V Corps was headed for frustration, surprise, and heartbreak; and the few miles of German territory forward of the West Wall was all it was going to get for a long time. Thirty-five miles to the north, VII Corps, also of First Army, crossed the border out of Belgium and took Roetgen on the 12th. No metropolis, Roetgen, sandwiched between the border and the forward edge of the West Wall, normally had a population of 2,500.

First Army was operating in what the Germans call the *Dreilaenderecke*, the corner where the boundaries of Germany,

Belgium, and the Netherlands meet. On the German side, the city of Aachen sits in the corner astride a corridor between the Maas (Meuse) River on the northwest and the Huertgen Forest on the south which opens toward Cologne on the Rhine forty miles to the east. VII Corps proposed to pass between Aachen and the Huertgen Forest, encircle the city with an assist from XIX Corps on the north, and be on its way via Dueren to Cologne. By 16 September, it had driven a wedge ten miles deep and twenty miles wide into Germany south of Aachen. In this sliver of territory—which was, however, two-fifths of the total area SHAEF forces would occupy in Germany before 1945—military government began when temporary detachments were stationed in Roetgen on 15 September, and on the 18th in Monschau, the first *Landkreis* capital to be captured. In the next several days military government took over in six other communities, Kornelimuenster, Lammersdorf, Rott, Schevenhuette, Vicht, and Zweifall. In the planning, only Monschau had been considered. The others were not administrative centers.

The civil affairs detachments of the 1st European Civil Affairs Regiment (ECAR), which had come through France with First Army, inaugurated military government in Germany, beginning with D8B1 at Roetgen. They were integrated detachments, each having one British officer, and were scheduled to be withdrawn and reorganized into military gov-

---

[1] Charles B. MacDonald, *The Siegfried Line Campaign,* United States Army in World War II (Washington, D.C., 1963), p. 3.

POSTING THE ORDINANCES

ernment teams which would be exclusively American. The procedure was the same everywhere, as it was to be throughout Germany. First came the posting of the Supreme Commander's proclamation and the ordinances. Here a temporary hitch had developed. SHAEF had sent out the proclamations on 10 September but had to withdraw them promptly for revision when Washington raised objections to the language. Until the first week of October, 12th Army Group substituted a "Notice to the Population" announcing the occupation.[2]

The second step was to find the *Buergermeister* (mayor) or, if he could not be found or was obviously a Nazi, appoint one and thereby establish a link to the population.

Next came a series of security actions. The first was to collect weapons, ammunition, and explosives in civilian possession and confiscate radio transmitters and other means of communicating with the enemy, including pigeons. The orders to surrender prohibited items were followed by house-to-house searches, which in fought-over areas

[2] Joseph R. Starr, U.S. Military Government Operations During the Rhineland Campaign, p. 34, in Hist Div, EUCOM, U.S. Military Government in Germany, CMH file 8–3.1 DE.

CIVILIANS TURN IN WEAPONS AND CAMERAS

frequently turned up sizable collections of arms that the civilians had not turned in, probably more out of fear than malice. For convenience and for security, the civilians also had to be kept out of the way of the tactical troops.

Often the commanders would have preferred to have the civilians removed altogether; in early October V Corps tried evacuating a five-by-ten-mile area in the Eupen-Malmédy sector where the inhabitants were nominally Belgian although real loyalties were difficult to determine. V Corps' G–5 thought little of the experiment at the beginning, and even less later. It appeared only to prove what military government doctrine had assumed all along, namely, that people could be controlled best at home. Moving them was expensive; imposed hardships on the old, the young, and the ailing; made the evacuees economic charges of the occupation forces when their own crops and property were lost or damaged; and probably allowed dissidents to conceal themselves more easily.[3]

From the start military government—and, after the V Corps' experience, the tac-

[3] Hqs, V Corps, ACofS G–5, After Action Report, 4 Nov 44, in SHAEF G–5, 17.11, Jacket 1.

tical commands too—preferred to rely on circulation restrictions and the curfew. The stringency of both tended to depend somewhat on the tactical situation and the whim of the local commander since 12th Army Group did not have a uniform policy. In general, no one was allowed to travel more than three miles from his home, and gatherings of more than five people, except in food queues and in church, were prohibited. The curfew was always at least from sunset to sunrise, and very often local commanders extended it through the daylight hours as well, giving the men an hour in the morning and evening to go to and from work and the women an hour or two during the day to fetch food and water.

The key to population control was knowing who was being controlled; this problem usually provided the detachments with their first big job. Every adult civilian had to be registered and issued a registration card, which would give military government a permanent hold on him. In the towns occupied in September, however, there appeared at first to be almost no one to register. The German authorities, to avoid the propaganda embarrassment of having Germans under Allied rule, had ordered all inhabitants to evacuate to the east. The towns seemed empty for several days after being occupied, until those who had disobeyed the order felt safe enough or became hungry and thirsty enough or just curious enough to leave the cellars and woods. None of the places occupied in 1944 had their usual populations, but on the average, excluding Aachen, about a third of the people stayed behind which, after the war had passed through the communities, was more than most of the towns could house or the land could support.

On 21 September, Companies G and H of the 2d ECAR arrived at First Army,

and a week later Detachment I4G2, commanded by Capt. Robert A. Goetcheus, took up its station in Monschau, becoming the first detachment to reach its pinpoint location in Germany. Upon seeing the military government detachments, First Army developed a sudden strong preference for going into Germany with the civil affairs detachments that had accompanied it across France. The military government detachments, First Army complained, were understrength and the personnel were misclassified and not satisfied with their assignments; and they were particularly short on interpreters and public safety officers. Of twenty-four officers assigned to public safety, First Army G–5 reported, only nine had police experience. The European Civil Affairs Division (ECAD) explained that the detachments had been set up in a hurry, and some of the omissions had been deliberate to leave vacancies for experienced officers from the civil affairs detachments being disbanded.[4]

Since the bulk of the detachments were not yet needed in Germany, First Army billeted them in barracks at Verviers, Belgium, which it designated as the MASTER (code name for First Army) Military Government Center, and sent them back to school. First Army G–5 believed it still had something to teach even to officers who had already been shunted from school to school for a year or more. In following the German Army through France, it had become unhappily aware that the stereotype of the German officer as smart and efficient and the American as sloppy and careless could not be shrugged off as Nazi propaganda when faced with civilians who had ample

<hr>

[4] Memo, Hqs, 12th AGp, ACofS G–5, Opns Br, for ACofS G–5, 12th AGp, sub: Opns Meeting, Civil Affairs, 29 Sep 44, in SHAEF G–5, 17.16, Jacket 1.

experience from which to make exact comparisons. Military government was competing with the image left behind by the enemy. In this competition, First Army G–5 had concluded, moral superiority and technical expertise needed to be backed by what Americans too often regarded as superficial appearances: offices arranged not only to be worked in but to look efficient, flags prominently displayed, officers who looked and acted their parts.[5]

The staffs were not much better prepared for the move into Germany than the detachments were. G–5, 12th Army Group, after coming to the Continent in the first week of August, had been on the run ever since to keep up with the front: to Periers and Laval in August, to Versailles in early September, and to Verdun at the middle of the month. In these weeks, while the entry into Germany approached at express train speed, ECAD had to be brought over from England and the civil affairs detachments in France regrouped and retrained for Germany. The latter was itself a monumental job, not the least part of which was separating the British officers from the detachments and recalling the U.S. officers attached to British detachments with 21 Army Group.[6]

ECAD, out of the picture aboard ship off UTAH Beach when the first detachments went into Germany, was badly situated at Rochefort-en-Yvelines, either to keep in touch with the detachments at the front or to reorganize and train those that stayed behind. The division headquarters occupied the "only chateau on the only hill in the village," a moderately elegant structure with an elaborate stone staircase outside, formal gardens, a park, and no heating. For reasons of health rather than rank, officers over forty-one years old were billeted in the chateau. The remaining officers and the enlisted men lived in tents and shelter halves in the adjacent woods. Because of the blackout, lights and fires were prohibited after dark, and the days were beginning to get short and the nights cold.[7]

G–5, First Army, was, after G–5, V Corps, the oldest U.S. civil affairs–military government section in continuous existence, having been activated on 5 November 1943 by Col. Damon M. Gunn, then the civil affairs officer and later the G–5, and his executive officer, Maj. James S. Thurmond. Unfortunately, at the army level, seniority had not been much of an advantage. Gunn and his officers had spent months getting civil affairs accepted as a legitimate staff function, and as long as SHAEF's plans for military government in Germany were unsettled, which was until D-day and beyond, little guidance had filtered through to 12th Army Group and even less to First Army. The Army G–5 historian has recorded as a towering event in the preinvasion planning the receipt of 150 copies of FM 27–5 on 16 March and of an approved table of equipment on the 17th. Only one copy of the field manual had been available in the whole army until then. The Standard Policy and Procedure had come in earlier, but it took a full month to travel the 114-mile distance from London to the army in Bristol.[8] As part

---

[5] Memo, Hqs, First Army, ACofS G–5, for All Concerned, sub: Military Government Conferences 9–10 Nov 44, 16 Nov 44, in SHAEF G–5, 17.11, Jacket 3.

[6] Hqs, 12th Army Group G–5, to SHAEF G–5, sub: Narrative Reports of G–5 Section for the Months of August and September 1944, in SHAEF G–5, 17.16, Jacket 1.

[7] Det E1C3, War Diary, in OMGUS 413–2/3, decimal 314.81.

[8] First Army G–5, History of G–5, First U.S. Army, Nov 43–Mar 44, in SHAEF G–5, 17.11, Jacket 2.

GERMANS READ THE PROCLAMATION AND ORDINANCES

of the highest U.S. headquarters in continuous action since D-day, G–5, First Army, had accumulated much practical experience in civil affairs and was confident of its ability to install military government in Germany; but the front was at the German border before copies of the handbook arrived from SHAEF and the first directive for Germany came down from 12th Army Group.

The Germans

The Germans were easier to understand in the abstract and from a distance than as flesh-and-blood people in their own communities. The French had been friends and allies—even if frequently not very friendly. The Germans were enemies and alleged inveterate disturbers of world peace; but how well they lived up to their image seemed to depend on the angle and distance from which they were observed. G–5, First Army, was struck by their orderly behavior and reported that they kept to their homes but seemed to be watching the troops with great interest while attempting to conceal their curiosity. On the streets, the army reported, the men saluted the American soldiers or tipped their hats politely. The children were more friendly. Many of them ventured to wave at passing soldiers, which their elders allowed them to do.[9] Further removed, Headquarters, ECAD, described the Germans as outwardly blank, stolid, and indifferent, while inwardly harboring "subdued, latent hostility mixed with fear." Most of them, ECAD claimed, shied away from anyone in uniform and remained stubbornly taciturn under questioning.[10] An observer from the Psychological Warfare Division of SHAEF, who actually entered the occupied area, reported:

the crossing of the German frontier is something of a shock. Even in Nazi Germany the cows have four legs, the grass is green, and children in pigtails stand around the tanks. Self-indoctrination by years of propaganda make it a shock to rediscover these trivialities. All the officers with whom we spoke reinforced this. The people left behind in this area are human beings with a will to survive. Just because we are conquerors and they know it, they are in certain ways easier to handle than the liberated Belgians or Frenchmen. They know they must obey our orders, and if they are allowed to survive and reconstruct their lives by self-help, they do not of themselves cause any trouble. Behind the front line, for instance, every road and byway is littered with cables, telephone lines, *etc.* Minor sabotage would be child's play. It has not happened because the people are not interested in the war but looking after themselves.[11]

On one score everyone agreed: the German civilians were not causing trouble. In the first three weeks of the occupation not a single serious act against the Allied troops was reported. One officer said he had been doused with hot water from a farmhouse at night. Some sniping was going on, but the military government officers were convinced it was the work of German troops since it occurred only in the areas closest to the front.[12]

One question that could not be answered was whether the Germans in the occupied areas were typical. Probably, they were not. The out-and-out Nazis could be assumed to have obeyed the evacuation order. On the other hand, the citizens who had stayed could not be shown to be particularly anti-Nazi. If asked, most admitted that they had stayed because they did not want to leave their homes and property and that they had not considered what they did an act of defiance. Their strongest motive for staying, next to looking after property, was apparently their desire to get out of the war.

While the military government officers could leave analysis of the German character in general to a time when they had more leisure, they had to make decisions on the character of certain Germans immediately, namely, those whom they appointed to administrative posts in the occupied communities. Such decisions were almost never easy. It was one thing to be determined to eliminate nazism, another to single out a man from an always small contingent of candidates, none of whom inspired genuine confidence. One of the first and most frustrating discoveries was that administrative ability usually went hand in hand with political taint; the Nazi party had been thorough in enlisting able men one way or another. The Germans themselves had unintentionally helped solve what was probably the easiest part of the problem, getting rid of Nazi incumbents, by evacuating almost the entire civil ad-

[9] Hist Rpt, G–5, First Army, 1–30 Sep 44, in SHAEF G–5, 17.11, Jacket 1.

[10] Hqs, ECAD, General Intelligence Bulletin No. 23, 2 Nov 44, in SHAEF G–5, 25, Jacket 2.

[11] SHAEF, PsyWar Div, Mr. R–H. S. Crossman, Impressions of a Brief Tour of Occupied Germany, 4 Nov 44, in SHAEF SGS 091.4/1.

[12] Hqs, ECAD, General Intelligence Bulletin No. 23.

ministration, including the police and fire departments; but they had also either destroyed or taken along the local records, which left military government nothing to go on in reconstructing the governments or in checking on the people who had stayed behind. One information source the Germans had overlooked was the Church. Since the occupied area was overwhelmingly Catholic, the priests knew nearly everyone and a great deal about local politics. In the early weeks, before both became a bit more wary of each other, the detachments relied heavily on the priests for advice, and a few priests became temporary *Buergermeisters* in their communities.

The first appointments were impromptu and usually also impermanent. One morning in October in Wuerselen, a coal mining town of 16,000 inhabitants northeast of Aachen, while fighting was still going on in the outskirts, a Herr Reuters stepped out of his cellar refuge onto an almost deserted street, just where an American major had stopped his jeep. Reuters, fifty-eight years old, had worked all his adult life as a cashier at one of the coal mines. His salary had been too small to support a wife but sufficient for him as a bachelor to cultivate middle class appurtenances, such as a wing collar and a frock coat, without which he never appeared in public, not even on that morning in the wake of battle. While the major, taking him for a more distinguished citizen than he was, questioned, him about candidates for appointment as *Buergermeister,* a miner happened along and told the major that Reuters himself would make a good mayor. The major continued up the street and questioned a few other people who agreed that Reuters was a decent enough fellow; the next day a soldier delivered a document to Reuters' door appointing him mayor of Wuerselen. The ap-

pointment was only the second political experience of his life, but there had been another and it was to be his undoing. One day in 1937 he had received a notice to pay the Nazi party initiation fee and begin paying his monthly dues. Afraid of losing his job, he had paid and been a party member ever since, without attending any meetings or benefiting from his membership, as his economic circumstances amply attested. His term in office under the occupation lasted eighteen days. On being dismissed he said sadly that he had hoped "to dedicate the last days of my life to the American *Herren*." His successor, Herr Jansen, a bookkeeper in the Singer sewing machine factory in Wuerselen, was not a Nazi. He had not joined for two reasons: he had not been asked and his boss had not joined. He had no discernible political convictions and did not want to be mayor. The military government officers wondered who was the better man.[13]

In Stolberg, another mining town, the 3d Armored Division uncovered a bona fide Nazi *Buergermeister,* Dr. Ragh, who had been in office since 1935. Under the Weimar Republic, he had been a leading member of one of the middle class parties, the *Deutsche Volkspartei*. After the other parties were abolished in the spring of 1933, he had joined the Nazis. He had secured the appointment in Stolberg through the influence of *Gauleiter* Josef Grohe of Cologne, who Ragh said had chosen him not because he was an active Nazi but because he had come to respect him while they were political opponents in Cologne. Under Ragh, the government of Stolberg had been markedly less Nazi than those of the surrounding towns, reportedly to the

---

[13] OSS, Research and Analysis Br, European Political Report, vol. II, No. 1, 5 Jan 45, in SHAEF G–5, 7.32.

annoyance of the local party leaders. People questioned about him said he had done his job well and had made it clear that his party membership was a formality, necessary for being in office. While conceding that he was the kind of man who would probably win in a free election, military government dismissed him. His successor, Dr. Deutzmann, was just the opposite type. His ability as an administrator was unproven, but he was not a Nazi. He had supported the republic in the 1920s and had not switched after Hitler came to power. He had been a primary school principal slated for promotion. When the Nazis came in, he was demoted to the rank of ordinary teacher. In appointing him to replace Ragh, military government had deliberately chosen political character over administrative efficiency, no doubt both out of moral conviction and out of knowledge that a *Buergermeister* with Ragh's past service under the occupation would make headlines in the press from London to San Francisco. The local clergy and reportedly the people seemed to support the sacrifice of efficiency for character. For military government the Ragh case, nevertheless, raised qualms about determining who were "active Nazis or ardent sympathizers."[14]

For the detachments, the chance to get some experience with authentic Germans was exhilarating in itself. In October, Detachment E1H2, slated for Cologne when the front got that far, moved into Alsdorf, another mining town north of Aachen. Alsdorf, with a usual population of 12,000, less than half of whom were in evidence when E1H2 took over, was no Cologne but a challenge nevertheless, since the town was at the front itself and since the detachment had a special job to do. The two local coal mines, named Anna I and Anna II, were in danger of flooding, and the detachment had to extract enough coal from them to generate power to keep the pumps running. To accomplish this task, the detachment had to have a bulkhead built to seal off one shaft that ran behind the German line.

Being among the first in Germany was something to write about and one of the detachment officers exulted:

It's just like the book, putting up the proclamations, taking over the best place in town, and calling in the *Buergermeister* to lay down Uncle Ike's rules of the game. The *Buergermeister* is just like the book too—a middle-aged, efficient public servant. I don't know if he's prompted by fear or gratitude at being freed of the Nazi yoke, but he's been most cooperative, and has gone out of his way to make us comfortable. Our offices are set up in a neat 4-room apartment, and after swapping desks for beds and maps and signs for knickknacks we're the darndest combination of comfort and order you ever saw. We've even hired a cook-charwoman who builds the fire, cleans, and then serves our noon meal in the vacant apartment above. Today we found linen, china, silver, and even flowers on the table. She had borrowed them from the *Buergermeister*. After three days of having people clicking their heels at me and calling me "Herr My-yor" I'm beginning to feel like God Inc.[15]

Working practically at the front added something that military government personnel did not expect to experience often. E1H2's billets were located forward of the nearest regimental command post. Day and night the town shook from the blasts of both U.S. and German artillery, and the detachment members acquired a soldierly

---

[14] Memo, 12th AGp G–5, Government Affairs Branch in the Field, for Chief, Government Affairs Branch, sub: Government Affairs in Stolberg, Kornelimuenster, Breinig, 2 Oct 44, in SHAEF G–5, 17.16.

[15] Ltr, E1H2 to ECAD, Maj Clemens to Maj Howard Gunlocke, 21 Oct 44, in SHAEF G–5, 17.12, Jacket 5.

skill at distinguishing by sound between mortars and antitank guns and between .50- and .30-caliber machine guns. Nobody was shooting at them specifically, but the front did not move for nearly a month, and the Germans occasionally dropped a few rounds on the town. On the morning of 17 November, Capt. Arthur K. Olsen was killed and Tech. 5 John H. Bergmann wounded by a shell that hit in the street outside the detachment headquarters.[16]

After the nonfraternization order appeared, 12th Army Group wanted to know what the troops thought about the Germans. It gave the job of finding out to Maj. Arthur Goodfriend, editor in chief of *Stars and Stripes,* who was going through the replacement system incognito as an enlisted man anyway looking for story material. Opinion on the Germans, Goodfriend concluded, could be compressed into a few typical G.I. vignettes:

These Germans aren't bad people. We get along with them O.K. All you've got to do is treat them good and you have no trouble.

These people aren't real Germans—they're Catholic. This part of Germany is all Catholic. They're good people and don't have any of this Nazi feeling toward us.

Hell, these people are cleaner and damned sight friendlier than the Frogs. They're our kind of people.

One military government officer interviewed by Goodfriend estimated thirty days as the interval before the onset of complete fraternization. Goodfriend doubted it would take that long. The temptation, he said, was great; the opportunity was also great; and the American soldier was "by nature kindly and generous in his treatment of other peoples, friend and foe alike." Nonfraternization, Goodfriend was convinced, established a standard difficult to define and pursue that was "beset every inch of the way by the attractiveness of many Germans, especially women and children, which tends to weaken the strongest determination to be aloof." Furthermore, the officers were not setting an example, he observed. They were subject to the same temptation as the enlisted men and shared their confusion and conflicts.[17]

Apparently as a by-product of Goodfriend's tour in the enlisted ranks, military government in Germany received its first blast of press criticism. Aside from one or two allusions in London papers to Nazis retained in office and pictures showing alleged fraternization, the civilian press had so far not taken much interest, critical or otherwise, in the occupation. The big news was at the front. But, on 20 October, *Stars and Stripes* ran a three-column article under the headline "Don't Get Chummy With Jerry." The gist was in the opening paragraphs:

Here's what's going on around Aachen:
1) German civilians are giving Yanks the V-sign, the glad hand, free beer, big smiles, plenty of talk about not being Nazis at heart, and hurray for democracy.
2) Some G.I.s and plenty of officers are returning the smiles, flirting with the *Frauleins,* drinking the beer, and starting to think what nice folks the Germans really are.
3) German civilians are being removed from Aachen and driven two miles in U.S. Army trucks to Luetzow Barracks, in Brand, a suburb of Aachen. To move them out is a matter of strict military necessity, but these Nazis are being quartered in the best build-

---

[16] Det E1H2, Report of Operations 16 Oct–17 Nov 44, 16 Nov 44, in SHAEF G–5, 17.12, Jacket 5.

[17] Memo, Editor in Chief, *Stars and Stripes,* for Ch, Sp Inf Services, sub: Fraternization Between Germans and American Officers and Men [no date], in SHAEF G–1, 250.1–1.

AACHEN EVACUEES ARRIVING AT BRAND

ings outside Aachen. They are being brought there in Army vehicles. There are canvas covers over them [the vehicles]. They have already received 20 tons of Army food.[18]

Whether the first two paragraphs would do more to arouse indignation or to stimulate envy among the troops not yet in Germany was no concern of military government. The third paragraph, however, implied that the Germans were getting soft treatment from military government at the expense of the U.S. soldiers. Aachen was then encircled; and as the troops pushed

into the heavily damaged city, First Army G–5 had undertaken to evacuate the civilians found in cellars and bomb shelters to the barracks in the suburb Brand to get them out of the way. Fortunately, Col. Gustav C. Dittmar, executive officer of First Army G–5, witnessed the evacuation, and he was able to assure the higher headquarters that all of the civilians who were able—men, women, and children—walked the two miles to Brand; only the aged and sick were moved in trucks; and the trucks had canvas tops because the weather was rainy and they were also being used to haul

[18] *Stars and Stripes,* 20 Oct 44.

supplies. The food for the civilians, he reported, came not from Army stocks but was either requisitioned locally or taken from captured German depots.[19]

As instruments for shaping relations between the population and the occupation forces, military government courts were regarded as most important. They were expected, on the one hand, to enforce sternly the authority claimed in the proclamation and ordinances and, on the other, to point up for the Germans the difference between nazism and democracy by giving fair and impartial trials to all accused. Modeled after Army courts martial, the military government courts convened on three levels: summary(one officer), intermediate (one or more officers), and general (not less than three officers). Summary courts could impose up to one year in prison and fines in marks up to $1,000; intermediate courts, ten years in prison and fines to $10,000; and general courts, the death penalty and unlimited fines.

The first summary court in Germany opened in Kornelimuenster late in September. The judge, an Army captain, presided behind a kitchen table on the ground floor of the town inn. In the first case, military police accused four women of returning, in defiance of notices posted throughout the town, to homes in a restricted military area from which they had been evacuated four days earlier. The charges, read in German and English, were explained to the accused by a former court interpreter from Aachen. The German lawyer who represented the women pleaded that they had returned to their homes to get more clothing. The hearing lasted fifteen minutes. Each of the women was fined 2,000 marks (reduced to 200 on review) and given thirty days to pay or six months in jail.[20]

In October, also in Kornelimuenster, the first intermediate court tried a woman, Maria Jensen, for concealing records of the *NS Frauenschaft* (the Nazi women's organization). She was sentenced to six years' imprisonment.[21] In early November, First Army G–5 held the first general court at the MASTER Military Government Center in Verviers to give the detachments training there a chance to observe. The court tried two men from Stolberg charged with harboring German troops. The defense argued that the area was not occupied, only patrolled, at the time the German soldiers were found, and that the soldiers were deserters being sheltered in response to Allied radio appeals. The two men were acquitted.[22]

During September and October, summary and intermediate courts tried twenty-three cases involving twenty-nine persons. Twenty-five of the accused were convicted. More than half of the offenses were minor circulation and curfew violations. The Germans were living up to their reputation for orderliness.

Aachen

Col. Gerhard Wilck, the last German commander in Aachen, surrendered the city at noon on 21 October, but shells from behind the German line not much more than a mile away continued to fall for days afterward. The garrison had been completely encircled for five days and had been under ground and air attack for more than

---

[19] Memo, ACofS G–5, First Army, for ACofS G–5, 12th AGp, sub: Editorial in *Stars and Stripes,* 22 Oct 44, in SHAEF G–5, 17.11, Jacket 1.

[20] Hqs, ECAD, General Intelligence Bulletin No. 23.

[21] Starr, U.S. Military Government Operations During the Rhineland Campaign, p. 94.

[22] Hist Rpt, G–5, First Army, 1–30 Nov 44, in SHAEF G–5, 17.11, Jacket 3.

AACHEN AFTER THE BATTLE

a month. The city, which had already been heavily bombed half a dozen times earlier in the war, was 85 percent destroyed. Of the 160,000 inhabitants, First Army had found and removed 5,000 to Brand and Homburg. A few thousand more turned up in the ruins after the surrender and in surrounding communities, eventually raising the total to 14,000. Some of the rest, no doubt, were dead and buried under the rubble; most had either followed the evacuation orders or dispersed into the countryside to areas not yet captured.

The Aachen detachment, F1G2, moved in on the day after the surrender. Its thirty-five officers and forty-eight enlisted men had by then been running the Brand refugee camp for a week and a half and had begun screening men for municipal posts—without much luck, since almost all the qualified candidates also had relatives on the German side and feared reprisals against them. After some searching for buildings in usable condition, the detachment set itself up in a former *Gestapo* headquarters and a courthouse. The city was virtually empty. The SS had evacuated the fire and police departments, including the fire engines, and the municipal records had been removed. Stores and *Wehrmacht* food dumps were unguarded and being rifled by the troops and the few Germans left in the city.[23]

To restore order, VII Corps assigned the 690th Field Artillery Battalion as military government security police. In their own areas the divisions formed roving squads mounted on ¾-ton weapons carriers. At the military government center in Verviers, First Army G–5 began an experiment in training captured German policemen for work under the occupation. After evacuating them, the Germans had put many of the Aachen police at the front, and some had been captured. As prisoners of war they could not be used, but since they had been captured in police, not *Wehrmacht,* uniforms, First Army decided that they were not actually prisoners of war. Starting with two dozen of these policemen, First Army had nearly a hundred in training by the end of October. The experiment was a qualified success. Only ten of the recruits turned out to be professional policemen; the rest had come to the police force late in the war from nonessential occupations; and the ten professionals all had been Nazi party members. However, they were better than nothing. First Army kept the professionals as instructors and put the others on duty after they had some training.[24]

F1G2 was a regional detachment that expected to assume supervision of all detachments in the Aachen *Regierungsbezirk;* but the whole *Regierungsbezirk* was not occupied yet, and the control that did exist was in the hands of the G–5's of the tactical units. Moreover, the division and regimental boundaries shifted frequently, at times almost every day, and each new command seemed to have its own concept of how military government ought to be conducted. Nevertheless, after F1G2 settled in Aachen, military government officials in the area occupied so far, which would not be greatly increased before the end of the coming winter, began to take the measure of the job that lay ahead. Sooner or later the front would move on, but military government would stay. For this one corner of Germany, the war seemed to be over and the permanent occupation beginning.

In one respect this prospect was awesome. Aachen lay on the western fringe of the Ruhr industrial complex, and even in ruins it was a highly sophisticated area. The Public Relations Branch, G–5, First Army, gave the following description:

Germany is different from France. France was mostly small towns that received water from wells. Except for Paris, power was supplied by small, widely separated stations. The section of Germany now before us is Pittsburg, Youngstown, Detroit, and Toledo rolled into one. The telephone system is automatic and probably better than at home, having a complete underground cable system where long distance calls can be dialed to almost every city in the country. The large industrial cities, like Aachen, are served by tremendous power and gas systems.[25]

Under the rubble, the utility systems were still almost intact. The Germans apparently had not had the heart to destroy them. But if the systems had been more primitive, they might have been more useful. The

[23] Hist Rpt, G–5, First Army, 1–31 Oct 44, 3 Dec 44, in SHAEF G–5, 17.11, Jacket 1.

[24] When the school moved to Aachen in the spring of 1945, the ex-Nazi instructor raised a popular stir and brought a flurry of denunciations to military government. Office of the Chief Historian, EUCOM, Occupation Forces in Europe Series, Public Safety, 1947, CMH file 8–3.1 CA 18.

[25] Memo, Hqs, First Army, ACofS G–5, for All Concerned, sub: Military Government Conferences 9–10 Nov 44, 16 Nov 44, in SHAEF G–5, 17.11, Jacket 3.

men who could have repaired and run them were gone.

Winter was coming, and life in Aachen was not going to be easy. The most optimistic prediction First Army G–5 would venture was that the area might just be able to feed itself through the winter from local stocks and from what could be gathered in the countryside provided "no more people return."[26] Privately the military government officers worried that the area might be picked clean before the winter came. The detachments reported persistent looting by the troops. Each new unit passing through cut a swath, taking along "radios, food, bicycles, crucifixes, doors, cooking utensils, and cattle." When questioned, the soldiers expressed the belief that having fought for the property, they were entitled to it, particularly since the Germans had acquired so much wrongfully.[27] Paradoxically, the troops also seemed to be the best guarantee that the German civilians would survive. Maj. Gen. J. Lawton Collins, commanding VII Corps, declared that the Germans would have to be fed one way or another because the American soldier would not permit women and children to starve while he was well fed.[28]

SHAEF policy was to turn the problems of their existence over to the Germans themselves. After moving into Aachen, F1G2 created a new functional subdivision, the Special Branch of Public Safety, to screen the political backgrounds of candidates for municipal offices. The Special Branch was going to become a permanent and pervasive fixture in the occupation, as was also its chief weapon against nazism, the *Fragebogen*. A deceptively simple-looking questionnaire, the *Fragebogen* required the respondent to list all his memberships in National Socialist and military organizations and to supply a variety of other information concerning his salary, associations, and employment back to the pre-Hitler period. With the information in the *Fragebogen* military government expected not only to be able to detect overt Nazis but also sympathizers, militarists, and individuals who had benefited materially from the Nazi regime. The Special Branch in Aachen opened with no public records with which to verify the information in the *Fragebogen* and only one agent-investigator from the Counterintelligence Corps (CIC); consequently, the branch resorted—as most Special Branches did later—to hiring Germans to check on Germans.

On 30 October, F1G2 installed Franz Oppenhoff as *Oberbuergermeister* (chief mayor) of Aachen. His was the most important appointment yet made in Germany and one that was certain to attract attention on both sides of the front. Military government was concerned over press and political reactions in the United States and England; Oppenhoff was concerned for the safety of his relatives in unoccupied Germany and for his own life. Earlier in the month the SS newspaper, *Das Schwarze Korps,* had written that there would be no German administration under the occupation because any official who collaborated with the enemy could count on being dead within a month.[29]

Oppenhoff was a native of Aachen and a prominent Catholic layman. He was an

---

[26] Hist Rpt, G–5, First Army, 1–31 Oct 44, 3 Dec 44, in SHAEF G–5, 17.11, Jacket 1.

[27] Det E1H2, Report of Operations 16 Oct–17 Nov 44, 16 Nov 44, in SHAEF G–5, 17.12, Jacket 5.

[28] SHAEF, PsyWar Div, Mr. R–H. S. Crossman, Impressions of a Brief Tour of Occupied Germany.

[29] Press and Information Office, The Federal Republic of Germany, *The Bulletin,* 12 May 70.

expert on Nazi law, had been legal representative for the Bishop of Aachen, and had defended some cases for Jewish firms. Knowing that the *Gestapo* was interested in him, he had taken refuge in Eupen, across the border in Belgium, in the first week of September, taking his wife and three daughters with him. When he returned to be sworn in as mayor in Aachen, he was alone.[30]

On the day F1G2 moved in, the Monuments, Fine Arts, and Archives (MFA&A) Branch of First Army G–5 began a survey. With a history dating to Charlemagne and a special position as the coronation city of medieval German kings and emperors, Aachen had been known particularly for its architectural treasures. Of these only four—the cathedral, the Ponttor (the fourteenth-century city gate), the Frankenberg Castle, and the Haus Heusch (an old patrician dwelling)—could be described as "to a degree spared." The most important was the cathedral, which housed the coronation chair, the so-called throne of Charlemagne. The cathedral was in rather surprisingly good condition after what it had been through: five fires and a direct hit by a heavy bomb, which, had it not been a dud, would surely have demolished the whole structure. A six-man fire-fighting force had stayed with the building through the bombings and the siege; when the Americans arrived, they were still there, on guard against fires that might be started by German shells falling in the city. The archives, library, and movable treasures had been taken out early in the war, and the heavy coronation chair was intact inside a mas-

onry shield, the floor beneath it reinforced against the bombing by temporary brick arches and shoring.[31]

The most sensational "find" of treasure was not in Aachen—there practically everything of value had been removed several years before—but at Rimburg Castle in the northern outskirts. Lt. George F. Stout, MFA&A, First Army, and Lt. James B. Larwood, MFA&A Officer, Detachment E1H2, made an inventory in the castle in the third week of October. By then the war had passed through the old place with a vengeance. The SS had taken away the owner, Siegfried von Brauchitsch, a cousin of the former commander in chief of the German Army, after the 20 July 1944 attempt to assassinate Hitler. Subsequently the Germans had used the moated structure as a field hospital and to billet troops and had constructed a pill box in one of the buildings on the grounds. During the fighting for Aachen, German infantry had holed up behind the stone and brick walls for a short but bitter exchange with troops of XIX Corps coming across the Wurm River out of Holland. When Stout and Larwood arrived they found every window broken and the masonry holed by artillery and bazooka shells. Inside, the furniture, paintings, and art objects were in fairly good condition considering what had been going on around them. The two biggest discoveries were a diamond and platinum tiara and a collection of ancient coins, which apparently neither the Germans nor the Americans had previously suspected were there.[32]

---

[30] (1) Hist Rpt, G–5, First Army, 1–31 Oct 44, 3 Dec 44, in SHAEF G–5, 17.11, Jacket 1. (2) OSS, Research and Analysis Br, European Political Report, vol. 1, No. 40, 8 Dec 44, in SHAEF G–5 7.32.

[31] SHAEF G–5, MFA&A, to ACofS G–5, sub: Report on MFA&A for Feb 45, 31 Mar 45, in SHAEF G–5, 130.1, Jacket 2.

[32] Memo for Record, Ninth Army, ACofS G–5, sub: Additional Art Treasures at Schloss Rimburg [no date], in Ninth U.S. Army, 17.14, Jacket 1.

Monschau

Monschau in peacetime had been a quiet border town tucked into the valley of the Roer River and framed on the east and west by wooded ridges. Its medieval-looking, beamed and stuccoed, three-story houses huddled over narrow streets had made it a local tourist attraction until the *Organisation Todt,* the German military construction agency, built the West Wall around it. As a *Landkreis* capital it had the appurtenances of a moderately elevated status, a jail, a courthouse, a *Kreissparkasse* (county bank), two hotels, and the office of the *Landrat,* the chief administrative officer of the *Kreis.* When the Americans came in the third week of September they were vastly less interested in viewing the scenery than in cracking the West Wall and breaking out into the open country lying northeast of Monschau between the Roer River and the southern edge of the Huertgen Forest. The 9th Division took the ridgeline on the west and pushed its outpost line into the valley and out to the eastern edge of the town, but the Germans held on to the heights on the east. In the succeeding months while the Americans and Germans shelled each other from the ridges and the Germans sporadically dropped rounds into the town in the valley, Monschau added to its other modest attainments a place in the history of the occupation.

When Detachment I4G2 was given Monschau as its pinpoint assignment, no one suspected that such a thoroughly average I detachment of two officers, a warrant officer, and six enlisted men would have anything but a routine career in a backwater *Landkreis.*[33] Goetcheus, the com-

mander, as a captain, held the average rank for detachment commanders.

While waiting to move into Monschau, I4G2 established itself for several days in Roetgen, six miles to the north, which was by three or four hundred inhabitants actually the largest community in the *Landkreis.* Roetgen provided an unvarnished introduction to the small towns of western Germany. It had a flour mill and a police department consisting of one man, age sixty, who made his rounds on a bicycle and presided over a jail with one cell and a toilet. It also had a civil defense organization and a volunteer fire department; each house had a stirrup pump and a box of sand, but there had not been any fires in recent years as Roetgen had not been on the bombing schedule. The MFA&A function reached its fullest possible scope in Roetgen with the posting of off-limits signs on a hunting lodge outside town, which contained some paintings of uncertain value. Roetgen was, as a detachment stationed there later reported, "a typical rural village in which the residents obey the rules—no brothels, no reports of a black market, no intoxicating liquors sold, and all military routes free of civilian traffic."[34]

In Monschau, I4G2 opened its headquarters in the movie theater building. Herr Scheibler, the acting *Landrat,* already broken in, reported for his instructions every morning at ten. On 29 September the registration of civilians started, and the U.S. flag was raised at the headquarters, the detachment believed for the first time in Germany. A day earlier the electricity had been turned on again. Monschau received its electricity from a small water

---

[33] Besides the commander, Lt. William F. Schmidt, WO (jg.) Jack E. Milner, Cpl. Ralph C. Most, Tech. 5 Herbert P. Franz, and Pfc.'s Floyd S. Eisner, Eilert H. Fredricks, and Heinz Jauch.

[34] Det Hist, Det G1H2, 21 Oct–30 Nov 44, in SHAEF G–5, 17.11, Jacket 4.

BUILDING A BRIDGE IN MONSCHAU. *Captain Goetcheus second from the left.*

power plant on the Roer River. The 9th Division's outpost line looking into enemy territory was four blocks from detachment headquarters, and artillery shells going both ways rumbled and whistled overhead.

In its subsequent daily reports the detachment interwove the drama and triviality of the occupation:

1 Oct: The *Buergermeister* of Muetzenich reported enemy patrols contacting civilians for food and threatening the lives of him and his family.

6 Oct: All civilians ordered evacuated from Kalterherberg to Malmedy within the next two days. No transport being provided by tactical units, and the movement involves 1,100 persons. The people at Kalterherberg knew about the evacuation 5 hours before the tactical units told the MG detachment.

Enlisted men escorted a civilian truck to Roetgen to get 4,000 lbs. of rye there to be ground into flour.

7 Oct: Ten enemy soldiers surrendered at detachment headquarters. Among them was a soldier with relatives in Monschau. Before being taken to the PW enclosure he was allowed to visit his mother, sister, and brother. Photos taken.

8 Oct: *Buergermeister* of Muetzenich reports U.S. soldiers broke into his office in the schoolhouse and stole 12 cameras, 7 pair binoculars, 15 sabers, all of which he had been retaining by order of a tactical unit now gone. Wanton destruction of gardens also re-

ported. This serious because the Germans depend on them for food.

Provisional MG police detachment has moved to Kalterherberg to protect the evacuated village from looting and plundering.

9 Oct: Capt. Goetcheus requested arrangements for Protestant church services for civilians and U.S. soldiers.

10 Oct: Capt. Goetcheus held a summary court to try four civilians for violation of circulation. Two were convicted and fined. Two were dismissed on technicalities of borders and insufficient evidence.

11 Oct: Capt. Goetcheus went to Kalterherberg to confer with the C.O. of the MG police detachment. While there noticed two sides of beef hanging in a schoolyard CP of the local tactical unit. Also a local farmer reported loss of a heifer. Investigation requested.

12 Oct: Evacuation of the part of Monschau outside the tactical outposts but inside the city limits was ordered on recommendation of the tactical troops owing to possible subversive activity by small, roving enemy patrols.

Two German soldiers of a patrol were killed. Bodies taken to the local cemetery and *Buergermeister* ordered to have them buried.

13 Oct: *Buergermeister* of Muetzenich reports U.S. troops using public bathing facilities in local schoolhouse using up the available water supply at an alarming rate.

14 Oct: [Report on the missing heifer from Det. "A: 20th Engineer Bn.] MG officer, Monschau, said he saw a cow hanging in the vicinity of VANITY [28th Division] Rear Headquarters. Capt. Welch investigated, but cow had been butchered, so he could not identify it. Lieutenant at the headquarters knew nothing about the cow. First sgt. knew about the cow but did not know how it got there—except that it had been brought in by some men who found it wounded from artillery fire. Lt. Anderson of this detachment observed a live cow standing in the back of a 2½ ton truck on 12 Oct.

16 Oct: Woman prisoner received from Aachen to be confined in local jail.

18 Oct: Three boys, 13, 14, and 15 years old, tried for attempted theft of U.S. property consisting of chocolate bars and cigarettes. One convicted. Two acquitted.

Woman from Zweifall taken into prison for six months for possession of firearms.

19 Oct: During the night all windows on one side of the MG building were shattered when an enemy shell burst on the roof of a building 50 feet away.

Having trouble with CIC. Do not believe security threatened so have concentrated on assuring food, proper administration, and property protection on the assumption these will prevent unrest. Have done these at the expense of looking into past activities of present civil servants.

21 Oct: First Protestant services held. Many soldiers attended. Arrangements made to obtain 1,500 kilos of soap and 500 kilos of salt from Stolberg.

22 Oct: During the night another artillery shell struck the same building struck three days ago.

28 Oct: During the night an enemy patrol demolished the interior of the schoolhouse being used as the *Buergermeister's* office in Muetzenich.

German policemen in Muetzenich reported four U.S. soldiers in a jeep climbed through a window and stole 2,150 RM [Reichsmarks], 3 gold bracelets, 2 gold wristwatches, a necklace, and a ring. People were at the time attending church.[35]

1 Nov: Went to Stolberg to buy soap. Two civilian trucks with military escort.

2 Nov: One enlisted man escorted civilian truck to Stolberg for salt. On return dropped some salt at Roetgen and picked up shoes for Monschau.

3 Nov: Another trip for salt and soap to Stolberg.

Capt. Goetcheus went to Roetgen to make arrangements for shoes from supply at Roetgen.

Submitted requisitions for food. 6,500 civilians in the *Landkreis* now. Requisitioned food for two months. No sugar or salt has been available for two months. Salt is needed for slaughtering cattle. Local vegetables normally not enough for the population, and this

---

[35] Periodic Reports, Det I4G2, 4–28 Oct 44, and Rpt, Det A, 20th Engineer Bn, to CO, V Corps Provisional MG Police Bn, sub: Activities of the Det. at Kalterherberg, 14 Oct 44, in V Corps 205–5.1.

CIC CHECK IN MONSCHAU

year the crops are rotting in the fields because the people have not been allowed to go out to get them. No hay or other fodder for the cattle.

7 Nov: Civilian truck and enlisted escort went to Stolberg with a load of beef. Returned with soap for Roetgen and from Roetgen brought back 10 sacks of meal to be used as cattle feed.

8 Nov: First snow. Seventeen artillery shells fell on Monschau during the night.[36]

Snow fell again on the 11th and continued falling for the next three days. What

was left of the summer's crops, potatoes especially, was buried and frozen. In normal times *Kreis* Monschau was no more than 20 percent self-sufficient in grain and potatoes and imported 200,000 tons. Now not even the potatoes in the fields, which would not have been enough to last the winter, could be dug. Roetgen had enough grain to make up the bread ration for nine more weeks, provided the mill could be kept running. F1G2 in Aachen undertook to administer a barter system for the distribution of food between the occupied communities, but the most that such an

---

[36] Periodic Reports, Det I4G2, 1–8 Nov 44, in V Corps 205–5.1.

arrangement could do in the long run was equalize the shortages.[37]

One deficiency the Germans were not likely to suffer during the coming months was in supervision. *Landkreis* Monschau had two detachments permanently assigned and others coming and going on training assignments. (The whole occupied area, which had been slated to have four detachments at most, had twenty-one detachments deployed on 1 November.) It was good training, and the detachments of themselves did the Germans no visible harm. Monschau, because of the peculiarity of its position, also attracted visitors from higher staffs, war correspondents, and waves of CIC teams. These teams seemed to regard Monschau as a bottomless pit of subversion, each refusing to accept the judgments of its predecessors and usually locking up some Germans who had previously been screened and passed. On one day, a CIC team carried off as suspected prisoners of war six men, including the town's only dentist and the man who operated the power plant. Goetcheus retrieved both—the dentist on the condition that he be kept locked in the town jail during curfew hours.[38]

In the second week of December, CIC and G–2, First Army, performed a full-scale security check in Monschau to discover and arrest unregistered persons and to discourage would-be spies. Fifty-four three-man teams descended on the town before dawn on the morning of the 9th. At every house, one member of a team stood guard outside, one gathered all the residents in one room and checked their registration, and the third secured all the keys to locked doors and drawers and searched the building from top to bottom. Everybody checked was found to be registered. The contraband picked up amounted to a few cameras and binoculars, some pieces of German military uniforms, and some U.S. rations. No one was arrested.[39]

Shells continued to fall in Monschau, more frequently in the latter half of November: twelve on the 20th, nine the next day, and nine the day after. One round hit between the military government headquarters and the building next door causing in the former a short circuit in the electrical wiring and a fire. The civilian volunteer fire department put the fire out. At first the casualties were few and all civilians, who were taken to the hospital in Eupen in Army ambulances. Goetcheus thought the enemy was trying to break the civilians' morale because the shells came mostly in the early morning when the people were either on the way to or at Mass. On the 25th, three hit the Catholic church during the service, but no one was injured. The shellfire kept the detachment busy finding lodging for civilians and billets for troops driven out of damaged buildings. In the early afternoon on the 29th, three shells hit one of the hotels causing casualties among the troops quartered there, and that evening another half-dozen shells hit a schoolhouse wounding several soldiers seriously.[40]

Battle of the Bulge

Winter came early to western Germany in 1944. After the heavy snow in the mid-

---

[37] Memo, Det G1H2, sub: Report of Conference of *Buergermeisters* in Monschau, 18 Nov 44, V Corps 205–5.1.

[38] Memo, ECAD G–2 for CO, ECAD, sub: Report of Mission Performed 15–21 Nov 44, 21 Nov 44, in SHAEF G–5, 17.12, Jacket 5.

[39] Hqs, First Army, ACofS G–2, Counterintelligence Report No. 15, 9 Jan 45, in SHAEF G–5, 17.11, Jacket 4.

[40] Periodic Reports, Det I4G2, 15–29 Nov 44, in V Corps 205–5.1.

dle of November, rain alternated with sleet, snow, and cold. Clouds brushed the tops of the evergreen forest and sent swirls of mist and fog down to the ground beneath. The Eifel, the German extension of the Ardennes Forest, could hide an army or two or three with all their troops, artillery, tanks, and supplies. Hitler knew this. On the morning of 16 December, three armies—half of the entire German forces in the west—attacked along a fifty-mile front in the Ardennes from Monschau south to Echternach. They were aiming for Antwerp to cut off Eisenhower's whole left flank and, Hitler hoped, force the Western Allies to come to terms. The result was the Bulge, a sixty-mile-deep wedge driven through the Ardennes almost to the Meuse River. First Army's VIII Corps took the worst of the attack east of Bastogne. V Corps was hit hard too but held on to its anchor at Monschau.

The half dozen military government detachments deployed in Germany south of Monschau all escaped. I8G2, which had been stationed at Winterscheid, fought its way out with the troops of the 14th Cavalry Group. I4H2 at Buellingen had to leave its equipment behind. But Civil Affairs Detachment D6G1 at Clervaux, Luxembourg, was overrun, and its eight officers and men were captured.[41] Monschau was in the midst of the two-hour artillery barrage that preceded the attack on the morning of the 16th. I4G2 had permission to leave Monschau on the 17th but decided to stay:

. . . detachment vehicles and trailers were brought to the west side of the Roer River.

All personnel were instructed to pack and hold it ready out of sight of civilians. The civilian population was ordered to stay indoors in lower and western sides of buildings. Conference of detachment officers resulted in a decision to evacuate only in the most extreme necessity for the following reasons: (1) presence in town assists the local tactical unit; (2) departure would be obvious to civilians who have already seen a group and a battalion headquarters leave and would have serious effect on morale possibility resulting in a mass evacuation that would be difficult for tactical units to control; (3) military government would be handicapped in the future in the *Kreis* if the unit departed leaving those who had cooperated at the mercy of the German military.[42]

Monschau had never been a routine assignment, and Goetcheus was not surprised a week later when a civilian brought him the following letter:

Dear Sir,

22 December

I tried to meet German troops near Monschau. As I could find there no German troops, I surrender because I am hurt and ill and at the end of my physical forces.

Please be kind enough to send me a doctor and an ambulance as I cannot walk.

I am lying in a bed at Mr. Bouschery's and am awaiting your help and orders.

> Freiherr von der Heydte
> Lt. Col.
> Commanding German paratroops
> in Eupen-Malmedy area.

I4G2 took von der Heydte prisoner and eventually ran its score of captured German paratroopers to twenty-five, most of them brought in by local civilians.[43]

For a month the battle and the winter swirled around Monschau, the latter at times appearing in the detachment reports as almost the worse:

[41] (1) Hist Rpt, First Army G–5, 1–31 Dec 44, in SHAEF G–5, 17.11, Jacket 4. (2) Hqs, ECAD, to SHAEF G–5, sub: Activities of the ECAD, 1–31 Jan 45, 14 Feb 45, in SHAEF G–5, 17.12, Jacket 6.

[42] Periodic Report, Det I4G2, 17 Dec 44, in V Corps 205–5.1.

[43] Periodic Report, Det I4G2, 22 Dec 44, in V Corps 205–5.1.

18 Dec: Town shelled continuously for twenty-four hours. Population told to stay close to homes. Capt. Goetcheus made several trips to investigate areas shelled and assist in obtaining first aid by tactical unit and removal of injured civilians. Two civilians dead.

19 Dec: Population of Monschau remaining calm and cooperative.

Three-fourths of population of Muetzenich evacuated themselves on 18 and 19 Dec across the Belgian border toward Eupen. Muetzenich had been under heavy artillery fire for three days. The people were led by the acting *Buergermeister* and police.

21 Dec: Pfc. traveled to Brand to obtain supplies six days overdue and found Company G headquarters had moved to Holland. C.O., G Company, stated supplies and mail would be sent 22 Dec.

Detachment is grateful to VISUAL [99th Division]. As other tactical units evacuated on the 16th and 17th and bridges were prepared for demolition the population became apprehensive. The outward attitude of officers and men of VISUAL was helpful in restoring confidence in U.S. troops being able to defend the town.

24 Dec: Five hundred head cattle and horses face starvation because of no fodder. Oats has been used for humans. Some has been sent to try to save the horses which will be needed in the spring. Restrictions in travel make it impossible to get fodder. Tactical units say present situation renders any relaxation impossible.

Capt. Goetcheus asked permission for people to go out and feed cattle. No passes to be issued under any circumstances.

26 Dec: Col. Gunn, G-5, 1st Army, and Lt. Col. Pharr, G-5, V Corps . . . went to I4G2 and talked to Capt. Goetcheus about evacuating Monschau, Kalterherberg, and Muetzenich. At end recommended no evacuation be made.

29 Dec: Supply of fat for baking bread exhausted. German artillery shells continue to fall.

30 Dec: Men from the security guard relieved cattle feeding situation by hauling seven loads of hay to Reichenstein and Monschau.

3 Jan: Large amounts of organizational equipment, ammunition, and jerricans were left behind by units that evacuated on 16 Dec. Private property, including stoves, typewriters, and furniture were taken in lieu of issue U.S. Government property and equipment when troops departed.

8 Jan: Heavy snow for past 36 hours. Civilian trucks that have been driven by security guards to haul food for civilians cannot operate. Request two 6 × 6 2½ ton trucks.

Twelve-year-old girl killed by shell. Some civilians killed almost every day.

11 Jan: German Civilian Ration Report, Period 70: Daily allowances—normal not to exceed 1,400 calories, actual 977 calories.

Electric supply cut in half. Flow of Roer River has decreased so there is not enough water to turn the generators fast enough to get necessary voltage.

13 Jan: Two U.S. 6 × 6's travelled to Aachen and Stolberg to get oats and rye flour for the *Landkreis*. Two head of slaughtered beef taken to Stolberg in trade for rye flour.

19 Jan: Capt. Goetcheus went to Aachen to arrange nine tons soap—scabies increasing.

Almost a blizzard. Military government trucks could not move. Monschau shelled. All electric service stopped—lack of water.[44]

The German Ardennes offensive was the severest test of civil affairs–military government since D-day. The detachments had thought they were about at the stage where they could relinquish direct control and confine themselves to supervision of German agencies. The civilians had seemed convinced that for them the war was over, and the fear of Nazi reprisals against those who collaborated with the occupation had abated. The German offensive struck hard at both those impressions. The civilians suddenly realized that far from being out of the war, they were back in the thick of it. Seeing the roads filled day and night with convoys of troops and supplies going

[44] (1) Periodic Report, Det I4G2, 18 Dec 44–20 Jan 45, in V Corps 205–5.1. (2) Periodic Reports, 9th Division, OMG, to ACofS G–5, First Army, 30 Jan 45, in V Corps 205–5.1.

COLLECTING BEDSHEETS DURING BATTLE OF THE BULGE

in all directions and not knowing what was happening, they were gripped with fear that the Nazis might return and take vengeance on them. Military government detachments, often not much better informed than the civilians, had to supply courage and stamina to thousands of frightened people, suppress hysteria where it threatened to break out, control refugees, keep the roads open for military traffic, and in some places, provide security against German paratroops and partisans.

As they did at Monschau, the German civilians in the occupied area, while freely admitting that they were inwardly terror stricken, remained outwardly calm and orderly. There were no reports of civilian acts against the occupation forces. The majority of defendants in military government courts were charged with minor circulation and curfew violations. Everywhere, including Monschau, bank deposits increased.[45] The fear did not degenerate into panic. The police stayed at their posts, including those trained at Verviers, some of whom had been brought into Aachen a week before the attack, where, for secur-

---

[45] Ninth Army, ACofS G–5, sub: Bi-weekly Casum, 13 Jan 45, in SHAEF G–5, 17.14, Jacket 2.

ity reasons, they were lodged in the jail. The city officials in Aachen, plainly the most prominent candidates for reprisals, declared their willingness to continue at work, even though they knew they might be risking their lives. To accept Germans as allies would have been awkward, but 12th Army Group did instruct the detachments confidentially to take along the Germans who had collaborated with the occupation if evacuation was necessary.[46]

Military government learned some lessons that, had they been heeded, could have made the whole occupation a less unhappy experience. A detachment in Merkstein ordered all radio sets turned in for security reasons. It got 400 sets—and a flood of wild speculation. In Herzogenrath, when bicycles were ordered turned in, min-

ers stopped going to work and doctors and nurses could not make their rounds; rumors of various sorts of impending requisitions sprang up as the news spread. On the other hand, when camouflage snowsuits failed to arrive for the troops and the tactical units sent soldiers from door to door collecting bed sheets, one corps collected 60,000 in a few days. The soldiers explained what they would be used for, and most civilians co-operated without grumbling.[47]

The battle of the Bulge put a period to a phase in the occupation. Dreams of an early victory evaporated, and the Aachen experience of the fall of 1944 slipped out of mind. The victory would come, as would the occupation, but on harder terms. Hitler had bought a four months' lease on life, and the German people would pay.

---

[46] Monograph, SHAEF G–5, Hist Sec, sub: Civil Affairs, Military Government in a Defensive Operation, May 45, in SHAEF G–5, 60, Jacket 3.

[47] SHAEF, PsyWar Div, Weekly Intelligence Summary, No. 19, 3 Feb 45, in SHAEF, 7.35.

CHAPTER XI

Getting Ready for "The Day"

ECAD

Headquarters, ECAD, moved to Troyes, eighty miles east of Paris, in October 1944. There, at Camp Tank, in the concrete and steel buildings of a former Daimler-Benz automotive assembly and repair shop, the headquarters had space enough to billet itself comfortably—after the windows blown out in battle were reglazed. In the move, the units of ECAD went separate ways never to be assembled together in one place again: Headquarters, 2d ECAR, and its company headquarters dispersed to various locations in Belgium and northeastern France nearer their detachments, most of which were by then with tactical units; 3d ECAR went to Chartres. The detachments of 1st ECAR were being disbanded and their personnel transferred to the other two regiments as rapidly as they could be released from civil affairs assignments in France and Belgium.[1]

ECAD was beginning to show two serious flaws in its conception: its relationship with the detachments tended to become ineffectual after they were attached to tactical commands; while, on the other hand, ECAD's existence created a hiatus in the tactical commands' responsibility for the detachments. When Maj. Milton W. Buffington, G–2, ECAD, undertook an inspection of the detachments in November,

he first had to get travel clearance from 12th Army Group, which complied only with the understanding that similar clearances would have to be secured from each of the armies and corps. The G–5's of First Army and VII Corps granted the clearances, after expressing unhappiness over the spirit and ability of the detachment officers. G–5, XIX Corps, flatly denied permission to visit its detachments in Germany and added a demand for a copy of all communications between ECAD and the detachments. At the MASTER Military Government Center in Verviers, the senior detachment commander said he was under orders not to communicate outside the center except through First Army G–5.[2] As an E detachment commander he had expected to have some continuing contact with his subordinate teams; he had none. Only a week before, however, VII Corps G–5 had complained of the "headache" caused by having to supervise fourteen detachments in Germany.[3]

For the detachments still under ECAD control, being stationed in France was becoming a repeat of Shrivenham and Manchester. Detachment E1C3, Lt. Col. James R. Newman commanding, and its thirty-one H and I detachments went to Chartres

[1] Hqs, ECAD, to SHAEF G–5, sub: Activities of the ECAD 1–31 Oct, 17 Nov 44, in SHAEF G–5, 17.12, Jacket 5.

[2] Memo, ECAD G–2 for CO, ECAD, sub: Report of Mission Performed 15–21 Nov 44, 21 Nov 44, in SHAEF G–5, 17.12, Jacket 5.

[3] Memo, First Army, ACofS G–5, for All Concerned, sub: Military Government Conference 9–10 Nov 44, 16 Nov 44, in SHAEF G–5, 17.11, Jacket 3.

with the 3d ECAR. E1C3 and the detachments—the military government contingent for Wuerttemberg—would have a long wait ahead of them. In November they were back at daily lectures and language classes which, as they continued through the winter, spawned a crushing boredom. Newman resorted to periodic appeals. During the Bulge he tried self-interest, comparing the comforts of Chartres with the hardships being endured by the frontline troops. Later, he attempted to rouse the officers by urging them to devise ways for the enlisted men to pass the time constructively. Finally, he was reduced to recommending reading, study of current events, and physical fitness for all.[4]

Memorable events were rare everywhere in ECAD. Lt. Col. D. I. Glossbrenner, the division's executive officer, put together a saxophone sextet which was remarkable because it proved quite popular and also because it was the second such ensemble Glossbrenner had organized, the other having been formed while he served with the 42d Infantry Division in France in World War I. Even more notable was a mission performed by the Division Service Company in October. In a convoy of twenty-five dump trucks, fifty-eight men of the Service Company and Headquarters Company, 3d ECAR, under Maj. Arthur M. Cory, moved 1¼ billion Allied military marks from London to the vaults of the Bank of France in Paris and other depositories in France. The fifty-four tons of money, worth $122,352,000, was the most valuable single cargo to pass through the SHAEF supply line in the campaign.[5]

ECAD also received some publicity. For six weeks beginning in early January 1945, Congressman Albert Gore of Tennessee served incognito as a private with various types of military government detachments. Later, many newspapers picked up a part of his report to the Congress that described some of the men in military government as having been transferred there because they were surplus or misfits elsewhere. Fewer newspapers, however, printed the complete statement in which Congressman Gore characterized military government personnel on the whole as carefully selected, competent, and qualified.[6]

In November, Detachment A1A1 joined ECAD in Troyes, setting up its headquarters in the city hall of the *faubourg* Saint Savine. A1A1, the U.S. Berlin detachment designate, came on orders from SHAEF and was not entirely happy to be in Troyes. The detachment commander, Col. Frank L. Howley, had wanted to go to the more comfortable and quieter summer resort of Barbizon in the forest of Fontainbleau outside Paris. Under Howley, who was an advertising executive in civilian life and a cavalry officer until a back injury sent him into the Civil Affairs Training Program (CATP), A1A1 had become the premier U.S. civil affairs detachment and had held the two most glamorous and demanding assignments in the war so far, Cherbourg and Paris. In Paris it had supervised twenty-three detachments with 136 officers and 220 enlisted men. It moved to Troyes with 16 officers and 48 enlisted men.[7] At Troyes, as the detachment historian stated, "A1A1 ceased to be a mere detachment attached to the 1st ECAR and attained

[4] Det E1C3, War Diary, Oct 44–Mar 45, in OMGUS 413-2/3, decimal 314.81.

[5] Memo, ECAD G–2, sub: Report on Mission of SHAEF Det. No. 63, 28 Dec 44, in SHAEF G–5, 17.12, Jacket 6.

[6] Draft ECAD History, Sep 45, in USFET CAD, Hist Doc file.

[7] A1A1, History: Paris, in SHAEF G–5, 17.23, Jacket 2.

military status as Detachment A1A1, ECAD."[8] The detachment also began rebuilding to its authorized strength for Berlin, 77 officers and 150 enlisted men.[9] Howley set as the first training objectives complete self-sufficiency in operations, down to cooking and housekeeping, and a state of discipline superior to any other unit in the Army. Dr. Walter L. Dorn, attached as an OSS (Office of Strategic Services) civilian expert adviser, developed a program of instruction on Germany and built up a specialized library on Berlin largely from materials recently captured in Germany.

Practice and Policy

One of the most disconcerting experiences of the early occupation was the discovery that the policies emanating from Washington would not only have to be imposed on the Germans but on the Americans as well. What seemed to be elementary justice in the White House, and hence also in the CAD and possibly even in SHAEF, did not automatically seem so on the ground in Germany. Here the Germans, alleged nation of sinners against peace and human decency though they might be, became people who could be sick, hungry, and frightened, old and young, pretty and pitiable, guilty and innocent. Even though they might accept the idea of German collective guilt, the American soldiers did not feel at ease as agents of collective retribution.

Nonfraternization, no doubt, was the policy that met the earliest, strongest, and in the long run most successful resistance. It was resented as a physiological frustration and in its prohibition of any kind of unofficial contact with Germans, including shaking hands and giving candy to children, as an awkward and irksome social quarantine. Generals as well as privates found it hard to have to ignore children.[10] Worse, in a way, were attempts to defend the policy, which either sounded arbitrary or seemed to disparage the American intelligence, or both, as in the following effort by ECAD:

American forces occupied the Rhineland after the last war. At first the Germans hated them, but later the attitude was more friendly, even subservient.

This time it will be different. Many German towns and cities are in ruins already and many more will be before the end of the fighting. The Nazis plainly mean to hang on to the bitter violent end, then go underground and cause all the trouble and casualties they can.

The majority of the Germans support the Nazis. They hold democratic ways in contempt. They will try to make friends with us to try to get favors, to create sympathy for the "poor downtrodden" German people, to make us disagree among ourselves, or just to get a good chance to slip a knife into an Allied soldier. They will try to stir up ill-feeling and mistrust between the British and Americans and between both and the Russians. They will try to make the occupying forces feel sorry for themselves and undermine their will to finish the job. DON'T BE A SUCKER FOR GOEBBELS' ECHOES!

It will be especially difficult for personnel of military government to avoid friendly relations with Germans. But nonfraternization is the rule. It will be strictly followed.[11]

---

[8] A1A1, History of A1A1 Detachment, *Die Stadt,* First Phase, in SHAEF G–5, 17.23, Jacket 3.

[9] Hqs, ECAD, to SHAEF G–5, sub: Activities of the ECAD 1–30 Nov 44, in SHAEF G–5, 17.12, Jacket 5.

[10] Memo, First Army, ACofS G–5, for All Concerned, sub: Military Government Conference 9–10 Nov 44, 16 Nov 44, in SHAEF G–5, 17.11, Jacket 3.

[11] Hqs, ECAD, sub: Conduct of Members of This Command in Occupied Germany, 28 Oct 44, in SHAEF G–5, 17.12, Jacket 5.

After two months of the occupation, the nonfraternization problem began to settle down in at least one respect. The fines for violations were becoming standardized: $10 for conversing with a German in the open, $25 for unauthorized presence in a German dwelling, and $65 for cohabitation with a German woman. The last fine, a month's pay for a private, could be higher for other ranks, but up to 15 December only one such fine had been imposed—which, perhaps, reveals much about enforcement of the policy.[12] No one denied that enforcement, particularly in the matter of what was coming to be called the $65 question, was a problem. A major difficulty was that fraternization was a punishable offense for American soldiers but not for the Germans against whom, the commanders in the field concluded early, enforcement would probably be easier and more effective. SHAEF found itself having to point out repeatedly that nonfraternization was meant to represent an attitude of Allied troops toward the Germans, not one of the Germans toward the Allies or one which in any sense depended on the cooperation of the Germans.[13]

The nonfraternization policy had one virtue: its meaning was clear. The same could not be said of most of the other policies coming out of Washington. In the first place, they came late. The SHAEF and 12th Army Group interim directives of September, which had not included the latest policies, were not replaced until November.[14] Until then the only guidance the armies and lesser commands had was contained in the four points on the flyleaf of the handbook. More important though was the apprehension in SHAEF, after the flyleaf and the directive were out, that the spirit of the new policies was not taking hold. The military government officers showed dismaying persistence in doing a good job according to the standards by which they had been trained.

The first point in the flyleaf, also included in the SHAEF directive, prohibited "steps looking toward economic rehabilitation of Germany." As a practical matter, there was almost nothing military government could have done in the fall of 1944 even if it had wanted to, but it had taken one small step. On 5 October, Detachment I4G2 had reopened the *Kreis* bank in Monschau. In the following weeks others were opened at Roetgen, Stolberg, Buesbach, and Aachen. The purpose, psychological rather than economic, was to give the occupation an appearance of permanence and stability. SHAEF had misgivings from the beginning, and Colonel Bernstein went to First Army to talk to Colonel Gunn:

Col. Bernstein: We are not supposed to meddle too much in the financial structure of Germany. . . . We have no program for banks. . . . Our job is to observe. Can we assume the responsibility of solving Germany's problems in a half-baked way? No. All we can do is let the Germans do it—and if anything goes sorry it is their responsibility. Our job is not to protect and build up the financial structure for the country as a whole. Col. Gunn: I do not think we are trying to do this. . . .

Col. Gunn: Is an orderly regime of life in our rear areas necessary? Just answer that one question.

---

[12] Ninth Army G-1, Operational Extract of Journal, 1–15 Dec 44, in Ninth Army 109–1.
[13] DF, First Army, ACofS G–5, sub: Orders Prohibiting Fraternization with Allied Troops by German Civilians, Germany, 14 Dec 44, in SHAEF G–5, 17.11, Jacket 6.
[14] SHAEF, Office of CofS, to Hqs, AGps 21, 12, 6, sub: Directive for Military Government of Germany Prior to Defeat or Surrender, 9 Nov 44, in AFHQ G–5, Directives.

Col. Bernstein: In terms of finance now—if they cannot clear their checks through banks, will it hurt anything?

Col. Gunn: I'm not referring to that. I mean lack of riots, lack of need to hold supplies, lack of need for troops to patrol streets—is this necessary?

Col. Bernstein: I do not think it is necessary to have an orderly regime to the extent that the Germans had one before the war. . . .

Col. Gunn: I mean the barest elements of order.

Col. Bernstein: . . . For the moment at least, we are not planning to give the Germans the type of treatment we are giving Italy or France. We are bound to be blamed for the inevitable financial chaos in Germany. Our responsibility is to our armies and to our people; and to carry out the affirmative policies of our President and of Mr. Churchill.

Col. Gunn: Do you think it is necessary to have a regime where it isn't necessary to have soldiers policing every block?

Col. Bernstein: The answer to that is obvious. . . .[15]

SHAEF's concern deepened when military government reported a considerable success in its banking operations. Deposits everywhere consistently exceeded withdrawals—at Monschau even during the hectic days of the Bulge. The bank at Aachen received 617 new accounts and deposits of over a million *Reichsmarks* in the first three weeks it was open. In December it loaned a half million *Reichsmarks* to the city of Aachen and 50,000 to the bishopric.[16]

G–5, First Army, with satisfaction, took the success of the banks as a gauge of the effectiveness of the occupation. SHAEF, without satisfaction, apparently did too.

Actually, both seem to have overlooked one point: the Germans could do almost nothing with their money except put it in banks. There was nothing to buy that was not rationed and very little that was.

By December, one thing seemed clear to SHAEF: the recent developments in the philosophy of the occupation had not penetrated to military government in the field. As General McSherry stated, "This is clearly understandable in view of the fact that these military government officers received their training at Shrivenham and elsewhere without the benefit of the most recent CCS policy. . . ."[17] A corrective was needed, and G–5, SHAEF, supplied it in the following letter to the army groups and ECAD:

The essence of . . . policy is that no effort will be made to rehabilitate or succor the German people. Rather, the sole aim of military government is to further military objectives.

All planning, direction, and instruction by U.S. elements concerning military government should be guided by this policy which reflects firm U.S. views as known in this headquarters. Principal points to be emphasized are the following:
   a. Germany will not be "liberated" but occupied as a defeated nation.
   b. The German people will be made to realize that all necessary steps will be taken to prevent any further attempt by them to conquer the world.
   c. No steps will be taken looking toward the economic rehabilitation of Germany.

Reports from the field indicate that military government detachments and G–5 staffs of subordinate formations are inclined to try to do too much too relieve the problems of the German people. There seems to be a disposition to approach the administration of Germany with the idea that it is our job to

---

[15] Notes of Conference in Col. Gunn's Office, 11:30–11:45, 14 Nov 44, in SHAEF G–5, 17.11, Jacket 3.

[16] Hist Rpt, First Army G–5, Dec 44, in SHAEF G–5, 17.11, Jacket 4.

[17] Ltr, Brig Gen Frank McSherry to Brig T. Robbins, 21 Dec 44, in SHAEF G–5, 803/1, Jacket 1.

make Germany a "happy land" again. It is essential that all military government personnel be disabused of this concept.[18]

Eclipse Plans

In the outline plan issued on 10 November 1944, SHAEF described ECLIPSE as plans and preparations for operations in Europe in the event of a German surrender. ECLIPSE succeeded RANKIN and TALISMAN. Strictly speaking, since it incorporated the work done since summer, ECLIPSE was the same as TALISMAN and would have continued to be called such had SHAEF not learned in October that the meaning of the code word "TALISMAN" was known to the enemy.[19] But ECLIPSE was actually more than just a substitute for RANKIN or TALISMAN renamed. RANKIN and TALISMAN had assumed a formal surrender either before Allied troops had crossed the German border or before they were deep into Germany. ECLIPSE defined the surrender in two ways: as an instrument formally signed by a German government or the German High Command, or as a decision to be taken by Eisenhower when the majority of the German forces had capitulated or been overpowered. By introducing this second and at the time seemingly more likely possibility, ECLIPSE, although it purported to be a military operation, became actually more a designation of a state or condition, namely, the end of hostilities and the beginning of the occupation.

The outline plan specified a primary phase in which the SHAEF forces, after the collapse or surrender would consummate OVERLORD by a rapid advance deep into Germany. The plan also contained the hint of a race for Berlin; but the ECLIPSE planning, as it continued into the winter, never did get down to the staging of an operation. In late January, an airborne strike to seize Berlin was nominally on the agenda for ECLIPSE; but although such a strike would have taken weeks, possibly months, to mount, nothing had been done to prepare it. SHAEF obviously expected to execute only the second phase: the routine deployment of forces in the western zones. Consequently, ECLIPSE planning became almost exclusively concerned with five objectives set for the second phase: (1) primary disarmament and control of the German forces; (2) enforcement of the terms of surrender or the will of SHAEF in the event there was no surrender; (3) establishment of law and order; (4) beginning of the total disarmament of Germany; and (5) redistribution of Allied forces into their national zones.[20]

In the second phase, ECLIPSE became not an operation but an administrative plan for establishing the occupation in Germany. As such it had a singular deficiency: SHAEF was a combined command, yet no combined policy existed for the posthostilities period or was likely to be issued. All Eisenhower had were the CCS presurrender instructions. The five objectives for the second phase were handcrafted to avoid any encroachment on the existing policy vacuum; therefore, the objectives also practically omitted a mission for military government, the establishment of which would logically be SHAEF's primary function in ECLIPSE. The only feasible remedy was

---

[18] Ltr, SHAEF G–5 to CG's, 6 and 12 AGps, and CO, ECAD, sub: Policy in Occupied Germany, 7 Dec 44, in SHAEF G–5, 803/1, Jacket 1.

[19] SHAEF AG, sub: Codewords, 28 Dec 44, in SHAEF G–5, 115.25A, Jacket 2.

[20] SHAEF (44) 34, Operation ECLIPSE, Appreciation and Outline Plan, 10 Nov 44, in SHAEF G–5, 115.25A, Jacket 3.

to assume an extension of the CCS presurrender policy into the postsurrender period. Consequently, in its ECLIPSE planning, SHAEF G–5 took on the following additional objectives from the SHAEF presurrender directive of 9 November: care, control, and repatriation of displaced persons; apprehension of war criminals; establishment of property and financial controls; elimination of nazism and militarism; and preservation of a suitable civil administration to accomplish all the objectives.[21]

In writing the outline plan, SHAEF predicted that German resistance to ECLIPSE would be low. The Germans, the planners expected, would know they had been overwhelmingly defeated and would be too physically and spiritually exhausted to continue the struggle. Some sabotage might be attempted and some of the Nazi leaders might attempt a dramatic last stand, perhaps in the Bavarian Alps, though it was most unlikely.[22] Instinct regarding the Germans was better in November 1944 than it would be a half year later. (See below, p. 255.)

The Carpet and Static Plans

Whether military government went into Germany after a surrender, as TALISMAN assumed, or, as ECLIPSE supposed, in the wake of the last battle, its first mission would be to seize governmental control in all areas occupied by SHAEF forces. In this respect the planning for military government in Germany had differed from the planning for civil affairs in liberated countries. Under RANKIN the concept of pinpointing—the assignment of specific detachments to specified localities—had been introduced for Germany. In liberated territory, detachments would be assigned where they were needed; in Germany they would be assigned to assert Allied control. RANKIN, however, said nothing about how detachments would get to their pinpoint assignments. The war remedied this omission. By the end of summer 1944, the armies were either at or approaching the German border and would most likely sweep across Germany in the deployment they then had, whether the Germans surrendered or not. For military government the effect would be like unrolling a carpet: control would be extended across Germany from the border eastward as the armies advanced, the pinpointed detachments taking up their stations as the locations were uncovered.

The carpet made its appearance in the 1,186 South Plan Amended, which ECAD issued on 13 September 1944 and which thereafter went by the more convenient name Carpet Plan.[23] Two ECAR's, the 2d and 3d, with 213 detachments and 1,428 functional military government officers were to provide the carpet. The area to be covered, at first the U.S. zone plus the Rhineland from the zone boundary north to Duesseldorf, was later increased in the ECLIPSE planning to include the whole southern third of the British zone. The carpet was a thin one. I detachments (four officers and six enlisted men) were assigned areas with populations up to 100,000. To provide coverage for the northward extension, four companies of detachments pinpointed for southern and eastern Bavaria had to be transferred north and given tem-

---

[21] SHAEF G–5, ECLIPSE Memo No. 13, Digest of Military Government Considerations for Germany, 13 Dec 44, in SHAEF G–5, 115.25A, Jacket 3.

[22] SHAEF (44) 34, Operation ECLIPSE, Appreciation and Outline Plan, 10 Nov 44, in SHAEF G–5, 115.25A, Jacket 3.

[23] ECAD G–3, Organizational Development per G–3 Records [no date], USFET CAD 322.

porary second assignments in Westphalia and Hanover in the British zone.[24]

Devised for TALISMAN, the Carpet Plan was adapted to ECLIPSE and retained during the advance into Germany in 1945, somewhat less satisfactorily at each successive stage. The carpet was primarily a method of quickly providing area military government, but after September the movement into Germany was anything but fast. Consequently, the armies found themselves having to set up and maintain military government centers for detachments they would probably not soon be able to deliver and could not use for anything else. In the fall an irksome and seemingly endless round of detachment transfers began as operational plans and tactical boundaries changed. In the detachments—separated from their parent organization, ECAD, and not integrated into the armies—morale sagged.

The least satisfactory aspect of the Carpet Plan was that it did not resolve the problem of the transition from SHAEF's anti-AMGOT philosophy of military government in the combat phase to the regional approach projected for the permanent occupation. In a fast, unopposed sweep like the one anticipated in TALISMAN, the problem could have been expected to resolve itself quickly; the carpet would be laid and regional administration established in a matter of weeks at most. Not so under the conditions that would prevail. Furthermore, although the Carpet Plan assigned regional detachments, the SHAEF directive of 9 November reconfirmed military government as a command responsibility and only projected the regional system as the ultimate form of military government.

While the carpet was being laid the combat commands would direct military government, each within its own tactical boundaries which would rarely if ever coincide with the German regional boundaries.[25]

Since the Carpet Plan was concerned with the whole area that U.S. forces would occupy on the advance into Germany, and not specifically with the U.S. zone, ECAD at the end of October also submitted a Static Plan to provide for permanent deployment into the zone. In the first stage of the Static Plan the detachments stationed outside the final U.S. zone would be withdrawn. In the second stage, 250 detachments would be deployed in the U.S. zone to provide complete coverage down to the *Landkreise* and *Stadtkreise,* and the permanent occupation would begin. To complete the Static Plan, thirty-seven new detachments would be needed—thirty-nine after Bremen and Bremerhaven were added.[26]

The change from the mobile phase of the Carpet Plan to the static phase would require a command reorganization. When the carpet had been laid and active operations ceased, Headquarters, 6th Army Group, which in September 1944 moved in on the right flank of the front after making the drive through southern France, would be withdrawn; and 12th Army Group would assume command of the entire U.S. zone. The tenure of 12th Army Group was also likely to be short. When the combined command was dissolved, the U.S. element of SHAEF would become the

[24] USFET, General Board, Study No. 32, Civil Affairs and Military Government Organization and Operations, 15 May 46, in Hist Div, Hqs, ETO, 97–USF 5–03.0, p. 112.

[25] SHAEF, Office of the CofS, to Hqs, AGps 21, 12, 6, sub: Directive for Military Government of Germany Prior to Defeat or Surrender, 9 Nov 44, in AFHQ G–5, Directives.
[26] (1) Hqs, ECAD, to SHAEF, sub: Activities of the ECAD 1 Nov–30 Nov 44, 19 Dec 44, in USFET CAD 314.7, ECAD. (2) General Board Study No. 32, p. 97.

Headquarters, U.S. Forces in the European Theater (USFET); Eisenhower as theater commander and military governor would use the theater staff in the zone and the U.S. Group Control Council to carry out his tripartite obligations in Berlin.[27] In the shift to the Static Plan deployment, the armies would become military district headquarters. Originally there were to have been four military districts, but after 12th Army Group pointed out that the whole zone was actually only about the size of the state of Mississippi and that Bavaria would have to be arbitrarily split in half to provide the fourth district, the number was reduced to two. Bavaria would become the Eastern Military District, and the Western Military District (later to be reduced by transfer of territory to French control) would include the *Laender* Hesse, Hesse-Nassau, Wuerttemberg, and Baden.[28]

Since the zone and military district boundaries followed German administrative boundaries, the transition to the Static Plan would make possible the installation of regional military government detachments. The SHAEF presurrender directive envisioned this development and authorized a G–5 technical channel of command on matters which did not "affect tactical operations or concern the security of Allied troops." But military government would also remain a command responsibility of the military district commanders, who, with their corps and division commanders,

if the security of their forces was threatened and who were to be informed of all military government technical instructions. The military district commander could suspend such instructions "when in his judgment conditions within his district require."[29]

The Carpet and Static Plans put ECAD in the peculiar position of experiencing an acute personnel shortage at a time when most of the personnel it had were not employed. In November, ECAD and 12th Army Group submitted separate requests to Washington for increased officer and enlisted allotments. The War Department, which had since D-day already raised ECAD's authorized strength (including other than detachment personnel) to 2,768 officers, 120 warrant officers, and 5,366 enlisted men, was reluctant to approve an increase when the end of the war might soon make thousands of men available in Europe.[30] In December, McSherry went to Washington to promote a boiled-down request for 740 officers, 16 warrant officers, and 1,071 enlisted men. When the War Department told SHAEF that it had no unallocated troops from which to make an increase, Smith replied, "What the hell am I going to do to handle this personnel problem . . .?" He asked for at least an allotment of grades and ratings, saying, "[We] will secure the bodies over here," and implied that the "bodies" would be secured "from the backdoors of hospitals" if necessary.

In February, the War Department approved a temporary overstrength up to the number SHAEF had requested, thereby re-

---

[27] (1) Memo, SHAEF, CofS, for 6th AGp, 12th AGp, sub: Responsibility During Post-Surrender Period, 11 Oct 44, in USFET SGS 322. (2) Memo, ETOUSA, CofS, for CG's, Army Groups; Acting Dep, US Gp CC; CG, Com Zone, sub: U.S. Organization and Planning for Occupation of Germany, 16 Dec 44, in SHAEF SGS 322.3.

[28] Memo, Hqs, 12th AGp, for SHAEF, sub: Territorial Organization of the U.S. Zone, 4 Jan 45, in SHAEF G–5, 20.1.

would be charged with taking direct action

[29] SHAEF, Office of the CofS, to Hqs, AGps 21, 12, 6, sub: Directive for Military Government of Germany Prior to Defeat or Surrender, 9 Nov 44, in AFHQ G–5, Directives.

[30] Hqs, ECAD, to SHAEF G–5, sub: Activities of the ECAD 1–31 Dec 44, in SHAEF G–5, 17.12, Jacket 6.

lieving for the moment one pressure on ECAD while intensifying another.[31] Because ECAD did not have a fixed table of organization, promotions had been difficult. After ECAD also became an overstrength organization, promotions were doubly difficult since theater regulations all but prohibited promotions in overstrength units.[32]

The Displaced Persons Executive

During the early months of OVERLORD, neither the displaced person (DP) nor refugee problems materialized to the extent that had been feared. The western Europeans, by then wise in the ways of war, for the most part stayed close to their homes. The eastern Europeans encountered were nearly all Soviet nationals forced into German service after being captured on the Eastern Front. The question of their status was a delicate one that would not be answered until the Yalta Conference, but in the meantime the German uniform guaranteed them prisoner of war treatment. SHAEF handled civilians under the Outline Plan for Refugees and Displaced Persons (4 June 1944), which placed the responsibility on the local governments and restricted the military involvement to relief where it was essential and to prevention and control of disease that might also threaten the health of the military forces.[33]

The flood of displaced persons, however, was still expected when Germany collapsed or when the Germans weakened and could no longer control the millions of forced laborers within their boundaries. The DPs were there, and something would have to be done about them sooner or later. The questions were, what and how much. The German handbook and early SHAEF policy proposed to make them a responsibility of the German authorities who would care for them in centers until their own governments arranged repatriation. Whether the Germans, even under Allied supervision, could be proper guardians for people they had so long oppressed, however, was doubtful; and SHAEF G-5 concluded shortly after D-day that some kind of special DP teams would be needed and that the United Nations Relief and Rehabilitation Administration (UNRRA) was the logical source of such personnel, since to set up military teams in ECAD would dissipate military government strength.[34]

For SHAEF G-5 in the summer of 1944 the most ominous aspect of the DP problem was, as always, the nightmare possibility of millions of people streaming out of Germany, clogging roads, creating an avalanche of economic problems for the war-weakened liberated countries, and spreading disease, typhus in particular, across Europe. Furthermore, the critical stage, the start of the mass DP movement, would most likely come at a highly inopportune moment, namely, when German control broke down and SHAEF forces were not yet on the scene. If the DPs were to be persuaded to stand fast, it would have to be done in advance by an order or by an appeal. General Gullion and the DP Branch, SHAEF, did not believe either

---

[31] Cable, SHAEF Main from McSherry to AGWAR for Hilldring, 30 Dec 44; Cable, AGWAR to Com Zone, 14 Jan 45; Memo, McSherry for Smith, 28 Jan 45; Cable, AGWAR to SHAEF, 25 Feb 45, in USFET SGS 200.3.
[32] General Board Study No. 32, pp. 100–102.
[33] USFET, General Board, Study No. 35, Displaced Persons, Refugees and Recovered Allied Military Personnel, 11 May 46, in Hist Div, Hqs, ETO, 97–USF 5–03.0, p. 12.

[34] (1) SHAEF G-5, Hist Sec, Analysis Sheet [no date], sub: G-5 ETOUSA memo, 6 Jun 44, in SHAEF G-5, 601. (2) General Board Study No. 35, p. 12.

method had much chance of succeeding with people who would experience their first taste of freedom in years; but in July they decided to try an appeal through psychological warfare channels for what it might be worth. A standfast order seemed to be ruled out, for the time being anyway, since SHAEF's authority to issue orders to Allied citizens, Soviet nationals in particular, was in doubt. Consequently the appeal merely informed the DPs that they would receive food and shelter and help in getting home and concluded with "Stay Where You Are!"[35]

TALISMAN and ECLIPSE and the possibility of a German collapse in the fall of 1944 lent urgency to the DP planning even though the DP problem was nonexistent in the early stage of the Rhineland campaign. The Germans still had a tight hold on the people behind their front, and the movement was eastward rather than westward. At the end of January 1945, the Aachen DP center housed only twenty-nine displaced persons, all of them Poles, and intelligence reports (which later proved correct) indicated that the Germans were moving the forced laborers out of the Rhineland.[36] Nevertheless, in SHAEF planning during the same period, the DPs advanced to top priority among the concerns of the occupation, and, notably, the emphasis shifted from control to welfare. A mass migration was still to be feared, but henceforth it could, at least, probably be confined to the boundaries of Germany.

The presurrender directive for military government made care, control, and repatriation of United Nations DPs the second of seven major military government objec-

tives.[37] As such it became a command responsibility, one which SHAEF further defined in a memo, "Displaced Persons and Refugees in Germany," issued on 18 November. The DPs from liberation to repatriation were to be cared for as a direct military concern, and commanders were to employ all available resources to this end. To the maximum extent, the German authorities would be required to provide food, shelter, medical attention, and wages and, in all of these matters, give the DPs priority over the German population. During the opposed advance into Germany, military government detachments operating in the normal military chain of command would be detailed to work with the DPs. In the later stages and in the static phase the Displaced Persons Executive (DPX) would take over.[38]

In creating the DPX, SHAEF conferred on displaced persons a distinctive status in the occupation and established an administration for them that was separate to some extent from both military government and the tactical commands. Within SHAEF, the DPX became the first example of a new form of organization that cut across existing organizational as well as national lines to co-ordinate work in a specific functional area. In the 18 November memorandum SHAEF contemplated using officers from the U.S. and British Control Council groups and the Women's Army Corps; and on 25 November Eisenhower concluded an agreement with Governor Lehman, Director General of UNRRA, authorizing UNRRA teams to be recruited in Belgium, Luxembourg, the Netherlands, Norway,

---

[35] SHAEF G–5, Hist Sec, Analysis Sheet, 2 Aug 44, in SHAEF G–5, 111.05.

[36] Hist Rpt, 12th AGp G–5, Jan 45, 31 Jan 45, in SHAEF G–5, 17.16, Jacket 5.

[37] SHAEF, Office of the CofS, to Hqs, AGps 21, 12, 6, sub: Directive for Military Government of Germany Prior to Defeat or Surrender, 9 Nov 44, in AFHQ G–5, Directives.

[38] General Board Study No. 35, pp. 13–15.

and France to assume "to the maximum extent" the handling of the DPs.[39] These groups would be associated in the DPX with the G–5 branches in SHAEF and its subordinate staffs, the military government DP detachments, and combat and service personnel detailed to DP work.[40] In the ECLIPSE planning, SHAEF lowered considerably its estimate of the number of DPs from the 21 million talked about earlier, but still expected them to number close to 10 million in all of Germany and over 3½ million in the western zones. The work of the DPX would be to persuade the DPs by every means to stand fast, move them into assembly centers where they could be given food, shelter, and medical care, and arrange their orderly and early return to the countries of their origin.[41]

War Crimes

The post–World War II prosecution of war criminals had its formal beginnings in the Moscow Declaration of 1 November 1943 and the United Nations War Crimes Commission, which began its work in London in January 1944. The Moscow Declaration pledged the three major allies, speaking in the interest of all the United Nations, to seek out Axis war criminals and return them for punishment to the countries in which the atrocities had been committed. The declaration implied further that major war criminals, whose offenses were not restricted to a geographical area, would in some manner be punished jointly by the Allied governments.[42] The War Crimes Commission was charged with gathering evidence and compiling lists of Axis war criminals.

War crimes had been a lingering concern of the anti-Axis nations throughout the war, a concern that in part reached back to 1919 and the Paris Peace Conference where provisions for trying accused Germans had been written into the Treaty of Versailles but not enforced. Before November 1943, the U.S. President, the British Prime Minister, and the governments in exile had issued numerous warnings aimed particularly at deterring the Germans from executing hostages and from mistreating and murdering Jews. That many crimes against Allied soldiers were also to be expected could be inferred from Hitler's "Commando" order of 1942, which refused quarter to enemy troops on raids or missions behind the German lines, and from the official encouragement, beginning in 1943, of civilian attacks on downed U.S. and British airmen. The victims of such policies, civilian and military, could number in the millions and the perpetrators in the tens of thousands.

In spite of their seriousness, war crimes were for a long while a subject on which the U.S. authorities spoke sternly but acted with elaborate caution, both for good reasons. As long as hostilities lasted, verbal deterrence—the promise of punishment—was for the U.S. government the only feasible approach. The other possibility of actually trying war criminals as they were captured, although a more positive deterrent, could also bring reprisals against U.S. prisoners of war in German hands, and American public opinion was especially sensitive to

---

[39] SHAEF Admin Memo No. 39, sub: Employment of UNRRA Personnel with Military Forces, 25 Nov 44, in USFET SGS 334.

[40] General Board Study No. 35, p. 14.

[41] SHAEF G–5, ECLIPSE Memo No. 14, Control of DPs, 13 Dec 44, in SHAEF G–5, 115.25A, Jacket 3.

[42] Department of State, *Foreign Relations, 1943*, vol. I, p. 768.

the welfare of prisoners of war. In November 1943, while Eisenhower was still commanding in the Mediterranean, Secretary of State Hull urged and Eisenhower agreed that no publicity should be given to the capture of war criminals or to evidence collected against them. Hull even advised against any actions that might reveal individuals to be under suspicion, and Eisenhower, to be on the safe side, forbade not only trials in the theater but all publicity on the subject.[43] In December, when the Soviet Union tried and condemned three German soldiers at Kharkov for gas van atrocities, Hull announced that the United States did not regard "direct handling of war criminals" as falling within the terms of the Moscow Declaration.[44] When the Germans threatened to try captured British and American airmen (reprisals against Soviet prisoners of war being somewhat superfluous since neither the Germans nor the Soviet Union recognized any rules in their war against each other), the State Department assured the Germans through the Swiss of continuing U.S. strict observance of the Geneva Convention.[45]

In the plans for OVERLORD, both the Standard Policy and Procedure and CCS 551, the presurrender military government directive, made the arrest of war criminals an objective of the occupation. CCS 551 directed Eisenhower to have arrested and "held for investigation and subsequent disposition" Adolf Hitler, his chief Nazi associates, and all war crimes suspects, including those on the War Crimes Commission

lists.[46] Neither document, however, applied outside the German borders, and procedure for dealing with war crimes developed slowly. On 20 August 1944, SHAEF established a standing court of inquiry in G–1 to collect and preserve evidence "only in cases involving Allied military personnel." The court of inquiry was not mobile and could only hear witnesses and receive evidence brought to it.[47] In the first week of September, just before the first troops crossed the German border, SHAEF instructed the army group commanders to take all war criminals into custody "so far as the exigencies of the situation permit," but the army groups were not given instructions on the investigative procedures for another three months.[48]

A good part of the reason why little had been done at SHAEF up to the late summer and fall of 1944—apart from the concern for reprisals which was always predominant—was that equally little was being done in Washington. In August the Joint Chiefs of Staff were just beginning to work on a war crimes directive, JCS 1023, which at that stage constituted mainly a definition of war crimes.[49] The law as to the nature and punishment of war crimes was far from precise. The Responsibilities Commission of the Paris Peace Conference in 1919 had listed thirty-two specific war crimes. In 1943, the War

---

[43] Department of State, *Foreign Relations, 1943,* vol. I, p. 427.

[44] Department of State, *The British Commonwealth, Eastern Europe, The Far East* in "Foreign Relations of the United States, 1943," vol. III (Washington, D.C., 1963), p. 849.

[45] Department of State, *Foreign Relations, 1944,* vol. I, p. 1128.

[46] CCAC 69/5, Directive for MG in Germany Prior to Defeat or Surrender, 29 Apr 44, in OPD, ABC 387, sec. 4–A.

[47] (1) Rpt, EUCOM, Dep JA for War Crimes, for Period Jun 44–Jul 48, 29 Jul 48. (2) USFET, General Board, Study No. 86, War Crimes and Punishment of War Criminals, 15 May 46, in Hist Div, Hqs, ETO, 97-USF 5–03.0, p. 7.

[48] General Board Study No. 86, p. 7.

[49] Chief of Counsel for War Crimes, *Final Report to the Secretary of the Army on the Nuernberg War Crimes Trials Under Control Council Law No. 10* (Washington D.C., 1949), p. 2.

Department's Judge Advocate General had identified forty-four crimes.[50] JCS 1023 accepted the following as a general definition: "The term 'war crimes' covers those violations of the laws and customs of war which constitute offenses against persons or property, committed in connection with military operations or occupation, which outrage common justice or involve moral turpitude."[51] Neither the two lists nor the definition extended the concept of culpability beyond the commission of specifically identifiable acts, and whether such acts could even be successfully tried was doubtful. Although the Judge Advocate General had found no bar to trying war criminals during hostilities, the United States was obviously not inclined to exercise that prerogative.[52] As a further obstacle, FM 27–10, *Rules of Land Warfare*, appeared to give most defendants an easy plea by providing that members of armed forces would not be punished for crimes "committed under orders or sanction of their government or commanders."[53]

Nevertheless, late summer 1944 was as crucial a period in the U.S. thinking on war crimes as it was in other matters concerning the occupation. In the outline of his plan for Germany which Morgenthau sent to Stimson on 6 September, he included a proposal for dealing with war criminals which specified that a list be made beforehand of the "arch criminals . . . whose obvious guilt is recognized" and that after being captured and identified they be executed by firing squads

without trial. Specific crimes "leading to or causing the death or persons" were to be tried by military commissions.[54] Morgenthau had talked to Hilldring about the proposal some days earlier, and Hilldring had wondered how people would get on the list, a question Morgenthau seems never to have answered to his own satisfaction. Stimson, in his memo to the President on 9 September, ranked the proposed war crimes policy almost equally with the economic provisions in his objections to the Morgenthau Plan. The accused, he insisted, would have to be charged, heard, and allowed to call witnesses in their defense; the punishment would have to be accomplished in "a dignified manner consistent with the advance of civilization" for the sake of "the greater effect on posterity." He proposed that an international tribunal be set up to try the "chief Nazis" and that the other war criminals be returned to the scenes of their crimes as the Moscow Declaration required.[55]

Although Stimson subsequently withdrew from the argument on the economic future of Germany, he became more passionately involved with the war crimes question as time passed, not only continuing to argue for orderly trials but making himself a leader in the development of the legal philosophy on the whole subject. His first reaction to the Morgenthau proposals seems to have been that all charges against major as well as lesser criminals would have to based on violations of existing laws of war. Much as he abhorred them, he said, he did not see how crimes committed in Germany or committed before the war began, such as the killing of Jews, could be considered crimes which the United

---

[50] Department of State, *Foreign Relations, 1944,* vol. I, p. 1272.
[51] Chief Counsel for War Crimes, *Final Report,* p. 2.
[52] Department of State, *Foreign Relations, 1944,* vol. I, p. 1269.
[53] Rpt, EUCOM, Dep JA for War Crimes, for Period June 44–Jul 48, 29 Jul 48.

[54] *Morgenthau Diary (Germany),* vol. I, p. 548.
[55] (1) *Ibid.,* pp. 486 and 612. (2) Stimson and Bundy, *On Active Service,* p. 584f.

States could punish "any more than Germany would have a right to intervene in our country to punish people who are lynching the Negroes."[56]

After the Quebec Conference, when he heard that the President and Prime Minister had leaned toward the idea of executions without trials, Stimson appointed a panel of War Department lawyers to study the question.[57] Although he remained opposed to mass summary executions, his thinking on what constituted punishable offenses changed. From the study, which continued to the end of the year under Stimson's active leadership, a plan emerged for a grand conspiracy trial not only of individuals but of organizations as well, such as the SS and *Gestapo*. The charge would be conspiracy to dominate the world "by means wholly contrary to international law."[58] The law would be less the rules of war than the prewar international agreements which had sought to outlaw war itself, particularly the Kellogg-Briand Pact. Stimson was encouraged when, after telling Roosevelt the story of a conspiracy case he had tried against the American Sugar Refining Company in 1906, the President "gave his very frank approval to my suggestion . . . that conspiracy with all of the actors brought in from the top to the bottom, or rather with all classes of actors brought in . . . would be the best way to try it. . . ."[59]

In the fall, spurred by Secretary Stimson's interest, the War Department began to acquire organizations for dealing with war crimes. At the end of September, on instructions from Stimson, the Judge Advocate General established a war crimes office which some weeks later, by agreement with the Navy and State Departments, became the National War Crimes Office.[60] The mission of the office was to collect evidence of "cruelties, atrocities, and acts of oppression" against members of the U.S. Armed Forces or other Americans and to apprehend, try, and execute sentences on persons against whom cases were developed.[61] Stimson kept the handling of policy in his own office, naming Assistant Secretary of War McCloy as his representative "in all matters involving war crimes" and charging G–1 with staff supervision of plans and policies.[62] In November, FM 27–10 was revised to eliminate the plea of superior orders.[63]

By year's end some of the new thinking in Washington was beginning to reach Europe. The JCS had submitted 1023 to the Combined Chiefs of Staff in October but, when the scope of the U.S. approach expanded shortly thereafter, did not press for its conversion into a combined directive. Consequently, Eisenhower, as Supreme Commander, could only continue under the limited guidance he had received earlier. The War Department, however, could issue instructions to him independently as

---

[56] (1) Memo for Record, H.L.S., 9 Sep 44, in ASW 370.8. (2) *Morgenthau Diary* (Germany), vol. I. p. 612.

[57] Stimson and Bundy, *On Active Service*, p. 585. See also Department of State, *Cairo and Tehran*, in "Foreign Relations," p. 400.

[58] Memo, Brig Gen Adam Richmond for SHAEF G–1, sub: War Crimes, 23 Dec 44, in SHAEF G–1, 000.5–.8.

[59] Stimson and Bundy, *On Active Service*, p. 586.

[60] (1) Chief Counsel for War Crimes, *Final Report*, p. 2. (2) Department of State, *Foreign Relations, 1944*, vol. I, p. 1392.

[61] Department of State, *Foreign Relations, 1944*, vol. I, p. 1392.

[62] Chief Counsel for War Crimes, *Final Report*, p. 2n.

[63] The elimination was not complete, however. Paragraph 345.1 provided that acts under orders "may be taken into consideration in determining culpability, either by way of defense or mitigation of punishment."

Commanding General, ETOUSA, and on 25 December the Judge Advocate General directed the theater judge advocate general to set up a war crimes office similar to the one recently created in Washington. To Eisenhower, G–1 explained, "Mr. Stimson regards the investigation of war crimes as a subject of top importance."[64] The theater war crimes branch was to be charged with investigating war crimes alleged against Americans and, for transmission to the appropriate governments, also crimes against nationals of other United Nations; but no war criminals were to be tried.[65]

PsyWar

The Psychological Warfare Division, SHAEF, which liked to call itself PsyWar but went more conservatively and correctly by the initials "PWD," originated as one of two new general staff divisions, G–5 and G–6, in February 1944. In the April 1944 SHAEF reorganization, G–6 was abolished and its functions were divided between two special staff divisions, Public Relations and Psychological Warfare. Brig. Gen. Robert A. McClure, who had been Assistant Chief of Staff, G–6, during its brief existence and before that Eisenhower's chief of information and censorship in the Mediterranean, became the director of PWD. As such he was blessed—not entirely happily—with four deputies, each of whom represented a powerful U.S. or British civilian agency, namely, the Office of War Information and Office of Strategic Services (U.S.) and the Political Intelligence Department and Ministry of Information (British). The U.S.

operating personnel had been selected on the basis of language knowledge and occupational background and were mostly graduates of the Psychological Warfare School at Camp Ritchie, Maryland.

Psychological warfare during OVERLORD had two broad purposes: to undermine the enemy soldier's will to fight and to influence civilian opinion in ways useful to SHAEF. The first objective, which often had to be attuned to the immediate combat situation, was delegated to the army groups by PWD. The second objective, over which PWD retained direct control, took several forms: propaganda to friendly peoples still under German occupation, so-called consolidation propaganda in liberated countries, and propaganda to the German people. This last form was going to make PWD an important agency in the occupation because SHAEF planning assumed from the beginning—though it is not clear why—that the mission to conduct propaganda to the Germans during the war naturally also embraced control of information in Germany under the occupation.[66] Military government, charged with executing all other aspects of occupation policy, was thereby excluded from the propaganda mission. As a result, military government tended always to look on the occupation as primarily an exercise in governmental administration, while PWD and its successors regarded it as an operation on the German mind. Both were valid approaches, but undoubtedly they would have been more effective combined rather than competing with each other.

Public information policy developed

---

[64] Memo, Brig Gen Adam Richmond for SHAEF G–1, sub: War Crimes, 23 Dec 44, in SHAEF G–1, 000.5–.8.

[65] Ltr, War Dept, AG, to CG, ETOUSA, sub: Establishment of War Crimes Offices, 25 Dec 44, in SHAEF G–1, 000.5–.7.

[66] (1) SHAEF, PWD, An Account of Its Operation in the Western European Campaign, 1944–45, Sep 45, in OMGUS 242–2/5. (2) OMGUS, ICD, History, 8 May 45–30 Jun 46, in OMGUS 242–1/5, pp. 1–3.

slowly. It did not figure in the military government plans, and PWD was engrossed throughout 1944 with its operational responsibilities. CCS 551, while setting freedom of speech and press as essential, authorized only a negative program of censorship and control in the interest of military security and to prevent Nazi propaganda. JCS 1067 ordered the German information services, including moving pictures, to shut down completely, presumably pending an overhaul and subsequent establishment of free speech and press. But the order said nothing about how these freedoms would be accomplished, and it was not a combined directive.

As the armies drove into Germany in the fall of 1944, PWD's chief concern was with the Germans on the other side of the front, to sell them unconditional surrender if possible and, in any case, to condition them for the military government to come. Restrictions imposed from Washington reduced appeals for both purposes to a portrayal of military government as stern and all-powerful but just—a combination that made unconditional surrender about as attractive as Judgment Day.

The lack of something to say became painfully evident after PWD acquired a first-class vehicle for reaching the Germans, the 150-kilowatt Radio Luxembourg transmitter, one of the most powerful in Europe. The Germans demolished the main control room in Luxembourg City on 1 September while U.S. troops were still sixty miles away; but at the transmitter outside the city a civilian technician, who knew where spare tubes had been hidden away, convinced the German chief engineer that smashing the tubes in the transmitter would do a permanent enough job. On the 10th, the 5th Armored Division captured the transmitter. Four days later the spare tubes

were recovered, and on the 23d Radio Luxembourg went back on the air.[67] Getting two national and several civilian agencies and military staffs to agree on what to broadcast was a great deal more difficult, as was also the attempt to explain a policy to the Germans that was not clear to SHAEF itself. After two months, one of McClure's British deputies thought things were almost hopeless enough to warrant giving up and reverting to "purely tactical leaflet and radio work."[68]

After military government moved into the Aachen area, PWD's mission with regard to the Germans took on a new and unforeseen aspect. No need to control or sanitize the press existed because there was no press; and without electric power much of the time, the Germans could not listen to their radios. The implications for the future were clear: occupied Germany was not going to be a hotbed of resurgent Nazi propaganda; it was going to be an information desert. Experience soon showed that the one could be as potentially dangerous as the other. If the occupation had no voice, the people would live on rumors. The pressures of the time were too great for them to exist in an information vacuum.

In November, PWD began publishing a weekly paper, *Die Neue Zeitung* (*The New Newspaper*), at its headquarters in Luxembourg. The press run of 23,000 copies was enough to supply about one copy for every five persons in the occupied area. PWD apparently proposed to relieve the information drought and simultaneously give the Germans their first lesson in democratic journalism, hence the title

---

[67] SHAEF, PWD, An Account of Its Operation in the Western European Campaign, 1944–45, Sep 45, in OMGUS, 242–2/5.

[68] Memo, Mr Crossman for Gen McClure, 10 Dec 44, in SHAEF, PWD 014.1.

and the pictures, maps, and feature articles in the first issue. *Die Neue Zeitung* would have its day but not for almost a year. The second issue came out in austere format as *Die Mitteilungen* (*Communications*). SHAEF had declared it would not let its resources be used to provide anything for the Germans other than official military government communications.[69]

In January, SHAEF public information policy for the occupation began to take form. SHAEF added Military Government Law No. 191 to the proclamation and ordinances which military government posted in every occupied community. The law ordered a shutdown of all media of public expression: press, radio, moving pictures, theater, and musical performances. Television and sound recordings, overlooked at first, were later added to the list. The Germans would have to get along on Radio Luxembourg, *Die Mitteilung*, and the so-called *Mitteilungsblaetter* (information sheets) that SHAEF authorized the army groups to publish as needed. All three would carry only official announcements and summaries of international news. General McClure said, "It is PWD policy *not* to entertain the Germans."[70] To avoid making the Army a permanent press service for Germany—and, contrary to some opinion in PWD, only incidentally to begin the democratic reorientation of the German information media—PWD would, when conditions permitted, license carefully selected individual Germans as publishers. Neither corporations nor associations would be licensed because they were difficult to call

to account. Eventually Germans would operate the newspapers and other media and be controlled through the licensing power.[71]

A Place for the Control Council Group

The U.S. Group Control Council was guided by three sources: the EAC "Agreement on Control Machinery in Germany," JCS 1067, and SHAEF. Under the EAC agreement, the U.S. Group Control Council was actually the nucleus of what was to be called the Control Staff, since the Control Council would consist of the three commanders in chief and the Co-ordinating Committee of their deputies, who had not yet been appointed. In November, the group reorganized into twelve divisions provided for in the EAC agreement: military; naval; air; transport; political; economic; finance; reparations, deliveries, and restitution; internal affairs and communications; legal; prisoners of war and displaced persons; and manpower.[72] To these divisions were added an intelligence section in the headquarters staff, a public relations service, and an information control service, the latter two to be headed by Brig. Gen. Frank A. Allen, SHAEF's public relations chief, and General McClure when they had finished their duties with SHAEF. The majority of the divisions, in fact, had temporary or acting directors, pending civilian appointments in some cases and release of designees from SHAEF in others. The projected nucleus group strength was 1,200 officers; the actual strength in November was 175 officers and 15 civilians.[73]

[69] Hqs, 12th AGp G–5, ACofS G–5, Public Relations, sub: Draft Report on German Language Army–Sponsored Newspapers, Jun 45, in SHAEF G–5, 17,16, Jacket 14.
[70] Harold J. Hurwitz, Press Reorientation, vol. I, p. 28, in Hist Div, EUCOM, U.S. Military Government in Germany, CMH file 8–3.1 DE.

[71] OMGUS, ICD, History, 8 May 45–30 Jun 46, in OMGUS 242–1/5, pp. 2–4.
[72] Senate Committee on Foreign Relations, *Documents on Germany, 1944–1959*, 8 May 59, p. 7.
[73] OMGUS, ICD, History, 8 May 45–30 Jun 46, in OMGUS 242–1/5, pp. 9–11.

JCS 1067, as the U.S. Group Control Council's Bible, was a formidable test in exegesis. On the other hand, the group was under orders to make its plans in accordance with EAC recommendations to the three governments, and in the absence of these to be guided by U.S. views pending before the commission; but the EAC had not made any recommendations to the governments beyond the surrender instrument and those on the zones and control machinery. The War Department regarded JCS 1067 as a U.S. view to be put before the EAC, but it was being revised in Washington and had not yet been submitted. Already, however, the original JCS 1067 seemed to conflict with the agreement on control machinery in one instance. The agreement required the twelve divisions of the Control Staff, as one of their chief functions, "to control the corresponding German Ministry or Central Institution"; and Strang, Winant, and Gousev had assumed in their report that there would be at the outset some sort of German central administration through which the Control Staff would operate.[74] JCS 1067 required the immediate dismissal of all members of the Nazi party and all "ardent supporters." It was difficult to conceive how anyone working in a German ministry could fail to qualify as at least an ardent supporter.[75]

The agreement on control machinery had given the Control Council a role in the postwar administration of Germany, but pending the surrender and actual establishment of tripartite control, definition of the role was left to SHAEF, which was where the War Department wanted it to be. Defining a mission for the Control Council groups raised several problems. The Control Council would be a tripartite body, hence any planning should have been on a tripartite basis from the start. The Russians had said they were selecting their personnel and would send them to London; they had thereafter subsided into silence.[76] The U.S. and British groups were in London but not co-ordinating their work except through SHAEF, which could hold a tight rein on the Americans but not on the British. What the Control Council groups had to plan for was also in question. That SHAEF would be dissolved soon after the surrender had become accepted thinking. However, SHAEF would be responsible for inaugurating the occupation, which SHAEF interpreted to include "responsibility for control of the German forces, military government, and disbandment and disarmament in its widest sense." Furthermore, SHAEF had instructed the army groups to make no agreements on policy with the Control Council groups without its concurrence and to hold no meetings with them without SHAEF representatives present.[77] Exactly what the Control Council groups would plan for the period after SHAEF was dissolved was also in doubt.

In the first week of December, in a staff memorandum which superseded the so-called Treaty of Portsmouth and became known as the Treaty of Versailles, SHAEF set some doubts to rest, at least to its own satisfaction. During the presurrender period, the Control Council groups would be separate—the British under their own government, the Americans under Eisenhower

---

[74] Department of State, *Foreign Relations, 1944,* vol. I, p. 405.

[75] OMGUS, ICD, History, 8 May 45–30 Jun 46, in OMGUS 242–1/5, p. 17.

[76] Department of State, *Foreign Relations, 1944,* vol. I, p. 379.

[77] Ltr, SHAEF, AG, to CG's, AGps, sub: Relationship between Army Groups and Control Commission (Council), 15 Nov 44, in OPD 336 (sec. III) (Cases 51–   ).

as Commanding General, ETOUSA—but they would work "in closest liaison with each other" to assure that their plans and SHAEF's were in agreement. Until the governments decided to disband SHAEF, it would be responsible for the occupation in Germany and would execute policies transmitted to it through the Combined Chiefs of Staff. The Control Council groups would advise on control machinery and on "measures to be taken to implement established policies." Any of their personnel in Germany during the SHAEF period would be under SHAEF command.[78] Later, SHAEF also gave the U.S. Group Control Council two planning missions: to plan for the control of the German ministries and central agencies and to plan for the U.S. participation in the Control Council and its subordinate bodies. Plans for the U.S. zone, however, were to be worked out in the U.S. element of G–5, SHAEF.[79]

The over-all bleakness of the immediate future of the Control Council groups was relieved somewhat by Plan GOLDCUP. In late September, SHAEF had rather vaguely agreed to let a small ministerial control team enter Berlin after the city was occupied to do some preliminary reconnaissance for the Control Council.[80] Later in the fall, when it still seemed that the British and Americans would enter Berlin first, the idea was expanded and given the code name GOLDCUP. Under GOLDCUP, the U.S. and British Control Council groups would furnish officers and enlisted men to form an Advanced Ministerial Control Group. Under SHAEF's command, the Advanced Ministerial Control Group would supply a mobile control party for each of the German ministries and central agencies. The control parties would be ready to move in and take charge of German ministerial personnel and records as soon as they were uncovered, presumably in Berlin but anywhere in Germany in case the government dispersed.[81] By the time the control parties were organized in January 1945, when or whether they would enter Berlin had become doubtful.

---

[78] Staff Memo No. 130, SHAEF, AF, sub: Relationship Between SHAEF and the U.S. and British Elements of the Control Commission/Council for Germany, 5 Dec 44, in OPD 336 (sec. III) (Cases 51–   ).
[79] (1) Hqs, US Gp CC, Planning Directive No. 34, 18 Dec 44, in OMGUS 12–1/5, v60–11/1. (2) Ltr, Wickersham to Smith, 1 Jan 45, and Ltr, Wickersham to Hilldring, 12 Jan 45, in SHAEF SGS 014.1.

[80] SHAEF G–5, Opns/Fwd/803, sub: Agreements Reached on Military Government of Berlin, 28 Sep 44, in SHAEF G–5, 31.
[81] (1) Hqs, US Gp CC, Planning Directive No. 29, sub: Advanced Ministerial Control Group, 12 Dec 44, in USFET SGS, 381. (2) Hist Rpt, US Gp CC, 1–31 Dec 44, in SHAEF G–5, 17.05.

CHAPTER XII

The Rhineland Campaign, 1945

The Hard Winter

On New Year's Day 1945, eight German divisions attacked south out of the Saar attempting to trap Eisenhower's thinned-out flank in Alsace. In the Ardennes, the Battle of the Bulge was at its height. During the next few days the fighting around Bastogne was as bitter as any since D-day. On the other hand, as for getting to his strategic objective, Antwerp, or anywhere near it, Hitler no longer had a chance. His chief of the Army General Staff, Generaloberst Heinz Guderian, had told him as much at Christmas and had also told him that the Russians along the Vistula were ready to unloose their most powerful offensive of the war. Calling the report on the Russians a colossal bluff, however, Hitler refused for a week to concede that the breakthrough to Antwerp could not be made. He then waited five more days before taking his spearhead force, Sixth Panzer Army, out of the front in the Ardennes, and took another week making up his mind to dismantle the rest of the buildup in the Bulge.

When Hitler returned to Berlin from his Western Front headquarters on 15 January, the Vistula line in Poland was collapsing. Two weeks later the Russians were on the Oder River at Kuestrin, thirty-five miles from Berlin. On the 26th, Marshal Georgi K. Zhukov reportedly told Stalin he could be ready to attack toward Berlin in four days.[1] In the west, the U.S. armies were barely back to the line in the Ardennes that they had held in December, and in Alsace the Germans were still fighting hard. Who would arrive in Berlin first seemed not to be a question anymore. At the speed they had moved in January, the Russians could have been first on the Rhine.

In and around Aachen the occupation was nearly four months old. Most of the civilians in the city were living in cellars, air raid shelters, or bunkers without heat, electricity, gas, or running water. The main thoroughfares had been cleared for military traffic; elsewhere the snow cover had softened but could not entirely conceal what was "a fantastic, stinking heap of ruins."[2] Cabbage soup and potatoes were the standard diet. On the ration, each adult was entitled to half a pound of meat and bones, a quarter pound of butter, and one loaf of bread a week, when available. In Stolberg, the second largest occupied community, three-quarters of the population was eating at soup kitchens and getting 900 to 1,000 calories a day. The few trucks owned by the cities were being used to collect food in the countryside. To pay for city services, such as they were, and make pension and relief payments, Aachen was selling off the abandoned property of evacuees.[3]

[1] S. Shtemenko, *"Kak planirovalas poslednaya kampaniya po razgromu gitlerovskoy Germanii,"* *Voyenno-istoricheskiy Zhurnal* (May 1965).

[2] Office, Allied Naval CinC, to SHAEF G–5, sub: German Civilians and Military Government Control, 1 Apr 45, in SHAEF G–5, 803, Jacket 3.

[3] Hist Rpt, 12th AGp, G–5, Feb 45, 28 Feb 45, in SHAEF G–5, 17.16, Jacket 6.

The economy was prostrate. In Stolberg no stores were open. The municipal labor office in Aachen had registered all able-bodied inhabitants for work at clearing rubble and repairing roads. The work was unpaid, and for one job on which 200 workers were called, seventeen appeared, a typical turnout. For all jobs the only workers to be found were boys under sixteen or old men. Military government was under orders not to concern itself with reviving the German economy, but it had an interest in coal, which in winter ranked next to food as a necessity of life. The Aachen mines had formerly employed 20,000 men. In February 1945 there were 1,000 working in the mines; and they had a 33-percent rate of absenteeism, because the ration was not enough to sustain a man at heavy work in the mines, and miners could not buy anything with their pay. The workers easiest to secure and most reliable were those employed by the Army. Army employees received a noon meal—something which was going to prove a major attraction for many Germans in the coming months and years. The meal was prepared and served on the job partly for the sake of economy but also because if the worker was allowed to take the food home, it usually went to his family.

The civilians' feeling of relief at being out of the war was beginning to give way under the hardships of the winter to a subdued resentment.[4] But the resentment was not at a level approaching resistance to the occupation. Of 487 cases tried in Ninth Army military government courts up to the end of January, three-quarters were for minor circulation and curfew violations. In the two most serious cases, one defendant got twenty years for spreading rumors prejudicial to Allied interests and the other got fifteen years and a 10,000 *Reichsmark* fine for disobedience to military government orders. The other cases were sometimes interesting but hardly evidence of a threat to military security. Even harboring German soldiers, a serious crime, usually turned out not to have been motivated by malice. In one instance a mother wanted to keep her son at home; in another a homeowner needed someone to fix his house and the soldier was handy with tools; and in a third a soldier turned himself in after a lovers' quarrel with the woman with whom he was living. He went to a prisoner of war camp, she to jail for fifteen months. In Schaffenberg, outside Aachen, a man was sentenced for holding a public meeting. He had hired a carpenter to repair his house and a crowd had gathered to watch the carpenter work. In Brand a summary military government court fined a civilian 100 marks for calling the *Buergermeister* a thief and a Nazi. The review board reversed the sentence on the ground that civilians should be encouraged to comment on public officials.

Nonfraternization cases against civilians continued to trouble the courts. In Stolberg, a summary court found three women guilty of acting in a manner prejudicial to the good order of members of the Allied forces. The military policeman who made the arrest stated he had entered an apartment and found the three listening to a phonograph with two U.S. soldiers. The review board took the position that the soldiers might have been guilty of fraternization, but in the absence of immoral conduct, the women could not be charged. In Aachen, a summary court found two girls guilty of inviting two American soldiers into a house marked "off limits." A

---

[4] Office, Allied Naval CinC, to SHAEF G–5, sub: German Civilians and Military Government Control, 1 Apr 45, in SHAEF G–5, 803, Jacket 3.

TRIAL IN A MILITARY GOVERNMENT COURT. *The two German women were convicted of illegal border crossing.*

review board set aside the convictions because the off-limits signs had been posted solely to prevent fraternization and therefore constituted an attempt to shift responsibility for nonfraternization from the military to civilians.[5]

---

[5] (1) Hqs, Ninth Army, ACofS G–5, sub: Biweekly CASUM, 27 Jan 45, in SHAEF G–5, 17.11, Jacket 2. (2) Hist Rpt, Hqs, First Army, ACofS G–5, 1–28 Feb 45, in SHAEF G–5, 17.11, Jacket 7. (3) Hist Rpt, Hqs, Ninth Army, 1–28 Feb 45, in SHAEF G–5, 17.11, Jacket 3. (4) Hist Rpt, Hqs, First Army, ACofS G–5, 1–31 Mar 45, in SHAEF G–5, 17.11, Jacket 9.

In January, Aachen became the first city in the occupation to have a licensed newspaper, the *Aachener Nachrichten*. Partly for the experience and partly in the belief that it was time to get on with re-educating the Germans, the Psychological Warfare Division sent a press control team into Aachen to set up a plant and find a licensee. The plant did not prove to be much of a problem. The building and press of the former Aachen newspaper had survived the battle fairly well, and some newsprint was on hand. Finding a publisher was more difficult. The press control officers interviewed every newspaperman in Aachen but could not come up with one who, besides being professionally qualified, had an unclouded political past. Determined not to compromise politically for the sake of competence, they finally settled on a 70-year-old ex-composing room foreman, Heinrich Hollands, who had been unemployed since 1933 because he was a Social Democrat. Hollands had no experience at writing or editing and neither did the other Germans on the staff; so for the first months the paper was mostly a product of the U.S. and British officers on the press control team. SHAEF eased its restrictions on what could be printed to permit local news but not features or editorials, which nearly confined the paper to the stereotype format of *Die Mitteilungen*. Hollands had other troubles as well. The electricity went on and off, and when it went off the metal in the typesetting machines hardened and had to be reheated; furthermore, the curfew interfered with distribution and newsgathering. The local news helped military government to stifle rumors but sometimes inadvertently increased discontent. The people of Stolberg, for instance, began to complain when they found out that the curfew in Aachen was an hour later than theirs and when they read that the Aachen residents were getting extra sugar and marmalade rations.[6]

Oberbuergermeister Oppenhoff entered his third month under the occupation in Aachen in January. So far he had survived the threatened Nazi vengeance and had become almost a hero by volunteering to stay in the city through the worst of the Ardennes offensive, an act that may have been more dangerous than he imagined since Hitler at one time was close to switching the objective from Antwerp to Aachen. But Oppenhoff had also become a political liability. His appointment ranged back to the days when a recommendation from the Catholic clergy was the best a man could have, and he had the backing of the Bishop of Aachen. But a closer look revealed that the Church had been not so much anti-Nazi as neutral and, having so survived Hitler, was inclined to remain the same during the occupation.[7] Oppenhoff and his fourteen department heads, all his choices, proved to have a similar bent. Except for one nominal party member, they had not been Nazis, and like Oppenhoff, the *Gestapo* had from time to time had an eye on them; but they had apparently not sacrificed or risked very much during the Nazi regime. In fact, all of them had prospered. Several, including Oppenhoff, prided themselves on having rejected the war and avoided military service. Their method, however, had not been one to inspire in American minds much confidence in their motives. They had helped each other—as they sometimes seemed to be doing again in the city government—into draft-exempt managerial jobs in the Nazi-owned Veltrup armament works in Aachen.[8]

Politically the men in the Aachen city administration baffled and chagrined the

[6] (1) SHAEF, PWD, Weekly Intelligence Summary No. 21, 17 Feb 45, in SHAEF G–5, 7.35. (2) Hqs, 12th AGp, ACofS G–5, Public Relations, sub: Draft Report on German Language Army-Sponsored Newspapers, Jun 45, in SHAEF G–5, 17.16, Jacket 14. (3) OMGUS, ICD, History, 8 May 45–30 Jun 46, in OMGUS 242–1/5, p. 18f.

[7] Hqs, Ninth Army, ACofS G–5, sub: Bi-weekly CASUM, 27 Jan 45, in SHAEF G–5, 17.14, Jacket 2.

[8] Hqs, 6th AGp, sub: German PW opinion of Allied MG, 28 Feb 45, in SHAEF G–5, 17.18, Jacket 4.

Americans who had come into Germany expecting to decide a clear-cut issue— democracy versus Nazi totalitarianism. These Americans felt that every German who was anti-Nazi must be either a democrat, a willing convert to democracy, or at worst a Communist—the last, in the spirit of the wartime alliance, being equated with a democrat. Oppenhoff, by his own definition, was anti-Nazi, but he was also quite frankly antidemocratic, and he admitted to having chosen a staff and appointed city workers whose views agreed with his own.[9] He was an authoritarian, apparently of the Bismarckian school. Some of his colleagues were proponents of the *Staendestaat,* a semifacist class state of the kind the Austrian chancellor Engelbert Dollfuss had organized in Austria in the early 1930s. Oppenhoff disliked fanatical Nazis but saw nothing wrong with employing those who had changed their minds or who had joined the party for business or professional reasons.[10]

Although disenchantment with Oppenhoff's administration set in early, the sometimes peculiar circumstances of the time gave him a surprisingly solid hold on his office. Competent non-Nazis were among the rarest commodities everywhere in Germany, not only in Aachen; in the managerial and professional groups they were practically nonexistent. In Strassburg, 6th Army Group captured the personnel files of the *Deutsche Aerztebund* (medical association) of *Land* Baden. Of its membership, which comprised all of the doctors and dentists and many of the public health officials in Baden, less than a quarter had

no or only slight party connections.[11] The medical profession had one of the highest percentages of Nazis, but law, teaching, and public adminstration were not far behind. Bona fide political opponents of the regime, if they had survived at all, were generally old men, like Hollands. Oppenhoff and his colleagues were competent, perhaps irreplaceable, and consequently appeared indispensable, to the Americans more than to the Germans. To their fellow Aacheners they represented a new elite, not of money (Oppenhoff's salary was 450 marks a month) or real power (the Americans held the power) but of survival. They had eluded the Nazis painlessly and somewhat profitably and they seemed to be handling the consequences of defeat in the same way. They were not living elegantly but they fared a great deal better than the average cellar or bunker dweller. To the occupation forces, they represented stability. The tactical commands in Aachen changed from week to week and, in crises such as the Bulge, sometimes from day to day. Within six weeks in December and January, the over-all command shifted from First Army to Ninth Army and then back again; the military government detachment had three commanders before the end of December. By the time Oppenhoff had been in office three months, he knew more about running Aachen under the occupation than any of the Americans.

Oppenhoff himself was no problem. He and all the Germans who worked under him served entirely at the pleasure of military government and, whatever their politics, executed only American policies. He was, however, a reminder that despite all planning, the purpose of the occupation

---

[9] Hist Rpt, First Army, ACofS G–5, 1–28 Feb 45, in SHAEF G–5, 17.11, Jacket 7.

[10] Saul K. Padover, *Experiment in Germany* (New York: Duell, Sloan and Pearce, 1946), p. 244.

[11] Hqs, 6th AGp, ACofS G–5, sub: The German Medical Profession in Baden, 20 Jan 45, in SHAEF G–5, 17.18, Jacket 5.

was still obscure and the method of achieving it in doubt. To destroy the Nazi regime was an often stated United Nations war aim dating back to the Atlantic Charter; but did this policy mean the elimination of every party member, even at the price of inconvenience to the occupation forces? Military government had assumed that as long as hostilities continued, its first responsibility was to the combat commands, which would benefit most from an orderly and efficient civil administration. Was denazification to be pushed to the point where it might impair military government's effectiveness and so affect the interests of the troops? Men like Oppenhoff and his colleagues raised a still more difficult question: Was it the business of the occupation to bring democracy to Germany? The Americans considered themselves individually and collectively as natural apostles of democracy. The occupation plans were devised to demonstrate, in the court system for instance, the differences between totalitarian and democratic methods. Neither the policy nor the plans, however, provided for an active democratization program. On the other hand, democratization was so compellingly logical an objective, so much what the war ultimately was all about, that it was bound to become the standard against which the occupation was measured.

The Psychological Warfare Division, SHAEF, did not have the same priorities and responsibilities as military government. Its job was to create an image of the occupation in the German mind, and to do so PWD wanted to get on with the business of democratization. For this purpose, the Oppenhoff administration was not ideal raw material. In January, three captains from Psychological Warfare, Saul K. Padover, Paul Sweet, and Lewis F. Gittler,

investigated the Aachen city government and were dismayed. Their report charged military government with having allowed a new elite to emerge—one "made up of technicians, lawyers, engineers, businessmen, manufacturers, and churchmen," and one which was perhaps not Nazi but certainly did not fit the American picture of democracy.[12] The report, according to Padover, reverberated throughout the European Theater of Operations.[13] The three captains from PWD had signaled the arrival of a powerful ally for radical denazification, the traditional American demoncratic idealism.

On a staff tour in January, however, Brig. Gen. Eric F. Wood, director of the Prisoner of War and Displaced Persons Division, U.S. Group Control Council, found the trend in 12th Army Group G–5 to be away from a rigid interpretation of the denazification provisions of JCS 1067. The G–5 believed that some Nazis would have to be used because otherwise the field commanders could not be given what they wanted most from military government, an efficient civil administration. Experience so far, the G–5 officers pointed out somewhat ruefully, had shown that most local Nazi officials had acquired their positions through experience and ability, not by virtue of party membership alone.[14] The trend noted by General Wood was shortlived. The Aachen experience had demonstrated how difficult it was to defend the appointment of even some non-Nazis. The newspaper correspondents were still concentrating on the fighting war, but at least

---

[12] Padover, *Experiment in Germany,* p. 222.
[13] *Ibid.,* p. 262.
[14] Memo, US Gp CC, PW and DP Div, for Distribution, sub: Trends in Allied MG and Admin, 28 Jan–5 Feb 45, 8 Feb 45, in OMGUS, PW and DP Div War Diary, OMGUS, 314.81, CMH files.

one, Max Lerner, writing for the New York paper PM, had already echoed the criticism expressed in the PWD's report on Aachen.[15] In early March, 12th Army Group ordered all Nazis removed from public offices and other positions of trust and influence. A few weeks later, 6th Army Group followed suit.[16]

In Aachen, First Army began weeding out the city's administration after it resumed control in February. Oppenhoff was regarded as being of dubious value but was not dismissed.[17] On Sunday night, 25 March, while Oppenhoff was visiting his neighbor, Herr Faust, whom the Americans had recently removed as *Buergermeister* for Industry, three men dressed in German paratrooper coveralls entered Oppenhoff's house. They awakened the maid and ordered her to fetch him home. When he returned with Faust, they told him they had jumped from a plane, were on their way back to the German lines, and needed food and shelter. According to Faust, Oppenhoff objected that aiding them would jeopardize his position with the Americans and urged them to surrender. When an argument developed, Faust slipped away— to get help, he said. The next morning Oppenhoff's body was found crumpled up in the hallway. He had been shot through the head. During the same night, a tank destroyer unit billeted near Oppenhoff's home discovered that its telephone had gone dead. Two men sent out to look

for a break found the line had been cut. The officer in charge then sent out a third man to stand guard while repairs were made. While the first two were working, the guard saw three men walking toward him from Oppenhoff's house. When he ordered them to halt they turned, ran into some bushes at the side of the road, and disappeared. A search the next morning turned up a German belt and a musette bag hanging from a fence nearby, apparently abandoned after it became entangled in the wire.[18]

Oppenhoff died as many Germans did that spring, unmourned and without many questions asked. The Americans found it hard to see Oppenhoff as an anti-Nazi martyr, and one favorite theory was that his disgruntled and recently discharged colleagues, of whom Faust was one, had committed the murder.[19] Six months later, after the war was over and Oppenhoff nearly forgotten, intelligence investigators uncovered the true story. The order for the murder had come from Himmler and been carried out by border police to set an example for the *Werwolf,* the allegedly spontaneous, Nazi-sponsored, German guerrilla and underground resistance organization.[20] The staged killing, ordered in January and planned by an SS general as if it were a major operation, was probably the *Werwolf's* most sensational achievement.

On the Move

For the detachments sidetracked in the army military government centers, the winter seemed worse than the previous one in

[15] SHAEF, ACofS G–5, G–5 Weekly Journal of Information No. 6, 28 Mar 45, in SHAEF G–5, 17.16, Jacket 8.

[16] (1) Hqs, 12th AGp, G–5 Operational Instructions No. 5, 11 Mar 45, in SHAEF G–5, 17.16, Jacket 6. (2) Memo, Hqs, 6th AGp, for CG's, 7th and 1st French Armies, sub: Disqualification from Office of Nazis and German Militarists, 30 Mar 45, in SHAEF G–5, 17.18, Jacket 5.

[17] Hist Rpt, First Army, ACofS G–5, 1–28 Feb 45, in SHAEF G–5, 17.11, Jacket 7.

[18] Hist Rpt, Hqs, First Army, ACofS G–5, 1–31 Mar 45, in SHAEF G–5, 17.11, Jacket 9.

[19] Padover, *Experiment in Germany,* p. 247.

[20] CSDIC/WEA BAUR, Weekly Intelligence Summary No. 4, 2 Oct 45, in OMGUS 3/35, decimal 350.09.

Shrivenham. The front had not advanced any farther into Germany after November. Meanwhile, the pinpoint assignments had changed so often to keep pace with shifts in plans that it was hard to believe anyone was going anywhere. The latest strategy gave the priority to Montgomery's army group which included only the U.S. Ninth Army. Third and Seventh Armies apparently might be parked on the German border indefinitely, and First Army's prospects were not much brighter. In the third week of February, Ninth Army, the one with the most substantial mission, was standing on the bank of the Roer River waiting for the water to go down. The Germans had opened the dams upstream and flooded the valley down to the Meuse. First Army had taken the dams, but the Germans had done their work well and blown the gates in time to get maximum effect from the millions of tons of water pouring into the valley.

Nevertheless, the dams were no longer a threat. The flood crested, and when it began to recede, the war changed. In the early morning darkness, behind a 2000-gun barrage, Ninth Army crossed the Roer on 23 February. Nine days later the army had a spearhead on the Rhine opposite Duesseldorf. First Army joined in on the south and at the end of the first week in March got what Ninth Army had wanted and not found, a bridge on the Rhine, at Remagen. Against crumbling German resistance, Third and Seventh Armies then cleared the southern Rhineland during the first three weeks of March.

Ninth Army found scarcely a soul in the first ten miles east of the Roer but had uncovered half a million civilians by the time it reached the Rhine. Except for the evacuated zone along the Roer and the cities where the bombing had caused many inhabitants to seek safer places, more Germans were staying home this time, with Nazi party blessings. The Nazi leadership did not even try to conceal its nightmare: a refugee wave raised by the Russians in the east meeting a similar wave from the west somewhere between the Rhine and the Oder. If such a meeting took place, nothing would move in Germany, military or civilian. The *Gauleiters* had encouraged the civilians, women and children especially, to stay, excepting only those whose skills could give advantage to the enemy.[21]

Ninth Army, advancing from Aachen northeastward toward the Rhine, had the first look at the Germany of 1945, and it was a dismal sight. Detachment I3G2 entered Juelich on the third day. Lying on the right bank of the Roer, the city had been bombed from the air and blasted by artillery. The people were gone. The physical destruction was put at 100 percent, probably a wartime record for cities in Germany. What the bombs had spared, the shells had churned into complete uselessness. With nothing to govern, the detachment turned to directing traffic. The other communities less than ten miles beyond the Roer were in a similar, if not quite as bad, condition.

Muenchen-Gladbach, about halfway between the Roer and the Rhine, was a different case. It was a study in contrasts—some districts badly damaged, others almost intact except for the windows—the work of the air bombardment. Craters in the streets showed where recent bombs had hit. Gravel patches revealed where older craters had been. Buildings were sliced in two, and frequently where a wall had col-

---

[21] (1) SHAEF G–5, CA–MG Weekly Field Report No. 42, 31 Mar 45, in SHAEF G–5, 17.16, Jacket 9. (2) SHAEF, ACofS G–5, G–5 Weekly Journal of Information No. 6, 28 Mar 45, in SHAEF G–5, 17.16, Jacket 8.

lapsed, the furniture could be seen in place in rooms on upper floors.[22] The walls left standing were covered with slogans: *Dein Gruss—Heil Hitler!* (Your Greeting—Heil Hitler!); *Tapfer und Treu!* (Brave and Loyal); *Die Front fuer die Heimat! Die Heimat fuer die Front!* (The front for the Homeland! The Homeland for the front!); *Erst jetzt Recht!* (Now more than ever!). Here and there, grim-faced older civilians could be seen painting out the slogans with whitewash.

In Krefeld on the Rhine, 100,000 of the 169,000 population had stayed behind in the huge concrete air raid shelters to await the invaders. As soon as the front passed, more inhabitants began drifting in from the countryside. The local newspaper, the *Rheinische Landeszeitung,* had published its last issue on 1 March, the day before the Americans came. Its headline had read, "Enemy Attempts at Breakthrough in the West Repulsed." The *Landeszeitung* building was among the few still standing in the center of the city, and its roof was gone. The local Labor Front chief had had an apartment inside. He had obviously left in a hurry. The breakfast table was set, and his personal stationery was in place in his desk. The street outside had been called the *Adolf Hitlerstrasse* since 1939. Within hours the residents had reverted to calling it *Rheinstrasse.* In some places, civilians looting abandoned stores and homes fell to arguing among themselves, oblivious to the American tanks and trucks rolling east.[23]

Ninth Army's Psychological Warfare Section took the first of innumerable public opinion samplings in Muenchen–Gladbach a few days after the occupation began. The Germans professed to be relieved that the Americans had come, because the occupation meant an end to the bombings. One fifteen-year-old boy added that for him it meant he could play soccer and not have to attend Hitler Youth meetings; and he liked American chewing gum. Many inhabitants also professed to be anti-Nazi for various reasons. Some claimed religious objections. Others seemed simply to be unhappy that after all their sacrifices, Hitler had lost the war. Some wanted to reserve judgment until they saw how the Americans treated them. Nearly all said they expected hard times. Nevertheless, they complained about the rations they were getting and about having to give up their homes to troops.[24]

The workhorses of military government on the move were the I detachments, composed of three or four officers apiece, five enlisted men, and two jeeps with trailers. Except in the big cities, these detachments represented the occupation to the Germans, at once the harbingers of a new order and the only stable influence in a world turned upside down. They arranged for the dead in the streets to be buried, restored rationing, put police back on the streets, and if possible got the electricity and water working. They provided care for the displaced persons and military government courts for the Germans. If troops needed to be billeted, they requisitioned the houses. If the army needed labor, they secured it through the labor office. Under the more stringent denazification directives put out in March, they were responsible for getting everything done without using Germans who were

[22] Hist Rpt, Ninth Army, ACofS G–5, 1–31 Mar 45, in SHAEF G–5, 17.14, Jacket 6.

[23] Hqs, Ninth Army, P and PW Sec, sub: Extract of PsyWar Civilian Interrogation Report: Krefeld, 5 Mar 45, in Ninth Army, P and PW Sec 109–39.

[24] Hqs, Ninth Army, P and PW Sec, sub: The People of Muenchen–Gladbach after Occupation, 17 Mar 45, in Ninth Army, P and PW Sec 109–39.

U.S. OFFICER SWEARS IN A BUERGERMEISTER AND FIVE POLICEMEN

tainted by nazism. "Busy" was the word that described these detachments best—busy with getting local government running again and with streams of Germans reporting to be registered, wanting favors, wanting passes, or reporting rapes and looting, confident that the omnipotent military government would be able to ferret out the guilty from among thousands of soldiers.[25] For the civilians, living and eating and staying out of jail all depended on a military government officer's signature on their registration cards and on any passes they might need to be out during the curfew hours or to travel beyond the three-mile limit. One detachment commander claimed to have signed his name 540,000 times in less than a month.[26]

Since, in an opposed advance, predicting when specific localities would be reached was impossible, the armies sent out spearhead detachments in the first wave—I detachments whose pinpoint assignments were east of the Rhine. Their job was to move with the divisions in the front, stopping only long enough to post the procla-

[25] Hist Rpt, Ninth Army G–5, 1–31 Mar 45, in SHAEF G–5, 17.14, Jacket 6.

[26] SHAEF G–5, DP Br, sub: Report of Visit by Col. Gary, 27 Mar 45, in SHAEF G–5, 2748/4.

A Spearhead Detachment at Work

mations and ordinances, issue circulation and curfew orders, and remove the most obvious Nazis. They sometimes appointed an acting *Buergermeister* who would then frequently have to be left to struggle with the new rules on his own until the next unit came along and, as often as not, dismissed him for incompetence.

One spearhead detachment was I11D2, commanded by Capt. Lloyd La Prade and pinpointed for *Landkreis* Friedburg north of Frankfurt. In the first week of March, I11D2 crossed the Roer River behind First Army. On the 9th, the detachment took over Bruehl outside Cologne, appointed a

Buergermeister, received orders on the same day to double back to Euskirchen, and on the way was diverted to Linz am Rhein in the Remagen bridgehead. Sunday morning, 11 March, the detachment ran the "hot corner" at Remagen and crossed the bridge safely, becoming the first detachment across the Rhine. La Prade set up his headquarters in the town hall at Linz, which happened to be a mile upstream from the bridge and directly in line with it. The German planes on bombing runs came in low overhead, and on the second day one dropped its bombs short, wounding one officer and an enlisted man. On the

29th, having counted 200 bombing sorties and evacuated some thousands of Allied prisoners of war and displaced persons to the west side of the river, I11D2 turned Linz over to its assigned detachment and headed south to join Third Army, which was then closing in on Frankfurt. Four days later, after helping to quell riots among political prisoners at Diez and Butzbach near Frankfurt, the detachment moved to its station at Friedburg.[27]

In the big cities the pinpoint detachments moved in immediately, sometimes before the fighting ended. First Army began clearing Cologne, the largest city in the Rhineland, on 6 March, and Detachment E1H2 arrived on the 9th. At the last minute before the Americans came, the Nazi *Gauleitung* had sent criers through the streets directing the women and children and men over sixty to cross over to the east side of the Rhine; but, except for party big shots who left wearing *Wehrmacht* greatcoats over their party uniforms, few followed the directions because they would have had to go on foot with only the possessions they could carry in their hands. Some, women and children in particular, had left earlier either to escape the bombing or avoid the occupation. First estimates put the number who stayed at 100,000 to 150,000, but for weeks there was no way of telling how many were living in cellars or hiding in the outskirts. The most significant change in comparison with communities occupied earlier was a great increase in *Wehrmacht* deserters, *Volkssturm* men, and policemen who had stayed behind in civilian clothes. According to a strong rumor, a hundred *Gestapo* agents, called *"die raechende Schar"* (the avenging band), had also stayed, to kill anyone who collaborated. If the rumor was true, the agents must have put caution before vengeance, because they were never heard from.

The first Americans into Cologne pronounced their welcome "terrific." They had not seen anything like it in Germany. The days were bright and sunny. Beerhalls and restaurants offered free beer and wine; people on the streets looked at the troops as if they were heroes; and to those who could understand German and to the many who could not the civilians said, *"Endlich seid Ihr gekommen. Seit Jahren haben wir auf Euch gewartet."* (At last, you have come. We have waited years for you.) When the weather became dreary two or three days later, the mood appeared to fade, and the Americans decided upon reflection that the joy had been "patently false" anyway.[28]

Finding the city a wreck and over 70 percent destroyed was no longer a surprise, but the cellar life that had sprung up under the constant threat of air raids continued to astonish the Americans. The average citizen seemed to find spending his life underground entirely normal. A typical cellar contained bedding, a stove, a cabinet, and some decorations to give the place a homey touch. In the cellars, the inhabitants had even developed a brisk trade and social life. Many were hesitant about coming up into the daylight and facing the new risks of the occupation, but most were out in a few days scavenging among the ruins. The military government officers observed, as they had elsewhere, that the first reaction seemed to be to regard all unguarded property as free for the taking.

For E1H2 and its commander, Lt. Col.

[27] Hist Rpt, Det G–34, LK Friedburg, 17 Sep 44–31 Jul 45, in OMGUS 8–2/5.

[28] SHAEF, ACofS G–5, G–5 Weekly Journal of Information No. 6, 28 Mar 45, in SHAEF, G–5, 17.16, Jacket 8.

IN THE WAKE OF BATTLE *a German woman surveys the wreckage of her property.*

R. L. Hyles, the big problem was to rebuild the city administration under 12th Army Group's recent and rigid directive against employing Nazis and without letting a clique like the one in Aachen emerge. The detachment had to do more of the work of running the city, handpicking the officials at all levels, not only at the top, and supervising those who did qualify since, if they were up to the new standard of political purity, the chances were their other qualifications were weak. Hyles' prize appointee was Dr. Konrad Adenauer, who had been *Oberbuergermeister* of Cologne from 1915 to 1933 when the Nazis forced him out. He had been in jail for several months after the 20 July 1944 attempt to assassinate Hitler and, after his release, was prohibited from returning to Cologne. To wait out what was left of the war, Adenauer had settled in Rhoendorf on the right bank of the Rhine five miles downstream from the Remagen bridge. In his seventieth year, he had done poorly at choosing a refuge from the war but brilliantly in setting the stage for a late political career. When the bridgehead front passed Rhoendorf, military government brought him to Cologne and reinstalled him as *Oberbuerger-meister,* in secret for the first two months because his three sons were in the Wehrmacht.[29]

Cologne demonstrated on an ominously large scale something that had been observed earlier at Aachen: the helplessness and hopelessness of a city cut off from its lifelines to the outside. The city administration, German and American, could do practically nothing about getting the railroads, the power grid, or the food distribution system functioning again. Fortunately, the breakdowns in these services antedated the occupation, and the civilians had adjusted to them. The cellars contained stocks of food and coal, and the city had seventy-five wood-burning trucks. Electricity came in sporadically over the German grid. When it was on, the civilians could tune in their radios and hear the German stations across the Rhine broadcasting that the new chief of police in Cologne was a "cocky Jew," that the Americans were forcing women to bury the dead dug out of the rubble, and that hundreds of Negroes were standing guard over German civilians and forcing them to clean up the streets.[30] The detachment believed that the population benefited by being able at last to compare the Nazi propaganda with reality.

Third Army's 10th Armored Division entered Trier on 1 March, and Detachment F2G2 moved in two days later. Lying close to the West Wall, Trier had been under artillery fire and air bombardment for months. The people, except for about

4,000 of the normal 88,000, had either moved east or gone into hiding. Electricity and water were out. When the detachment, under Lt. Col. S. S. Sparks, arrived they found that most life had settled in the Kemmel Caserne (barracks) on the heights above the city, which was beginning to fill up with displaced persons filtering in from the east. In the first week, Sparks appointed Friedrich Breitenbach as civil leader in Trier—avoiding the more dangerous title of *Buergermeister*—and registered the population, which by the time the registration was completed had risen to nearly six thousand. As long as the count did not go above ten thousand, the city promised to be in relatively good shape for the time being. People who stayed had stocked up on food in advance, and although the city was 80 to 90 percent destroyed, the housing was adequate. The big problem, as it would be in most heavily bombed cities, was water. The only reliable sources were three Army chlorination tanks and a trickle still running in an ancient Roman aqueduct. When the detachment discovered it could get a little electricity by tapping the German power grid, it began work on getting the big pumps that served the city water system back in operation. The reservoir and the pumps were in good condition, but troubles soon began to multiply. First the electric lines serving the pumps were dead. The trouble was eventually traced to a switch house that an Army photo group had decided to convert into a baggage room. When the pumps were turned on, the leaks began to show. The geysers in the streets were spectacular, but worse were the breaks deep underground which were hard to locate and repair. Restoring the water system would take months. For a while, what was left of the city seemed likely to burn up before the water was

[29] Konrad Adenauer, *Erinnerungen* 1945–1953 (Stuttgart: Deutsche Verlags-Anstalt, 1965), p. 15–22.

[30] (1) Hist Rpt, First Army, ACofS G–5, 1–31 Mar 45, in SHAEF G–5, 17.11, Jacket 9. (2) 5th Information and Historical Service, The Rehabilitation of Cologne, Germany, 16 May 45, in CMH files.

COBLENZ, MARCH 1945. *In the background the forts at Ehrenbreitstein.*

turned on. Careless soldiers and roving displaced persons caused so many fires that the army had to send in the 1240th Fire Fighting Platoon to help the local volunteer fire department. The first day without a fire was 29 March which, Sparks noted in his report, was also the first day the displaced persons had not been allowed to leave the Kemmel Caserne.[31]

The detachments at Cologne and Trier did not have to contend with enemy shell-

fire or counterattacks. At Coblenz, on the Rhine at the mouth of the Mosel, the situation was different. Lt. Col. M. W. Reed took Detachment F3G2 in behind the assault troops on 20 March. He opened his headquarters in a hospital on the bank of the Mosel near where the assault boats landed and moved to the city hall in the afternoon after it was secured. The inhabitants were even less a problem than at Trier. In the first place there were only about 4,000 people in the city, and few ventured out to bring their complaints or requests for passes to the detachment. Ger-

---

[31] Hist Rpt, Third Army, ACofS G–5, 1–31 Mar 45, in SHAEF G–5, 17.10, Jacket 4.

MILITARY GOVERNMENT HEADQUARTERS, COBLENZ

man forts on the heights at Ehrenbreitstein across the Rhine kept nearly the whole city under observation, and anything that moved, even individual persons, drew artillery or sniper fire. At night, from the gun platform of Fort Constantine in the city, the detachment could watch one artillery duel going on downstream between First Army and the Germans around the Remagen bridgehead and another closer at hand upstream between Third Army's artillery and the guns at Ehrenbreitstein. Overhead the tracer and mortar fire, accompanied by the thunder of the American howitzers

firing farther back, made a permanent fireworks display. On the 25th, a German patrol raided downtown Coblenz and sent some civilians and a smaller U.S. patrol running to the city hall for safety.[32]

Before the end of March, 150 detachments were deployed in Germany, almost two-thirds of the total ECAD strength. Ninth and Third Armies had committed all the detachments assigned to them, except for some E detachments. Not all of these detachments would be needed perma-

---

[32] *Ibid.*

nently in the Rhineland, but all were busy. H and I detachments were holding areas three and four times the size they had been designed for, and an average small town was getting only about four or five days of actual military government in a month. To help the detachments keep order, among the troops and displaced persons as much as among the Germans, the armies converted field artillery battalions to security guard duty and began authorizing them to appoint *Buergermeisters* and post the proclamations and ordinances.[33] The speed of the advance threatened to make ECAD's predicted personnel shortage an imminent reality; and the War Department's temporary overstrength allotment, which reached SHAEF in late February, did not reach ECAD until March. Then the officers and enlisted men still had to be found, trained, and organized into detachments. One modest piece of good luck helped. On 22 February, ECAD opened a school at Romilly Sur Seine to give Air Force and airborne officers two weeks' training in military government liaison. At the end of the first course, nineteen graduates requested transfers into the division, having been advised "without proselytizing or promises" how to go about it. In the second course the school shifted to training both officers assigned to ECAD and ECAD enlisted men nominated for field commissions as second lieutenants under the recent allotment.[34]

Shorthanded or not, military govern-ment was propelled onto center stage in March 1945. The war would not wait. Training and practice were over and the real occupation was on. The nation that had almost conquered Europe was being brought as low as any of its victims had been. Germany's long-range future, if it had one, was undecided; the immediate future was in the hands of the G–5's and military government detachments, and even they were unsure of what it was to be. For the moment, what they saw most clearly were the approaching shadows of two relentless companions of war, disease and hunger.

The Germans were not starving, yet. In the cities, reduced populations and cellar stocks combined to make the short-term outlook deceptively bright. Searches in the basements of abandoned dwellings regularly turned up small reserves, mostly potatoes and home-canned vegetables. In Germany flour milling was still a local industry, and the mills usually had some unground grain on hand, which could be extended by setting the extraction rate up to 90 percent. Some places had lopsided surpluses. Alzey, in the fertile Rhine plain, had 5,000 excess tons of potatoes but no meat other than horse meat and not much of that. One thing was certain everywhere: the Germans were better off in March 1945 than they were likely to be again any time soon. The Rhineland, like all western Germany, was a food deficit area. Normally, the half of the Rhineland south of the Mosel imported a half million tons of food every day, equivalent to one fifty-car trainload; but no trains were running, nor was there enough transportation to ensure the movement of local produce. A survey

---

[33] (1) Hqs, ECAD, sub: Activities of the ECAD, 1–31 Mar 45, 7 May 45, in SHAEF G–5, 17.12, Jacket 6. (2) Hqs, Ninth Army, Bi-weekly CASUM, 24 Mar 45, in SHAEF G–5, 17.14, Jacket 6. (3) Hqs, V Corps, ACofS G–5, to CO, Military Government Security Guards, 196th FA Bn, sub: MG Opns, 15 Mar 45, in V Corps 205–5.5.
[34] Hqs, ECAD, sub: Activities of the ECAD,

1–28 Feb 45 and 1–31 Mar 45, 17 Mar 45 and 7 May 45, in SHAEF G–5, 17.12, Jacket 6.

showed sufficient livestock to provide half the minimum monthly meat tonnage; enough chickens to supply one egg per person per month, "provided 300,000 people do not like eggs"; enough milk to give each child under ten a pint a week; and enough butter to provide each consumer with a half pound a month.

The statistics, however, were less chilling than what the detachments had reported during their march to the Rhine. In the countryside, fields were unplowed and practically no one was at work on the farms. The young men were gone; the registrations showed that 90 percent of the males were over fifty years old. The foreign workers and prisoners of war who had made up the bulk of the agricultural labor force quit and took to the roads as soon as the front passed. There were too few horses. They, like the men, had been drafted into the *Wehrmacht*. Finally, thousands of acres of land were mined and too dangerous to work.

Famine lurked in the unplowed fields. Military government told the Germans that what they expected to eat during the next winter they would have to raise themselves. For what it was worth, the armies ordered the troops not to use local food, and military government tried to persuade the foreign workers to stay on the farms. In a more practical vein, SHAEF instructed the army groups to restrict the farmers' movements as little as possible. As a result, most units limited the curfew to the hours between sunset and sunrise, and in the *Landkreise* many allowed free circulation throughout the *Kreis* during daylight. The speed of the drive to the Rhine brought one unexpected dividend: the retreating Germans did not have time to get all their horses across the river. By the end of the month the armies had rounded up several

thousand and were turning them over to the farmers.[35] Under the pressure of the war and existing policy restrictions, military government could not do more. To provide for acute emergencies and for the displaced persons, 12th Army Group moved 80,000 tons of relief supplies into Germany during March; by the end of the month Third Army alone had issued over 7,000 long tons of food to displaced persons.[36]

In cold logic, hunger was the Germans' problem. It could be argued that whatever befell them was their own doing. But the *rickettsia* microorganism, which causes typhus, did not trouble itself to distinguish between victor and loser. It accompanied war but was not concerned with justice or with causes, any more than was the body louse on which it traveled. On the drive across the Rhineland all the armies discovered cases of typhus. The 6th Army Group found several in a camp for Russian forced laborers near Saarbruecken. Some inmates had wandered off, and, predictably, the disease also began appearing in surrounding DP camps. In Cologne a small epidemic had begun from two separate sources before the Americans arrived. In January, a doctor and several SS guards escorting political prisoners eastward had fallen ill and entered the hospital in Cologne. In the confusion of war and the continuous bombing, they were at the hospital two weeks

[35] (1) Hist Rpt, 6th AGp, ACofS G–5, 1–31 Mar 45, in SHAEF G–5, 17.18, Jacket 4. (2) Hist Rpt, First Army, ACofS G–5, 1–31 Mar 45, in SHAEF G–5, 17.11, Jacket 9. (3) Hist Rpt, Ninth Army, ACofS G–5, 1–31 Mar 45, in SHAEF G–5, 17.14, Jacket 6. (4) Hist Rpt, Third Army, ACofS G–5, 1–31 Mar 45, in SHAEF G–5, 17.10, Jacket 4. (5) 5th Information and Historical Service, sub: Food and Agriculture, XXIII Corps Area, 14 Jun 45, in Fifteenth Army 115–2.
[36] Hqs, 12th AGp, ACofS G–5, to CofS, sub: Present Status of Military Government, in SHAEF G–5, 17.16, Jacket 8.

DP Being Dusted With DDT

before their cases were diagnosed as typhus. By then they had infected several nurses and others on the hospital staff. The second source was the Klingelputz prison where, owing to overcrowding and neglect, the Germans did not detect the disease until after it had passed from the prisoners to the guards and been carried outside the walls. Having seen at first hand what the disease could do, the army and army group G–5's reported that they could not prevent its spread to the troops with the resources they had, and SHAEF issued orders making public health a command responsibility and the concern of all U.S. medical officers in Germany. SHAEF also began shipping in enough vaccine to inoculate all displaced persons. ETOUSA, charged with maintaining the communications zone across France, set up a *cordon sanitaire* on the Rhine from the Netherlands to the Swiss border and allowed no civilians to cross without an examination and DDT dusting. Persons going west into France were dusted with DDT at the border control stations. At the end of the month authorities were far from certain that the disease was being stopped. Cologne still had 185 suspected cases, and there was no way to isolate carriers among the displaced persons, short of a rigid and probably unenforceable stand-fast order.[37]

Monuments, Fine Arts, and Archives

The Monuments, Fine Arts, and Archives branch (MFA&A) had not developed even to the modest proportions envisioned in early 1944. SHAEF and 12th Army Group had MFA&A sections in the G–5, and each "E" detachment had space for one MFA&A officer. In the advance in March and April 1945, the armies employed one officer apiece on detached service from the E detachments.[38] On the other hand, the monuments multiplied as the front moved into Germany. The monuments, including archives, in the SHAEF official list totaled 1,055 for all Germany. By late March, 12th Army Group had identified 600 in the path of its advance alone. SHAEF had listed 15 monuments in Aachen. After the city was captured, the number rose to 66. The list made no provision at all for art collections, libraries, and archives evacuated from the cities and deposited in remote places to keep them safe during the bombing; and 12th Army Group had found or knew about 115 items in this category before the end of March.[39]

Because of the nature of the war, even having many more MFA&A officers could not have prevented the most extensive losses. The bombs had generally done their work days, weeks, or months before the first Americans appeared on the scene, and MFA&A had left to itself the sad task of assessing what had survived and what was gone for good. In the old city of Trier, for instance, the only structures found undamaged were the Roman ruins. The bombers had obviously tried to avoid the churches but were only partially successful. The cathedral, the oldest Romanesque church in Germany, had taken one direct hit, and the bell had shaken loose and fallen through the tower. The Liebfrauenkirche, an early Gothic structure dating from the thirteenth century, was badly damaged, and the eighteenth century Paulinuskirche had a hole in its roof. In both structures, all the windows were blown out. The most that could be done was to make the buildings weathertight to prevent added damage from the elements. In buildings so old, whatever was left was valuable, and close inspection revealed that some things, such as the paintings in the interior pillars of the Liebfrauenkirche, had survived practically intact.[40]

Muenster, fifty miles east of the Rhine, was the only city in Ninth Army's path on the first leg of its march across the north German plain. It was bombed and burned on Sunday, 25 March 1945. Capt. Louis B. LaFarge, Ninth Army MFA&A officer, wrote its epitaph:

The greater part of the old city of Muenster is gone for good. It is little better than rubble with the towers of the medieval churches alone standing to mark what the city once was. All the fine fourteenth to eighteenth century buildings are gone.

The cathedral sustained direct hits on the western porch and the nave, and an unexploded bomb lies near the sacristy door. The nave is roofless, and much of the north wall is gone. The south face remains standing and

[37] (1) Hist Rpt, 12th AGp, ACofS G–5, 1–31 Mar 45, in SHAEF G–5, 17.16, Jacket 8. (2) Hist Rpt, 6th AGp, ACofS G–5, 1–31 Mar 45, in SHAEF G–5, 17.18, Jacket 5. (3) 5th Information and Historical Service, The Rehabilitation of Cologne, Germany, 16 May 45, in CMH files.

[38] USFET, General Board, Study No. 36.

[39] Hist Rpt, 12th AGp, ACofS G–5, 1–31 Mar 45, in SHAEF G–5, 17.16, Jacket 8.

[40] Hist Rpt, Third Army, ACofS G–5, 1–31 Mar 45, in SHAEF G–5, 17.10, Jacket 4.

is surprisingly untouched. The towers have lost their roofs. The more precious moveable property is bricked up in the bottom story of the towers. The approaches to both towers are so covered with rubble that the treasures are as safe as they can be.

There is little that can be done at present. The *Domprobst* [prior] responsible for the treasure is dead, and a new one has not been appointed. The architect is old, ill, absent, and useless; and a new appointment must be made. The bishop and the vicar general have migrated to the village of Sendenhorst, and the only resident canon who had concern in the matter is an old man of somewhat defeatist views.[41]

Probably the least necessary casualties were the castles, of which the Rhineland had a large number. Most, generally located in isolated spots, had come through the bombing well; but castles have military associations, and sometimes the artillery could not resist laying in a few rounds. Castles also were rumored to have fabulous wine cellars, which made them magnets for thirsty troops. They also made attractive command posts and billets, often the only ones for miles around. Unfortunately, because they were generally safe from bombing, the Germans had done nothing to protect the castles or their contents and had used them to store art work and archives evacuated from the cities. From experience, MFA&A officers ranked them as the least safe depositories, after ordinary country houses and far below churches, monasteries, and hospitals. After the experiences at Rimburg Castle and a castle of the *Deutschorden* at Siersdorf near Aachen, where a division had set up its command post and moved valuable carved panelling from the Aachen *Rathaus* (city hall) out into the weather, units had been ordered to inven-

tory all valuables and store them under lock and key; but such orders were notoriously hard to enforce in a fluid situation.[42]

One castle which had not escaped the air raids was the *Schloss* Augustusburg, located in Bruehl. Augustusburg had been a fine example of baroque architecture, complete with a grand staircase, chapel, gardens, and outlying lodge. On 10 October 1944, a single bomb destroyed the north wing. On 28 December, several bombs had hit near the chapel, and the concussions smashed the plaster baroque and rococo interior. On 4 March, two days before the castle fell into American hands, three artillery shells struck the main building. Testimony taken later indicated that no German troops had been in or near the building. One shell blew a corner off the roof. The other two detonated inside and did extensive damage. Before the military government detachment arrived in Bruehl, troops bivouacked in the *Schloss* and caused more damage. Again it was a case of trying to salvage something from the wreckage. Detachment I1D2 found an architect, a master carpenter, and a dozen carpenters and laborers and put them to work patching the roof, shoring up the walls, and putting cardboard in the windows. Material had to be scavenged from other ruins in the city. The detachment stationed two German policemen on the grounds, but they had no authority over U.S. soldiers who continued to go in and out as they pleased.[43] Augustusburg seemed likely to suffer the same treatment as Rimburg. Ninth Army G–5 had inspected Rim-

---

[41] SHAEF G–5, MFA&A Sec, to ACofS G–5, sub: Report on MFA&A for the Month of April 1945, in SHAEF G–5, 130.21.

[42] (1) *Ibid.* (2) Hist Rpt, 12th AGp, ACofS G–5, 1–28 Feb 44, in SHAEF G–5, 17.16, Jacket 6.

[43] Det I1D2, sub: Survey of Damage to Schloss Augustusburg, Report on Measures Taken to Safeguard It, 27 Mar 45, in SHAEF G–5, 130.5.

MFA&A Posts Room in Which Museum Pieces Are Stored

burg Castle again in late February and found the furniture and art work scattered about, some thrown into the moat, and the locked rooms broken into and rifled.[44]

Lt. Col. Webb, SHAEF's MFA&A adviser, toured the two British armies and U.S. Ninth Army in March. Pillage and wanton destruction, he concluded, were at least a combined effort, being as prevalent among the British and Canadians as among the Americans. At Juelich, he saw slashed pictures and cases of books from the Aachen library broken open and their contents strewn about by souvenir hunters. Aware that the prevailing mood was not one of kindliness toward Germans or their property, he pointed out that the German collections also contained looted art work which the Allies had pledged to restore to their rightful owners, and these pieces too were threatened. SHAEF G–5 forwarded Webb's report, adding, "It is appreciated that a certain amount of 'toughness' may be desirable in occupied territory and it is not suggested that we should instruct our troops to act in Germany as they have usually in liberated territory; nevertheless, it

---

[44] Journal, Ninth Army, ACofS G–5, 1–28 Feb 45, in SHAEF G–5, 17.14, Jacket 3.

is important that Allied troops should not desecrate churches and should not destroy works of art looted from our allies."[45] It was, in fact, not a good time to attempt to convert the troops into guardians of German culture. General Smith passed the Webb report on to the army groups with the slightly equivocal comment that looting had to be considered a less despicable offense on enemy territory than on liberated territory but ought to be discouraged for the sake of the restitution policy and "to impress on the inhabitants the fact that their conquerors are superior to them not only in military prowess but in their moral standards."[46]

The DP Flood Begins

In January 1945, the twenty-nine Poles in the camp at Brand were the only displaced persons held by SHAEF in Germany. On 31 March, the army groups reported 145,000 on hand in centers and 45,000 shipped out to France, Belgium, the Netherlands, and Luxembourg, the latter mostly repatriated citizens of these countries but also including eastern Europeans. Many thousands more had not reported to the centers or had not yet been evacuated from the division areas. The number of DPs on hand had doubled in the last week of the month and, wherever the Rhine was crossed, multiplied with every mile that the front moved east. By the time the Remagen bridgehead attained an area of fifteen

square miles, it contained 3,500 DPs, 235 for every square mile taken.

The intelligence reports of the previous fall had been correct. The Germans had moved many forced laborers out of the Rhineland. The number of persons recovered, therefore, was less than half the total that had been there as late as September 1944, which was lucky, since the DP problem even with those who were left was bigger than had been anticipated. Nobody was hugely surprised when the DPs ignored SHAEF's appeals to stand fast. The DPX, however, had expected those on farms, where lodging and food were assured, to stay at least several weeks; they had not. Like the others, they had taken to the roads as soon as they knew they were liberated. On bicycles, on wagons, and on foot, displaced persons streamed away from the rural districts at the same time others were leaving towns and cities—many, the Russians and Poles especially, heading no place in particular other than away from where they had been. Cut loose from the German economy and unable to provide for themselves, they became the charges of the first U.S. unit they met. In a fairly typical instance, the 5th Infantry Division, on one day, 27 March, found 190 DPs in three towns in its sector, 400 more on the roads behind the front, and another 300 in the area uncovered in the day's advance—together, enough to fill a good-size camp. Assembly centers run by the armies quickly reached populations of 10,000 or more. Western Europeans could be kept moving toward home, but on 12 March SHAEF closed the border to the Poles, Russians, and other eastern Europeans for fear of wrecking the already weak French economy. The eastern Europeans, who made up more than half of all the DPs, hereafter became an unanticipated long-term respon-

[45] Memo, SHAEF G-5, MFA&A, for Ch, Internal Affairs Br, sub: Pillage and Wanton Damage by Allied Troops, 20 Mar 45; Memo, SHAEF G-5, Internal Affairs Br, for G-1, sub: Pillage and Wanton Damage by Allied Troops, 22 Mar 45, in SHAEF G-1, 250/2-2.

[46] Memo, SHAEF, CofS, for CG's, 21, 6, 12 AGps, sub: Looting by Allied Troops, 28 Mar 45, in USFET SGS 250.1.

RUSSIAN DPs PREPARE MEAL IN CAMP AT TRIER

sibility of the occupation forces. Unanticipated too was the amount of care and supervision they needed. Homeless, without jobs, knowing neither English nor German, elated at being free but uncertain about the future, sometimes restless, sometimes apathetic, they caused problems in more than just feeding, housing, and road-clearing, as the DPX sadly discovered. SHAEF had proposed to turn the DPs over to UNRRA teams, but in March only seven teams appeared. The H and I detachments did the work; they were sometimes reorganized with a doctor, U.S. or French welfare workers, and Allied liaison officers attached, and often operated without assistance and as a sideline to their military government assignments.

The two largest DP assembly centers established during the Rhineland campaign were at Brand, outside Aachen, and at Trier. Both were in former German army barracks. The Brand camp, after being used in the fall of 1944 for German refugees, had later been used as a hospital. Kemmel Caserne, outside Trier, had been a German *Stalag* (prisoner of war camp). It had no water supply, and when First Army surveyed it on 7 March it was pronounced too foul for anything but emer gency use; by then, however, the DPs were arriving by the hundreds and there was no other place to put them. Some came on foot; most were brought back by supply trucks returning from the front. Within days Brand reached a population of 15,000, Trier 12,000. The Belgians, Dutch, and French could be sent across the border toward home as fast as they arrived, and 700 to 1,000 a day were processed through the camps. After SHAEF closed the border to eastern Europeans, the Russians and the Poles became permanent inmates. Maj. Melvin B. Vorhees, who was with F1G2 in Aachen, remembered them vividly when he wrote the detachment's report a year later:

In Aachen there were thousands of Russian DPs. . . . They lived in a huge *caserne,* and it must be said they were filthy in the highest degree. They ruined the light wires every time they were installed; telephones were ripped out; windows were broken as soon as they were installed; fires broke out "accidentally"; a liaison officer was murdered; and the camp was in a constant state of chaos. The tactical troops assumed "responsibility" for the camp. They issued passes every afternoon for a group of DPs to visit the town. The visits were looting expeditions. The DPs would leave the camp with empty baskets and briefcases and return at nightfall loaded down like camels with all manner of goods.

Murders, rapes, and robberies abounded. Several Russians were put in prison, but they caused so much trouble they had to be turned over to the penitentiary in Ebrach. Everything was run on a hands-off kidglove policy, which was not conducive to discipline.[47]

Third Army began phasing out the camp at Trier after it captured Baumholder, which had once accommodated 50,000 German troops, and other *Casernes* in the

Mosel and Rhine valleys. S. Sgt. C. M. Tipograph saw the camp at the height of the campaign before better accommodations were found:

The Camp

High on a hill overlooking the blighted city of Trier, the camp consists of a number of bleak greystone barracks disposed around a parade ground. At a distance the buildings still seem to retain some of their former military primness and neatness. However, on closer inspection they present a spectacle of confusion and human degradation which is difficult to describe.

Literally thousands of former German slaves of all nationalities are constantly arriving or departing. The camp is administered only by three officers and six enlisted men, aided by two female members of the French Army.

Sanitary Conditions

Appalling. As soon as I arrived I became unpleasantly aware of the stench of human excrement. I myself witnessed occupants of the camp who in plain view were defecating in the shrubbery in their barracks. No facilities for bathing or washing existed except for water hauled in containers from nearby tanks and pumps. The interiors of the buildings, except one—where French PWs are housed— are indescribably filthy and disorderly; all sorts of litter from broken bottles to articles of clothing lie strewn about on the floor. The occupants live in extremely crowded and unsanitary conditions and there exists a grave danger of disease of epidemic proportions—a danger not only for them, but also for American troops in the city where the occupants are allowed to circulate.

The occupants for the most part have no change of clothing and pitiably few other belongings. I assume from the fact that many of them continually scratched themselves that the existence of body lice is widespread.

It must be admitted that the DPs themselves do little or nothing to alleviate their own miserable situation. With a bit of initiative and organization, having plenty of time, they could easily tidy up the place. Yet, just this spark of initiative and organization seems to be lacking. It must be recognized that the

---

[47] Hist Rpt, Det A–210, 2 Jul 44, in OMGUS 83–1/10.

camp is only a very temporary makeshift stopping place, with which none of the occupants identifies himself, each hoping to be off on his way home in a day or so. Even so, the sanitary conditions are such that they could only be tolerated by people who have lost their sensitivity for the niceties of civilization and have had their powers of self-reliance undermined.

The Russians

The Russians seem to have suffered the worst degradation of all the DPs in the camp. They apparently are often drunk in the daytime as well as at night, and they are not above vomiting on the passageways or in the sleeping quarters. They loll around in the sun, conduct love affairs, or go down the hill and wander through the city, of which they have free run. They take delight in pillaging or destroying German property. I saw one Uzbek in the town who was systematically slashing an upholstered sofa. When I asked him, in my halting Russian, why he was doing it, he smiled and said, "*Nyemitsky* (German)," and continued industriously at his work.[48]

SHAEF's policy was to guarantee the DPs and RAMPs (recovered Allied military personnel), the latter in the Rhineland mostly French and Russian prisoners of war, adequate food, shelter, and medical care—at the Germans' expense to the maximum extent, and out of Army resources whenever necessary. Military barracks provided the most efficient housing, but where there were no barracks, military government requisitioned hotels, schools, factory buildings, or private homes. At a small place called Lauterecken in the Third Army area, the *Buergermeister* failed to arrange space for DPs as ordered. One night a truckload of thirty-five arrived, and military government moved them in with

him.[49] The DPs received 2,000 calories subsistence per day; the RAMPs received a U.S. private's ration, 3,600 calories. Local German officials were told how much food was needed and that if they did not provide it, military government would step in and take what was needed from stores, warehouses, or any place else it could be found. The Germans got what was left, on the average about 1,100 calories. The camp at Brand used 300,000 rations in its first ten days, consisting of two-and-one-half tons of vegetables obtained from the Germans locally and captured *Wehrmacht* stocks trucked in from a depot at Liège. The two meals a day each took four hours to serve. Two smaller camps at Duisdorf issued a quarter million rations in March, and six thousand blankets and eight tons of Red Cross clothing.[50] At Krefeld, a military government private, first class, Irving Stern, ran a camp for 3,000 DPs in a prison. To feed them he supplied flour to the Krefeld bakers and made them bake bread and secured coffee from the troops, milk for children from farms, meat from German warehouses, and potatoes and barrels of sauerkraut from the prison cellar.[51] Possibly the most elegantly appointed camp was at Anrath in the Ninth Army area. It was situated in a large former prison and supervised by an I detachment and a sanitary collecting company. The 3,000 DPs were fed from captured stocks that included butter, honeybutter, flour, rice, prunes, macaroni, spaghetti, meat, ersatz coffee, cocoa, sugar, soup stock, and dried vegetables. The prison farm a short distance away sup-

---

[48] Memo, SHAEF, PWD, S Sgt C. M. Tipograph for Capt D. V. McGranahan, sub: Impressions of Displacement Camp in Trier, 16 Mar 45, in SHAEF G-1, 383.7.

[49] Hist Rpt, Third Army, ACofS G-5, 1–31 Mar 45, in SHAEF G-5, 17.10, Jacket 4.
[50] Hist Rpt, First Army, ACofS G-5, 1–31 Mar 45, in SHAEF G-5, 17.11, Jacket 9.
[51] Hist Rpt, Ninth Army, ACofS G-5, 1–31 Mar 45, in SHAEF G-5, 17.14, Jacket 6.

plied potatoes and milk. A bed factory delivered mattresses, and in a crockery factory, the detachment turned up enough cups, bowls, and plates to feed 20,000 persons.[52]

The care and feeding of the Russians was carried out from the beginning—as it would be to the end—to the accompaniment of nightmarish political overtones. Before D-day, knowing that the Germans had recruited captured Russians into collaborator military units, SHAEF had asked the Soviet government what it wanted done with its nationals captured in German uniform. Moscow had blandly replied that the problem would not arise because there were no such persons. In France, the armies had begun picking up Russians serving with German units, but it was October 1944 before the Soviet Military Mission at SHAEF admitted their existence.[53] Having made the admission, it demanded that the Russians no longer be regarded as prisoners of war and be segregated and accorded special status as "liberated Soviet citizens." When SHAEF complied, the Soviet desires concerning ration scales, pay and privileges, and working conditions became progressively more exacting, culminating after the turn of the year in a demand that Soviet civilians, of whom some thousands were in SHAEF's hands, be given identical treatment with the prisoners of war. In the meantime, owing to constant Soviet interference, discipline had become almost impossible to maintain among the "liberated Soviet citizens," and in January SHAEF

asked the War Department to assign two 3,000-space troopships to take the Russians home.[54] But they were not going to be disposed of that easily. On a closer look, the SHAEF Provost Marshal concluded that the United States did not have a right under the Geneva Convention to transfer Russians captured in German uniform to Soviet custody. Under the convention, the uniform, not a man's actual nationality, determined his right to prisoner of war status; consequently, if any of the Russians were later killed or mistreated, the United States could be held responsible and its troops subjected to German reprisals. That the Russians would not be given such preferential treatment at home as their government demanded for them from SHAEF was readily deducible from a recent British experience. The British had repatriated about 10,000 Russians captured in the Mediterranean theater and had seen them marched away under heavy guard as soon as they landed on Soviet soil.[55]

By early February, when the Big Three met at Yalta, the Soviet armies had overrun camps holding Western prisoners of war, including Americans and British, in Poland and eastern Germany. The main objective of the American and British negotiators thus became to secure good care and a safe and speedy return for their own men. The chief Soviet interest was to get all of its citizens back whether they wanted to return

---

[52] SHAEF G–5, DP Br, sub: Report of Visit by Col. Gary, 27 Mar 45, in SHAEF G–5, 2748/4.

[53] The Soviet Army had 204 officers, including several general officers, attached to SHAEF. The only liaison the Soviet government permitted with its forces, however, was through the Military Mission, Moscow, which had a tenuous access to the Soviet General Staff.

[54] (1) Memo, SHAEF AG for Com Zone, sub: Russian Nationals Captured While Serving in German Armed Forces, 18 Oct 44; Cable, SHAEF Main to Military Mission, Moscow, 7 Nov 44; and Cable, SHAEF Main to AGWAR, 12 Jan 45, in SHAEF G–1, 383.618. (2) Memo, US Gp CC, PW and DP Div, for Distribution, sub: Trends in Allied MG and Admin, 28 Jan–5 Feb 45, 8 Feb 45, in OMGUS, PW and DP Div War Diary, OMGUS, 314.81, CMH files.

[55] Ltr, Reckord to Barker, 24 Jan 45, in SHAEF G–1, 383.618.

or not. The Soviet negotiators demanded that all their nationals—those captured in German uniform, liberated prisoners of war, and civilian DPs alike—be regarded as forming a single group of "liberated Soviet citizens" for repatriation and for treatment while under SHAEF's control. In a protocol signed on 11 February the Russians had their way: they would get back all their citizens in a trade for a much smaller number of Western prisoners of war liberated by them. The meaning of the article on repatriation did not have to be faced right away but the meaning of the article on treatment did. Strictly interpreted, the article appeared to entitle former Soviet military personnel, either prisoners of war or those captured in German uniform, to treatment equal to that given U.S. troops of the same rank and entitled Soviet DPs to at least the standard of living of U.S. privates.[56]

Since SHAEF was already practically committed to giving the former Soviet military personnel treatment comparable to its own troops, the most remarkable feature of this aspect of the agreement was the provision linking the Soviet DPs to the scale for privates which, SHAEF told the Combined Chiefs of Staff, would impose impossible supply requirements. In terms of food alone, raising the rations for an estimated 1.4 million Soviet DPs from the planned 2,000 calories to the 3,600 calories of a U.S. private would require an additional 110,000 long tons of supplies. Furthermore, to raise the ration for Russians and not for other DPs would be administratively diffi-

cult and politically dangerous; but to guarantee all DPs 3,600 calories would require at least half a million additional tons of supplies.[57] As it was, SHAEF was having trouble getting shipping for the supply commitments it had and was not certain it could maintain a 2,000-calorie scale for DPs.[58] The DP ration stayed at 2,000 calories, which appeared to be consonant with the protocol after SHAEF decided that the sense of the agreement had been to provide for adequate food, clothing, housing, and medical treatment—not to establish a fixed standard.[59]

SHAEF conceded that the DPs had a special claim on SHAEF resources and, as the most numerous and obvious victims of Nazi exploitation, on German resources as well. They were to be among the first to witness the dawning new age promised in the Atlantic Charter. In the plans the DPs were a convenient abstraction; dealing with them in the flesh, however, quickly proved to be an altogether unanticipated experience. For one thing, the designation "DP" turned out to be almost synonymous with "Russian" (with an admixture of Poles and other eastern Europeans). They were the majority, the real slave laborers, the ones most in need of care, and the most

---

[56] (1) JCS 1266/2, U.S.–Soviet Reciprocal Agreement on Liberated Prisoners of War and Civilians, 18 Feb 45, in CCS 383.6 (7–4–44), sec. 4. (2) Cable, SHAEF Main to AGWAR for CCS, sub: U.S.–Soviet Agreement Dated 11 Feb 45, 24 Feb 45, in SHAEF G–5, 658.

[57] The U.S. Group Control Council estimated the required extra tonnage as 680,000 tons. Rpt No. 6, US Gp CC, PW and DP Div, 23 Feb 45, in OMGUS, PW and DP Div War Diary, OMGUS, 314.81, CMH files.

[58] Cable, SHAEF Main to AGWAR for CCS, sub: U.S.-Soviet Agreement Dated 11 Feb 45, in SHAEF G–5, 658.

[59] SHAEF also decided later that Article 3 of the protocol in stipulating one basis for privates, noncommissioned officers, and officers did not require exact equality with U.S. personnel in the same ranks. (1) Memo, SHAEF ACofS for CG, Com Zone, sub: U.S.-U.S.S.R. Agreement Relative to DPs and PWs, 23 Mar 45, in USFET SGS 363.6/11, vol. I. (2) Department of State, *Malta and Yalta,* in "Foreign Relations," p. 896.

exasperating to care for. PWD investigators sent out during the campaign pronounced them "astonishingly well-behaved" and dismissed German complaints of looting and unruly behavior as "a mixture of hypocrisy, impudence, and subtle propaganda."[60] The military government detachments dealt with them more intimately, and their judgments uniformly ran along the lines cited earlier from Brand and Trier and the following from a camp for Russians at Neustadt:

Lacking direction the majority of these DPs live voluntarily in the dirtiest conditions imaginable, and it is difficult to induce them to clean their quarters. In the camp at Neustadt a "mayor" and a "police force" were appointed and the "mayor" was instructed to have the place cleaned up before they were fed. Looting of wine cellars and the resulting drunken orgies have created trouble. . . . Heated arguments and loss of tempers have caused two murders to be committed here. The bodies were thrown out of the building, and it was only after specific orders were given that they were buried. It is impossible to find out which Russians killed the others.[61]

The dawn of the bright new world was clearly not going to be serene.

The G–5 Field Survey

In the third week of the campaign SHAEF G–5 Forward canvassed 12th Army Group and its armies and concluded, "The strictly tactical theory of military government has broken down of its own weight under pressure of practical considerations. . . ." The armies, the intended chief beneficiaries of the tactical system, conceded that an area as large as the Rhineland could not be administered for long within arbitrary unit boundaries, which sometimes divided cities in two, as the First Army–Ninth Army boundary did at Aachen. The detachments were being showered with regulations by tactical commands above them and could find themselves simultaneously taking orders from platoon commanders and army headquarters or any staff in between. One I detachment was under two corps and three divisions within five days. However, some functions, mainly agriculture and food distribution, were too broad for the armies to control. The 12th Army Group was having to take a hand in co-ordinating the armies' operations, and SHAEF G–5 expected the early result to be a compromise between the tactical and territorial systems, probably to be achieved by installing the regional E detachments.[62] At the end of the month, however, after the front had moved across the Rhine, the compromise was achieved without abandoning the principle of tactical control. Headquarters, Fifteenth Army, which SHAEF had been using for odd jobs, moved in to set up a blocking line on the river and assumed territorial G–5 responsibility for the Rhineland.

The field survey also found a deficiency in political guidance which it predicted could have "calamitous results in the not too distant future." All military government activities had political implications, but the guidance from the top was so meager that policy development—such as it was—was being left to the detachments in the field. The SHAEF policy so far was all negative: to destroy nazism and milita-

[60] Hist Rpt, First Army, ACofS G–5, 1–31 Mar 45, in SHAEF G–5, 17.11, Jacket 9.

[61] Wk Rpt, Hqs, XXI Corps, to CG, Seventh Army, 31 Mar 45, in SHAEF G–5, 17.18, Jacket 5.

[62] SHAEF G–5 Forward to DACOS G–5, sub: Field Survey, 12–22 Mar 45, 4 Apr 45, in SHAEF G–5, 204.

rism. Nothing had been decided about what to put in the place of nazism: yet, just by appointing people, military government was creating a political complexion. Without guidance, the detachments were following their own political likes and dislikes or relying on the German clergy, which meant that in the Rhineland the political outlook of the Catholic Church was becoming predominant.[63]

[63] *Ibid.*

CHAPTER XIII

After Yalta

The Fate of JCS 1067

Secretary of State Edward R. Stettinius, Jr., dispatched JCS 1067 to Ambassador Winant in London on 13 January 1945 with instructions to present it in the European Advisory Commission as the U.S. proposal for an over-all directive for Germany.[1] As revised in the SWNCC (State-War-Navy Co-ordinating Committee), the document had undergone an important change. In the September 1944 version it had been an interim directive for the period between the surrender and the establishment of the tripartite authority. The revision extended it into the period after the tripartite authority was established and implied that it would stay in force until the governments had formulated long-range policies. Consequently, the revised JCS 1067 was, in addition to being a statement of occupation policy, a charter for the commanders in chief as members of the Control Council.

JCS 1067 was agreed U.S. policy, but as far as the State Department was concerned, the agreement was less than half-hearted. James W. Riddleberger, the chief of the Division of Central European Affairs, who had worked on the revision, complained about the "intransigent attitude" of the War Department representatives and described the document as "substantively . . . the same as drafted by

the Treasury Department some months ago." He had recommended that "if for various reasons the Department thinks it must . . . approve JCS 1067 for submission to EAC . . . Winant be advised by us that he should not insist upon JCS 1067 to a point where it will unduly prolong the negotiations."[2] The Advisor on German Economic Affairs, Emile Despres, who had also worked on the revision, while conceding that the War Department acted in its own interest and not the Treasury Department's, found the policy equally unpalatable.[3] Winant and his political adviser, Philip E. Mosely, declared JCS 1067 unsatisfactory in general and objected to most of its particulars. The discontent acquired an intercontinental dimension when Leon Henderson, former director of the Office of Price Administration and the State Department and Foreign Economics Administration choice as adviser on economic affairs in the occupation, returned from Europe "in a highly critical frame of mind with regard to plans and preparations . . . for military government in Germany" and acutely unhappy with the economic implications of JCS 1067.[4] Among the multitude of State Department objec-

---

[1] Mr. Stettinius had succeeded Cordell Hull as Secretary of State on 1 December 1944.

[2] Department of State, *Foreign Relations, 1944,* vol. 1, p. 420f.

[3] Department of State, *European Advisory Commission; Austria; Germany,* in "Foreign Relations of the United States, 1945," vol. III (Washington, D.C., 1968), p. 413.

[4] Ltr, Hilldring to Smith, 24 Feb 45, in SHAEF SGS 334.

tions to the document, three predominated: namely, that it was an infringement by the Departments of War and Treasury of the State Department's policy-making function; that it emphasized the authority of the zone commanders to the practical exclusion of the Control Council; and that the Morgenthau Plan lurked in the economic provisions only faintly disguised.

On the eve of the Yalta Conference the State Department's opposition to JCS 1067 smoldered in deepening frustration; the only way out took a perilous course directly through the White House. Hilldring wrote to Smith, "It [JCS 1067] is at present the policy of the United States, approved on the highest level, and so long as that is true, we will, of course, as good soldiers, base our plans on it."[5]

The Yalta meeting, being chiefly concerned with other matters, was not expected to define an occupation policy for Germany, and, in fact, it did not; but the protocol did include partial decisions on reparations, war crimes, dismemberment, and a seat on the Control Council and zone for France. The conferees also agreed in principle on close co-ordination of laws and administration between the zones, removal of active Nazis from positions of importance, dissolution of Nazi institutions, and confiscation of German external assets.[6] Two weeks after the conference, the President turned over the potpourri to Stettinius and instructed him as Secretary of State to take responsibility for seeing that the "conclusions" were carried forward.[7] Sud-

denly, the pall of frustration in the department lifted.

On 10 March, citing his responsibility for the conclusions reached at Yalta, Stettinius sent the President a State Department draft directive for Germany. It came back three days later with an "OK FDR."[8] On the 14th, in the SWNCC, the War and State Department representatives talked about rewriting JCS 1067 in light of the new directive, knowing that the two could not survive side by side. From the Army point of view, the heart of JCS 1067 was the latitude it gave the zone commander in his own zone. The revision had stated: "The agreed policies of the Control Council shall be determinative throughout the zones. Subject to such policies the administration of military government in each of the zones of occupation shall be the sole responsibility of the Commanders-in-Chief of the forces occupying each zone."[9] The 10 March directive, however, specified: "The authority of the Control Council shall be paramount throughout Germany. The zones of occupation shall be areas for the enforcement of the Council's decisions rather than regions in which the zone commanders possess a wide latitude of autonomous power."[10] For the Army, these four sentences were the issue.

But there was another issue, namely, the degree to which the zone commander would be charged with maintaining controls on the German economy. In the revised JCS 1067 as in the original, in response to Eisenhower's desire not to be required to sustain an economy he thought was bound to collapse, the Army had insisted on making the Germans solely responsible for all controls on prices, food

---

[5] *Ibid.*

[6] Memo, McSherry for CofS, sub: Military Government Problems Requiring Immediate Agreement with the Russians, 27 Jan 45, and Ltr, H. Freeman Matthews to Smith, 15 Feb 45, in USFET SGS 014.1.

[7] Department of State, *Foreign Relations, 1945*, vol. III, p. 433.

[8] *Ibid.*

[9] *Ibid.*, p. 379.

[10] *Ibid.*, p. 434.

distribution, employment, production, reconstruction, distribution, consumption, housing, and transportation.[11] The March 10 directive made economic controls a responsibility of the occupation authorities and assigned the power to formulate policy to the Control Council.[12] The second issue was double-barreled, aimed at the Army's desire to avoid an onerous and potentially impossible mission, but even more at the Morgenthau philosophy of promoting German economic weakness.

The President's okay and initials made the State Department directive a powerful document but, as Stettinius quickly found out, not an unassailable one. The weakness was in a sense congenital. In the charge to him, the President had stated, "you will, I know, wish to confer with other officials of this Government on matters touching upon their respective fields." In forwarding the directive to the White House, Stettinius had reported that he intended to establish "an informal policy committee on Germany under the chairmanship of the Department of State and including representatives of War, Navy, Treasury, and the Foreign Economic Administration."[13]

On the 15th, Stettinius met in his office with Stimson, Morgenthau, Assistant Secretary of the Navy H. Struve Hensel, and Assistant to the Foreign Economic Advisor Henry H. Fowler to acquaint them with the 10 March directive and have them name their departments' members to the Informal Policy Committee on Germany (IPCOG), which was to be chaired by Assistant Secretary of State for Economic Affairs William E. Clayton. Stimson, who had not seen the document before, said it appeared to place "a good deal of empha-

sis" on centralization, in regard to both policy formation and administration. He had no quarrel, he said, with the assumption that Germany ought to be treated as one nation or with centralized policy formation, but he did not believe that administration should be "handed over to a central office." Morgenthau had not seen the document either, but he had heard about it from McCloy earlier in the day, as Stimson probably had also. To McCloy he had been noncommittal, saying, "it's up to Stimson to take the lead on this thing."[14] At the meeting, however, he demanded to be told "just how much . . . of the present German centralized government" was to be continued. His impression was, he said, that "the German Empire is to be continued through the medium of a central unit in Berlin."[15]

Afterward, apparently following a cabinet meeting on the 16th, Stimson talked to the President and told him the State Department directive would prevent the soldiers from doing their job in Germany. The Army, he said, was trained for a zonal operation and the zone commander had to have "complete residual authority" in matters the Control Council did not take over and handle centrally. To McCloy, Stimson indicated he still felt badly about the turn that policy on Germany had taken at the Quebec Conference and was not pleased with the State Department's interpretation of Yalta but was determined to keep himself and the War Department out of policy decisions. He instructed McCloy as the War Department's chief negotiator to leave political and economic questions to others. The Army would carry out any agreed pol-

---

[11] Ibid., p. 387.
[12] Ibid., p. 436.
[13] Ibid., pp. 433–34.

[14] Morgenthau Diary (Germany), vol. II, p. 976.
[15] Department of State, Foreign Relations, 1945, vol. III, pp. 452–56.

icy on these matters, provided they were administratively feasible.

Stimson's talk with the President was inconclusive but on one point highly enlightening: the President told him that he did not remember the State Department directive and, to his knowledge, had not read it.[16] The Secretary forwarded a report of the talk to McCloy and then withdrew from the affair, leaving McCloy to defend the Army's case in IPCOG. An interdepartmental committee at the assistant secretary level, however, was not the place to perform major surgery on a document bearing presidential approval, as McCloy had helped demonstrate during the revision of JCS 1067 in the SWNCC. If necessary, McCloy apparently proposed to attempt to get JCS 1067 and the 10 March directive recognized in IPCOG as co-ordinate policy statements without materially altering either one.[17] This potentially fascinating piece of sleight of hand was not going to be necessary, however, because McCloy had an ally whose reach went far beyond the subcabinet level, Secretary of the Treasury Morgenthau.

Theirs was a strange alliance. Stimson remained totally aloof from it, and McCloy could only participate in it to promote the War Department's limited objectives. Morgenthau, on the other hand, had to produce a substantial victory for the Army if he was going to salvage any part of his own occupation philosophy. For him JCS 1067 was a compromise, hardly more than an entering wedge for the Morgenthau Plan, but he had to fight to save it if he wanted to preserve any chance of the full-fledged plan being put into effect. Above all, he had to scuttle the State Department directive. In doing so he was impervious to the scruples that had bothered Stimson. Writing to Stettinius on 20 March he attacked the views in the directive as "completely opposed to the Treasury's views on these issues" and as "contrary in major respects to decisions made by this Government prior to Yalta; and . . . opposed in their most important implications to the views which I understand the President holds on Germany."[18] At a luncheon in the White House that same day, Morgenthau persuaded the President to reconsider the 10 March directive, which the President again said he did not remember signing.[19]

Two days later the President summoned Acting Secretary of State Joseph C. Grew, Under Secretary of War Patterson, and McCloy to the White House. Assistant Secretary of State Clayton and Mr. Roosevelt's son-in-law, John Boettiger, were also present. No Treasury representatives were included, but Morgenthau had presented his views in writing at the luncheon, and McCloy believed these papers were on the President's desk during the meeting. The President said there were many elements in the 10 March directive that he did not like, and he wanted the directive rewritten.[20]

He seemed to want to compromise on the main issues between the departments. He said the State Department directive placed too much emphasis on centralized administration, but he wanted provisions for central administration of some national public services, such as telephone and transportation. He did not want military government to administer economic con-

---

[16] *Morgenthau Diary (Germany),* vol. II, p. 1043f.

[17] Department of State, *Foreign Relations, 1945,* vol. III, p. 469f.

[18] *Ibid.,* p. 460.

[19] *Ibid.,* p. 469.

[20] *Morgenthau Diary (Germany),* vol. II, pp. 1070–73.

trols, such as rationing, but he believed the Germans ought to be required to maintain them. He suggested, as a possibility, appointing three-man German committees, which would be told what was required and if they failed would be taken out and shot. Neither did he believe that the occupation authorities should undertake to preserve a minimum standard of living for the Germans above the starvation level. He talked again about soup kitchens but did not object to the disease and unrest formula. He alluded several times to the deindustrialization features of the Morgenthau Plan, saying repeatedly that he did not want to eliminate German heavy industry. He had made a mistake at Quebec, he said, and he blamed it on Churchill, who in drafting the memorandum had used the word "pastoral," which the President said he would never have thought of using. He did not believe in such things as ruining the mines or destroying industry and specifically would be willing to let the Germans have machine tool and locomotive industries, as long as they used them for their own internal needs.[21]

On the morning of 23 March, the State, War, and Treasury members of IPCOG met in Morgenthau's office to write a directive for Germany based on the guidance received the day before. The result read as follows:

The authority of the Control Council to formulate policy with respect to matters affecting Germany as a whole shall be paramount, and its agreed policies shall be carried out in each zone by the zone commander. In the absence of such agreed policies, and in matters exclusively affecting his own zone, the zone commander will exercise his authority in accordance with directives received from his own government.

---

[21] *Ibid.*, pp. 1070–73 and 1116–18.

The administration of affairs in Germany should be directed toward the decentralization of the political structure and the development of local responsibility. The German economy shall also be decentralized, except that to the minimum extent required for the purposes set forth herein, the Control Council may permit or establish central control of (a) essential national public services such as railroads, communications, and power; (b) finance and foreign affairs, and (c) production and distribution of essential commodities. There shall be equitable distribution of such commodities between the zones.

Controls may be imposed upon the German economy only as they may be necessary (a) to carry out programs of industrial disarmament and demilitarization, reparations, and relief for liberated areas as prescribed by higher authority and (b) to assure the production and maintenance of goods and services required to meet the needs of the occupying forces and displaced persons in Germany, and essential to prevent starvation or such disease or civil unrest as would endanger the occupying forces. No action shall be taken, in execution of the reparations program or otherwise, which would tend to support basic living standards in Germany on a higher level than that existing in any one of the neighboring United Nations. [Here follow financial provisions related to reparations, which are omitted.]

In the imposition and maintenance of economic controls, German authorities will to the fullest extent practicable be ordered to proclaim and assume administration of such controls. Thus it should be brought home to the German people that the responsibility for the administration of such controls and for any breakdowns in those controls, will rest with themselves and their own authorities.

The Nazi party and its affiliated and supervised organizations and all Nazi public institutions shall be dissolved and their revival prevented. Nazi and militaristic propaganda in any form shall be prevented.

There shall be established a coordinated system of control over German education designed completely to eliminate Nazi and militarist doctrines and to make possible the development of democratic ideas.

Nazi laws which provide the basis of the

Hitler regime or which establish discriminations on grounds of race, creed or political opinion, shall be abolished.

All members of the Nazi party who have been more than nominal participants in its activities, and all other persons hostile to Allied purposes will be removed from public office and from positions of responsibility in private enterprise.

War criminals and those who have participated in planning or carrying out Nazi enterprises involving or resulting in atrocities or war crimes, shall be arrested, brought to trial and punished. Nazi leaders and influential Nazi supporters and any other persons dangerous to the occupation or its objectives, shall be arrested and interned.

A suitable program for the restitution of property looted by Germans shall be carried out promptly.

The German armed forces, including the General Staff, and all paramilitary organizations, shall be promptly demobilized and disbanded in such a manner as permanently to prevent their revival or reorganization.

The German war potential shall be destroyed. As part of the program to attain this objective, all implements of war and all specialized facilities for the production of armaments shall be seized and destroyed. The maintenance and production of all aircraft and implements of war shall be prevented.[22]

The War Department supplied most of the language in the directive. Yet, on the chief points of contention it was a compromise, as Clayton and McCloy agreed, based on the President's statements of the day before. The central administration was weaker than the State Department had wanted, but the authority of the Control Council was "paramount," not merely "determinative," as in JCS 1067, and the zone commander's authorities would not administer economic controls, but they would

make sure that the Germans did. JCS 1067 had left such controls entirely up to the Germans. JCS 1067 had not specified a deliberate reduction of the German economy in the sense of the Morgenthau Plan, and neither did the new directive. Morgenthau was disappointed with the paragraph on the German war potential but said he would not urge anything that McCloy and Clayton thought went beyond what the President had specified, especially since he was certain that the President was "so committed to a program reducing the size of German heavy industry" that he was certain to issue more detailed instructions later.[23]

In the afternoon, Morgenthau and Grew took the directive to the White House where the President signed it and, at Morgenthau's prompting, added the words, "This supersedes March 10th." After the signing, the President's secretary, Grace Tully, brought in a memorandum containing a single paragraph that the President added as the third paragraph of the directive. It read: "Germany's ruthless warfare and fanatical Nazi resistance have destroyed the German economy and made chaos and suffering inevitable. The Germans cannot escape responsibility for what they have brought on themselves."[24] When the paragraph later headed the list of basic military government objectives in Germany in the final version of JCS 1067, it read like an ominous echo of the Morgenthau Plan. In the White House office that day, Morgenthau had no idea where it came from. McCloy explained later that he "guessed it originated in John Boettiger's brain." He thought, and Morgenthau agreed, it was "sort of pretty good—pretty

[22] (1) Summary of U.S. Initial Post Defeat Policy Relating to Germany 22 Mar 45, Initial FDR 23 Mar 45, in OPD 336 (Section V) (Cases 104–154). (2) Department of State, *Foreign Relations, 1945,* vol. III, pp. 471–73.

[23] *Morgenthau Diary (Germany),* vol. II, p. 1120.
[24] *Ibid.,* p. 1079.

good propaganda."[25] Neither saw any significance in it beyond that.

The 23 March directive went to Winant in London the next day with an explanation that it superseded the 10 March directive—and that JCS 1067 would be withdrawn—but without clear instructions that it was to be submitted in the EAC. After a heated discussion in IPCOG when the War, Treasury, and Foreign Economic Administration members learned that Winant had not been instructed to present the directive and after Winant asked what he was to negotiate, if anything, Grew told him to negotiate the directive as a protocol of agreement as "a matter of highest priority."[26] JCS 1067—also, if less explicitly superseded—went to IPCOG to be rewritten as IPCOG 1 and become the directive to the U.S. commander in Germany.

Part I (Political and General) and Part III (Financial) of IPCOG 1 were written within a week from War Department drafts which incorporated much of the detail from JCS 1067. Part II (Economic) took almost another four weeks as the Treasury members attempted to write in provisions making the Germans entirely responsible for economic controls.[27] In the final version, the implication that the zone commander would require the Germans to maintain controls was less clear than in the 23 March directive, but not completely eliminated as the Treasury wanted.[28]

In the meantime, on 12 April, Harry S.

Truman succeeded to the Presidency. On the 26th, IPCOG approved and sent to him a complete draft of IPCOG 1. The following morning the members of IPCOG and Grew and Morgenthau, who at the White House conferences always stood in for the Treasury member, Harry Dexter White, went to the President's office to explain IPCOG 1 and the 23 March directive, which he had not yet seen. Mr. Truman said he wished to study the papers and asked the committee to get the directive ready quickly for final approval.[29]

The JCS gave its concurrence to IPCOG 1 on 10 May with a proviso that the directive be amended to allow Eisenhower to continue the production of synthetic rubber and oil, aluminum, and magnesium to meet the needs of the occupying forces. The President, informed that Morgenthau wanted to have such plants destroyed but that the War and State Departments believed Eisenhower ought to keep at least the synthetic oil plants to save on U.S. imports, said he entirely disagreed with Morgenthau.[30] Four days later, approved by the President with the JCS amendment, the directive went to Eisenhower as JCS 1067/8.[31]

---

[25] Ibid., p. 1079f.

[26] (1) Ibid., p. 1103. (2) Department of State, Foreign Relations, 1945, vol. III, pp. 473 and 479.

[27] Morgenthau Diary (Germany), vol. II, p. 1173.

[28] JCS 1067/6, Directive to the Commander in Chief U.S. Forces of Occupation Regarding the Military Government of Germany, 26 Apr 45, in CCS 383.21 (2–22–44), sec. 7.

[29] (1) Department of State, Foreign Relations, 1945, vol. III, pp. 483–503. (2) Harry S. Truman, Memoirs, vol. I (New York: Doubleday and Company, Inc., 1955), pp. 101 and 105.

[30] Department of State, Foreign Relations, 1945, vol. III, p. 509f.

[31] Although JCS 1067/8 was the final version, the directive continued to be referred to as JCS 1067. The version made public in October 1945 and subsequently cited in most works on the subject was JCS 1067/6 of 28 April 1945, which did not contain the amendment concerning the aluminum, magnesium, and synthetics plants. See James K. Pollock and James H. Meisel, Germany Under Occupation (Ann Arbor: G. Wahr Publishing Co., 1947), pp. 100–15, and Hajo Holborn, American Military Government (Washington: Infantry Journal Press, 1947), pp. 157–72.

War Crimes

By the turn of the year 1944–45, the war crimes question was becoming urgent without having been brought measurably closer to a solution. The War, State, and Navy Departments had worked since November on a recommendation to the President for a grand conspiracy trial. As the War and State Departments drew closer to agreement on the wording, the Navy became increasingly uninterested and finally withdrew altogether, stating that its interest was limited to the traditional concept of war crimes as single identifiable acts. The Treasury, also consulted, refused to give its concurrence without provisions that would have allowed any of the United Nations, as a matter of first priority, to claim and dispose of alleged German war criminals as they saw fit. Where the President stood and how he would react to the approach of the War and State Departments had been uncertain all along but appeared particularly so in December when he appointed Judge Samuel I. Rosenman as his special adviser on war crimes.[32]

Simultaneously, the time for influencing the President was becoming threateningly short. The Big Three meeting at Yalta was scheduled for early February, and a decision on war crimes was likely to be made there. The British government was already pressing for an answer to a question that could scuttle the conspiracy trial before it was even properly launched. In late September, the United Nations War Crimes Commission had proposed a United Nations court to be created by treaty and be charged with trying all war crimes cases.[33]

The British government vehemently opposed the idea of a treaty court, ostensibly on the grounds that setting up such a court would take intolerably long; it wanted a strict interpretation of the Moscow Declaration of 1943, under which each nation would try the persons accused of having committed crimes against its subjects or on its territory. In an *aide memoire* of 30 October, the British had asked the U.S. government to join in communicating these views to the War Crimes Commission.[34] The difficulty of organizing a treaty court could not be denied, but an international tribunal was essential to the War Department's concept of a conspiracy trial, and an affirmative answer to the British could have been a crippling blow to it. The State Department delayed answering, but by late December the continued silence was beginning to arouse suspicion in the War Crimes Commission that the United States and United Kingdom were not interested in the problems at all, and the British were talking about presenting their views independently.[35]

In the first week of January a break appeared when the President, on the 3d, asked the Secretary of State for a report on the status of proceedings in the War Crimes Commission, particularly concerning the approach the U.S. representative was taking, and indicated he believed a conspiracy indictment and an indictment for waging aggressive warfare ought to be included.[36] During the next three weeks, in meetings with Judge Rosenman and Justice Department representatives Stimson

---

[32] R. A. Winnacker, Draft MS, History of the Office of the Secretary of War, ch. 6, War Crimes, pp. 25, 33, in CMH files.

[33] Department of State, *Foreign Relations, 1944,* vol. I, pp. 1370–76.

[34] *Ibid.,* pp. 1389–91.

[35] *Ibid.,* p. 1406f. The Soviet Union was not a member of the United Nations War Crimes Commission, having refused to join because it was not allowed seats for each of its sixteen republics.

[36] Department of State, *Malta and Yalta,* in "Foreign Relations," p. 401.

and McCloy, with the State Department agreeing, succeeded in getting the War Department thinking on war crime trials written into a memorandum for the President. Two days before the last draft—the twelfth written since November 1944—was completed, Stimson repeated his views to the President but was not "sure whether it registered."[37]

The memorandum went to the White House on 22 January. In it the concept of criminality was broadened, particularly vis-a-vis Stimson's original thinking, to include "pre-war atrocities and those committed against their own nationals, neutrals, and stateless persons, as well as the waging of an illegal war of aggression with ruthless disregard for international law and the rules of war." Such crimes as those committed inside Germany before or during the war which could not be classified as offenses against international law or existing German law would, nevertheless, be tried and punished because to do so was declared United Nations policy and because postwar security, the rehabilitation of the German people, and the demands of justice required such action. The trials would be carried out in two stages. To conduct the first stage of trials, an international court would be created by executive agreement, thus avoiding the cumbersome process of establishing a treaty court. The highest ranking German leaders would be brought before the tribunal both as individual defendants and as representatives of Nazi groups and organizations. They would be charged with specific crimes and with "joint participation in a broad criminal enterprise which included and intended

these crimes, or was reasonably calculated to bring them about." The tribunal would adjudicate not only the guilt of the persons brought before it but also the complicity of the organizations included in the charges. In the second stage, other courts would try the rank and file members of organizations that the international tribunal had found to be criminal. Where specific acts or atrocities could not be proved, membership in the proscribed organization would be considered ample evidence to sustain a conviction, and the nature and extent of the individual's participation would determine the severity of the sentence.[38]

The memorandum included a draft executive agreement for an international tribunal. Stettinius carried a copy with him to Yalta, but, contrary to State and War Department expectations, war crimes were barely mentioned at Yalta aside from the customary press releases promising swift punishment and a statement in the protocol submitting the question to the foreign secretaries for a report in due course.[39] The President had not acknowledged receiving the memorandum before he left for the conference, and after he returned, gave no sign that he approved it or, indeed, that he had read it. Mounting speculation in the newspapers on the war crimes question, talk in Congress about its taking the lead, and soundings in the White House by the War and State Departments concerning the memorandum all failed to bring a response.[40]

The silence had not been broken on 6 March when the British Ambassador, Viscount Halifax, reminded Acting Secretary of State Grew that the *aide memoire* of

---

[37] (1) Stimson and Bundy, *On Active Service,* p. 587. (2) Winnacker, Draft MS, Hist of OSW, p. 35.

[38] Department of State, *Malta and Yalta,* in "Foreign Relations," pp. 402–11.
[39] *Ibid.,* p. 979.
[40] Winnacker, Draft MS, Hist of OSW, p. 43.

30 October 1944 had not yet been answered. The British government, he added, believed a discussion of war crimes and war criminals would be mutually advantageous and, therefore, invited Brig. Gen. John Weir, director of the War Department (National) War Crimes Office, and Green H. Hackworth, Legal Advisor to the State Department, and any other officials the State or War Departments wanted to send, to a meeting in London at the middle of the month. The invitation was at once an opportunity and a potential pitfall: an opportunity to solicit a presidential opinion on the memorandum; a pitfall in that if the attempt failed, the Americans would have a hard time persuading the British to accept an approach that was not even adopted in Washington. Presumably, the British would not have issued the invitation without knowing what they wanted to do. The assumption could also be made that what the British wanted would differ considerably from what the Americans intended to propose. At Yalta, Prime Minister Churchill had said—as he apparently also had at Quebec four and a half months before—that he preferred to have the major criminals shot without trial.[41] That President Roosevelt did not lean more toward Churchill's thinking than toward Stimson's and the War Department's was by no means certain.

All in all, the outlook for a satisfactory meeting in London was not bright, and ten days had elapsed before the State Department informed Mr. Roosevelt of the British invitation, asking him to authorize Judge Rosenman to head the U.S. delegation and hinting that a decision on the January memorandum would help get the war

crimes program moving. The copy returned from the White House carried an okay, but whether it could be construed as applying to the brief résumé of the January memorandum included in the message was doubtful. The State Department waited until late in the month to tell Lord Halifax that Judge Rosenman, already in Europe on other business, would conduct the discussions in London together with General Weir and Col. R. Ammi Cutter, whom the War Department was sending.[42] The War Department representatives, wary of going unprepared into talks with the British, had used the interval to work up a detailed agenda and a summary of the U.S. point of view.[43]

After two meetings, on 4 and 5 April, the negotiations in London were deadlocked. The British insisted on having the worst half-dozen or so offenders, including Hitler and Mussolini, sentenced by "political" means. The farthest they would go, even tentatively, was to permit an arraignment stating the offenses to be drawn up and presented to an inter-Allied tribunal. The tribunal would pass on the truth of the arraignment without considering whether what was charged was "a crime by any law," and the Allied governments would determine the sentences.[44] For the next week, while the British negotiators awaited new instructions from the War Cabinet, the Americans consulted with Washington by cable. Stimson's first reaction was that the British proposal deprived the trial of the judicial character he considered essential. Judge Rosenman inclined toward accepting the British approach pro-

---

[41] Department of State, *Malta and Yalta,* in "Foreign Relations," pp. 400 and 849.

[42] Department of State, *Foreign Relations, 1945,* vol. III, pp. 1155–57.
[43] Winnacker, Draft MS, Hist of OSW, p. 45.
[44] Department of State, *Foreign Relations, 1945,* vol. III, pp. 1158–61.

vided the tribunal was military rather than civilian, the sentencing was done by the court, and the arraignment was fully documented (the British wanted it "in somewhat general terms"). Stimson believed Judge Rosenman's conditions were essential, as was also an inclusion of the conspiracy charge in the arraignment; but he remained fearful that the British procedure would diminish the effect on world opinion. The talks broke off on 12 April when President Roosevelt's death forced Judge Rosenman to return home. They probably would not have gone on in any case, since the War Cabinet on the same day decided unanimously against court trial in any form.[45] McCloy, who had been in France and arrived in London on the 15th, saw no way of reopening the discussion at this stage even though he brought with him General de Gaulle's agreement to the American position.

In Washington, the uncertainty over the war crimes question was greater than ever—but only for the moment. On the 17th, Judge Rosenman gave President Truman a report on the talks in London. The President at once said he did not believe in a political disposition of the chief criminals and approved the stand the U.S. negotiators had taken, asking Rosenman to carry the matter forward at the forthcoming meeting in San Francisco to draft the United Nations Charter, which the Allied foreign ministers would attend.[46] With the White House backing, the War, State, and Justice Departments decided on the 20th to stand firm on the January memorandum at San Francisco and, if the British balked, to approach the Russians separately. They decided also to underscore their stand by

beginning to set up the U.S. element of the court. McCloy suggested several candidates to head the prosecution for the United States, among them Supreme Court Associate Justice Robert H. Jackson. On 2 May, Mr. Truman made public Justice Jackson's appointment as Representative of the United States and Chief Counsel for the Prosecution of War Crimes. The trial procedure, the President added, "Will be expeditious . . . but one which is in keeping with our tradition of fairness towards those accused of crime."[47] In San Francisco the next day, Judge Rosenman explained the American proposal to the British and Soviet delegations. To the surprise of McCloy and Colonel Cutter, who were also present, and of Judge Rosenman himself, Foreign Secretary Anthony Eden said the British position had recently changed. The War Cabinet, Eden added, still saw objections to a formal trial for the most notorious Nazis, but if the United States and the Soviet Union wanted such a trial it was willing to bow to them in the matter.[48]

After Justice Jackson's appointment, War Department concern with the major war criminals rapidly became peripheral. Justice Jackson, as the President's personal representative, carried out the lengthy negotiations after San Francisco. On Secretary Stimson's orders, McCloy set up in his own office, separate from the Army Staff, the Office of the Chief Counsel. Its main functions were to give Jackson administrative assistance and help him assemble a staff. McCloy kept in touch with the negotiations through the summer, but by then he had less to do with influencing the Allies

---

[45] Winnacker, Draft MS, Hist of OSW, p. 47.
[46] Truman, *Memoirs,* vol. I, p. 284.

[47] EO 9547, 2 May 45.
[48] Department of State, *Foreign Relations, 1945,* vol. III, pp. 1161–64.

than with smoothing the way for Justice Jackson with the U.S. occupation authorities in Germany, who were not inclined to welcome independent agencies into their bailiwick.[49]

While the trial of the major criminals was no longer a direct Army concern, the apprehension and eventual trial of offenders against specific laws and usages of war still were Army responsibilities, as would be the members of organizations found guilty under the conspiracy charges. The number of cases in these categories was bound to be vastly larger than at the top; yet, in early 1945, almost no machinery existed for dealing with them. SHAEF and the army groups were engrossed in the final drive against Germany, and it was the last week of February before Headquarters, ETOUSA, set up under the theater judge advocate a war crimes branch, the War Crimes Group, in accordance with the December 1944 instructions from Washington.

The ETOUSA letter of 24 February announcing the War Crimes Group did, at least, envision more than just another ineffectual staff agency. The War Crimes Group was to work through the army groups and armies to collect evidence and to "arrange for apprehension and prompt trial of persons against whom a *prima facie* case is made and for execution of sentences which may be passed."[50] Plans called for nineteen war crimes investigating teams, each consisting of four or five officers, including a legal examiner, and five enlisted men, a court reporter, a photographer, and interpreters. Their mission would be to follow up reported crimes and prepare cases, without as yet proceeding to the trial stage.[51]

The beginning had been made, but it was only that. The war was moving at full speed, and the expert personnel that the War Crimes Group needed was next to impossible to find. The number of courts-martial was at its wartime high, and men with legal training, particularly court reporters, were in short supply; and a check turned up only five pathologists in the entire European theater.[52] Consequently, the investigating teams materialized slowly. Only seven were organized before the war ended. The intelligence agencies, charged with locating and detaining suspects, were engaged in innumerable higher priority enterprises. Commands changed; units moved; and in the shuffle even suspects in custody were lost or forgotten. To become lost among the faceless thousands in the prisoner of war and detention camps was not difficult. The turmoil and confusion at the end of a war was just not conducive to orderly legal processes. In the second week of March, SHAEF added to the confusion and to the potential work load of the War Crimes Group by ordering the automatic arrest of entire categories of Germans: the *Gestapo*, the *Sicherheitsdienst* (SS intelligence), SS officers and senior noncommissioned officers, all members of the SS *Totenkopfverbaende* (concentration camp guards), Nazi party officials down to *Ortsgruppenleiter* (Local Group Leader), Hitler youth officials, and sundry others including all female members of the

---

[49] Winnacker, Draft MS, Hist of OSW, p. 52.

[50] Seventh Army, Judge Advocate Sec, War Crimes Br, sub: History of War Crimes Br. From Creation to 31 May 45, 21 May 45, in Seventh Army 107–25.

[51] (1) *Ibid.* (2) EUCOM, Dep JA for War Crimes, Report of the Dep JA for War Crimes, June 1944–July 1948, 29 Jul 48, ETOUSA files, p. 21.

[52] General Board Study No. 86, p. 8.

SS.[53] The individual offender became almost too rare to waste time on.

In large part, as late as the end of February 1945, the extent of the war crimes problem was still unappreciated. At first the War Crimes Group was thought of as being directly concerned only with acts against U.S. troops and U.S. nationals. The great majority of the crimes, presumably, were those the Germans had committed on occupied territory, and they would eventually be the concerns of the restored governments. What had been and would be going on in Germany was not yet actually seen, and the overdone World War I atrocity propaganda had left an enduring legacy of skepticism on the subject.

Consequently, the true criminality of the Nazi regime, for all that had been said about it, was an enormous shock and surprise when it was uncovered in the last two months of the war and the doubts evaporated. Combat Photographers recorded countless atrocity scenes in still and motion pictures, but no war crimes personnel were there to document the crimes. Unfortunately, having evidence of the crimes on film was a far cry from being able to identify and convict the criminals.

In magnitude the German crimes vastly overshadowed crimes committed in Germany by U.S. troops, but they did not completely obscure them. Looting was so widespread as to be regarded as a soldierly sport. The USFET General Board cautioned that its study of war crimes issued in the spring of 1946 should not be construed to imply "that conduct among American troops was always beyond reproach." Aside from looting, the board was aware of "substantial charges" of mistreat-

ment of prisoners of war, including one general court-martial proceeding against Americans accused of murdering prisoners of war. In the latter instance, the evidence had been held insufficient to sustain a conviction without, in the board's opinion, leaving any assurance that the accused were innocent.[54] Of the crimes committed by U.S. troops, the best—though by no means most accurately—documented was rape, and it showed a "spiral increase" in the closing months of the war. Between July 1942 and October 1945, 904 rape cases were charged in the European theater, 552 of them in Germany. All told, 487 soldiers were tried for rapes allegedly committed in the months of March and April 1945. By no means all the incidents were reported or, of those reported, brought to trial, and the conviction rate was relatively low. The Judge Advocate, Seventh Army, referred 84 cases to trial in April and May 1945. More than half, 47, were tried, resulting in 24 acquittals and 23 convictions. Tolerance on the part of the courts was probably less a factor than the weight of the penalties and the difficulties of proof. The convictions in Seventh Army resulted in eleven death sentences, seven life sentences, and several for twenty and fifteen years. The legal requirement, a manifest lack of consent by the victim, was missing in so many cases that at last some courts began to hold that "a man who enters a strange house, carrying a rifle in one hand, is not justified in believing he has accomplished a seduction."[55] If not all the crimes or even a large percentage were

---

[53] Ltr, SHAEF AG to Distribution, sub: Arrest and Detention in Germany, in SHAEF G-5, 000.5-2.

[54] *Ibid.*, p. 6.
[55] (1) USFET, JAG, History, Branch office of the Judge Advocate General, 18 Jul 42–1 Nov 45, in Admin Hist Collection, ETOUSA, Nr. 559A, vol. I, p. 249. (2) Seventh Army, Judge Advocate Sec Rpts, 1 Dec 44–31 May 45, in Seventh Army 107–25.

punished, some were, and these severely. Moreover, as the General Board later pointed out, there was a difference between the individual offenses of the U.S troops and the systematic, officially sponsored Nazi criminality.[56]

In the last weeks of the war, influenced by what was being seen in Germany, the war crimes program gathered momentum. In April, the armies began setting up war crimes branches and sending out field investigating officers with clerks and interpreters to gather evidence at the scenes of crimes as they were uncovered. Suspects could not yet be segregated, but three prisoner of war enclosures in the Normandy Base Section, Communications Zone, were set apart where they and unfriendly witnesses could be congregated.[57] At Spa, Belgium, SHAEF opened ASHCAN, a holding and interrogation center for top Nazis and military officers.[58] At its rear headquarters in Versailles, SHAEF set up the Central Registry of War Criminals and Security Suspects (CROWCASS). CROWCASS was to maintain wanted lists, particularly of persons who might be turned up in prisoner of war camps. In three weeks the registry accumulated 70,000 names.[59]

A Mission for the U.S. Group Control Council

The EAC agreements on zones and control machinery made one radical change in the planning concept for the administration of occupied Germany: they added in effect a fourth phase to the three phases SHAEF had used as a planning basis since Slash 100. According to Slash 100, military, that is, SHAEF, control would end in the second phase and the permanent occupation take over in the third. The EAC agreements added a third temporary and still military period, that of the Control Council. Upon the inception of the Control Council, SHAEF would be disbanded, but Eisenhower would remain as military governor in the zone, commander of the U.S. occupation forces, and a member of the Control Council. Replacing his two staffs, SHAEF and ETOUSA, he would have one, the Headquarters, U.S. Forces in the European Theater (USFET), which would absorb ETOUSA and the U.S. side of SHAEF.

During the Control Council period, then, SHAEF would no longer exist, but USFET would continue and inherit the U.S. side of SHAEF G-5 and the question of its relationship to the U.S. Group Control Council. The answer to this question was bound to hinge on two considerations: one, the built-in reluctance of a bureaucratic organization to contemplate its own demise; the other, the War Department view of the Control Council's role in the occupation. With regard to the first, in the fall of 1944, the U.S. element of SHAEF G-5 was powerfully situated to protect its future in USFET. It was a full-fledged, functioning, and—most important—decision-making organization. The U.S. Group Control Council was not. As far as the second consideration was concerned, War Department CAD opinion at least could hardly have been more favorable toward the projected G-5, USFET. Hilldring, writing to Smith on 2 November 1944, took for granted that the theater G-5 would be the operating military govern-

[56] General Board, Study No. 86, p. 6.
[57] EUCOM, Dep JA for War Crimes Report, p. 20.
[58] Memo, SHAEF AG for CG, 12th AGp, sub: Establishment of Special Detention Centers, 27 May 45, in SHAEF G-2, 383.6-4.
[59] Ltr, SHAEF, G-1, to AG, 7 May 45, in SHAEF G-1, 000.5-2.

ment agency in the U.S. zone.[60] Thus encouraged, Smith accepted a staff study two weeks later in which Eisenhower's two military government staffs were assigned separate roles: the U.S. Group Control Council, policy-making in Berlin; and the G–5, USFET (see above, p. 166), implementation in the zone.[61]

At the same time, the talk about appointing a civilian high commissioner for Germany that accompanied the advent of the Morgenthau Plan and the seeming imminence of the end of the war brought up the question of the appointment of the deputy military governor, who would head the U.S. Group Control Council. McCloy proposed that the deputy ought to be a regular officer of standing. The War Department particularly did not want, at least for the initial period, a high powered civilian commissioner working outside the military chain of command. Eisenhower agreed but was willing to accept a civilian as his deputy, especially if the civilian were McCloy or Assistant Secretary of War Patterson, whose name had been mentioned as a candidate. Eisenhower agreed, too, that the deputy probably ought to begin working himself into the job soon but added that Wickersham was doing an "extremely good job" and could carry the planning through to the end. Apparently, if he could not get McCloy, for whom he had already asked early in the year, Eisenhower would rather have waited until he could spare a senior general from SHAEF.[62]

When Wickersham returned from Washington in November, he brought back, for Eisenhower's and Smith's information only, the name of Maj. Gen. Lucius D. Clay as the War Department's choice for the deputyship, Clay, who as Director of Matériel, Army Service Forces, supervised the military production program, had recently commanded for a time the Normandy Base Section, at Eisenhower's request, to speed the flow of supplies through Cherbourg. After only a three weeks' stay in France, he had returned to Washington to report for Eisenhower on a threatening heavy-ammunition shortage.[63] Eisenhower had wanted to retain him in the theater and was willing to have him as the deputy for military government. Stimson, however, decided that as long as German resistance continued, the ammunition problem was more important and therefore assigned Clay for at least sixty days to the Office of War Mobilization and Reconversion. When Hilldring proposed appointing an interim deputy and alluded to "disquieting reports" that the U.S. Group Control Council's work was "more or less aimless and ineffective," Smith assured him that Eisenhower would be willing to wait sixty days, that no change in the U.S. Group Control Council was necessary, and that he did not agree with Hilldring's views on the "ineffectiveness of our staff work."[64]

---

[60] Cable, Hilldring to Smith, 2 Nov 44, in USFET SGS 334/2.

[61] Memo, Maj Gen R. W. Crawford for Gens Bull, Barker, Holmes, Wickersham, McSherry, sub: Organization of the ETO for the Occupation of Germany, 16 Nov 44, in SHAEF SGS 322.3.

[62] Ltr, McCloy to Eisenhower, 24 Oct 44, and Ltr, Eisenhower to McCloy, 1 Nov 44, in USFET SGS 334/2.

[63] Lucius D. Clay, *Decision in Germany* (New York: Doubleday and Company, Inc., 1950), p. 3.

[64] Cable, Hilldring to Smith, 5 Dec 44, and Cable, Smith to Hilldring, 7 Dec 44, in USFET SGS 334/2. Hilldring had visited London in October and returned to Washington convinced that the job as acting deputy had "developed beyond Wickersham's capabilities." He had described the U.S. Group Control Council as "drifting aimlessly" and attributed "95 percent of the trouble to vacillating leadership." Eisenhower and Smith did not

During the winter, the U.S. Group Control Council worked on its Basic Preliminary Plan which, together with its elaborations and supplements, eventually made up a file that General Clay later described as being "beyond the ability of one man to comprehend."[65] SHAEF, in the meantime, completed one "final" G–5 reorganization for Germany at the end of February and another in late April. Together, they did finally end the separation of policy and operations within G–5 and abolished the remnants of the special staff. Henceforth the G–5 functional branches were responsible for policy, planning, and operations.[66] On the other hand, the U.S. side of SHAEF G–5, at least, was now intent on applying the distinction between policy and operations to the U.S. Group Control Council and the future theater G–5.

In March, the U.S. Group Control Council moved to Versailles, leaving a rear echelon in London to maintain contact with the EAC and the British Control Council element. The move brought the American Control Council personnel in contact with events on the Continent—and under closer G–5 scrutiny. One particular weakness G–5 had found in the Basic Preliminary Plan was "some tendency to assume [on the part of the Control Council] power to give orders to the U.S. zonal staff

and subordinate echelons."[67] This tendency was corrected in two directives—one issued on 31 March, the other on 29 April. The first directive limited the U.S. Group Control Council to negotiating in the Control Council and developing policies "consistent with approved U.S. views in conjunction with the joint theater staff."[68] Wickersham managed later, with some effort, to get the words "in conjunction with" changed to "in consultation with."[69] The second directive defined the two staffs' functions as follows:

1. The U.S. Group Control Council will be the U.S. element of the Control Authority.
2. The theater staff will be specifically charged with execution, implementation, and supervision within the zone of approved U.S. and Control Council policies.[70]

In Washington, however, the War Department had, in the President's 23 March directive and the revised JCS 1067, accepted the Control Council's authority as paramount; and Hilldring thereafter concluded that in the long run Eisenhower would clearly have only one staff for military government in Germany, the U.S. Group Control Council.[71]

While the staffs were jockeying for position, one genuinely crucial step toward deciding the future of the occupation was

agree, possibly because whatever drifting the Control Council group was doing was not aimless as far as SHAEF was concerned. In Smith's view, the main purpose of the group for the time being was to "assemble a corps of experts on the civil side." He wanted to hold open the jobs in the executive staff for "outstanding commanders and staff officers here, who are now conducting the war." (1) Cable, Hilldring to Smith, 2 Nov 44, in USFET SGS 334/2. (2) Ltr, Smith to Hilldring, 3 Mar 45, in CAD 014, 7–10–42, sec. II.
[65] Ltr, Clay to Hilldring, 7 May 45, in OMGUS 177–1/3.
[66] General Board, Study No. 32, pp. 52–54.

[67] OMGUS, Control Office, Historical Branch, History of Military Government in Germany, 8 May 45–30 Jun 46, in OMGUS 21–215, ch. VIII, p. 25f.
[68] Hqs, US Gp CC, Planning Directive No. 21, 31 Mar 45, in OMGUS 12–1/5, V60–11/1.
[69] US Gp CC, Staff Meeting of Division Directors, 2 Apr 45, in OMGUS 12–1/5, V60–12/1.
[70] Memo, Hqs, ETOUSA, CofS, for Distribution, sub: Relationship of Dep. Mil. Gov. and U.S. Gp. CC to Theater Staff, 29 Apr 45, in USFET SGS 322/3.
[71] History of the CAD, bk. VI, ch. XII, p. 66.

taken—the appointment of the Deputy Military Governor. After December 1944, the discussion of the appointment, never very enthusiastic on the European side anyway, had faded. Writing to Hilldring in early March, Smith mentioned the need for a deputy but said Wickersham could carry on until one was appointed. He was more concerned at the time with finding a chief for the theater G–5, whose job he described as being "as important or more important" than that of the deputy; he suggested Clay.[72] Hilldring had told Smith a week earlier that the War Department was actively engaged in selecting a deputy but promised only "some official word . . . before long" and did not mention Clay or any other candidates.[73] Consequently, Clay's appointment as Deputy Military Governor at the end of March, which was a surprise to Clay, equally surprised Eisenhower and Smith when he appeared at SHAEF headquarters on 7 April.[74]

Upon his arrival at SHAEF Forward in Reims, Clay, as he relates in his memoirs, had a title without a job.[75] Military government was all in the hands of G–5, SHAEF, and the welcome Smith gave him was less than warm. But he had ironclad credentials: a presidential send-off arranged by his former chief in the Office of War Mobilization and Reconversion, Justice James F. Byrnes; a commitment from the War Department that he would be Eisenhower's deputy in fact and not be buried somewhere in the general staff; and a promotion

to lieutenant general in the offing. On 18 April ETOUSA created the post of Deputy Military Governor and announced Clay's assignment to it. A week later he took command of the U.S. Group Control Council.[76] The 29 April directive on the relationship between the U.S. Group Control Council and the theater G–5 appeared still to leave some ambiguity in Clay's position as Deputy Military Governor: he was to be in direct charge of the U.S. Group Control Council; he would represent the Commanding General, USFET, on the co-ordinating committee of the Control Council when it was established; and he would be "adviser" to the Chief of Staff and the Commanding General USFET, for military government within the U.S. zone in Germany. In this last capacity he would "secure coordination directly through" the theater G–5.[77] But the 29 April directive was less authoritative than Clay's own definition written on 11 April. In it he proposed to "work directly through the G–5 Divisions with the several command echelons" and as he later told Hilldring claimed as Deputy Military Governor "full charge for the commander in Berlin and in addition . . . staff supervision over G–5 activities within the U.S. zone."[78]

Not everyone knew yet but the struggle for power was over and General Clay had won.

---

[76] OMGUS, History of Military Government in Germany, ch. VIII, p. 25. General Wickersham became Assistant Deputy Military Governor until 26 May when he asked to be relieved from duty for reasons of family health.

[77] Memo, Hqs, ETOUSA, CofS, for Distribution, sub: Relationship of Dep. Mil. Gov. and U.S. Gp. CC to Theater Staff, 29 Apr 45, in USFET SGS 322/3.

[78] (1) Department of State, Foreign Relations, 1945, vol. III, p. 934. (2) Ltr, Clay to Hilldring, 7 May 45, in OMGUS 177–1/3.

---

[72] Ltr, Smith to Hilldring, 3 March 45, in CAD 014, 7–10–42, sec. 11.

[73] Ltr, Hilldring to Smith, 24 Feb 45, in SHAEF SGS 334.

[74] (1) Clay, Decision in Germany, pp. 4–7. (2) Summary Sheet, Director, CAD, to OPD, sub: Personnel for U.S. Gp. CC, 28 Mar 45, in OPD 336 (sec. 11–A).

[75] Clay, Decision in Germany, p. 8.

CHAPTER XIV

Eclipse

The Ruhr Pocket

All the armies had crossed the Rhine before the end of March. On the 28th Eisenhower set Ninth Army on the north, and First and Third Armies, on the south, moving to snare the Ruhr in a sweeping envelopment that would reach east 120 miles to the Weser River. Later in the day, in a cable addressed "Personal to Marshal Stalin," Eisenhower told the Russians, as he had already informed the British and U.S. Chiefs of Staff, that he proposed to close an encirclement of the Ruhr in the vicinity of Kassel and then turn the armies east to meet the Russians, probably in the Leipzig–Dresden area. Subsequently, to keep the Germans from setting up a redoubt in the Bavarian and Austrian mountains, he would send forces south to link up with the Russians on the Danube between Regensburg and Linz.

Having lost the West Wall and having failed to hold on the Rhine, the German armies, reinforced by over-age and under-age *Volkssturm* men, were nothing like the opponents they had been even a few weeks earlier. On the southern arm of the encirclement, First and Third Armies were already halfway between the Rhine and the Weser by nightfall on the 28th. Ninth Army drove east and south, met the First Army point at Lippstadt on 1 April, and closed the noose tightly around German Army Group B in the Ruhr the next day.[1]

---

[1] For a complete tactical description see Charles

The two PWD captains, Gittler and Padover, followed behind Ninth Army and described the scene:

The traffic keeps going endlessly to the east. Streaming back are the huge COM Z trucks bearing the prisoners. They smile, wave, stare with awe at the busy Americans building bridges, patching roads, unloading, loading, bearing forward. You can stand on an intersection and count the prisoners by the thousands. When they look at the ruined towns where there had been resistance, they just stare and shake their heads.

Past the main cities of resistance, past the broken roads and shattered farmhouses and torn-up fields, we suddenly come upon towns that stand intact and fields that are green and farmers who are at their job working. There was no fighting in these areas, and the people have profited. Then in the open country behind Muenster and south to Paderborn, you see thousands and thousands of liberated foreign workers and prisoners of war from every army in Europe. Mingling with them are German workers walking back home from the Ruhr. This is the great migration. When you talk with them you see the senseless, desperate measures the Nazis took to transport labor back and forth across the land during the last six weeks.

In Lippe, where the Germans were surprised and surrendered by the thousands, the ancient picturesque beauty of the towns and countryside is preserved. The towns operate normally; the fields are rich with cattle. The farms and houses stand as before. Rarely do you see American soldiers in these towns. Nevertheless, there is order and tranquillity, even without German or Allied authority.

B. MacDonald, *The Last Offensive*, (Washington, 1973).

Allied proclamations, however, are posted in every village all the way up to the most forward lines. German children wave as you pass by and the old people smile. Everyone falls over himself to give you help and information and directions.

From Lippe you suddenly come to Paderborn. And again appear the familiar ruins and broken life; people searching in the rubble for some trinket or possession. Here there had been resistance and the city had paid for it. We talked to a saddlemaker who was trying to clear away the debris around his business. He is angry and apologetic. "We should have used our hunting guns on the Nazi *Lieter*," he says. "Then this would not have occurred and we would have saved something."[2]

Had death not all too often still been waiting around the next corner, the war would have been little more than a sour joke by April 1945. At Arolsen, when an SS officer candidate school pulled out the day before the Americans came, the people hurried to fill in the antitank ditches around the town. The 9th Panzer Division troops detailed to defend Olpe drove themselves to a prisoner of war cage in their own trucks.[3] In one small town, a military government public safety officer, called to quell a disturbance, found a displaced person beating a German over the head with a yard-square, framed picture of *Der Fuehrer*.[4] When ECAD Tech. 4 Kenneth Dennis found himself the only American in a German town, he commandeered a bicycle from a rack in front of a cafe and rode down the street shouting: *"Achtung. Amerikanische Bomben."* While the Germans, including three officers whom he

saluted out of habit, scrambled for cover, he pedaled through town and back to the American line.[5]

Third Army's 5th Division captured Frankfurt on 29 March. Caught in a narrowing pocket between First Army on the north and Third Army on the south and east, the people had known what was coming for nearly a week. The *Gauleiter* ordered the men to leave the city on the 24th. Some did; many did not, preferring to wait out the end in the cellars and air raid bunkers. The next day was Palm Sunday. On Monday artillery shells began to fall in the city, and at night, when the firing subsided, the roar and rattling of American tanks carried across the Main River from the south. The weather was fine, more like May than March. The city went on a spree as looters plundered the property of those who had left. The shopkeepers tried to sell out their stocks. Butter, scarce since before the war, could be bought by the case and wine sometimes by the bucketful, and the butchers gave out four or five times the legal meat ration. On Thursday the Americans came: the scouts and skirmishers first, keeping under cover close to buildings and behind the rubble piles lining the streets; and then the columns with rifles slung on their shoulders.[6]

The war was over for Frankfurt. After twenty air raids, the bombing was ended. The sirens would not be heard again, nor the antiaircraft guns. But the city was all but dead. The business district was a brick and stone wilderness in which the old residents could hardly find their way around. No trains were running and no streetcars.

---

[2] Lewis F. Gittler and Saul K. Padover, "Up the Weser River," in SHAEF G–5, 17.11, Jacket 9.

[3] Hqs, 12th AGp, P&PW, Daily Summary of Intelligence, 13 Apr 45, in SHAEF G–5, 17.11, Jacket 9.

[4] Hist Rpt, 12th AGp, G–5, Apr 45, in SHAEF G–5, 17.16, Jacket 10.

[5] Hqs, ECAD, to SHAEF, sub: Activities of the ECAD, 1–30 Apr 45, in SHAEF G–5, 601.

[6] Madlen Lorei and Richard Kirn, *Frankfurt und die drei wilden Jahre* (Frankfurt a. M.: Verlag Frankfurter Buecher, 1968), pp. 11–17.

U.S. TANK CRASHES THROUGH RUINS OF A GERMAN TOWN

The telephones were out, and the electric lines and water and gas mains would take months to repair. The Chief Military Government Officer, Lt. Col. Howard D. Criswell, Detachment F2D2, found a non-Nazi former editor of the *Frankfurter Zeitung,* Wilhelm Hollbach, and had him sworn in as *Oberbuergermeister.* In the railroad yards, Germans and displaced persons raided stranded *Wehrmacht* supply trains, and seventy Russians died from drinking methyl alcohol taken in a raid. Of the 31,000 Jews who had inhabited Frankfurt, one of the oldest Jewish communities in Germany, military government officers found 140. They had been employed under the Nazis in cemeteries and at cleaning toilets. Living in segregated houses, one family to a room, they had in the past three years not received any egg, meat, milk, white flour, wine, tobacco, or clothing rations. Military government requisitioned houses and a hospital for them.[7]

On the edge of the Grueneburg Park in Frankfurt stood a marvel, a spacious highrise office building belonging to the I. G. Farben cartel, untouched by bombs and

[7] *Frankfurter Presse,* 10 May 45, in SHAEF G–5, 17.16, Jacket 12.

with hardly even a window broken. It seemed likely to be the only building big enough to house SHAEF (and USFET) left standing in western Germany, and Smith cabled Washington to make sure that Frankfurt, which might be considered for assignment to the French zone, was kept in the U.S. zone.[8] The Germans later suspected that the U.S. Air Force had spared the building deliberately. More likely, the antiaircraft batteries in the Grueneburg Park and the adjacent Palm Garden had influenced the bomber pilots to pick less hazardous targets.

Advancing north from Frankfurt, Third Army cut into the future Soviet zone when it occupied the western tip of Thuringia. On 4 April, the 90th Infantry Division took Merkers, a few miles inside the border in Thuringia. On the morning of the 6th, two military policemen, Pfc. Clyde Harmon and Pfc. Anthony Kline, enforcing the customary orders against civilian circulation, stopped two women on a road outside Merkers. Since both were French displaced persons and one was pregnant, the MPs decided rather than to arrest them to escort them back into the town. On the way, as they passed the entrance to the Kaiseroda salt mine in Merkers, the women talked about gold that the Germans had stored in the mine—so much gold, they said, that unloading it had taken local civilians and displaced persons who were used as labor seventy-two hours. By noon the story had passed from the MP first sergeant to the chief of staff and on to the division's G–5 officer, Lt. Col. William A. Russell, who in a few hours had the news confirmed by other DPs and by a British sergeant who had been employed in the mine as a pri-

soner of war and had helped unload the gold. Russell also turned up an assistant director of the National Galleries in Berlin who admitted he was in Merkers to care for paintings stored in the mine. The gold was reportedly the entire reserve of the *Reichsbank* in Berlin, which had moved it to the mine after the bank building was bombed out in February 1945. When Russell learned that the mine had thirty miles of galleries and five entrances, the division, which had already detailed the 712th Tank Battalion to guard the Merkers entrance, had to divert the whole 357th Infantry Regiment to guard the other four.

The next morning, after having steam raised in the boilers overnight to generate electricity for the lifts and ventilators, Russell went down into the mine with a party of division officers, German mine officials, and Signal Corps photographers. Near the entrance to the main passageway they found 550 bags containing a half billion in paper *Reichsmarks*.[9] A steel vault door

[8] Cable, SHAEF Forward to AGWAR (Hull), 16 Apr 45, in SHAEF G–3, Ops. 387-15.

[9] The discovery that Germans had possibly removed money recently raised suspicions concerning the uses to which it might be put. Dr. Werner Veick, a *Reichsbank* official who gave himself up to military government in Merkers on 8 April, insisted, however, under intensive questioning, that the money was being taken out for normal circulation because the *Reichsbank's* printing presses had broken down. As Veick explained, he and several other bank employees had loaded 1,000 bags of money in a railroad boxcar on 3 April. The next morning they had decided to unload the car again when they learned that it could not leave Merkers because of a blown bridge. They were about half finished when they heard that the Americans were less than two miles away. The senior official then decided that he was badly needed back in Berlin, locked the vault, and drove off by car while Veick went to get his suitcase. When Veick returned to the mine, the Americans were there. They searched him, asked what he was unloading, looked at the money, and moved on. He and the laborers then finished unloading the money and stacked it in the passage outside the vault.

SOLDIERS ADMIRE MANET PAINTING IN MERKERS MINE

on the entrance to the tunnel said to contain the gold was locked. In the afternoon, after having tried unsuccessfully to open the door, the party left the mine without having seen the treasure.

The next day was Sunday. In the morning, while Colonel Bernstein, Deputy Chief, Financial Branch, G–5, SHAEF, read about the find in the New York *Herald Tribune's* Paris edition, 90th Infantry Division engineers blasted a hole in the vault wall to reveal on the other side a room 75 feet wide and 150 feet deep. The floor was covered with rows of numbered bags, over 7,000 in all, each containing gold bars or gold coins. Baled paper money was stacked along one wall; and at the back—a mute reminder of nazism's victims—valises were piled filled with gold and silver tooth fillings, eyeglass frames, watch cases, wedding rings, pearls, and precious stones. The gold, between 55 and 81 pounds to the bag, amounted to nearly 250 tons. In paper money, all the European currencies were represented. The largest amounts were 98 million French francs and 2.7 billion *Reichsmarks*. The treasure almost made the 400 tons of art work, the best pieces from the Berlin museums, stacked in the mine's other passages seem like a routine find.

On Sunday afternoon, Bernstein, after checking the newspaper story with Lt. Col. R. Tupper Barrett, Chief, Financial Branch, G–5, 12th Army Group, flew to SHAEF Forward at Rheims where he spent the night, it being too late by then to fly into Germany. At noon on Monday, he arrived at Gen. George S. Patton's Third Army Headquarters with instructions from Eisenhower to check the contents of the mine and arrange to have the treasure taken away. While he was there, orders arrived for him to locate a depository farther back in the SHAEF zone and supervise the moving. Bernstein and Barrett spent Tuesday looking for a site and finally settled on the *Reichsbank* building in Frankfurt. Wednesday, at Merkers, they planned the move and prepared for distinguished visitors by having Germans tune up the mine machinery. The next morning, Eisenhower, Bradley, Patton, and Maj. Gen. Manton S. Eddy took the 1,600-foot ride down into the mine. When they stepped out at the foot of the shaft, the private on guard saluted and, in the underground stillness, was heard by all to mutter, "Jesus Christ!"

The move began at 0900 on Saturday morning, 14 April. In twenty hours, the gold and currency and a few cases of art work were loaded on thirty ten-ton trucks, each with a 10 percent overload. Down in the mine, jeeps with trailers hauled the treasure from the vault to the shaft, where the loaded trailers were put aboard the lifts and brought to the surface. At the vault entrance an officer registered each bag or item on a load slip, and at the truck ramps an officer and an enlisted man checked the load slips and verified that every item that left the vault was loaded on a truck. Finally, the officer recorded the truck number and the names and serial numbers of the

driver, the assistant driver, and the guards assigned to the truck.

The convoy left Merkers on Sunday morning for the 85-mile trip to Frankfurt with an escort of five rifle platoons, two machine gun platoons, ten multiple-mount antiaircraft vehicles, and Piper cub and fighter air cover. All this protection, however, was not enough to prevent a rumor, which surfaced periodically for years after, that one truckload of gold (or art work) disappeared on the way to Frankfurt. On Sunday afternoon and throughout the night the trucks were unloaded in Frankfurt, each item being checked against the load lists as it came off a truck and again when it was moved into the *Reichsbank* vault. Two infantry companies cordoned off the area during the unloading.[10]

The same procedures, except that a hundred German prisoners of war did the work, were followed in loading the art objects aboard a second truck convoy on Monday, and a similar security guard escorted the trucks to Frankfurt the next day. After the main treasure was removed, the mine was still a grab bag of valuables. Reconnaissance of the other entrances had turned up four hundred tons of German patent office records, *Luftwaffe* material and ammunition, German Army High

---

[10] The gold remained in the *Reichsbank* vault under Army control until 24 January 1946 when control and responsibility for it passed to the Inter-Allied Reparation Agency. The agency was charged with returning the gold on a prorated basis to governments having claims on it and with making a substantial amount ($25 million in monetary gold, plus all "non-monetary gold" and all so-called heirless funds, according to a subsequent agreement of 14 June 1946) available to "non-repatriable victims of German action." The latter amount went mostly to compensate and resettle Jewish victims of nazism. The Soviet Union was not included in the distribution, since it had relinquished all claims to captured gold in the Potsdam Agreement.

Command records, libraries and city archives (including 2 million books from Berlin and the Goethe collection from Weimar), and the files of the Krupp, Henschel, and other companies. The patent records in particular were potentially as valuable as the gold; but Third Army needed its trucks, and Bernstein had to settle, on 21 April, for a small seven-truck convoy to move the cream of the patent records, samples of the Krupp and Henschel files, and several dozen high quality microscopes.

Leads found in the *Reichsbank* records at Merkers also helped uncover a dozen other treasure caches in places occupied by U.S. forces that brought into the vault in Frankfurt hundreds more gold and silver bars, some platinum, rhodium, and palladium, a quarter of a million in U.S. gold dollars (the Merkers mine set the record, however, containing 711 bags of U.S. $20 gold pieces, $25,000 to the bag), a million Swiss gold francs, and a billion French francs.[11]

The front moved on; the troops read about the treasure in *Stars and Stripes* or *Yank* and probably only vaguely remembered they had been in or near Merkers. Another spot was more likely to stick in the memories of those who passed through it in early April 1945. On the 6th, the 4th Armored division took Ohrdruf, thirty miles east of Merkers, a small city hardly touched

[11] (1) SHAEF, G–4 Functions in ETOUSA Operations, Merkers–Herringen–Frankfurt Areas of Germany, 9 Apr to 22 Apr 45, in CMH files. (2) Hist Rpt, 12th AGp, ACofS G–5, 1–30 Apr 45, in SHAEF G–5, 17.16, Jacket 10. (3) Rpt, SHAEF, G–5, Col Bernstein to Brig Gen F. J. McSherry, sub: Developments in Removal of Treasure from Kaiseroda Mine at Merkers, Germany, 18 Apr 45, in SHAEF, G–5, 1/13. (4) Cable, SHAEF Main, Eisenhower for CCS, CCAC, 6 May 45, in SHAEF G–5, 1/13. (5) Cable, SHAEF to AGWAR, 18 Apr 45, in USFET SGS 123.3.

by the war. Atop a hill on the outskirts stood a row of empty stone SS barracks. On a nearby hill was a cluster of low, dirty, and weather-beaten wooden buildings. This was Ohrdruf–Nord, work camp for the Buchenwald concentration camp. When the troops entered, they found twenty-nine bodies on the ground in front of the administration building. A short distance away was a gallows and not far beyond it a shed in which fifty-two naked bodies were stacked in tiers of four, covered with what appeared to be powdered lime. They apparently had been awaiting transportation to pits in the forest where between two and three thousand others had been buried during the six months the camp had existed. Most had died of disease, but most also had marks on their faces and heads and bruises on their bodies. A third group, nine charred torsos, lay among ashes under a rough incinerator made of railroad ties and rails. Those in front of the administration building were the most recently dead—all shot in the back of the neck.

Ohrdruf–Nord was not a proper concentration camp. It had no gas chamber or high-performance crematorium. The deaths there were caused by disease and neglect, helped along by overwork and brutality. The inmates had been employed at digging a tunnel, probably as a site for an underground factory. A thousand had been there a week before the Americans came. In the succeeding days the guards had marched those who could walk away to the east. At noon on the 6th two busses had come to take out the bedridden sick. By then American artillery fire could be heard coming close, and the commandant lost his nerve, sent the busses away empty, and shot the prisoners with his pistol. A dozen men had hidden in the camp buildings and survived to tell about the last days at Ohrdruf-Nord and to identify the dead, among whom was an American pilot who had been imprisoned there after being shot down nearby and had contracted typhus.

Among the first persons that Lt. Col. James H. Van Wagenen, the 4th Armored's military government officer, took on a tour of the camp was Albert Schneider, *Buergermeister* of Ohrdruf. Schneider had been a party member since 1933, but he had also been an honest and conscientious mayor, and he had not skipped town ahead of the Americans as other Nazi officials were doing. He was shocked by what he saw. Admitting there had been rumors in the town, he claimed simply not to have believed Germans capable of such atrocities. On Van Wagenen's orders, he agreed to summon twenty-five prominent men and women who were to be taken to view the camp the next morning. In the morning, a soldier who had been sent to fetch him after he failed to appear at the stated time found him and his wife dead in their bedroom, their wrists slashed. G–2 investigators concluded the Schneiders' suicides were motivated by sincere shock and regret over what had happened in their town. One of the most frustrating psychological problems of the early occupation was going to be how to make the German people realize the horror of the concentration camps. In Ohrdruf, however, after the Schneiders' suicides and after others had been taken to see the camp, the citizens seemed to be convinced.[12]

The Turn to the East

The closing of the Ruhr pocket in the first week of April opened a 125-mile-wide

hole in the center of the German front. Generalfeldmarshall Walter Model's Army Group B, the 400,000 troops who should have been there, were locked in the pocket and hardly counted anymore in Bradley's decision to send his three armies' main forces racing eastward into the gap. By the week's end, Ninth and First Armies were heading across the Weser River toward Magdeburg and Leipzig. Third Army, already somewhat farther east, waited for the other two to come abreast before beginning its drive toward Chemnitz and Dresden.

V Corps jumped off from Kassel on 5 April. Like Aachen and Cologne before it, the heart of the city was bombed out. Among the ruins, the remaining 30,000 inhabitants of what had been a quarter million population rummaged for lost belongings, their own or other people's, or waited passively for what would come next. Four days later and twenty-five miles farther east, V Corps took Goettingen. Except for some bomb damage in the railroad yards and to the power plant, the war had not touched the city. The *Buergermeister* performed a formal and quite unnecessary surrender on the city hall steps. The only German troops in town were 10,000 hospitalized sick and wounded. An attempt to mobilize the local *Volkssturm* had collapsed several days before when the city commandant called such a move crazy, after learning that the men had only had ten days' training in the past six months. Swollen by refugees from Kassel and Berlin, the population was up to 70,000 from its normal 50,000 inhabitants. The University of Goettingen was open and holding some classes, until G–5, V Corps, ordered it closed in compliance with SHAEF's standing orders.

The only recorded exchange of fire in Goettingen was not between Americans

---

[12] (1) Hist Rpt, Third Army, G–5, 1–30 Apr 45, in SHAEF G–5, 17.16. (2) Hqs, 12th AGp, P&PW, Daily Summary of Intelligence, 12 and 15 Apr 45, in SHAEF G–5, 17.11, Jacket 9.

TROOPS ADVANCE THROUGH SURRENDERED TOWN

and Germans but between a German general and the *Gestapo*. General der Infanterie Friedrich Hossbach, once Hitler's adjutant but recently dismissed under a cloud for having attempted to order a breakout from East Prussia, was under treatment in the university clinic for an ear infection. Illnesses that needed to be treated in out-of-the-way places were common among German generals in those days, but Hossbach had not been forgotten. An hour before the Americans arrived, an SS major, a uniformed policeman, and two men in civilian clothes rang the doorbell of his house. Warned by friends to expect the

Gestapo, Hossbach ran out on an upstairs balcony and engaged his callers in a pistol duel until they—obviously pressed for time—ran to a car they had parked at the corner and drove off. The Americans were rather pleased to have turned up a general who had been against Hitler, not so pleased when they discovered he was "a Prussian of the old school" who despised the democracy Germany had under the Weimar Republic. Nevertheless they decided to let him keep his pistol for the time being in case his visitors returned.[13]

---

[13] (1) After Action Report, V Corps, ACofS

GERMANS DIG GRAVES *for concentration camp victims at Nordhausen.*

Nordhausen, on the edge of the Harz Mountains, is thirty-eight miles east and south of Goettingen. First Army's VII Corps, moving fast, took the town on 11 April. Again the Americans were astonished and shaken by what they uncovered: a concentration camp with 3,000 rotting, unburied bodies and 2,000 survivors all sick and nearly all in the last stages of starvation; a slave labor camp; two complete underground factories; and a treasure mine

with unusual contents. The corps G–5 rounded up several hundred German civilians to bury the dead in the concentration camp and evicted several hundred others from their homes in the town to provide accommodations for the survivors. The 23,000 displaced persons and prisoners of war in the slave labor camp had been employed in the *Mittelwerk,* one of the underground factories. In the last months they had been dying at the rate of 150 a week; and 9,000 were sick, 1,000 with tuberculosis. The *Nordwerk,* the other factory, was an assembly plant for jet aircraft engines. The *Mittelwerk* had all the equipment

G–5, Apr 45, 6 May 45, in V Corps, 205–5. (2) Hqs, 12th AGp, P&PW, Daily Summary of Intelligence, 13 and 14 Apr 45, in SHAEF G–5, 17.11, Jacket 9.

Entrance to Nordhausen V–2 Plant

needed to manufacture V–2 rockets, from the components to the completed projectile, and the Germans had left behind enough finished parts to make 250 rockets. The Berntrode Mine, outside Nordhausen, contained the remains of Frederick the Great, Frederick William I of Prussia, and Paul von Hindenburg and his wife; the Prussian royal regalia, scepter, orb, crowns, helmet, broadsword, and seal; over two hundred regimental standards; the best books from the Prussian royal library; several dozen palace tapestries; and 271 paintings, all valuable, among them several by Lucas Cranach. The MFA&A officers could find

only one defect in the mine as a storage place: although it was dry and had a constant temperature, it had been used since 1937 to house a munitions factory and still held 400,000 tons of ammunition, some of it in highly doubtful condition.[14]

Between Goettingen and Nordhausen, First Army had crossed into the future Soviet zone, as Ninth Army also did at the

---

[14] (1) Hist Rpt, 12th AGp, ACofS G–5, May 45, in SHAEF G–5, 17.16, Jacket 11. (2) Hist Rpt, First Army, ACofS G–5, 1–30 Apr 45, in SHAEF G–5, 17.11, Jacket 10. (3) Memo, Hqs, USFET, sub: Nordhausen Caverns, 7 Jun 45, in USFET SGS 600.6, vol. 1.

same time on its drive to Magdeburg. The military government carpet had been getting thinner since the beginning of the month because it had been stretched east and north at the same time that the pinpoint locations in the south were being uncovered. When they entered the Soviet zone, the armies ran completely out of trained detachments, and from the zone border west to the Rhine they could not achieve even the planned minimum of one I detachment for every two *Landkreise.* ECAD had begun training its officer overstrength, but the first hundred would not be available until the third week in April, and the last hundred not until late May. The armies resorted to provisional detachments and drew the personnel from their own tactical troops. Ninth Army set up the Ninth Army Military Government Unit, modeled on an ECAD regiment, with 3 companies, 49 detachments, and 900 officers and men. The detachments trained for two weeks. First Army put a thousand officers and men into fifty-two provisional detachments, two more than the total of its regular military government detachments, and assigned one trained ECAD officer to each provisional detachment. Third Army's three corps used antiaircraft, field artillery, and signal troops to put together a dozen detachments apiece, and the army G–5 ran fifty officers through "Charlottesville in three days" in Frankfurt. In all armies, the corps and division G–5 staffs took over detachment functions. The 80th Infantry Division G–5, for instance, in mid-April conducted military government in Erfurt, Weimar, Jena, and Gera.[15]

A 4th Armored Division tank column heading east past Weimar on 11 April encountered one of the strangest sights of the war. Two PWD observers, 1st Lt. Edward A. Tennenbaum and Egon W. Fleck, a civilian, described what they saw.

[We] turned a corner onto a main highway and saw thousands of ragged, hungry looking men marching in orderly formation, marching east. The men were armed and had leaders at their sides. Some platoons carried rifles. Some platoons had *Panzerfausts* on their shoulders. Some carried hand grenades. They laughed and waved wildly as they walked. Their captains saluted gravely for them. They were of many nationalities, a platoon of French followed by a platoon of Spaniards—platoons of Russians, Poles, Jews, Dutch. Some wore striped convict suits, some ragged U.N. uniforms, some shreds of civilian clothes. These were the inmates of Buchenwald walking to war as tanks roared by at twenty-five miles per hour.[16]

The tank officers ordered the marchers to turn back, and Fleck and Tennenbaum left the column to have a look at the camp. There they found another fantastic scene. Armed inmates stood guard at the main gate, a two-story, wooden structure bearing in large letters across the entrance the motto *"Recht oder Unrecht, mein Vaterland"* (Right or wrong, my Fatherland). Inside, wildly cheering prisoners rushed to shake their hands. Others were busy throwing binoculars manufactured in the camp shops over the barbed wire fence to troops passing by outside. Armed guards in prison clothes patrolled the grounds, and a few words from them were enough to quiet the excited crowds. The Americans noticed at once that the guards looked healthier than the others and later learned why: they were mostly German communists who had sur-

[15] (1) After Action Report, First Army, 1–30 Apr 45, in First Army, 101–0.3. (2) Hist Rpt, Hqs, Third Army, ACofS G–5, Apr 45, in SHAEF G–5, 17.10. (3) Hqs, Ninth Army, ACofS G–5, Bi-weekly CASUM, 8 May 45, in Ninth Army G–5, 109–5.

[16] Hqs, 12th AGp, P&PW, sub: Buchenwald, a Preliminary Report, 24 Apr 45, in SHAEF G–5, 17.11, Jacket 10.

SURVIVORS OF BUCHENWALD

vived by helping the SS manage the camp as they were now helping the Americans.

Opened in 1937, Buchenwald was a camp with a history reaching back into the prewar Nazi era. Inside one building, Fleck and Tennenbaum saw a thousand sealed tin cans containing the unclaimed ashes of prisoners who had died in the 1930s. Such niceties had long ago stopped being observed. In the SS offices and quarters they saw lamp shades, bookends, and other bric-a-brac decorated with tanned, tattooed human skin, products of one of the hobbies of former commandant Karl Koch's wife. The Koch regime, which ended in 1943, had been the most bestial. Since then the camp had been run to get maximum work from the prisoners with minimum food and maintenance. At the end the death rate was about two hundred prisoners a day; but the 50,000 who died there in the eight years before 1945 were not enough to rank Buchenwald with Auschwitz or the other extermination camps.

In appearance Buchenwald was everything, and more, that the Americans had imagined a concentration camp to be. An immense barbed wire fence, screened on the outside by a dense pine forest, enclosed the rows of one-story hutments of the main camp and the twenty-seven low, wooden barns encircled by barbed wire that were known as the little camp. The "little camp" was the quarantine station for new prisoners, permanent quarters for Jews, and the assembly area for transports to the death camps. Tennenbaum and Fleck noticed when they arrived that the gates to this section were closed and guarded. The "aristocrats" in the main camp did not allow the little camp to join their freedom celebration. To the right of the main gate, off the edge of the parade ground where the prisoners (as many as 90,000 in 1944) had stood for morning and evening roll call, was the crematorium, separately enclosed by a high board fence. The incinerator, a model of technical efficiency, could reduce a "charge," eighteen bodies, to ashes in about twenty minutes. The basement housed the furnace and the "strangling room," a novel installation even in the macabre world of concentration camps. At ground level, condemned prisoners were hurried through a door into a short, narrow corridor with a four-by-four-foot opening in the floor at the far end. Through the opening they fell thirteen feet to the concrete basement floor where, if the fall did not kill them as it often did not, SS men garroted them and hung the bodies on hooks along the wall until the incinerator crew was ready for them upstairs. The crematorium had been shut down for a time in March, when the coal supply ran out, but had been running again in April. The SS guards had not had time to clean up the evidence before they fled the camp on the 10th, and they left behind a truckload of naked corpses in the yard and unconsumed bones and skulls on the incinerator grates.

There were 21,000 prisoners in Buchenwald at the liberation, about half the number that had been there a week earlier. The SS had marched the others east, toward Leipzig. U.S. fighter planes were keeping the columns in view but could not fire without endangering prisoners.

The 12th Army Group had assigned responsibility for the concentration camps to the Displaced Persons Executive (DPX), and on the day after liberation 1st Lt. Walter F. Emmons, commanding DP Detachment 10, took charge in Buchenwald. He had food and clothing brought in from German stocks in Weimar and Jena and set up an emergency hospital in the SS barracks, where inmate physicians gave seventy blood transfusions from the American blood bank the first day. On the fourth and fifth days, to reduce the death rate, which was far less than before but was still about twenty a day, the 66th Medical Battalion and a complete 500-bed evacuation hospital came in with enough medical supplies to treat the 5,000 cases needing immediate attention. By then 700 cases had been treated, and Germans had been put to work improving the sanitation.

A particular problem for Emmons and his detachment was the multitude of visitors that descended upon them and their charges. The tactical troops, as always, moved on quickly, but after them came newspaper reporters and visitors from other headquarters and from Allied governments and armies. Buchenwald had been an international camp, and among the thirty-one nationalities represented there were men prominent in various fields in their own countries. The prisoners' desire to be away from the place and the visitors' eagerness to do something for them resulted in numerous unauthorized departures; before long, reports were coming back of cases in which former inmates died before reaching home. Finally, 12th Army Group had to prohibit visits to liberated concentration camps without approval of the army commanders.[17]

In the second week of April the dam broke. Until then, the Germans had herded as many displaced persons and prisoners of war as they could eastward, as they had done earlier in the Rhineland. Between the Weser and the Elbe they ran out of space. The Soviet advance to the Oder River had also raised a wave of refugees, prisoners of war, and displaced persons that had filled central Germany and was continuing westward. Ninth Army encountered columns of American and British prisoners who had been on the road since January, first marching west from camps in Poland and then recently headed east again. The other RAMPs (recovered Allied military personnel) were mostly mixed with the civilian DPs, both groups having been used as ordinary industrial and farm labor.[18]

Maj. Philip Shafer, head of the DPX, Third Army, had one officer and two enlisted men under him on 1 April. In the field he had twelve DP detachments (eighty-seven officers and men); thirteen French *Mission Militaire Liaison Administrative* (MMLA) welfare teams, each with one officer, a male driver, and two or three enlisted women; and a scattering of French, Belgian, Dutch, and Polish liaison and medical officers. Totaling 230 individuals, they were soon having to deal with 1,500 times their own number of DPs and RAMPs. A dozen UNRRA teams and eleven emergency DP detachments added during the month were barely enough to keep the ratio from going higher.[19] The armies formed fifty-one DP detachments, received forty-three UNRRA teams and a like number of MMLA teams, and still had to divert tactical units ranging up to the size of a division (the whole 29th Infantry Division for instance) to DPX duties. By 16 April they had uncovered a million DPs, and they would pass their second million before the month was out. Ninth Army issued 200,000 rations a day; First Army, over a million a week. The food came mostly from captured stocks, but First Army also requisitioned 20,000 tons of imported military government relief supplies. Ninth Army used four seven-story buildings in a former German Army complex near Muenster as its supply center. The 12th Army Group reported 350 camps established with capacities between 3,000 and 30,000 persons.[20]

As had happened in the Rhineland, the DPs' first impulse was to get away from where they were; and once they did, they seemed beset with the desire to keep moving. The former prisoners of war, especially the French and Belgians, who remembered the lessons of 1940, kept off the roads. To reduce the flow of the others, the armies set up checkpoints and patrols on the main roads and had them turn over the DPs to the nearest village *Buergermeister* with orders to house and feed them from local resources. The rivers, from the Rhine eastward, helped somewhat to keep the DPs' wanderings compartmentalized.

[17] (1) Hist Rpt, Third Army, ACofS G–5, Apr 45, in SHAEF G–5, 17.11. (2) SHAEF, G–5, Hist Sec, sub: Report on German Concentration Camp for Political Prisoners at Buchenwald by Lt. Col. F. van Wyck Mason, in SHAEF G–5, 60, Jacket 3. (3) USFET, General Board, Study No. 35, p. 20. (4) Eugen Kogon, *The Theory and Practice of Hell* (New York: Farrar, Straus, 1950), pp. 48–57.
[18] After Action Report, Hqs, Ninth Army, ACofS G–5, 1–15 Apr 45, in Ninth Army 109–1.

[19] Hist Rpt, Hqs, Third Army, ACofS G–5, Apr 45, in SHAEF G–5, 17.11.
[20] Hist Rpt, 12th AGp, ACofS G–5, Apr 45, in SHAEF G–5, 17.16, Jacket 10.

Expecting that they could be started on their way home soon after a junction with the Soviet forces was made, the DPX wanted to hold the eastern Europeans as far east as possible. The French, Belgians, and Dutch were repatriated as fast as transportation could be found, as many as 5,000 a day from each of the armies (46,000 from Ninth Army in April and 74,000 from Third Army). When, as the front advanced to the east, the armies were less and less able to spare their own trucks to haul the DPs back to the railroads, the DPX secured fifty French truck companies to keep the repatriates moving; and on 11 April, Third Army began a westbound DP airlift from Frankfurt.

The psychology and behavior of the DPs, if no longer a shock, were as much a puzzle and a problem as they had been in the Rhineland. The PWD observers again were the least alarmed. Padover and Gittler reported:

On the German highways and byways one sees a veritable *Voelkerwanderung*—thousands, tens of thousands of men, in small groups and large, carrying bundles, carrying suitcases strapped to their backs, carrying bulging handbags, are marching east and marching west. Many wear shabby green uniforms—they are Red Army PWs. Frenchmen and Belgians also still wear their old army uniforms, now almost in tatters. Poles and Dutchmen and Serbs wear any kind of rags. Their German masters had not kept them in clothes. They were surprisingly cheerful, surprisingly orderly.

Now they all march . . . in the direction of home. Occasionally they help themselves to chickens or loaves of bread or a pair of pants, but they are orderly and obedient, even the French. There seems to be no vengeance in these people, no lust for destruction, no desire to make the Germans pay for what they have done to them, to their countries.

There is much talk about looting. German farmers say the Eastern workers are stealing their chickens. German workers say that the Russians are breaking into homes and helping themselves to necessities. German middle-class people say that Russians are animals. The truth is that the Eastern workers are astonishingly well-behaved.[21]

On the other hand, in half the military government court cases tried in the Ninth Army area during April, the accused were DPs. Looting often declined dramatically in the vicinity of tightly controlled camps, but not all the DPs wanted to live in the camps. Some preferred to experience their new found freedom to the fullest. Others were not exactly the innocent victims of nazism that the Americans presumed them to be and did not want to risk being recognized. Many wandered cross-country or along back roads living on what they could beg or steal. Sometimes they formed armed gangs of thirty or forty men and turned to outright banditry. Such groups would not hesitate to skirmish with patrols sent to flush them out, and on at least one occasion AWOL U.S. soldiers were caught with them. The military government reports agree, however, that the DPs, including the most restless and unruly among them, were completely friendly to Americans and that the trouble they caused was vastly less than it might have been had they chosen to use the power inherent in their numbers to take organized vengeance on the Germans.

Among the DPs, the former prisoners of war were usually the easiest to handle. They knew the necessity for discipline and, after years in captivity, wanted to refurbish their self-esteem by contributing to the victory. In the camps and assembly centers, the French usually were quick to establish order among themselves. The Russians were less ready to organize independently,

---

[21] Gittler and Padover, "Up the Weser River," in SHAEF G-5, 17.11, Jacket 9.

and the camp detachments often had to call on the Soviet liaison officers, as Detachment H1G3 did in the following:

5 April 1945

Col. Niccolai Lischnevsky of the Russian Army visited the camp on an inspection tour and was advised by Maj. [George B.] Mehlman that the Russian leader was very conscientious and hard working but that he lacked the ability to obtain obedience or discipline from the Russian group. Maj. Mehlman requested the Russian colonel to appoint a new leader and vest in him the authority of his office. Col. Lischnevsky ordered that all the Russians be assembled in one group in order that he might speak to them. When they had been assembled, the colonel harangued them at length on the fact that they were being placed under the protection of the U.S. military and that he was directly ordering them to obey all orders given them and that he was going to appoint new leaders and establish within the Russian group regular Russian Army discipline and that he was forming battalions, companies, and squads and that discipline and obedience must be rigidly enforced. Col. Lischnevsky ordered all the former Russian Army officers and NCOs to fall in, dismissing the rest. He personally interviewed and selected from the group of former Russian officers a new Russian leader and staff, battalion commanders, company commanders, company officers and NCOs.[22]

The detachments learned early that the Russians and other eastern Europeans were frequently quite willing to settle down to the good life in camps that offered welfare programs and luxuries, particularly liquor and radios. The trouble was that their expectations escalated rapidly, and their demands kept increasing. Since the luxuries had to come from the Germans, limits were soon reached. During the month, First Army provided each of its DP detachments with a security guard detail, which was by far the most effective, if not the most desirable, means of DP control.[23]

While the DP flood had come later than expected, that of the surrendering German troops came earlier. The plans had anticipated U.S. prisoner of war holdings to reach about 900,000 by 30 June 1945. On 15 April 1.3 million prisoners were in U.S. hands. Another 600,000 captures were expected in the next two weeks and at least that many more in May. Legally they were all entitled to the basic rations and quarters furnished to U.S. troops of the same rank. In fact, however, SHAEF had never contemplated extending such treatment to so many German soldiers. Expecting the big wave of prisoners to come with the surrender or collapse, SHAEF proposed to take advantage of the EAC surrender provisions and create the category "disarmed German troops," which would make the bulk of the *Wehrmacht* a German responsibility pending disbandment. In April, however, the war was still on; American prisoners were still in German hands; and 30,000 Germans were already surrendering every day. By mid-April, SHAEF had allocated 50 U.S. officers, 4,000 enlisted men, and 13 antiaircraft battalions to prisoner of war guard duty. Just west of the Rhine, 12th Army Group was settting up four huge enclosures which could hold 50,000 men each but which would not have shelters "or other comforts" until the prisoners themselves built them from local materials.[24]

---

[22] H1G3, War Diary, Mar–Jun 45, in OMGUS 413/3/3.

[23] Hist Rpts, 12th AGp, First Army, Third Army, and Ninth Army, Apr 45.

[24] (1) SHAEF, G–1, PWX Br, sub: Report on Enemy POWs, 19 Apr 45, in SHAEF G–1, 383.6/1. (2) Cable, SHAEF Main, Eisenhower to AGWAR for CCS, sub: Armistice, Control and Disposal of German Armed Forces, 10 Mar 45, in SHAEF G–1, 387.4/1. (3) Cable, CofS SHAEF to AGWAR for Hull from Smith, 16 Apr 45, in USFET SGS 371, Germany, vol. II. (4) Cable, SHAEF, G–1, to AGWAR, sub: Equalization of

CAPTURED GERMANS IN AN IMPROVISED STOCKADE

On April 15, Lt. Col. F. Van Wyck Mason, SHAEF G–5 historian, and Capt. Jesse C. Beesley, civil affairs historian for the Communications Zone, set out from Luxembourg in a recon car to follow the route Third Army had taken into Germany. For Mason the "first point of interest" was Bad Kreuznach, twenty miles west of the Rhine crossing at Mainz. As he described it:

The military government detachment commander had his largest attacks not from the local population, but from the demands of

PWs Under 50/50 Agreement, in SHAEF G–1, 383.6/3–19.

the high brass in our own army. His time was so taken up with finding dachshund puppies for General Blank and locating people to cut the lawn for Colonel So-and-so that he was hard put to administer the town.

I had a look at the jail which was well supplied with Nazis and suspects. Then went on to the PW cage on the edge of town. We arrived at sunset and saw a breathtaking panorama, 37,000 German, Hungarian, and other Axis prisoners roaming in a caged area of about half a square mile. They certainly were not coddled there. They slept on the bare ground with whatever covering they had brought with them. They got two "C" rations a day and that was all. There was a separate enclosure for officers where they were so tightly packed they had barely room to lie down, and more trucks kept coming up every few minutes. Adjoining it was another enclosure for about 500 German WACs and non-medical personnel that were surprisingly good looking on the whole. Fortunately for them the weather was good and continued to be good for some time afterwards.

In command of the camp was a 1st Lt. of infantry with less than 300 men. The boys looked a bit serious as they crouched behind their machine guns, for there was only one strand of wire and no search lights for night time. Periodically some Germans did try to get loose, but they were always cut down before they got 50 yards distance.

From Frankfurt, the historians drove to Weimar on the *Autobahn,* and Mason found the trip a great pleasure "after bumping one's backside over the incredibly rutted and ruined roads of France." Between Frankfurt and Weimar they passed into the area in which Third Army had run out of trained military government detachments, and they "sensed that something was amiss the moment we hit Weimar":

The feeling of something being amiss was not lessened by finding German policemen in full uniform and carrying loaded carbines in front of the town hall, where apparently military government of some kind was being set up. Investigation revealed the reason. The acting Military Governor was a completely untrained Lt. Col. of the field artillery who had been firing in the line 56 hours before.

Lt. Col. Billingsley, the officer in question, seemed infinitely relieved to have trained military government officers suddenly appear, and he urgently requested that I break our trip and lend a hand in setting up military government in Weimar. This we did, among the first acts being to disarm the police and bring him up to date on directives concerning displaced persons. It appears that the whole area was under Lt. Col. Billingsley, and none of his officers had the least grounding in the responsibility and powers of military government.

Further to assist Lt. Col. Billingsley, Capt. Beesley and I undertook to visit various de-

tachments of his post in the surrounding country. In this connection we visited Erfurt, Langensalza, Mulhaus, Apolda, and Jena. All of these cities, with the exception of Apolda, had suffered from 25 to 40 percent damage. It was interesting to observe the difference in the attitude of the inhabitants in those towns which had been smashed and those which had not. Those in the unhit towns were arrogant and hostile. Such was the condition of Apolda where we found an artillery 1st Lt. and 40 men holding down a city of 70,000 normal population and at least 15,000 transients. Lt. Hurtz was doing a fine job under the circumstances but lacked knowledge of his rights. When we told him he was "Caesar" in that town, he was pleased and immediately issued orders for the arrest of the Nazi mayor and equally Nazi police chief. He listened attentively to all we said and when he realized his powers, he was a much happier boy than he had been a couple of hours earlier. Because of the attitude of the inhabitants, we arranged to station a particularly hardboiled battalion of infantry in that town.[25]

While Mason and Beesley were at Weimar, First Army's V Corps on 19 April took Leipzig, the fourth largest city in Germany. To control the city, swollen by DPs and refugees from its normal 700,000 population to over a million, the corps designated Col. Jim Dan Hill, Commanding Officer, 190th Field Artillery Group, as military commander of Leipzig and gave him three field artillery battalions, four security guard detachments, and Provisional Military Government Detachment A. Detachment A had sixteen officers and twenty-four enlisted men, but only two of the officers had even a small amount of previous military government experience. Hill and his troops entered Leipzig on the 19th while fighting was still going on in the Napoleon Platz around the Battle of the Nations Monument, which in its cav-

---

[25] SHAEF, G–5 Hist Sec, "Germany—April 1945," 5 May 45, in SHAEF G–5, 60.

SCENE OF THE ATROCITY AT THEKLA

ernous stone base provided cover for a die-hard German colonel and a company or so of soldiers. Some sections of the city were destroyed. Other sections were untouched, however, and in them the electric service continued without a break, water service could be restored in a few days, and the streetcar system required only minor repairs to wire and track. The Nazi *Ober-buergermeister*, his deputy, and their families had committed suicide. Hill divided the city into three military police zones and put a battalion in each zone; the Germans, however, were not as much a threat to order as the Allied liaison

officers who, he complained, "tend to get emotional with the DPs and get them all stirred up." His main difficulty with the Germans was getting them adjusted to doing common labor. They had become accustomed to having foreign workers do the menial jobs.[26]

At Thekla, just outside Leipzig, V Corps uncovered a small concentration camp. On the afternoon of the day before, the guards had herded over three hundred inmates

---

[26] Hqs, 190th FA Gp to CG ,V Corps, Report of Military Commander, Stadtkreis Leipzig, 7 May 45, and After Action Report, Hqs, V Corps, Apr 45, 6 May 45, in V Corps 205–5.

into a wooden barracks building, doused it with gasoline, and set it on fire with thermite grenades. Those who ran from the building were shot. When the Americans entered, the fire was still burning, and seventy-five bodies were hanging on the concertina wire and electrically charged barbed wire surrounding the camp. Somehow about a hundred had managed to escape to freedom. In accordance with standing instructions from Eisenhower to make the Germans bury atrocity victims in the most prominent and suitable spot in the nearest town, military government ordered the newly appointed Leipzig *Buergermeister* to supply seventy-five caskets and two hundred German civilians to dig the graves. The site was the parkway along the main road into Leipzig's most beautiful cemetery, the *Suedfriedhof*. The city also had to provide a cross and a wreath for each grave, and all city officials and a hundred other prominent citizens were required to attend the funeral. Three U.S. chaplains, representing the three faiths, conducted the service. Several hundred DPs dropped flowers on the graves as, a reporter noted, "did a few of the nearly 900 Germans who attended voluntarily."[27]

Mason and Beesley saw Leipzig the day after it was taken:

There were plenty of dead bodies and still burning houses in the suburbs. The troops carried their arms in very handy positions. Rivers of prisoners were driving out of Leipzig in supply trucks, going back empty to the railheads. Leipzig was terribly smashed in the center but some of the suburbs seem to be in pretty fair shape. The *Buergermeister* and the *Oberbuergermeister* committed sui-

cide together with their families. We saw the latter group at the office—the father, the mother, and a very pretty 18-year old daughter.

The police problem in a city of this size was of a special interest to me, so we spent the bulk of our time with Colonel Green, Public Safety Officer on Colonel Hill's staff. He had, of course, disarmed [the police] and required them to wear uniform caps, trousers, and boots but with civilian coats. He said it was necessary because so many trigger-happy "doughfeet" were loose and had shot half a dozen of his men the day before thinking they were soldiers. The uniforms were distinctly similar. Such police as remained were stolidly obeying orders and arresting their previous bosses just as happily as they had political victims a few days earlier.

Colonel Hill invited us to join him in listening to the nomination of a new *Buergermeister* for Leipzig. It was a solemn bunch of Boche who appeared. One thing they were very anxious to know—would the Russians gain eventual possession of their city?[28]

The two staff historians had, half seriously, hoped to end their trip in Berlin. Mason, a World War I veteran, regarded this occasion as his second attempt to get there, but he was disappointed again. Ninth Army was stopped on the Elbe, not much more than a day's march from Berlin, but Eisenhower had decided that the army would go no farther. When Mason and Beesley started back from Leipzig, they also missed what could have been the next best finale for their trip, the American-Soviet link-up on 25 April at Torgau on the Elbe River, thirty miles east of Leipzig. A night stop at Muenden, north of Kassel, however, produced a rare experience, a reasonably bona fide encounter with the *Werwolf* organization:

That evening, Squadron Leader Gordon Freisen [the local military government de-

[27] Hist Rpt, First Army, ACofS G–5, 1–30 Apr 45, and Press Release, First Army, G–5 PRO, sub: Burial of Atrocity Victims [no date], in SHAEF G–5, 17.11, Jacket 10.

[28] SHAEF, G–5 Hist Sec, "Germany—April 1945," 5 May 45, in SHAEF G–5, 60.

tachment was British] . . . invited us to assist in the interrogation of a pair of Hitler Jugend toughs caught with a notched pistol and a supply of explosives near one of our bridges. Their attitude was typical, at first openly defiant, then as hunger and fatigue began to work, more and more malleable. The amusing thing about these youths and the Nazis we subsequently questioned was their complete willingness to betray one another once they were convinced that a friend had tattled, and it required very little persuasion to convince them that they had been betrayed. To the disappointment of some of our men, it was quite unnecessary to become physical in the interrogation.

As a result we organized a raiding party of four officers and six enlisted men. We picked up three Nazis in possession of illegal arms. All of them lied like troopers to start with, but invariably would lead us to where the weapons were hidden—generally under the eaves of an outbuilding. It was very picturesque because of the full moon and the light it threw from the helmets and weapons of the men. . . .

We topped off the evening with a raid on an inn in the suburbs which had been established as a sort of headquarters for the local "werewolves." One of the Hitler youths had admitted that there were four female military personnel at the inn, one of which was his sweety. He betrayed her quite cheerfully. The result was, we swooped down on the inn and ransacked the place thoroughly. Among other things, flushing a G.I. who was certainly qualified for the sixty-five dollar question.[29]

The next day Mason and Beesley crossed into Luxembourg "where people smiled and waved, and one could look at a pretty girl without having that sixty-five dollars in the back of one's mind."

Into the Redoubt

Seventh Army's primary mission during the first three weeks in April was to cover the 12th Army Group's south flank. In doing so the army bore east and slightly

north across northern Baden and Wuerttemberg and into Bavaria. The German defense on the Rhine had been weak, and at the end of March, Seventh Army held a bridgehead that tied in with Third Army's on the north and reached south across the Neckar River and embraced the cities of Mannheim and Heidelberg.

The pinpoint detachments were standing by. F1E2, under Lt. Col. Charles D. Winning, moved into badly damaged Mannheim on 28 March, and I2E2, Capt. Albert Haskell in command, took over in Heidelberg two days later. Having become accustomed in the Rhineland to seeing nothing but flattened cities, the Americans were surprised to find Heidelberg completely undamaged. The university was intact, and the shops and banks stayed open while the city changed hands. The *Buergermeister* and the city officials were at work, except for the police chief who had disappeared along with the men of his force. The war had not completely bypassed Heidelberg however. Its electric power came from Mannheim, and until the lines and plants were repaired there would not be any, nor would there be any water, because the pumps in the water system were electric. The people, 24,000 more than the 86,000 peacetime population, looked well fed, but the food situation was close to catastrophic. The whole municipal reserve was one trainload of potatoes, flour, and canned beef fat that had become stranded in the railroad yards after the bombing had cut all the rail lines.[30]

East of Heidelberg, the Germans seemed determined again to show they had some bite left in them. Heilbronn held out under bombing and artillery fire from 5 to 12

---

[29] *Ibid.*

[30] Wk Rpt, Hqs, XXI Corps, to CG, Seventh Army, 31 Mar 45, in SHAEF G–5, 17.18, Jacket 5.

HEIDELBERG, MARCH 1945

April, and so many people were buried in the ruins "that Heilbronn had a noticeable stench all during the summer of 1945."[31] At Nuremberg, eighty-five miles farther east, the Germans put up a four-day fight, from 16 to 20 April, that brought down a final wave of destruction on the already badly bombed old city—a wave which unfortunately hit the medieval relics much harder than it did the banal structures in which the Nazis had staged their prewar party rallies.

[31] History of Military Government in Land Wuerttemberg–Baden to 30 June 1946, pt. I, p. 124, in OMGUS 409–3/3.

Lt. Col. Delbert O. Fuller took Detachment E1B3, fifteen officers and ten enlisted men, into Nuremberg on the 21st. The population was a third its normal 450,000. A hunt for the city officials turned up the *Oberbuergermeister* and the *Gauleiter* of Franconia dead in the *Gestapo* headquarters. They had killed themselves. Only a few city employees responded to the order to report for work that was broadcasted by sound trucks. The police headquarters was demolished, and nearly all the police were prisoners of war. Germans and DPs looted food warehouses undeterred by the 225 streetcar conductors that the detach-

NUREMBERG, APRIL 1945

ment had drafted as temporary police, and reports of rape and robbery by U.S. troops piled up on the public safety officer's desk. An MFA&A survey showed that thirty-two of sixty-five listed artistic monuments had been totally demolished and another eighteen badly damaged; fragments of valuable, centuries-old stonework and sculpture mixed in with the rubble promised to make the clean-up job in the city unusually long and painstaking.[32]

The fight for Nuremberg was a last flicker in a dying war. From the Rhine to the Elbe, Germany was subdued, and the staffs were polishing the ECLIPSE plans. (See above, p. 163.) Although it could not begin as an operation until either the Germans surrendered or Eisenhower declared them defeated, ECLIPSE was already in effect as a condition for the greater part of the SHAEF area in Germany.[33] GOLD-CUP (see above, p. 177) was ready, but that it could be put into effect was becoming increasingly doubtful. The most recent planning had added to GOLDCUP the SHAEF Special Echelon, 287 officers and

---

[32] Hist Rpt, Det B–211, 20 Jun 46, in OMGUS 81–3/10.

[33] SHAEF, G–3, ECLIPSE Memorandum No. 1, 25 Apr 45, in SHAEF SGS 387/2.

869 enlisted men, charged with making contact with the Soviet element of the Control Council and beginning to set up the central Allied authority for Germany; thus far, however, the Russians had not given any sign of being willing to establish direct contacts. The Special Echelon's destination was presumed to be Berlin, but as to how the force would get there, SHAEF could only say, "It is . . . probable that the forces of SHAEF will only enter Berlin on Soviet invitation, possibly as a result of negotiations at the governmental level."[34] The Ministerial Control Group, broken up into seventy control parties, had a more promising future. SHAEF had attached ministerial control parties to the T (Target) Sub-Division, G–2, which was sending its own teams across Germany behind the armies to gather scientific and industrial intelligence. When the teams came upon documents or personnel of possible political value, they called forward the appropriate ministerial control party. Experience was bearing out, to a greater degree than had been expected, the assumption that the German government would be dispersed outside Berlin. Bits and pieces of governmental agencies were turning up in widely scattered locations, such as Army High Command records in the Merkers mine and the cryptographic section of the Foreign Ministry in a castle outside Leipzig. Most were valuable finds for various reasons but, nevertheless, were only fragments, not the substance of government.[35]

On 22 April, Seventh Army and Third Army turned south into the area of the redoubt. From the outset the operation had more the character of ECLIPSE than of OVERLORD. The Germans were finished and neither in the condition nor in the mood to make a last ditch stand anywhere, even in the mountain strongholds of Bavaria. Seventh Army's 10th Armored Division took twenty-eight towns in a single day on 23 April. By the 27th, both armies had crossed the Danube, and the cities of Ulm, Augsburg, and Regensburg were in their hands. Where pinpoint detachments were available they generally moved in on the same day as the combat troops. Ulm, for its size the most heavily bombed city in the south, was a ruin. Water-filled bomb craters covered blocks where factories and houses had once stood. The streets were rough paths through the rubble. But the 500-year-old Gothic cathedral still stood, towering above the flattened city around it.[36] At Augsburg, a German civilian, Franz Hesse, driving his own automobile, led the tanks of 3d Battalion, 15th Infantry, through the roadblocks and into the city to receive the garrison commander's surrender.[37]

Third Army's march took it across the border into Czechoslovakia, where, being on liberated territory, military government again became civil affairs but, as civil affairs, functioned more in the manner of military government because the Sudeten Germans outnumbered the Czechs by ten to one. On entering Czechoslovakia, Third Army encountered a new problem, German DPs. A quarter million Silesian Germans fleeing the Russians took refuge in the U.S.-occupied area before roadblocks were set up to stop them. They were in desperate straits, having no place to turn for assis-

[34] SHAEF, G–3, Plan GOLDCUP, 18 Apr 45, in SHAEF G–3, 21550/2/3.
[35] Memo, SHAEF, ACofS G–2, for Distribution, sub: Ministerial Control Parties, in SHAEF G–5, 803/2.

[36] History of Military Government in Land Wuerttemberg-Baden, pt. I, p. 126.
[37] CO, 15th Infantry, to CG, 3d Infantry Div, 30 Apr 45, in OMGUS 76–1/10.

MASS FUNERAL *for concentration camp prisoners murdered by their guards in the last days of the war.*

tance. Military government put some in camps and billeted others with the Sudeten Germans and gave them subsistence from captured German rations.[38] At the Flossenburg concentration camp, ten miles from the Czech border, 186 typhus cases raised the threat of an epidemic, especially from the 16,000 prisoners that the SS guards were marching south, ahead of the front. 26th Division G–5 kept track of the exodus by the trail of bodies and hastily dug mass graves the prisoner columns left behind.[39]

The Germans were conquered and their property was "liberated." Looting had become something of an art. Soldiers stationed themselves outside military government offices and intercepted civilians bringing in weapons. Tactical units posted their own contraband lists in which they included items as various as automobiles and jewelry, and the military government de-

---

[38] After Action Report, Hqs, V Corps, ACofS G–5, May 45, in V Corps G–5, 205–5.

[39] Hist Rpt, Third Army, ACofS G–5, Apr 45, in SHAEF G–5, 17.11.

GERMANS AND DPs CARRYING LOOT

tachments acquired a new and, for the most part, unwelcome function as tactical commands and individual high-ranking officers requisitioned items of doubtful military usefulness through them. The retreating *Wehrmacht* troops had confiscated many bicycles and automobiles. The U.S. troops took most of the rest.[40] In the last week of April SHAEF stopped accepting *Reichsmark* currency for exchange into

dollars because tremendous amounts dubiously acquired were known to be in the hands of the troops.[41]

Since the U.S. troops, German civilians, and DPs all looted, there was some debate over whose behavior was the most reprehensible. In the DPs defense it was frequently said that they took only food, clothing, and items for their own comfort. The Americans could claim the sanction of military custom. But the Germans stole from each other. On the other hand, the

[40] (1) History of Military Government in Land Wuerttemberg–Baden, pt. I, p. 127. (2) Hist Rpt, Det I4B2, 14 May 45, in SHAEF G–5, 17.11, Jacket 7. (3) War Diary, Det HIG3, Mar to Jun 45, in OMGUS 413–3/3.

[41] SHAEF, ACofS G–5, Financial Br, Report of Conference Held at SHAEF Forward, 25 Apr 45, in SHAEF G–5, 1.

urge to loot was shortest lived among the Germans, and the military government detachments discovered that in their home communities the Germans lacked the anonymity and mobility of the troops and the DPs and could often be prevailed upon to return what they had taken. In Ansbach, the *Landkreis* food officer put out an order demanding the return of all looted stocks and got back more than he knew had been taken. In Bensheim, the German police chief recovered a hundred tons of *Wehrmacht* supplies by hinting that he was about to begin making arrests.[42]

Dachau, fifteen miles northwest of Munich, was the largest concentration camp captured by U.S. forces. Its rolls listed 65,000 prisoners—32,000 in the main compound and the rest in satellite work camps. The Americans came on 29 April, a Sunday. Work had stopped in the camp on Wednesday, and an evacuation was being organized. One transport of 4,000 prisoners was able to get away, but the 45th Infantry Division covered the forty miles from the Danube faster than the Germans expected. At noon on Sunday the camp was quiet, and the SS guards were at their posts in the towers when the cry "Americans!" went up. A prisoner rushed toward the gate, and a guard shot him. Outside, a single American soldier stood looking casually at the towers while the guards eyed him and others who were two or three hundred yards away. When the Americans opened fire, the guards in the gate tower came down, hands in the air. One held a pistol behind his back, and the first American shot him. In the next few minutes a jeep drove up; in it were a blond woman war correspondent and a chaplain. The chaplain asked the prisoners, now crowding

to the gate, to join him in the Lord's Prayer.[43]

Dachau, dating back to 1933, was among the first concentration camps set up in Germany and the only one with an unbroken existence through the whole Nazi period. It had all the appurtenances: the motto over the gate (*Arbeit macht Frei*, Work Liberates), the electrically charged barbed wire fence, the gas chamber, the crematorium, the starved prisoners, and the presence of death in the form of human bodies piled like logs. Bad as it was, the prisoners considered Dachau to be superior to hard labor camps like Ohrdruf and vastly superior to death camps like Mauthausen.[44] Most Americans found such distinctions hard to comprehend but not those who also saw Mauthausen when it was uncovered a week later.[45]

Seventh Army G–5 had prepared for Dachau. On the morning after liberation two batteries of the 601st Field Artillery, three truckloads of food and medical supplies, and a public address sound truck arrived. Col. Kenneth E. Worthing, G–5, XV Corps, took command, and Detachment I13G3 assumed military government responsibility for the camp and the city of Dachau. The 3,500 bodies stacked in several places inside the compound were left until after a war crimes investigation team made its survey. On the third day, two 400-bed evacuation hospitals, the 116th and 127th, moved in. The prisoners' daily

---

[42] Hist Rpt, Third Army, ACofS G–5, Apr 45, in SHAEF G–5, 17.11.

[43] Hqs, Seventh Army, ACofS G–2, Dachau Report [no date], in Seventh Army 107–2.0.

[44] SHAEF, PWD, Report on Dachau Concentration Camp, 12 May 45, in SHAEF G–2, GB1/C1/CS/383.7–1, Folio 2.

[45] In Mauthausen, the center of a camp complex around Linz in Austria, prisoners were worked to death in stone quarries. Third Army evacuated the 23,000 prisoners as quickly as they could be moved and burned the disease- and vermin-infested buildings to the ground.

rations, 600 calories each when the Americans arrived, was raised immediately to 1,200 and within two weeks to 2,400 calories.[46]

The small city of Dachau was, in a way, more of a discovery for the Americans than the camp itself. It had existed side by side with the camp for twelve years. The tracks on which trains brought in prisoners and carloads of corpses for the crematorium ran through the city along the Nibelungen Strasse, and the guards frequently marched prisoner work details through the streets. Asked whether they realized that in the last three months at least 13,000 people had lost their lives barely a stone's throw from them, the citizens of Dachau claimed shock and surprise and answered, *"Was koennten wir tun?"* (What could we do?). Asked whether they had seen the prisoners come in on the railroad, they insisted that the trains all came at night and that the cars were sealed. The camp had brought prosperity to Dachau, and many had profited directly from it. Those who had not benefited were more willing to talk. They said that people knew what was going on and were disturbed by it but had been afraid to say anything for fear of economic retaliation and even more afraid to do anything because the shadow of the camp also hung over them. Seventh Army G–2 reached, for the time, a remarkably charitable conclusion:

No citizen of Dachau is without a deep sense that something was wrong, terribly wrong, on the outskirts of their town. Those who really did not give a damn were few. Those who did show opposition should be

honored. But it should be pointed out in justice to the others that they were people who could seclude themselves from the community without harming their sources of income.[47]

The 45th Infantry Division troops who liberated Dachau in the afternoon on 29 April were fighting in Munich the next morning and by nightfall had, along with XV Corps' other three divisions, captured the city that was the capital of Bavaria and the birthplace of nazism. Not an industrial center, its association with nazism had, nevertheless, made Munich a target for air attacks, and in the end 80 percent of the city was damaged or destroyed. The Munich military government detachment, F1F3, under Lt. Col. Eugene Keller, arrived in the morning on the 30th. As befitted a pinpoint detachment with a year's training for its assignment, the 52-man truck and jeep column drove straight to the Marienplatz and wheeled to a stop before the city hall. A few apprehensive Germans, selected from "white lists" of non-Nazis and anti-Nazis and notified to be present, were waiting at the entrance. Keller told one to act as temporary *Buergermeister*. Some detachment officers went out in their jeeps to inspect the water, gas, sewage, and electric plants. Others inspected the police and fire departments, interviewed the leading Catholic and Lutheran clergy, or questioned educators and welfare workers. The banks were closed and the newspaper offices and radio stations seized. Sound trucks broadcasted instructions and essential world news to the population. The smart and efficient performance of the detachment was marred by only one hitch. It was one that almost all the detachments were experiencing: the

[46] Memo, Hqs, XV Corps, to CG, Seventh Army, sub: G–5 Report, Concentration Camps, Dachau, 5 May 45; Memo, SHAEF G–5, Ch, DP Br, to ACofS G–5, sub: Visit to Dachau, 19 May 45; Msg, CG, Seventh Army, to SHAEF, 9 Jun 45, in SHAEF G–5, 2711/7.3.

[47] Hqs, Seventh Army, ACofS G–2, Dachau Report [no date], in Seventh Army, 107–2.0.

MARIENPLATZ, MUNICH. *On the left, the city hall.*

tactical units habitually dumped their prisoners of war on the nearest military government office's doorstep. For the first week, the members of F1F3 shared their quarters in the city hall with a disconsolate and confused collection of prisoners.

As the cradle of nazism, Munich had been slated for especially rigorous military government, but the city from the outset proved to be as tractable as any other in Germany. In fact, Munich could claim something that the Americans had not found anywhere else in Germany, an active anti-Nazi resistance. Two underground groups, the *Freiheitsaktion Bayern* and the *Bayerische Hilfspolizei 0–7*, had staged an uprising two days before the U.S. troops arrived. Although they had not been overwhelmingly successful against the Nazis even at that late date, they were more than willing to relieve the Americans of the burden of running the city. After accepting a number of their nominees for appointments, however, military government learned that anti-Nazis could in some ways be as troublesome to handle as Nazis.[48]

---

[48] (1) Annual Hist Rpt, Det E–213, 3 Jul 46, in OMGUS 78–1/10. (2) Hqs, EUCOM, Hist Div, Special Studies, vol. 1, no. 3, Military Government in Munich, 1945–47, in CMH files.

MUNICH'S MAIN RAILROAD STATION, MAY 1945

The redoubt, if it existed, was expected to lie in the mountains south of Munich, probably centered on Hitler's vacation retreat at Berchtesgaden. To a degree, this estimate was correct. In mid-March, Hitler had belatedly given orders to set up a fortress in the mountains, and since then trainloads of goods and material had been funneled by the hundreds into southern Germany—partly because they had nowhere else to go. At war's end there were over 8,000 locomotives south of the Main River, twice the number ordinarily operating there. Loaded boxcars blocking the ramps and stations had contributed to the railroad breakdown. The Munich division of the *Reichsbahn* had a 14,000-car jam that was not fully unsnarled as late as June 1945.[49] The buildup, such as it was, had centered at Berchtesgaden where Hitler had contemplated establishing his headquarters if he was driven out of Berlin. He had spent several months each year during the war in his retreat on the Obersalzberg and had a communications center nearby that was

---

[49] (1) Hist Rpt, OMGB, Transportation Br, Jun 46, in OMGUS 65–11/0. (2) OMGUS, Control Office, Hist Br, History of U.S. Military Government in Germany, 8 May 45–30 June 46, Jul 47, in OMGUS 23–1/5, Folder XIV–6.

as good as the one the Army maintained for him at Zossen outside Berlin. On the night of Hitler's birthday, 20 April, Reichsmarschall Hermann Goering, assorted lesser Nazi big shots, and sections of the armed forces, army, and air force staffs had moved to Berchtesgaden expecting Hitler to follow in a few days, since the Russians had by then almost encircled Berlin. Thousands of laborers had worked day and night for a month building fortifications, and weapons, ammunition, and food had rolled in as fast as the railroad marshalling yards could handle them. It was all wasted effort however. Hitler decided to end his career in Berlin, and in twenty minutes, beginning at noon on 25 April, Allied bombers smashed the fortifications. After the bombing, the erstwhile defenders of the redoubt headed south looking for refuge in the Austrian Tyrol.

Goering, whom Hitler had at the end stripped of all his titles and offices including that of Reich Game Keeper, emerged from the mountains some days later to return briefly to the limelight as a figure in the most publicized fraternization incident of the war. He surrendered—by arrangement—on a country road to Brig. Gen. Robert Stack, Assistant Division Commander, 36th Infantry Division, who was photographed shaking hands with him. At the division headquarters, the press reported, the division commander, Maj. Gen. John E. Dahlquist, interviewed Goering in private, gave him time to bathe and to change his uniform, ate chicken with him at lunch, and provided him and his wife with a night's lodging in a castle.[50]

On the morning of 4 May, when U.S. 3d Infantry Division troops crossed into *Landkreis* Berchtesgaden, the *Landrat*, Emil Jacob, was the most important official left. Even the local party leaders, the *Kreisleiter* and the *Ortsgruppenleiter*, had taken to the mountains. At two o'clock in the afternoon, Jacob drove in his car to meet the Americans and surrender the town. Detachment I3G3, under Capt. R. A. Bryand, arrived the next morning and suffered the only casualties known to have been incurred in Berchtesgaden, two men injured when a time bomb exploded in one of the *Kreis* headquarters offices.[51] Berchtesgaden would have been just a small town with some fine scenery had it not been for two reminders of the past: the Adlerhorst, Hitler's elaborate guest house on the Kehlstein, reached by an elevator run through a 400-foot copper-lined tunnel in the mountain; and the Berghof, Hitler's home on the Obersalzberg, now bombed, burned, and looted—an appropriate monument to the Third Reich.

---

[50] Cable, Marshall to Eisenhower, sub: Goering Friendliness, 13 May 45, and Cable, Eisenhower to CG's, 12th AGp, Third and Seventh Armies, 14 May 45, in USFET, SGS 250.
[51] Annual Hist Rpt, Det E–311, Jun 46, in OMGUS 77–1/10.

CHAPTER XV

The Victory Sealed

Surrender at Reims

Hours before dawn on the morning of 7 May 1945, a cluster of correspondents and press and newsreel photographers waited at one end of the G–3 war room at SHAEF forward headquarters in Reims. In the center of the room stood a large, empty table. At 0230, ten Allied officers entered and took seats around three sides of the table. Generals Smith and Morgan headed three-officer U.S. and British delegations; Gen. François Sevez represented France; and Maj. Gen. Ivan Souslaparov, a colonel, and a lieutenant were the Soviet contingent. When all were seated, Morgan called in the Germans, Generaloberst Alfred Jodl and two others. They entered, clicked their heels, and gave small military bows. At the table nobody moved except Smith, who waved the Germans to seats on the unoccupied side of the table where they sat facing a large wall map showing the Allied forces' latest dispositions. Maj. Gen. Kenneth W. D. Strong, SHAEF–2, acting as interpreter, stood behind the Germans and read out the surrender terms, more for the benefit of the press than for the Germans, who were familiar enough with them already. After Strong finished, Jodl rose and declared, in the name of the German Army, Navy, and Air Force, that he surrendered unconditionally. The document was then signed, and Jodl and his party left the room.[1]

SHAEF's wartime mission was completed, but with a last-minute twist. What the Germans signed at Reims was the "Act of Military Surrender," written three days before in the SHAEF G–3, not the painstakingly negotiated EAC surrender instrument. The chief author of the surrender document signed at Reims was a British colonel, John Counsell, an actor and theatrical manager in civilian life, who had cheerfully "cribbed" much of it from the terms for the German surrender in Italy (2 May) published in *Stars and Stripes*.[2] Its six short paragraphs—none more than two sentences long—simply affirmed the German High Command's unconditional surrender, to take effect fifty-nine minutes before midnight on 8 May.[3]

SHAEF had included the EAC surrender instrument in the ECLIPSE plans and had assumed it was the document the Germans would sign if they signed one at all, which by the time Jodl arrived had begun to seem unlikely. The EAC was by then at work on an Allied proclamation of the German defeat, and nothing had been done to clear up several deficiencies in the surrender instrument that had developed since it was approved by the governments. One slipup was that, although SHAEF had received copies of the sur-

---

[1] Memo, SHAEF, ACofS G–5, for All Branches,

sub: Unconditional Surrender, 7 May 45, in SHAEF G–5, 10.

[2] John Counsell, *Counsell's Opinion* (London: Barrie and Rockliff, 1963), 148–50.

[3] Pogue, *The Supreme Command*, p. 488.

render instrument, none had been sent officially through its channel of command, the CCS. When Winant tried to correct this omission on 4 May, he ran into another complication. At Yalta, Roosevelt, Churchill, and Stalin had added a single word, "dismemberment," to the rights the victorious powers reserved for themselves with regard to Germany. The change had not been communicated to the French.[4] Finally, the surrender instrument required the signature of the "highest German civilian authority" as well as the highest military authority. Hitler had killed himself on 30 April. Grossadmiral Karl Doenitz had announced himself as Hitler's appointed successor two days later and had initiated the negotiations for the surrender; but the Allies did not recognize him as head of state, and his authority, except possibly over the armed forces still fighting, was doubtful. Berlin, the capital, had fallen to the Russians on 2 May, and nearly all the rest of Germany was already occupied by one or the other of the Allies. When Winant talked to Smith on the 6th, Winant agreed that the Act of Military Surrender would accomplish the purpose with the "least controversy and delay." At his request, Smith had included in the short document a sentence obligating the Germans to accept the EAC terms as well, if they were imposed.[5]

SHAEF had sent drafts of the Act of Military Surrender to Washington, London, and Moscow on 6 May and received reactions from Churchill and Winant before the signing but not from Washington

or Moscow.[6] Moscow's response reached Reims on the morning of 7 May, six hours after the Germans had signed. It practically accused Eisenhower of making a truce with the Germans that would allow them to continue the war against the Soviet Union; and it insisted—too late by then—that there be only one signing and that in Berlin. SHAEF had proposed signing first at Reims and later at Berlin to save time and lives.[7]

The second signing was held, amidst obvious evidence of Soviet pique, in Berlin shortly before midnight on the 8th. Excepting perhaps the Germans, the least happy man of those who had been present during the surrender at Reims was General Souslaparov. He was recalled to Moscow on the same day. Colonel Counsell saw him leave the SHAEF senior officers' mess after he received the order—"an old man, sagging at the knees, his face drained of all color, his eyes expressionless."[8]

President Truman and Prime Minister Churchill announced the surrender on 8 May. The Soviet government withheld its announcement until early on the 9th, after the ceremony in Berlin. In Germany, the troops and displaced persons had vented

---

[4] Department of State, *Foreign Relations, 1945,* vol. III, pp. 266–71.

[5] (1) *Ibid.,* pp. 284 and 289f. (2) Memo for Record, signed L.H.S., sub: Surrender Terms Negotiated in EAC, 11 May 45, in OPD, ABC 387, sec. 1–D. (3) Ltr, War Dept, signed Ed, to Smith, 11 May 45, in SHAEF SGS 387.

[6] Department of State, *Foreign Relations, 1945,* vol. III, p. 284. The strongest reaction from Washington after the signing came from Assistant Secretary of War McCloy, who was at the United Nations Conference in San Francisco until after V–E Day. He said it was "incredible" that the EAC surrender instrument had "been simply forgotten and ignored." His concern was mostly personal, however; in early 1944 he had strongly advocated a short surrender document and believed he would be suspected of "having put one over on State and gotten Smith to use his terms." (1) Department of State, *Foreign Relations, 1945,* vol. III, p. 290. (2) Memo, G.A.L. for Gen Hull, 12 May 45, in OPD, ABC 387, sec. 1–D.

[7] Cable, Military Mission Moscow to SHAEF FWD, 7 May 45, in SHAEF G–3, Opns. A, 384.1–1.

[8] Counsell, *Counsell's Opinion,* p. 155.

their enthusiasm in a premature celebration on the night of the 5th; the Germans themselves had little to celebrate. The military government detachments noted the occasion in forms similar to the following entry from the journal of H1A2, Saarbruecken:

8 May Tuesday
   0700 first call; 0730 breakfast; 0830 officers' call. Lt. Larsen to cover property control duties and received what information he could from Mr. Leathart. Lt. Vogel sent Preble to Friedrichsthal on procurement for 1282d Engineer Construction Battalion. Lt. Harris investigated complaints of looting on the part of DPs, German civilians, and French and U.S. troops; investigated the escape of a Russian prisoner from the DP hospital. Lt. West checked warehouses for chloride of lime needed for sanitary purposes in DP camps. Capt. Young investigated the agricultural situation in Saarlautern *Landkreis*. Capt. Laid conferred with local industrial leaders. Churchill spoke over the radio and declared the war in Europe is over. In Saarbruecken, it was just another day, with the German people going about their business as usual. Cpl. Pfluger celebrated by shooting himself in the heel and was hospitalized.[9]

As far as the Americans could tell, the emotional impact on the Germans was slight. Their faith in victory had been undermined by the defeat at Stalingrad in 1943 and shattered by the Normandy landing. Few had retained any real hope for a German victory after the Allied forces reached the western border. In contrast to the reaction after the Armistice in 1918, they clearly recognized the fact of a complete military defeat. On the other hand, SHAEF's Psychological Warfare Division, during interrogations after V–E Day, found a pervasive tendency among the Germans to disclaim personal responsibility for the disaster. They retreated to an intense preoccupation

with purely private affairs, resorted to the argument of the *"Kleiner Mann"* (the little man), and endlessly repeated the phrase *"belogen und betrogen"* (lied to and deceived).[10]

After the surrender was signed, the remaining question for the Allies to decide was what, exactly, had been accomplished. The General Board concluded later that the German state was extinguished at Reims and the victors acquired sovereignty over the German people. It cited Grotius, who defined unconditional surrender as "pure surrender . . . which makes the one who surrenders a subject and confers the sovereign power on him to whom the surrender is made."[11] Immediately after V–E Day, Eisenhower was not so certain. The Act of Military Surrender had procured the submission of the German armed forces but not necessarily of the German government, which was just the opposite of what had happened in 1918 when the civilians had signed the Armistice and the military had not. Neither did the Act of Military Surrender provide for Allied assumption of supreme authority in Germany. Also missing was authority to exclude the surrendered German forces from the prisoner of war provisions of the Hague and Geneva Conventions.[12] The EAC was aware of these omissions, too, and on 12 May submitted to the governments a draft "Declaration Regarding the Defeat of Germany and the Assumption of Supreme Authority by the Allied Powers" that combined the essentials of the Act of Military Surrender,

---

[9] Det H1A2, Daily Journal, May 45, in SHAEF G–5, 17.25.

[10] SHAEF, PWD, Weekly Intelligence, Summary No. 33, 14 May 45, in SHAEF G–5, 7.3.
[11] General Board, Study No. 85, p. 42.
[12] (1) Memo, SHAEF, ACofS G–5, for CofS, sub: Assumption of Supreme Authority in Germany, 13, May 45, in SHAEF G–5, 627. (2) Cable, Eisenhower to CCS, 14 May 45, in SHAEF G–3, Opns. C, 387–1.

the EAC surrender instrument, and the proclamation of the German defeat that the EAC had worked on just before the surrender. When the governments approved, the declaration was to be issued over the signatures of the commanders in chief in Germany.[13]

Flensburg Interlude

The third sentence in the EAC declaration read, "There is no central Government or authority in Germany capable of accepting responsibility for the maintenance of order, the administration of the country, and compliance with the requirements of the victorious Powers."[14] This statement was not yet quite accurate. On the Flensburg Fiord, close to the Danish border, in a former navy torpedo school at Muerwick, Admiral Doenitz held a potentially arguable claim to the headship of the German state. In a political testament, written on the night before his death, Hitler had conferred on Doenitz the presidential powers under the Weimar Constitution that Hitler himself had assumed in 1934 after Hindenburg died. Doenitz had not received the testament, but he had authenticated transcripts of radio messages from Berlin informing him of the appointment, and he had begun preparing a "white book" to defend his claims.[15] In negotiating the surrender, SHAEF had studiedly ignored

Doenitz while at the same time dealing with him, indirectly at least, and tolerating his government's existence.

Doenitz had surrendered northern Germany, including Schleswig-Holstein and Denmark, on 5 May, thus making himself and his people virtual prisoners of Montgomery's 21 Army Group; however, from a little island of territory around Flensburg and Muerwik, Doenitz continued to conduct governmental and military affairs, as far as he was still able, up until the general cease-fire and for some days thereafter. The Soviet General Staff protested acidly SHAEF's having permitted the German negotiators at Reims to use terminology such as "new government" and "German Government" in their messages to Doenitz because, the Russians said, they preferred to "do business with the German High Command and not with the German Government, which in actuality does not exist."[16] The Russians, however, who had been the first to learn about Hitler's death and the testament, had at one point offered to allow Doenitz to assemble his government in Berlin.

After V–E Day, the small area around Flensburg–Muerwik became an enclave in the otherwise totally occupied country. Armed German soldiers marched in the streets and stood guard outside the offices and residences of the members of the government. The Reich's war flag still flew over Doenitz's headquarters, and Allied officers who had business there avoided appearing to give orders. As a government, Doenitz and his associates lacked nearly all the essentials, above all, contact with the people they proposed to govern. Albert Speer, Hitler's armament and munitions minister

---

[13] Department of State, *Foreign Relations, 1945,* vol. III, p. 289.

[14] Department of State, *Treaties and Other International Acts Series,* No. 1520.

[15] (1) Draft White Book, in OKW 1892. (2) Memo, SHAEF Control Party at OKW, sub: Meeting between Maj. Gen. Lowell W. Rooks [and others] and Grossadmiral Doenitz in Flensburg on 18 May 45, in SHAEF G–3, GCT 322.01–2/GPS. See also Walter Luedde-Neurath, *Regierung Doenitz* (Goettingen: Musterschmidt Wissenschaftliche Verlag, 1951).

[16] Cable, Military Mission Moscow to SHAEF FWD, 7 May 45, in SHAEF G–3, Opns. C, 384.1–1.

AN ERA PASSES *as Germans exchange street signs.*

who had become Doenitz's minister of economics and production, proposed that they
close up shop completely after the surrender was signed to escape becoming a
laughing stock; but Doenitz and the others
believed that they represented at least the
continuity of the Reich.

The one resource Doenitz had in plentiful supply was executive talent—though
not often the kind that was likely to find
Allied acceptance. Like Speer, many others
from the upper and middle reaches of the
Nazi governmental hierarchy had made
their way to the Flensburg Fiord. From
among the less tainted, Doenitz found

enough men to assemble a complete, even
elaborate, cabinet of experts, all suffering
from the same disability however: the organizations they had headed were smashed
and the records and people scattered all
over Germany.[17] When the British troops
surrounding the enclave did not move in
to arrest them after the surrender, a wild
hope sprang up that maybe they could survive by making themselves indispensable to
the Allies. Doenitz put the specialists to

[17] (1) Karl Doenitz, *Zehn Jahre und Zwanzig
Tage* (Bonn: Athenäum-Verlag, 1958), p. 471.
(2) Albert Speer, *Erinnerungen* (Berlin: Propyläen-
Verlag, 1969), p. 499.

work writing proposals, and Jodl began to talk about "overwhelming" the Allies with memoranda, letting them "break their teeth off" on the big problems, and eventually playing the Russians and the Western Allies off against each other.[18] On an emotional binge, the cabinet met every day to work on polishing its own organization; it even acquired an official photographer. Doenitz took to riding the five hundred yards between his quarters and his office in one of Hitler's big Mercedes limousines that had turned up in Flensburg.[19]

On the morning of 12 May, Maj. Gen. Lowell W. Rooks arrived at the OKW (*Oberkommando der Wehrmacht,* High Command of the Armed Forces) in Flensburg at the head of the SHAEF Control Party with orders "to impose the SCAEF's will on the German High Command."[20] After taking up quarters for himself and his party aboard the *Patria,* a passenger ship docked in the harbor not far from the torpedo school, Rooks called in Doenitz and ordered him to arrest Generalfeldmarschall Wilhelm Keitel, Chief, OKW, and turn him over as a prisoner of war in reprisal for an alleged failure of some German troops to cease resistance against the Soviet forces at the specified time.

Despite its ominous beginning, Doenitz considered the meeting highly encouraging. He believed it constituted a recognition of him as the head of state.[21] Rooks reported only a great desire on the part of Doenitz and his group to create the impression

"that they are the best people to issue orders."[22] What Doenitz interpreted as recognition was apparently mostly uncertainty on the part of Rooks and SHAEF as to what to think of or do with this strange military-political menage that had drifted up out of the wreckage of the Third Reich.

Rooks may have had instructions to explore the possibility of using Doenitz and his people as an instrument of Allied control.[23] If so, he did not tarry long over his decision. On the 15th he told Smith, "It is quite obvious that this headquarters is a rapidly decaying concern with little knowledge of present events and practically no work to do." He suggested, subject to the needs of SHAEF and the army groups, disbanding the OKW as soon as possible. On the 17th, Rooks, his British deputy, Brig. E. J. Foord, and the SHAEF Political Adviser, Ambassador Robert D. Murphy, jointly recommended abolishing "the so-called acting government" immediately. The next day they questioned Doenitz about the manner of his appointment, but only to satisfy their curiosity. SHAEF had already requested Moscow's agreement to the arrest of Doenitz and the others with him who were in the automatic arrest cate-

---

[18] *Kriegstagebuch des Oberkommandos der Wehrmacht* (Frankfurt a.M.: Bernard and Graefe, 1961), vol. VI, pt. 2, pp. 1499–1507.

[19] Speer, *Erinnerungen,* p. 499.

[20] Memo, SHAEF, CofS, for Maj Gen Lowell W. Rooks, sub: Supreme Hqs Control Party, OKW, 11 May 45, in SHAEF G–3, Opns. C, 387–7.

[21] *Kriegstagebuch des Oberkommandos der Wehrmacht,* vol. VI, pt. 2, p. 1493.

[22] Cable, SHAEF Control Party at OKW to SHAEF FWD, 13 May 45, in SHAEF G–3, Opns. C, 387–7.

[23] Prime Minister Churchill, who usually found ways to communicate his ideas to SHAEF, was talking about "letting things slide for a while" and using the Doenitz government as "a handle with which to manipulate this conquered people." In his first postsurrender meeting with Eisenhower on 16 May, he said he would not be averse to using suitably qualified Germans to reorganize and handle German problems, possibly "some of the German generals already in our hands." (1) Winston S. Churchill, *Triumph and Tragedy* (Boston: Houghton-Mifflin Company, 1953), p. 756. (2) War Cabinet, Chiefs of Staff Committee, Minutes of Conference Held 16 May 45, in SHAEF G–3, 1/GPS.

gories and had instructed Rooks to "take all steps short of arrest" to insure that Doenitz ceased executive functions.[24]

The Americans were, in a way, more interested in a Soviet OKW control party, under Maj. Gen. Trusov, who arrived several days after them, than they were in the Germans. No other element of the elaborate GOLDCUP and SHAEF Special Echelon organizations had so far made contact with the Russians. To Murphy, Trusov gave the impression that the Russians wanted a co-ordinated administration in Germany but had not yet formed anything like the U.S. and British Control Council groups.[25] Rooks saw in the Russians' behavior a latent threat to SHAEF's still-cherished nonfraternization policy. The Russians, he reported, "fraternized wholeheartedly." The enlisted men talked to German women on the streets. The crew of the plane that brought the Russians got drunk with German officers in Flensburg and ended up kissing them. The pilot tried to bring back a German woman to the airfield on a motorcycle. On board the *Patria* a Soviet officer had been seen drinking and laughing with three German officers in his cabin.[26]

On the 19th, the Soviet command having agreed, SHAEF ordered 21 Army Group to arrest the Doenitz government and the OKW. Col. C. W. Stewart, Jr., described the arrest as it occurred on the morning of the 23d:

At 10 A.M., Admiral Doenitz, General Jodl, Admiral von Friedeburg and three other officers came marching down the dock and were escorted up to the ship's bar where a long table had been prepared with chairs on both sides, very much in the same way the war room in Rheims was arranged. If ever a man with a field marshall's baton looked unhappy, Doenitz did (after he came out). Rooks must have taken almost no time to deliver his message. The Germans were marched off and put into cars to take them home to pack.

By the time Doenitz emerged from the interview, the main street of Muerwik was filled with British tanks and with troops rounding up the Germans. The German barracks were looted, and, Stewart reported, "the complexion of the town changed overnight from being optimistic to sullen quiet."[27] Before the day's end, Doenitz, Speer, Jodl, and the other top war crimes suspects were moved to ASHCAN. Generaladmiral Hans Georg von Friedeburg, who had made the partial surrender to Montgomery and who had been at Reims with Jodl, at Berlin with Keitel, and finally on the *Patria* with Doenitz, shot himself.

Meeting in Berlin

Since the unconditional military surrender had already been accomplished, the most significant passage in the Declaration Regarding the Defeat of Germany and the Assumption of Supreme Authority by the Allied Powers was that pertaining to the assumption of supreme authority. It read as follows:

---

[24] (1) Cable, SHAEF Control Party at OKW to SHAEF FWD, 17 May 45; Cable, SHAEF to Control Party, 18 May 45, in SHAEF G–3, Opns. C, 387–9. (2) Cable, SHAEF Main (Eisenhower) to AGWAR to CCS, 18 May 45, in SHAEF SGS 250.3.

[25] Cable, Murphy to Sec of State, 21 May 45, in CAD 014, 7–10–42, sec. 13.

[26] Memo, Rooks for Smith, sub: Nonfraternization Policy, 26 May 45, in SHAEF G–1, 250.1–10.

[27] Memo, Col C. W. Stewart, Jr., for Gen Crawford, sub: Dissolution of the OKW (Nord) and the So-called Acting German Government, 24 May 45; Memo, SHAEF, G–3 Opns, for ACofS G–5, sub: Arrest of Acting German Government, 23 May 45, in SHAEF G–3, Opns. C, 387–9.

The Governments of the United States of America, the Union of Soviet Socialist Republics and the United Kingdom, and the Provisional Government of the French Republic, hereby assume supreme authority with respect to Germany, including all the powers possessed by the German Government, the High Command and any state, municipal, or local government or authority. The assumption, for the purposes stated above, of the said authority and powers does not affect the annexation of Germany.[28]

The second sentence mitigated the traditional ultimate effect of unconditional surrender, the permanent extinction of the defeated state. Under the declaration, however, the German state, nevertheless, did cease to exist, even if only provisionally. The law of belligerent occupation also no longer applied to Germany. The Allied sovereignty was complete, limited only by its own decision, and the relationship was that of conqueror and subject. The declaration was written to be issued by the representatives of the Allied supreme commands on the authority of their governments and in the interests of the United Nations.

President Truman approved the declaration on 14 May, and the War Department instructed Eisenhower to arrange to have the four commanders in Germany issue it.[29] McCloy commented that, since one slipup had already been made, SHAEF should be careful not to make another and should therefore take no action not approved beforehand by the four governments.[30] The other governments submitted their formal approval within a week.

In the meantime, however, although the declaration remained a formality, an almost superfluous statement of a *de facto* condition, it had become entangled in a knot of tangential problems. One problem was that Gousev wanted to add the Soviet-sponsored Polish government as one of the Allies who would be given advance copies of the declaration. Seven European Allied governments, including neither the Polish exile government in London nor the Polish "Lublin" (later Warsaw) government, had been consulted in writing the original surrender instrument and would be shown the declaration. The British wanted to add to this number the Dominions, India, and Brazil. When Strang raised the question in the EAC on 10 May, Gousev at once proposed including the Warsaw government, which neither the United Kingdom nor the United States recognized.[31]

While the EAC negotiated the Polish question, the Americans and the British debated some other subjects among themselves. Both groups assumed, in fact hoped, that the signing of the declaration would automatically bring the Control Council into being, since the signatories would also be the members of the Control Council. Activating the Control Council, however, could force decisions concerning SHAEF's existence and the SHAEF-held territory in the Soviet zone—decisions on which opinion was both mixed and divergent. Eisenhower made a strong case for keeping SHAEF until the forces were redisposed in their national zones and the Control Council was operating effectively—which, his staff predicted, would take at least three months.[32] The British, who had long de-

---

[28] Department of State, *Treaties and Other International Acts Series*, No. 1520.

[29] Department of State, *Foreign Relations, 1945*, vol. III, p. 293.

[30] Cable, Marshall to Eisenhower, 14 May 45, in CAD 104, 10–7–42, sec. 12.

[31] Department of State, *Foreign Relations, 1945,* vol. III, p. 286.

[32] (1) Pogue, *The Supreme Command,* p. 511. (2) Memo, SHAEF, ACofS G–3, for CofS, sub: Redeployment of U.S., British, French, and Soviet Forces into Zones of Occupation in Germany, 14 May 45, in USFET SGS 370.5/3.

sired SHAEF's early disbandment, opposed prolonging the combined command formally because existence of the command would logically require the declaration to be signed only by Eisenhower as Allied Supreme Commander and Marshal Zhukov as Soviet Supreme Commander. On the other hand, however, they apparently did not want to see SHAEF formally disbanded before a decision was made regarding the SHAEF-held Soviet territory.[33]

Truman had proposed, in late April, making the troop and boundary adjustments as soon as a government declared itself ready to take over its assigned territory. But Churchill had objected both to "letting the Russians . . . order us back at any point they might decide" and to "yielding up . . . an enormous territory . . . while all questions of our spheres in Vienna or arrangements for the occupation of Berlin remain unsettled." The President and the Prime Minister had finally agreed to propose setting up the Control Council first and then redisposing the troops in the zones. Stalin acknowledged the message but, except for agreeing to a "temporary tactical demarcation line," ignored the proposal.[34]

Talking to Eisenhower on 16 May, Churchill indicated that he did not want to see any decision made on SHAEF's status that would give the Soviet Union an excuse to press for a withdrawal from its zone; therefore, on the 24th the British argued in Washington for separating the decisions on SHAEF and the Soviet territory from the declaration and the activation of the Control Council. They wanted

to make the withdrawal from the Soviet zone in particular, they later explained, contingent on the settlement of the "whole question of future relations" between the Western Allies and the Soviet Union in Europe. The State Department indicated the U.S. government was interested above all in getting the Control Council established and working and would not delay the withdrawal from the Soviet zone if the Russians made it an issue but would "defer" the decisions on SHAEF and the Soviet zone temporarily—presumably at least long enough to gauge the Soviet reaction.[35]

In the end it was Eisenhower who brought the matter to a head, though not by his or the U.S. government's choice. On 29 May, Winant recommended in the EAC having the commanders in chief meet in Berlin on 1 June, sign the declaration, form the Control Council, and put the protocols on zones and control machinery into force. The EAC had by then solved the Polish question. It would transmit the declaration to the original seven Allied governments through its Allied Consultation Committee, and the British government would give copies separately to the Dominions and India, the U.S. government to Brazil, and the Soviet government to Poland. Gousev's instructions from Moscow were slow in coming, but not unusually slow for the Russians, and on 4 June he reported that his government had accepted Winant's recommendation and wanted to hold the ceremony in Berlin the next day.[36] Eisenhower, meanwhile, had asked on 2 June how he was to respond in case the Russians raised the question of their zone, as they seemed likely to do. The JCS told him that the withdrawal from the Soviet zone "should

---

[33] War Cabinet, Chiefs of Staff Committee, Minutes of Conference Held 16 May 45, in SHAEF G–3, 1/GPS.

[34] Department of State, *Foreign Relations, 1945,* vol. III, pp. 240, 241, 244, 245, and 259.

[35] *Ibid.,* pp. 304, 305, and 308.

[36] *Ibid.,* pp. 314, 315, and 323.

not be a question precedent to establishment of the Control Council." If the Russians raised the point, he was to say that it was "one of the items to be worked out by the Control Council."[37]

On 3 June, Eisenhower sent to the JCS his proposed agenda for the first meeting of the Control Council, which he expected would take place after the formal signing of the declaration. He expected to discuss a location for the Control Authority, either in Berlin or elsewhere, and, if in Berlin, the questions of transit and communications to the city. He would talk about moving the U.S forces out of the Soviet zone if the Russians brought it up, but he would not make any commitments without consulting the JCS. If the Russians asked, he would explain SHAEF's continuing existence as an interim arrangement for the period in which the U.S., British, and French forces were being redistributed to their zones.[38]

The planes carrying Eisenhower and his party landed at Tempelhof airport in the late forenoon on the 5th. After reviewing a battalion-size honor guard, he was taken by car to the southeastern Berlin suburb Wendenschloss, as were also Montgomery and the French commander in chief in Germany, General Jean de Lattre de Tassigny, when they arrived—separately, of course, to emphasize their status as representatives of their respective countries. The drive through Berlin, along streets lined with Soviet troops and with scarcely any Germans to be seen, showed the city to be heavily damaged; but in Wendenschloss, wooded and lying between two lakes, the war had missed the expensive villas, until recently the property of movie stars and important Nazis. Zhukov lived in one of the villas, and he assigned one to each of the Western commanders for the day. At a private meeting, Eisenhower presented Zhukov with the Chief Commander grade of the Legion of Merit and then returned to his quarters expecting to be called for the signing ceremony shortly, since the time set, noon, was already past.

Hours passed without anything more being heard from or seen of the Russians other than the household staffs, who seemed not even to know what the gathering was for in the first place. Finally, when Eisenhower and Montgomery threatened to leave without signing, they and de Lattre were called to the yacht club where the ceremony was to take place, only to discover when they arrived that the Russians insisted they could not sign because the wording of Article 10 of the declaration could be construed as requiring them to arrest Japanese nationals found in Germany, and they were not at war with Japan. Eisenhower ordered the passage taken out, which amazed Zhukov, who had to check with Moscow before accepting the deletion. By the time the Russians were ready it was approaching five o'clock, and Eisenhower, who intended to return to Frankfurt that day before dark, was again becoming impatient.

The signing took only a few minutes. Seated at a large round table, in a blaze of arc lights and photographers flash bulbs, each commander in chief signed four copies of the declaration: in English, French, Russian, and German. When finished, they adjourned with their interpreters and a few

---

[37] (1) JCS 1374, Withdrawal of U.S. Forces from Russian Zone in Germany as a Corollary to Establishment of the Control Council, 4 Jun 45, in CCS 334 (6–20–44), sec. 3. (2) Truman, *Memoirs*, vol. I, p. 301. (3) Cable, Hqs ETOUSA, to Eisenhower, 4 Jun 45, in SHAEF G–3, GCT 384.1–2/GPS.

[38] Cable, Eisenhower to JCS, 3 Jun 45, in SHAEF G–3, Opns. C, 387–1.

Marshal Zhukov (*Center*) Pours a Toast *at the 5 June 1945 meeting in Berlin. General Eisenhower* (*left*) *departed immediately after the toast. On the right are Field Marshal Montgomery and General de Lattre de Tassigny.*

aides for a private talk on the clubhouse porch.[39] After a brief preliminary conversation, Eisenhower, apparently assuming from the EAC's agreement that they now constituted the Control Council, asked Zhukov whether the control staffs could begin work.[40] Zhukov replied that they could not. When Eisenhower talked about an agenda and schedule for Control Council meetings, Zhukov said the troops should be established in their proper zones first because he could not study questions relating to Germany while he did not con-

[39] (1) Harry C. Butcher, *My Three Years With Eisenhower* (New York: Simon and Schuster, 1946), p. 857. (2) Clay, *Decision,* pp. 20–23. (3) Bernard Law Montgomery, *The Memoirs of Field-Marshal Montgomery* (New York: New American Library, 1958), pp. 336–39. (4) Alexander Werth, *Russia at War* (New York: E. P. Dutton & Company, 1964), pp. 983–85.

[40] The EAC statement, which Eisenhower received before he departed for Berlin, read, "Upon signature of the declaration the four representatives will constitute the Control Council in order to deal with matters affecting Germany as a whole. . . ." Cable, Winant to Eisenhower, 4 Jun 45, in SHAEF G–3, Opns. C, 387–1.

trol his own zone. On remarks by Montgomery about the difficulties of sorting out the tangle created by the war and getting the troops into their zones, Zhukov commented blandly that the war was over and he wanted to know how long the redeployment would take. When Montgomery estimated three weeks, Zhukov said that was "very satisfactory"; in the meantime they could gather their Control Council staffs. Since Eisenhower's and Montgomery's instructions did not allow them to make commitments on the withdrawal, the meeting ended with only a decision to refer the question to the governments.[41]

The Russians had an elaborate banquet planned, but Eisenhower declined to stay, the occasion having become a contest in stubbornness on both sides. Shortly after six o'clock, Eisenhower and his party, which included General Clay and U.S. Group Control Council personnel who had planned to stay in Berlin, departed. The Russians had given no sign of being willing to accommodate Clay and his people in Berlin even overnight.

Summing up his impressions a day later in his report to Washington, Eisenhower said he believed the Soviet Union would join some form of Control Council and would allow the Western Allies' troops to take over their zones in Berlin when the withdrawal from the Soviet zone was accomplished. (Zhukov had said at the meeting that he had no objection to establishing the Control Authority in Berlin.) Eisenhower added, however, that the Control Council could possibly "become only a negotiating agency and in no sense an overall government for Germany." To prepare for this contingency, he suggested two alternatives: administering the U.S. zone as an independent economic unit or establishing three-power control in the western zones and administering them as a unit.[42]

---

[41] OMGUS, History, Office of Military Government for Germany, ch. III, p. 2f.

[42] Daily notes, Allied Declaration on German Defeat, 6 Jun 45, in OPD, ABC 387, sec. 1–D.

CHAPTER XVI

Germany in Defeat

The Carpet

By V–E Day the military government carpet was laid in dimensions larger than any plan had contemplated. It stretched across the Rhineland and the Ruhr into central Germany to the Elbe and the Mulde Rivers, into western Czechoslovakia to Pilzen, and south into Austria past Linz, Salzburg, and Innsbruck. The carpet was a thin one, 250 ECAD military government detachments and about 200 provisional detachments drawn from the combat troops.[1] Although the movement and the fighting had ended, military government command was still entirely in tactical channels—from division to corps to army to army group. Fifteenth Army controlled the Rhineland. On 11 May, when First Army became nonoperational, Ninth Army assumed military government responsibility for the area east of the Rhine and north of the Main River and for the Bremen enclave. Third Army held northern and eastern Bavaria, the western Sudetenland in Czechoslovakia, and a dozen *Landkreise* in Austria. Seventh Army straddled half of Bavaria (including Munich, the capital), Wuerttemberg, and Baden. Headquarters, 12th Army Group, took command of Seventh Army on 16 May and therewith became responsible for military government in all U.S.-occupied Germany.

The U.S. Group Control Council, resigned to a delayed entry into Berlin, enjoyed an advancement from the rearward ranks of SHAEF Main, at Versailles, to a spearhead position with SHAEF Forward, in Frankfurt. When SHAEF Forward opened in the I.G. Farben building in Frankfurt after V–E Day, the U.S. Group Control Council set itself up in a Farben plant in nearby Hoechst. Hoechst, a Farben company town, was ideally suited to a military occupation. The houses had been designed for assignment to Farben employees according to rank. Headquarters, ECAD, moved from Troyes to Bad Homburg, ten miles northwest of Frankfurt, and settled into a collection of resort hotels spared from the bombing because they had been used as hospitals during the war.

The E detachments, after their long winter's wait, were in Germany and working, though not yet exercising the regional supervision for which they had been designed. Some detachments, like E1C3 (*Land* Wuerttemberg) and E2C2 (*Land* Bremen and the enclave), had entered their areas in April not far behind the combat troops. Others, like E1F3 (*Land* Bavaria), took up their stations after V–E Day. All had problems, among which inadequate personnel—in numbers and in specialized skills—was the most common. The *Land* detachment commanders learned, as Col. Charles E. Keegan did when he took E1F3 into Munich on 14 May, that the govern-

---

[1] Memo, Hqs, ETOUSA, ACofS G–5, for CofS, sub: Personnel Requirements [no date], in USFET SGS 200.3.

ments they had come to supervise were practically nonexistent. In Munich, the government buildings were badly damaged; the ministries had either been bombed out or evacuated; the *Reichsstatthalter* (head of government under the Nazis) had reportedly been kidnapped by the SS; and, for the near future at least, the Seventh Army–Third Army boundary cutting through Bavaria was more important than the *Land* political boundaries.[2] Col. Bion C. Welker, commanding E2C2, had a tight, if entirely artificial, area in the Bremen enclave, but he shared it with two major generals, one commanding the 29th Infantry Division, the other the Bremen Port Command.[3]

Military government operations, with few exceptions, were being conducted as they had been during the combat phase, by the local detachments under the supervision of the tactical commands and sometimes in competition with the security troops. Among the exceptions, E1F3, as one of its first acts, appointed a German food and agriculture administrator for Bavaria, thereby recognizing a regional problem though by no means solving it. In two directives affecting the entire U.S.-occupied area, 12th Army Group authorized the reuniforming of the German police and the reopening of lower courts. The police, in old *Wehrmacht* uniforms dyed some color other than field gray, could not be armed but could carry nightsticks. The courts were to make a beginning at clearing up the backlog of ordinary civil and criminal cases accumulated before the surrender, provided judges and lawyers

could be found. At least 80 percent of the members of the legal profession had been Nazis. Twenty-five German courts were operating by the end of May. The opening of the German courts did not affect the jurisdiction of military government courts, which had tried 16,000 cases by V–E Day, 70 percent on curfew and circulation charges.[4]

MFA&A was one of the first military government functions to be centrally coordinated. Because of the shortage of personnel, its functions had not been delegated to lower staffs to the extent others had; moreover, it had become the trustee for a greater quantity of art treasures than had ever been captured by any other army in history. At the time of the surrender, although they did not know it yet, the U.S. armies held the contents of all the major German art repositories except the Hamburg museums and, apparently, nearly all the art work the Nazis had looted in the countries occupied by Germany. The march into the south had uncovered dozens of caches, among them *Einsatzstab* Rosenberg loot at Neuschwanstein, the Rothschild collections at Herrenchiemsee, Nazi Foreign Minister Joachim von Ribbentrop's collection at Gaibach, and, in Austria, mines at Laufen and Alt Aussee—the first mine containing the collections of the Vienna *Kunsthistorischesmuseum,* and the other holding the best of the *Einsatzstab* Rosenberg loot, probably intended originally for the great museum Hitler had planned to build in his hometown, Linz.

In neighboring salt mines at Heilbronn and Kochendorf, Seventh Army made finds that rivaled those of Third Army at Merk-

---

[2] Wk Rpt, Det E1F3, 21 May 45, in SHAEF G–5, 17.16, Hist Rpts, 12th AGp, Jacket 14.
[3] Functional History of Military Government, 27 April 1945–30 June 1946, Bremen Enclave, in OMGUS 39–3/5, p. 7f.

[4] (1) Hqs, 12th AGp, Legal Br, to ACofS G–5, sub: Branch Activities, 18 Jun 45, in SHAEF G–5, 17.16, Jacket 11. (2) General Board, Study No. 85, p. 32.

GERMANS QUEUE UP *for information and advice at a military government detach-ment headquarters.*

ers. When the MFA&A officer, Lt. James J. Rorimer, went into the mines in late April, he saw, in cavernous galleries 700 feet below the surface where the temperature never varied from 67° Fahrenheit in winter or in summer, thousands of paintings and works of sculpture, millions of books, all the stained glass from the Strassburg Cathedral, the crown jewels and throne of the Grand Duchy of Baden, and, in addition, an I. G. Farben poison gas factory, a Heinkel jet plane factory, locomotives, fireworks, and stores of oil and aluminum.

On into June, depositories came to light almost daily. By the end of the month, the number reported to Headquarters, 12th Army Group, came to 849. The MFA&A job was to locate the caches, identify their contents, check on their condition, and see to their preservation and safekeeping. The 12th Army Group established collecting points at Marburg, Wiesbaden, and Munich; but getting the objects to these points was a massive undertaking. Maj. Louis B. LaFarge estimated that just moving the contents of the Alt Aussee mine to

Munich would take the sixteen trucks at his disposal six weeks.[5]

Organizationally, military government was most advanced in the area longest occupied, the Rhineland. After the Ruhr pocket collapsed in mid-April, Fifteenth Army converted itself into a predominantly military government headquarters by assigning military government functions to all its staff sections—religion and welfare to G–1, public safety and censorship to G–2, finance to the inspector general, and so on. The army's two corps, XXII and XXIII Corps, took over subareas—XXII Corps in the Duesseldorf–Aachen–Cologne districts, and XXIII Corps from Trier and Koblenz south. Early in May, the army brought in Detachments E1A2 and E1G2 to organize German provincial and district governments and at the middle of the month installed Dr. Hans Fuchs as head of the German administration for the entire Fifteenth Army area, then designated as the Rhine Province Military District. For a brief time Fuchs became the highest ranking German official in the western zones (his province was soon to be divided between the British and French zones).

Finding men for the higher posts who had no Nazi involvement was an arduous business. Fuchs had held a similar position under the U.S. Army of occupation after World War I and had been president of the Prussian *Rheinprovinz* under the Weimar Republic; he had been in forced retirement during the twelve years of the Nazi regime and was seventy years old.[6]

The other appointees were, like Fuchs, men who had not worked under the Nazis at all or, if they had, had held much lower ranks. Some were women, for whom the Nazi discrimination against their sex was proving an advantage under the occupation. The search for candidates had required the combined efforts of military government and the Counterintelligence Corps (CIC), and at the end of May some positions were still unfilled. At Coblenz, the hunt had not yet turned up enough qualified persons to begin establishing a district administration.[7] The recruiters had not only to weed out Nazis but also to steer clear of overinvolvement with other political factions. They found it especially hard to determine when Catholic priests were making recommendations "as public-spirited gentlemen of the clergy" and when as "leaders of the Center [Catholic] Party seeking posts for their candidates."[8]

Four days after the surrender, Eisenhower reminded the army group commanders that the purpose of military government was to control German governmental authorities, not to govern—if for no other reason, because the military forces themselves could not provide the manpower to run the government under any circumstances. He instructed the commanders to relax the circulation and travel restrictions enough to allow German officials to function beyond the local level (Fifteenth Army had reopened the intercity telephone system in the Rhineland for its German officials), and to put in the E detachments at once with the mission to reestablish German administrative machinery

---

[5] (1) SHAEF, MFA&A, to ACofS G–5, sub: Report of MFA&A, 9 Jul 45, in SHAEF G–5, 130.21. (2) Hqs, 12th AGp, ACofS G–5, sub; Narrative Summary, Jun 45, 9 Jul 45, in SHAEF G–5, 17.16, Jacket 13. (3) History of Military Government in *Land* Wuerttemberg-Baden, vol. I, ch. IX, sec. III.

[6] Hist Rpt., 12th AGp, ACofS G–5, May 45, 29 Jun 45, in SHAEF G–5, 17.25, Jacket 3.

[7] Hist Rpt, XXIII Corps, 10–23 May 45, in XXIII Corps, 223–0.3.

[8] Hist Rpt, 12th AGp, ACofS G-5, May 45, 29 Jun 45, in SHAEF G–5, 17.25, Jacket 3.

at the regional level.[9] By the end of the month the E detachments arrived east of the Rhine and began to organize German administrations up to the *Land* level.

But Eisenhower's instructions did not affect the so-called tactical theory of military government that SHEAF G–5 had criticized in the field survey in March. From top to bottom in the SHEAF-occupied area, military government remained tightly locked into the tactical command channels. This arrangement meant that, except in the Rhineland where Fifteenth Army had assumed the characteristics of a military government staff, military government and the German administrations had to function within unit boundaries, not German political boundaries, and that down at least to the regiment and battalion level, tactical commanders had more military government authority than any military government detachment. The E detachments could organize German administrations, but the chances of their authority, to say nothing of the German officials' authority, reaching across the nearest corps boundary were not good. Although, with the war over, units no longer were constantly on the move, they still moved frequently and cultivated their own, sometimes idiosyncratic, concepts of military government.

For their own reasons, the tactical commands, from the army groups on down, were also finding fault with the "tactical theory." The 12th Army Group complained in April and again in May that its responsibilities exceeded its resources, particularly in matters that reached beyond even its farflung boundaries, such as production control, operation of the railroads, and maintenance of the electric power sys-

tem.[10] XV Corps protested that the plans had never called for corps to conduct regional military government. Its three-officer G–5 section was responsible for supervising twenty *Landkreise* and two *Stadtkreise* in southern Bavaria and in Austria, and all the regional administrative centers for these *Kreise* were outside the corps boundaries.[11] On the other hand, at the top, the reasons for having put military government in the tactical channels in the first place seemed not to have lost their force. Late in May, Hilldring told Clay to watch military government: "The G–5 boys have a tendency to fall under British influence in setting up . . . on what they call a territorial basis, but which really means outside normal military channels. Whatever the theoretical justification, if in practice the military government officer (a lt. col.) sitting in the same town as a division commander (maj. gen.) is independent, God help the lt. col. and your military government."[12]

The Country

Whatever else the defeat may have meant to the Germans, it meant that they were going to go hungry, probably for a long time; and they were hungry already. The SHAEF maximum daily ration for normal consumers was 1,550 calories, but the amounts actually being issued ranged from 804 calories in Hesse and Hesse-Nassau to 1,150 calories in parts of the Rhineland. The normal consumers were the new

---

[10] Hist Rpt, 16h AGp, ACofS G–5, May 45, in SHAEF G–5, 504. (2) Memo, Hqs, 12th AGp, Col W. A. Bailey, for CofS, sub: Questions to be Discussed with SHAEF, 27 Apr 45, in USFET SGS 322.

[11] Memo, Hqs, XV Corps, G–5, for CG, sub: Military Government Operations, 20 May 45, in XV Corps, 215–5.3.

[12] Ltr, Hilldring to Clay, 21 May 45, in OMGUS 177–1/3.

---

[9] Msg, SCAEF to CG's 21, 6, and 12 AGps, 11 May 45, in SHAEF G–5, 803, Jacket 3.

proletariat of the occupation. The gentry were the "heavy" and "very heavy" workers, railroad workers and miners for instance, who could get up to 2,800 calories. The out-and-out aristocrats were the self-suppliers, that is, the farmers, who did not have to trouble themselves with ration cards. The normal consumer was not starving, but if he subsisted entirely on his ration, which no one really expected him to do, he was very close to it. A typical week's ration issued during May of 1945 consisted of the following: bread, 3 pounds; meat, 4 ounces; butter and fat, 2 ounces; sugar, 7 ounces; marcaroni and spaghetti, 5 ounces; potatoes, 6 pounds; some cereal (added to the children's ration), 6 ounces; milk (only for children up to six), 1 quart. The total was less than 1,000 calories per day, and the difference was made up by adding a few ounces of green vegetables "provided trucks can be found to haul them and provided the people can eat rhubarb without sugar."[13]

The 6th and 12th Army Group surveys indicated that there might be enough food in Germany to feed the Germans until the next harvest at the existing ration scales, if the necessity for feeding large numbers of displaced persons and disarmed German troops did not last too long into the summer. The spring planting for 1945 was about 90 percent of normal, but it had been done late and the results were doubtful. Military government had helped. XXIII Corps distributed 10,000 tons of seed potatoes in its area. Fifteenth Army secured 10,000 tons of German and 2,000 tons of imported farm and garden seeds, most of them transported in Army trucks. Military government set up farm machinery and automotive repair shops in the *Landkreise*. The shops could make one usable truck out of two or three wrecks. In the towns and cities, military government worked to protect the food resources of the people and to get the processing plants running again. In Erlangen, the detachment allowed Germans whose houses had been requisitioned as troop billets to have access to their gardens. In Ansbach, the detachment distributed garden seed. By the end of May, mills in Freising were producing 20 tons of flour a day for Munich, and a creamery was processing 50,000 quarts of milk. In June XXIII Corps listed salt, flour, meats, cereals, potatoes, and bread as not to be requisitioned from the Germans for feeding displaced persons. Third Army, by using central repair and strict surveillance, raised the number of vehicles available for civilian transport in its area from 7,500 in May to 25,000 in June.[14]

SHAEF G–5's estimate of the German food situation was, if anything, more pessimistic than that of the army groups. It predicted sporadic starvation in urban areas before the harvest unless food was imported. The most obvious reason for this prediction was that normally the SHAEF area was only 60 to 70 percent self-sufficient. The difference had come from im-

---

[13] (1) Hqs, 12th AGp, Legal Br, to ACofS G–5; sub: Branch Activities, 18 Jun 45, in SHAEF G–5, 17.16, Jacket 11. (2) 5th Information and Historical Service, sub: Food and Agriculture, XXIII Corps Area, 14 June 45, in Fifteenth Army, 115–2.

[14] (1) Hqs, 12th AGp, Legal Br, to ACofS G–5, sub: Branch Activities, 18 Jun 45, in SHAEF G–5, 17.16, Jacket 11. (2) Hist Rpt, 6th AGp, ACofS G–5, May 45, in SHAEF G–5, 5–4. (3) Hist Rpt, Third Army, ACofS G–5, May–Jun 45, in ETOUSA, Admin Hist, Nr. 146. (4) Hist Rpt, Fifteenth Army, ACofS G–5, Apr 45, in SHAEF G–5, 17.25, Jacket 1. (5) Memo, Hqs, XXIII Corps, for CG, Sub-Areas, sub: Feeding of DPs, 26 Jun 45, in XXIII Corps, 223–0.3.

ports and from eastern Germany, now in Soviet hands. The western sections that had produced some surpluses, Bavaria and Schleswig–Holstein for instance, were having to feed populations swollen by refugees. The big city populations were often half of normal, but the rural towns and villages had as much as two and a half times the usual number of people. Furthermore, the freeing of the displaced persons had cut the farm labor force in half; the bombing had destroyed processing machinery and impaired the distribution system; and because of the bombing, which had prevented the east-west movement of grain during the past winter, western Germany had begun the year with a food shortage. SHAEF's program was to encourage agriculture to the utmost—one of the few areas in which the Germans would be given Allied encouragement. SHAEF had granted permission to restart the agricultural machinery, fertilizer, and insecticide industries; and 12th Army Group had released 237,000 prisoners of war as farm labor by 1 June and would release over 200,000 more later in the month. Whether the effort would succeed was doubtful.[15] However, the Germans would have to be fed. As General Stearns, ETOUSA G–5, said, "While we can say they brought it on themselves and to hell with them, the fact remains that the Supreme Commander, who will be Military Governor of Germany, will be forced by public opinion at home to take at least minimum steps to prevent starvation."[16] Although the decision was not an easy one—all of Europe was short on

food—SHAEF began importing 650,000 tons of wheat for Germany in June.[17]

Competing with the food shortage for the status of number-one crisis was the state of German coal production. In May, a group of U.S. and British experts, the Potter–Hyndley Mission, surveyed the European coal requirements and concluded, "Unless drastic steps are taken, there will occur in Northwest Europe and the Mediterranean next winter a coal famine of such severity as to destroy all semblance of law and order, and thus delay any chance of reasonable stability."[18] This chilling prediction extinguished whatever life was left in the Morgenthau Plan's proposal for closing the German mines; but the outlook for Germany was dark nevertheless. The anticipated coal deficit for northwest Europe excluding Germany in the year from June 1945 to June 1946 was 25 million tons, unless coal could be gotten from Poland, which was highly unlikely, from the United States, which would require four hundred 16,000-ton ships full time and so was impossible, or from Germany. The Potter-Hyndley Mission recommended taking coal from Germany "without any regard for the consequences to Germany." The question was, the mission report conceded, whether German production could be raised to anywhere near 25 million tons. Either way, the Germans would suffer. At the time, production was 30,000 tons a day, 3 percent of normal, and 24,000 of these tons were being used to run the mines. The mines had over 5 million tons on hand but only enough

[15] SHAEF, ACofS G–5, Weekly Journal of Information, No. 15, 16 Jun 45, in SHAEF G–5, 131.11.
[16] Hqs, Com Zone, ETO, Command and General Staff Conference, 4 May 45, in ETOUSA, Admin Hist Collection, Nr. 146.

[17] (1) SHAEF, ACofS G–5, Weekly Journal of Information, No. 15, 16 Jun 45, in SHAEF G–5, 131.11. (2) Hqs, Com Zone, ETO, Command and General Staff Conference, 31 Jul 45, in ETOUSA, Admin Hist Collection, Nr. 146.
[18] Report by the Potter-Hyndley Mission, 7 Jun 45, in USFET SGS 463.3, vol. I.

transport to move 19,000 tons a day.[19] A SHAEF solid fuels conference in April had estimated 12th Army Group's coal requirements alone at 200,000 tons a month.[20] Not much was going to be left for the Germans, who were dependent on coal for heating, electricity, railroads, food processing, and even running water. In Wiesbaden, military government took coal from the gas works and scraped the coal dealers' bins to generate enough electricity to keep the city water system working. By the end of April, practically the whole power grid south of the Main River could have been operating had there been coal, but the railroad freight service had to be restored in order to bring in the coal, and it would need coal itself. The miners had to be fed much more than the average 1,000 calories a day if they were to do their work; and even if they dug the coal, Germany would have last claim on it. If the coal famine was going to result in acute unrest somewhere, the Potter–Hyndley Mission preferred to see it in Germany and said so in its report: "Should it become necessary to preserve order by shooting, it would surely be better for this to occur in Germany than elsewhere."[21]

In the midst of shortages the Germans were rolling in money. In May, 3,000 banks were open in the 12th Army Group area, and they had a total 3 billion *Reichsmarks* on deposit. Deposits exceeded withdrawals by so much that the banks were in trouble; they had no place to invest. In military government courts, the defendant who could not pay a thousand-mark fine out of his pocket was rare. Everybody had

money from high wartime wages and from compensation for bomb damage. The Nazi government, to sustain morale, had paid bomb damage claims promptly and without many questions asked. As the owners of the German 450-billion-mark war debt, however, the banks and the people were bankrupt. In April, the mark had sold (in Spain) for 4½ cents. SHAEF maintained an exchange rate of ten to the dollar for the Allied military marks when they were exchanged by U.S. personnel, and none for *Reichsmarks*. What value the *Reichsmark* had was derived from its being accepted in payment of fines and taxes and for rationed goods. For the purchase of such goods its value was about 30 cents, maintained by government subsidies to the producers, whose reluctance to accept the money even with the subsidies was increasing and, no doubt, contributed to shortages.[22]

One direction, other than agriculture, in which military government was willing to give the Germans encouragement and assistance was education. Some military government officers believed the schools ought to be left closed and the Germans kept in ignorance; but the predominant opinion was that properly regulated instruction of children would be the best foundation for the future. Schools were also a means for preventing juvenile delinquency which, as the threat of active German resistance faded, became one of the chief public safety concerns of military government. In May 1945, all the schools were closed; some had

[19] *Ibid.*

[20] Hist Rpt, 12th AGp, ACofS G–5, Apr 45, in SHAEF G–5, 17.16, Jacket 10.

[21] Donnison, *Civil Affairs and Military Government, Northwest Europe,* p. 405.

[22] (1) Hqs, 12th AGp, Legal Br, to ACofS G–5, sub: Branch Activities, 18 Jun 45, in SHAEF G–5, 17.16, Jacket 11. (2) Hqs, Fifteenth Army, ACofS G–5, CA & MG Summaries, No. 1, 2, and 96, 11 May–4 Jun 45, in SHAEF G–5, 17.25, Jacket 6. (3) U.S. Senate, Special Committee Investigating the National Defense Program, Executive Session Testimony, 5 Apr 46, in OMGUS 177–1/3.

already been closed for several months and some, like those at Aachen, since September 1944. In the defeated country, about all the children had in abundance were temptations. Before the surrender, military government had picked up reports of nationally organized adolescent gangs going by such names as Snake Club, Red X, and *Edelweisspiraten*. Their activities had ranged from listening to swing music and wearing zoot suits, to laughing and applauding in the wrong places at Hitler Youth meetings, to draft dodging and petty gangsterism. They were likely to find new things to do and many recruits if the occupation left the children unsupervised.

Like everything else in postsurrender Germany, reopening the schools was not easy. SHAEF required that before they could be opened, suitable buildings had to be readied, non-Nazi teachers certified, and new textbooks printed. Many school buildings had been destroyed, and those that had not were nearly all being used as DP camps, troop billets, or hospitals. Many teachers could not survive the first hurdle, the denazification *Fragebogen*. None of the old textbooks were considered suitable, and just to reopen the first four grades in the 12th Army Group area would require printing six-and-a-quarter-million new textbooks. Since it was not difficult to imagine the publicity effects of slips in the textbooks or the appointment of a few stray teachers with questionable political antecedents, military government would have to provide intensive supervision, which it was not ready to do. The E detachments had spaces for three education officers in their tables of organization and the F detachments spaces for two; in May, however, only one E detachment and no F detachment had an officer who carried education as his first assignment. During the war, the

education officer's sole function had been to close the schools, and this task did not require a full-time educational specialist.

In Aachen, F1G2 had been working since early in the year getting ready to reopen the schools. The detachment had plates for new textbooks made in England. The first set of plates disappeared on the way from London to Paris, and a second set had to be made. In April, 40,000 textbooks were printed. By May, F1G2 had found a superintendent of schools who had not been a member of the Nazi party, because he was half Jewish, and twenty-six teachers, twenty-four of whom were women in their forties and fifties who had been housewives during the Nazi period and so escaped party involvement. Finally, on 4 June, grades one to four in Aachen, with a thousand students, became the first to reopen in postwar Germany.[23]

"The Nazi Party," 12th Army Group G–5 reported in the third week of June, "seems almost to have vanished from the earth."[24] This was almost literally true. The Army security services were arresting the most prominent and dangerous Nazis by the thousands. At the end of June, 50,000 were in jails and camps. The arrests of the Doenitz government and of Goering and other prominent Nazis in southern Bavaria filled up the detention center known as ASHCAN, which had moved from Spa to Mondorf Les Bains in Luxembourg. Military government, working to bring new people to the fore, installed its appointees

---

[23] (1) Hqs, ECAD, General Intelligence Bulletin No. 40, 24 Mar 45, in SHAEF G–5, 17.16, pt. I, Jacket 8. (2) Hist Rpts, Hqs, 12th AGp, ACofS G–5, Apr, May, Jun 45, in SHAEF G–5, 17.16, Jackets 10 and 11. (3) Hist Rpt, Hqs, Fifteenth Army, ACofS G–5, Jun 45, in SHAEF G–5, 17.25.
[24] Hqs, 12th AGp, Legal Br, to ACofS G–5, sub: Branch Activities, 18 Jun 45, in SHAEF G–5, 17.16, Jacket 11.

SCHOOL OPENS IN AACHEN

with much ceremony and all the trappings of office. Its star was Dr. Konrad Adenauer who, after he openly assumed office as *Oberbuergermeister* of Cologne, quickly became the most prominent and most popular political figure in the Rhineland. On 31 May, military government permitted Corpus Christi Day celebrations and parades in Catholic communities; and the local officials attended, something the people had not seen in the twelve years of Nazi rule. Although the Nazis were no longer a danger, they could still be an embarrassment. ASHCAN was in a ninety-room resort hotel outside Mondorf. The

furniture had been taken out. Each room had one canvas cot with two blankets and no pillow, one straight-back chair, and wire netting across all the windows—more to keep the prisoners from jumping than to prevent their escape. They ate prisoner of war rations, usually C and K rations. Although ASHCAN was secret, a SHAEF inspector who visited it in the second week of May, while the Goering fraternization incident was prominent in the U.S. press, recommended moving it. The outside appearance was too sumptuous, and he shuddered at the thought of what some newspaper reporter might make of the name "Palace" chiseled in stone in eighteen-inch-high letters over the entrance.[25]

Housing themselves looked like a hopeless job for the Germans. The troops and the displaced persons always had first choice, and the population was totally out of joint. Southern Bavaria, which had been a favorite refuge from the bombing, had an estimated two and a half million people more than its normal population. About half of an estimated seven million refugees who had escaped from eastern Germany ahead of the Soviet winter offensive were in SHAEF territory. Undamaged towns and cities had a third to a half again as many people as normal. In the heavily bombed big cities the populations were increasing—in Cologne, for instance, at a rate of 2,000 people a day during May—but the cities could not accommodate all their former residents and were beginning to discourage the return of those who did not have needed skills or assured places to live. Military government did not regard where or how the Germans lived as its concern, although it provided some indirect relief by moving the newly arriving Sudeten refugees out of overcrowded Bavaria and by preventing residents of the area that would be handed over to the Russians from moving west. The worst consequence of unsettlement and overcrowding, a typhus epidemic, did not materialize. Serious outbreaks in the concentration camps—over four thousand cases in Dachau alone—led 12th Army Group to send out typhus-finding teams and dusting teams. By the end of May they had deloused a million persons and had used fifteen tons of DDT, and reports of new cases had decreased. Tuberculosis and venereal diseases, however, were on the rise.[26]

The worst off of the Germans were the refugees who had no homes to return to and the most pitiable were the children who had been evacuated from the bombed cities. The refugees were consigned indefinitely to living on the charity of communities in which they were, to say the least, unwelcome. The children, who had been kept in camps in isolated spots, were sometimes found abandoned and hungry. Although military government did not provide relief for German refugees, at this stage not even for starving children, it did compel the frequently reluctant local German governments to assume responsibility for them. The military government detachment in *Landkreis* Ebersberg southeast of Munich acquired an unusual brood, 200 babies, all less than three months old, in the Heim Hochland, an SS *Lebensborn* establishment barracks. In the barracks were a hundred women, "all attractive, perfect physical specimens," blood-typed in the SS fashion, and some pregnant. The babies, offspring of women like these and SS fathers, had been destined to become children of the state.[27]

Understanding the Germans was not easy. Military government seemed to have the strongest popular support in the places

[25] (1) Hqs, USFET, sub: U.S. Security Search for Nazis, 14 Jul 45, in Admin Hist, ETOUSA, No. 155. (2) Hqs, Fifteenth Army, ACofS G–5, CA & MG Summary No. 96, 11 May 45, in SHAEF G–5, Jacket 3. (3) War Diary, Det I1A2, May 45, in SHAEF G–5, 17.25, Jacket 5. (4) Memo, SHAEF G–5 Forward for ACofS G–4, sub: Inspection of ASHCAN, 15 May 45, in SHAEF G–2, 383.6–4.

[26] (1) Hqs, 12th AGp, Legal Br, to ACofS G–5, sub: Branch Activities, 18 Jun 45, in SHAEF G–5, 17.16, Jacket 11. (2) Hqs, Fifteenth Army, ACofS G–5, Weekly Military Government Survey No. 1, 28 May 45, in SHAEF G–5, 17.25, Jacket 3. (3) Hist Rpt, Det B-261, 26 Jun 46, in OMGUS 80–3/10.

[27] Hist Rpt, Det E-361, 29 Jun 46, in OMGUS 77–2/10.

HOUSING WAS A PROBLEM

where denazification was the most thorough. The commonest complaint against denazification was that it did not reach all of those who had profited from the Nazi system and the war. Instead of underground political activity against the occupation, a kind of belated anti-Nazi uprising seemed to be developing.[28] The number of persons "willing, even eager," to act as informers was not entirely a pleasant surprise. Military government had expected that the displaced persons and those who had suffered under the Nazis would want to get even, but many Germans with no such motives came forward to denounce their neighbors as Nazis and "to tell where the loot was hidden."[29] Rumor-mongering was a national mania. Most of the stories concerned wildly oppressive regulations supposedly about to be imposed by the Allies, an alleged impending Soviet takeover of western Germany, and an imminent war

[28] Hqs, 12th AGp, Legal Br, to ACofS G–5, sub: Branch Activities, 18 Jun 45, in SHAEF G–5, 17.16, Jacket 11.

[29] Hist Rpt, 6th AGp, ACofS G–5, May 45, in SHAEF G–5, 504.

between the Western Allies and the Soviet Union. Least understandable was the people's apparent indifference to the suffering of their fellow countrymen, especially the stranded refugees and the jail and concentration camp inmates. In Bavaria in May, a few Catholic priests were the only ones doing welfare work among the refugees. Up to the end of the first week in May, SHAEF PWD observed, "no German individual or civil organization has expressed the slightest concern" for the concentration camp victims, and no voluntary offers of food, clothing, or medical aid had been made.[30]

Aside from the military government detachments, SHAEF had two lines of communication to the Germans, Radio Luxembourg and PWD-produced newspapers. Both forms provided an austere fare of news, military government instructions, and atrocity stories, although the strictures originally imposed on *Die Mitteilungen* had been relaxed enough in the spring to allow PWD to print papers with a slight local cast. By V–E Day, *Die Mitteilungen,* with a press run of 300,000, was overshadowed by a dozen Army-published "name" papers, largest of which were the *Frankfurter Presse* (900,000), *Hessische Post* (980,000), and *Koelnischer Kurier* (850,000). At the end of May, the papers had a combined circulation of over 5 million. All were weeklies and, except for their names and some local news, were standardized in makeup and content. The one semi-licensed paper, the *Aachener Nachrichten,* printed 37,000 copies. Distribution was no problem: the news-hungry Germans constituted an insatiable market. The lim-

itations were paper, ink, presses, and transportation.[31]

After the surrender, PWD became suddenly and uncomfortably aware that it had a rival in the east, the Soviet-operated Radio Berlin. The Germans were listening to it more than would have been expected even considering that Radio Berlin was on the air in German nineteen hours a day while Radio Luxembourg's German-language broadcasts were limited to about four hours a day; and PWD listened, too, to find out why. What it heard were variety programs, music, friendly chats with listeners, and announcements of movies and theaters reopening and of alleged special coffee and tea rations. One morning music program was entitled "Let's Start the Day With a Gay Heart," and the announcer advised his listeners, "For greater pleasure, you should listen on your balcony amid flowers." On 22 May, the day the Russians put Berlin on Moscow time, the announcer who read the notice concluded with "Therefore, my dear listeners, you must not forget to set your clock forward an hour before going to sleep." The PWD monitors noted a sharp contrast with U.S. policy announcements and an even sharper contrast in tone.[32] When PWD asked 12th Army Group how extensive the popularity of Radio Berlin was and what could be done about it, the army group replied that the Soviet programs were the main topics of conversation of Germans in all walks of life.

---

[30] (1) Hist Rpt, B–261, 25 Jun 46, in OMGUS, 80–3/10. (2) SHAEF PWD, Weekly Intelligence Summary No. 32, 7 May 45, in SHAEF G–5, 7.35.

[31] The papers were delivered in Army trucks, and PWD figured one truck was required for every 70,000 copies printed. (1) Hqs, 12th AGp, ACofS G–5, Public Relations, Draft Report on German Language Army-Sponsored Newspapers, Jun 45, in SHAEF G–5, 11.16, Jacket 14. (2) SHAEF PWD, Weekly Intelligence Summary No. 36, 4 Jun 45, in SHAEF G–5, 7.35.

[32] SHAEF PWD, Weekly Intelligence Summary No. 35, 28 May 45, in SHAEF G–5, 7.30.

TROOPS DISTRIBUTE GERMAN-LANGUAGE NEWSPAPERS

They liked the entertainment and were impressed by the stories of rapid reconstruction in the Soviet-occupied territories. The programming for Radio Luxembourg, the army group's reply concluded, needed to take into account the enormous hunger for escapist entertainment in Germany and needed to put a better face on SHAEF occupation policy.[33] Subsequent army group and army assessments agreed that Radio Berlin increased discontent in western Germany. The Germans praised the Soviets' apparent willingness to distinguish between Nazis and non-Nazis and complained about the "dour and grim" quality of Radio Luxembourg and the "dishwater taste" of SHAEF's press and radio output; however, few said they would prefer to live under the Soviet occupation.[34]

[33] Cable, SHAEF, from McClure to 12th AGp, 26 May 45; Cable, 12th AGp to SHAEF for Mc-Clure, 28 May 45; and US Gp CC, Information Control Service, Special Report, 16 Jul 45, in USFET SGS 091.412.

[34] (1) Memo, Hqs, 12th AGp, ACofS G-5, Public Relations Br, sub: Military Government and Russian Radio, 12 Jun 45, in SHAEF G-5, 17.16, Jacket 14. (2) Hqs, Ninth Army, ACofS G-5, Weekly Military Government Summary No. 2, 4 Jun 45, in SHAEF G-5, 17.14, Jacket 9. (3) SHAEF, SGS, sub: Report of Harry J. Schneiders, 9 Jun 45, in USFET SGS 091.412.

The Question of Policy

During the week the war ended, Col. Joe Starnes, on a mission for SHAEF, finished a two weeks' tour of Germany. He had traveled two thousand miles and talked to military government officers from the army group G–5's on down to the spearhead detachments. He had seen more of Germany than any other Western observer so far, and he reported to General Smith:

Germany's military power is destroyed. The Nazi Party is dead. More than 20 million Germans are homeless or without adequate shelter. The average basic ration is less than 1,000 calories.

The ability to wage war in this generation has been destroyed.[35]

Military government, Starnes said, was applying the presurrender directives with common sense, but it would be severely handicapped by the lack of a constructive postwar policy. He recommended setting five objectives for immediate postwar policy at the highest level: (1) revival of agriculture; (2) restoration of transportation and communication; (3) resumption of coal and iron production; (4) revival and conversion of industry for civilian production; and (5) adequate housing.[36]

In one of his first letters to the CAD from Europe, Clay told Hilldring on 7 May, "The progress of the war in Germany has been much more destructive than most people at home realize." Therefore, he said, he hoped that his directives from Washington would be kept "flexible and general" until enough information was gathered to "enable you people at home to develop sound policy." He added that being "hard on Germany" did not call for unnecessary destruction of the economy. What was

needed could only be accomplished in the long run if the Germans were allowed a "decent standard of living" under controls that would prevent the expansion of industries adaptable to war production.[37] Although he did not say so directly, Clay had the limiting economic provisions of JCS 1067 in mind when he asked for a flexible directive. He had not read JCS 1067 before he arrived in Europe, and he either did not know about or was not impressed with SHAEF's earlier desire to be relieved of responsibility for the German economy. He agreed with his financial adviser, Lewis W. Douglas, that the Germans, "the most skilled workers in Europe," ought to be used to produce all they could "for a continent which is short of everything." After writing to Hilldring, he sent Douglas to Washington to argue their viewpoint with the CAD.[38]

Hilldring answered two weeks later, after he had talked to Douglas He said he felt, as Douglas did, that at the moment it would be easier not to have an economic directive such as the one in JCS 1067, but "in the long pull," it would be best to administer Germany along lines laid down by the government. While he was convinced that long-range policy "must bubble up from the facts you discover" and that he and McCloy had "planted the seed of this idea" in JCS 1067, Hilldring also felt that it would not be in the Army's or Clay's interest for Clay to be personally responsible for formulating economic policy. JCS

---

[35] Ltr, Col Joe Starnes to W. B. Smith, 5 May 45, in USFET SGS 014.4.

[36] Ibid.

[37] Ltr, Clay to Hilldring, 7 May 45, in OMGUS 177–1/3. See also letter dated 26 April cited in John Gimbel, The American Occupation of Germany (Stanford: Stanford University Press, 1968), p. 6.

[38] (1) Robert D. Murphy, Diplomat Among Warriors (Garden City: Doubleday and Company, Inc., 1964) p. 251. (2) Gimbel, The American Occupation of Germany, p. 7.

1067, Hilldring wrote, put the U.S. government behind the occupation. Without it, Clay's greatest problem might be "the flanking fire that will fall on you from U.S. sources." Hilldring predicted that soon a "bright light" of public scrutiny was going to shine on Germany, and when it did, Clay was going to need two assets "tucked away in your knapsack: . . . the support of the Government" and "the best public relations counselor in Christendom."[39]

Since JCS 1067 was a U.S. directive, and hence technically not in force during the period of the combined command, SHAEF was in fact exercising some of the flexibility Clay wanted. In the last week of April, SHAEF had established the Production Control Agency. Under G–4 at all levels, the agency had a strength of 1,400 officers and 5,800 enlisted men—not a great deal less than the entire strength of military government—and a two-fold mission: to secure industrial production both for Allied military needs and for German civilian needs. Nearly everyone tacitly agreed that a third stated mission, to hold German civilian production to the minimum, was meaningless; with the economy at a standstill, the whole idea was to get it going again. In May, production control groups and sections at army and lower levels worked to restart industries, giving priority to agricultural machinery and supplies, food processing machinery, medical supplies, textiles, and construction materials, and, of course, coal, liquid fuels, and lubricants.[40] In May, on Clay's advice,

SHAEF established the Economic Control Agency. Under G–5, the Economic Control Agency was to deal with prices, rationing and distribution, imports and exports, agriculture, fisheries, and "determination of essential civilian requirements for all commodities."[41] The agency's instructions did not specify assistance for the German economy, but setting it up for any other purpose would have been pointless.

The DPs Homeward Bound

After V–E Day, SHAEF G–5 reckoned the total number of displaced persons uncovered in SHAEF-held territory, including those already repatriated as well as liberated prisoners of war, to be 5.2 million. All but about a million were in the areas of the two U.S. army groups. They were being cared for by 102 UNRRA teams, about an equal number of French MMLA teams, and, wherever necessary, by the local military government detachments. The western Europeans were leaving as fast as transportation could be provided. In April the repatriation rate had been 35,000 persons a week; in May it jumped to over 200,000 a week.[42]

Willing though SHAEF was to have the displaced persons off its hands, some would have to stay a while, particularly the two million Soviet citizens, because their government had not indicated when or where it would receive them. For those who stayed, SHAEF ordered "the conditions of

[39] Ltr, Hilldring to Clay, 21 May 45, in OMGUS 177–1/3.

[40] (1) SHAEF, Staff Memo No. 148, 14 Apr 45, and Memo, SHAEF, ACofS G–4, for CofS, sub: Production Control in Germany, 24 Apr 45, in USFET SGS 091.3/1. (2) Hist Rpt, Seventh Army, Hist Sec, 30 Sep 45, in Seventh Army, 107–3.0.

[41] (1) Memo, SHAEF, Actg Dep CofS, for Gen Smith, 9 May 45, and Memo, SHAEF, ACofS G–5, for CofS, sub: German Economic Control Agency, 8 May 45, in USFET SGS 091.3. (2) ETOUSA, 6093, 14 May 45, in ETOUSA, Admin Hist Collection, No. 146.

[42] (1) SHAEF, ACofS G–5, Min of Meeting with Branch Chiefs, 9 Jun 45, in SHAEF G–5, 3573, Jacket 2. (2) General Board, Study No. 35, p. 38.

Westbound DPs Board a Train *in the yards at Weimar.*

living . . . improved to a standard as high as resources permit and without consideration of any adverse effect on the living conditions of the Germans."[43] While the German ration fell below 1,000 calories a day, military government held the DP ration everywhere at 2,000 calories or more, even when this requirement meant, as it did in the Fifteenth Army area, drawing food from U.S. Army stocks.[44] In the cities, the detachments moved thousands of Germans (10,000 in Munich for instance) out of their homes to make room for the displaced persons, and sick and wounded German soldiers were transferred out of hospitals to provide beds for them. However, the armies found SHAEF's repeated advice not to confine the DPs too closely easier to accept in principle than to carry out in practice. The best camps continued to be those in which the residents were kept under fairly strict control.[45]

[43] Hist Rpt, 6th AGp, ACofS G–5, May 45, in SHAEF G–5, 504.

[44] Hqs, Fifteenth Army, ACofS G–5, Military Government Summary No. 2, 4 Jun 45, in SHAEF G–5, 17.25, Jacket 6.

[45] Hist Rpt, 6th AGp, ACofS G–5, May 45, in SHAEF G–5, 504.

For the western displaced persons, the DPX did its best to speed them on their way home. Third and Seventh Armies sent their DPs by train to Metz and to Luxembourg City where the trains were separated, some going north to Belgium and Holland, the others continuing on into France. Ninth Army routed its trains to Liege, where Civil Affairs Detachment A1F1 operated around-the-clock sorting centers in which the repatriates were separated by nationality and rerouted to their destinations. Although all DPs were dusted with DDT powder at the 12th Army Group's *cordon sanitaire* on the Rhine and at least once more when they crossed the German border, a few persons infected with typhus made their way into Belgium and France. SHAEF's "case-finding teams" traced them and dusted their contacts to prevent the spread of the disease.[46] At Lauterecken on the most heavily traveled line, the one to Metz, XXIII Corps maintained a rest and feeding point for the DPs. The corps engineers built box latrines along the tracks and laid a quarter mile of water pipe with outlets every twenty feet. Medical personnel ran a delousing station and provided first aid and ambulance service. Every passenger received two-thirds of a day's ration, consisting of canned fish or meat, canned biscuit, and chocolate; and expectant mothers, babies, and obviously undernourished persons were also each given a can of U.S. evaporated milk.[47] The record days at Lauterecken were 27–31 May, when almost 55,000 displaced persons passed through.

In the camps, the eastern Europeans predominated. Baumholder, the former German Army training center northwest of Trier, had 17,000 Russians. The Army provided general supervision—interior and exterior guards to control the DPs and regulate traffic—and supplied the food—staples and processed foods from the Army Quartermaster Depot in Trier and vegetables, butter, and milk requisitioned from the Germans. Soviet liaison officers ran the camp on a military basis. Each barracks had a leader who took roll once a day. The DPs operated a shoe shop, tailor shop, and bakery and cooked their food in big German Army kettles. An UNRRA DP team handled the paper work, ran a kindergarten and a school for older children and staged concerts and shows in which the DPs performed. Nevertheless, Maj. Marvin A. Jones, 161st Field Artillery Battalion, the U.S. officer in charge, was appalled by the Russians' cavalier attitude toward life and believed the relatively low mortality rate only proved that the Russians had "constitutions of iron." Seventeen DPs, however, had died from drinking wood alcohol. Patients in the hospital, he said, "started running around" as soon as they felt a little better. The Russian nurses did not know how to plot a fever chart, and the Russian doctors mixed typhus and tuberculosis patients in the same wards.

The 110th Infantry took over a camp with 7,400 Russians at Bad Homburg on 1 May. The regimental executive officer, 1st Lt. Donald V. Taverner, reported, "People . . . were running wild, going into town and killing Germans, then coming back again." After the regiment turned the internal administration over to a Soviet liaison officer, Captain Patrizuk, it reported that from then on there was "never any friction between the Russians and the Americans." Patrizuk organized the DPs into three regiments of three companies

[46] General Board, Study No. 35, p. 38.

[47] XXIII Corps to AG War Dept, sub: Report of Operations, 10–31 May, 5 Jun 45, in XXIII Corps, 223–0.3.

RUSSIAN DPs GIVE DEPARTING COMRADES A SEND-OFF

each; gave them physical training and military training and drill; and set up guard and police forces and a jail. At the end of May, when repatriation to the Soviet Union began, the Homburg camp became a transit stop. The eastbound trains were loaded at the Homburg railhead, and each day trucks from other camps brought in DPs scheduled for shipment out the following day. During their overnight stay they were given a medical check and some entertainment. The next morning, they boarded trains to the accompaniment of Russian band music. The Army provided four days' U.S. rations, water, and medical supplies, and the

men of the 110th Infantry collected toothpaste, chewing gum, candy, and cigarettes to give to the DPs.

As they had during combat, Army enlisted men frequently played an important part in managing the DPs. Sgt. Edward Beatle of the 5th Ranger Battalion organized a mixed camp of Czechs, Poles, and Russians—a formidable job—in a former concentration and work camp at Poeckeing, and even succeeded in getting the Poles and Russians to work together on the camp police force. Third Army awarded Pfc. Frank Rykowski the Bronze Star for helping the DPs in a camp at Fuerth to run their own mess, clinic, and entertainment program.[48]

For three weeks after the surrender the only Soviet nationals being repatriated were the 28,000 captured in German uniform during 1944. The shipment, which had started in late March, went by boat from England and from Marseille to Odessa. The ships returned with troops of the Western Allies whom the Soviet armies had liberated, including 2,858 Americans.[49] On Soviet insistence, SHAEF exchanged the Russians' German uniforms for U.S. clothing before embarkation.[50] To carry out its obligations under the Geneva Convention, and also because of qualms over the reception the men would get in the Soviet Union, SHAEF had ordered that the Russians would be returned only on a voluntary basis. Until the surrender, SHAEF also had to be concerned about giving the Germans a possible excuse for reprisals against the U.S. prisoners they held. On 10 May, through the Military Mission Moscow, Lt. Gen. K. D. Golubev, Soviet Deputy Plenipotentiary for Affairs of Repatriation, complained about the "abnormal attitude toward Soviet citizens." The Russians, he said, were being asked such questions as " 'Who wants to go home?' . . . I especially insist," he concluded, "on the return of all Soviet citizens without depending on their agreeing to return home."[51] SHAEF

then revised its procedure and permitted the men only to be asked whether they claimed Soviet citizenship and were willing to relinquish their prisoner of war status.[52]

In the first week of June, Eisenhower reported to the JCS that the number of Soviet citizens captured while serving in the German forces and still under SHAEF control was under a thousand. He proposed, since the "danger of German reprisals on our own prisoners" no longer existed, to turn them over to the Soviet Union; and in the following week he ordered "German prisoners of war . . . who are claimed to be Soviet citizens and whose citizenship as such has been established will be transferred to Soviet authorities for repatriation."[53] He did not, however, broach the obvious next question, whether force was to be used against those who could not be repatriated any other way; it was a question that would also have to be answered sooner or later for some of the DPs and for the additional thousands of Russians in German service who had come into SHAEF's hands after the surrender. The 12th Army Group, for example, was holding a contingent of 45,000 Cossacks and 11,000 of their camp followers who had surrendered with the German armies in Austria. In Czechoslovakia, Third Army had 7,000 Russians who had fought on the German side and could claim prisoner of war status because they had surrendered before V–E Day.[54]

From beginning to end, probably the

---

[48] (1) Fifteenth Army, 5th Information and Historical Service, sub: Displaced Persons, 14 Jun 45, in XXIII Corps, 223–5.0. (2) Hist Rpt, Third Army, ACofS G–5, May–Jun 45, in OMGUS 76–3/10.

[49] The Exchange with the Soviet Forces of Liberated Personnel—World War II, in CMH files, pp. 4 and 9.

[50] Memo, Hqs, ETOUSA, Provost Marshal, for G–1, sub: Uniforms for Liberated Soviet Citizens, 1 May 45, in SHAEF G–1, 383.618–8.

[51] Cable, Military Mission Moscow to SHAEF Main, Opns Div, 10 May 45, in SHAEF G–1, 383.6/8.

[52] Cable, SHAEF Main to Military Mission Moscow, 15 May 45, in SHAEF G–1, 383.6/9.

[53] Cable, SHAEF Forward, Eisenhower to AGWAR for JCS, 5 Jun 45, and Cable, SHAEF Main to ALFNOR, 10 Jun 45, in SHAEF G–1, 383.6/8–8.

[54] (1) Cable, SHAEF Forward to AFHQ, 12th AGp Msg, 17 May 45, in SHAEF G–1, 383.6/3–19. (2) XII Corps, Report of Operations, 9 May–27 Oct 45, in XII Corps, 212–0.3.

least edifying aspect for SHAEF of having Soviet citizens of any variety in its custody was the endless shower of carping complaints from the Soviet authorities. Already before V–E Day, SHAEF had investigated so many baseless charges from the chief Soviet liaison officer, Maj. Gen. V. M. Dragun—among them one that 850 Russians bound for Odessa had been diverted to North Africa and forcibly enlisted in the Foreign Legion—that it refused to accept any more without some evidence to substantiate them. In May, Moscow took over. On the 2d, *Pravda* printed an interview with Col. Gen. P. I. Golikov, the Plenipotentiary for Affairs of Repatriation, in which Golikov asserted that all Soviet-liberated U.S. and British troops, "except for small groups," had been repatriated but that the Americans and British were holding Russians in camps and mistreating them. Subsequently, his deputy, Golubev, alleging "rude" violations of the Yalta agreement, leveled a series of charges at SHAEF: Soviet citizens were being kept in prisons, given "miserable" rations, denied medical treatment, poisoned with methyl alcohol, and fed poisoned food.[55]

On 16 May, Maj. Gen. Ray W. Barker, SHAEF G–1, went to Halle, twenty miles northwest of Leipzig, to meet General Golubev, coming from Moscow via Berlin, and to arrange with him a system for exchanging DPs and liberated prisoners of war across the demarcation line. Barker had with him Brig. Gen. Stanley R. Mickelsen, Brig. R. H. S. Venables, and a small party of technical services officers. Golubev

came with forty officers, including six major generals, and fifty enlisted men in a convoy that included a U.S.-built armored car and a fully equipped radio truck. The Russians were armed with pistols, submachine guns, and rifles. The next morning, at their first meeting, Barker proposed sending airplanes at once to bring out the U.S. and British prisoners of war. After making some excuses about there not being serviceable airfields—which Barker knew was not true and said so—Golubev made it "very clear that neither now, nor any time in the future, would they permit Allied Airplanes to be used for movement into or out of their territory of prisoners of war or DPs. . . ." The Russians then brought out their plan for the exchange. Obviously written in Moscow, it was cast as a legal document, and its tenor was "to extract compliance to the last degree" with its provisions and with the agreements made at Yalta. Among its specific provisions were some that would have allowed Soviet repatriates to take with them unlimited amounts of "personal effects" and up to 600 pounds of food per person, that would have required SHAEF to provide each repatriate with three days' rations at the exchange point, and that would have prohibited any movement of the repatriates on foot as long as they were on SHAEF territory.

When Barker insisted that he had not come to renegotiate the Yalta agreements but to work out the technicalities of the exchange, Golubev agreed to have a drafting committee set up to work out a plan. The committee met all day and all night on the 17th and into the morning of the 18th and accomplished nothing. The Soviet members were obviously not allowed to depart even in details from the text they had brought with them. Thereafter, Barker ne-

---

[55] (1) Cable, SHAEF Main to Military Mission Moscow, 15 May 45, in SHAEF G–1, 383.6/9. (2) Memo, SHAEF, Political Adviser, for CofS, 2 May 45, in SHAEF G–1, 383.6/8–8. (3) Cable, Military Mission Moscow, from Deane to Eisenhower, 7 Jun 45, in SHAEF G–1, 383.6/8.

gotiated directly with Golubev. The going was slow, since Golubev himself apparently could not make substantive decisions without approval from Moscow. On the 19th and 20th, the talks stalled for twenty-four hours on the question of how far the Soviet repatriates could be required to walk. Finally, in the early morning hours on 22 May, Barker and Golubev completed and signed a plan. Under it, SHAEF would set up reception–delivery points on its side of the demarcation line at Wismar, Wustmark, Ludwigslust, Stendal, Magdeburg, Leipzig, and Plauen; and the Russians would set up points at corresponding locations on their side. As the plan worked out, the Soviet repatriates did not have to walk very much. SHAEF agreed to transport them to its delivery points by rail, truck, and air and to carry them across the line to the Soviet reception points by truck.[56]

During the talks at Halle, Barker proposed converting his and Golubev's groups into a permanent committee to deal with repatriation questions. Golubev refused but announced that he wanted to send Maj. Gen. S. Y. Vershinin and 162 Soviet contact personnel into western Germany to minister to the "hundreds of thousands of Soviet citizens [there] under difficult conditions and more than ever in need of the support of our officers." When Barker asked him whether he would let the French, for example, do the same on Soviet territory, Golubev was noncommittal. Barker later told General Deane at Military Mission Moscow, "A scheme such as this amounts to creation of a Soviet empire in the SHAEF area, which would give them boundless opportunity for criticism—also intelligence." When Golubev, several days later, cabled from Moscow to "demand insistingly an immediate decision," Barker told him that General Dragun, the chief Soviet liaison officer, already had 153 Soviet liaison officers under him and no new organization was needed.

After the Halle conference, Golubev toured five DP camps in SHAEF territory. He had agreed to let one of Barker's officers tour five Soviet camps on the same day, but when the U.S. officer visited the first camp, the Soviet major accompanying him produced an order with Golubev's signature limiting the tour to that one camp only. Later Golubev cabled from Moscow that he had not found the treatment of Soviet citizens satisfactory in a single one of the five camps he had visited.[57]

The exchange had begun before the Halle agreement was signed. On 20 May, the Soviet forces turned over 2,000 liberated U.S. and British prisoners of war. By the 26th, 60,000 eastbound DPs had passed through the SHAEF delivery points, and by the 28th, all of the 28,662 liberated U.S. troops reported in Soviet hands had been returned.[58] In June the rate of repatriation of Soviet DPs reached 250,000 a week, and on 9 June, SHAEF G–5 reported that the repatriation of all DPs had passed the halfway mark. As of 1 July, 1,390,000 Soviet citizens had gone east, and the Soviet forces had delivered 300,000 western European DPs and prisoners of war. The western

---

[56] (1) Memo, SHAEF, ACofS G–1, for CofS, sub: Report on Conference with Russian Officials, 23 May 45, in SHAEF G–1, 337/2. (2) SHAEF, G–5 Div, DP Br, DP Report No. 32, 28 May 45, in SHAEF G–5, 6.

[57] Cable, Military Mission Moscow to SHAEF Main, 5 Jun 45; Ltr, Barker to Golubev, 9 Jun 45; Ltr, Barker to Deane, 9 Jun 45; and Cable, Military Mission Moscow to SHAEF Main, 18 Jun 45, in SHAEF G–1, 383.6/8.
[58] The latter figure includes those returned earlier through Odessa.

Europeans still in camps under 12th Army Group control were then down to 6,583. The number of Soviet citizens left in western Germany was below 700,000 and being reduced fast, leaving 871,000 Poles, the largest national DP group. The Soviet authorities had not included them in the east–west exchange, and the Warsaw government had so far not made any arrangements to have them returned.[59]

The Wehrmacht

In the last week of the war, on orders from Admiral Doenitz, the main objective of the German troops still fighting had been to surrender to the Western Allies, which they had done by the hundreds of thousands. What was left of the German Army Group Vistula after its retreat from the Oder River and Berlin took refuge behind the 21 Army Group and Ninth Army lines. Third Army, in Czechoslovakia, let in 125,000 German troops before the surrender. Austria was jammed with the remnants of the armies that had been on the southern flank of the Eastern Front. Meanwhile, the U.S. troops were rounding up and herding into makeshift cages what was left of the Wehrmacht in southwestern Germany, and Montgomery's armies were acquiring the entire garrisons of Holland, north Germany, and Denmark. When SHAEF G–1 added up the totals, the figures came close to 5 million prisoners of war and disarmed enemy troops in SHAEF custody, well over 3 million of them being held by U.S. forces.[60]

The discrepancy between the numbers of prisoners in U.S. custody and in British custody was a lingering point of contention between the U.S. side of SHAEF and the British War Office. Under the Fifty-fifty Agreement, made in 1944, the British and Americans had each undertaken to assume responsibility for half the prisoners no matter who captured them. After February 1945, the U.S. forces had made the most captures, but the British had refused to take their half, arguing that they did not have places to keep them or men to guard them on the Continent and that moving them to England would arouse public resentment and adversely affect British troop morale. After V–E Day, Eisenhower repeatedly tried to get the British to take at least several hundred thousand prisoners, with remarkable lack of success. When Seventh Army negotiated with the British command in Austria for 9,000 Wehrmacht horses, the British said they would have to send along enough prisoners to care for the horses; they sent 82,000. On 1 June, Eisenhower informed the War Office that the shortage in the British "account" up to then amounted to 25 million prisoner-days' rations and was growing at the rate of 900,000 rations every day.[61]

---

[59] (1) SHAEF, ACofS G–5, Min of Meetings with Branch Chiefs, 9 Jun 45, in SHAEF G–5, 3573, Jacket 2. (2) Memo, SHAEF G–5, DP Br, sub: Russian DPs, 9 Jul 45, in SHAEF G–5, 29.2. (3) Hqs, 12th AGp, ACofS G–5, Narrative Summary for Month of June, 9 Jul 45, in SHAEF G–5, 17.16, Jacket 13.

[60] Reports of the Military Governor, U.S. Zone, give a total of 7.7 million German military personnel disposed of by U.S. forces between 8 May 1945 and 15 July 1945, including Volkssturm and other paramilitary groups, camp followers, and prisoners returned from Norway, Italy, and camps in the United States and England. (1) Memo, ACofS G–1 for Staff, sub: Disbandment Directive No. 5, 14 Jun 45, in SHAEF G–1, 383.6. (2) OMGUS, Demilitarization Cumulative Review, in Monthly Report of the Military Governor, U.S. Zone, 20 Aug 46.

[61] (1) Cable, AGWAR, from Marshall to SHAEF Main, 25 Mar 45; Cable, SHAEF G–1 to AGWAR, 21 Apr 45; and Cable, SHAEF For-

PRISONER OF WAR COLUMN *marches through Munich.*

Food was the problem. Registered prisoners of war were entitled to 2,000 calories a day, and working prisoners, 2,900 calories. The disarmed enemy troops could be given the normal German consumer's ration; therefore, SHAEF had intended to transfer all German troops inside Germany to disarmed enemy status after the surrender, but the legality of this move was in doubt at least until after the Berlin Declaration was signed.[62] According to the

ECLIPSE plan, the disarmed enemy troops were to be fed, like the DPs, from German sources; but while the DPs were scattered in groups of thousands and could theoretically live off the local economies, the troops were concentrated, sometimes in the hundreds of thousands. On 16 May, Bradley cabled Eisenhower that the *Wehrmacht* stocks the Seventh Army had been using to feed its disarmed enemy troops would run out that day. In another four days

ward to War Office, 1 Jun 45, in SHAEF G–1, 383.6/3–19. (2) Memo, Hqs, Seventh Army, 6 Jun 45, in Seventh Army, 107–0.19.

[62] Msg, Com Zone to SHAEF Forward, 2 Jun

45, and Cable, SHAEF Main, Eisenhower to AGWAR for CCS, 10 Mar 45, in SHAEF G–1, 387.4/1.

Seventh Army would have used up all it could get from civilian sources in its area. The other armies could not help because they were in much the same position. "These disarmed forces," he maintained, "will either have to be fed or released." He asked for immediate authority to discharge the disarmed enemy forces and for U.S. Army or military government rations to feed them until the discharge could be completed.[63] SHAEF could not authorize a "blanket release" of German forces, Eisenhower replied, because their discharge had to be "strictly controlled in order to prevent widespread disorder, or other conditions which military government agencies will be unable to cope with"; the release of the categories already approved (see below) would "tax the administrative machinery for a considerable time. . . . Until such time as indigenous resources can meet the needs," he concluded, 12th Army Group could use imported military government food for the disarmed forces. Preferably it should use the imported food for feeding the DPs, and the indigenous food could thus be saved for feeding the German troops.[64] Imported food, however, was not a real solution either. Brig. Gen. Robert M. Littlejohn, Chief Quartermaster, Communications Zone, pointed out that there was a food shortage in the United States and in the theater. Including the prisoners of war, his ration strength was over 7 million, and he was having to reduce the rations of U.S. officers and enlisted men by ten percent to meet it. Moreover, the War Department had made no provision for clothing and camp equipment for the

prisoners. Littlejohn recommended "settling down to 500,000 in three months."[65]

SHAEF issued three disbandment directives in May. Disbandment Directive No. 1 authorized the release of agricultural workers, coal miners, transportation workers, and others in key occupations. No. 2 authorized the discharge of women, and No. 3 of men over fifty years of age. Directive No. 4, put out in early June, released the Belgians, French, and Dutch who had served in the *Wehrmacht* to their governments.[66]

A G–1 inspection in early June revealed, however, that the attitude of the armies was "to discharge as many as possible as fast as possible without a great deal of attention to categories." The average rate for 12th Army Group was 30,000 a day; Third Army alone had released over a half million disarmed enemy troops by 8 June. The armies were working against time. Unless the British accepted the prisoners and troops due on their account or unless a large number were released, the rations, according to G–5 estimates, would run out within the month.[67]

The discharge procedure was simple and generally similar to that devised by CCA of 12th Armored Division under Brig. Gen. Riley F. Ennis, which got the job of disbanding the 82,000 troops sent by the British with the horses from Austria. The

---

[63] Cable, Hqs, 12th AGp, to SHAEF Forward, 16 May 45, in SHAEF SGS 370.01.
[64] Cable, SHAEF to 12th AGp, 18 May 45, in SHAEF G–3, GCT 388.3–1/GPS.

[65] Ltr, Com Zone, Ch, QM, to SHAEF, ACofS G–4, 23 May 45, and Cable, ETOUSA, Com Zone, to SHAEF Main, 23 May 45, in SHAEF G–1, 383.6/3.
[66] (1) Memo, ACofS G–1 for Staff, sub: Disbandment Directive No. 5, 14 Jun 45, in SHAEF G–1, 383.6. (2) Memo, SHAEF, ACofS G–1, for AG, sub: Disbandment Directive No. 5, 29 Jun 45, in SHAEF G–1, 387.4/12.
[67] Memo, SHAEF G–1, Asst G–1, for Ch, German Affairs Div, sub: Report of Trip, 9 Jun 45, in SHAEF G–1, 387.4/1.

separation center was an old cavalry school. The men lined up in the stable compound. On entering the building, they removed their shirts and raised their arms to be inspected for the SS blood-type tattoo. (SS men were held either as prisoners of war or, if they had enough rank, under automatic arrest.) After they were inspected, German doctors gave them superficial physical examinations and separated any who were obviously sick. Next, the men filled out counterintelligence questionnaires and were interviewed briefly to determine whether they were subject to automatic arrest or had technical skills of intelligence interest. Those who fell into neither category were given slips stamped with a "B" and could be discharged. Those with an "A" slip were put under automatic arrest when they reached the end of the line. With a "C" they were held as prisoners of war. The next step was to fill out the so-called P–4 form, on which the soldier was required to give his name, the names of his close relatives, and his place of residence. After completing the form, he turned his *Soldbuch* (pay book) over to a German clerk and received a discharge form and instructions on how to act. If he was going to a place in the Seventh Army area, he was also given half a loaf of black bread and about a pound of lard, his rations for the trip, and could leave the stable to wait for a truck to take him home. CCA had five truck companies working day and night hauling those discharged. If his destination was outside the army area, the soldier went to one of several small temporary camps to await transportation. Outside the center, CCA set up sixty guard posts to block all roads and paths leading in, less to keep those inside in than to keep others out. Upon learning of the center's existence, German soldiers who had deserted late in the war or had been captured and turned loose by U.S. troops tried to infiltrate the center to get themselves officially discharged.[68]

On 29 June, SHAEF G–1 sanctioned what the armies were already doing and in Disbandment Directive No. 5 authorized a general discharge of German nationals held as prisoners of war and disarmed enemy troops, excepting those in automatic arrest categories, SS men, war criminals, or residents of the Russian zone. The last group would have to be held until the Soviet authorities agreed to receive them.[69] From then on, the separation centers ran at full tilt until the middle of August when the glut of prisoners seemed about to become a shortage. SHAEF had contracted in July to provide 1.3 million prisoners for labor in France and smaller numbers for Belgium, Holland, and Luxembourg; and the U.S. forces were using over half a million in Military Labor Service Units. For the next several months, the numbers on hand plus the contingents to be returned from the United States (370,000) and from Norway and Italy were just about enough to meet the commitments.[70] After the summer's rush was over, the presence of prisoners of war threatened to become a permanent feature of the occupation. For the U.S. forces, they were a useful source of labor as well as a willing one, since they were better fed than they would be on the

[68] Memo, Hqs, Seventh Army, 6 Jun 45, in Seventh Army, 107–0.19.

[69] (1) SHAEF G–1 to AG, sub: Disbandment Directive No. 5, 29 Jun 45, in SHAEF G–1, 387.4/12. (2) memo, SHAEF G–1 for SHAEF Staff, sub: Disbandment Directive No. 5, 14 Jun 45, in SHAEF G–1, 383.6.

[70] (1) Ltr, SHAEF G–1 to SHAEF AG, sub: German PW Labor, 13 Jul 45, in SHAEF G–1, 383.6/3. (2) Final Report, Seventh Army [Mar 46], in USFET, Historical Program Files, T 167/5.

outside; furthermore, no matter how many disbandment directives were published (the last, No. 26, was issued on 29 November 1945), there seemed always to be thousands of ineligibles: the sick and disabled, war crimes suspects, SS men, who might be charged as members of a criminal organization, and members of the General Staff.[71]

The General Staff officers, including also all generals, appeared for a time to be the likeliest candidates for permanent detention. Because their appointments had been for life, SHAEF had ordered all active and retired General Staff officers arrested, "not so much to punish them for their misdeeds as to ensure that their opportunities for planning and making preparations for future war . . . are reduced to a minimum."[72] One recurring proposal, last submitted by SHAEF G–2 on 27 April 1945, was to "exile all General Staff officers and all generals forever in a group and imprison them for life in an area under the control of one or all of the United Nations."[73]

The future of the General Staff officers and generals was going to be substantially different from the one G–2 proposed for them, which in fact never went beyond the talking stage. In Washington, the War Department G–2 Historical Branch, later the Historical Division, War Department, and eventually the Office of the Chief of Military History, needed information on German operations for the war histories it was going to write. Col. S. L. A. Marshall, chief of the Historical Division, ETOUSA, needed the same kind of information for his division's history of the European theater. In the spring and summer of 1945, however, German military records were only just being uncovered and war crimes and intelligence investigators would have first call on them for a long time. Interviews seemed to offer a useful substitute, and in July 1945, the Historical Branch, G–2, sent Dr. George W. Shuster, President of Hunter College, to Europe at the head of a mission charged with interviewing high-ranking Germans. The transcripts of eighty interviews that Maj. Kenneth Hechler, a member of the mission, conducted with German officers held at ASHCAN so impressed Colonel Marshall that he authorized Major Hechler to transfer some key German officers to a prisoner of war enclosure at Versailles, where the theater historians would have a better opportunity to interrogate them. After the theater historical activities were moved to Frankfurt in early 1946, the Historical Division, USFET, took over Disarmed Enemy Forces Enclosure 20 at Allendorf, Hesse. The division assembled there all of the German generals and General Staff officers in U.S. custody whose personnel records indicated that they would be able to provide information pertinent to the history of U.S. campaigns in western Europe. Later, prisoners with knowledge of the Mediterranean theater and the German campaigns against the Soviet Union were also included. Under the former chief of the General Staff, Generaloberst a. D. Franz Halder, the officers were put to work writing studies for use in the Army historical program and in the training courses at service schools. After nearly all were released from prisoner of war status in July 1947,

---

[71] Memo, Hqs, USFET, Dep CofS, for Major Commands, sub: Status of Enemy Prisoners of War, 26 Sep 45, in USFET SGS 383.6/3.

[72] Memo, SHAEF for CG's, 12th, 21, and 6th AGp, sub: Treatment of Senior German Commanders and Staff Officers, 29 Apr 45, in SHAEF G–3, 387.4–5.

[73] Memo, SHAEF, ACofS G–2, for CofS, sub: Disposal of Officers of the German General Staff, 27 Apr 45, in SHAEF G–1, 387.4/1.

many continued to work full or part time under General Halder and a control group of senior German officers, turning out hundreds of historical manuscripts and providing information for Army historians. By the time the program terminated in 1959, most of the younger officers had found managerial positions in industry or had resumed their military careers in the *Bundeswehr* of the German Federal Republic.[74]

---

[74] (1) Bell I. Wiley, Historical Program of the U.S. Army, 1939 to Present [no date], in CMH files. (2) Draft of paper "The Use of Captured and Related Records in Official Military History" delivered by Detmar Finke at the National Archives Conference on Captured Records, 13–14 Nov 1968, in CMH files.

CHAPTER XVII

Zone and Sector

Access to Berlin

After the ceremony at Wendenschloss, Prime Minister Churchill on 9 June made one more attempt to have the American and British withdrawal from the assigned Soviet zone put off until the Russians came to terms on the other questions pertaining to Germany and Austria. President Truman replied that because of the existing agreement on the zones, he could not "delay the withdrawal of American troops from the Soviet zone in order to use pressure in the settlement of other problems."[1] By cable on the 14th, Truman told Stalin he was ready to issue instructions to the U.S. troops to begin withdrawing into their own zone on 21 June "in accordance with arrangements between the respective commanders, including in these arrangements simultaneous movement of the national garrisons into Greater Berlin and provision of free access by air, road, and rail from Frankfurt and Bremen to Berlin for U.S. forces."[2] To the President's surprise Stalin asked for a postponement. Marshal Zhukov and the other Soviet commanders, he said, would be in Moscow for a victory parade on the 24th and for a meeting of the Supreme Soviet and would not be able to return to Germany until the end of the month. He suggested, instead, starting the movements on 1 July and added that by

then the work of clearing mines in Berlin would also be completed. Truman agreed, with the proviso that enough U.S. troops be in Berlin before 1 July to carry out preparations for the forthcoming Big Three conference scheduled to begin in Berlin in mid-July.[3]

In early June, Maj. Gen. Floyd L. Parks became Commanding General, Headquarters, Berlin District (U.S. Sector).[4] On the 15th, SHAEF began trying to arrange for Parks to take a reconnaissance party to Berlin to survey the site and start work on the accommodations for the U.S. delegation to the Big Three conference. Six days later, after a combined effort by the Military Mission and the Embassy in Moscow and, finally, after a strong hint that otherwise the conference might have to be delayed, the Russians grudgingly agreed to let Parks and his party go to Berlin.[5]

Parks and an advance party of a dozen

---

[1] *Foreign Relations, 1945,* vol. III, pp. 132–34.
[2] *Ibid.,* p. 135f.

[3] (1) *Ibid.,* p. 137. (2) Truman, *Memoirs,* vol. I, p. 305.
[4] On 20 May, SHAEF had designated the Headquarters, First Allied Airborne Army, as the combined Berlin District headquarters. In June, under Parks, the U.S. Elements of Headquarters and Headquarters Company, First Allied Airborne Army, became the U.S. Berlin District staff, (1) Memo, SHAEF, AG, for Distribution, sub: Organization of Hqs, Berlin District, 16 May 45, in SHAEF G–5, 115.05. (2) SHAEF, General Orders No. 9, 17 Jun 45, in USFET SGS 322.
[5] Department of State, *The Conference of Berlin (Potsdam), 1945,* in "Foreign Relations of the United States," vol. I (Washington, D.C., 1960), pp. 108–14.

officers landed at Tempelhof airfield in Berlin on the afternoon of the 22d; the Russians took them through the city to Babelsberg in the southwestern suburbs. The main element, designated the Preliminary Reconnaissance Party for Berlin, was to come by road the next day. Col. H. G. Sheen, who was in the Parks group, recorded what he saw:

The bomb damage in the heart of the city is difficult to describe. In certain areas the stench of unburied dead is almost overpowering. From Tempelhof to the Wilhelmsstrasse not one undamaged building is standing; roofs, floors, and windows are gone, and in many cases the fragments of only one or two walls are standing. Many of the streets remain passable, but rubble covers the sidewalks and large numbers of streets are still blocked off because of bomb craters and debris.[6]

At Babelberg—the mostly undamaged former German film colony where the Russians had chosen to billet the delegations to the Big Three meeting—Parks met his Soviet host, Col. Gen. Sergey N. Kruglov, Stalin's security chief. Kruglov showed him the houses reserved for the President and the U.S. conferees and the Cecilienhof Palace in Potsdam where the meetings would be held; in the evening he sent a case of wine and some champagne. He refused to talk about the entry of U.S. troops into Berlin, however, saying his authority extended only to arrangements for the conference, which were confined to the Babelsberg-Potsdam area. Having been warned by the Military Mission before he left Frankfurt that he might have some trouble if he tried to open the Berlin question, Parks did not press the point.[7]

On the return flight the next afternoon, Parks followed the Berlin-Halle *Autobahn* looking for the truck convoy of the Preliminary Reconnaissance Party for Berlin. It was supposed to have crossed the Elbe early in the morning and should have reached Babelsberg before he left. When he spotted the head of the column, it was three miles east of the Elbe and still fifty-five miles away from Berlin. Colonel Howley, commanding the convoy, had reached the Elbe bridge at Dessau in the morning on time. With him he had 100 trucks, the 136 enlisted men and 85 officers of his Detachment A1A1, and several dozen officers and 175 enlisted men detailed to work at the conference site. At the bridge, the Russians had refused to pass more than 50 trucks, 37 officers (actually a total of 50 but minus the officers with Parks), and 175 enlisted men—the exact number specified in the instructions from Moscow. Howley, after arguing with successive Soviet generals for seven hours, had finally crossed the river with the numbers the Russians stipulated. He had left A1A1 behind, which made him and three other officers the only military government personnel in the part of the convoy allowed to continue.

The Americans had learned something about the Russians at the Dessau bridge; they learned more on the road that day. Howley described the scene:

The trip from the Elbe River to Babelsberg was an experience out of this world. Russian displaced persons who had gaily marched across the bridge at the Elbe were seen wearily struggling on foot toward the railhead at Berlin. Horsedrawn convoys dotted the road. Each vehicle was drawn by 3 or 4 horses with a number of spares tied to the side. Often young foals tottled along in back

[6] Memo, SHAEF G–2, CI Sub Div, for Brig Gen T. J. Betts, sub: Report of Visit to Berlin, 27 Jun 45, in SHAEF G–2, GB I/CI/CS/091.1–4.
[7] (1) Department of State, *Conference of Berlin* (*Potsdam*), in "Foreign Relations," pp. 127–32. (2) Cable, Military Mission Moscow, Deane to ETOUSA, 22 Jun 45, in SHAEF SGS 510/2.

BERLIN, MAY 1945

of the mares. The Russian boatlike wagons were piled high. They were driven by one mustached Russian with another sleeping on top of the wagon. These were supply trains reminiscent of our Civl War. Thousands of horses were in the fields guarded by Russian soldiers. The troops were dirty and disinterested in our progress. They looked as earthy as our own combat troops at the end of three weeks in the mud. The country was deserted. Fields were unattended, and no Germans were in sight.[8]

The reconnaissance, such as it was, ended at Babelsberg. The Russians refused to

allow the party members to enter Berlin, and guards prevented them from leaving the U.S. compound at Babelsberg. No one would even have set eyes on the city had Howley not secured permission on the 26th for himself and his deputy, Lt. Col. John J. Maginnis, to make a two-hour trip to Tempelhof airfield to confer with a U.S. air crew due to arrive there. When the Soviet NKVD (secret police) officer, who went along to make certain the Americans did not stray from their stated mission, showed that he did not know the shortest way to the airfield, Howley and Maginnis had the small satisfaction of laying out a

---

[8] OMG, Berlin District, Military Government Report, 4 Jul 45–3 Jan 46, in CMH files.

route that took them across five of the six boroughs in the U.S. sector.[9] On the 28th, the military government officers went back to Halle, as Howley remarked later, "convinced that we would never be sent to Berlin for any military government work."[10]

The frustrations would indeed never end, but the wait to get into Berlin was not going to be as long as Howley feared. On 27 June, General Deane cabled to General Marshall from the Military Mission Moscow, "Soviet General Staff has just informed me . . . that instructions have been given to appropriate commanders regarding free access to Berlin and Vienna."[11] At the same time, he informed Eisenhower that Zhukov was back in Berlin "with full power to settle all questions on the spot."[12]

General Clay and Lt. Gen. Sir Ronald Weeks, Montgomery's deputy military governor, went to Berlin on the 29th to confer with Marshal Zhukov. Zhukov, whom Clay afterwards described as cordial but unpredictable, demonstrated both qualities at the outset.[13] He accepted the agenda Clay and Weeks had brought with them as the basis for discussion and turned at once to the first point, which concerned arrangements for the U.S. and British forces to enter and take over their sectors in Berlin. After some desultory discussion about how many troops the Western Allies would bring in, however, he asked how long the Americans would take to evacuate the parts of the Soviet zone they held. When Clay said the plan was to begin on 1 July and to complete the turnover in nine days, Zhukov wanted to know why it would take so long. The Soviet forces, he said, could take over the entire area in twenty-four hours, and, he added, the quicker the move out of the zone, the quicker the Western Allies could enter Berlin. Coldly, he let it be seen that what was important for him was a trade: the approximately 16,400 square miles of the Soviet zone that SHAEF held in exchange for the 185 square miles of the western sectors in Berlin. Obviously not expecting SHAEF to agree to so lopsided an exchange if it could be avoided, he furthermore specified that reconnaissance parties might enter Berlin on 1 July but that the main body of the occupation troops would have to wait until the day the movement out of the Soviet zone was completed. When Clay asked why, if the U.S. forces released a third of the territory they held to the Soviet forces on the first day, one-third of the Berlin force could not move in on that day, Zhukov simply replied that such an arrangement was impossible. The most he would allow, after Clay had agreed to the complete U.S. evacuation of the Soviet zone by midnight on 4 July, was that the U.S. and British forces could begin moving across the Soviet zone toward Berlin on the 3d.

The remaining items on the agenda primarily concerned road, rail, and air access to Berlin. SHAEF asked for two highways, three rail lines, and open access by air in an arc bounded by lines drawn from Hamburg and Frankfurt to Berlin. Zhukov, saying that one road and one railroad ought to be enough for the 50,000 troops the British and Americans had said they would

---

[9] John J. Maginnis, *Military Government Journal: Normandy to Berlin* (Amherst: University of Massachusetts Press, 1971), pp. 257–59.

[10] OMG, Berlin District, Military Government Report, 4 Jul 45–3 Jan 46, in CMH files.

[11] Cable, Military Mission Moscow, Deane to Marshall for Eisenhower, 27 Jun 45, in USFET SGS 370.5/3.

[12] Cable, 30 Mission to SHAEF Main, 27 Jun 45, in USFET SGS 370.5/3.

[13] OMGUS, History, ch. III, p. 7.

have in Berlin, offered the *Autobahn* Berlin–Magdeburg–Hanover, the railroad paralleling it, and one twenty-mile-wide air corridor from Berlin to Magdeburg and west. The air corridor, he agreed after some argument, would be divided in two over Magdeburg, one lane bearing southwest toward Frankfurt, the other west toward Hanover. Clay reserved the right to reopen the access question in the Control Council, and Zhukov coolly replied that possibly all points discussed at the meeting might be changed. When Clay asked for unlimited use of the roads, Zhukov said he did not understand just what the British and Americans desired. It would be necessary, he stated, for vehicles to be governed by Russian road signs, military police, and document checks, but there would be no cargo inspection; the Russians were not interested in what was being hauled, how much was being hauled, or how many trucks were moving.[14] Eventually, Clay would come to think he had been "mistaken in not . . . making free access to Berlin a condition to our withdrawal into our occupation zone."[15] At the moment, however, under instructions from McCloy in Washington not to press controversial matters to the point of dissension, he was most concerned with getting the Control Council established and working. To McCloy he reported after the meeting, "I still feel that with patience and understanding we will be able to work out central controls over a long period of time."[16]

Howley, after his Babelsberg trip, had requisitioned a farm outside Halle, and he planned to move Detachment A1A1 into camp there on Sunday, 1 July. On Saturday, he received orders to proceed to Berlin instead. In the morning, in battle dress and with full field packs, the detachment headed east across the Elbe. The convoy moved through the Russian control points without a hitch, and by nightfall, A1A1 was bivouacked in the Grunewald, the parklike wooded area on the southwestern outskirts of Berlin.

On Monday morning, Parks, Howley, and Maj. Gen. Lewis O. Lyne, the British Berlin district commander, met Col. Gen. Aleksandr V. Gorbatov, the Soviet city commandant, at his headquarters. In spite of some stiffness—most of the morning was spent just trying to reach Gorbatov by telephone—the meeting resulted in two important decisions: that the U.S. sector would comprise six boroughs (*Verwaltungsbezirke*) in the southwestern part of the city, Zehlendorf, Steglitz, Tempelhof, Schoeneberg, Kreuzberg, and Neukoelln; and that the Americans would assume control in their sector at midnight on 4 July. Gorbatov agreed to allow U.S. military government officers to reconnoiter the boroughs they would control and, after the tour, invited the British and Americans to a tea, which turned out to be a full-course dinner.[17] The Russians accepted Parks' invitation to a formal ceremony of occupation to be held by the U.S. forces in Berlin on the afternoon of the 4th.

The 2d Armored Division, which together with First Airborne Army paratroops formed the main Berlin occupation force, began to move out on the morning

---

[14] (1) *Foreign Relations, 1945*, vol. III, pp. 353–61. (2) Msg, SHAEF Main to U.S. Headquarters, Berlin District, 28 Jun 45, in SHAEF G–5, 803. (3) SHAEF G–5, Draft Notes on Meeting at Berlin on Friday, 29 June, 29 Jun 45, in SHAEF G–5, 803/1.

[15] Clay, *Decision in Germany*, p. 26.

[16] OMGUS, History, ch. III, p. 7.

[17] Hist Rpt, OMG, Berlin District, 1 Jul 45–30 Jun 46, in CMH files, vol. I, p. 22.

ALLIES MEET IN BERLIN. *Soviet troops greet Signal Corps photographer who was one of the first Americans into the city on 4 July 1945.*

of Tuesday, the 3d, expecting to close to Berlin by midnight on the 4th. The armored division passed through Halle, which would come under Soviet control on the 4th. Zhukov had said the division could use the Halle-Dessau-Berlin *Autobahn,* but only until the 7th. After this date, the road would be closed because of the conference. The Russians stopped the lead convoy for a half day at Dessau, however, claiming that a bridge ahead was unsafe. To be out of Halle on time, the division then had to make a hasty detour sixty-five miles north

to Helmstedt to get on the Magdeburg-Berlin *Autobahn,* only to find itself caught there in a traffic jam with British units to whom the Russians had given a similar excuse when they forced them off a road farther north.[18] The railroad proved to be totally unusable; the bridge at Magdeburg was out. The line had been double-tracked, but the Russians had torn up and taken

—————————

[18] (1) Msgs, Hqs, Berlin District, to SHAEF Main, 4 Jul '45, in SHAEF G–5, 803/1, Jacket. 5. (2) Donnison, *Civil Affairs and Military Government, Northwest Europe,* p. 269.

away one track and all the signal equipment; the first military train did not get through until the end of July.

On the afternoon of the 4th, Parks held the occupation ceremony in the Adolf Hitler Caserne in Berlin with as much of the 2d Armored Division as had arrived. After the parade, which some Russians had attended, he received a message from Zhukov stating that the Americans would not be allowed to take over their sector at midnight as agreed but would have to wait until the Kommandatura was set up. The Americans, by then tired and thoroughly irritated, suspected the Russians were stalling for time to finish stripping the western sectors, and Parks, after failing to reach Zhukov, told Howley to take over the sector anyway, adding, "But don't get into too much trouble."[19]

Howley's borough teams moved in early the next morning. By nine o'clock, they had raised the American flag in each borough, posted the proclamation and ordinances, set up summary military government courts, and notified the *Buergermeisters* to obey orders. The Russians were late sleepers, and it was eleven before they came around to protest. The language difference hampered discussion somewhat, but both sides had essentially only one point to make: the Russians, that Marshal Zhukov said "No"; and the Americans, that General Gorbatov said "Yes." The Russians said that they had their orders, and the Americans said that they had theirs. In the end the Americans stayed and the Russians stayed. In a day or two, when the Russians learned they would not be punished for having failed to expel the Americans, some of them became quite friendly. Inter-

views generally were conducted with much headshaking over the conflicting orders and ended with elaborately cordial handshakes.[20]

The Americans at last had a chance to see what they were getting. What they saw were mostly the effects of the 75,000 tons of bombs the U.S. and British air forces had dropped on the city during the war. In all Berlin only 300,000 dwelling units out of what had been a million and a half remained undamaged. To haul away the rubble, they estimated, would take sixteen years at a rate of ten fifty-car trainloads a day. Of the once great Berlin bus fleet, thirty-seven vehicles were still running. Steam engines were being used to haul the streetcars to save electricity, and less than a tenth of the subway cars were operable. The bridges over the city's many canals had nearly all collapsed under the bombing and artillery fire or had been blown up by the retreating German troops. Sewers hanging under the bridges had fractured and were pouring their sewage into the canals, which were stagnant and covered with scum, breeding places for billions of flies and mosquitos. Graves marked by crude wooden crosses could be seen everywhere, even in the public squares and along the streets; and thousands of corpses lay unburied under the rubble. The people were getting 64 percent of a 1,240-calorie daily ration. The Russians had put Germans, mostly women, to work on the mountains of rubble, using some debris to fill in the craters in the streets and arranging the rest in less obtrusive patterns.

The Germans seemed relieved to see the Americans arrive. Although the Soviet command had not imposed nonfraterniza-

---

[19] OMG, Berlin District, Military Government Report, 4 Jul 45–3 Jan 46, in CMH files.

[20] (1) Hist Rpt, OMG, Berlin District, vol. I, p. 24. (2) Earl Ziemke, *Battle for Berlin* (New York: Ballentine Books, 1968), p. 145.

RUSSIANS LEAVE THE U.S. SECTOR OF BERLIN

tion in the stringent form the Americans and British were still trying to enforce on themselves, the Russians' official arbitrariness and individual unpredictability had aroused insecurity and fear that persisted even though they also often displayed personal generosity and kindness, and even though looting and plundering had subsided and rape had become an unnecessarily strenuous way of attaining what hundreds of women in the almost starving city were willing to provide for small considerations.[21]

Clay, Murphy, Parks, Howley, and a battery of interpreters went, together with their British counterparts, to talk to Zhukov in the Soviet headquarters in Berlin-Pankow on the 7th. The spirit of the meeting was not at all friendly. Zhukov said he was willing to set up the Kommandatura, but there were matters of food and fuel supplies to be settled before the Soviet authorities turned over the western sectors. The Americans and British were going to occupy their sectors and in doing so, he said blandly, they would also have to assume responsibility for feeding the people.

[21] Ziemke, *Battle for Berlin*, pp. 149–53.

According to his figures there were nearly 800,000 Germans in the American sector and 900,000 in the British sector, and they would require 40,000 tons of food per month. Berlin's normal supply system, he maintained, had broken down completely and was not likely to be restored soon. He also insisted on the Western Allies' supplying nearly all the city's coal, because, he claimed, Upper Silesia, formerly the chief source of coal for Berlin, had been transferred to Polish control and was no longer part of Germany. Since the British and Americans had expected to get food for their zones from the primarily agricultural eastern zone, and not to have to ship it there, and since neither the United States nor the United Kingdom had recognized the Soviet transfer of Upper Silesia to Poland, the western representatives, badly shaken, broke off the meeting to consult their governments.

Clay, nevertheless, came away somewhat encouraged by Zhukov's apparent willingness to set up the Kommandatura. He thought this attitude might establish a pattern for the Control Council, and to preserve it he and his party and Weeks and his party returned three days later prepared to assume responsibility for the food and coal pending subsequent decisions to be made either at the Potsdam Conference or by the Control Council when it came into being. Zhukov agreed to keep Berlin supplied until the Western Allies could begin to get shipments in—with a commitment to repay him, of course; the conference then moved on to the organization of the Kommandatura. Clay tried again to get the original U.S. view accepted that the city should be administered as a unit. Both the British and the Russians objected, and in the end the system that was proposed for the Control Council was also adopted for

the Kommandatura. This body would be responsible for central administration, but each nation would have full control in its own sector; furthermore, it was to be quadripartite, Zhukov having agreed to let the French commander-designate, Brig. Gen. Geoffrey de Beauchesne, sit as an observer until a French sector was assigned. On questions of municipal administration the western representatives were once more at a disadvantage; while the Russians had detailed knowledge of conditions in the city, they had practically none. Consequently, they felt forced to let the Soviet organization and legislation remain in effect even though they knew that the rule of unanimity in the Kommandatura would make changes difficult later.[22]

On the 11th, the members of the Kommandatura, Parks, Lyne, Gorbatov, and de Beauchesne, met to decide how they would operate. To the first question on the agenda, when the Kommandatura would begin to function, Parks answered, "This is the first meeting." The others approved, and they elected Gorbatov chairman for the rest of July. At nine o'clock the next morning, the Soviet military government detachments withdrew from the western sectors.[23]

---

[22] For a description of how the Soviet authorities had used their two months of exclusive control in Berlin to organize the municipal administration in their own interest, see Wolfgang Leonhard, *Child of the Revolution* (Chicago: Henry Regnery Co., 1958), pp. 287–338.

[23] (1) Cable, SHAEF to War Dept, 9 Jul 45, in CAD, 014 Germany, 7–10–42 (1), sec. B. (2) Department of State, *Conference of Berlin (Potsdam), 1945,* in "Foreign Relations," pp. 631–34. (3) Cable, WARCOS to CG, USFET, for Clay, 11 Jul 45, in OMGUS 3/35, dec. 322. (4) Historical Summary of the Agreement and Events Which Preceded the First Meeting of the Allied Control Council [no date], in OMGUS 358–1/5. (5) Hist Rpt, OMG, Berlin District, vol.

Rolling the Carpet

Military government called the operation "rolling the carpet." The tactical commands used the term "redisposition" to avoid "redeployment," which was reserved for the troop movements from Europe to the war in the Pacific. For both, the withdrawal to the final U.S. occupation zone was a massive job. On V–E Day, the U.S forces held 43 percent (78,000 square miles) of the area within the 1937 German boundaries, which was the whole (with minor exceptions) of the assigned U.S. zone (41,400 square miles) plus an area almost as large in the British and Soviet zones.[24] The carpet would have to be rolled and the tactical units redisposed from the west, east, north, and south, and within the zone the boundaries of Third and Seventh Armies would have to be readjusted, before the armies could become the military district commands. The obscure behavior of the Russians and belated decision on the boundaries of the French zone added complications.

The movement out of the British zone was completed by stages in June. Fifteenth Army relinquished the northern half of the *Rheinprovinz,* and Ninth Army evacuated southern Hanover, Braunschweig, Westphalia, and the part of the Soviet zone contiguous to the British zone.[25] Simultaneously, Third and Seventh Armies redisposed their troops within the U.S. zone to give Third Army complete control of Bavaria. The day after this move was accomplished (15 June), Headquarters, Ninth Army, closed down, and Seventh Army assumed command of its troops and territory, by then mainly the U.S. part of the Soviet zone but including also the Bremen enclave and, temporarily, the Headquarters, Berlin District.[26]

When Clay and Zhukov talked in Berlin on 29 June about the withdrawal from the Soviet zone, Zhukov said he wanted it done fast and without ceremony. He did not desire formal reliefs, he said. In fact, he wanted a two- or three-mile gap between his advance guards and the U.S. rear guards.[27] The Commanding General, Seventh Army, Lt. Gen. Wade H. Haislip, arranged the details with Col. Gen. Vassily I. Chuikov in a meeting at Wiesbaden on the 30th. Accordingly, the Russians sent reconnaissance parties to selected points on 1 July. For the next three days, both forces moved to an agreed phase line each day; the last line, reached at midnight on 4 July, was the Soviet zonal border. The Russians refused to take over any prisoners of war, and SHAEF had to rush at the last minute to evacuate 40,000 hospitalized prisoners. Chuikov also said his orders were not to accept any displaced persons other than Soviet citizens; SHAEF's instructions, however, were to leave all DPs who wanted to stay. The question, which had been left hanging, turned out to be immaterial in any case, since practically no DPs other than Soviet citizens—and not even all of them—wanted to stay. Before the exchange began, SHAEF had emptied the Merkers and Nordhausen mines and the *Mittelwerk*

I, pp. 47–50. (6) OMGUS Control Office, Quadripartite Access to and Control of Berlin, vol. II [no date], in OMGUS 23–2/5, folder V205–3/2A.

[24] *Ibid.,* (6).

[25] (1) Cable, 12th AGp to Ninth Army, 19 May 45, in SHAEF G–5, 803/1. (2) Hqs, Fifteenth Army, ACofS G–5, Military Government Summary No. 4, 18 Jun 45, in SHAEF G–5, 17.25, Jacket 6.

[26] Seventh Army, G–3 Diary, 2 and 10 Jun 45, in Seventh Army, 107–0.3.0.

[27] SHAEF G–5, Draft Notes on Meeting at Berlin on Friday, 29 June, 29 Jun 45, in SHAEF G–5, 803/1.

and had resettled 600 German scientists and their families in the final U.S. zone.[28]

The last to be evacuated was the French zone, and the movements out of the other two zones were nearly completed before the final decision on its boundaries was made. In February 1945, anticipating the action of the Yalta Conference, the French Provisional Government had asked for a zone composed of the German territory on the left bank of the Rhine from Cologne south and, on the right bank, Baden, Hesse–Darmstadt, Hesse–Nassau, and Hesse–Kassel.[29] Such a division, while no doubt very satisfactory to France, would have been highly inconvenient to the United States, since it would have interposed a broad band of French-occupied territory between the British and American zones, thereby reopening the question of access routes to Bremen, and it would have cut the U.S. zone off entirely from the Rhine River. After Yalta, the de Gaulle government attempted to press its desires as a matter of right, and as time passed, SHAEF found reasons why it also could not relinquish other areas. Frankfurt could not be let go because it was the only suitable site for the Supreme Headquarters. Eisenhower for a while thought he could give up Baden and Wuerttemberg, but then he found that he needed Mannheim, in Baden, as a Rhine port and the Karlsruhe-Stuttgart-Ulm *Autobahn* and railroad. What he then had left to offer the French were the southern halves of Baden and Wuerttemberg and a bridgehead east of Koblenz. These areas,

together with what the British offered on the left side of the Rhine, made a wasp-waisted zone about two-fifths the size of either the British or the U.S. zone. The French were not pleased and argued for control of at least the whole state of Baden or, failing that, at least Karlsruhe, the administrative center of Baden. It was the first week of July before the French accepted the zone as offered, with a provision for a review of the boundaries later. The signing of the amended zones protocol was then delayed until 26 July by uncertainty over the French sector in Berlin, which eventually comprised two boroughs of the assigned British sector, Reinickendorf and Wedding, the Soviet Union having refused at Potsdam to relinquish any of its territory.[30]

The exchange with the French was the only one in which the U.S. forces acquired new territory. Stuttgart, Karlsruhe, and some of the surrounding *Kreise* had been under French administration since April. Detachment H1E2 recorded its experience on moving into Karlsruhe as follows:

The policy of the French seemed to be to remove everything that could be moved. When their vehicles were not enough they asked for U.S. help, and the detachment was directed by the *Regierungsbezirk* detachment to supply its one truck. During the week following entry into Karlsruhe every officer spent most of his time trying to stop the "equipment repatriation" that extended even to our own personal billets. On one occasion we had to alert the security troops who, at the point of a machine gun, blocked the attempted removal of the city's fire engines.[31]

In Karlsruhe the population grew by 21,000 people in the week after H1E2 ar-

---

[28] (1) Draft Notes on a Meeting at Wiesbaden on 30 Jun, 2 Jul 45, in SHAEF G–5, 803/1. (2) Msg, SHAEF G–2 to 12th AGp, 16 Jun 45, in SHAEF G–5, 803, Jacket 4. (3) Memo, US Gp CC, FIAT, for CG, USFET, 16 Jul 45, and Memo for CofS, 6 Apr 46, in OMGUS 3/35.
[29] Department of State, *Foreign Relations, 1945,* vol. III, p. 182.

[30] (1) *Ibid.,* pp. 261, 322, 340, 344, 363, 364n, and 365. (2) CAD History, ch. VII, pp. 61–63.
[31] Hist Rpt, Det H1E2, 14–31 Jul 45, in OMGUS 410–2/3.

rived. Detachment H3G3 under Maj.
Joseph I. Taylor had been in *Landkreis*
Esslingen for ten days at the end of April
and had turned the area over intact to the
French. When H3G3 returned on 8 July,
the *Kreis* was "stripped . . . of work
horses, automotive equipment, machinery,
and food and medical supplies" but not
of Nazis; the French had removed only the
Buergermeister of Esslingen.[32] On Sunday
morning, 8 July, Detachment E1A2 sent
a cleaning detail to work on the buildings
it was going to occupy in Karlsruhe. When
the French departed later in the morning,
they took the detail's truck, paint, pails,
brushes, and ladders with them.[33] West of
the Rhine the exchange was carried out
more ceremoniously. Maj. Gen. H. J.
Gaffey, commanding XXIII Corps, received General de Joslard de Monsabert
with a fifteen-gun salute and a guard of
honor and formalized the transfer of the
southern Rhineland with the hoisting of the
French flag.[34]

When the last exchanges with the
French were completed in 10 July, Seventh
Army was wholly within the territory it
would administer as the Western Military
District (the U.S.-held portions of Hesse,

Baden, and Wuerttemberg plus the Bremen
enclave). Third Army held all of Bavaria,
the Eastern Military District, but it also
still had two corps in Czechoslovakia. Although the Czech government had stated
a desire to have both the U.S. and Soviet
forces leave its territory, it had privately
asked the Americans to stay as long as the
Russians did. Eisenhower had told Marshall that he could begin the withdrawal
from Czechoslovakia any time but added,
"If Czech independence is to be maintained it seems undesirable that Russia
should be left in sole occupation."[35]

Settling in the Zone

After 10 July, U.S. forces did not occupy
any territory in Germany that was not part
of the U.S. zone; military government
entered what was termed the intermediate
status, that is, between the mobile phase,
which ended with the redisposition to the
zone, and the final static phase, which,
owing to changes in the Static Plan, had
yet to be achieved. Although the zone
would be reduced by the territory to be
ceded to French control, ECAD had concluded before V–E Day that because of the
unanticipated increase in the population of
the U.S. zone, the 250 pinpoint detachments contemplated in the 1944 Static
Plan would not be enough. In staff studies
in March and April, ECAD projected a
second "final" static phase "to effect a
more complete and thorough coverage of
the U.S. zone."[36] In late June, Clay ap-

---

[32] Hist Rpt, Det G–23, 9 Jul 45–15 Jan 46, in OMGUS 1–10/5.
[33] History of Military Government in Land Wuerttemberg–Baden to 30 June 1946, pt. I, p. 151, in OMGUS 409–3/3.
[34] Upon the transfer of the XXIII Corps area to French control, Fifteenth Army's mission in the occupation ended; and the army's headquarters, headquarters company, and special troops, under Lt. Gen. Leonard T. Gerow, became the staff of the USFET General Board charged with preparing a detailed analysis of the strategy, tactics, and administration employed by the U.S. forces in Europe during the war. (1) Opns Rpt, Hqs, XXIII Corps, 20 Jul 45, in XXIII Corps, 223–0.3. (2) Memo, Hqs, USFET, G–3, for CofS, sub: Continuation of General Board, 12 Oct 45, in USFET SGS 322 TGB.

[35] Cable, Marshall to Eisenhower, 13 Jun 45; Cable, Eisenhower to Marshall, 16 Jun 45; and Cable, JCS to Eisenhower, 4 Jul 45, in USFET SGS 370.5/3.
[36] (1) Memos, G–1, 2, 3, 4, for CO, ECAD, 24 and 26 Mar 45, in USFET CAD, ECAD 322. (2) Memo, Hqs, ECAD, for G–5 SHAEF, sub: Recommendations for Static Plan (Second Phase), 4 Apr 45, in USFET CAD, MG Plans.

CHART 2—U.S. MILITARY GOVERNMENT RELATIONSHIPS (STATIC PHASE, AUGUST–DECEMBER 1945)

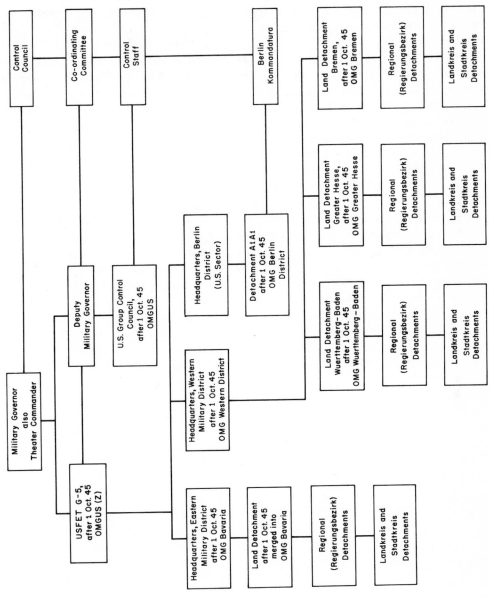

proved an ECAD proposal to use the officers and men of the approximately two hundred provisional detachments, all of which by then had at least six weeks' experience in military government, to increase the number of detachments in the zone to 419 and provide at least one detachment in each *Landkreis* and one in every town with a population over 5,000.[37] (*Chart 2*)

Consequently, the intermediate status at first seemed likely to culminate in almost a doubling of the number of detachments to be stationed in the zone; by 15 July, 346 detachments were deployed. In the meantime, however, ECAD surveys and conferences with the army G–5's had developed requirements for fewer but stronger detachments. During the rest of the month and the first two weeks of August, ECAD disbanded the provisional detachments and some I detachments, using their personnel to augment the larger detachments. When the static phase began on 15 August, the number of detachments was down to 269, one for each of the 4 *Laender*, 12 *Regierungsbezirke*, 44 *Stadtkreise*, and 209 *Landkreise* in the zone. The number of detachment officers, however, had increased from 2,600 in mid-July to 2,887 on 15 August.[38]

The conversion from the intermediate status to the static phase rang down the curtain on ECAD—no doubt, in the opinion of many of its members, none too soon.

In June, three USFET officers, Col. Henry Parkman, Jr., Col. Harry P. Cain, and Lt. Col. Mitchel Wolfson, made a general inspection of the military government detachments in the U.S. zone. They concluded that "the usefulness of ECAD is at an end so far as detachments in the field are concerned." The most common complaint of the detachment personnel, both officers and enlisted, was stagnation in grade. In the I detachments, for instance, almost everyone was at least one step below his table of organization grade or rating and had been for two years or more. The fundamental trouble, as the USFET inspectors discovered and the detachment members had known for months, was that ECAD was too remote physically and too often excluded from actual military government to exercise competent authority over the detachments. After reading the inspector's reports, Brig. Gen. Clarence L. Adcock, Assistant Chief of Staff G–5, USFET, on 10 July ordered ECAD "washed out," effective 1 September. On 15 August, control of the civil affairs regiments passed to the military district commands, the 2d ECAR going to the Western Military District and the 3d ECAR to the Eastern Military District. The detachments were reassigned and renumbered, the designation being by type and number only. The *Land* detachment for Wuerttemberg-Baden, for instance, E1C3, became E–1; the *Land* detachment for Bavaria, E1F3, became E–201.[39]

The G–5 inspection cast doubt as well on the whole concept of organization and training for military government adopted in World War II. The inspectors rated the

---

[37] Memo, Hqs, ETOUSA, G–5, for CofS, sub: Personnel Requirements for MG Activities [no date], in USFET SGS 200.3.

[38] (1) EGAD G–3, ECAD Organization and Development 1945 [no date], USFET CAD 322. (2) General Board, Study No. 32, pp. 117–22. (3) EUCOM, Office of the Chief Historian, Organization and Administration of the European Theater and Its Headquarters, 1947, in CMH, 8–3.1, CA5, p. 144.

[39] Col Henry Parkman, Jr., to ACofS G–5, USFET, sub: Notes on Military Government in Bavaria, 22 Jun 45, and Memo, Hqs, USFET, ACofS G–5, for Branch Chiefs, sub: Col Parkman's Report, 10 Jul 45, in SHAEF G–5, 602.

morale and spirit of the detachments as "surprisingly good . . . considering the exasperatingly long wait and repeated training in various pools and schools before finally getting down to the real job for which they came overseas." However, noting that company grade officers recruited from the tactical troops and given short periods of training had performed well, they recommended recruiting more "with the view not only of filling shortages but to the gradual replacement of older military government officers who have grown tired or stale or otherwise proved unsatisfactory in performance."[40] Military government officers in the field sometimes put the problem less equivocally, as in the following:

Many officers and enlisted men have worked for the detachment. Those coming from tactical units have often done more efficient and honest work than those trained for months in ECAD schools. The series of pools in which military government officers were forced to stagnate for over a year was as vicious a system as can be conceived. There is hardly a man who has passed through it who has not given concrete evidence of demoralization in the most exact sense of the word. The long, sterile inactivity and the theoretical, half fish half fowl military training killed all enthusiasm in officers and men, and many became subject to a complete moral breakdown.[41]

The trouble was most serious in the lower level detachments, which suggests that the weakness was not inherent in Colonel Hunt's vision of a trained military government force but rather in the World War II interpretation of it, which insisted on equal preparation at all levels and resulted in overtraining, overorganization, and underemployment.

Settling military government into the Eastern Military District posed no problems. The district and the Bavarian *Land* boundaries coincided, and all of Bavaria was in the U.S. zone. When the *Land* detachment established itself in Munich and E and F detachments took over the major political subdivisions, the framework for regional control was complete.

The Western Military District was a different case altogether. Its external boundaries were in doubt until after the final decision on the French zone, and internally it was a clutch of administrative anomalies. From north to South (excluding Bremen) the district was made up of the Prussian provinces of Kurhessen and Hesse-Nassau, *Land* Hesse, northern Baden, and northern Wuerttemberg. Across its middle, dividing it in two, stretched a curious creation, the SHAEF enclave. When the idea of the enclave was born in April 1945, the rationale apparently had been that SHAEF as the combined command ought to have a degree of separate territorial status, and the original proposal had been to set aside the seventy-five square miles of the Frankfurt *Stadtkreis*.[42] By the time SHEAF Main moved to Frankfurt on 15 June, the enclave had grown to embrace the *Stadtkreise* Frankfurt, Hanau, and Offenbach and five *Landkreise* in Hesse-Nassau and *Land* Hesse. No military or civilian agencies could billet there without SHAEF approval, and the administration of military government in the enclave, delegated to

---

[40] Col Henry Parkman, Jr., to ACofS, USFET, sub: Notes on Military Government in Bavaria, 22 Jun 45, in SHAEF G–5, 602.

[41] Hist Rpt, Det E–232, May 45–Jun 46, in OMGUS 77–2/10.

[42] In military government the opinion persisted, and was difficult to refute, that the only reason for the enclave was to provide a kind of personal fiefdom for the Headquarters Commandant, SHAEF. See Harold Zink, *American Military Government in Germany* (New York: The Macmillan Company, 1947), p. 98.

12th Army Group and the armies in the rest of the U.S.-occupied territory, was transferred to Brig. Gen. Robert Q. Brown, Headquarters Commandant, SHAEF.[43]

Clay's first thought was to make a single *Land* of the Western Military District, but it would still have been split in two by the enclave; furthermore, Ambassador Murphy objected because the creation of a single unit conflicted with the Allied policy of decentralization. The next best solution was to set up three *Laender:* Hesse-Nassau (Kurhessen and Hesse-Nassau, less the territory transferred to French control), Hesse (the old *Land* Hesse), and Wuerttemberg-Baden (the northern halves of these two *Laender*). This arrangement left the Western Military District with six separate administrative centers: Bremen, Marburg (for Hesse-Nassau), Darmstadt (for Hesse), Stuttgart (for Wuerttemberg-Baden), Frankfurt (for the SHAEF enclave), and Heidelberg (the military district headquarters).[44]

In the new Wuerttemberg-Baden the populations of the two former *Laender* had at least one thing in common; they both regarded the division of their states between the U.S. and French zones as the greatest misfortune that had befallen them as a result of the war.[45] The two states of Hesse, however, had offended the American sense of administrative efficiency. Economically they and the SHAEF enclave formed a single unit, and there was no good reason for

their separate existences—as, indeed, there had not been since 1866 when the Czar of Russia, Alexander II, who was married to a Hessian princess, had intervened to prevent Prussia from uniting them. What the German governments thereafter had been unable to do, military government accomplished rather quickly and easily. The big obstacle was the SHAEF enclave, which at first seemed destined to be taken over by USFET and become permanent. In the second week of July, however, after SHAEF had been disbanded, G–3, USFET, recommended to the Chief of Staff that the enclave be abolished because "Control by the Headquarters Commandant . . . is beyond his ability." Smith agreed, and in the conversion to the static phase, military government control in the former enclave passed to the Western Military District. In September, arguing that the merger would promote local patriotism and thus serve the decentralization policy, G–5, USFET, secured an order to combine Hesse-Nassau, of which the former SHAEF enclave had been made a part, and *Land* Hesse in a new *Land* Greater Hesse.[46]

The establishment of the military district, *Land,* and regional boundaries in July and August completed the framework for territorial military government, and in August, Seventh and Third Armies relieved their corps and divisions of command functions with respect to military government. The chain of command then passed directly from the army commanders (as military district commanders) to the *Land,* regional, and *Kreis* detachments. Third

---

[43] (1) Memo, no source, sub: MG Procedure in the SHAEF Enclave, 9 Apr 45, in SHAEF G–5, 803/1. (2) Memo, SHAEF for CG, 12th AGp, sub: Directive on SHAEF Enclave, 3 Jun 45, in OMGUS 3/35.

[44] (1) US Gp CC, Min of Special Meeting with Gen Haislip, 22 Jun 45, in SHAEF G–5, 803/1. (2) History of Military Government in Land Greater Hesse, 1945–46, in OMGUS 42–1/5.

[45] Hist Rpt, Det E1A2, 1 Jul–30 Sep 45, in OMGUS 9–3/5.

[46] (1) Memo, Hqs, USFET, ACofS G–3, for CofS, sub: SHAEF Enclave, 19 Jul 45, in USFET SGS 371.2. (2) Memo, Hqs, USFET, ACofS G–5, for CofS, sub: Organization of Western Military District, 16 Sep 45, in USFET SGS 322. (3) OMGUS, Org Br, Organization of Western Military District, 22 Mar 47, in OMGUS 21–1/5.

Army went a step further and combined the *Land* detachment for Bavaria with the Army G–5. At the district and theater levels a G–5 technical channel to the detachments was authorized. The instructions specified, however, that at theater and district levels the military command channel would "always be controlling" and that the advent of territorial military government in no way removed from a corps, division, or subordinate commander "the responsibility for taking direct action in military government matters when the security of forces under his command is prejudiced."[47]

The conversion from tactical to territorial military government control was more easily accomplished on paper than in the *Landkreise* and *Stadtkreise*. A year later, Maj. Gen. Oliver P. Echols, talking about the problem, which was still very much alive, told the Senate Special Committee Investigating the National Defense Program, "Military government had a hard time taking over. When fighting troops take an area they consider that they own it."[48] After four months of the occupation, Seventh Army G–5 complained, "Most tactical units, troops and commanders alike, do not know what military government is or what it is supposed to do." Even the new units coming in as replacements, while slow in comprehending the functions of military government, were

quick to assume the prerogatives their predecessors had held during the war.[49] As Hilldring had predicted, a military government detachment commander—at most a colonel and more often a captain or major—whatever his authority on paper, was no match for a major general commanding a division when the two occupied the same bailiwick. Always, the division commander determined when the security of his forces required an intervention in military government. Colonel Parkman's report on the inspection of military government cited the difficulty of getting the tactical commands to limit their interpretation of the word "security."[50]

The tug of war between the tactical commands and military government unfortunately could not be conducted entirely out of the sight of the Germans. Sometimes the result was only harmless embarrassment, as when Detachment E1C3 had to relinquish the Villa Reitzenstein, which had traditionally been the governor's residence in Stuttgart, to Headquarters, 100th Infantry Division.[51] At other times, the conflicts among the Americans threatened to undermine the authority of the occupation. The German civilian officials were often caught between military government, which had appointed them but did not have the power to protect them, and the tactical troops, who either ignored them or treated them as if the war was still going on and they were all Nazis. In Amberg, in northern Bavaria, after being repeatedly called on the carpet by the 4th Armored Division, the civilians asked the military government de-

---

[47] (1) Hqs, ETOUSA, Organization for Military Government of U.S. Zone, 13 May 45, in SHAEF G–2, GBI/CI/CS/322. (2) Memo, 12th AGp for SCAEF, sub: Assumption of Responsibility for Certain Functions of Military Government, 19 Jun 45, in SHAEF G–5, 803/1. (3) Memo, 12th AGp, Internal Affairs Br, G–5, for ACofS G–5, sub: Report of Field Inspection, 5 Jul 45, in SHAEF G–5, 17.16, Jacket 14. (4) General Board, Study No. 32, pp. 120–22.
[48] U.S. Senate, Special Committee Investigating the National Defense Program, Executive Session, 5 Apr 45, in OMGUS 177–1/3.

[49] Hist Rpt, Eastern Military District, 15 Sep–14 Oct 45, in OMGUS 76–3/10.
[50] Hist Rpt, Third Army, G–5, 1 Jul–14 Aug 45, in OMGUS 76–3/10.
[51] History of Military Government in *Land* Wuerttemberg-Baden pt. I, p. 150, in OMGUS 409–3/3.

tachment not to issue any more orders without clearing them first with the tactical
commands.[52]

At Ingolstadt, part of the staff of the 9th
Infantry Division became involved in a plot
with German civilians to overthrow the city
government.[53]

The Spoils

One of the earliest lessons of World War
II was the potential crucial importance of
technology. From the beginning the governments—fortunately the Allies more than
the Germans—expected scientific and technical proficiency to influence heavily and
perhaps even decide the outcome of the
war. A new scientific device or a new industrial process, they believed, could be
worth divisions or even armies; and battles,
perhaps even the war, could be won or lost
in the laboratory or factory. In occupied
enemy territory, scientific and technical intelligence might reveal the state of the
enemy's advancement in particularly dangerous areas such as atomic fission and
might uncover processes or devices that
could be converted to Allied use.

During the planning for the invasion
SHAEF set up the T (Target) Sub-Division in G–2 to plan for intelligence exploitation of scientific and industrial targets.
It was at first composed of five U.S. and
three British officers and thirteen enlisted
men and women. In February 1945, on
the eve of the advance into Germany,
SHAEF created the Special Sections Sub-
Division to co-ordinate the operations of
the T Sub-Division and several other G–2

sections and subdivisions with related missions. T Sub-Division, meanwhile, had acquired a field element, the 6800 T Force,
which would reach a 1,700-man strength
in April and, with the later addition of the
GOLDCUP ministerial control parties, went
well over 2,000. During May and June, the
force put another 1,000 investigators into
the field.

Among its high priority targets the T
Force listed synthetic rubber and oil cata-
lysts, new designs in armored equipment,
V (rocket) weapons, jet and rocket propelled aircraft, naval equipment, field
radios, secret writing chemicals, aero medi-
cine research, gliders, and "scientific and
industrial personalities." During the drive
into Germany and the first weeks after the
surrender, T Force examined some 3,000
planned targets and uncovered 2,000
others. The grand prize target, of course,
was the *Mittelwerk,* the V–2 plant at Nordhausen; but to the scientific and technical
specialists, documents, patent records,
optical devices, high pressure pumps, gear
grinders, tire cord twisters, and supersonic
wind tunnels were often almost as sensational. When large numbers of German scientists and economic and industrial experts
began to be discovered in late April, Special Sections Sub-Division set up the
Enemy Personnel Exploitation Section to
manage and interrogate them. For its most
important charges, the Enemy Personnel
Exploitation Section established a detention
center, DUSTBIN, first in Paris and later in
Kransberg Castle outside Frankfurt. DUST-
BIN was the scientific and industrial–economic counterpart of ASHCAN, and some of
its inmates, such as Albert Speer and
Hjalmar Schacht, were candidates for both
centers.

The top technicians and leaders of the
German rocket development program, 450

---

[52] (1) Hist Rpt, Eastern Military District, 15
Sep–14 Oct 45, in OMGUS 76–3/10. (2) Annual
Report, Det E–236, 1 May 45–30 Jun 46, in
OMGUS 77–3/10.

[53] Annual Report, Det E–237, May 45–Jun 46,
in OMGUS 77–3/10.

of whom had been evacuated to southern Bavaria late in the war and had there surrendered to U.S. troops, formed a special group. In July, the Secretary of War approved Project OVERCAST, the shipment of 350 German specialists—mostly in rocketry but also including some in other fields of military significance—to the United States. What use might be made of these specialists, aside from their possibly being able to contribute something to the war against Japan, was uncertain, and one of the most compelling arguments for bringing them to the United States seemed at the time to be simply to put them beyond the reach of Soviet recruiters. The Russians had captured Peenemuende, the German rocket research station, and acquired the *Mittelwerk* in the redisposition of forces but had missed out on the research and development personnel. Had the leaders of the rocket group, Professor Wernher von Braun and Gen. Walter Dornberger, not decided for themselves that in the long run the United States was the best place to carry on their work and had they not held their colleagues together, OVERCAST might have come to nothing. The War Department insisted all OVERCAST personnel be volunteers, sign contracts for one year, and agree to leave their families behind in Germany, in order to forestall complaints from U.S. soldiers who could not bring their families to Europe. Under these conditions, few volunteered. Those who had families refused to leave them to face the hardships of the first postwar winter alone; and it was not until the late fall, after USFET agreed to provide housing and a 2,300-calorie ration for the dependents, that OVERCAST began to progress.[54]

Although the GOLDCUP teams did not uncover any intact parts of the German government, at least none considered worth salvaging, they had by the end of May collected 750 tons of documents and nearly a thousand German ministerial personnel. To house and exploit the documents and personnel, Special Sections Sub-Division in June opened the Ministerial Collecting Center in a former munitions plant at Hessisch-Lichtenau outside Kassel. In the summer, the center's holdings increased to 1,420 tons of documents, 46 tons of microfilm, and 1,300 Germans.[55]

Early in 1945, foreseeing a vastly increased military and civilian interest after hostilities ended in Germany, Secretary of War Stimson had sent his scientific consultant, Dr. E. L. Bowles, to Europe to help set up a single high-level scientific and technological intelligence organization. Later, in April, among his other assignments, General Clay had acquired the job of

---

USFET admitted that it had touched off a second psychological crisis among the potential recruits by failing to give adequate housing of the families of the first men who left. (1) Memo, ASF for CofS, 17 May 45, and Cable, AACofS, OPD, to CG, USFET, 19 Jul 45, in OPD, 236, Germany, sec. V, Cases 104– . (2) Cable, AGWAR to USFET, 22 Jul 45; Cable, AGWAR to USFET, 6 Sep 45; and Memo, USFET, ACofS G–2, for CofS, sub: Project OVERCAST, 1 Nov 45, in USFET SGS 383.6/4. (3) Hqs, USFET, Theater Commander's Weekly Staff Conference No. 27, 26 Jun 46, in USFET, 97–USF9–0.5. (4) See also James McGovern, *CROSSBOW and OVERCAST* (New York: William Morrow & Co., Inc., 1964).
[55] (1) Lt Col Joseph S. Piram, Background and History of Field Information Agency, Technical, 8 Jul 44–30 Jun 46, in EUCOM, T 298–1/2. (2) OMGUS, 7771 Document Center, General History, 28 Apr 47, in OMGUS 21–1/5. (3) Memo, SHAEF, AG, for CG, 12th AGp, sub: Ministerial Collecting Center, 13 Jun 45, in SHAEF G–2, GBI/CI/CS/091.1–3. (4) Memo, SHAEF, AG, for CG, 12th AGp, sub: Special Detention Centers, 27 May 45, in SHAEF G–2, 383.6–4.

---

[54] Even so, at the end of June 1946, only 195 men had been shipped under OVERCAST (by then renamed PAPERCLIP for security reasons).

working with Dr. Bowles in carrying out the mission from the Secretary of War. Since the new organization would have to be combined for as long as SHAEF existed, Clay had selected as its chief Brig. R. J. Maunsell (British), who was already chief of the Special Sections Sub-Division, and as the deputy chief Col. Ralph M. Osborne (U.S.). Clay also gave the organization a name, Field Information Agency, to which Maunsell added the word "Technical" to make a pronounceable acronym, FIAT.

FIAT was from the first conceived as a posthostilities agency. It would inherit from the Special Sections Sub-Division a military mission and, in the search for information to use against Japan, also a wartime mission; but in the long run it would be oriented at least equally toward civilian interests. Chief among its interests would be "the securing of the major, and perhaps only, material reward of victory, namely, the advancement of science and the improvement of production and standards of living in the United Nations by proper exploitation of German methods in these fields."[56] FIAT's scope was therewith extended to take in scientific and industrial processes and patents having civilian as well as military applications.

Although Clay, Bowles, and Maunsell envisioned FIAT as having exclusive "control and actual handling of operations concerning enemy personnel, documents, and equipment of scientific and industrial interest," they discovered before long that to set up an agency with such sweeping authority in the bureaucratic thickets of SHAEF was not possible. Direct control of operations was already in the hands of various long-established SHAEF elements and would remain there—except for DUSTBIN, which came under FIAT along with its parent agency, the Special Sections Sub-Division, on 1 July, and the 6800 T Force, which by the time it passed to FIAT (on 1 August) had practically finished assessing its assigned and uncovered targets. The one new T Force operation in the FIAT period was conducted in Berlin in July and August.[57] In its charter, issued at the end of May, FIAT was authorized to "co-ordinate, integrate, and direct the activities of the various missions and agencies" interested in scientific and technical intelligence but prohibited from collecting and exploiting such information on its own responsibility.[58]

Never the high-powered intelligence unit Stimson had wanted and, after SHAEF was dissolved, an orphan shared administratively by the U.S. Group Control Council and USFET without being adopted by either, FIAT eventually came by its distinctive role in the occupation almost inadvertently. In the summer of 1945, from its office in Frankfurt and branches in Paris, London, and Berlin, it provided accreditation, support, and services to civilian investigators from the Technical Industrial Intelligence Committee (Foreign Economic Administration) then arriving in Europe in large numbers to comb German plants and laboratories for information on everything from plastics to shipbuilding and building materials to chemicals. As military units that had been engaged in gathering

---

[56] Memo, SHAEF, ACofS G–2, for CofS, sub: Establishment of a Field Information Agency, Technical, 2 Jun 45, in OPD, 336, sec. V, Class 104–.

[57] OMGUS, Control Office, Historical Br, History of Field Information Agency, Technical, 8 May 45–30 Jun 46, in OMGUS 20–3/5.

[58] (1) SHAEF, CofS, to distribution, sub: Establishment of FIAT, 31 May 45, in OPD, 336, sec. V, Class 104–. (2) Memo, Hqs, US Gp CC, for Distribution, sub: Establishment of FIAT, US Gp CC, 14 Jul 45, in USFET SGS 322.

technical intelligence were redeployed beginning in the late summer, FIAT frequently also became the custodian of the documents and equipment they had collected.

Meanwhile, in June, President Truman had established the Publications Board under the Director of War Mobilization and Reconversion and instructed it to review all scientific and technical information developed with government funds during the war with a view toward declassifying and publishing it. In August, after V-J Day, the President also ordered "prompt, public and general dissemination" of scientific and industrial information obtained from the enemy and assigned this responsibility as well to the Publication Board.[59] At first informally and later, in December, by War Department order, FIAT acquired the responsibility for the Publication Board program in Germany and a mission, which was the same one in fact that had been foreseen for it in June, namely, to exploit Germany's scientific and industrial secrets for the benefit of the world. As the military intelligence projects were completed and phased out in late 1945 and early 1946, the volume of civilian investigations increased; FIAT microfilming teams ranged across Germany, and the Frankfurt office screened, edited, and translated reports before shipping them to the United States. By the end of the first year of the occupation, FIAT had processed over 23,000 reports, shipped 108 items of equipment (whole plants sometimes were counted as single items), and collected 53 tons of documents.[60]

Exit SHAEF

SHAEF's wartime mission ended on V-E Day. The last residual mission, the redisposition into the zones, was completed on 10 July, and the Supreme Command terminated on the 14th. Headquarters, USFET, under Eisenhower as Theater Commander and Smith as Chief of Staff, had opened in Frankfurt on 1 July; and when its increments from ETOUSA, SHAEF, and 12th Army Group were fully assembled, it was, with 3,885 officers and 10,968 enlisted men, an imposing organization in its own right. USFET commanded only U.S. troops, but its sphere of responsibility extended outside the zone in Germany into England, France, Belgium, Norway, and Austria. Two military government staffs, the U.S. Group Control Council and the theater G-5, would provide the U.S. element of the quadripartite administration for Germany and govern the zone. The 12th Army Group ceased its operations on 25 July, and thereafter USFET also assumed direct command of the occupation forces.

SHAEF had used its authority to bring into being a number of combined agencies which, while they did not constitute a central administration for the western zones, were a more substantial step in this direction than would be made again for several years. The agencies included the Allied Printing and Paper Control Board, the Rhine Navigation Agency, the Resources Allocation Board, the Production Control Agency, the Economic Control Agency, the

---

[59] EO 9568, 8 Jun 45, and EO 9604, 28 Aug 45, in *Federal Register*, vol. 10, pp. 9568 and 10960.

[60] With Department of Commerce financial support and personnel, FIAT continued investigations until 30 June 1947 and continued microfilming until 30 September of that year. (1) Piram, Background and History of Field Information Agency, Technical, 8 Jul 44–30 Jun 46, in EUCOM, T 298-1/2. (2) Memo, Actg Ch, CAD, for Sec War, sub: Termination Date for FIAT, 11 Jun 47, in CAD, 014.

Combined Evidence Collecting Center for War Crimes, the DPX, FIAT, and CROWCASS. The functions of the agencies concerned with economic matters went to the Control Council and to the zonal administrations. The Combined Evidence Collecting Center, CROWCASS, and some other organizations that could not be divided or assigned either to the British or U.S. commands passed temporarily to a Combined Administrative Liquidating Agency. FIAT separated into its British and U.S. components, but the British FIAT stayed in Frankfurt. The two components occupied the same building, at 69 Burgerstrasse, Frankfurt, and later the Director's Building in the I. G. Farben plant at Hoechst, and continued to work closely together.[61]

The Displaced Persons Executive (DPX) was a special case. In the month of July, UNRRA had 2,656 persons in 332 DP teams deployed throughout the western zones. It planned to more than double its personnel, set up a central headquarters for Germany near Frankfurt, and then take over entirely the care and supervision of the displaced persons from the military authorities. For the interim, which was expected to be about three months, the DPX continued as the Combined Displaced Persons Executive (CDPX), operating under the existing SHAEF directives but without authority to make new policy.[62]

Along with SHAEF, the Combined Chiefs of Staff and Combined Civil Affairs Committee also virtually passed out of the picture as far as Germany was concerned. The USFET channel of command from Washington was IPCOG, the SWNCC, and the JCS. Soon, this changed also. On 16 July at Potsdam, the President assigned "the necessary direction of our activities and negotiations pertaining to the treatment of Germany and Austria" to the War Department and the State Department—State to deal with policy, and War to deal with "the executive and administrative aspects." IPCOG, in which the Treasury Department and Foreign Economic Administration were represented, subsequently ceased to exist.[63]

As a kind of housewarming for the zone, USFET planned and, in forty-eight hours beginning at daybreak on 21 July, executed a check and search operation code-named TALLYHO. The objectives were to check the credentials of all persons in the zone, civilian or military; to search all premises and individuals for prohibited articles, such as firearms and stolen U.S. government property; and to search for evidence of black-marketeering. Staged in secret, to the extent that an operation employing 163,000 troops in the Western Military District alone could be kept a secret, TALLYHO apparently did at least take most Germans by surprise. It raised a fast-traveling wave of rumors: that there had been a jailbreak, that an American officer had been shot, that the Americans were making a last minute search for loot before turning the zone over to the Russians. After

[61] EUCOM, Office of the Chief Historian, Organization and Administration of the European Theater and Its Headquarters, 1947, in CMH file 8–3.1, CA 5.

[62] (1) Cable, SHAEF Main to CG, 12th AGp, 6 Jul 45, in SHAEF G–5, 2772. (2) Cable, USFET to AGWAR, sub: Fifth Report on Status of UNRRA, 20 Jul 45, and Memo, USFET, ACofS G–5, for CofS, sub: Summary of UNRRA/Military DP Programs, 21 Jul 45, in USFET SGS 334.

[63] (1) Memo, Asst Dep CofS, OPD, for Sec JCS, sub: Communications with CINC's, U.S. Forces of Occupation, Germany and Austria, 21 Jul 45, in OPD, ABC 387, sec. 4–E. (2) Memo, James F. Byrnes for the President, sub: Termination of IPCOG, 30 Aug 45, in CAD, 014, Jul 45–14 Sep 45.

SOLDIERS CHECK PAPERS OF A CIVILIAN

the surprise wore off, which took no more than four hours, the Germans became quite co-operative; and some of them began to arrange their property in neat displays, as if for "showdown inspection." The search brought in 2,747 illegal small arms, 2,658 miscellaneous items of Army clothing and equipment, 340 AWOL soldiers, and evidence for 23 fraternization cases. The confiscated black-market goods amounted to 100 gallons of gasoline, 1,000 pounds each of sugar and flour, 75 pounds of coffee, 138 automobile tires, and 300 pairs of shoes, which in total, USFET G–2 concluded with not quite flawless logic, constituted "no evidence of an organized black market." Of the 83,000 Germans arrested, 77,000 were held for nothing more than improper identification papers. In the end, however, USFET believed TALLYHO was a success in that it impressed German population "with the serious intention of the American troops."[64]

---

[64] Memo, CG, USFET, to Army Cmdr's, sub: Co-ordinated Security Control Check and Search Operation, 1 Jul 45, and Hqs, USFET, ACofS G–2, Report on Operation TALLYHO, 18 Sep 45, in USFET SGS 333.5.16.

CHAPTER XVIII

The Occupation Troops

Army-Type Occupation

On V–E Day, Eisenhower had sixty-one U.S. divisions, 1,622,000 men, in Germany, and a total force in Europe numbering 3,077,000.[1] When the shooting ended, the divisions in the field became the occupation troops, charged with maintaining law and order and establishing the Allied military presence in the defeated nation. This was the army-type occupation. A counterpart of the military government carpet, its object was to control the population and stifle resistance by putting troops into every nook and cranny. Divisions were spread out across the countryside, sometimes over great stretches of territory. The 78th Infantry Division, for instance, for a time after V–E day was responsible for an area of 3,600 square miles, almost twice the size of the state of Delaware, and the 70th Infantry Division for 2,500 square miles. Battalions were deployed separately, and the company was widely viewed as the ideal unit for independent deployment because billets were easy to find and the hauls from the billets to guard posts and checkpoints would not be excessively long. Frequently single platoons and squads were deployed at substantial distances from their company headquarters.

The occupation troops manned border control stations, maintained checkpoints at road junctions and bridges, sent out roving patrols to apprehend curfew and circulation violators, and kept stationary guards at railroad bridges, Army installations, DP camps, jails, telephone exchanges, factories, and banks. In the first months troops were plentiful and almost everything of importance—and some not so important—was guarded.[2] In effect, the combat forces became military government security troops.

The army-type occupation was comprehensive and showed the Germans that they were defeated and their country occupied. This type of occupation was presumably capable of squelching incipient resistance since none was evident. On the other hand, it employed a much larger number of troops than would be available for the permanent occupation and did so at considerable cost in combat potential and discipline. The larger units lost their cohesiveness, and in the platoons and companies discipline weakened. Ironically, the supposed chief beneficiary, military government, concluded after two months' experience that the better plan would have been to form the occupational police battalions General Gullion had asked for and been refused in 1942. The tactical troops thought in terms of military security and therefore often followed different priorities

---

[1] Memo, Hqs, ETOUSA, for Gen Eisenhower, sub: Strength of the U.S. Forces, 30 Apr 45, in USFET SGS 320.3/2.

[2] (1) EUCOM, Office of the Chief Historian, Troop Basis and the Disposition of Forces, 1947, in CMH file 8–3.1, CA 20, p. 3. (2) EUCOM, Hist Div, U.S. Military Government in Germany, Operations from Late March to Mid-July 1945, 1950, in CMH file 8–3.1, DF, pp. 79–93.

than would have been most useful to military government. The public safety officer in Marburg, for instance, complained that he was having to spend most of his time explaining to the tactical troops why they should, besides protecting potential sabotage targets and checking passes, also supply guards for the $200-million worth of art work, 400 tons of German Foreign Office records, and 84 tank cars loaded with mercury, all of which were in military government custody.[3]

The most obvious defect of the blanket occupation was its impermanence. The vast majority of the troops were going to be redeployed either to the Pacific or home for discharge. Their work in Germany was finished the day the war ended. Some troops would be there for weeks, some for months, but all would be almost constantly on the move outward. In July, after the withdrawal to the zone was completed, SHAEF published a revised deployment plan. It was based on an assumed permanent occupation force of 8 divisions: 3 for the Western Military District, 4 for the Eastern Military District, 1 (less 1 regiment) for Berlin, and 1 regiment for Bremen. The army-type occupation would be retained but revised. Two regiments, one armored and one airborne, would be trained and held ready as a mobile striking force. The others would be static and engage in occupation duty but would be stationed in regimental concentrations near main administrative centers and not again dissipated by battalions and companies.[4]

Non-Fraternization

The ban on fraternization had been in force eight months by V–E Day—long enough in the opinion of those who had to enforce it and, no doubt, too long to suit those required to observe it. After his tour of occupied Germany in late April, Colonel Starnes recommended revising the nonfraternization orders "to a common sense basis immediately [after] hostilities cease. . . . A non-fraternization policy anywhere," he told Smith, "with any people with whom we are not at war will appear childish, senseless, and in a very short time all of us will be ashamed that we ever behaved in such a manner."[5] Three days after the surrender Bradley and Smith talked about modifying the policy; at almost the same time in Washington, Marshall was talking to Elmer Davis, Director of the Office of War Information. The subject was the Goering case and the alleged friendly treatment of other high-ranking Germans which, Davis said and Marshall reported in a cable to Eisenhower, had aroused "an intense public reaction, approaching and in many cases reaching bitterness." Smith later sent a copy of the cable to Bradley with the comment, "It seems to me that this is a fairly good answer to our conversation."[6]

For two months thereafter, SHAEF wrestled with itself, trying desperately to enforce the nonfraternization policy and, just as desperately, to get rid of it. Deluged with letters, telegrams, and editorials protesting the Goering incident, Marshall ordered Eisenhower on 14 May to "stimu-

---

[3] Memo, SHAEF, ACofS G-5, Public Safety, sub: Tactical Troops in Support of Military Government, 6 Jul 46, in OMGUS 177–2/3.
[4] (1) Cable, Eisenhower to District CG's, 29 Jul 45, in OMGUS 3/35, dec. 320.2. (2) Memo, USFET, ACofS G-3, for CofS, sub: Distribution of Occupational Ground Forces, 14 Aug 45, in SHAEF SGS, 370.

[5] Ltr, Col Joe Starnes to Gen W. B. Smith, 5 May 45, in USFET SGS 014.4.
[6] Cable, Marshall to Eisenhower, 11 May 45, and Ltr, Smith to Bradley, 12 May 45, in USFET SGS 250.

late stories and pictures showing the stern attitude of American military personnel" toward German prisoners of all ranks. For a start, Eisenhower issued a public statement disapproving all forms of fraternization and an order to the U.S. commands threatening to deal summarily with any future incidents.[7] A week later, however, he asked Clay's opinion on a switch to the milder nonfraternization policy stated in the 1944 War Department's "Guide to Germany." In his reply, Clay summed up the dilemma in one sentence: "While it is recognized that discipline in the Army should not be governed by public opinion, we cannot completely forget the effects of public opinion. . . ." He believed that to relax the nonfraternization policy, except possibly with respect to small children, would be "misunderstood by the press and the public." However, he was apparently convinced that the "Guide" policy was the only feasible one, and he recommended having a study made to determine how it could be put into effect after the combined command terminated.[8]

Meanwhile, arrests were being made, cases were being tried, and good combat soldiers were getting bad records. As a deterrent, the judge advocates frequently tried the cases as violations of standing orders under the Articles of War, which could result in as much as six months' confinement and two-thirds' loss of pay. While no one imagined that any calculable percentage of the offenses was being detected, the number of trials held was not insignificant. The 28th Infantry Division, for example, had sixty cases on its docket in mid-June and was going to try every one by court martial under the Articles of War. In May, the XXIII Corps' judge advocate tried twenty-five cases against enlisted men and two against officers.[9] The Inspector General, Seventh Army, investigated four cases involving ten generals. The generals probably fared better than the enlisted men similarly charged. Generals Dahlquist and Stack and Brig. Gen. Walter W. Hess were found to have "engaged in social contact" with Goering, and Maj. Gen. Frank W. Milburn, Maj. Gen. F. A. Prickett, and Brig. Gen. W. H. Maris to have "engaged in friendly contact" with Field Marshal Gerd von Rundstedt in violation of the nonfraternization policy. The other two cases were declared not to have constituted fraternization. The investigation took almost three months and, the nonfraternization policy being all but defunct by then, ended with a recommendation to take no further action in any of the cases.[10]

A curious myth associated with the non-

---

[7] Cable, Marshall to Eisenhower, 13 May 45; Cable, Eisenhower to Marshall, 14 May 45; and Cable, Eisenhower to CG's, 12th AGp, Third and Seventh Armies, U.S. Air Forces, 14 May, in USFET SGS 250.

[8] Memo, Gen Eisenhower to Gen Clay, 22 May 45, and Memo, US Gp CC, Office of Deputy Military Government, for Gen Eisenhower, sub: Nonfraternization Policy, 23 May 45, in USFET SGS 250.

[9] Rpt, Fifteenth Army, 5th Information and Historical Service, sub: Nonfraternization Policy, XXIII Corps Area, 22 Jun 45, in XXIII Corps, 223–5.0.

[10] In the other two cases, the Seventh Army inspector general found that Maj. Gen. Maxwell D. Taylor, Brig. Gen. Gerald J. Higgins, and Brig. Gen. William N. Gilmore "engaged in contact with" Field Marshal Albert Kesselring but did not fraternize and that Maj. Gen. Robert T. Frederick, "being unaware of the fact that the Excelsior Hotel in Munich was fully occupied by American personnel," did not engage in fraternization when he gave orders that resulted in some American officers and enlisted men being evicted in the middle of the night during a rain storm to make room for a party of German generals. Memo, Hqs, USFET, ACofS G–1, for CofS, sub: Fraternization by General Officers, 6 Aug 45, in USFET SGS 250.

NONFRATERNIZATION

fraternization problem was the belief that the ordinary soldiers objected most to the ban on friendliness to young children. On 2 June, Eisenhower reported to Marshall, "Continuing surveys among our troops show that non-fraternization rules are fairly well observed except in the case of small children." Because the American soldier could not be stern and harsh with young children, Eisenhower continued, "the fear of all commanders is that the breaking down of the order with respect to the child will eventually have its effect on the whole proposition and upon discipline in gen-

eral." After some discussion as to what constituted a small child (Eisenhower proposed twelve years as the age limit, but Marshall wondered "how a soldier is going to tell the age of a child before being kind to it?") and after Marshall decided that public reaction would be favorable, Eisenhower announced the lifting of the ban on fraternization with children on 11 June.[11]

The soldier's urge to befriend small chil-

<hr />

[11] Cable, Eisenhower, Personal, to General Marshall, for eyes only, 2 Jun 45, and Cable, Marshall to Eisenhower, eyes only, 4 Jun 45, in SHAEF G–1, 250.1–6.

dren, however, was not the real issue. Of five provost marshals interviewed in June, none mentioned children as figuring in his fraternization cases—or, for that matter, any other Germans except women. Maj. William Hill, 28th Infantry Division, said: "Soldiers are going to have their fling regardless of rules or orders. If they are caught they know what the punishment will be. However, that is not stopping them and nothing is going to stop them." Maj. Hal N. Briggs, 35th Infantry Division, added, "There is a lot of fraternization going on and we know it, but to catch them is a different thing."[12]

Exactly how widespread fraternization was no one in authority seemed to know or want to know. Ninth Army reported that German girls and U.S. soldiers were sometimes seen walking in parks. The 6th Army Group noted a "surprisingly large number of young women"—Wacs, their French equivalent, and DPs—appearing in the company of U.S. soldiers. Few of the girls, according to the army report, were in uniform, and most of them spoke German which "made it impossible to tell whether a soldier was violating the rule or associating with an Allied National."[13] The soldiers were more candid. They joked about the opportunity being given the Germans "to see Americans engaged in the most widespread violation of their own laws since Prohibition" and about putting on French uniforms so that they could fraternize without a guilty conscience.[14]

One thing could not be ignored: in attempting to force on its troops a wholly artificial standard of conduct, the Army was putting itself in a position that was both ludicrous and potentially dangerous. No amount of pious exhortation could, once the fighting had ended, convince the soldiers that they were not the chief and possibly intended victims. Some said that "the policy is just to give the brass the first crack at all the good looking women." Others saw "the German soldier getting a discharge, donning civilian clothes, and making love to the women while they [the U.S. troops] are the ones virtually in prison."[15] Staffs that had engineered the defeat of the *Wehrmacht* were having to match wits with their own soldiers and were losing. The powerful Headquarters, 12th Army Group, struggled with the problem of how to tell a female DP from a German *Frauelein* and came up with the following solution: "an armband four inches wide, made of materials in the colors of their respective nations will be worn on the left arm by Allied DPs as a symbol of recognition."[16] One unit tried issuing buttons to the DPs, and the unit newspaper announced the move under the headline "Button, Button, Who's Got the Button." In the Fifteenth Army area, a CIC detachment was reportedly sent to watch a security guard detachment that had been detailed to shadow an MP private who was suspected of flirting with a German girl.[17] The Germans, SHAEF PWD reported ruefully, could hardly fail to notice that some-

[12] Rpt, Fifteenth Army, 5th Information and Historical Service, sub: Nonfraternization Policy, XXIII Corps Area, 22 Jun 45, in XXIII Corps, 223–5.0.

[13] (1) Hist Rpt, Ninth Army, ACofS, G–5, May 45, in SHAEF G–5, 17.14, Jacket 8. (2) Hist Rpt, 6th AGp, ACofS G–5, May 45, in SHAEF G–5, 504.

[14] Rpt, Fifteenth Army, 5th Information and Historical Service, sub: Nonfraternization Policy, XXIII Corps Area, 22 Jun 45, in XXIII Corps, 223–5.0.

[15] *Ibid.*

[16] Ltr, Hqs, 12th AGp, to CG's, Armies, sub: Enforcement of Nonfraternization, 15 Jun 45, in SHAEF G–1, 250.1–1.

[17] New York *Times,* 13 Jun 45.

thing had gone wrong "when large signs 'Don't Fraternize' have to be displayed every 50 yards or so." In Frankfurt, where barbed wire preserved the monastic seclusion of the SHAEF compound, the Germans were remarking that the Americans were a people who built concentration camps and put themselves in them.[18] Lastly, the venereal disease rate was rising and with it a knot of contradictions. The SHAEF Judge Advocate pointed out:

The very establishment of prophylactic stations and the directives requiring reports of the contraction of veneral disease are indicative of the realistic view which the Army has heretofore taken of this problem. Soldiers will fraternize in the manner indicated, in spite of any rules to the contrary, and should they, fearful of being tried by court martial for such fraternization, avoid the use of prophylaxis or checkup, venereal disease may become rampant and completely out of control.[19]

On 4 June, SHAEF, with desperate illogic, published orders stating: "Contraction of venereal disease or the facts concerning prophylactic treatment will not be used directly or indirectly as evidence of fraternization. . . ."[20]

Fittingly, nonfraternization did not end, it disintegrated. On 19 June in Washington, Eisenhower said that there could be no fraternization in Germany until the last Nazi criminals had been uprooted. Two days later at a press conference in Abilene he talked about abating the nonfraternization policy "as soon as the criminals and

dangerous elements [among the Germans] are sorted out." On the 25th, in a group interview at the Waldorf-Astoria Hotel in New York, Generals Jacob L. Devers, Joseph T. McNarney, and William L. Simpson, all recently returned from important commands in Germany, agreed that "non-fraternization must and will be relaxed in the near future."[21] On 10 July, SHAEF announced that nonfraternization would continue except in special cases. Relations with German girls and the German public, the announcement explained, were only part of the picture. Security was more important, and there might be serious trouble in the coming winter; therefore, the troops could not be permitted to fraternize.[22] Four days later, Eisenhower announced, "In view of the rapid progress which has been made in carrying out Allied de-Nazification policies . . . it is believed desirable and timely to permit personnel of my command to engage in conversation with adult Germans on the streets and in public places."[23]

Joyously dubbed "the fraternization order" by the troops, the Eisenhower revision went into effect on the 15th, a Sunday. Gladwin Hill, correspondent for the New York *Times,* described the scene in Schierstein on the Rhine River:

There was a new watch on the Rhine today—by handholding American GI's and German girls taking advantage of the relaxed restrictions on fraternization.

In the hot sunshine of a Sunday afternoon they sat on grassy riverbanks, chugged up and down stream in American boats, and zipped around streets with the zest of a child

---

[18] Memo, SHAEF, PWD, Int Sec, for Ch, PWD, sub: Possible Relaxation of Fraternization, 30 May 45, in SHAEF G–1, 250.1–11.

[19] Staff Minute Sheet, SHAEF, JA, to G–1, 17 May 45, in SHAEF G–1, 250.1–10.

[20] Memo, SHAEF, ACofS G–1, for Distribution, sub: Policy on Relations Between Allied Occupation Forces and the Inhabitants of Germany, 4 Jun 45, in SHAEF G–1, 250.1–2.

[21] New York *Times,* 19, 23, and 25 Jun 45.

[22] *Ibid.,* 10 Jul 45.

[23] Memo, SHAEF, ACofS G–1, for Director, Pbulic Relations Div, sub: Partial Relaxation of Nonfraternization Policy, 13 Jul 45, in SHAEF G–1, 250.1–11.

FRATERNIZATION

diving into a box of candy previously accessible only by stealth.[24]

Seventh Army reported an immediate free and open mingling of soldiers and German civilians and asked for clarification of the announcement because its commanders and MPs had no instructions concerning which types of contact were permissible and which were not.

Taking its guidance from Eisenhower's message to the commands and the War Department, which stressed the limited nature

of the modification, SHAEF G–1 prepared a clarifying directive. In it, G–1 defined public places as parks and streets or enclosures such as railroad stations, concert halls, theaters, art galleries, market places, shops, and city halls. In such places soldiers could engage in conversation or exchange "customary forms of greeting" with adult Germans, and walk and sit with them.[25] General Patton, the Third Army com-

---

[24] New York *Times,* 16 Jul 45.

[25] Memo, USFET, ACofS G–1, for Theater Cmdr, sub: Amendments to Directives on Nonfraternization, 19 Jul 45, in USFET SGS 250.

mander, however, urgently requested permission to hold organizational dances with German girls as invited guests, while Generals Clay and Adcock proposed to extend the G–1 definition of public places and exclude only private homes, hotel rooms, brothels, and Army-sponsored social events such as the dances Patton wanted to give. This last event, they maintained, could not be considered public. G–1 protested that the Clay-Adcock definition could possibly allow soldiers to consort with undesirable women in cabarets while prohibiting sponsored dances "under controlled conditions." At the end of the month, the problem went to Eisenhower; he responded with, "The Theater Commander wishes you to be advised that he considers his major commanders fully competent to interpret and define the term 'public places' within the spirit of his intentions and that he does not wish to publish any further definitions or interpretations in this connection."[26]

Although nonfraternization had still not positively been pronounced dead, from then on the USFET staff was concerned only with arranging the funeral. The debate over the definition of public places rumbled on sporadically, but in the meantime enforcement ceased. When the Control Council, at USFET's urging, ended the ban entirely, effective 1 October (even though the Control Council had not imposed it and the French and Russians had not observed it), the only prohibitions left were those against marrying Germans and billeting in German homes.[27] By then the subordinate commands had even begun to sponsor fraternization. Quite a few experimented with systems of social passes. The passes were issued to girls of presumed good character and admitted them to unit social events. Unfortunately, some implications of being registered made it difficult to interest the kinds of girls the commands wanted most.[28]

In November, after six months of the occupation and nearly three months of tolerated fraternization, USFET surveyed soldier opinion on the Germans. Nearly 80 percent of the soldiers interviewed said their impression was favorable. They most liked the Germans' cleanliness and industriousness and most disliked their "air of superiority and arrogance." Although exactly half still liked the English best, 28 percent said they preferred the Germans and only 11 percent the French. Less than half (43 percent) blamed the German people for the war and fewer (25 percent) imputed to the people responsibility for the concentration camp atrocities. The soldiers were also asked how much time they had spent during the previous seven days and seven nights "talking" (including contacts "other than those of purely conversational nature") with Germans. Few had associated at all with older Germans and fewer still with men their own age, while 56 percent had spent some time "talking" with German girls, 25 percent for ten hours or more.[29]

[26] Memo, CG, Third Army, for CG, USFET, sub: Enlisted Men's Dances, German Girls, 21 Jul 45; Memo, USFET, ACofS G–5, for CofS, sub: Amendments to Directive on Nonfraternization, 23 Jul 45; Memo, USFET, ACofS G–1, for Theater Cmdr, sub: Amendments to Directives on Nonfraternization, 26 Jul 45; and Memo, USFET, Dep CofS, for Distribution, sub: Social Association with Germans, 1 August 45, in USFET SGS 250.

[27] Memo, USFET, ACofS G–1, for CofS, sub: Nonfraternization Policy, 29 Sep 45, in USFET SGS 250.

[28] Hist Rpt, Seventh Army, 8 May–30 Sep 45, in Seventh Army, 107–3.0.

[29] Hqs, USFET, I&E, Research Staff, Study No. 1, The American Soldier in Germany, Nov 45, in USFET SGS 250.

Redeployment and Readjustment

Wartime planning had assumed that a large part of the forces required to defeat Japan would come from Europe after hostilities ended there. In early November 1944, Lt. Gen. Brehon B. Somervell, Commanding General, Army Service Forces, had told Eisenhower: "The European Theater of Operations . . . will in fact become a base, the location of resources which we will wish to divert to use in the Pacific. . . . We are going to place immediate demands on you to put your machine in reverse and this at a time when you will have to be laying out your billeting areas, lines of communications, ports, railroads, and other facilities for your job of maintaining order in Germany."[30] Subsequently, with the Battle of the Bulge and the drive into Germany still months ahead, redeployment planning groups had gone to work in the Pentagon and at Headquarters, ETOUSA.

By the third week in March 1945, SHAEF anticipated having to release a million and a half troops for the Pacific and having to send another 600,000 men home for discharge.[31] Concerning the shipment home, General Marshall cabled to Eisenhower:

It is becoming increasingly apparent that the task of readjusting the Army and promptly releasing to civilian life those people who are surplus to the needs of the Japanese war is one that will demand the most unselfish and conscientious efforts on the part of everyone. I fear that the weight of public opinion in the U.S. will be such that unless the task is handled properly we may be forced to take measures that will interfere with redeployment and result in a prolongation of the Japanese war.

Marshall stipulated that the units to be shipped to the Pacific were to contain only the troops least eligible for discharge, and those being sent home were to be only the most eligible. He remembered, he said, that in World War I the unit shipped out first was often the one most convenient rather than most deserving.[32]

What would determine whether a man stayed in the occupation forces in Germany, went to the Pacific, or went home to be discharged was the Adjusted Service Rating. The rating was calculated individually for every enlisted man in the theater on the basis of one point for each month of service since September 1940, one point for each month of overseas service since September 1940, five points for each decoration or battle star, and twelve points for each child under eighteen up to a maximum of three. Eisenhower informed the commands that they would have to be ready to release the men with high scores "when the bell rings. . . . The fairness and speed," he stated, "with which the redeployment is carried out will be reflected in public support of the Pacific campaign, in the future attitude of the public to the Army, and in the confidence of the returned soldier in the Army command."[33]

The bell rang sooner than anyone in Europe anticipated. ETOUSA had expected to have about a month after the

---

[30] Ltr, Somervell to Eisenhower, 4 Nov 44, in USFET SGS 370, vol. I.

[31] SHAEF, G–3, Redeployment Brief, 18 Mar 45, in USFET SGS 370, vol. I. For a discussion of evolving War Department and JCS redeployment plans in late 1944 and the spring of 1945, see Robert W. Coakley and Richard M. Leighton, *Global Logistics and Strategy* (Washington: United States Army in World War II, 1968), pp. 539–46, 577–79, and 584–91.

[32] Cable, Marshall to Eisenhower, 17 Apr 45, in USFET SGS 370, vol. I.

[33] Ltr, Eisenhower to Lt Gen Lewis H. Brereton, 19 Apr 45, in USFET SGS 370, vol. I.

surrender to get ready and then eighteen months to complete the shipments. On 8 May, the War Department announced 12 May as R–day, the day full redeployment and readjustment would begin. The Adjusted Service Ratings would have to be calculated by midnight on the 12th, and thereafter they would determine all enlisted assignments (officers were not yet included). On the night of V–E Day the War Department reduced the completion time from eighteen months to twelve and raised the shipping quota for June from 60,000 troops to 240,000. Two days later the department called for 17,500 men eligible for discharge to be shipped by air or water in May and ordered a minimum of 35,000 in June.[34]

The critical score was 85 for enlisted men (44 for enlisted women). Those with 85 or more points on the Adjusted Service Rating were eligible for discharge. Those with fewer points— pending reduction in the score—would serve either in the occupation or be redeployed to the Pacific. For these men and women in particular the War Department released a film entitled "Two Down and One To Go." All movements were to be made by complete units, which necessitated a reshuffling of personnel throughout the theater and the classification of all units into four categories. Category I units were those scheduled to stay in the occupation, Category II units were those to be redeployed to the Pacific, and Category III units were those being reorganized either

for the Pacific or the occupation. Categories I, II, and III would contain no men with point scores of 85 or over. Category IV units would have only men with 85 or more points and would function as vehicles for returning them to the United States. In northeastern France, between Reims and Chalons-sur-Marne and the Aisne River, ETOUSA established an assembly area to accommodate 250,000 men in tent camps. Other camps, capable of housing up to 60,000, were built in staging areas near the embarkation ports of Le Havre, Marseilles, and Antwerp. The camps were named for brands of cigarettes, such as Herbert Tareyton, Wings, Lucky Strike, and Twenty Grand.[35]

For the first two months the shipments out exceeded the original War Department quotas. Nearly 90,000 men were shipped out in May, almost 70,000 of them had high scores.[36] Units went into the assembly areas and on to the staging areas with minimum essential equipment to eliminate the necessity for packing and loading heavy items. Although they were supposed to be traveling light, ETOUSA orders permitted the troops to carry war trophies "to the fullest extent practicable," excepting only explosives and nonmilitary articles removed from enemy dead. The 28th Infantry of 5,000 men embarked with 20,000 souvenir weapons.[37]

No matter how high the rate of departures, however, hundreds of thousands of

---

[34] (1) Cable, Marshall to Eisenhower, 8 May 45, in USFET SGS 383.3. (2) Memo, USFET, Dep ACofS G–3, for Dep CofS, sub: Redeployment "Ups" and "Downs," 5 Nov 45, in USFET SGS 370, vol. V .(3) Memo, ETOUSA, Redeployment Coordinating Group, for Dep CofS, sub: Early Return of U.S. Personnel, 13 May, in USFET SGS 370, vol. I.

[35] (1) Cable, Hqs, ETOUSA, to Distribution, 10 May 45, in USFET SGS 383.3. (2) Hqs, USFET, ACofS G–3, Outline Plan of Functions and Operation of Redeployment Assembly Area, no date, in USFET G–3, 370.

[36] EUCOM, Office of the Chief Historian, Redeployment, 1947, in CMH file 8–3.1, CA 20, pp. 82 and 83.

[37] Cable, Com Zone, to USFET, 13 Jul 45, in USFET SGS 330.11.

men were going to have to wait months before their turns came. Since they could have constituted a monumental morale problem, especially while the nonfraternization policy was in force, the redeployment plans included provisions for training, education, and recreation programs throughout the theater.

The training program, which was to have prepared the low-score units for combat in the Pacific, never started. After R–day, the units were continuously occupied reshuffling personnel and moving into the redeployment "pipeline"; consequently, Headquarters, 6th Army Group, which was to have become the Redeployment Training Command, found it impossible to schedule even short courses. About the only units likely to be in one place for a few consecutive weeks were those in the assembly areas waiting for ships, and they by then had turned in their equipment and might be rushed off to board ship at any time.[38]

The education program, aside from sustaining morale, was conceived also as a means of smoothing the transition to civilian life and of compensating soldiers who had had their educations interrupted by the war. The showplaces were the Shrivenham American University (capacity 4,000), Biarritz American University (capacity 12,000), and the Warton American Technical School (capacity 4,000). In addition, the theater secured spaces for 32,000 soldier-students at thirty-five European civilian colleges. The instructors for the two American universities were required to have M.A. or Ph.D. degrees or their equivalent; about half were hired from U.S. colleges and universities. The two-month

courses, in fields including agriculture, commerce, education, engineering, fine arts, journalism, and liberal arts, were to be conducted in a near-civilian atmosphere, reveille being the only required military formation. The students began assembling at Shrivenham in the second half of July after Eisenhower called on the commands to give the program vigorous support and fill their quotas with "men who are qualified and interested" because "the eyes of America are on this program."[39] The first course began at Shrivenham, in the former American Schools Center, on 1 August and at Biarritz, in a group of resort hotels, three weeks later. The Warton American Technical School opened in mid-September at Warton in Lancashire, England, which was later than the other two because of the time required to install machinery and instructional equipment—about $10 million worth in all.[40]

For those who could not meet the admission requirements of the theater-level schools, the plans provided command schools to be operated by units down to battalion level. The instructors were qualified military personnel and civilians, including, after the nonfraternization rules were relaxed, English-speaking Germans. The command schools were a massive undertaking. Seventh Army issued packs of 10,000 textbooks to each of its divisions and supplied hundreds of microscopes, transits, levels, phonographs, and other instructional items. In August, Seventh Army alone operated 134 schools, offering 133 courses to nearly 44,000 students.[41] By

---

[38] EUCOM, Office of the Chief Historian, Training, 1947, in CMH file 8–3.1, CA 23, pp. 3–9.

[39] Ltr, Eisenhower to Major Commands, 17 Jul 45, in USFET SGS 353.
[40] EUCOM, Office of the Chief Historian, Education and Information, 1947, in CMH file 8–3.1, CA 21.
[41] Hist Rpt, Seventh Army, 8 May–30 Sep 45, in Seventh Army, 107.3–0.

Ice Cream Parlor, *intended to boost morale during redeployment and readjustment.*

October, the theater total was nearly 300 schools. Soldiers could also take free courses for high school or college credit through the U.S. Armed Forces Institute, which had its main office in Madison, Wisconsin, and a European branch in Cheltanham, England. Between May and September, over 93,000 soldiers were enrolled in USAFI courses.[42]

Entertainment and recreation programs, considered important to morale during the war, were continued after the German sur-render. The sixty-six USO (United Services Organizations) shows in the theater on V–E Day played to three-quarters of a million men a month. Stars such as Jack Benny, Bob Hope, Raymond Massey, and Shep Fields continued to perform, but the lesser known professionals became notice-ably more tempermental after the war was over and career opportunities at home beckoned. USFET also had to point out that the USO performers were there to entertain the enlisted men and not to act as social companions for high-ranking officers. Jeep Shows and Soldier Shows, using Army personnel, provided additional

---

[42] TSFET, Progress Report, Nov 45, in Admin Hist Collection, ETOUSA No. 448.

live entertainment. Three- and four-man Jeep Show teams performed and helped units stage their own shows. The Soldier Show companies were large enough to put on Broadway plays. At first they were limited, as they had been during the war, to plays with all male casts, such as *Golden Boy* and *Brother Rat*. In the summer their repertoires expanded when USFET provided funds for hiring civilian actresses, who were somewhat astringently designated "Civilian Actress Technicians."[43] During the summer, Seventh Army operated a Soldier Show School giving sixty-man classes instruction in staging, casting, and directing complete shows. As had been the case during the war, the most available and most heavily attended form of entertainment was the motion picture. Out of a total attendance of 32 million people at all types of entertainment in May 1945, 26 million were at motion pictures. An estimated eight out of every ten soldiers saw at least three movies a week.[44]

To provide active and passive diversions, USFET Special Services stocked 21,000 basketballs, 100,000 dozen table tennis balls, and nearly 350,000 decks of cards and issued, by November 1945, 1443 libraries (each containing 1,000 cloth-bound books), close to 15 million paperback books, and over 44 million magazines. The most popular spectator sport was football. A survey showed that 305 basketball teams had drawn 21,250 spectators, 1,200 touch football teams a mere 1,200, and 90 football teams 379,000.[45] Best evidence of increasing participation in one unplanned

leisure time activity was the veneral disease rate, which went up from 50 cases to 190 per 1,000 troops per year in the first three months of the occupation (and to over 250 by the end of 1945). The Army had anticipated this problem, but a check in Munich, where approximately one hundred new venereal disease cases were occurring each week, showed that the three main prophylactic stations were giving at most three treatments a day.[46]

Furlough travel appeared to be the best prop for morale. It offered contact with civilian society, relief from the military routine and the supposed strain of nonfraternization, instructive experience, and a taste (with a marked GI flavor) of what had formerly been the life of the privileged. Before V–E Day, ETOUSA opened the Riviera Recreational Area in southern France, with 18,000 accommodations at Nice (for enlisted men) and Cannes (for officers). Inexpensive tours in France, England, Belgium, Holland, and Switzerland were offered after hostilities ended. Paris attracted the most soldier-sightseers by far, and visits there had to be limited to forty-eight hours throughout the summer of 1945.

The U.S. zone in Germany, in spite of the war damage, offered a variety of tourist attractions. (A standard military government joke was that the Russians had received the agriculture, the British the industry, and the Americans the scenery.) In the summer of 1945, USFET Special Services opened a rest and recreation center at Berchtesgaden that rivaled the one on the Riviera. Civilian guides conducted tours for three hundred men a day at Heidelberg.

[43] EUCOM, Office of the Chief Historian, Recreation and Welfare, 1947, in CMH file 8.3–1, CA 22, pp. 36–60.

[44] *Ibid.*, p. 36.

[45] TSFET, Progress Report, Nov 45, in Admin Hist Collection, ETOUSA No. 448.

[46] Hqs, TSFET, Office of Theater Chief Surgeon, sub: Venereal Disease, Eastern Military District, 15 Nov 45, in USFET SGS 720.

The most popular tours in Germany were the Rhine tours. From three riverside hotels at Assmanshausen, parties of soldiers were taken on motor rides to points of interest in the Rhine valley. The climax of the three-day tour was a seven-hour boat ride from Mainz to Koblenz. At Sechenheim, near Mannheim, Seventh Army maintained the "Special Service City," which housed the Soldier Show School as well as other athletic and music schools and provided billets and messes for Red Cross workers, USO troupes, and soldier-tourists. It could accommodate nearly 2,000 persons a night and served 45,000 meals per week. At Karlsruhe, the main junction for leave trains going to France, the Karlsruhe Hotel could billet 1,000 persons a night and serve 5,000 meals a day. The most unusual hotel was at Kassel where a large aid raid shelter had been converted into an underground hotel with accommodations for two hundred people. Possibly the most elegant hotel was the Castle Schoenstadt near Marburg.[47]

By mid-summer 1945, the search for morale-sustaining devices was being stretched to, and perhaps somewhat beyond, the limits of feasibility. In July, General Marshall visited Paris and the Berchtesgaden center and pronounced the efforts being made there for morale "splendid," but he came away worried that the enlisted men were still not getting the "feeling of independence which all Americans crave." He proposed that each regiment, for a week at a time, give trucks, rations, and gasoline allowances to small groups of about ten men and let them go anywhere they pleased except into the Soviet zone. Eisenhower thought the idea was good and,

rather gingerly, passed it along to the Army commanders with the comment that he would "like to see such excursions permitted insofar as local conditions will permit." The result was the establishment of a category known as Military Vacation Tours, of which few were taken. Confronted with a steeply rising traffic accident rate and a growing black market, commanders, much as they might have agreed with the spirit of General Marshall's proposal, could not bring themselves to turn loose on the roads of western Europe small groups of men in trucks with no supervision.[48] In September, USFET's WAC Staff Director, Lt. Col. Mary A. Hallaren, proposed revoking the prohibition on social contacts between enlisted personnel and officers of opposite sexes as a means of boosting the morale of enlisted women. To this proposal USFET G–1 gave short shrift, saying the interest of high-ranking male officers in enlisted women would undermine the WAC officers' authority. Besides, G–1 felt the problem would soon go away because all Wacs were to be redeployed by 1 April 1946.[49]

In spite of the offerings in education, entertainment, and recreation, surveys conducted in July indicated that the high-score men wanted above all to go home. An Army-wide survey revealed that in the Pacific particularly, delays in getting the eligible men home were generating dissatisfaction with the whole point system. In Europe, where the war was over at least,

---

[47] (1) EUCOM, Recreation and Welfare, pp. 129–31. (2) Hist Rpt, Seventh Army, 8 May–30 Sep 45, in Seventh Army, 107.3–0.

[48] (1) Ltr, Marshall to Eisenhower, 31 Jul 45; Ltr, Eisenhower to Marshall, 17 Aug 45; and Ltr, Eisenhower to Major Commands, 18 Aug 45, in USFET SGS 330.11. (2) EUCOM, Recreation and Welfare, p. 162.
[49] Memo, Hqs, USFET, ACofS G–1, for CofS, sub: Policy Governing Off-Duty Associations Between Commissioned and Enlisted Personnel, 20 Sep 45, in USFET SGS 330.11.

outright disgruntlement was less evident; but almost half the men complained that their officers had given them no explanation for the delay in their departures. Most correctly assumed that the cause was a shortage of shipping space but said that they had not been so informed. Shocked to discover that all the effort and expense might go for nothing because of a simple failure to communicate, Eisenhower ordered: "Both officers and enlisted men will be fully informed of the reasons for delay in connection with their return home and no frivolous answers will be given to any inquiry on this subject."[50]

The second atomic bomb was dropped in Japan on 9 August, and the next day Marshall told Eisenhower to be ready, as soon as Japan capitulated, to reverse the redeployment–readjustment priorities. First priority, he said, should go to the men eligible for demobilization, those with 85 points, and plans should also be made for moving out the men with at least 75 points. When Eisenhower asked for a month to clear the pipeline of more than 380,000 low-score men already processed and awaiting shipment, Marshall replied: "The pressure here is terrific. The demands for termination of Selective Service increase daily, a wait of a month before men begin to pour into the U.S. will greatly accentuate our difficulties."[51] On 15 August, the War Department directed Eisenhower to reverse the priorities immediately and prepare to ship out 1,716,000 men by the end of January 1946. Marshall informed Eisenhower

that he could not expect to have any men with scores over 45 left in the theater after 1 April 1946 and therefore should screen out from among the low-score men in the pipeline as many men with less than 45 points as he could.[52]

Since R–day, the decisive element in the long-range planning for the occupation had been the Occupational Troop Basis, the total number of troops to be left in Germany (and Austria) after the redeployment and readjustment were completed. The original Occupational Troop Basis was 404,500, to be reached a year and a half after the surrender. In May, the War Department reduced the time to one year. In August, it reduced the number of troops to 370,000, with a strong indication that the final figure would be substantially lower. The shipping schedule set in August would bring USFET's strength down to this number by the end of January 1946. The low point would be reached in the middle of the first postwar winter, when civil unrest, if it occurred at all, was to be expected in Germany and when the Army would probably still have to care for about a half million DPs and guard many thousands of war prisoners and internees. After USFET pointed out that it would take 100,000 troops just to guard and maintain the $8 billion (six million tons) of surplus property left in the theater, the War Department in September approved a liquidation force of 337,000 troops, which could be used to postpone the reduction to the Occupational Troop Basis until 1 July 1946. Concerning the efficiency and quality

[50] Memo, Office of the Chief of Staff [U.S. Army] for the Chief of Staff, sub: MPR Section 10, 23 Aug 45, and Memo, Hqs, USFET, G–1, for CofS, 1 Sep 45, in USFET SGS 330.11.

[51] Cable, Marshall to Eisenhower, 10 Aug 45; Cable, Eisenhower to Marshall, 13 Aug 45; Cable, Marshall to Eisenhower, 15 Aug 45, in USFET SGS 370, vol. III.

[52] (1) Cable, Marshall to Eisenhower, 14 Aug 45, in USFET SGS 370, vol. III. (2) USFET, G–3, Weekly Summary of Activities, 31 Aug 45, in USFET SGS 319.11/6, vol. I. (3) Memo, USFET, Dep ACofS G–3, for Dep CofS, sub: Redeployment "Ups" and "Downs," 5 Nov 45, in USFET SGS 370, vol. V.

of the troops, however, either in the Liquidation Force or the Occupational Troop Basis, the War Department had nothing to offer. The point score was to be the sole determinant of whether a man went or stayed, and all high-score men would go. Until January some relatively experienced men would be available while awaiting shipping. Thereafter public opinion would determine how many troops of any kind stayed, and Marshall told Smith, "It will be difficult for the Army to explain each case arising without a thorough investigation."[53]

The War Department supplied enough ships to transport over 400,000 men in September and proposed to do the same in October; but in that month it had to return the *Queen Elizabeth* and *Aquitania* (each capable of transporting 20,000 troops a month) to British service and had to loan the British ten Victory ships in order to keep the *Queen Mary*. In November, the troop number again went over 400,000 when Liberty and Victory ships were sent back in ballast from U.S. east coast ports—to the accompaniment of threatened dock workers strikes—and the battleship *Washington*, three heavy cruisers, four light aircraft carriers, and the captured German liners *Europa* and *Vulcania* were pressed into service as troop transports. At the end of December the theater strength was down to 614,000 troops and was 93,000 below the combined total of the Occupational Troop Basis and Liquidation Force.[54]

When the war was over everyone wanted to go home faster than any feasible schedule could move them and with an intensity that was not going to be diverted by any amount of persuasion. On V–J Day the students at Shrivenham American University stayed away from classes and asked to be sent home. When some who failed the midterm examinations were returned to their units, there was a rash of attempted failures. Shrivenham and Warton both closed at the end of their second term. Biarritz went into a third term with its enrollment down by half.[55] The Riviera Recreational Area had more French civilian employees (7,000) than soldier-guests (5,600) in October. Paris held up well as an attraction, but there the length of stay could be increased in October from forty-eight hours to a full week. USFET Special Services ran a contest for Soldier Shows in which the best show was to be given a three months' tour in the United States and individual performers would receive prizes from Hollywood stars. The contest drew three entries.[56] The loss of the two British liners and a related failure to get all 80-point men out before the end of October brought a plunge in morale in spite of detailed explanations from both the War Department and USFET.[57]

Within three months after V–J Day, the

[53] (1) Draft, TSFET, ACofS G–3, Redeployment Briefing, 3 Sep 45, in USFET G–3, 370. (2) Cable, Handy to Smith, 30 Aug 45, in EUCOM, Staff Message Control, Jul–Dec 45. (3) Cable, Smith to Marshall, 24 Oct 45, in USFET SGS 400.74. (4) Cable, AGWAR, WARCOS to Smith, 5 Nov 45, in USFET SGS 370, vol. IV.
[54] (1) Draft, TSFET, ACofS G–3, Redeployment

Briefing, 3 Sep 45, in USFET G–3, 370. (2) Cable, AGWAR, WARCOS to USFET, 23 Oct 45, in USFET SGS 370, vol. IV. (3) Memo, Hqs, USFET, Redeployment Co-ordination Gp, for Dep CofS, sub: Monthly Rpt, 1 Dec 45, in USFET SGS 322.
[55] EUCOM, Education and Information, pp. 31, 46, and 78.
[56] EUCOM, Recreation and Welfare, pp. 60, 130, and 132.
[57] Cable, USFET Rear to USFET Main, 17 Oct 45, and Cable, AGWAR, WARCOS to USFET, 23 Oct 45, in USFET SGS 370, vol. IV.

army that had defeated Nazi Germany was no more. In a November 1945 combat efficiency assessment, Smith reported operational understrengths of officers and enlisted men and high percentages of personnel "poorly trained in their duties. . . . A trained, balanced force of infantry armor, and air and supporting combat troops" he continued, "no longer exists. As a result, the forces within this theater are today unable to perform any serious offensive operations. The capability to carry on limited defensive operations is slightly better. Ability to perform . . . occupational duties, to control the German population, and to suppress local uprisings is rated as satisfactory."[58]

Currency Control

Currency trouble began even before the troops were properly deployed in Germany. In March 1945, First and Ninth Armies' finance officers turned in $52,875.60 worth of Reichsmarks that they had exchanged into dollars for U.S. troops before the Roer River crossing.[59] Neither the Reichsmarks nor Allied military marks were convertible for the Germans, but both were accepted from U.S. personnel at the rate set for Allied military marks, ten to the dollar. The Reichsmarks were already obviously worth a great deal less. In an attempt to head off a possible flood of Reichsmarks, ETOUSA, on 15 March, limited the dollars an individual could send home to an amount equal to his month's pay. Since dollar conversions of German currency were only made for transmissions to the

United States, the troops would hopefully at least be discouraged from accumulating excessively large amounts of Reichsmarks.[60]

The advance into Germany not only expanded the troops' opportunities for black market dealing in Reichsmarks—with fraternization as an inevitable byproduct—but put the Army in the questionable moral position of converting looted German money into American dollars. Haunted, too, by the nightmare of someday having troops attempting to convert a cache like the one recently uncovered at Merkers, ETOUSA on 19 April stopped exchanging and disbursing Reichsmarks altogether and ordered the post offices and PX's to stop accepting them for purchases.[61] The action was effective, particularly in relieving the Army of the embarrassment of legitimizing illegally acquired and probably worthless money. After V–E Day, however, the theater command apparently assumed that the currency control problem was about to disappear; in early June it began allowing soldiers to convert and send home savings and gambling profits in addition to their month's pay. A perfunctory oath was sufficient to qualify almost any amount as gambling profits.[62]

In the meantime, after the surrender, the value of the Reichsmark on the black market had dropped to 200 to the dollar. For the Germans the Allied military marks were worth about the same since they could only exchange them one-for-one for Reichsmarks; but the American soldier, who sold rations, cigarettes, candy, or any of a mul-

---

[58] Cable, Smith to Hull, 17 Nov 45, in EUCOM, Staff Message Control, Jul–Dec 45.

[59] Walter Rundell, Jr., *Black Market Money* (Baton Rouge: Louisiana State University Press, 1964), p. 33.

[60] EUCOM, Office of the Chief Historian, Currency Control, 1947, in CMH file 8.3–1, CA 6, p. 10.

[61] Memo, USFET, ACofS G–1, for CofS, sub: Currency Exchange Control, 29 Aug 45, in USFET SGS 123.5.

[62] EUCOM, Currency Control, p. 10.

titude of things (including government property) that the Germans were willing to buy at black market prices, could convert the Allied military marks at ten to the dollar. Dealing in Reichsmarks, he soon learned, was only slightly more inconvenient. While the Reichsmarks could not be converted directly, the G–5 Currency Section periodically put blocks of new Allied military marks into circulation and accepted Reichsmarks in exchange.[63] Probably no army ever had so many successful "gamblers." They could hardly miss, of course, with the odds pegged at twenty to one in their favor.

In the eastern zone, the Russians were paying off their troops, most of whom had not been paid for many months, in Allied military marks printed from the duplicate plates given to them in 1944. Unlike the U.S. soldier, the Soviet soldier did not have a choice as to how much of his pay he wanted to take in marks and how much in rubles, and the Soviet authorities would not convert either the Reichsmarks or Allied military marks. The soldiers had to spend the money or risk being transferred out of Germany and losing it. In the first weeks after the surrender, while the border was almost hermetically sealed to everything else, the Soviet marks began coming across in exchange for cigarettes and candy; some said the Soviet troops were even giving the money away. Doubting at first that the Soviet-printed marks could be identified except by experts, SHAEF told the War Department that the whole mone-

tary program was endangered. The danger was indeed there but not because the money was unidentifiable. Someone, probably in the Bureau of Engraving and Printing in Washington, D.C., had arranged that the plates the Russians received were not exact duplicates; the Soviet-printed currency could be easily identified by a dash printed ahead of the serial number.[64]

SHAEF's foreboding, nevertheless, became reality in July after the U.S. garrison entered Berlin. Soviet soldiers willingly paid as much as 10,000 Allied military marks for wristwatches and nearly as fantastic prices for cigarettes, candy, soap, and almost anything the U.S. troops wanted to sell. On 24 July, the Berlin District stopped selling postal money orders and war bonds; the troops had drawn a million dollars in pay during the month and had sent four million dollars home.[65] How much more money the troops had nobody knew. When Infantry Reorganization Company K, 400 men being redeployed from Berlin, arrived at Camp Lucky Strike in the last week of July, every man had some Soviet marks; one private had 70,000.[66]

For USFET the question was, Where would the dollars to convert the marks come from? Presumably, in the long run a deficit could be passed to the Germans along with the other occupation costs; but in the meantime, if the total amount the troops sent home exceeded the amount they drew in pay, the excess dollars would be

---

[63] Memo, USFET, ACofS G–1, for CofS, sub: Currency Exchange Control, 29 Aug 45, in USFET SGS 123.5. G–5 also opposed the ban on the convertibility of Reichsmarks to dollars, apparently because it tended to further depress the value of the indigenous currency. See Rundell, *Black Market Money,* pp. 33–35.

[64] (1) Cable, SHAEF Forward, Eisenhower, for CCS, 24 May 45, in SHAEF G–5, 115. (2) Memo, USFET, ACofS G–1, for CofS, sub: Currency Exchange Control, 29 Aug 45, in USFET SGS 123.5.
[65] (1) Cable, CG, Berlin District, to USFET, 24 Jul 45, in USFET SGS 123.5. (2) EUCOM, Currency Control, p. 12.
[66] Msg, Chanor Base Section to USFET Rear, 25 Jul 45, in USFET SGS 123.5.

ones the theater did not actually have. A check showed that the Berlin District's dollar overdraft in July was covered in the theater totals. It also showed, however, that the margin was getting thin. In March 1945, in the midst of the war, the troops had drawn $50 million more in pay than they sent home, in July only $17 million more.[67]

The answer—namely, to stop converting Allied military marks—was clear but not easy. The Allied military marks were evidence of U.S. determination to administer Germany as a single economic unit. The Soviet Union, although it was not converting, had not repudiated the Allied military marks as the occupation currency; it had merely made the money practically worthless to its own troops. USFET could either do the same—with readily predictable troop and press reactions—or adopt some other currency for its forces, thus leaving itself open to accusations of having been the first to break the principle of economic unity. The Russians, of course, could have raised the same charge if only their marks were not converted. Unfortunately, to preserve the principle, USFET had to ignore the fact that there was no other solution able to withstand the pressures, and ingenuity generated among the troops by the prospect of fantastic profits.

Effective at the end of the first week in August, USFET restricted the amount that could be sent out in any one month to the sender's pay plus ten percent and required commanding officers to verify and certify the transmittal.[68] The object was to remove the free-wheeling gambling profits allowance, which could have been accomplished had the unit commanders been able and

willing to enforce the restriction; but with redeployment in full swing, many had nothing to go by except a soldier's word that he had not already sent out his month's pay plus ten percent, perhaps several times over. Other commanders took much the same attitude as they had toward looting, that the soldiers were entitled to a tangible share in the victory. This attitude also seems to have been shared by the theater command, until the situation reached a point where the troops sent home more dollars than had been appropriated for their pay. This point was fast being reached. In August the excess of pay over dollar transmittals shrank to $6 million. The excess was a million dollars higher in September, but, no doubt, only because more troops were in the redeployment pipeline and stationed outside Germany. In Germany alone the deficit was probably already substantial. In Frankfurt, the USFET Headquarters Command personnel sent home nearly three-quarters of a million dollars more than they drew in pay in September.[69] When USFET, for reasons not cogently explained, lifted all restrictions on dollar transmittals in October as a preliminary to instituting a system of currency control books, $36 million more left the theater than had come in as pay. The War Department hastened to inform Eisenhower, "Whatever use of dollars is sanctioned by your theater, either directly or indirectly through inadequate controls, to meet the conversion of foreign currencies in excess of those amounts derived from pay and allowances or from dollar instruments is entirely the responsibility of your theater. . . ."[70]

---

[67] EUCOM, Currency Control, p. 66.
[68] Ibid., p. 13.

[69] Memo, USFET, Hqs Comdt, for Dep CofS, sub: Transmittal of Funds, 16 Oct 45, in USFET SGS 123.5.
[70] Cable, AGWAR, WARBUDIV, to CG,

Currency control books were introduced on 10 November. Each officer or enlisted man was given a book in which were entered his cash and bank deposits held in the theater, net cash pay for the last three months, and amounts sent out during this period. Subsequently, all pay and allowances and other legally acquired funds would have to be entered, and any amounts sent home would be deducted. When an individual left the theater he was entitled to exchange currency only up to the balance in the book. The enlisted men's books were held by certifying officers, who were required to initial each entry; officers held their own books.[71]

Some weaknesses of the currency control books were obvious from the outset; others took more time to emerge. The books, for instance, enabled every person in the theater to send all his pay home if he wished and live entirely off black market profits. They also enabled those who had not gotten their profits out during October and the first ten days of November to legitimize substantial amounts in their initial entries. In the 504th Paratroop Regiment, forty-four enlisted men had drawn $12,000 in pay and allowances in the three months before the introduction of the books, and they had sent $8,000 home; yet their first declarations totaled $21,000.[72] The enterprising also quickly discovered that the books, which were printed on single sheets of plain white paper and folded to make

four pages, could easily be counterfeited. They learned very soon, too, that initials could be forged and entries altered and that loopholes still existed. For several months, the telegraph companies, for instance, did a booming business in telegraphed flowers. The companies accepted marks, which they expected USFET to convert, and the florists delivered not flowers but money, for a commission.[73] Nevertheless, the books did, at least temporarily, cloud the full and free enjoyment of black market profits. In November, the theater was short $17 million, but during each of the next two months the troops converted $2 million less than they drew in pay.[74]

Police-Type Occupation

The nine-division permanent occupation force planned for Germany soon began to look like an outright extravagance after Japan surrendered. The Army expected to be down to two million men by 30 June 1946 and to have "utmost difficulty in obtaining manpower to sustain even that strength." For the whole European theater, the War Department forcasted a probable strength of five divisions, with further reductions likely after 1 July 1946.[75] In October, Marshall asked Eisenhower to consider going over to a police-type occupation similar to one being devised for Japan, in which a native Japanese police force under American supervision and backed by U.S. tactical units would take over practically the entire responsibility for security and order in the country. He also suggested considering whether foreign manpower—Ger-

USFET, 24 Oct 45, in USFET SGS 123.5. The full story of the overdraft, which eventually grew to nearly a quarter billion dollars, extends well beyond the scope of this volume. It did, however, remain the responsibility of the theater and was finally liquidated there without supplemental appropriations. See Rundell, *Black Market Money*, p. 88f.
[71] *Stars and Stripes*, 12 Nov 45.
[72] EUCOM, Currency Control, p. 34.

[73] *Ibid.*, p. 31.
[74] *Ibid.*, p. 66.
[75] Cable, Handy to Smith, 30 Aug 45, in EUCOM, Staff Message Control, Ins and Outs, Jul–Dec 45.

GENERAL HARMON INSPECTS A CONSTABULARY DETACHMENT

man, Polish, Norwegian, Danish, or Dutch—could be substituted for American manpower in the police force and in the tactical units "to reduce requirements for U.S. manpower and expense." Eisenhower accepted the idea of a police-type occupation but objected to using Germans on the ground of adverse public reaction, anticipated in both Europe and the United States. The War Department thereafter raised the possibility of recruiting other Europeans several times during the succeeding months before finally dropping the whole idea because of various difficulties, among them expense, language problems, and danger of

increasing the pressure for the withdrawal of all U.S. forces.[76] In the meantime, USFET undertook to devise a police-type occupation of its own.

A beginning had already been made in September, when G–2, USFET, recommended creating security forces for each military district (and Berlin and Bremen) to be composed of MPs, CIC detachments,

---

[76] (1) Cable, AGWAR, WARCOS to USFET, 17 Oct 45, in USFET SGS 371.2 (2) U.S. Constabulary, Hist Subsec, G–3, Maj James M. Snyder, The Establishment of the U.S. Constabulary, in Hist Div, Hqs, ETO, 97–USF8–0.1, pp. 3–5 and 22–25.

and district constabularies. The district constabularies would be mechanized cavalry groups taken from the tactical units, given special instruction in military government laws and ordinances, trained in conducting raids and searches, and employed as quick, mobile security reserves. G–2 also proposed a distinctive uniform, but G–4 could not supply any special items of dress; and when the districts activated their constabularies in November, the only distinguishing marks were the letters "DC" painted in yellow on the front of the helmet liners.[77]

From the idea of the district constabularies, USFET in the fall of 1945 evolved the concept of the United States Constabulary, a self-sufficient security force for the whole zone. Calculating on the basis of one constable (plus signals, supply, and air reconnaissance) for 450 Germans, Eisenhower informed the War Department that a constabulary of 38,000 men would be enough to establish police-type control by 1 July 1946, assuming that by then the surplus property, DP, and prisoner of war burdens would have been substantially eliminated. The estimated savings in the Occupational Troop Basis would amount to 81,000 spaces, since the supporting tactical troops could be reduced to three divisions and one army headquarters.[78]

The organizational plans, completed at the turn of the year, provided for a Headquarters, U.S. Constabulary, comparable to a corps headquarters; three brigade headquarters, one for each *Land* capital; nine regimental headquarters, one for each

Regierungsbezirk; and twenty-seven squadrons, located so as to cover one or more *Kreise.*[79] Each squadron would have three mechanized and two motorized troops (thirteen men to the troop) equipped with M5 armored cars mounting 37-mm. cannons (the mechanized troops only), quarter- and half-ton trucks, .30-caliber light machine guns, Thompson submachine guns, rifles, pistols, and code and voice radios. The U.S. Constabulary was to be an elite force of handpicked men, distinguishable from the other troops by their highly polished paratroop boots, service coats in place of the standard Eisenhower jacket, gold silk scarves, Sam Browne belts, and lacquered helmet liners circled with a half-inch blue stripe flanked by two half-inch yellow stripes and with the constabulary insignia (a gold disc bordered in blue with the letter "C" in blue pierced by a bolt of lightning in red) on the front.[80]

As late as mid-February 1946, however, the U.S. Constabulary consisted only of a plan and a headquarters. When Maj. Gen. Ernest N. Harmon was appointed commanding general on 10 January, he was for a time the sole member of the constabulary. By mid-February, he had selected a headquarters staff; on the 16th, a constabulary school opened in the former Adolf Hitler Schule at Sonthofen to train members of a cavalry reconnaissance squadron as teachers for the main body of the constabulary yet to be assigned.

---

[77] (1) Memo, Hqs, USFET, G–2, for Major Cmdrs, sub: Organization of Security Forces, 10 Sep 45, in USFET SGS 371.2. (2) Snyder, Establishment of Constabulary, pp. 9–11.

[78] Snyder, Establishment of Constabulary, pp. 14–16.

[79] The U.S. Constabulary did not function in Berlin, the Bremen enclave, or Frankfurt, all of which had static security forces directly responsible to USFET.

[80] (1) Hqs, USFET, to CofS, War Dept, sub: Police-Type Method of Occupation, 22 Dec 45, in Hist Div, Hqs, ETO, 97–USF8–0.20. (2) Snyder, Establishment of Constabulary, pp. 32–36 and 52–54.

CHAPTER XIX

Potsdam Germany

Quadripartite Control

The occupation entered the quadripartite phase shortly after noon on 30 July 1945 when the Allied commanders in chief assembled in the conference room of the U.S. Group Control Council headquarters in Berlin for their first meeting as the Control Council. At the same time, Truman, Stalin, and Clement Attlee, who had replaced Churchill two days earlier, were about to begin their final meetings at the Cecilienhof in Potsdam. Because the conclusion of the Potsdam Conference had been delayed somewhat by the change in the British government and by an illness of Stalin's, the Control Council could not yet transact any significant business. The Russians had tacitly made their participation in the four-power body dependent on a satisfactory—for them—outcome of the talks among the heads of state; and Zhukov, even at this late date, would agree only to set a schedule for future meetings (on the 10th, 20th, and 30th of each month) and to establish a rotating chairmanship, with Eisenhower taking the chair for the first month. When Eisenhower proposed activating the control machinery, which was composed of the Co-ordinating Committee (formed by the deputy military governors) and the directorates, the bodies that would do the day-to-day work of running Germany, Zhukov demurred. He would have to get his government's ratification, he said.

The Potsdam Conference protocol, signed on 1 August, gave the Control Council its charter and it missions. The commanders in chief, individually in their own zones and jointly as members of the Control Council, would exercise supreme authority in Germany. They would also, as directed by their governments, be responsible for developing occupation policies; the European Advisory Commission would be dissolved.[1] In addition to administering and observing agreed policies, such as demilitarization, decentralization, and denazification, the Control Council received two missions: one was crucial from the U.S. point of view, the other from the Soviet point of view. The first mission, which President Truman had put before the conference at its opening session, was to administer Germany as an economic unit.[2] Truman, no advocate of the Morgenthau Plan, had accepted Secretary of the Treasury Morgenthau's resignation on 5 July after refusing to have him at Potsdam.[3] The President's own thinking was closer to that of Stimson, who had written to him the day before the conference opened, "The problem which presents itself . . . is how to render Germany harmless as a potential aggressor, and at the

---

[1] Questions affecting the settlement of the war and an eventual peace treaty with Germany were assigned to the Council of Foreign Ministers established by the conference.
[2] Truman, *Memoirs,* vol. I, p. 345.
[3] *Ibid.,* p. 327.

SESSION AT POTSDAM. *President Truman is at the far side of the table with Secretary Byrnes and Admiral Leahy on his right.*

same time enable her to play her part in the necessary rehabilitation of Europe."[4] To accomplish both purposes, Stimson had urged treating Germany as an economic unit and stimulating her peacetime production while eliminating her war potential. The President, no doubt, wished also to avoid the political consequences of a divided Germany as well as the economic consequences to the American taxpayer of having to maintain a zone that had no prospect of being able to support itself. As an earnest of U.S. commitment to the principle of economic unity, he was willing to assume a share in financing supply imports for all four zones on a basis to be determined by the Control Council; and on 29 July, he assigned the procurement and financing responsibility for such a program to the War Department.[5] The conference protocol accepted economic unity as a principle and charged the Control Coun-

---

[4] Department of State, *The Conference of Berlin (Potsdam), 1945* in "Foreign Relations," vol. II, p. 756.

[5] (1) *Ibid.*, vol. I, p. 492f; vol. II, p. 821f. (2) The President to the Secretary of War, 29 Jul 45, in OPD 336, sec. V, Cases 104–

cil with setting up central German departments for finance, transport, communications, foreign trade, and industry. The predominant—possibly exclusive—Soviet concern was with reparations, not from its own zone where it was already collecting on a scale to suit itself but from the western zones. After long, frequently sharp debate, the conference gave the Control Council the second mission of establishing a level of industry for Germany, that is, determining how much of its existing productive capacity the country would need to subsist without being able to threaten the peace again. Any excess would become available for reparations, with 25 percent from the western zones going to the Soviet account.[6]

The Control Council held its second meeting on 10 August in its permanent quarters, the building in which a year earlier the infamous Nazi People's Court had tried the participants in the 20 July plot against Hitler. In the high-ceilinged, newly redecorated sessions chamber where the Nazi judge, Roland Freisler, had handed down his sentences, the military governors, flanked by their deputies, political advisers, and secretaries, took seats around a large oval table. Interpreters sat behind each delegation, and recorders occupied tables in the corners of the room. The resolution activating the control machinery was quickly adopted, and the meeting proceeded in an atmosphere of great personal amiability; but when the responsibilities acquired as a result of the Potsdam Conference came under consideration, the French member, Gen. Pierre Joseph Koenig, announced that he would have to "reserve his position" with regard to the Potsdam decisions.[7]

The subsequent meetings were conducted, in the words of one observer, with "few dissensions, all things considered," but with "a tone of fatality."[8] France, not having been represented at Potsdam, did not regard itself as bound by the agreements made there; and in the Control Council, General Koenig vetoed the proposed central economic agencies one by one as they came up, eventually including also a proposal to establish a post office department and a law allowing German trade unions to organize nationally. In early October, Gen. Charles de Gaulle told the French press: "France has been invaded three times in a lifetime. I do not want ever to see the establishment of a Reich again."[9] The Russians seemed to want to see the economic agencies created, but when the War and State Departments authorized Clay, in October, to enter into a trizonal arrangement, neither the Russains nor the British would agree.[10] The U.S. representatives returned then for almost another year to the futile task of trying to secure economic unification on quadripartite terms; and the Control Council remained, as Clay predicted it would, a negotiating rather than a governing body, capable of enacting legislation but completely dependent on the separate zonal authorities for enforcement.

While the French attitude alone was enough to cripple the Control Council, it in fact only masked a fundamentally more formidable obstacle to the treatment of Germany as an economic unit, namely, the

[6] B. U. Ratchford and W. D. Ross, *Berlin Reparations Assignment* (Chapel Hill: University of North Carolina Press, 1947), p. 43.

[7] OMGUS, History, ch. III, pp. 14–17.
[8] *Ibid.*, p. 16.
[9] *Ibid.*, p. 19.
[10] OMGUS, Control Office, Hist Br, sub: Civil Administration in Germany, 16 Dec 46, in OMGUS 21–2/5, folder VII-2 ABC.

Soviet insistence at Potsdam that, as Mc-Cloy put it, "anything anybody captured does not count as reparations." In other words, the Russians proposed to take whatever they liked out of their zone without regard for the level of industry and without including their acquisitions in the total of their reparations account; thus, eastern Germany could become an economic desert capable of endlessly soaking up economic assistance for the exclusive benefit of the Soveit Union. President Truman, McCloy told the members of the U.S. Group Control Council, was adamant against allowing the United States to be put in the position of financing reparations for the Soviet Union.[11] Hope of reasonable Soviet co-operation in administering Germany as an economic unit dimmed further after September when work began in the Control Staff on the level of industry plan. Determined to have the maximum capital assets from the western zones made available for reparations, the Russians were ready to strip the whole German economy to the bone and, in attempting to do so, plunged the negotiations into a tangle of conflicting statistics.[12]

Potsdam and Policy

Since JCS 1067 and its expansion by USFET into a military government directive (issued on 7 July 1945) were held under security classification until the end of the first week in August, the Potsdam Communiqué of 2 August was the first official knowledge the German people had of the Allied plans for their country and for their own future under the occupation.

For them, the news was a stunning blow. The territory east of the Oder and Neisse Rivers was lost; factories would be dismantled for reparations; and with what was left of its land and economy, the country would have to support added millions of Germans about to be expelled from Poland, Czechoslovakia, Austria, Hungary, and Rumania. An allusion in the communiqué to "primary emphasis" on "the development of agriculture and peaceful domestic industries" appeared to echo the Morgenthau Plan; the main purpose of the occupation seemed to be to convince the Germans of their "total military defeat" and leave them to endure the "chaos and suffering" they had brought upon themselves.[13]

The austere program and hard language of the Potsdam Communiqué was not new to the U.S. occupation authorities. Much of it had also appeared in JCS 1067 and was taken almost verbatim from the Summary of U.S. Initial Post Defeat Policy Relating to Germany of 23 March 1945.

To military government, however, the Potsdam decisions signaled the beginning of a positive program for the occupation. Although the tone of the 23 March summary emerged strongly from the Potsdam Communiqué, the content was significantly altered in the document that the President presented to the conference as the U.S. proposal for initial control policy in Germany and was further modified in the version approved by the conference. The decision to administer Germany as an economic unit and another to provide uniform treatment for the German population appeared to eliminate dismemberment as a possible

---

[11] War Diary, US Gp CC, PW and DP Div, 1 Aug 45, in OMGUS 314.81, CMH files.

[12] Ratchford and Ross, *Berlin Reparation Assignment,* pp. 86–103.

[13] (1) Cable, Eisenhower to JCS, 7 Aug 45, in USFET SGS 000.7. (2) State Department, *The Conference of Berlin (Potsdam),* in "Foreign Relations," vol. II, 1502–07.

Allied aim. More important for current military government operations, Potsdam opened the way for a political rehabilitation of Germany that would enable the Germans "in due course to take their place among the free and peaceful peoples of the world" and "allowed and encouraged" democratic political parties, local self-government (to be extended up to the *Land* level "as rapidly as may be justified"), and free trade unions. Harsh as the economic provisions of Potsdam appeared to be to the Germans, they were more moderate than some proposed and existing U.S. policies. Whereas JCS 1067 put the ceiling on the German standard of living at the lowest level among the neighboring nations, Potsdam set it at the average of the European countries, excluding Britain and the Soviet Union.[14] Potentially, then, the Germans could become eligible for relief at a level considerably above the disease and unrest formula.

The President, the JCS, and Eisenhower also made individual decisions in July that would be as important to the Germans in the U.S. zone as the provisions of Potsdam. In one decision, while assigning responsibility to the War Department for procuring and financing imports to Germany, the President specified that the authorization would remain in force "whether or not an agreed program is formulated and carried out by the Control Council." He thereby opened the way for a separate relief program in the U.S. zone.[15] In another deci-

sion, accepting the conclusions of the Potter-Hyndley Mission, the JCS ordered Eisenhower as a member of the Control Council to advocate the export of 25 million tons of German coal during the period ending April 1946, although recognizing that "this may delay industrial resumption [in Germany], cause unemployment, unrest, and dissatisfaction among Germans of a magnitude which may necessitate firm and rigorous action."[16] In a third decision, Eisenhower, at a USFET G–5 conference on 19 July, stressed the need to help the Germans prepare for the coming winter and authorized the use of Army trucks and military drivers to bring in the harvest.[17]

On 6 August, Eisenhower became the first prominent Allied figure to talk directly to the Germans by radio. After three months, he said, the occupation and denazification had progressed enough to allow him to speak to them about plans for the future. The months ahead would be hard. There would be food and transportation shortages and no coal for heating during the coming winter. Damaged houses would have to be repaired. The Army was providing transportation, but otherwise the Germans would have to solve these problems themselves. They would have to work and help each other. As a token of a brighter future to come, he told them that they would be allowed to form trade unions and engage in local politics when they showed readiness for healthy exercise of these privileges."[18] Bleak as the message was, it was a first—some would later think

---

[14] Hqs, US Gp CC, Analytical Section, sub: Notes on Differences Between Agreed Report of Tripartite Conference of Berlin and JCS 1067/6/8, 14 Aug 45, in OMGUS 358–2/5.

[15] (1) Summary Sheet, ACofS OPD to CofS, sub: German Interim Financing, 5 Aug 45, in OPD, 336, sec. V, Cases 104– . (2) Cable, AGWAR to USFET, 5 Oct 45, in USFET SGS 091.3.

[16] Cable from U.S. Forces, Berlin, from JCS to USFET, 26 Jul 45, in USFET SGS 463.3, vol. I.

[17] Memo, Hqs, USFET, ACofS G–5, for CofS, 19 Jul 45, in USFET SGS 451.1.

[18] Msg from General Eisenhower to the German People in the U.S. Zone, 6 Aug 45, in Admin Hist Collection, ETOUSA, No. 155.

a false—ray of hope. The war, at last, was over. The enemy commander had become a concerned and responsible administrator.

The Subjects of the Policy

Berlin in the summer of 1945, though only tenuously restored as the capital, was more than representative of the nation's woes. Divided, occupied by foreign troops, and isolated, the city was an island of 3¼ million people in a country for which it had once been the economic as well as political hub. For most of July, until the railroad bridge on the Elbe River at Magdeburg was repaired, food and coal trains from the western zones had to be unloaded at the river and reloaded onto Soviet-manned trains on the other side. The first U.S. train did not arrive in Berlin until the end of the month, and passenger service would not resume until November.[19] In the U.S. sector, as in the others, the Russians had dismantled and hauled away 95 percent of the industrial machinery. What was left was buried under rubble or was useless owing to lack of coal and electricity to run it and raw materials with which to work. The first firm to operate in Tempelhof, in the U.S. sector, sharpened used razor blades. In the fall a radio manufacturer began turning out a maximum dozen sets a day, and several metal fabricators, on orders from military government, started making stoves and cooking utensils out of salvaged materials.[20] The most visible part of the work force in the summer and fall—and for many months to come—were the *Truemmerfrauen,* women who scavenged usable bricks and other building materials from the rubble.

Bombing, destruction of bridges in the final battles, and the breakdown of the transportation system had reduced the city to a sprawling cluster of villages, each a block or two of habitable or nearly habitable buildings in which possibly a store or two remained open. In daylight the residents sallied out on foot in search of black market goods and firewood. Few went out after dark. Nighttime was the Russians' favorite time for picking up political suspects, as it had been with the Nazis, and they were not particular about sector boundaries or about whom they victimized.[21] Ruined as the city was, it still attracted German refugees from east of the Oder River and from Czechoslovakia. More than three-quarters of them were women and children; they came by the thousands in the summer of 1945, sometimes bringing disease with them. Disease was nothing new in Berlin, however, which in the first months of the occupation was swept by waves of dysentery, typhoid fever, and diphtheria, all spread by sewage leaking into the water system from fractured sewer pipes. Usually the adults and older children survived, but the first wave of dysentery, which the Berliners called hunger typhoid, killed 65 percent of the newborn babies.[22]

Clay described Berlin as "the world's largest boarding house, with all of the population on relief."[23] After the bridge at Magdeburg was reopened and the food trains began running into the city regularly, the daily civilian ration rose gradually from

---

[19] OMGUS, Control Office, Hist Sec, Quadripartite Access to and Control of Berlin, vol. II, in OMGUS 23–2/5, folder V205–3A.

[20] Hist Rpt, OMG, Berlin District, pp. 88–90.

[21] Hqs, Seventh Army, ACofS G–2, G–2 Bulletin No. 90, 28 Nov 45, in Seventh Army, Opns Rpt, Annex No. 3.

[22] OMG, Berlin District, Military Government Report, 4 Jul 45–3 Jan 46, in CMH files.

[23] Memo, OMGUS, Dep Military Governor, for CG, USFET, sub: Supply of Food to Civilians in Berlin, 3 Oct 45, in USFET SGS 014.1.

WOMEN SALVAGE BRICKS

less than 800 calories supplied in July to 1,250 calories, which the Russians had set as the maximum ration for normal consumers before the Western Allies arrived. The 1,250-calorie ration was more than the Germans in the western zones were getting; but the Germans in these zones, even those who lived in the large cities such as Frankfurt and Munich, could sometimes forage in the countryside, trading personal belongings to the farmers for potatoes, eggs, or meat. Berlin was an island, cut off from the outside, and the Berliners had to live on the ration, or on the black market. Col. M. D. Jones of Clay's Redeployment Co-ordinating Group reported what he saw on a visit to Berlin in September:

A typical meal consisted of 1 serving spoonful of canned stew, 2 or 3 boiled potatoes the size of golf balls, 1 handful of hardtack crumbs, 1 cup black coffee made from leftover grounds from U.S. messes, and 1 spoonful of watery gravy. [Jones was describing the meals served to a relatively small and fortunate group, those who had jobs with the Army.]

A meal two maids were eating in the billet I occupied, which they claimed was their only food for the day besides the meal described above, consisted of 1½ thin slices of bread, 2 small half-green tomatoes, 2¼ small

BERLINERS RECEIVE BREAD RATION FROM A TRAILER *because there is no transportation to business areas.*

potatoes, and 1 onion half the size of one's thumb.

On several occasions I saw children and old people gathering grass in a park, they said for food.

Although many children looked healthy, I also saw many covered with sores. The sores, I was told, were the result of an inadequate diet—the slightest bruise would fester.

I saw no fresh vegetables in the markets and was told there were none in the U.S. Sector. Only 3 out of 15 meat markets I visited had any meat at all. One had 20 lbs. which was rationed ⅓ lb. to the customer.[24]

Artists and entertainers, especially the latter, lived better than almost anyone else. Out of respect for "culture," the Russians had put them in the highest ration category, 2,500 calories per day; such a ration was otherwise restricted to very heavy workers. As a result, the normal consumers in Berlin were well entertained if poorly fed. Next best off were the manual laborers on essential jobs, who could thus qualify for increased rations. Public officials worked under the eye of military government for presurrender salaries and stood near the bottom on the ration scale. On the black market, of course, after the Ameri-

---

[24] USFET, Redeployment Co-ordination Group, Gp Ch, Observations in Berlin, 8–12 Sep 45, in USFET SGS 014.1.

cans came everything could be had: butter, Spam, cheese, canned meats, and liquor. The prices in marks ran into the thousands for small quantities. Among the Germans, American cigarettes were the preferred currency, because they had an intrinsic value. A carton of any American brand, which cost the U.S. soldiers 50 cents in the PX, was worth 150 marks, $15 at the U.S. rate of exchange, and in Berlin could bring several hundred dollars in marks. Matches were the small change.[25]

In the U.S. zone proper, the military government economic specialists watched for small sparks of life in the industrial machine that had enabled Germany to wage war for six years against half the world. Out of their wartime profits, factory owners could afford to clean up and put their plants in order; but afterwards all they could do was wait for coal, electricity, and materials. In July, military government allocated coal to run one newsprint paper mill and in September enough coal to reopen a rolling mill to make sheet metal for cooking and heating stoves. The first window glass was produced in Bavaria in September, and a month later one chemical plant in Wuerttemberg-Baden began making soda ash needed for glass and soap, while another started to produce calcium cyanamid for nitrogen fertilizer. The plants were using leftover and scavenged materials, however, and when these were exhausted they would have a hard time getting new stocks.[26] Of the whole industrial establishment in the U.S. zone about 15 percent was in working condition in August and was running at about 5 percent of capacity. Output was meager. All the soap produced in July, for instance, amounted to no more than an ounce and a half per person.[27] One-time sales of a spool of thread per person and, with the use of ration coupons, of 10 German-made cigarettes (or 2½ cigars) were events covered in the newspapers.[28]

Coal was the key. In July and August, the output was 15 percent of the 1935–1936 monthly average. Every industry restarted increased the shortage. The amounts that arrived were always smaller than those shipped. Of 120 carloads consigned to Nuremberg, 70 carloads arrived. Another 1,000 tons of coal disappeared completely en route from Munich to Nuremberg.[29] In his 6 August radio speech Eisenhower told the Germans to cut wood for the coming winter because there would be no coal for heating, and during the late summer and fall military government embarked on a wood-cutting program throughout the zone. The Army supplied power saws and axes and military trucks to haul the wood in areas the German trucks could not reach. Wood-cutting progress became a required subject of military government detachment reports, but many detachments found that the idea did not really catch on with the Germans until after the first spell of cold weather in October.

The Transportation Corps' Military Railway Service, supervising the German *Reichsbahn,* had 90 percent of the first-line railroad track in the zone open by Septem-

[25] Hqs, Seventh Army, ACofS G–2, G–2 Bulletin No. 90, 28 Nov 45, in Seventh Army, Opns Rpt, Annex No. 3.

[26] OMGUS, Econ Div, Occupation Report, Industry, Sep 47, in OMGUS 358-2/5.

[27] JCS 1517, Summary of the Jul 45 Report of the Military Governor, 19 Sep 45, and JCS 1517/1, Summary of the Aug 45 Report of the Military Governor, 18 Oct 45, in CCS 383.21 (2–22–44), sec. 9.

[28] *Weser Bote* (Bremen), 13 and 16 Oct 45.

[29] Hist Rpt, Det B–211.

ber and had a through train running from Frankfurt to Paris. But except for city and suburban lines, which were essential to get the German civilians back and forth to work, the railroads carried only U.S. troops, DPs, and military supplies. The cars ran with leaking roofs and broken windows because new glass and tar paper always disappeared on the first run.[30] Civilian goods, mostly farm produce and firewood, moved by truck; and the 100,000 trucks and busses in the zone had been so diminished by requisitionings of both the *Wehrmacht* and the U.S. forces that less than a quarter of them were operable. In September, the Army released 12,500 surplus military trucks for sale to the German authorities.

Even without transportation, as the travel restrictions within the zone gradually eased and finally were abolished altogether in August, the Germans became a restlessly mobile people. By truck, by horse and wagon, or on foot carrying their possessions on their backs, they crisscrossed the countryside looking for relatives or for places to live. For the city dwellers, periodic trips into the country with spare pairs of shoes, rugs, or other household furnishings and pieces of clothing to trade for food were becoming necessary to survival.[31]

When the U.S. Group Control Council took a survey during September in Frankfurt, Nuremberg, Kassel, and Stuttgart, the Germans most frequently mentioned food and housing as their main worries. A check of the inhabited dwellings showed that three-quarters needed repairs. More than half had no windows; a third had damaged

roofs, and a quarter unsound walls.[32] In Frankfurt alone, 173,000 persons lived in basements, shacks, and ruins that would not be habitable in winter. Although military government ordered homeowners to rent out spare rooms and promoted programs for salvaging building materials from the debris of the bombing, continuing requisitions for troop and DP billets actually decreased the living space available to the Germans. In Wuerttemberg-Baden, a fifth of the population was inadequately housed, even by prevailing German standards. In Wuerzburg, Bavaria, one of the most heavily bombed cities, the 55,000 population were nearly all living in ruins. In Bremen, 62,000 persons lived in the basements of bombed-out houses; others lived in flimsy shacks, in air raid bunkers without light or ventilation, and in rooms without doors, windows, or roofs. When cold weather approached in October, military government initiated a forced exodus to the country districts of 30,000 people from Heidelberg, 10,000 from Wuerzburg, and similar numbers from other cities.[33]

Although, contrary to SHAEF G–5's earlier prediction, the Germans were not starving in the summer of 1945, malnutrition was undoubtedly a contributing cause of some deaths, particularly in Berlin. The U.S. Group Control Council interrogators concluded that the Germans were not as undernourished as they looked; on the other hand, military government in Bavaria believed the Germans looked better physically than they should have, considering the

---

[30] OMGUS, Control Office, Hist Br, US MG in Germany, Rail Transport, Jul 47, in OMGUS 23–1/5, folder XIV–6.

[31] Cumulative Hist Rpt, Military Government, *Land* Bavaria, 30 Jun 46, in OMGUS 436–2/3.

[32] Hqs, Seventh Army, ACofS G–2, G–2 Bulletin No. 91, 6 Dec 45, in Seventh Army, Opns Rpt, Annex No. 3.

[33] (1) Hist Rpt, Eastern Military District, 15 Nov–15 Dec 45, in OMGUS 76–3/10. (2) History of Military Government in *Land* Wuerttemberg-Baden, vo. I, in OMGUS 410–1/3. (3) *Weser Bote*, 17 Nov 45.

MANY LIVED IN SHACKS AND RUINS

rations they were getting. At the end of August, the USFET Chief Surgeon, Maj. Gen. Morrison C. Stayer, reported that nutritional survey teams had found that 60 percent of the Germans were living on a diet that would inevitably lead to diseases caused by malnutrition. Surveys, he said, already showed vitamin deficiencies and weight loss in both adults and children. Because the issued ration, which varied downward from 1,150 calories per day, was not enough to sustain life, and the additional 400 to 500 calories that the average German was assumed to be getting from cellar stocks, home gardens, and the black market were not enough to sustain productive labor, Stayer recommended raising the ration to 2,000 calories per day. In September, Clay applied to the Combined Food Board in Washington for an import allotment for Germany, expecting "to get our share but not at all sure it will be enough to supply the 2,000 calories recommended by the health officer."[34] Clay said he could not ask the Food Board "to accept as a

[34] (1) Final Rpt, Seventh Army, ACofS G–5, 25 Mar 46, in USFET, Hist Div, 11068/100. (2) Memo, OMGUS, Dep Military Governor, for CG, USFET, sub: Supply of Food to Civilians in Berlin, 3 Oct 45, in USFET SGS 014.1.

TROOPS SEARCH LUGGAGE FOR BLACK MARKET GOODS

premise that food should be supplied to Germany on a scale equal to or greater than that supplied to other countries of the world who have suffered from but did not initiate aggressive war."[35] Moreover, the requirements for Germany would be large. The total agricultural output of the U.S. zone from November 1945 to September 1946 would only be enough to supply 938 calories per day to the normal consumer. An increase to 1,500 calories would require 543,000 tons of imported food, and an increase to 2,000 calories would require nearly twice as much.[36]

On the black market, in the zone as in Berlin, all kinds of goods were available at astronomical prices in marks and often only in exchange for items of value, such as cigarettes, sugar, butter, and coffee—all of which functioned more as currency than as consumable commodities. The "banker" for one large black market ring was carry-

[35] *Ibid.*, (2).

[36] (1) JCS 1517/4, Summary of Nov 45 Report of the Military Governor, 14 Jan 46, in CCS 383.21 (2–22–44), sec. 10. (2) Cable, OMGUS to AGWAR for WARCOS, 1 Nov 45, in OMGUS 12–1/5, v60–20/1.

ing nearly $300,000 in diamonds when he was arrested. The DPs, because of their privileged status, and the U.S. troops, UNRRA employees, and Red Cross workers, because of their access to U.S. goods, figured prominently in the black market. The Germans partly depended on it for their subsistence and partly used it as a means for converting their money into material goods as a hedge against inflation. Because search operations like TALLYHO consistently failed to turn up sufficient evidence, USFET and the military districts for several months persuaded themselves that the black market was nothing to worry about. In September, on the apparent assumption that the people involved were mostly soldiers wanting to trade cigarettes or chocolate bars for souvenirs and Germans wanting to oblige them, USFET opened officially sponsored barter markets in Stuttgart and Frankfurt—thus contributing to the further undermining of confidence in the currency. In the fall, certain by then that a black market existed, USFET began to concern itself with the professional operators who were definitely criminals and might also be Nazis using the black market to support themselves in the underground and who dealt heavily in U.S. goods and supplies pilfered from Army dumps; by the end of the year an average of $10,000 worth of supplies a day was disappearing from the Quartermaster depot at Ludwigsburg alone. In October, military police searched two passenger trains coming into Bremen and confiscated a truckload of illegal goods, mostly Army property and black-market slaughtered meat.

Certainly the most numerous and probably the most successful black marketeers were not the professionals but the farmers. They were required by law to deliver all their produce, except subsistence allowances for themselves and their families, at fixed prices to authorized distributors. Under the Nazi regime the Reich Food Estate had kept records on the productivity of every farm down to the last egg and quart of milk; but in the many places where these records had not survived the war, military government had a much looser hold on production. In Bavaria in the fall of 1945, the legal butchering of hogs was 50 percent below normal, and six sugar beet processing plants had to be closed down because the farmers had diverted the beets to the black market. The farmers argued that they in turn had to barter to get tools and equipment, but the people in the cities widely suspected that most were well on the way to acquiring enough property to be able to carpet and furnish their cow barns like parlors if they wanted.[37]

Except for black marketeering, some thefts of food and firewood, and petty violations of military government ordinances, the German civilian crime rate was low, sometimes almost disconcertingly low for the Army agencies charged with ferreting out and suppressing resistance. In October, after five months of occupation, Seventh Army G–2 believed Germany to be a "simmering cauldron of unrest and discontent" and claimed to have detected a "mounting audaciousness in the German population"; but as concrete evidence G–2 could only cite some illicit traffic in interzonal mail (then still prohibited), a "strongly worded"

[37] (1) Memo, Hqs, Seventh Army, ACofS G–2, sub: The Black Market in Seventh Army Area, Mar 46, and Memo, Hqs, Seventh Army, ACofS G–5, sub: G–5 Report on Black Market, 11 Mar 46, in Seventh Army, CofS files. (2) EUCOM, Office of the Chief Historian, Public Safety, 1947, in CMH file 8–3.1, CA 18, pp. 109–13. (3) *Weser Bote,* 5 Oct 45.

Werwolf threat to one military government officer in the Western Military District, and a protest against denazification from the Evangelical Church of Wuerttemberg.[38] Patrols occasionally found decapitation wires stretched across roads, ineptly it would seem, since no deaths or injuries resulted from them. Military government public safety officers from scattered locations reported various anti-occupation leaflets and posters, some threats against German girls who associated with U.S. soldiers, and isolated attacks on soldiers. Although not a single case was confirmed, possibly the most talked about crimes against the occupation were the alleged castrations of U.S. soldiers by German civilians. When the commanding officer of Detachment E3B2, in Erbach, Hesse, was asked to investigate one such rumor, he reported that not only had there been no castration but that there had not been a single attack on U.S. military personnel in over four months of occupation.[39] The most pressing concern of public safety officers was often with getting the German police out of their traditional nineteenth century Prussian drill sergeant uniforms and into American styles, usually modeled on the uniforms of the New York City police. Wherever troops were stationed, especially in towns and smaller cities, prostitutes and camp followers were a moral problem, placed added strain on food supplies, housing, and medical facilities (frequently also on jails), and raised mixed feelings of disgust and jealousy among the other civilians. In quarrels with other civilians and with the police, the prostitutes did not hesitate to call on their soldier friends.[40]

The Germans attributed all violent crimes to the DPs; and military government reluctantly came close to agreeing with them. Of 2.5 million DPs originally in the U.S. zone, all but 600,000 had been sent home by the end of September, and General Wood reported the repatriation problem "substantially solved."[41] But those who stayed were becoming a special problem, being a hard core of largely nonrepatriable stateless persons. About half were Poles, for years the most mistreated of the Nazi forced laborers and now torn between their desire to go home and their apprehension about the future awaiting them in Communist Poland. The rest were Balts, non-German Jews, eastern Europeans other than Poles, and—although many fewer than there had been—Soviet citizens, most of whom tried to claim special status as Ukrainians. USFET policy made repatriation entirely voluntary for all DPs except those who came from within the pre-1939 boundaries of the Soviet Union; many had legitimate reasons for not wanting to return, principally fear of political or religious persecution. As the total number of these displaced persons de-

---

[38] Hqs, Seventh Army, ACofS G–2, Weekly Intelligence Summary No. 15, 24 Oct 45, in Seventh Army, Opns Rpt, Annex No. 2.

[39] Weekly Summary, Det E3B2, 20 Oct 45, in OMGUS 7–3/5.

---

[40] The tension was greatest in areas where Negro troops were stationed, since they, already feeling discriminated against by both the Army and the Germans, frequently interpreted efforts to curb prostitution as another form of discrimination. In Kuenzelsau, Wuerttemberg, Negro soldiers of the 350th Field Artillery Battalion beat up the local jailer when he refused to release prostitutes being held for venereal disease treatment. Later the whole police in Kuenzelsau tried to resign after being threatened that they would be killed if they interfered with the prostitutes. Memo, Hqs, USFET, Internal Affairs Br, for CG, Western Mil Dist, sub: Opns Rpt on Det H–52, in OMGUS 10–2/5.

[41] War Diary, US Gp CC, PW and DP Div, 29 Sep 45, in OMGUS 314.81, CMH files.

Tanks Move In *to keep order in Yugoslav DP camp.*

clined, however, the percentage of doubtful types among those who remained, such as criminals and Nazi collaborators, constantly increased, as did their influence on the others. A questionnaire, similar to the *Fragebogen* used for the Germans, tried on 240 DPs in a camp at Regensburg, Bavaria, revealed that 40 percent, if they had been Germans, would have been in the mandatory removal category, that is, unemployable in responsible positions and possibly subject to arrest.[42]

Among all categories of DPs, uncertainty about the future, free rations and lodging without having to work for them, privileged status under the occupation, and virtual immunity from the German police bred indolence, irresponsibility, and organized criminality. Their access to Army, UNRRA, and Red Cross supplies made them potent operators in the black market; the camps provided havens for black market goods and bases for criminal gangs; and the Army-issue clothing that most of them wore was excellent camouflage for the criminal elements and an effective

[42] EUCOM, Office of the Chief Historian, Public Safety, p. 119.

means of intimidating the Germans.[43] The 100,000 or more DPs who did not live in camps or who drifted in and out of them at will constituted the nucleus of a kind of Army-sponsored underworld. Even the former concentration camp inmates were becoming an annoyance. Many persisted in wearing their convict uniforms and were willing to regale any newspaper reporter who would listen with supposed new atrocities being inflicted upon them by the Army. Some were trying to make their privileged status permanent by having official-looking documents drawn up and badges made.

At the same time, stories about the DPs in U.S. newspapers were making them objects of particular public and official sympathy. In the summer the U.S. representative on the Intergovernmental Committee on Refugees, Earl G. Harrison, visited the camps as President Truman's special emissary and recommended setting up separate camps for Jews. Later, after Saul S. Elgart of the American Joint Distribution Committee surveyed the Jewish camps, UNRRA undertook to distribute Red Cross packages to the Jews, thereby raising their ration to over 3,000 calories a day. In September, Eisenhower personally inspected several DP camps and announced that general officers would inspect all camps. Al-

though the inspections showed the camps in general to be adequate and the larger ones often excellent with kindergartens, chapels, medical facilities, electric lights, flush toilets, and average food rations above 2,100 calories a day, the press and public concern did not abate. In late September, Eisenhower ordered the military government and military authorities to requisition housing for DPs from the Germans without any hesitancy, prohibited any restrictions on the DPs' freedom of movement, and made food and sanitation in the camps a concern of all responsible officers.[44] As a consequence, the Office of Military Government for Bavaria reported later, "there were so many inspections by generals, public health officers, correspondents, and other privileged emissaries of interested organizations that the objects of scrutiny themselves cried for a respite."[45]

Upon hearing of the order to let the DPs come and go as they pleased, the detachment in charge of 15,000 in a camp at Wildflecken, Bavaria, observed that considering the marauding and looting which had taken place when only 1 percent a day were allowed to leave, it looked to the future "with great concern."[46] The detachment's apprehension was not unfounded. DP depredation was the chief reason for rearming the German police in September; until then, they had only carried nightsticks. Military government recorded 1,300 DP raids against Germans in Bavaria during one week in October, and in some country districts people were afraid to leave

[43] Eisenhower believed that the wearing of these uniforms by the DPs and other groups, including some German prisoners of war, was also a major cause of declining troop morale in the late summer of 1945, and he proposed outfitting the U.S. soldiers with the 1938 blue dress uniform for off-duty wear. General Marshall replied that he understood the problem but believed the procurement of the required amounts of cloth and leather would provoke civilian protests at home, where both commodities were in short supply. USFET efforts to provide the DPs with clothing dyed some other color brought protests of discrimination from them. Ltr, Eisenhower to Marshall, 24 Sep 45, and Ltr, Marshall to Eisenhower, 5 Oct 45, in USFET SGS 421.4.

[44] (1) EUCOM, Office of the Chief Historian, Public Safety, p. 87. (2) Opns Rpt, Hqs, Seventh Army, 8 May–30 Sep 45, in Seventh Army, 107–3.0.
[45] Hist Rpt, Western Military District, 15 Nov–15 Dec 45, in OMGUS 76–3/10.
[46] Ibid., 15 Sep–14 Oct 45.

their houses even in the daytime. Many farm communities found a new use for old air raid sirens: to warn of approaching DP bands. In Munich, DPs constituted 4 percent of the population but were responsible for 75 percent of the crimes. Military government courts in Bavaria held 2,700 trials between 1 June and 30 October in which displaced persons were accused of serious crimes, such as murder, robbery, and looting; and in Bremen, a DP population of 6,000—3,500 of them males over fourteen years of age—committed 23 murders, 677 robberies, 319 burglaries, and 753 thefts. Organized gangs armed with pistols and automatic weapons operated out of the Bremen camps. When an eight-man gang murdered thirteen Germans during one night in November, soldiers of the 115th Infantry raided the camp from which they had come and uncovered large quantities of illegally slaughtered beef and U.S. property. Afterward, in protest, the DPs flew black flags and placed large signs at the camp entrance reading "American Concentration Camp for Poles."[47]

Next to the black market and the DPs, German youths were military government's most worrisome concern. Many children were completely adrift, orphaned by the war, unable to find their families, or simply abandoned. All were idle. Schools were closed; youth organizations, other than a few sponsored by the U.S. forces, were prohibited; and entertainment and recreation facilities were requisitioned for the U.S. troops. The worst off—and most dangerous in the eyes of military government—were those in their late teens. Although too young to have served in the *Wehrmacht* and experienced the sobering effects of defeat in the field, they were old enough to have absorbed Nazi attitudes. The *Freikorps* and the Nazi storm troops had found many recruits among a similar group after World War I. Under the occupation, these young people were becoming sidewalk loafers. They could not continue their educations or learn trades, and the only jobs being offered involved cleaning up rubble, which was not enticing in either the short or the long run. So they gathered out of the sight of the Americans, made up bawdy verses about the behavior of the U.S. soldiers and German girls, at times threatened to shear the hair of girls who had soldier friends, and sometimes, military government officers suspected, rigged decapitation wires or attempted acts of sabotage. Their activities were all quite amateurish but might not remain so once enough young, but more experienced, prisoners of war returned home.[48]

In the summer, though far from ready to democratize the German educational system and by no means certain how to go about it anyway, the detachments worked under USFET orders to get the schools open and the children and teenagers off the streets. Grades one through eight opened on 1 October with slightly more students than in 1939, but with about half the teachers and buildings. Since the teachers were as politically pure as military government and the CIC could get them, they

---

[47] EUCOM, Office of the Chief Historian, Public Safety, p. 119. (2) Det E2C2, Functional History of Military Government in the Bremen Enclave, Oct–Nov 45, pt. II, in OMGUS 39–3/5. (3) Functional History of Military Government, Bremen Enclave, 27 Apr 45–30 Jun 46, p. 95. (4) Hqs, EUCOM, Hist Div, Military Government in Munich, p. 15. (5) Memo [no source], sub: Offenses by DPs, 17 Nov 45, in USFET SGS 383.7.

[48] (1) EUCOM, Office of the Chief Historian, Public Safety, p. 102. (2) EUCOM, Hist Div, Military Government in Munich, p. 18. (3) Hist Rpt, Det G–42, Oct 45, in OMGUS 10–2/5.

PRINTERS ASSEMBLE DENAZIFIED TEXTBOOKS

were consequently often persons who had been away from the profession a long time or who were the products of crash courses in pedagogy that the detachments ran when too many professionals in their districts turned in unsatisfactory *Fragebogen*. The average age of the teachers in Munich was fifty-seven, and the pupil-teacher ratio was eighty-nine to one. Secondary schools were the most difficult to staff and did not begin opening until November and December. Although "pep talks" on democracy always accompanied the openings, the education officers' subsequent visits to the schools were more frequently in the in-terest of discipline. Nazi textbooks had been rigorously screened out, but their replacements, relics from the Weimar Republic, were sometimes not really antidotes to militarism and nationalism. The fifth-year reader contained items such as Frederick the Great's speech to his troops before the battle of Leuthen ("Let us beat the enemy, or let us be buried by his batteries. . . ."); a contemplation entitled "At the Funeral of My Friend Lieutenant Wurche, Killed in Action, 1915"; and Liliencron's "Ballad of the Battle of Kolin." The seventh-year arithmetic books used the economic and territorial losses under the Treaty of Versailles as problems. On the flyleaves, USFET included the disclaimer, "The fact of reprinting does not imply, seen from the educational and other points of view, that this book is absolutely without objection."[49]

The newspapers, as the following extracts from the *Weser Bote,* published in Bremen, demonstrate, mirrored a dark Germany:

3 October
Children under 18 and pregnant women will get an additional pound of apples or pears in their rations.

5 October
Count Bernadotte will arrive on Monday with General Eisenhower's permission to arrange for setting up soup kitchens to feed German children during the winter.

10 October (want ads)
Request information about D. Luerssen, last a member of the replacement battalion at Riga-Strand (Latvia).
Opera singer wants a piano, to buy or on loan for a man's suit.

13 October
Lida Barova, Czech movie actress who collaborated with the Nazis has been arrested and turned over to the Czech authorities.
Last night the street sign on Friedrich Ebert Street [recently renamed after the first president of the Weimar Republic] was painted over, and the newspaper kiosk at the main post office was smeared with Nazi slogans and swastikas.

16 October
General Clay said the American occupation would stay in Germany for many years. Asked if it could be as long as a generation, he said it could well be.
Who can give information concerning Corporal Claas Mueller?

Who can give information concerning *Flak* Auxiliary Gisela Slomberg?

30 October
Monika von Dittmar, daughter of General Kurt von Dittmar, Nazi radio commentator, was picked up wet and hungry on a street in Oberammergau. After her arrest she tried to commit suicide by jumping from a window.
In Bremen, SS General Count George Hennig von Bassewitz-Behr was arrested. He had been police chief of Hamburg and a friend of Heinrich Himmler.
The first Liberty Ship, *William F. Cody,* entered Bremen harbor.

3 November
Beer brewing has been stopped in Bavaria because the barley must be used to make flour.[50]

A Lesson in Democracy

JCS 1067 established as one of military government's basic objectives "the preparation for an eventual reconstruction of German political life on a democratic basis." Concerning politics, however, the directive instructed Eisenhower, "No political activities of any kind shall be countenanced unless authorized by you," and added, "You will assure that your military government does not become committed to any political group." Although the first sentence seemed faintly to affirm a controlled resumption of political activity, the second echoed a more fundamental premise, namely, that military government should be nonpolitical. FM 27-5, as published two years earlier, read, "Neither local political personalities nor organized political groups should have any part in determining the policies of military government."[51] SHAEF G–5, there-

---

[49] (1) JCS 1517/2, Summary of Sep 45 Report of the Military Governor, 13 Nov 45, in CCS 383.21 (2–22–44), sec. 10. (2) After Action Rpt, Eastern Military Government Staff, Sep 45, in OMGUS 72–3/10. (3) Annual Rpt, Det B–262, Jun 46, in OMGUS 10–1/5.

[50] *Weser Bote,* in OMGUS 39–3/5.
[51] War Dept, FM 27–5, *Army-Navy Manual of Military Government and Civil Affairs,* 22 Dec 43, p. 10.

fore, had assumed all along that the best way to keep military government out of politics was not to allow its practice and had planned to prohibit political activity, not to revive it.

The prohibition was almost totally effective in Germany after the surrender, no doubt because the twelve Nazi years had left little with which to renew political activity. No party, other than the Nazi party, had existed legally—or even illegally in any organized fashion—in Germany since 1933. The Communist and Social Democratic party leaders had either been jailed or had emigrated, and the leadership of the other parties had either been assimilated into the Nazi system or, with the help of the *Gestapo* where needed, reduced to complete impotence. The German people, never notably enthusiastic about party politics, remembered what had happened to the Marxist and bourgeois parties under Hitler and what was happening to the Nazis under the occupation. Consequently, when SHAEF G–2 undertook to investigate German political activity in early July 1945 it could not find any "in the traditional sense of the term. . . . Normal political issues," it concluded, were relegated "to the status of academic questions," the subject of low key discussion among a few scattered survivors of the old parties.[52]

On the other hand, in the field, military government had been learning since Aachen that politics was more than just parties and party rivalries. German appointees invariably represented social, religious, economic, and—with or without party labels—political outlooks. The absence of a positive political program meant

only, as the G–5 field survey pointed out in March, that political directions were determined by special interests such as the Church or by individuals and cliques. Hence, military government, willingly or not, was involved in politics, and most dangerously so because it would have to bear the entire responsibility for the political consequences of the acts and character of its supposedly nonpolitical appointees. General Clay, who had missed the Aachen affair, had his own lesson in June when a wilder storm broke over the appointment of the first postwar Minister President of Bavaria, Fritz Schaeffer (see below, pp. 384–86). Seeing military government in Bavaria trapped in a crossfire of press and public recriminations, Clay wrote to McCloy, "The experience in Bavaria seems to me to indicate the desirability of relaxing the ban on political activities as promptly as possible."[53]

The Potsdam decision to allow and promote democratic political parties in Germany was, therefore, not unwelcome to the U.S. occupation authorities; and the day after his 6 August speech, in which he told the Germans they would be permitted to engage in local political activities, Eisenhower instructed the military districts to begin licensing parties at the *Kreis* level.[54] The public reacted, the Western Military District reported, with "stunning apathy." A few survivors of the pre-Nazi parties, mostly Communists and Social Democrats, asked desultory questions about licensing procedures, which the military government officers could not answer because there were none. Representatives of would-be

---

[52] Memo, SHAEF, ACofS G–2, for Head, CI, sub: CI Report to be submitted to Gen Clay, 3 Jul 45, in SHAEF G–2, GBI/CI/CS/091.1, folio 3.

[53] Ltr, Clay to McCloy, 15 Jul 45, in OMGUS 410–2/3.
[54] Cable, Hqs, USFET, ACofS G–5, to CG's, Western and Eastern Military Districts, in USFET SGS 014.1/4.

movements occasionally drifted into detachment offices. In Munich, for instance, a group calling itself the League of German Culture proposed to rally politically the devotees of art and culture. The vast majority of the Germans, the detachments agreed, were occupied with other things, such as food, housing, and the other problems of existence in a defeated and devastated country. These Germans took Eisenhower's offer as evidence of approval, which they craved, but were willing to let the issue drop there, feeling that politics had brought on all their troubles in the first place. Those who had been pro-Nazi without having joined the party were congratulating themselves on a narrow escape and were not willing to risk another even remotely. In Kurhessen, the regional detachment put the majority of the farmers in the latter category and saw only the urban workers as expecting to benefit in any way from restored unions and political parties.[55] The torpid public response at least saved military government much of the embarrassment of not being able to actually license political parties. Neither USFET nor the military districts had worked out the procedures and, therefore, they had to put a freeze on the whole program for nearly two months.[56]

In the interim, although in no way evincing a ground swell of democratic enthusiasm, a party-political pattern began to emerge. In a limited sense, the Soviet zone provided the model. Already on 10 June, the Soviet Military Administration in the zone had granted permission to organize "all anti-fascist parties."[57] By the end of the month, four parties with national potential had secured licenses: the Communist party, the Social Democratic party, the Christian Democratic Union, and the Liberal Democratic party. Although the Soviet authorities would not have objected, none except the Communist party regarded itself as headquartered in the Soviet zone. All had roots reaching back into the pre-Nazi period and, except for the Communist party, were just beginning to feel their way into the new era. By being licensed in the Soviet zone, they acquired corporate existences but not much more.

The first parties on the scene in the U.S. zone were the Communists and the Social Democrats, in that order. They shared one big advantage: neither bore the Nazi taint. The Social Democrats could claim the distinction of having been the only one of the old parties (the Communists had been outlawed by then) to have voted against the granting of dictatorial powers to Hitler in March 1933. The Communists, while their record under the Weimar Republic showed them to be almost as lacking in respect for democracy as the Nazis, had been the party most ruthlessly persecuted by the Nazis; and since they were protégés of one of the victorious powers, they were also by definition democratic. In the U.S. zone, the Communists and the Social Democrats also had two common problems: the opposition of the Catholic Church and the absence of a working class majority. The Communists also had to contend with the negative effects of "rumors and reports from the Soviet Zone"; the Social Democrats had to deal with a left wing attracted by a So-

---

[55] (1) OMG, *Land* Bavaria, Cumulative Hist Rpt, 30 Jun 46, in OMGUS 436–2/3. (2) Hist Rpt, Det 205, Sep–Dec 45, in OMGUS 1–2/5.
[56] Wk Rpt, Det E 205, 28 Sep 45, in OMGUS 1–2/5.

[57] Beate Ruhm von Oppen, *Documents on Germany Under Occupation* (New York: Oxford University Press, 1955), p. 38.

viet-sponsored Communist bid for unity of the working class parties.[58]

Of the pre-Nazi middle class parties, the two showing strongest signs of life were the Center Party and its Bavarian counterpart, the Bavarian People's party. Traditional ties with the Catholic Church helped them to dissociate themselves from nazism, although their members were not always successful in doing so as individuals. U.S. military government, with some misgivings, had been relatively generous in appointing their potential leaders to administrative posts under the occupation, most notably Dr. Adenauer as *Oberbuergermeister* of Cologne and Fritz Schaeffer as Minister President of Bavaria. But these parties hesitated to enter postwar politics in their old Catholic stance, partly because their more progressive leadership wanted to give them a broader base of voter appeal and partly because—in the case of the Bavarian People's party especially—their actions under the Weimar Republic were not above reproach, but mostly because they were afraid they would not be able to compete against the Communists and Social Democrats. For this last reason, they would just as soon have seen the prohibition on political activity prolonged, and they were furthermore spurred to break with the past and take the lead in promoting "Christian" parties as soon as the Social Democrats and Communists began to organize.

The idea of a Christian party or parties uniting all confessions through their common opposition to Marxist atheism, after being written into a formal program in Adenauer's Cologne in March 1945, took hold more or less independently in all parts of Germany. Advocates of such a party in the Soviet zone gave it a name, Christian Democratic Union, on 25 June when they secured a license to form it. In the U.S. zone the name Christian Social People's party was more frequently used until September, when Christian Democratic Union (CDU) came into general use in the *Laender* of the Western Military District and Christian Social Union (CSU) was adopted in Bavaria. By the time they emerged in the U.S. zone, the CDU and CSU were, in the words of one observer, "a banquet for political gourmets." The CDU in particular attempted to embrace all elements opposed to communism or social democracy for religious or any other reasons, and even some that were not opposed. Its right wing catered to industrialists, big businesses, and large landowners, while its left wing looked for support from civil servants, small shopkeepers, and farmers and, in working class areas, endorsed socialization of some industries. The CSU additionally presented itself as a defender of the Bavarian way of life and as a staunch ally of the Catholic Church. Both parties also let it be known, to the marked annoyance of military government, that they were prepared to welcome repentant Nazis to their ranks, and both endorsed the view that denazification should be limited to the "real" Nazis, the small numbers in the top leadership. The rest they dismissed as *Mussnazis*, Nazis by compulsion.

The Liberal Democratic party, licensed in the Soviet zone in June, was a revival of the old German Democratic party. Similar offshoots of the German Democrats in the U.S. zone went by several names, most prominently the Democratic People's party.[59] Having a nineteenth century lib-

---

[58] (1) History of Military Government in *Land* Wuerttemberg-Baden, pt. I, p. 247. (2) Hist Rpt, Det E4C2, Sep 45, in OMGUS 7-3/5.

[59] The various "democratic" parties did not merge nationally until 1948, when they became the Free Democratic party.

eral outlook and being both defenders of private enterprise and private property and nonsectarian, they were closer to the average American's idea of a political party than the others. Their weaknesses were an appeal limited to the middle class and the need to find a middle ground between the Social Democrats and the CDU-CSU— both of whom stretched their programs so as to leave them practically no common ground. The Democratic People's party had a minor stronghold in Wuerttemberg-Baden, where one of its founders, Dr. Reinhold Maier, was the *Land* Minister President appointed by military government.[60]

Military government political analysts worried about the paucity of leadership talent in all parties. Too many good men, they believed, had either been killed, broken, or driven out of the country by the Nazis or were too old. Except for the few who had survived the concentration camps or other forms of Nazi persecution, those who were left had apparently been, at best, "political office boys," too insignificant to have attracted the Nazis' attention. However, the one major new political figure to appear in the U.S. zone, Dr. Josef Mueller, leading founder of the CSU, nonplussed the Americans. A prominent lawyer and member of a Munich patrician family, Mueller had the attributes of a typical Bavarian, including a double chin. He was also suspected of being an intriguer and a "double-triple-crosser." He cultivated good relations with the Americans but re-

portedly told his followers that, "in a pinch," it might be necessary to go over to the Soviet side. He gave information to U.S. intelligence agencies but was thought also to have contacts with Russians. While professing to reject the rightist outlook of the old Bavarian People's party, he argued for leniency toward nominal Nazis and accepted them into the CSU. His membership in the *Abwehr* (counterintelligence) during the war would ordinarily have been enough to put him in the mandatory removal, if not automatic arrest, category under the occupation; however, he had spent the last months of the war in a concentration camp, he had the confidence of the Catholic hierarchy in Bavaria, and he had a supportable claim to have been a go-between with the Vatican for the German resistance while he was in the *Abwehr*.[61] Perhaps, as the summer of 1945 wore on, Mueller's best attribute in the eyes of military government was that compared to his strongest rival, Minister President Schaeffer (see below, p. 385), he was beginning to look like a sterling champion of democracy.

Ready or not, however, the Germans in the U.S. zone were going to taste democracy soon—sooner than anyone expected. They were not going to get it because they wanted it or because they deserved it but because General Clay believed in learning by doing and—probably as much as for any other reason—because the end of the war in the Pacific inspired him to convert necessity into virtue. After V–J Day, USFET G–5 records showed that 40 percent of the officers and 50 percent of the enlisted men in military government would

---

[60] (1) Hist Rpt, *Land* Hesse, Jun 46, in OMGUS 42–1/5. (2) History of Military Government in *Land* Wuerttemberg-Baden, pt. I, pp. 247–53. (3) OMGB, Political Intelligence Br, Yearly Report of Political Activities in Bavaria, 1 Jul 46, in OMGUS 65–1/10. (4) Gerhart Binder, *Deutschland Seit 1945* (Stuttgart: Seewald Verlag, 1969), pp. 100–21.

[61] (1) Rpt on CSU [no source, no date], in OMGUS 65–1/10. (2) OMGB, Political Intelligence Br, Yearly Report of Political Activities in Bavaria, 1 Jul 46, in OMGUS 65–1/10.

be eligible for discharge by the end of 1945.[62] With this information in mind, on 16 September, Clay wrote to McCloy that he had worked out a program for local elections in the U.S. zone. He continued:

The Potsdam Agreements call for restoration of local self government as rapidly as consistent with the purposes of the occupation. If the Germans are to learn democracy, I think the best way is to start off quickly at the bottom. Besides, this will help us reduce the personnel needed for military government. With many officers returning to the U.S. in the coming months, we will not be able to staff a large number of local detachments. Yet, we can hardly withdraw the detachments until officials appointed by us have been replaced by others selected by the Germans.[63]

Four days later, orders went out to German *Land* governments to write election codes and to the military districts to prepare for elections in January 1946 in communities (*Gemeinde*) of less than 20,000 people, to be followed in March and May by elections in *Landkreise* and communities with 20,000 to 100,000 people. Elections, as it turned out, were announced ahead of the procedures for licensing political parties. The procedures did not reach the detachments until the first week of October.[64]

Apart from Clay and his staff, the consensus of the Americans and Germans was that the plan for elections was premature, dangerous, and potentially disastrous. Clay, in fact, told McCloy that some of his own

advisers were urging him to postpone the elections.[65] Doctrinally, Clay's decision appeared to be flaming heresy to most of military government. Although no such program existed, it had been a fundamental assumption of military government that the Germans would be subjected to an extensive period of education and training in democracy. President Roosevelt, after all, had talked in terms of a whole generation. To hold elections after eight months and without the German character having been remolded in any significant way could only be judged frivolous or cynical. Furthermore, as a practical matter, early elections appeared to offer nothing but disadvantages. At the end of October, local parties had been approved in only six of the Bavarian *Kreise*. In the important Munich *Stradtkreis,* the second party, the Social Democrats (the Communists were first), was not licensed until 17 November. In some *Kreise* not a soul showed up even to talk about founding a party. And USFET's rules did not exactly encourage would-be politicians or promote speed in the granting of licenses. The names of twenty-five sponsors were required on each application; and each sponsor had to submit a personal *Fragebogen*, which brought him to the attention of Special Branch and CIC investigators. The people, the politicians, and the military government detachments all wanted the elections postponed. When Louis P. Lochner, Chief of the Berlin Bureau, Associated Press, toured Bavaria in the second week of October, he reported that public and military government opinion was preponderantly against early elections. A quarter of those responding in a poll taken in Munich stated categorically

[62] Memo, Hqs, USFET, ACofS G–5, for CofS, sub: Program for Introduction of Classified Civil Service, 6 Sep 45, in USFET SGS 200.3.
[63] Ltr, Clay to McCloy, 16 Sep 45, in OMGUS 410–2/3.
[64] (1) History of Military Government in *Land* Wuerttemberg-Baden, pt. I, 254. (2) Annual Hist Rpt, Det E 213, 3 Jul 46, in OMGUS 78–1/10.

[65] Ltr, Clay to McCloy, 16 Sep 45, in OMGUS 410–2/3.

that they would not vote in any election. Even Adalbert von Wittelsbach, pretender to the Bavarian throne, vacant since 1918, indicated that he proposed to wait a while before attempting to revive the monarchist cause. The parties that had been licensed seemed to be campaigning against the elections as much as against each other. None of them wanted to risk their fledgling organizations in a test of strength; and since many of the prospective candidates were already military government appointees, they did not want to risk their jobs.[66] In mid-October, Clay himself told the CAD: "Except for [four] cities mentioned above

and some smaller cities where political parties are in the process of formation, complete political apathy is reported from nearly every section of [the] American Zone. . . . There is significant unanimity in reports from Military Government in stressing this fact and in observing that [the] German masses are entirely unready for self-government and ignorant of democratic processes and responsibilities."[67] Nevertheless, in a USFET directive of 23 November, he ordered the *Land* military governments to set firm dates for the *Gemeinde* elections in January and authorized them to license parties at *Land* level, a harbinger of more important elections to come.

[66] (1) OMG, *Land* Bavaria, Cumulative Hist Rpt, 30 June 46, in OMGUS 436–2/3. (2) Hist Rpt, *Land* Hesse, Jun 46, in OMGUS 42–1/5. (3) Annual Hist Rpt, Det E 213, 3 Jul 46, in OMGUS 78–1/10.

[67] *Foreign Relations, 1945,* vol. III, p. 981. The four cities were Stuttgart, Frankfurt, Kassel, and Munich.

CHAPTER XX

The First Freedom

ICD Organization and Policy

Of President Roosevelt's Four Freedoms the first was freedom of speech and expression. As it applied to the individual, freedom of speech was regarded by U.S. occupation policy as a natural right, although for the Germans somewhat circumscribed. Collectively, in regard to the communications media, it was to be granted to the Germans under tutelage after Nazi and other undesirable influences had been eliminated. The instrument to do both was the Information Control Division (ICD), USFET.

The ICD, headed by General McClure and composed of the personnel who had formed the U.S. side in the Psychological Warfare Division of SHAEF, was a Special Staff division of USFET.[1] Until December 1945, when it was transferred to the newly created Office of Military Government (U.S. zone), ICD functioned separately from military government, as had PWD, SHAEF. Its chief field agencies were two District Information Services Control Commands (DISCCs). The 6870th DISCC, pinpointed for the Eastern Military District, had been organized in January 1945.

The 6871st DISCC, assigned to the Western Military District, was formed in February around the press control team that had founded the *Aachener Nachrichten*. Later the ICD also created the 6840th Theater Information Services Control Command (TISCC) to supervise certain zonewide activities and the Information Control Section for the Berlin sector.[2]

The ICD and its subordinate commands had two missions: the first was to act as the communications link between the German people and the U.S. occupation authorities; the second was to control and reconstitute the German information services "as instrumentalities of a democratic, peace loving society."[3] These missions were to be accomplished in three phases. In the first, using the authority of Military Government Law No. 191, all media of public expression in Germany would be shut down, which was done as areas were occupied. In the second phase, PWD and ICD would operate selected instruments of public information, such as newspapers and radio stations, as "overt" organs of the occupation. The third phase called for a gradual revival and return of the media to German hands through licenses to be given to "carefully selected anti-Nazi, democratic-minded Germans."[4]

[1] A policy and planning staff, the Information Control Service (ICS), also under McClure, was organized as a special section of the U.S. Group Control Council. After a brief stay in Frankfurt, it moved to Berlin in August 1945 to take part in quadripartite information control planning which in the first year had little influence on operations in the zones.

[2] Hist Rpt, ICD, 8 May 45–30 Jun 46, in OMGUS 242–1/5, pp. 12–17.
[3] Memo, Hqs, USFET, ICD sub: Priority for ICD Activities, 7 Aug 45, in USFET SGS 091.412.
[4] USFET to CG's, Eastern and Western Military Districts, sub: Administration of Military Govern-

At the time of the surrender all SHAEF-occupied territory was in the second stage. Newspapers and radio stations were shut down and theaters, moving picture houses, and concert halls were closed. The information Germans received came from *Die Mitteilung,* other Army newspapers, and Radio Luxembourg. PWD's second phase policy was to "maintain and deepen the mood of passive acquiescence [to the occupation]," to encourage food production, and "to arouse a sense of collective responsibility for Germany's crimes." This last point was going to be a permanent—and permanently frustrating—element of U.S. information activities.

Undoubtedly influenced by the more dulcet timbre of Soviet-operated Radio Berlin, PWD relaxed its policy slightly at the end of May. In the press and radio, German anti-Nazi writers were to be given limited opportunities to express themselves on political subjects; and cultural activities, particularly music, were to be encouraged. Stories and broadcasts having to do with German guilt would differentiate between the Nazi criminals, who were to be punished, and the German people, who were to be told that they could atone "by hard work, national restitution, and a change of heart."

In late June, two events ushered in the third phase: on the 27th, Hollands, editor of the *Aachener Nachrichten,* received a license, and on the 28th, PWD authorized limited licensing of other newspapers. These papers were to be subject to prepublication censorship and their tone and content would be the same as those of the official papers, the rationale being that the Germans would be more willing to accept ideas from other Germans, especially the concept of collective guilt to which their resistance increased as more crimes were revealed.[5]

As it turned out, only one paper, the *Frankfurter Rundschau,* was licensed under the 28 June directive. The Potsdam promises of free speech and press and Eisenhower's offer in the 6 August speech to extend these freedoms "by a gradual process" to the Germans in the U.S. zone brought another directive on 9 August. In the directive, ICD authorized licensing of German information services to engage in reporting, editorial writing, and discussion on a "wide variety of subjects, provided military security is not jeopardized." Postpublication scrutiny supplanted prepublication censorship, and full freedom of speech and press were envisioned in future stages.[6]

Press Control

When the redisposition was completed and SHAEF dissolved in mid-July, the only newspapers being published in the U.S. zone were eight overt Army papers, all weeklies, with a combined circulation slightly over three million. They were slated to be phased out as licensed papers took over the areas they served; but in the meantime, in August, two more were added, one in Stuttgart, to serve the parts of Wuerttemberg and Baden acquired from the French, and the *Allgemeine Zeitung,* in Berlin. The *Allgemeine Zeitung* appeared three times weekly, alternating with

---

ment in the U.S. Zone in Germany, 30 Jul 45, in CCS 383.21 (2–22–44), sec. 9.

[5] (1) Hist Rpt, ICD, 8 May 45–30 Jun 46, in OMGUS 242–1/5, pp. 6–8. (2) OMGUS, ICD, ICD Joins Military Government, 22 Dec 45, in OMGUS 242–1/5.

[6] Hqs, USFET, ICD, Directive No. 4 for Information Control Services, 9 Aug 45, in USFET SGS 091.412.

First Licensed Newspaper Comes Off Press. *On the left Editor Hollands of the "Aachener Nachrichten." General McClure on the right.*

a British-published paper to give the western sectors in effect a daily newspaper. In September, reflecting the progress in licensing, the overt papers declined to five, and in late November the last of them stopped publishing.

The 6870th DISCC, under Col. Bernard B. McMahan, had moved into Munich at the end of April; and at the same time, 6871st DISCC, under Lt. Col. John Stanley, had settled at Wiesbaden in the Western Military District. Since the overt papers were edited centrally in PWD and ICD and printed and distributed by army press

teams, the DISCCs concentrated from the first on working with the Germans. Enforcing Law No. 191 was the least of their jobs. Although military government detachments, often unaware that information control was not one of their functions, sometimes briefly tolerated so-called black newspapers, the German newspaper industry was dead. The problem, preliminary reconnaissance showed, was going to be to recruit acceptable Germans and find enough plants and presses to resurrect the country's newspaper industry. Goebbels' Propaganda Ministry had kept a tight hold on all public information media, and few people who had worked during the twelve year Nazi period, practically none in journalism, could meet the DISCCs' political standards. In the bombed-out cities, the presses were still buried in the rubble.

Nevertheless, in the beginning, the licensing procedure influenced the pace of press revival more than the availability of people and presses did. The 28 June and 9 August directives made licensing possible, but the procedure required both ICD and DISCC clearances, and ICD alone had the authority to issue licenses. Under this system only two papers secured licenses, the *Frankfurter Rundschau* on 31 July and the *Rhein-Neckar Zeitung* in Heidelberg on 5 September. The program first began to move in earnest after 11 September, when ICD delegated the licensing authority to the military district commanders, who acted on the DISCCs' recommendations. During the month, five papers received licenses in the Western Military District, including one in Bremen. At the end of the month in Berlin, *Der Tagesspiegel* received a license; in the first two weeks of October, The Eastern Military District licensed five papers in Bavaria, beginning in Munich on the 6th with the *Sueddeutsche Zeitung*. By the end of the year, twenty-three papers, with a combined circulation of more than three million, were publishing in the zone, Bremen, and Berlin. Because of the paper shortage, all were restricted to twice-weekly publication except *Der Tagesspiegel* which was a daily.

After January 1946, redeployment, the paper shortage, and the dearth of qualified and acceptable German journalists increasingly made themselves felt, and in the next six months only twelve newspapers received licenses. Both DISCCs had begun the occupation with close to a hundred officers. In.

the first three months of 1946, redeployment reduced this strength by half. The pool of potential licensees had begun to run dry already in the fall of 1945, and the 6970th DISCC had had to look for emigré journalists in France. For three months beginning in February 1946, 6870th DISCC stopped licensing newspapers in Bavaria completely while it sent scouts to Switzerland, France, England, and the British and French zones.[7] USFET slowed the licensing program further after the turn of the year when, to save paper, it restricted the total press run for the zone to one paper for every five persons. Consequently, the papers licensed later were fewer and smaller. A dozen of the papers licensed in 1945 had allotted press runs of more than 100,000 copies. *Der Tagesspiegel*, the *Frankfurter Rundschau*, the *Sueddeutsche Zeitung*, and the *Stuttgarter Zeitung* printed 400,000 to 450,000 copies, and several others among the 1945 papers had circulations ranging from 150,000 to 300,000 copies. Among the 1946 papers only the *Badische Neueste Nachrichten*, in Karlsruhe, received a 100,000-copy allotment, a figure that was apparently not reached.[8]

Finding licensees was the press control officers' first and usually most critical task. Besides having newspaper editorial and management experience, the candidates had to have been anti-Nazi—not merely non-Nazi—and prodemocratic. ICD added one other requirement: that, as a rule, licenses be granted to groups of individuals representing different social, political, and religious outlooks rather than to single persons. Because no more than one paper could be licensed in a single area, ICD

---

[7] Hist Rpt, OMG, Bavaria, 1945, Jun 46, in OMGUS 436–2/3, vol. II, pp. 201–03.
[8] Hist Rpt, ICD, 8 May 45–30 Jun 46, pp. 21–24.

wanted each paper to represent several opinions, hoping thereby also to break the German habit of a partisan press.[9]

In setting up the *Sueddeutsche Zeitung* in Munich, the 6870th DISCC reduced a field of 250 applicants to three. The chief editor, Emil Goldschagg, had edited a Social Democrat newspaper in Munich before 1933, had been arrested by the *Gestapo* twice, and had been rejected as an Army reserve officer when he refused to sign a paper stating that he would abide by Nazi principles. August Schwingstein, the publisher, had been a member of a liberal peasant group and a leader in the anti-Nazi *Reichsbanner* movement during the 1920s and early 1930s, and before 1933 had published several provincial newspapers in southern Bavaria. The cultural editor, Franz Schoeningh, had edited the independent Catholic literary periodical, *Hochland,* until the Nazis put it out of business.[10]

In the long run, the most distinguished early licensee was Dr. Theodor Heuss, who was a founder of the *Rhein-Neckar Zeitung* and Minister of Culture in the first *Land* government for Wuerttemberg-Baden and later served two terms as President of the German Federal Republic.

Almost without exception, the licensees had been away from newspaper work for a decade or more and thus needed advice on content and makeup and help at turning out papers in plants where electricity, paper, ink, machine parts, and everything else were short. The DISCCs supplied the assistance, including technical advice on re-building plants and controlling circulation and supplies. In Wuerzburg, the 6870th DISCC brought in American civilian specialists to rebuild a plant out of a pile of rubble.[11] Censorship was not a problem. Possibly because the licenses were valuable (no paper failed to sell out every edition), the editors were elaborately careful to respect the limits on what they could publish, although some complained about having to hush up incidents involving U.S. soldiers.[12]

Since none of the licensees owned printing plants and the rule against licensing corporations limited their ability to acquire capital to buy plants, USFET permitted ICD to use the confiscation and requisitioning powers of the occupation to put them in business; these powers were not used in any other instance to benefit Germans. Plant owners, who in the first place had no choice and the second place could not use the plants without licenses anyway, usually were willing enough to turn over the property at a reasonable rent; but ICD had to be concerned also for the future when American protection was gone. Viewing low capital and plants acquired by forced rentals as poor foundations for a democratic press, ICD worked to assure the survival of the licensed papers. In the German *Land* governments it promoted tax exemptions and other favorable legislation, and it required the licensees to pay 20 percent of their gross receipts into a capital fund. Most important, ICD secured authority for the DISCCs, as custodians of requisitioned plants, to offer the licensees long-term leases with options to buy.[13]

---

[9] ICD authorized licensing second papers in cities over 100,000 population in April 1946, but only one such paper, the *Frankfurter Neue Presse,* received a license before 30 June 1946.

[10] Hist Rpt, OMG, Bavaria, 1945, Jun 46, in OMGUS 436–2/3, vol. II, p. 196.

[11] Hist Rpt, OMG, Bavaria, 1945, Jun 46, in OMGUS 436–2/3, vol. II, p. 198.

[12] History of Military Government in *Land* Wuerttemberg-Baden, vol. I, p. 1316.

[13] (1) Hist Rpt, ICD, 8 May 45–30 Jun 46, in OMGUS 242–1/5, pp. 6 and 25. (2) Hist

While attempting to put the press on a sound business footing, ICD also had to consider a personnel problem. As was the case in public service, the youngest licensees were in their midforties and most others were in their fifties and sixties. Qualified, politically acceptable younger men were scarce. To perpetuate a German democratic press, a new generation of journalists would have to be recruited and trained. Work on this enormous task began in 1945 in the *Deutsche Allgemeine Nachrichten Agentur* (DANA), the German General News Agency.

Late in June, in an attic room of a hotel in Bad Nauheim, two ICD lieutenants, four enlisted men and a half dozen civilians from the Office of War Information started the German News Service to provide a news file for the overt and licensed press. Because the initials, DND in German, looked and sounded too much like those of the Nazi news agency, DNB, they later changed the name to DANA. After the Allied Press Service, which SHAEF had operated in London, closed in September 1945, DANA became the exclusive source of world and national news for the licensed press in the U.S. zone. Although DANA thereafter quickly became a full-fledged news service, having contracts with the U.S. press services, exchange agreements with the New York *Times* and *Herald Tribune,* and teletype links to Frankfurt, Munich, Stuttgart, Wiesbaden, and Nuremberg, it consistently regarded training young Germans in journalism as a primary mission. Expecting to turn DANA over to German licensees, the Americans began recruiting young men in the summer of 1945, giving preference over those who had

worked on Nazi-era papers to those with no experience but anti-Nazi backgrounds. The first three recruits were hired on 31 July directly out of prisoner of war cages. By the end of the year, 130 were trained and working as reporters. Their average age was twenty-six.[14]

ICD Overt Operations

Although emotions (and policy) discouraged any thought of entertaining the Germans, much less courting them, during the first months of the occupation, ICD recognized from the outset the need to enlighten them and to maintain direct contact with them. Enlightenment could best be accomplished, after years of Nazi-dominated intellectual isolation, by giving the Germans a view of the outside world, especially of the United States. The first step, aimed specifically at widening their horizons, was the opening of the American Library in Bad Homburg on 4 July 1945 with a stock of 3,000 books, 100 U.S. periodicals, and 10 British and French periodicals. To reach a wider audience, a magazine, *Die Amerikanische Rundschau* (American Review), devoted to descriptions of American cultural life and edited and printed in New York, went on sale in August. For the time being, in the summer of 1945, radio and Army newspapers provided adequate links within Germany between the occupation authorities and the population. Looking ahead, the ICD also planned to maintain

---

Rpt, OMG, Bavaria, 1945, June 46, in OMGUS 436–2/3, vol. II, pp. 199 and 202.

[14] Arrangements had been made to have the licensed newspaper publishers take over DANA at the end of 1945, but difficulties over the Trading with the Enemy Act, which would have prohibited contracts with the U.S. press services, delayed the licensing until October 1946. (1) Hist Rpt, OMG, Greater Hesse, Oct 45, in OMGUS 42–3/5. (2) Hist Rpt, ICD, 8 May 45–30 Jun 46, in OMGUS 242–1/5, pp. 28–30.

one newspaper after the Army papers were phased out, as an organ of the U.S. forces and as a reminder to the licensed press that it could be replaced if its performance was unsatisfactory.[15]

When the Information Control Division succeeded PWD, its primary mission, as its title implied, was to control the German information services. Apparently the ICD assumed that any U.S. information to the Germans would come from other agencies, such as the Office of War Information, which published *Die Amerikanische Rundschau* and furnished materials from the American Library. The passive supervisory phase, however, barely outlasted the changeover. While emerging east-west strains in the wartime alliance increased the need to make the United States known to the Germans, practical advantages demonstrated the logic of having all U.S. information activities centered in Germany. ICD was on the scene, had experienced people, and had in Munich the *Voelkische Beobachter* printing plant which could produce all kinds of publications for the Americans as it had for the Nazi party. Materials printed abroad, however, had to be brought long distances through an uncertain transportation system. The Office of War Information printed an edition of a second magazine, *Heute* (Today), in London in June 1945, but because of transportation troubles the magazine did not go on sale in Germany until mid-September.

Die Amerikanische Rundschau, made up mostly of reprinted articles of well-known American writers, continued to be edited in New York but was printed in Munich after December 1945, when the volume of its quarterly issues was increased from 50,000 to 300,000 copies. *Heute*, a picture

magazine similar to *Life* and *Look*, moved its entire operation to Munich in December, where it published biweekly issues of 350,000 copies. *Neue Auslese* (New Selections), a *Reader's Digest* type of monthly, carried articles from Allied (including French and Soviet) publications and was edited in London; it also began printing U.S. zone editions of 300,000 copies in Munich in December.[16]

The American Library opened in Bad Homburg in July but moved to Frankfurt in September; two similar libraries were opened in November and December, one in Berlin and one in Munich.[17] Founded primarily as reference libraries for writers, educators, and other professionals, they proved so popular as soon as they opened that reader's cards had to be issued. The library in Munich, set up in three rooms in the University of Munich's medical library, issued 250 cards its first week of operation and had a waiting list of 500 people. After the turn of the year, the libraries, redesignated "U.S. information centers," admitted the general public as quickly as their facilities could be expanded, and the stocks of U.S. newspapers and periodicals, for which the Germans seemed to have an endless hunger, increased.

In the fall of 1945, as the licensing program gathered momentum, the Publishing Operations Section, ICD, began work on the permanent overt paper projected early in July, to which it gave the name used briefly in Aachen a year before, *Die Neue Zeitung* (The New Newspaper). The mast-

---

[15] US Gp CC, ICS, Special Report, 16 July 45, in USFET SGS 091. 412.

[16] (1) Hist Rpt, OMG, Bavaria, 1945, Jun 46, in OMGUS 436–2/3, vol. II, pp. 212–14. (2) Hist Rpt, ICD, 8 May 45–30 Jun 46, in OMGUS 242–1/5, pp. 37–39.

[17] Another five libraries opened in the first half of 1946 at Stuttgart, Marburg, Erlangen, Regensburg, and Heidelberg.

head of the first issue (18 October) announced it as "The American Newspaper for the German People." Although it was still an organ of the U.S. forces and a tacit admonishment to the licensed press, its concept had expanded since July: it was now also to provide an example for the German press of objective reporting and high journalistic standards and to widen the view of the readership, giving them information about the world and educating them "to the tasks which lie ahead of them." McClure also changed the orientation somewhat in November when he specified that 50 percent of the space be devoted to America and its viewpoints, 25 percent to world news, and 25 percent to German news of national interest.[18]

Printed in Munich on the *Voelkische Beobachter* presses, *Die Neue Zeitung* appeared twice a week, on Thursday and Sunday, in the U.S. zone, Berlin, and Bremen. At first produced entirely by U.S. personnel under Maj. Hans Habe and Maj. Hans Wallenberg, who had been newspaper editors in Germany and Austria before Hitler, *Die Neue Zeitung,* like DANA, later undertook to give opportunities and training to Germans. The circulation rose from 500,000 to 1,500,000 in two months without getting close to saturating the market. Dealers reported a demand for at least 3,000,000 copies, but the paper shortage held the press run to 1,500,000 after January 1946. In one survey, 50 percent of the people questioned said they read *Die Neue Zeitung,* often third, fourth, or fifth hand, in preference to any German paper because its quality was superior to that of the licensed press. While *Die Neue Zeitung* avoided financial competition with the licensed press by not carrying advertise-

ments, it admittedly had two important competitive advantages: better access to world and national news and freedom from the constraints, real and psychological, under which the licensed editors worked.[19] Nevertheless, it was probably the best and possibly the most effective of all the attempts to demonstrate freedom of speech and press as understood by Americans.

Other Media

In another branch of the press—book publishing—and in radio, film, theater, and music, ICD was also committed to the elimination of Nazi influences and the propagation of democracy through controls and licensing. Even more than the newspapers and periodicals, among which some scattered sparks of independence had stayed alive for a few years after 1933, these other media had been instruments of the Nazi regime. As nazism's intellectual and emotional props, they would have to be purged of undesirable people and of practically the entire previous twelve years' output of books and films. At the same time, Soviet competition and the Germans' need for escape from their everyday existences exerted strong pressures to sweeten the resulting cultural deprivation.

Books were a special problem. Normally, *per capita* German book consumption was at least four times that in the United States and after the bookdealers had cleared Nazi-influenced and other unacceptable works off their shelves, they had nothing left to sell.[20] ICD suspected that books influenced

---

[18] ICM, 9053, 28 Nov 45, in OMGUS 244–2/5.

[19] Hist Rpt, OMG, Bavaria, 1945, June 46, in OMGUS 436–2/3, vol. II, pp. 210–12.

[20] Before the war, the annual average of titles published in German was 17,000; in the United States it was 9,000. Although the German population was half that of the United States, the total number of copies printed was also larger.

AUTHOR SUBMITS MANUSCRIPT FOR ICD CLEARANCE

German opinion as much or more than any other medium, which increased the need to prevent Germans from reading the wrong material. In any event, getting rid of the old book industry, although it was more work than in the other media and successive inspections always turned up some objectionable volumes, was easier than getting the industry restarted on a new course. To avoid the stigma of Nazi-style book-burning, ICD issued strict orders against burning, arranged to have sample copies deposited in research libraries in the United States, and pulped the rest.

The cleanup opened the market, but the industry suffered from paper, ink, and machine shortages and most of all from a dearth of publishable manuscripts. Books took time to write, and the war and nazism had crippled the literary profession. ICD's insistence on the same political standards for book publishers as for newspaper licensees further slowed the revival, especially in comparison with the Soviet zone where the policy was to license the books rather than the publishers. ICD issued its first licenses in mid-July 1945, one to a publisher of religious literature in Munich and the other to a publisher in Heidelberg who proposed to issue general works. By

October, the DISCCs had received a thousand applications but granted only ten licenses. In the next three months they issued eight times as many, but the increase was not immediately reflected in production. The first eight books came off the presses in October, twenty-four more in November, and sixty-nine in December; but most were either technical or liturgical works or reprints. To help relieve the drought of general reading material, the Office of War Information had in the meantime supplied 35,000 copies each of twenty-five U.S. titles in translation.

During the early months of the occupation the film exhibitors were in as bad a situation as the booksellers. Although ICD had over 8,000 reels of feature film in vaults in Frankfurt, very few were likely to be approved for German postwar viewing; ICD's reluctance to sponsor entertainment for the Germans persisted longer with regard to films than to any other medium. ICD slowed the opening of movie houses through the summer of 1945 and, together with acute shortages of electronic equipment and raw film, delayed the licensing program for new productions throughout the whole first year. Although ICD held large, government-owned UFI (Universum Film G.m.b.H.) studios in Munich and Berlin, the only film made in them before 1947 was the U.S.-British newsreel *Welt in Film* (World in Film).

In mid-July 1945, the only movie houses open in the U.S. zone were the ten in Stuttgart that the French, less devoted to sanitizing the German mind than the Americans, had let stay in business with the films they had on hand. By then the DISCCs had inspected nearly a thousand movie houses in the zone but had approved very few for reopening. More than 80 percent of the exhibitors, they found, had been party

members; and while the exhibitors could not influence the content of the films they showed, ICD decided that, having profited from running Nazi propaganda, they should not also be allowed to profit under the occupation. At the end of July, ICD authorized a gradual reopening of movie houses, beginning with four in Berlin and eleven in the zone, all to show one-hour newsreel programs.[21]

The gradual approach would probably have persisted longer than it did if the advent of winter had not intensified the need to take the Germans' minds off the hardships of cold weather and to keep the young people off the streets. In late September less than a hundred cinemas were open; by the end of the year 350 were showing films and others were scheduled to open in the new year at a rate of two a day. In September, ICD released a dozen German-made films and acquired thirty-three American features.

However, not all the American films turned out to be suitable for German audiences. Some, comedies and fantasies in particular, were simply unintelligible to the Germans. Others seemed to confirm the Nazi propaganda picture of America. One such film, briefly exhibited and hastily withdrawn, was the *Maltese Falcon,* starring Humphrey Bogart, a lightweight thriller which, taken literally, seemed to glorify the underworld and demonstrate the ineptness of the American police. The audiences themselves preferred any kind of German film to the American products. After an undistinguished German picture called *Operette* consistently drew larger audiences than the American features by as much as 60 percent and after other films promised to do the same, ICD established a policy

---

[21] Hqs, USFET, Circular No. 120, 1 Sep 45, in Admin Hist Collection, ETOUSA, No. 73.

OUTDOOR CONCERT *in Heidelberg for Americans and Germans.*

requiring all exhibitors to show American films for two weeks before and after each run of a German feature.

Until 11 November 1945, when USFET returned the studios and transmitter to the Luxembourg government, broadcasting for the U.S. zone was centered at Radio Luxembourg. Radio Munich had started operating in May with 100 kilowatts. Radio Stuttgart, with 100 kilowatts, and Radio Frankfurt (first with 1 kilowatt and later with 20) went on the air in June, but until November all three received their programs from Radio Luxembourg. The three stations in the zone joined in the summer to form one network, the *Sueddeutsche Rundfunk,* but because of troubles with the land lines, the network did not function well in the early months, and Radio Munich finally withdrew to become an independent station.[22] The stations remained under Army control throughout the first year,

---

[22] Berlin had no U.S. radio service until February 1946 when a *Drahtfunk* system went into operation in the western sectors. The *Drahtfunk* programs were sent over the telephone lines. Listeners connected their sets either to their phones or to a telephone wire and could receive programs without disturbance to the regular telephone service. In Bremen, a one kilowatt U.S. station went on the air in December 1945.

while ICD negotiated legislation in the *Land* governments that would allow the stations to be turned over to independent broadcasting corporations.

The stern radio fare of the postsurrender weeks gave way in mid-July to more varied programing. Besides news and military government announcements, Radio Munich offered broadcasts of Sunday church services, concerts by the Munich Philharmonic orchestra, and various instructive features, such as "The Buergermeister Speaks" and "For the Farmer." In October, for the same reasons that had inspired a change in the policy on films, Radio Munich added a program for young people; an audience participation program "The Listener Speaks"; a comedy series; a popular song series and one of American folk songs; and "Ten of the Week," modeled on the U.S. program "Your Hit Parade," in which the German listeners chose the ten most popular American songs. Military government officers in the field still complained about the programming. One described Radio Munich as being "as popular as a flea on a dog's back," to which ICD retorted that the Bavarians probably did not want to listen to anything but yodeling. ICD's own surveys in late 1945 and early 1946 showed that the listeners preferred German music to any kind of American music, excepting possibly folk songs, and many were continuing to tune in the Soviet-operated Radio Berlin because it broadcasted more German music. However, a large majority preferred the U.S. stations for news, other than that of the war crimes trials.[23]

Music and the theater, although technically the easiest of the media to control, offered their own distinctive problems. Because the legitimate theaters, opera houses, and concert halls were usually located in the centers of cities, many had been destroyed in the bombing and those that had survived were requisitioned for U.S troops. ICD licensed 130 theater companies and musical groups by November 1945, but most had no place to perform regularly. In Wiesbaden, Army Special Services requisitioned the Deutsches Theater for the Red Cross. An antiaircraft artillery unit occupied the Prinzregenten Theater in Munich. In Nuremberg, the music-loving 610th Tank Destroyer Battalion monopolized the local opera company, which was fortunate for the performers since many of them were Nazis who would not have been permitted to perform for civilians anyway. The state opera house in Stuttgart was an American enlisted men's club, and the occasional German performances there played to the accompaniment of ping-pong games in the foyers.[24]

The denazification procedures in the two media required that not only certifiable Nazis be removed but also that performers and producers whose work had been closely associated with nazism be blacklisted and kept from working under the occupation. One of the most distinguished personalities on the blacklist was Wilhelm Fuertwaengler, conductor of the Berlin Philharmonic Orchestra. Very likely, the most thoroughly blacklisted individual—by a special quadripartite decision—was Norbert Schulze, composer of "Bombs Over England" and "Lili Marlene." On the whole, however, blacklisted performers fared better than the other subjects of denazification. To the

---

[23] (1) Hist Rpt, ICD, 8 May 45–30 Jun 46, in OMGUS 242–1/5, pp. 41–46, 49–58, and 75–85. (2) History of Military Government in *Land* Wuerttemberg-Baden, vol. I, pp. 1387–96. (3) Hist Rpt, OMG, Bavaria, 1945, Jun 46, in OMGUS 436–2/3, vol. II, pp. 230–38. (4) Hist Rpt, OMG, Greater Hesse, Oct 45, in OMGUS 42–3/5.

[24] Ingeborg Drewitz, ed., *Staedte 1945* (Duesseldorf: Eugen Dietrichs Verlag, 1970), p. 150.

lingering chagrin of ICD and DISCC, unit Special Service officers, looking for entertainment for the troops, were often all too willing to overlook the blacklists.

Music control officers had a special worry. SHAEF Music control Instruction No. 1 (19 July 1945) prohibited all military marches and all songs associated with the *Wehrmacht* or with nazism; furthermore, it cited a need to prevent performances of other types of "inflammatory" music as well, without seeming to resort to Nazi-style cultural regimentation. This instruction imposed on the DISCCs the large, and often pettifogging, job of scrutinizing concert programs in order to eliminate such Nazi-appropriated works as Siegfried's funeral march from the *Goetterdaemmerung* and the slow movements of Beethoven's *Third* and *Seventh Symphonies;* to prevent "musical sabotage," such as the playing of Beethoven's *Eroica* or Strauss's *Ein Heldenleben* on Hitler's birthday; and to identify and exclude non-German works that could "encourage dangerous tendencies," for example, Sibelius *Finlandia* or Chopin's *Revolutionary Etude* because of their intense nationalism.

With the appointment of *Pruefungsausschuesse* (examining boards), theater and music became the first entertainment and information media to acquire a degree of self-regulation. The first such board, made up of union delegates, *Land* and city cultural affairs representatives, and private citizens, began to function in Stuttgart in March 1946. The boards screened the *Fragebogen* of producers, performers, and theater owners and compiled lists of approved applicants. From these lists, after they were checked by the military government, the municipal authorities could select their theater companies and orchestras.[25]

---

[25] Hist Rpt, ICD, 8 May 45–30 Jun 46, in OMGUS 242–1/5, pp. 49–68.

CHAPTER XXI

Reckonings With the Past

Denazification

"The question who is a Nazi is often a dark riddle," Third Army G–5 reported more than a month after V–E Day, adding, "The question what is a Nazi is also not easy to answer."[1] In official terms, however, the questions were not difficult to answer at all. SHAEF had long ago worked out automatic arrest categories ranging from the top Nazi leadership to the local *Ortsgruppenleiter*, from the top *Gestapo* agents to leaders of the Hitler Youth, the Peasants' League, and the Labor Front. Furthermore, thousands of suspects were being arrested: 700 a day in May and June, and a total of over 18,000 in August. In September, 82,000 suspects were being held in internment camps, away from the political scene and available for possible trial and sentencing as members of criminal organizations.[2] They were all presumed to be confirmed Nazis and, with some allowance for excessive zeal on the part of the Counterintelligence Corps (CIC), the vast majority doubtless were. Usually, of course, they did what they could to conceal their identities and their pasts. Some succeeded no doubt, but most were not hard to find. Capt. Arthur T. Neumann, whose detach-

ment's out-of-the-way *Landkreis*, Alzenau in northwestern Bavaria, was a favorite refuge for those fleeing automatic arrest, reported that nearly all suspects, once they were identified, could be brought in by postcards telling them to report to the detachment office at a specified time.[3] Finding out who had been party members, whether important enough to merit arrest or merely rank and file, was also not difficult. The party had kept excellent records, which often passed into military government's hands intact. The detachment at Wasserburg am Inn, for example, had twenty-eight lists and rosters covering everything from party and Hitler Youth membership to deliveries of boots and uniforms.[4] The best evidence, the party's entire central registry of 12 million cards with photographs, turned up in Munich in a pile of wastepaper waiting to be pulped.[5]

It was on the gray fringes of denazification that the question of who and what were Nazis vexed military government, as much after V–E Day as when the first municipal appointments were made around Aachen nine months before. The cases of Reuters and Jansen at Wuerselen and Ragh and Deutzmann at Stolberg were being repeated all over the U.S. zone. Having been a party member did not prevent

[1] Hist Rpt, Third Army, ACofS G–5, May–Jun 45, in OMGUS 76–3/10.

[2] (1) JCS 1517/1, Summary of Aug 45 Report of the Military Governor, 18 Oct 45, in CCS 383.21 (2–22–44), sec. 9. (2) JCS 1517/2, Summary of Sep 45 Report of the Military Governor, in CCS 383.21 (2–22–44), sec. 10.

[3] Hist Rpt, Det A 330, 30 Jun 46, in OMGUS 82–2/10.

[4] Hist Rpt, Det E 283, 30 Jun 46, in OMGUS 78–2/10.

[5] *Weser Bote,* 27 Oct 45.

a man from being better at his job and having a more agreeable personality than someone who was not. Too often, in fact, the opposite seemed to be true. Frequently the Nazis had training, experience, energy, affability, and not a bad political record. The Americans respected efficiency and trusted the men who seemed to be friendly. In the words of one detachment commander, if "all the Nazis had been exceedingly unpleasant and rude, denazification would have been easy."[6] Moreover, the man who was individualistic enough to have stood out against the Nazis was probably not going to fit in easily with the Americans either. As the Aachen experience had shown, non-Nazi and anti-Nazi were not necessarily believers in democracy or even, to the American mind, very different from the Nazis in their thinking. A recurring suspicion among military government officers—acquired probably from the Germans they had talked to—was that many so-called non-Nazis were people who had wanted to join the party and been rejected, which made them worse in a sense than those who had joined out of expediency or under compulsion. The *Fragebogen,* the Bremen detachment pointed out, required disclosure of membership in the party and auxiliary groups but not of applications for membership or rejections.[7]

Whether they advocated passing a hard or a soft judgment on Nazis—a few argued for the latter—military government officers generally agreed that if they made a completely clean sweep of the party members, they were going to have to run the country with old men until the next generation grew up. The number of political acceptables between the ages of twenty and fifty who were also trained and competent was exceedingly small. In *Landkreis* Eichstaett, Bavaria, for instance, which was by no means an exception, when the 64-year-old *Landrat* had a stroke he could be replaced only by his deputy who was seventy.[8]

What most troubled military government officers in the field, however, was the absence of objective standards. They were blamed if they failed to find men to fill the jobs and, if they filled the jobs, for compromises they made while doing so. The policy-makers were in a different, but not better, situation. They had to contend with the field officers' desire to conduct efficient government as well as with the unanimous opinion of the public (German as well as American) press, and U.S. government that denazification was what the war had been about, and insistent on a ruthless and thorough clean up and half expecting to be duped and cheated. Consequently, policy wavered. In March 1945, SHAEF G–5 had informally established 1933 as a cut-off date for mandatory removal. Those who had joined the party after the Nazi takeover in January 1933 would not be dismissed or denied employment outright if they could show that they had not been active members and had joined solely to save their jobs.[9] By the end of the month, however, the press and public reaction to the Aachen affair had brought about a blanket prohibition on everyone who was or had been a party member at any time or who had been appointed "to an office

---

[6] Hist Rpt, Det E 232, 30 Jun 46, in OMGUS 77–2/10.

[7] Functional History of Military Government in the Bremen Enclave, 26 Apr–30 Sep 45, in OMGUS 48–1/6, pt. I, p. 15.

[8] Hist Rpt, Det B 262, 30 Jun 46, in OMGUS 10–1/5.

[9] Memo, SHAEF, ACofS G–5, Special Br, sub: Proposed Organization and Procedure, Mar 45, in SHAEF G–5, 17.16, Hist Rpts, 12th AGp, pt. I, Jacket 8.

of political importance" since January 1933.[10] After numerous detachments protested that under these rules they could not find enough people to begin reorganizing the German administration, SHAEF, on 11 June, ordered them to study the policy carefully and execute it "in accordance with its intent in such a manner as not to make impossible the establishment of administrative machinery."[11] Nobody knew what this order meant, but the army groups rescinded the directives they had based on the more stringent earlier policy, and Munich radio announced that post-1933 Nazis would again be acceptable.[12]

Recognizing the need for a clearer statement and taking its text from JCS 1967— which read, "All members of the Nazi Party who have been more than nominal participants, all active supporters of Nazism or militarism and all other persons hostile to Allied purposes will be removed and excluded from public office and from positions of importance in quasi-public and private enterprises"—ETOUSA, on 29 June, redefined denazification policy for the time when the Americans would be responsible only for their own zone. Public office was interpreted as extending down to *Buergermeisters,* police chiefs, and "legal personnel"; and all persons appointed to these or higher offices after 30 January 1933 would be unemployable. The term "persons of importance in quasi-public and private enterprises" was taken to cover executives in civil, economic, and labor organizations, in corporations, in industrial, agricultural, and financial institutions, in the press, and in education (including teachers). Nazis subject to mandatory removal were all persons who had held office in the party, had joined before 1 May 1937, or had joined later and were more than nominal members.[13]

The cut-off date of 1937, of course, immediately sparked a fresh debate. It had been chosen because after 1 May 1937 public employees had been required to join the party or lose their jobs. Those who joined earlier, even if not confirmed Nazis, were considered at least to have been opportunists, since they did not join under compulsion. The counterargument was that some, perhaps many, who had joined before 1937 or even before 1933 could have done so without realizing what nazism was; the same could not be said for anyone who joined after 1937.

Nevertheless, military government in the field was satisfied on the whole to have a specific, if stringent, denazification directive. The 1937 cut-off date at least did not force the firing of every person who had held a government job during the Nazi period, which would virtually have been the case under the March policy; but it did disqualify many who had been retained in the expectation that the earlier policy would collapse—as it did after 11 June— because of its sheer unworkability. Third Army G–5, whose detachments had reported 90-percent denazification at the end of June, dropped its estimate to 60 percent.[14] In July Seventh Army launched Operation LIFEBOUY (named for a brand of soap that claimed to be particularly effec-

[10] Hqs, 6th AGp, to CG's, Seventh Army and French 1st Army, sub: Disqualification from office of Nazis and German Militarists, 30 Mar 45, in OMGUS 411–2/3.

[11] Hist Rpt, 6th AGp, ACofS G–5, 1 Jun–16 Jul 45, in SHAEF G–5, 502.

[12] Hist Rpt, Third Army, ACofS G–5, May–Jun 45, in OMGUS 76–3/10.

[13] Hqs, ETOUSA, to CG, 12th AGp, sub: Removal of Nazis and Militarists, 29 Jun 45, in OMGUS 411–2/3.

[14] Hist Rpt, Third Army, ACofS G–5, May–Jun 45, in OMGUS 76–3/10.

tive at combating body odor). Under LIFEBOUY, Seventh Army CIC teams rechecked the entire Western Military District, *Kreis* by *Kreis*, in the light of the 29 June standards.[15] Three months later, USFET reported 100,000 persons dismissed from public employment in the U.S. zone—30,000 of them in July and August—and 20,000 removed from private enterprise.[16]

To decide administratively who—and, by implication, what—Nazis were, USFET discovered, was not going to be enough however. The emotional issues of denazification were not going to be settled that easily. They would have to be met under the bright light of public opinion that Hilldring had mentioned.

On 18 June in New York, the weekly news magazine *New Republic* ran an article under the headline "Bavarian Scandal," in which the author, Philipp Loewenfeld stated, "Democracy in Germany experienced its first setback with the appointment of one Friedrich [*sic*] Schaeffer as Minister President of Bavaria. . . ." Schaeffer's appointment was at the time just a day less than three weeks old. Loewenfeld accused Schaeffer and the Bavarian People's party (in which he had been a leading member) of supporting the Nazis in the 1920s and described Schaeffer as "one of the Weimar Republic's most diligent grave diggers." The article suggested that Colonel Keegan, who as commanding officer of Detachment E1F3 had selected Schaeffer and who was in civilian life a New York City council-

man, could have been acting under Vatican influence exercised through Democratic boss Ed Flynn of the Bronx.[17] After other U.S. papers picked up the story, Clay appointed a special board to investigate. The board found that all political outlooks were not equitably represented in the Bavarian government, particularly the liberals, but concluded that Keegan's selections had been made on the basis of professional qualifications and anti-Nazi convictions and had not been influenced by "any particular religious, political or social group." Clay at this stage apparently saw the affair as a public relations accident, to be best avoided, as he suggested to McCloy, by giving the Germans a voice in politics.[18]

On the whole, in July and August, denazification of public offices seemed to be going remarkably well. Mounting figures on dismissals brought approval even from the Germans, although some Americans suspected less for the policy than in the hope that an end would soon be reached. However, the denazification of private enterprises raised questions: what, for instance, were important positions in trade and industry? USFET, in the 29 June directive, used the size of the enterprise—capital over a million marks or more than 250 employees—but, the Germans themselves asked, what about the two-hundred-percent Nazis who were lucky enough not to be in the automatic arrest categories, in public employment, or in the specified range of private enterprise, who might not be employed at all but, nevertheless, had been vicious, petty tyrants and had profited mightily from the Nazi regime?[19] On 15

---

[15] (1) Hist Rpt, Seventh Army, ACofS G–5, 8 May–30 Sep 45, in Seventh Army, 107–3.0. (2) Hqs, Seventh Army, ACofS G–3, sub: Progress of Operation LIFEBOUY, 8 Nov 45, Seventh Army, 168–4/2.

[16] JCS 1517/2, Summary of Sep 45 Report of the Military Governor, 13 Nov 45, in CCS 383.21 (2–22–44) sec. 10.

[17] *New Republic,* vol. 112, no. 25, 18 Jun 45.

[18] Ltr, Clay to McCloy, 15 Jul 45, in OMGUS 410–2/3.

[19] Hqs, Seventh Army, Hist Sec, Report of Operations, 8 May–30 Sep 45, in Seventh Army, 107–3.0.

August, USFET broadened its definition to include people in business and professions, regardless of size, "whose standing in the community is one of prominence or influence."[20] If proven to be more than nominal Nazis, they were to be removed from their businesses, which, if they had been the owners, were to be taken under military government property control.

Four weeks later, the denazification of private enterprise broke into the news. Raymond Daniell reported in the New York Times, "Nazis still hold some of the best jobs in commerce and industry." Military government, he concluded, was concerned too much with preserving German industrial efficiency and too little with achieving the objectives for which the war had been fought. The article also brought an important figure into the controversy, General Patton, Commanding General, Third Army, and Military Governor of Bavaria. Patton, Daniell wrote, had asked a military government fiscal officer who was investigating Nazi bankers "if he did not think it silly to try to get rid of the most intelligent people in Germany."[21]

In the upper reaches of the U.S. command, Patton's views on denazification were already uncomfortably familiar. In a letter written on 11 August, he had suggested that Eisenhower pass "a word to the people responsible for civil government" to go more slowly on denazification because too many trained people were being removed and too many inexperienced or inefficient ones brought in. As far as nazism was concerned, he said, "It is no more possible for a man to be a civil servant in Germany and not have paid lip service to nazism than it is for a man to be a postmaster in America and not have paid lip service to the Democratic Party or Republican Party when it is in power."[22] Later in the month, in a meeting with Clay, he also proposed releasing the interned Nazis, many of whom, he said, "were either aged or pregnant."[23] In reply to the 11 August letter, Eisenhower reminded Patton that obliteration of nazism was a major U.S. war aim, that JCS 1067 specifically prohibited retaining Nazis for administrative necessity, convenience, or expediency, and that denazification was "a most delicate subject both here and at home" which "our governmental representatives as well as newspapers have been quick to seize upon. . . ."[24]

Meanwhile, as Clay told McCloy later, "things [were] not entirely smooth in Bavaria."[25] One of Schaeffer's ministers turned out to have been a general staff officer in German-occupied Poland, France, and Italy. Two others were also in mandatory removal categories, and another had falsified his Fragebogen. Forced to dismiss them, Schaeffer on 4 August entered a formal protest against the "hardship and injustice" of denazification.[26] Schaeffer insisted that one other official, Dr. Otto Gessler, Minister of War for a time under the republic and a leading figure in the German secret rearmament of the 1920s, was an "unofficial" adviser and refused to let him go, until military government for-

---

[20] Ltr, Hqs, USFET, to CG's Third Army and Seventh Army, sub: Removal of Nazis and Militarists, 15 Aug 45, in OMGUS 22–1/5.

[21] New York Times, 19 Sep 45.

[22] Ltr, Patton to Eisenhower, 11 Aug 45, in USFET SGS 000.1.

[23] US Gp CC, Staff Meeting of Div. Directors, 27 Aug 45, in OMGUS 12–1/5, v60–12/1.

[24] Ltr, Ike to George, 23 Aug 45, in USFET SGS 000.1.

[25] Ltr, Clay to McCloy, 16 Sep 45, in OMGUS 410–2/3.

[26] Hist Rpt, Third Army, ACofS G–5, 15 Aug–14 Sep 45, in OMGUS 76–3/10.

bade Gessler to set foot in the Bavarian government offices. When the Special Branch investigated the departments in August, it found 24 out of 39 *Fragebogen* missing in the Ministry of Food and Agriculture, 46 out of 51 missing in the Ministry of Interior, and 21 out of 31 missing in the Regional Economic Office; and six officials already ordered to be removed were still at their desks.[27]

In the first week of September, Col. Roy L. Dalferes, a Regular Army officer, replaced Colonel Keegan who was redeployed, although officers, particularly military government officers, were not then eligible. On the 11th, Eisenhower wrote to Patton:

I know certain field commanders have felt modifications to this policy [denazification] could be made. That question had long since been decided. We will not compromise with Nazism in any way. I wish you would make sure that all your subordinate commanders realize that the discussional stage of this question is long past and any expressed opposition to the faithful execution of the order cannot be regarded leniently by me. I expect just as loyal service in execution of this and other policies applying to the German occupation as I received during the war.[28]

Schaeffer by this time remained in office primarily because nobody could decide how to get him out. Although military government had the power, he was too prominent a figure to be dismissed arbitrarily. Besides, dismissal appeared to be exactly what he wanted, in order to sustain a future political reputation as a man who had

refused to kowtow to the Americans.[29] Like Oppenhoff in Aachen, Schaeffer was the kind of German with whom Americans were least prepared to deal. An organizer and good administrator and not a Nazi by any existing definition he was the sort of man they had believed they could use best. Yet the longer they observed him, the less he looked like a proponent of democracy. In the 1920s, he had belonged to the right wing of the already conservative Bavarian Peoples' party and, in at least one speech, had described the Nazis as "saviors of our Fatherland."[30] He had been at odds with the Nazis throughout their years in power and had ended up behind the barbed wire at Dachau, but his political outlook had not changed. Protesting his antinazism, he persisted in surrounding himself with men whose backgrounds were more doubtful than his own. A check in September disclosed sixteen officials still working in the Office of Food and Agriculture whose removal had been ordered the month before.[31] By mid-September the best the Americans could hope for from Schaeffer was that he would resign; and on the 16th, Clay announced without regret that he had, although the announcement turned out to be premature.[32]

Quite probably, Schaeffer actually would have "resigned" by the end of the month and thereafter the denazification

---

[27] Memo for Record, USFET, ACofS G–5, Adviser (Dr. Walter L. Dorn), sub: Min. Pres. Friedrich Schaeffer and the Tardy Denazification of the Bavarian Govt., 2 Oct 45, in USFET SGS 000.1.

[28] Ltr, Ike to George, 11 Sep 45, in USFET SGS 000.1.

[29] He may have succeeded, too. Elected to the *Bundestag* of the Federal Republic of Germany in 1949, Schaeffer was Finance Minister from 1949 to 1957 and thereafter Minister of Justice until 1961.

[30] Memo for Record, USFET, ACofS G–5, Adviser (Dr. Walter L. Dorn), sub: Min. Pres. Friederich Schaeffer and the Tardy Denazification of the Bavarian Govt., 2 Oct 45, in USFET SGS 000.1.

[31] *Ibid.*

[32] Min, US Gp CC, Staff Meeting of Div. Directors, 16 Sep 45, in OMGUS 12–1/5, v60–12/1.

controversy would have simmered more or less quietly had not USFET at midmonth lifted a wartime censorship prohibition on directly quoting general officers. On 21 September General Adcock, theater G–5, and his chief civilian adviser, Dr. Walter L. Dorn, with an interested following of newspaper reporters, went to Munich to have a personal look at the Bavarian government. On the 22d, talking to the reporters about his views on denazification, General Patton said, "The Nazi thing is just like a Democrat-Republican election fight."[33] The next day his words appeared in newspapers across the United States along with editorial comment questioning both his understanding of what the war had been about and the Army's ability to conduct military government. On the 28th, Schaeffer resigned or was dismissed; no one seemed to know, or want to say, which.[34] Dr. Wilhelm Hoegner, one of two Social Democrats in the cabinet, replaced him. In Frankfurt, Eisenhower conferred with Patton for two hours on the 28th, afterward declining to comment to reporters on what they had said.[35]

Several days later, Lt. Gen. Lucian K. Truscott stopped on the way from Italy to the United States to pay his respects to Eisenhower. At his next stop, Paris, Eisenhower called him back to Frankfurt, and on 5 October, Truscott took command of Third Army and the Eastern Military District. Patton became President of the General Board, USFET. In his first press conference a week later, Truscott told the re-porters, "I have left too many white crosses across North Africa, Italy, and France and I have seen too many young men wounded and maimed not to be in complete sympathy with any policy that designs to eradicate, root and branch, the evil force, Nazism, that loosed this holocaust on the world."[36]

Though perhaps for reasons more immediate than those Truscott gave, something like a root-and-branch eradication of nazism was in fact beginning in the U.S. zone. In the midst of the Patton and Schaeffer affairs, on 24 September, Clay told the U.S. Group Control Council staff that he was dissatisfied with the progress in denazification and that "A decision has been made that we are going to denazify all phases of German life."[37] Two days later, before any but the regional military government detachments had even gotten the news, the radio and newspapers announced Military Government Law No. 8, which prohibited employment of Nazi party members in business in any capacity other than common labor.[38] The law applied not only to executives and managers but also to private owners, including owner-operators such as grocers, barbers, bakers, and butchers.

For the Germans, Law No. 8 was the most ominous development yet. Complaints that denazification was not going far or fast enough suddenly stopped. The *Land* detachment in Wuerttemberg-Baden said the law "engendered a great fear." USFET used the words "bitterness and despair."

[33] New York *Times*, 23 Sep 45.

[34] A week later, Third Army reported to USFET that Schaeffer's resignation and those of his Ministers of Finance and Economics and Head of Food and Agriculture had been "accepted" on 28 September. Cable, Truscott to CG, USFET, 5 Oct 45, in USFET SGS 000.1.

[35] New York *Times*, 29 Sep 45.

[36] Diary, Hqs, XV Corps, 8 Oct–10 Dec 45, 12 Oct 45, in XV Corps, 215–0.3.

[37] Min, US Gp CC, Staff Meeting of Div. Directors, 24 Sep 45, in OMGUS 12–1/5, v60–12/1.

[38] Hqs, USFET, to CG's, Eastern and Western Military Districts, sub: Administration of Military Government in the U.S. Zone, Law, No. 8, 26 Sep 45, in OMGUS 411–2/3.

Rumors among the Germans arose that Law No. 8 was just the beginning of a plan to reduce the German economy to chaos; when the party members were removed, the Germans told themselves, next would be former members of the *Wehrmacht* and so on, until carrying on business of any kind would be a crime for Germans. Everyone feared an economic upheaval that would leave the country worse off than it already was.[39] The mood was not lightened when, in the first week of October, the U.S. zone was hit by a tidal wave of denazification, partly as a result of Law No. 8 and partly—as the law itself had been—as a reaction to the Patton and Schaeffer affairs. Within military government from top to bottom, the time for discussion was indeed past, at least temporarily. Some detachments closed down all the businesses in their areas and did not let them reopen until the Nazis were identified and removed. At military government offices everywhere, hundreds of Germans came to assert their nominal party membership or, in fewer but still numerous cases, simply to present the keys to their establishments.[40] Simultaneously another surge of denazification hit the public employees. On Sunday, 7 October, Seventh Army sent out special couriers to every detachment in the Western Military District with an order from General Keyes calling for the dismissal of every public employee in the mandatory removal categories by noon on Monday.[41] To be on the safe side, military government officers also immediately applied the common labor specification of Law No. 8 to public employment. The detachment in Wasserburg am Inn disqualified 20 medical doctors (very likely almost all there were), 15 dentists, 51 teachers, 10 mail carriers, and 20 rural policemen.[42] In *Landkreis* Alzenau, Detachment A–330 found only 3 out of 17 doctors politically clean.[43] The Bremen detachment dismissed a quarter of the 1,600-man police force; and some detachments reportedly got rid of their *Putzfrauen* (cleaning women) to reduce the chances of being caught with Nazis on the payroll.[44]

A shock for the Germans, Law No. 8 was almost as much a shock for military government, and Headquarters, USFET, itself was no exception. It had just released the *Ortsgruppenleiter,* the lowest and one of the most numerous automatic arrest groups, from the internment camps. When the incongruity of these certified active Nazis appearing on the streets at the same time their presumably less implicated comrades were being thrown out of their businesses and jobs became evident, as it soon did, USFET had to stage a special 24-hour sweep, Operation CHESTERFIELD, to get them back behind barbed wire.[45]

Military government officers everywhere had to deal with denazification in an entirely new context. All directives thus far had used the word "important" or some synonym to define the range of private occupations from which persons would be excluded. In the 29 June directive USFET

[39] (1) Hist Rpt, Det E1A2, 1 Jul–30 Sep 45, 15 Oct 45, in OMGUS 9–3/5. (2) Hqs, USFET, Rpts, and Inf Br, Political Intelligence Summary, 15 Jan 45, in OMGUS 418–1/3.
[40] (1) Hist Rpt, Det B 262, 30 Jun 46, in OMGUS 10–1/5. (2) Hist Rpt, Det E3B2, Oct 45, 8 Nov 45, in OMGUS 7–2/5.
[41] *Ibid.,* (2).

[42] Hist Rpt, Det E–283, 30 Jun 46, in OMGUS 78–2/10.
[43] Hist Rpt, Det A–330, 30 Jun 46, in OMGUS 82–2/10.
[44] Functional History of Military Government in the Bremen Enclave, Oct–Nov 45, in OMGUS 39–3/5, pt. I, p. 66.
[45] Opns Rpt, Third Army, 1 Oct–31 Dec 45, in Third Army, 66–98/25.

had used the size of an enterprise as the criterion; in the 15 August directive it had used prominence in the community. Law No. 8 dropped both these distinctions and established no others above the level of common labor. It affected potentially every person employed in work requiring skill or responsibility who had been a party member, and in effect it confiscated every Nazi-owned business establishment. Military government officers were often not far from agreeing with the Germans that the result would be chaos. Col. William W. Dawson, commanding the Wuerttemberg-Baden *Land* Detachment, reported: "Never before have Military Government measures been received with such open hostility and their wisdom questioned as today. The belief in the avowed purpose of encouraging the growth of democracy in Germany has been shaken and aspersions are being cast against the personnel of Military Government, the CIC, and other U.S. Army units."[46]

Regulation No. 1 of Law No. 8, issued in the first week of October, was as important to the future of denazification in the U.S. zone as the law itself. It laid a part of the responsibility for administering the law directly on the Germans. Each business was required to determine the status of its employees and owners, and none would be allowed to stay open or to reopen with former active Nazis in any capacity above common labor. Where owners were involved, the military government detachments would take the businesses under property control and appoint non-Nazi trustees. Nazi party membership before 1 May 1937 or participation in other party-directed activities would be grounds for immediate removal. If the persons affected wanted to argue their cases, they could do so later before appeals boards of non-Nazi Germans appointed by military government.[47]

The effects of Law No. 8 were most evident in the records of military government's property control offices. The detachments in Wuerttemberg-Baden took control of 93 Nazi-owned properties in November, 168 in December, and 919 in the first quarter of 1946. In Bavaria, military government took control of a record 1,912 properties in December; and by December, property control had become the largest single military government activity everywhere in the U.S. zone. As an index of the severity of Law No. 8, however, the fact should be noted that while 1,952 Nazi-owned properties were taken under property control in Wuerttemberg-Baden between November 1945 and May 1946, another 1,777 Nazi-looted, mostly "Aryanized" properties were recovered from Germans who had acquired them before 1945 in forced sales.[48]

From the beginning, Law No. 8 did not apply to agriculture, and the use of temporary revocable work permits made it virtually inapplicable in public health as well. Doctors and dentists, particularly, who lost their licenses because of party membership went on working with temporary permits, which were never revoked. Railroad employees, among whom were a large number of party members—some in the higher ranks actually in the automatic arrest categories—were already long past due for denazification, under the rules. The USFET

---

[46] History of Military Government, *Land* Wuerttemberg-Baden, in OMGUS 410–1/3, vol. I, p. 1440.

[47] Hqs, USFET, to CG's, Eastern and Western Military Districts, Regulation No. 1, 6 Oct 45, in OMGUS 411–2/3.

[48] (1) History of Military Government in *Land* Wuerttemberg-Baden, 8 May 45–30 Jun 46, in OMGUS 410–1/3. (2) Hist Rpt, Eastern Military District, 15 Dec 45–14 Jan 46, in OMGUS 76–3/10.

Service Forces, for whom they worked, regarded them as having vital, irreplaceable skills and had argued successfully that they were not public employees in the ordinary sense. At first they were also exempted from Law No. 8, but in early October, Clay extended the law's common labor provision to railroad workers. Two weeks earlier, he had pointed out to Lt. Gen. John C.H. Lee, commanding general of the Theater Service Forces, that "in view of the many attacks to which the entire occupation program has been subjected in the U.S. press," potential trouble lurked in the railroad denazification figures, which showed that fewer than 10,000 of 50,000 known party members had been removed. Nevertheless, the railroad employees came off better than most. Theater Service Forces secured the authority to retain them until their appeals were decided; in the end, less than 20,000 employees were discharged.[49]

In addition to imposing the burden of property control, the enforcement of Law No. 8 forced military government to play a running game of hide and seek with a sizable part of the German population. Since the law did not require outright removal of the persons affected, businesses tried to meet the law's technical requirements by merely changing job titles, and owners attempted to have relatives or friends appointed trustees or to make deals with those who were appointed. Many, no doubt, succeeded, and more would have

if they had remembered, as they should have after a dozen years under the Nazis, that the CIC was reading their mail.[50] Denunciations brought some to grief, but most employees—wisely on their part as it happened—did not share the Americans' faith in the permanence of denazification. (Where military government took the trouble to assign ousted Nazis to common labor in public works, medical insurance payments for heart ailments rose.)[51]

With notable reluctance almost everywhere, the local German appeals boards began to serve in November and December. At first military government officers believed the appeals procedure was unfair because it placed the burden of proof on the appellant. They soon changed their minds, however, when they discovered that the appeals boards, not being required to establish adverse cases, were perfectly content most of the time to hear only the evidence produced by the appellants, usually in the form of affidavits attesting to nominal membership in the party. In Landkreis Eggenfelden, Bavaria, the board classified the appellants in 810 of the 864 cases it heard as nominal Nazis and only 36 as active. In Landkreis Ebermannstadt, Bavaria, the board found 2 active Nazis in the first 80 cases it heard.[52] The detachment in Ingolstadt, Bavaria, dismissed the chairman of its appeals board after it discovered that he had not decided against the appellant in a single case, even though one case concerned a war crimes suspect.[53] At Bremen,

---

[49] (1) Memo, OCOT, TSFET, for G–4, TSFET, sub: Denazification of Transport Personnel, 24 Oct 45; Cable, Clay to Lee, 19 Oct 45; and Memo, Director, OMGUS (Z), to CofS, USFET, sub: Removal of Nazis and Militarists in the *Reichsbahn*, 5 Nov 45, in USFET SGS 000.1. (2) OMGUS, Control Office, Hist Br, History of U.S. Military Government in Germany, 8 May 45–30 Jun 46, Rail Transport, in OMGUS 23–1/5.

[50] Hqs, Seventh Army, ACofS G–2, Weekly Intelligence Summary No. 15, 24 Oct 45, in Seventh Army, Opns Rpt, Annex 2.
[51] Hqs, Seventh Army, ACofS G–2, Weekly Intelligence Summary, 15 Jan 46, in OMGUS 418–1/3.
[52] (1) Hist Rpt, Det D–302, 25 Jun 46, in OMGUS 79–1.10. (2) Hist Rpt, Det B–252, 2 Nov 45, in OMGUS 80–3/10.
[53] Hist Rpt, Det E–237, Jun 46, in OMGUS 77–3/10.

CONCENTRATION CAMP PRISONER IDENTIFIES SS GUARD

where the detachment kept a close watch on the boards and exercised its prerogative to review approved cases, the boards rejected 22 percent of the appeals and the detachment another 12 percent. The boards in Bavaria heard 90,000 appeals decided over 65,000 of them in favor of the appellant.[54] Those whose appeals were accepted—using the figures for Bavaria and Bremen as a guide, probably two out of

three—returned to their jobs and recovered their property. In February 1946 their ranks were increased substantially when businesses employing less than ten persons were exempted from Law No. 8.[55]

War Crimes Trials

The war crimes trials that were to be conducted under Army auspices in Germany and would last for four years began

---

[54] (1) Bremen Enclave, Functional History, 1 Feb–31 Mar 46, in OMGUS 48–3/6, pt. I, p. 8. (2) Hist Rpt, OMG, Bavaria, 1945, vol. III, p. 433.

[55] Hist Rpt, Det D–244, 20 Jun 46, in OMGUS 79–1/10.

in early April 1945 in the small Rhineland city of Duren, twenty miles east of Aachen.[56] There, on 7 April, a First Army military commission convicted a German officer, Capt. Curt Bruns, of having caused the murder of two American prisoners of war during the Battle of the Bulge. The Bruns case was entirely within the traditional concept of war crimes as specific acts against the laws and usages of war committed by soldiers during hostilities.

The second case tried under the U.S. occupation brought in another category of defendants. On 15 August 1944, an American pilot had bailed out over the village of Preist in the Rhineland. A rural policeman went to the spot where the airman landed to take him into custody. When the policeman arrived, two German soldiers home on furlough were helping the pilot out of his parachute harness. Before they had finished, Peter Back, a local Nazi *Blockleiter,* and a crowd of other civilians appeared on the scene. Back was carrying a pistol which he fired at the American, wounding him. The German soldiers protested, but Back ordered them to stand aside and shot the prisoner a second time. Back then called on the crowd to take revenge for a recent air raid on a nearby town, and two persons beat the dying pilot, one with a hammer, the other with a club. The policeman did not attempt to prevent the attacks. Military commissions sitting at Ahrweiler tried the policeman and two civilians on 1 June 1945 and tried Back after

he was captured two weeks later. Back and the two civilians received death sentences and the policeman life imprisonment. Similar cases in which downed U.S. airmen were the victims would make up the largest single category of trials involving crimes against Americans. By the end of summer 1945, war crimes investigating teams collected evidence in 800 such cases; the great majority charged to civilians or the police, very few to soldiers.[57]

The Back case was already extending the scope of war crimes to include nonmilitary acts committed away from the battlefield, when on 2 June Eisenhower asked the Combined Chiefs of Staff (CCS) to approve also the prosecution of concentration camp commandants and guards as war criminals. The Moscow Declaration, he pointed out, provided for returning Germans for trial and punishment to the countries in which their "abominable deeds" were done but said nothing about the crimes committed against United Nations citizens inside Germany. Swift punishment of these crimes, he believed, would have "a salutory effect on public opinion both in Germany and in Allied countries."[58] In reply, the CCS lifted all "previous restriction" on war crimes trials, "whether the offenses were committed before or after occupation . . . and regardless of the nationality of the victim."[59]

Although CCS lifted the restrictions on trials, many questions concerning the kinds of crimes to be tried remained undecided. The decisions were made before the end of 1945, but all the cases completed or

---

[56] The trials of lesser war criminals ended at Dachau on 30 December 1947; the Nuremberg Military Tribunal (U.S.) completed its last case on 14 April 1949; the Office, Chief of Counsel for War Crimes, was deactivated as an OMGUS division on 20 June 1949; and the War Crimes Branch, European Command, completed a final review of all unexecuted sentences in late 1951.

[57] General Board Study No. 86, pp. 3–5.

[58] Cable, Eisenhower to AGWAR, for CC's, 2 Jun 45, in SHAEF SGS 000.5/1.

[59] Cable, AGWAR, CCS, to Eisenhower, 19 Jun 45, in SHAEF SGS 000.5/1.

brought to trial in 1945 or the first months of 1946 fell within three categories: battlefield crimes, offenses against Americans no matter where they were committed, and crimes relating to concentration camps and similar institutions. The concentration camp atrocities were later treated as crimes against humanity, but at this time they were among those not fully defined. Consequently, the early cases were treated as conspiracies to commit offenses against the United Nations troops and citizens, and were hence war crimes.

The authority to try war criminals, however, did not automatically imply the ability to bring them to trial. Evidence had to be collected and suspects and witnesses taken into custody were scattered in camps all over Germany and in the liberated countries. The CROWCASS list of suspects, growing by the hundreds every day, would eventually reach 150,000 and take months just to put into usable form. The War Crimes Group in Paris was virtually out of the picture until July when it moved to Wiesbaden, and the war crimes branches of the armies, like military government locked into the tactical command channels, were out of touch with the war crimes group and with each other. Of the five armies, only two were going to be around long enough to contemplate staging more than a few trials.

After moving into the zone, Third and Seventh Armies began sorting out and segregating the suspects and hostile witnesses. Before they were through, they would have 15,000 altogether, not including the thousands more in internment and prisoner of war camps who might be charged as members of criminal organizations. Third Army lodged its share in the Dachau concentration camp, and Seventh Army put its share into Civilian Internment Enclosure No. 78

near Ludwigsburg.[60] Civilian suspects were usually fairly easy to identify by questioning witnesses at the scene, but soldiers, witnesses as well as perpetrators, had to be hunted among the anonymous millions in the prisoner of war cages, where they were likely to be found if they were not dead or prisoners of the Russians. Many, no doubt, were never found. Where names were known, the search was often surprisingly difficult. Where little more than the existence of the crime was known, the difficulties multiplied. One such instance was the Seventh Army's hunt for the SS men who had shot and killed 120 American prisoners of war in a field near Malmédy, Belgium, on 17 December 1944. The first step was to screen all the SS prisoners and identify those who had been members of the several elements of the 1st SS Panzer Division. This job alone would probably have been impossible if the suspects had been in the army rather than in the less numerous SS. Over several months, Seventh Army brought nearly a thousand SS men to Prison No. 1, an annex to Civilian Internment Enclosure No. 78. Among them were 400 men who had belonged to Combat Group Peiper, the unit in whose sector the massacre had occurred. These were kept isolated, totally out of communication with each other; the rest were returned to prisoner of war camps. Then began the long wait for uncertainty and isolation to take effect. Now and then, at intervals of weeks, a man would be convinced that somebody else had talked or would give himself away. Seventh Army had thought the case would be closed before the end of 1945. In March 1946, when

---

[60] (1) EUCOM, Dep JA for War Crimes, Report, passim. (2) Final Rpt, Seventh Army, G–1, Annex N, in USFET, Hist Program Files, 11068/100.

Headquarters, Seventh Army, left the theater, the search was still on and the suspects were transferred to Dachau, where the trial was not finished until October 1947.[61]

The Hadamar Hospital case in which German medical personnel were charged with having killed 45 Poles and Russians by injections, began on 8 October at the War Crimes Group headquarters in Wiesbaden, thus beginning the cases involving concentration camp and other mass atrocities. During the next month, Seventh Army began its trials at Ludwigsburg, and Third Army courts at Dachau began what was going to be a three-year session during which they would hear 489 cases against 1,672 accused and pass 297 death sentences.[62] The Hadamar case was tried under a military commission. All the subsequent cases were tried by special military government courts that had nothing to do with current offenses against the occupation, dealt exclusively with war crimes, and were more like military commissions than like regular military government courts. Procedurally, however, the distinction was significant. Military commissions operated under the elaborate regulations for courts martial. The regulations for military government courts, on the other hand, specified:

. . . rules may be modified to the extent that certain steps in the trial may be omitted or abbreviated so long as no rights granted to the accused are disregarded. Opening statements in particular may frequently be omitted. No greater formality than is consistent with a complete and fair hearing is desirable

and the introduction of procedural formalities from the Manual of Courts Martial or from trial guides based thereon is discouraged except where specifically required by these rules.

The military government courts, moreover, were held to have extensive powers where war crimes were concerned, "because a state adhering to the law of war as a part of international law is interested in the preservation and envorcement of it irrespective of when or where the crime was committed, the belligerency or nonbelligerency status of the punishing power, or the nationality of the victims."[63] With such streamlined procedures and extensive powers and the principle of common design, the Dachau concentration camp case, involving forty persons implicated in thousands of murders, was begun on 16 November 1945 and completed in four weeks.

While the early cases were being prepared and brought to trial, the categories of criminality were also being vastly expanded. In the London Agreement of 8 August 1945 (the charter for the International Military Tribunal), Justice Jackson and his British, French, and Soviet colleagues recognized four categories of crimes: war crimes, crimes against peace, crimes against humanity, and membership in groups which the International Military Tribunal might find to be criminal. Taken together, these categories made punishable the conduct of the war itself, all Nazi atrocities committed anywhere at any time, and mere membership in certain Nazi organizations such as the SS and the *Gestapo*.

The International Military Tribunal opened its trials of twenty-two major criminals and seven Nazi organizations on 20 November. After reconnaissance of Mu-

---

[61] (1) EUCOM, Dep JA for War Crimes, Report, p. 48. (2) USFET, JA, Report, 4 Apr 42–3 Apr 46, in ETOUSA file.

[62] Memo, Col G. Simpson for Sec Army, sub: Survey of Trials of War Criminals Held at Dachau, Germany, 14 Sep 48, in OMGUS 439–1/3.

[63] EUCOM, Dep JA for War Crimes, Report, p. 52–58.

nich, Heidelberg, and Nuremberg, SHAEF had selected Nuremberg several months earlier as the "best choice from the historical and accommodations points of view."[64] Third Army provided the Headquarters Command, International Military Tribunal, which took charge of the prisoners, supplied guards for the court, and furnished billeting, messing, and transportation for court personnel and correspondents. USFET supplied press, radio, and motion picture facilities and communications to meet Justice Jackson's requirement for "getting speedily and clearly to the world the record of evidence developed there."[65]

Before the international trials began, JCS 1023/10, dated 8 July 1945 but apparently not issued until September, assigned to USFET, the responsibility for trying lesser offenders (all those not tried at Nuremburg) in all four categories of the London Agreement for crimes, committed since 30 January 1933, including racial and religious persecution.[66] In December,

Control Council Law No. 10 made the London Agreement's provisions the uniform legal basis for prosecution of war criminals and similar offenders in the four zones and authorized the zone authorities also to try any major criminals not brought before the bar at Nuremberg.[67]

JCS 1023/10, in particular, and Control Council Law No. 10 laid a potentially mountainous new case load on the War Crimes Group. To investigate atrocities and crimes against humanity back to 30 January 1933 alone would probably have required a new organizational effort as least as extensive as that applied to war crimes since 1944; and trying the members of criminal organizations evoked a statistical nightmare. The Theater Judge Advocate, using 100,000 as the approximate number of persons in internment camps and assuming a three judge panel would take only one hour to try each person, figured that trying all the cases would take 375 judges four months. The OMGUS Denazification Policy Board, taking into account the SS, most of whom were held as prisoners of war, and the SA, the party storm troopers of whom only the leadership had so far been arrested, pointed out that the number to be tried might well be 500,000 rather than 100,000.[68]

After two months of often agonizing study in all offices concerned, talks in early December between USFET representatives and the Office, Chief of Counsel for the

---

[64] Cable, SHAEF Main to Justice Robert H. Jackson, 24 June 45, in SHAEF SGS, 000.5/1.

[65] The Army had no judicial responsibility in the trials, but until mid-September and even after, there was no assurance that it would not. On 17 September, Jackson informed President Truman that the Soviet government had just recalled its prosecutor and had not appointed a replacement and that so far the Russians had not produced either evidence or a staff. The whole project, he said, would "fizzle" if the United States did not "furnish everything including ideas, prisoners, evidence, billets, mess, and courthouse." Jackson recommended that the President appoint an American military commission to dispose of the charges if the delay lasted too long. (1) Memo, Third Army to CG, 1st Inf Div, sub: Hqs. Cmd. International Military Tribunal, 24 Nov 45, in USFET SGS 000.5/4. (2) Cable, Jackson to the President, 17 Sep 45, in USFET SGS 000.5/1.

[66] (1) JCS 1023/10, Directive on Identification and Apprehension of Persons Suspected of War Crimes or Other Offenses and Trial of Certain Offenders, 8 Jul 45, in CCS 000.5 (10–15–43), sec. 4. (2) Memo, Hqs, USFET, JA, from Ch,

International Law Sec, for TJA, sub: Organization for Proceeding Against Axis War Criminals, 16 Oct 45, in USFET SGS 000.5/1.

[67] Control Council Law No. 10, 20 Dec 45, in Ruhm von Oppen, *Documents on Germany Under Occupation, 1945–54*, pp. 97–101.

[68] Telford Taylor, *Final Report to the Secretary of the Army on the Nuernberg War Crimes Trials Under Control Council Law No. 10* (Washington, D.C., 1949), p. 16.

Prosecution of Axis Criminality (Justice Jackson's office), resulted in one conclusion, namely, "that literal compliance with JCS 1023/10 is in practice out of the question." They therefore produced a plan for compliance as far as it was feasible. The USFET War Crimes Group would retain responsibility for the kinds of trials it was conducting, that is, war crimes and concentration camps. The other atrocities since 30 January 1933 would be turned over to German courts as a "test of German regeneration." Jackson's office would prepare and, after the international trials, conduct the cases against the major offenders whom the International Military Tribunal did not try and against the members of criminal organizations.[69] Although the division of re-

sponsibility reduced the Army's direct share to a fraction of what it might have been under JCS 1023/10, it was still large and would in the end constitute the majority of the cases actually tried. As of January 1946, the War Crimes Group had referred 81 cases to trial and had 2,438 war crimes and 131 mass atrocity (concentration camp) cases on the docket.[70]

---

[69] By late January 1946, it became certain that the International Military Tribunal's findings were not going to permit convictions solely on the basis of membership in criminal organizations. Knowledge of the criminality and degree of involvement, at least, would have to be proved in each instance which made hundreds of thousands of trials clearly impossible. Consequently, Brig. Gen. Telford Taylor, Jackson's deputy, decided to let almost all the membership cases be handled under the denazification procedures. When the international

trials ended in October 1946, Taylor succeeded Jackson as Chief of Counsel for War Crimes and assumed responsibility for trying major offenders under Control Council Law No. 10. In the so-called Subsequent Proceedings, the Office, Chief of Counsel for War Crimes, prosecuted eleven cases against 185 persons before U.S. military tribunals sitting at Nuremberg. All defendants were charged with specific crimes, but a few who were acquitted of other charges were convicted of membership in criminal organizations. (1) Memo, CG, USFET, for CofS, Sub: Organization of Further Proceedings Against War Criminals and Certain Other Offenders, 5 Dec 45, in USFET SGS, 000.5/4. (2) SWNCC 237, Organization for Further Proceedings Against Axis War Criminals, 22 Dec 45, and JCS 1023/12, Organization for Further Proceedings Against Axis War Criminals, 21 Dec 45, in CCS 000.5 (10–15–43), sec. 4. (3) USFET, Prosecution of Nazi Crimes Against Germans, 15 Dec 45, in USFET SGS 000.5/1.

[70] USFET, JA, Report, 4 Apr 42–3 Apr 46, in ETOUSA file.

CHAPTER XXII

The Turning Point

Military Government in the Static Phase

After the carpet was taken up, the area in Germany remaining under U.S. military government control was about the size of the state of Kentucky but with five times the population.[1] The withdrawal into the zone had reduced the U.S.-administered area by more than two-thirds and the number of people by at least as much; however, the consolidation and additions of new personnel raised military government strengths at all levels. Between August and October 1945, although they were already under the shadow of redeployment, the detachments experienced a personnel explosion. The *Land* detachment for Bavaria went from a hundred officers and men (in May) to nearly five hundred. Detachment E2C2, which had taken over Hesse-Nassau in July with 35 officers and 36 enlisted men, had 94 officers and 134 enlisted men in September. A typical *Land* and *Stadtkreis* detachment, I7E3 at Ingolstadt, Bavaria, started out with 3 officers and 5 men and in September reached a strength of 10 officers and 30 men.

Although the planning at least as far

---

[1] The area of the U.S. zone, not including Bremen and Berlin, was 41,000 square miles. The total area of the four zones was 138,400 square miles. The 1939 population had been 13.7 million. A census in October 1946 reported a population of 16.9 million for Hesse, Wuerttemberg-Baden, and Bavaria and .5 million for Bremen. These figures included large numbers of refugees, expellees, and released prisoners of war taken into the zone after the fall of 1945, at which time the population was probably about 15.5 million.

back as the Standard Policy and Procedure in early 1944 had envisioned indirect control through German agencies, military government was still functionally locked in at all administrative levels. The stage when the detachments would supervise rather than operate seemed no closer than it had when Captain Goetcheus and I4G2 ran Monschau as an island between the German and American front lines. The main difference was that the number of functions and the scope of responsibilities had increased. When the Production Control Agency went out of existence in August 1945, its entire array of concerns passed from G–4 to G–5 and was shifted to military government down the line. Seventh Army G–5, for example, reorganized into two main branches, Economics and Industry and Internal Affairs. Economics and Industry was further subdivided into two sections: the Economics section (with subsections for labor; transportation; supply, food and agriculture; and trade and industry) and the industry section (with subsections for requirements and allocations; reports and statistics; oil; public utilities; building materials; construction; housing; forestry; and industrial control, which was further subdivided into machinery and equipment, metals, electrical equipment and instruments, chemicals, consumer goods, and coal and nonmetallic mines). Internal Affairs had ten subsections: civil government; public safety; posts, telephone, and telegraph; education and religious affairs; legal and prisons; finance and property control; displaced persons, refugees, and liaison; public welfare; public health; and monuments, fine arts, and archives.[2] Not all upper echelon functions were also functions of the *Kreis* detachments; but the *Kreis* detachments bore almost the entire burden of denazification and property control, which they could neither pass upward nor delegate to the Germans. The detachments were also experiencing no decline in the military government court cases. Black marketeering, DP crimes, and *Fragebogen* falsifications more than outbalanced a tapering off of circulation and curfew cases. By November, the military government courts in Munich had a backlog of 26,000 cases. Nearly all of the detachments were providing some direct services. In Munich, the detachment's public utilities experts, Maj. Elmer W. Price and Capt. Louis Wask, restored the city's gas service, which had been out since July 1944 when a bombing raid damaged the gas works and cracked the mains. Between May and August, using horse-drawn cars at first, they also put the streetcar system into good enough shape to transport 400,000 people a day.[3] In Bremen, the detachment's officers in charge of fisheries sent the first two trawlers out on 19 July with dust coal in their bunkers (which gave them a top speed of six knots, two knots less than the speed of an average fish). Two months later, twenty-one trawlers were operating out of Wesermuende with good coal and twenty-nine more were being reconditioned.[4]

Among the busiest men of the occupation were the MFA&A officers. The art treasures required painstaking care, and the monuments above ground had to be protected against weather damage, theft, and vandalism. In Nuremberg, Detachment B–211 used discharged Nazis who had artistic knowledge to sort through the rubble for fragments of old stone and iron work. The regulations against Germans having weapons or holding foreign currency posed a constant threat—from overly zealous or acquisitive U.S. troops—to antique arms and armor and to coin collections. New finds were still being made. Underground vaults in Nuremberg uncovered during the summer held the Neptune Fountain, which the *Wehrmacht* had looted from the grounds of the imperial palace in Leningrad, and the great fifteenth century Viet Stoss altar from St. Mary's Church in Cracow, Poland. Two months of detective work brought to light, buried behind two-foot-thick concrete walls and encased in airtight copper containers, the crown, the orb, the sceptre, and the two swords of the Holy Roman Empire. Two Nuremberg city officials who had stubbornly lied that SS troops had taken the imperial regalia out of the city in April 1945 received 25,000-mark fines and five-year prison sentences. By late summer, inquiries were coming in from experts and societies all over the world concerning the welfare and whereabouts of libraries and collections, the state of various castles and buildings, and in one instance, the condition of a unique specimen of an Indian shark preserved in a museum in Stuttgart.

The immense task of restoring looted treasures to their proper owners began in September when Seventh Army's special MFA&A team at the Heilbronn salt mines brought to the surface and turned over to

---

[2] Final Report, Hqs, Seventh Army, ACofS G–5, 25 Mar 46, in USFET, Hist Div, 11068/100.
[3] EUCOM, Hist Div, Military Government in Munich, 1951, OCMH 8–3.1, EA 3, p. 3.
[4] Functional History of Military Government in the Bremen Enclave, 26 Apr 45–30 Sep 45, in OMGUS 48–1/6, pt. I, p. 121.

French representatives the stained glass windows from the Strassbourg Cathedral. Thereafter, freight-car loads of books, art objects, and museum pieces were moved out of the mines, sometimes directly to their owners in France, Belgium, Holland, or Italy but more often to collecting points in Munich and Wiesbaden where they were photographed and identified before being returned to their owners. A special collecting point at Offenbach handled Jewish archives, books, and religious objects. Some two hundred of the most valuable German paintings were shipped to Washington in November for safekeeping, but they and all other German-owned works would be restored to their owners when they could be adequately housed.[5] A noteworthy example was the Stuppach Madonna by Mathias Gruenwald, a small work worth two million dollars, which MFA&A found in the Heilbronn mines and returned to its owner, a village parish church in Bavaria.[6]

Black marketeering and currency manipulation, no doubt, tempted military government personnel as much as the occupation troops, and military government had some temptations that ordinary soldiers did not. There is no reason to believe that the degree of resistance in military government ranks was markedly higher than in the U.S. forces at large, but instances of such complete capitulation as in the following account were rare. When Capt. Norman W.

Boring and Lt. Arnold J. Lapiner became the military government officer and deputy in Landkreis Laufen, Bavaria, in early 1946, they were flooded with claims for requisitioned jewelry, cameras, silverware, and radios, none of which could be traced since the detachment until then had kept practically no records of any kind. Among the detachment's civilian employees were typists who could not type and interpreters who knew no English. The detachment had been popularly known as the American Gestapo. In the monthly reports, the denazification sections were blank. An enlisted man in the detachment had held up the local post office for 35,000 marks. When asked why the theft had not been reported, the postmaster said the soldier had threatened to have him thrown in jail if he did and the general behavior of the detachment was such that he believed the threat.[7]

The detachments attempting to do their work conscientiously had, not surprisingly, various complaints, among which they unanimously agreed on two. One was the seemingly insatiable appetite of the upper echelons for reports. Every new development, such as the licensing of political parties and Law No. 8, added requirements for monthly, biweekly, and special reports. An average Landkreis detachment submitted 109 regular reports during the month of October 1945 and dispatched a total of 305 communications, or, as one detachment figured, 1.3 communications an hour, eight hours a day including Sundays.[8] More important, because it affected the detachments' image of themselves and their

---

[5] One collection not scheduled for return to German ownership was the Weltkriegsbuecherei, a privately endowed library of works pertaining to World War I. Described as consisting of 687 cases of books and 12 truckloads of uncrated materials, it was given into the custody of the Library of Congress.

[6] (1) History of Military Government in Land Wuerttemberg-Baden, vol. I, ch. IX. (2) Hist Rpt, Det G–28, Dec 45, in OMGUS, 10–1/5. (3) Hist Rpt, Det B–211, 20 Jun 46, in OMGUS 81–3/10.

[7] Hist Rpt, Det E–281, 30 Jun 46, in OMGUS 77–3/10.

[8] Wk Rpt, Det 205, 22 Nov 45, in OMGUS 1–2/5.

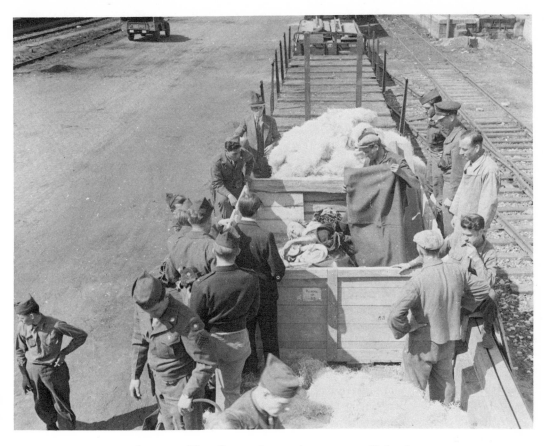

LOADING VEIT STOSS ALTAR *for return to Poland.*

prestige in the eyes of the Germans, was the not unfounded belief that they were the last ones to know about important decisions. Although not always, as some military government officers contended, but certainly too often, the Germans heard the news on the radio before the detachments received any official word; Law No. 8 was probably the most egregious instance. A good part of the trouble lay in the split between information control and military government. ICD received its information at USFET and, not having to co-ordinate with military government, could have it on

the air almost immediately. The same information going to the detachments had to pass through several intermediate headquarters, sometimes being revised along the way.[9] The existence of an essentially military government information agency that was separate from military government proved by the fall of 1945 to be a sufficiently glaring organizational weakness to become the subject of a report to the Presi-

---

[9] Memo, Hqs, USFET, IG, for CofS, sub: Delay in Transmission of Orders, 26 Dec 45, in USFET SGS 461/1.

dent.[10] However, the most embarrassing episodes, the announcement of Law No. 8 and the licensing of political parties, probably owed less to organizational lapses than to high-level efforts to exploit policies for publicity before they were ready to be put into effect.

Typically, military government did not lack critics in the summer and fall of 1945. The *New Republic* viewed the Schaeffer affair as demonstrating "the inability of the Army to run the civil affairs of an occupied country."[11] Raymond Daniell of the New York *Times* charged the officers responsible for denazification with having lost sight of the reasons for which the war was fought.[12] The Harrison report maintained that military government officers were timid about inconveniencing the Germans and more interested in getting German communities working soundly again than in caring for the DPs; furthermore, Truman told Eisenhower that the proper policies were not being carried out "by some of your officers in the field."[13] In October, during the aftermath of the Patton and Schaeffer incidents, the Army was completely on the defensive. Eisenhower wrote to Marshall about the "growing storm of discontent, even anger, among columnists and editors" that was giving the Army "a bad name when it is doing an overall good job."[14] Truscott talked to reporters about their "questioning the ability of the military mind to conduct civil affairs in occupied territory"; and Smith declared himself convinced that "the

American people will never take kindly to the idea of government exercised by military officers."[15]

In trouble with the press and publicly rebuked by the President (the White House released the President's letter to Eisenhower and the Harrison report on 31 August), military government's future was indeed murky—and that of the German people even more so. The important question of whether the Army was adequately performing its mission in Germany was being answered emotionally; and the more important question, in human terms, of what was going to happen to millions of Germans, both good and bad, was in danger of not being considered at all. Fortunately, on the day before he released the Harrison report, the President had sent Byron Price, who had been the Director of Censorship and who was an experienced newspaper man and former executive editor of the Associated Press, to Europe to "survey the general subject of relations between the American Forces of Occupation and the German people." After ten weeks in Germany, Price submitted a summary of what the occupation had done and not done since the surrender and a review of the problems ahead: hunger, economic reconstruction, and democratization. Concerning what had been done so far he concluded:

Taken altogether it [military government] seems to me a notable record of progress, whatever may be said by noisy backseat drivers. No one who knows the facts can fail to give General Eisenhower, his Deputy General Clay, and the staff of Military Government generally his continuing confidence and commendation. In no other zone of Germany

[10] In the Byron Price Report of 9 November 1945. See *The Department of State Bulletin*, 16 Sep 45, p. 891.

[11] *New Republic*, vol. 113, no. 15, 8 Oct 45.

[12] New York *Times*, 19 Sep 45.

[13] *The Department of State Bulletin*, 30 Sep 45, pp. 456–61.

[14] Cable, Eisenhower to Marshall, 13 Oct 45, in USFET SGS 000.7.

[15] (1) Diary, Hqs, XV Corps, 8 Oct–10 Dec 45, 12 Oct 45, in XV Corps, 215–0.3. (2) Memo, W. B. Smith for Byron Price, 14 Oct 45, in USFET SGS 014.113.

has greater progress been made toward the declared objectives of the Allied occupation.

As to the future, he warned, "The United States must decide whether we mean to finish the job competently, and provide the tools, the determination and the funds requisite to that purpose, or withdraw."[16] On 28 November, the President released Price's report to the press together with a letter to the Secretaries of State, War, and the Navy in which he directed them to "give careful consideration to this report, with a view to taking whatever joint action may be indicated."[17]

"Not a Job for Soldiers"

At his first meeting with the Army commanders on 21 June 1945, Clay told them that the War Department believed military government was "not a job for soldiers" and should, therefore, be "turned over to the political as soon as practicable."[18] President Truman had said, more than a month before, that he wanted control in Germany shifted to civilian hands as quickly as possible because he believed it was in the American tradition "that the military should not have governmental responsibilities beyond the requirements of military operations."[19] The President said he wanted the transfer made "as soon as the rough and tumble is over in Germany." Apparently he and Eisenhower felt that time was growing short when they met at Eisenhower's head-

quarters in Frankfurt in late July and agreed that Eisenhower should organize the military government in Germany so as to facilitate turning it over to civilian authority "at the earliest moment."[20]

The idea of organizing military government for a changeover to civilian control was of course not a new one. From the beginning the U.S. Group Control Council had been considered more a vehicle for future civilian authority than an element of Army-administered military government. In April 1945, in his first outline for military government organization, Clay proposed also to bring civilians into the theater G–5 so that both it and the U.S. Group Control Council could be "carved out of" the military command when the shift to civilian responsibility occurred.[21] A month later, in the organizational directive for military government, Clay stated, "This organization must become civilian in character as rapidly as consistent with efficient performance so that it may become at the earliest possible date a framework for the administration of political control in Germany by the appropriate U.S. civil agencies."[22] He told the army commanders at the 22 June meeting that he was "infiltrating highly qualified civilians" into the U.S. Group Control Council and the theater G–5; writing to McCloy three days later, he said he understood the creation of a supervisory body for Germany composed of civilians "to be my mission."[23]

Until the war ended in the Pacific, the

---

[16] Report of Byron Price to the President, 9 Nov 45, in *The Bulletin of the Department of State,* 2 Dec 45, pp. 885–92.

[17] *Ibid.,* p. 885.

[18] Min, US Gp CC, Staff Meeting of Division directors, 22 Jun 45, in OMGUS 12–1/5, V60–12/1.

[19] Memo by Acting Secretary of State Joseph C. Grew, 10 May 45, in *Foreign Relations, 1945,* vol. III, p. 509.

[20] Ltr, Eisenhower to President Truman, 26 Oct 45, in USFET SGS 114.113.

[21] Memo by Maj Gen Lucius Clay, 11 Apr 45, in *Foreign Relations, 1945,* vol. III, p. 934.

[22] Hqs, ETOUSA, Organization for Military Government of the U.S. Zone, 13 May 45, in SHAEF G–2, GBI/CI/CS/322.

[23] Ltr, Clay to McCloy, 25 Jun 45, in OMGUS 410–2/3.

numbers of military personnel available for military government assignments made civilianization below the top levels of the U.S. Group Control Council and USFET SGS G–5 an unnecessary luxury. Even in the U.S. Group Control Council, where the number of civilians increased from 83 on 1 May to 326 on 1 September, the relative progress in civilianization was slight since the numbers of officers and enlisted men went from 417 to 1,424 and from 553 to 4,012.[24] In the next two months, however, redeployment altered the proportions rapidly, and the military strength dropped by nearly 2,000 men while the civilians increased to 429. In the first week of September, Clay announced a program to induce officers in particular to convert to civilian status in Germany. On 1 October he initiated a civil service analysis of all military government jobs; and Eisenhower ordered the army commands not to "place any obstacles in the way of these people."[25]

The power struggle between the theater G–5 and the U.S. Group Control Council ended in June on Clay's terms. He and General Adcock, the theater G–5, agreed to integrate their staffs; the staff divisions would be located either in Frankfurt or Berlin depending on where they would be most effective. Adcock became in effect Clay's deputy. Clay indicated to McCloy on 25 June that he contemplated as the next step combining the two staffs into a single office of military government.[26] Since

the merger would remove the top military government echelon from the tactical command channels, it would logically do the same with military government down the line and would constitute a piece of radical surgery on a not entirely willing patient. The USFET and military district G–5's, having no functions that were not duplicated either in the U.S. Group Control Council or the *Land* detachments, would suffer most.

In mid-September, Clay made a choice between two directives: one would have immediately designated the U.S. Group Control Council as the military government authority and removed the G–5's from the chain of command; the other, which Clay approved, cut as deep but not as fast. As of 1 October, the U.S. Group Control Council became the Office of Military Government (U.S.) (OMGUS) and USFET G–5 became the Office of Military Government (U.S. Zone). The *Land* detachments became offices of military government for their *Laender*—Third Army G–5 merging with the Bavarian *Land* detachment to form the Office of Military Government, Bavaria—and Seventh Army G–5 became the Office of Military Government (Western District).[27] For USFET and the armies, however, and thus for the tactical concept of military government, the end was in sight. Other directives issued later in September and the first week of October ordered the armies to cease all military government activity after 31 December. USFET G–5, as the Office of Military Government (U.S. Zone), became the rear echelon of OMGUS upon notice that its functions and personnel would be gradually

[24] OMGUS, History, Office of Military Government for Germany, ch. II, p. 5.

[25] (1) Memo, Hqs, USFET, ACofS G–5, for CofS, sub: Program for Introduction of Classified Civil Service, 6 Sep 45, in USFET SGS 200.3. (2) Diary, Hqs, Seventh Army ACofS G–3, 2 Jun 45–25 Mar 46, 1 Oct 45, in Seventh Army, 107–0.3.0.

[26] Ltr, Clay to McCloy, 25 June 45, in OMGUS 410–2/3.

[27] Memo, Dep Military Governor for CG, USFET, sub: Organization of Military Government, 15 Sep 45, in OMGUS 177–2/3.

shifted from Frankfurt to the OMGUS headquarters in Berlin. Ironically, by then, since the Control Council had failed to establish even the most rudimentary German central authority, Frankfurt was a much better site for the zone military government headquarters than Berlin; however, having the headquarters in Frankfurt would have necessitated either withdrawing most of the personnel from Berlin, thus seeming to accept the division of Germany as permanent, or maintaining a large staff in Berlin without anything to do.[28]

The day after he approved the directive establishing OMGUS and the other offices of military government, Clay wrote to McCloy that the object was to convert military government to a civilian operation and separate it from the military forces as soon as possible.[29] On 1 October, Eisenhower told the army commanders "The Army must be prepared to be divorced from military government responsibilities on twenty-four hours' notice."[30] Clay did not anticipate quite so much speed; and when he read the preliminary draft of Byron Price's report to the President, which recommended as did the final report, complete civilianization and the appointment of a civilian high commissioner, he pointed out that the other three Allied governments would have to be consulted and that the complete conversion would probably take until 1 July 1946.[31] No doubt, however, considering the official and press criticism,

the Army would have liked to get out sooner. Smith directly expressed this view when he told Price that he frankly doubted whether civilians could do a better job than the military, but "from a purely selfish point of view, the sooner the Army is out of this very controversial job the better it will be for the military service."[32]

In Washington on 23 October, Secretary of War Patterson and Secretary of the Navy James V. Forrestal met with Secretary of State James F. Byrnes.[33] The subject was civilian control in Germany, which Patterson said he believed should be a State Department responsibility. They agreed that the shift, when it was made, should be to a single department; but Byrnes thought the Army had the best organization and that "it would be a great mistake to make the change now." If the State Department had to take over, he suggested postponing the "bad news" for eight or nine months.[34] Three days later in a letter to Truman, Eisenhower reminded the President of their conversion in July and, pointing out that the four occupying powers would have to agree, proposed making the transfer to civilian control no later than 1 June 1946.[35] On the 31st, the President released Eisenhower's letter to the press and announced that the shift from military to State Department civilian control in Germany would be made by 1 June 1946.[36]

---

[28] OMGUS, History, ch. I, pp. 63–67.

[29] Ltr, Clay to McCloy, 16 Sep 45, in OMGUS 410–2/3.

[30] Diary, Seventh Army, ACofS G–3, 2 Jun 45–25 Mar 46, 1 Oct 45, in Seventh Army, 107–0.3.0.

[31] (1) Byron Price, Preliminary Outline of a Report on Relations Between the American Army of Occupation and the German People, 4 Oct 45, in USFET SGS 014.1/3. (2) Memo, Clay for Price, 14 Oct 45, in OMGUS 177–3/3.

[32] Memo, Smith for Byron Price, 14 Oct 45, in USFET SGS 014.113.

[33] Under Secretary of War Patterson had succeeded Stimson when Stimson resigned in September 1945.

[34] (1) Memo, CAD, Econ Sec, for the Director, CAD, 1 Nov 45, in ASW, 370.8. (2) Foreign Relations, 1945, vol. III, p. 989.

[35] Ltr, Eisenhower to President Truman, 26 Oct 45, in USFET SGS 014.113.

[36] Memo, CAD, Econ Sec, for the Director, CAD, 1 Nov 45, in ASW, 370.8.

"We Don't Want the Low Level Job"

Expecting in mid-September to have to reduce military government in the field from its peak strength of close to 13,000 officers and men to around 4,000 by early 1946, Clay directed Adcock and USFET G–5 to work out a means of reducing military government supervision below the Land level. "We cannot," he said, "expect the Germans to take responsibility without giving it to them. We don't want the low level job; we want the Germans to do it." He added, "We are going to move a little fast. . . ."[37]

On 5 October, USFET announced:

It has always been the purpose of the U.S. Forces to permit the German people to develop a free government, shaped to fit the needs of Germany. Moreover, it is manifestly simpler to control Germany through German administrative machinery than by undertaking direct operating responsibilities. . . .

"In order to carry out this conversion," USFET ordered the Landkreis and Stadtkreis detachments to divorce themselves from direct supervision of the German civilian adminstrations by 15 November 1945 and the Regierungsbezirk detachments to do so by 15 December. After the last elections (and no later than 30 April 1946 in the Landkreise and 30 June in the Stadtkreise), the directive added, the Landkreis and Stadtkreis detachments would be disbanded and replaced with two-officer liaison and security detachments, which would observe and report on the German governments and act as the link between them and the occupation forces but have no authority, except in emergencies, to intervene in their operations.[38]

OMGUS, the Land offices of military government, the German Land governments, and a Laenderrat (council of ministers), consisting of the Land minister presidents and the Oberbuergermeister of Bremen, were to be the vehicles of authority in the U.S. zone. Bavaria had had a Land government since June. One Land government was installed in Wuerttemberg-Baden on 24 September and another in Greater Hesse on 8 October. On the 17th, Clay opened the first meeting of the Laenderrat in Stuttgart. Clay indicated, on the one hand, that he regarded the Laenderrat as a zonal substitute for the central authority that the Control Council had failed to establish. On the other hand, to avoid seeming to have accepted the Control Council's failure as final, he pointed out that the Laenderrat was neither a legislature nor a zonal executive but was only charged with co-ordinating legislation in areas where zonewide uniformity was necessary.[39] The Laenderrat began to function officially at its second meeting on 6 November. By then a joint co-ordinating staff composed of representatives of the Land ministeries, a permanent secretariat, and a U.S. advisory group—the Regional Government Co-ordinating Office (under Dr. James K. Pollock)—was established.

From the field, USFET survey teams described the reaction of military government officers as "100 percent" against the impending removal of the local military government detachments. Some officers saw

---

[37] Memo, USFET, Civil Admin Br, for CofS, sub: Proposed Directives, 4 Oct 45, in USFET SGS 014.1.

[38] Hqs, USFET, to CG's, Eastern and Western Military Districts, sub: Reorganization of Military Government Control Channels, 5 Oct 45, in USFET SGS 014.1.

[39] Hist Rpt, Det E1A2, Oct 45, in OMGUS 9–3/5.

GENERAL CLAY (*Second from left*) AT LAENDERRAT MEETING. *On his right Regional Government Co-ordinator, Dr. Pollock. On his left General Muller and Colonel Newman, Military Government Directors for Bavaria and Greater Hesse.*

the move as a kind of trick to reduce their staffs without reducing the work loads. Others protested that the German officials were too recently appointed and too inexperienced to have any idea of how to operate the governments on their own initiative. Many believed the Germans "would quickly revert to their old political, economic, and social customs"; and the Germans themselves reportedly feared a resurgence of Nazi elements and doubted the ability of the civilian officials to run the governments or to maintain public peace and order. OMGUS hoped that such pessimism could be written off as the natural reaction of a large organization threatened with a drastic reduction in its scope and activities, and Clay let the withdrawal of control from the *Kreis* detachments go ahead in mid-November. The organization was not going to be there much longer in any event. The detachments had lost an average of 50 percent, and in some instances as much as 80 percent, of their enlisted men in October. The officers, if held to the letter of their commitments, could have been retained six or eight months at most.[40]

On 21 November, USFET granted full executive, legislative, and judicial authority to the *Land* governments individually and extended to them all the powers formerly exercised by either the *Land* or the national governments. The offices of military government were told, "The initiative must be taken by the German authorities: the duty is theirs." All legislation issued by the *Land* governments was to be on their authority alone and "contain nothing to indicate that it was issued in the name of or having the approval of military government"; however, it was still subject to prior clearance through military government. Not later than 31 December 1945, U.S. orders and instructions would be issued only to the *Land* governments and would pass from them to the lower elements through German channels. Similarly, military government would intervene to correct mistakes or deal with violations only at the *Land* level.[41] Military government as conceived at Charlottesville, shaped at Shrivenham, and deployed under the Carpet and Static Plans had served out its time.

---

[40] (1) Hqs, USFET, OMG (U.S. Zone), Internal Affairs Div, Opns Br, sub: Opns Rpt of Det E–202, Oct 45, in OMGUS 1–2/5. (2) Hist Rpt, Det E–206, Oct 45, in OMGUS 1–3/5. (3) OMGUS, History, ch. I, pp. 68–70. (4) History of Military Government in *Land* Wuerttemberg-Baden, vol. I, p. 1459.

[41] Hqs, USFET, Director of Military Government (U.S. zone), to Directors of Military Government, sub: Action to Strengthen German Civil Administration in the U.S. Zone, 21 Nov 45, in USFET SGS 014.114.

CHAPTER XXIII

Winter

The Season of Despair

From the first sight in the spring of un-plowed fields, shutdown coal mines, and ruined cities, the winter to come had loomed ominously in the minds of those who would be responsible for administering the occupied country. In June, predicting a barren winter for Europe, the Potter-Hyndley Mission contemplated a possible need "to preserve order by shooting" in Germany.[1] When he talked to the Germans in August, Eisenhower warned them of the hardships in the months to come. By early autumn, the U.S. and British newspapers were printing stories about the approaching "Battle of the Winter," a battle against sickness, starvation, and cold. The occupation forces figured in some accounts as semiallies, in others as dispassionate observers of a people enduring the consequences of aggression, and not infrequently as the potential target of the unregenerate and the desperate. The third possibility occurred also to the U.S. command, and in October Eisenhower and Smith decided there was "a strong likelihood of incidents . . . in the winter" that would require "strong retaliation." At the end of the month, they instructed military government to warn German officials, from the minister presidents on down, that they and their communities would be held accountable for acts against the occupation forces.[2]

At first the Germans seemed too stunned and, as the summer wore on, too preoccupied with day-to-day existence to think about the future. When the harvest was in and the daily ration barely above 1,200 calories, when the weather turned cold and there was no coal, when the farmers and other producers became increasingly unwilling to part with their products for money, the people, as the Wuerttemberg-Baden Office of Military Government reported, sank "deeper and deeper into despair as they saw a cruel, cold, hungry winter ahead."[3] The harvest, all things considered, had been a good one but could not under any circumstances have been good enough to feed the zone population throughout the winter. Coal output in the British and French zones had increased, but the rail and water transport systems were only able to move about 60 percent of the coal away from the mines. The U.S. zone received half a million tons in August but only 150,000 tons more in December, just enough to run the railroads and essential public utilities. When cold weather came, military government in Stuttgart and other places requisitioned all coal supplies over a quarter ton, and throughout the zone children were required to bring a piece of firewood with them to school each day to heat the classrooms. To the excessive

[1] Donnison, *Civil Affairs and Military Government, Northwest Europe*, p. 405.
[2] Memo, Hqs, USFET, ACofS G-2, for ACofS G-5, sub: German Responsibility for Civil Order, 31 Oct 45 in USFET SGS 014.113.
[3] History of Military Government in *Land Wuerttemberg-Baden*, vol. I, p. 1428.

GATHERING FIREWOOD, *February 1946.*

amounts of paper *Reichsmarks* already in circulation the Allied military marks had added billions more and raised the fear of an uncontrollable inflation like that of 1923. Hardly able to buy with money anything that was not rationed, some people were investing in postage stamps; and in the cities, many workers reported for work only often enough to get their ration cards.

The news in November that the U.S. zone would receive two and a quarter million Germans expelled from eastern Europe between December 1945 and July 1946 deepened the despair. On instructions from the Potsdam Conference, the Control Council had worked out procedures for taking into the occupied territory 6,650,000 racial Germans who were to be expelled from Poland, Czechoslovakia, Hungary, and Austria.[4] The U.S. zone's share was 1,750,000 from the Sudetenland and 500,000 from Hungary. They were scheduled to come at a rate of a quarter million a month in December, January, and February and in larger numbers in the spring.[5]

---

[4] Cable, Hqs, USFET, to War Dept, AG, 20 Dec 45, in USFET SGS 091.1/1.
[5] After the State Department announced that XXII corps, the U.S. force in Czechoslovakia, would be withdrawn by 1 December, it looked

An agreement to exchange refugees between the zones plunged the refugees into gloom without raising the spirits of the native residents of the U.S. zone. The latter expected that relatively few refugees, particularly from the east, would go home—an opinion which later turned out to be correct.[6] Housing and feeding those Germans expelled from other countries was going to be entirely a German affair (with military government making sure this responsibility was being carried out), and no one denied that the Germans had reason to be worried. As the Chief of Staff, Third Army, Brig. Gen. Don E. Carleton, said: "I can't see with a couple more million coming in, how there is going to be room. Even stacking them on top of one another, the facilities are going to be really busting."[7]

It appeared for a time that USFET might also have to discharge upwards of 80,000 prisoners of war a month into the zone during the winter. The shipping schedule called for 80,000 to be returned from the United States in December and 85,000 each month in January and February. They were to have been part of the 1.3 million allotted to France for rehabilitation work, but in late September, the International Red Cross reported that 200,000 of the prisoners already in French hands were so undernourished as to be unfit for labor and likely to die over the winter. Eisenhower immediately ordered that food, clothing, and medical supplies be provided for the most needy prisoners and stopped all transfers of prisoners to French custody until the French were able to maintain them in accordance with the Geneva Convention. Since the U.S. forces were by then finding the 350,000 prisoners that they still held in labor service units to be more expensive than hired civilian labor, the shipments from the United States would probably have to be discharged as soon as they arrived, and the three-quarters of a million prisoners in France might also have to be brought back and either be discharged or otherwise made a German responsibility.[8]

By the first week in October, Clay knew almost for certain that he was not going to get enough food imports to raise the ration for the winter to 2,000 calories per day.[9] In the 28-day ration period beginning on 15 October, the scale would barely reach 1,250 calories; and he knew that in

---

for a time as if the Sudeten Germans might burst into the zone in an uncontrolled flood. Generals Carleton and Adcock discussed that possibility by telephone on 21 November:

Carleton: As soon as the Germans realize that Harmon's XXII Corps is going to move they will become more and more terrified, because actually he has been their god and protector up there.

Adcock: Yes. He has been the only one to keep the low level Czechs from raising hell with them. I am afraid they will turn white upon hearing that Harmon's corps is going to pull out. Word is being spread now.

Carleton: Yes. The congestion along the border area is becoming terrific. So far we have been able to handle it, but we don't look to the future with any real hope.

(1) Cable, Marshall to Eisenhower, 9 Nov 45, in USFET SGS 370.5/3. (2) Diary, XV Corps, 21 Nov 45, in XV Corps, 215–0.3.

[6] The May 1946 census showed over three quarters of a million refugees from other zones still in the U.S. zone. Annual Report OMG, Bavaria, Refugee Section, 9 Jul 46, in OMGUS 65–1/10.

[7] Diary, XV Corps, 21 Nov 45, in XV Corps, 215–0.3.

---

[8] (1) Memo, USFET, CofS, for Head of U.S. Forces Mission to France, 2 Oct 45, and Memo, Hqs, TSFET, Office of the Chief Surgeon, sub: Conference—POWs Under French Control, 4 Oct 45, in USFET SGS 383.6/1. (2) Memo, Hqs, USFET, Provost Marshal, for CG, Hqs, USFET, Sub: Disposition of POWs, 26 Dec 45, in USFET SGS 383.6/3.

[9] Memo, OMGUS, Dep Mil Gov, for CG, USFET, sub: Supply of Food to Civilians in Berlin, 3 Oct 45, in USFET SGS 014.1.

unheated dwellings this ration level would not be enough to sustain life through the winter. In the middle of the month, probably more to raise the Germans' spirits than in the belief that the few hundred extra calories would make any real difference, and not at all certain yet that he would have the imports to support the increase, he announced a zonewide 1,500-calorie ration to begin on 12 November, with 50 calories more to be added after 10 December.[10] A 1,500-calorie ration worked out daily to 5½ slices of bread, 3 medium-size potatoes, 3 tablespoons of oatmeal or other cereal, 1 teaspoon of fat, and 1 teaspoon of sugar. Of the total 1,500 calories, 1,200 were in the bread and potatoes. USFET authorized adding, when available—which no one expected to happen very often—a piece of meat or fish "one half the size of an egg" and three tablespoons of vegetables other than potatoes.[11] To conserve precious calories and provide hot meals for those who would be without fuel to cook their own, the offices of military government, sometimes using Army equipment, began setting up community kitchens. The kitchens in Bavaria alone were able to serve 4½ million meals a month. Except in Berlin, where the school children received 190-calorie hot noon meals, recipients were required to turn in ration coupons and, if they were not on relief, pay for the meals.[12] In the first week of December, the State Department authorized private U.S. agencies to ship relief supplies to Germany,

provided the supplies were distributed impartially in the areas of greatest need.[13]

The first postwar Christmas, dismal though it was, was not quite as bad as it might have been. The worst specimen of a goose for the holiday dinner cost at least a thousand *Reichsmarks,* when one could be had at all; and one black marketeer made a huge profit selling cans of old *Wehrmacht* sauerkraut relabeled goulash. The *Frankfurter Rundschau* described the scene in that city:

A few stalls stand on the wet pavement of the main square in the midst of the ruins. Cards are for sale, also a few red and blue pencils, some cardboard toys, a few pitiful things made out of wood, and lots of trashy and expensive ornaments. The old Frankfurter Santa Claus and his arks full of wooden animals is distant as a dream.[14]

In Stuttgart, the Christmas selection consisted mostly of small and expensive wooden toys and small quantities of powder, lipstick, and oilless face creams. A lighted Christmas tree atop the *Stuttgarter Zeitung* building, the first seen in the city since 1938, stood out painfully amidst the dark ruins.[15] The weather, however, was warm and springlike. The *Frankfurter Rundschau* reminded its readers what such weather meant in terms of survival and recalled also that the previous year had been

---

[10] Cable, OMGUS to AGWAR for WARCOS, 1 Nov 45, in OMGUS 12–1/5, v60–20/1.

[11] Hqs, USFET, Theater Commander's Weekly Staff Conference No. 14, 26 Mar 46, in Hist Div, Hqs, ETO, 97-USF9–0.5.

[12] (1) Cumulative Historical Report for *Land* Bavaria, 30 Jun 46, p. 109. (2) Hist Rpt, OMG, Berlin, 1 Jul 45–30 Jun 46, vol. I, p. 100.

[13] Germany had been closed to relief shipments until December on the grounds that they might tend to negate the policy of restricting the German standard of living to the average of the surrounding European nations. CARE package shipments to individuals remained prohibited until 5 June 1946. (1) Memo, European Section Theater Group, OPD, for L & LD, sub: Establishment of Civilian Director of Relief, 8 Dec 45, in OPD, ABC 336 (sec. IV) (cases 155–   ). (2) OMGUS, Control Office, Hist Br, History of U.S. Military Government in Germany, Public Welfare, 9 Jul 46, in OMGUS 21–3/5.

[14] *Frankfurter Rundschau,* 21 Dec 45.

[15] *Stuttgarter Zeitung,* 19 Dec 45.

FAMILY MEAL, *mostly of potatoes.*

different in two respects: the weather on 24 December had been cold and the sky clear, and a hail of bombs had fallen on the city. This year at least "no mother needs to pick up her child in haste and run to the cellar with it."[16]

The holiday was, in fact, not completely barren. Third Army reported "a certain aura of good feeling" associated with the season, and the food offices released extra rations of sugar and flour. Throughout the zone, the troops gave Christmas parties for

children. In *Landkreis* Wetzlar, for example, the local detachment and the occupation troops gave a bag of cookies and a candy bar to each of the several thousand school children. In Bad Aibling the officers and men of the guard for Prisoner of War Enclosure No. 26 distributed chocolate and candy in the town schools. In Heilbronn, the U.S. soldiers furnished candy, the prisoners of war in the local stockade contributed handmade toys, and the military government detachment recorded with satisfaction "the presence of a traditional Christmas tree in even the humblest cellar

[16] *Frankfurter Rundschau,* 21 Dec 45.

home." Some detachments noted, however, that the Germans who came around to them with holiday greetings were often small-time Nazis hoping to ingratiate themselves, while those who had nothing to fear or nothing to gain stayed away.[17]

Three days after Christmas, damp warm winds swept across the zone. In Frankfurt they reached gale force, blowing off roofing paper and temporary roofs and blowing down walls of damaged buildings. The next morning some streets were covered with as much rubble as if there had been an air raid. The weather stayed warm into the new year, however; and because it did and military government was able to maintain a 1,550-calorie ration, the Germans began to recover their spirit. The *Frankfurter Rundschau* reported on "a milliner who bathes in the kitchen serially, as, of course, everyone now does." The report concluded that several such baths taken in various standing, sitting, and reclining positions were in all respects as effective as one "general" bath.[18] The *Rhein-Neckar Zeitung* gave its readers directions for making briquettes out of industrial ash and clay, which when soaked in pitch or tar could be burned to give off "a noticeable amount of heat, approximately equivalent to not quite dry wood." The drawback was, the paper admitted, that the briquettes did not lose volume in burning, so the stove had to be emptied after each charge. In Stuttgart, students in the audience threw little potatoes at the actors in Georg Buechner's *Woyzeck*. The theater manager said they would have thrown rotten eggs, but they did not have any.[19]

In its most crucial aspects, the battle of the winter never quite materialized. Because the U.S. command insisted on heated trains for cold-weather transport of Germans expelled from other countries, the expected flood of people from eastern Europe was held to a trickle. The first trainload from Hungary did not arrive until 10 January, and the first load from Czechoslovakia was delayed until the 25th.[20] During January, USFET discharged almost a hundred thousand prisoners of war but, at the end of the month, having secured assurances the prisoners would be adequately cared for, resumed prisoner of war transfers to the French.[21] Above all, the winter was one of the mildest on record and the 1,550-calorie ration held firm. The quality of the ration even improved somewhat after rye flour ran low and had to be mixed half and half with wheat for baking bread. The best fed were the DPs, who averaged 2,600 calories a day, and the interned Nazis, who were getting 2,200. Both groups were somewhat overweight. The normal German consumers, who with black market purchases were thought to be actually getting about 1,900 calories a day, were underweight by as much as 20 percent and showing signs of malnutrition; however, they were not in such bad shape as they would have been had the weather been colder. In Berlin, where the food and fuel shortages had been expected to be the most severe, the death rate of children under one year dropped

---

[17] Hist Rpt, Eastern Military District, 15 Dec 45–14 Jan 46, in OMGUS 76–3/10. (2) Hist Rpt, Det G–34, Dec 45, in OMGUS 8–2/5. (3) Hist Rpt, Det G–41, Dec 45, in OMGUS 9–1/5. (4) Hist Rpt, Det G–28, Dec 45, in OMGUS 10–1/5. (5) Annual Hist Rpt, Det E–285, 30 Jun 46, in OMGUS 77–1/10.

[18] *Frankfurter Rundschav*, 24 Dec 45.

[19] *Rhein-Neckar Zeitung*, 1 Jan 45.

[20] Annual Hist Rpt, OMG, Bavaria, Refugee Section, 9 Jul 46, in OMGUS 65–1/10.

[21] Hqs, USFET, Commanders's Weekly Staff Conference No. 6, 29 Jan 46, in Hist Div, Hqs, ETO, 97–USF9–0.5.

to 100 per 1,000 in December. It had been 660 in July and 162 in December 1944.[22]

Probably, the rise in the food ration was more responsible than anything else for dispelling the fear of what the winter would bring. What the average German did not know was that the increase bore no relationship to the actual adequacy of the food supply in the zone. Supplies were obtained by drawing heavily on U.S. imports and could only be sustained by continued and increased imports. Fundamentally the food situation had grown worse, not better. By early March, the imported stocks were depleted to the point where, used at the rate required to support a 1,550-calorie diet, they would barely last another sixty days.[23]

DPs, The Resurgent Problem

When General Wood declared the DP problem substantially solved at the end of September, the Army expected that the 600,000 or so DPs left in the U.S. zone would also be off its hands within the next few months. Some DPs, Poles chiefly, would want to return home; the others, the so-called stateless nonrepatriables, Balts, Hungarians, some Poles, and some Jews, could be turned over to UNRRA. As a result of several trips to Warsaw and Prague, Wood had arranged to move as many as 6,000 Poles a day by train across Czechoslovakia to Poland beginning on 1 October. The U.S. forces would supply the cars, locomotives, and coal as far as Pilsen,

where Czech locomotives running on Polish coal would take over and make the haul the rest of the way to the Polish border. Wood had observed however, that there was "no love lost" between the Czechs and the Poles. The Czechs were not happy to have Poles on their territory even temporarily; and the Polish government, while propagandizing for a quick return of all its citizens, was actually not capable of receiving the numbers it claimed it wanted. The fifty-seven trains that made the run in October carried far less than 6,000 persons a day, and at the end of the month the Czechs stopped the movement entirely because Poland failed to supply the coal.[24] The Poles were not going to be sent home as fast as had been expected, nor was the Army going to be relieved of its responsibility for them and the other DPs as had also been expected. When the UNRRA council in London failed to assume supply, equipment, and transportation obligations for the DPs in October as had been projected, the JCS directed USFET to continue its over-all responsibility for them.[25]

The Soviet DPs, because of their special status under the Yalta Agreement, would have remained Army charges in any case. In number, they were an insignificant minority; USFET at the end of August reported the repatriation of Soviet citizens 99 percent completed.[26] Politically and psychologically, however, they were almost as

---

[22] (1) Hqs, USFET, Theater Commander's Weekly Staff Conference No. 1, 18 Dec 45, No. 8, 12 Feb 45, and No. 9, 19 Feb 45, in Hist Div, Hqs, ETO, 97–USF9–0.5. (2) Hqs, USFET, Rpts and Inf Br, Political Intelligence Summary, 15 Jan 46, in OMGUS 418–1/3, v37–10/1.

[23] Hqs, USFET, Theater Commander's Weekly Staff Conference No. 13, 19 Mar 46, in Hist Div, Hqs, ETO, 97–USF9–0.5.

[24] (1) War Diary, US Gp CC, PW &DP Div, 29 Sep 45, in OMGUS 314.81. (2) Memo, Hqs, USFET, ACofS G–4, Opns Br, sub: Report on Progress of Polish Repatriation Movement, 1 Nov 45, in USFET SGS 383.7, vol II.

[25] (1) Cable, Hilldring to Smith, 5 Oct 45, and Ltr, Hilldring to Smith, 26 Nov 45, in USFET SGS 334. (2) Ltr, Sec of War to Sec of State, 16 Dec 45, in OPD, ABC 336, (sec VI), (Cases 155–).

[26] ECOM, Office of the Chief Historian, Displaced Persons, p. 58.

much a burden as they had been when their numbers ran into the millions. Virtually everything about them was in dispute, including how many there were. Eisenhower said there were about 15,000 "self-styled Ukrainians," 400 Kalmuks, and 4,000 former members of the German forces, none of whom wanted to be repatriated. Gen. A. N. Davidov, chief of the Soviet repatriation group, said he had uncovered another 22,000 Soviet citizens in the U.S. zone living outside camps.[27] USFET itself did not attempt to track down Soviet citizens in the zone but did check the persons whom the Soviet repatriation group claimed and eventually put the total at just under 38,900.[28]

The end of the mass repatriation brought USFET face to face with the possibility of having to use force to send the remaining Russians home. Considering what probably awaited them on the other side of the demarcation line, a surprisingly large number—even of those who had served in the German forces—went, if not cheerfully, at least without overt resistance. No doubt, the preferential treatment the Soviet government secured for them at U.S. expense influenced some. Probably the extensive authority the Americans allowed the Soviet repatriation officers to exercise also convinced many more that resistance was useless. USFET had not granted police powers to the Soviet officers, however. The DPs who were left after August were mostly those who had already demonstrated that they were not open to persuasion or ordinary intimidation. They believed their fate

in Soviet hands would "be worse than death," and they declared they would resist repatriation "by all means including suicide."[29] The Soviet representatives, Eisenhower informed the JCS, were "most disturbed by the situation and claimed "this headquarters is violating Yalta."[30] At the time, while enlisting Soviet co-operation in the larger affairs of the occupation still seemed possible, resisting the Soviet demands to have all their people back by any means was as difficult as comtemplating the human consequences of forced repatriation. Legally the U.S. command regarded itself as obliged to return the Soviet citizens, and on political grounds it did not see how the eventual use of force could be avoided; but as men and soldiers, Eisenhower and his officers found the business more than they could stomach. Moreover, in the minor disturbances that had already occurred, U.S. troops had sympathized with the demonstrators; and forced repatriation was likely to provoke downright refusals to carry out orders.[31]

On 9 August, slightly anticipating the problem, USFET had issued a policy for forcible repatriation. All persons who were or could be proven, before boards of U.S. officers, to be Soviet citizens were to be transferred to camps under Soviet administration. In the camps, Soviet officials would be responsible for putting the repatriates aboard trucks and trains. Outside the camps, the U.S. forces would guard the transports. The extent to which the troops would be expected to use force was left unclear as was the time at which the policy

[27] Memo, Hqs, USFET, Director OMG, for CofS, sub: Release of Soviet Citizens, 14 Nov 45, in USFET SGS 383.6/11.
[28] Hqs, USFET, Theater Commander's Weekly Staff Conference No. 1, 18 Dec 45, in Hist Div, Hqs, ETO, 97–USF9–0.5.

[29] Cable, Hqs, USFET, Eisenhower, to JCS, 1 Oct 45, in USFET SGS 383.6/11.
[30] Ibid.
[31] Malcolm J. Proudfoot, European Refugees: 1939–1952 (Evanston: Northwestern University Press, 1956), p. 215.

would be put into action. In the first week of September, before any DPs had been shipped under it, USFET suspended the policy and referred the whole question of forced repatriation to the JCS. Seventh Army had asked how much actual force was to be used. The USFET policy had stated only that the U.S. troops would prevent riots and guard the transports and that military government would arrest and transfer to Soviet-administered camps persons whom the Soviet representatives could prove were their citizens. USFET asked the JCS to review the question of forced repatriation "in its entirety . . . since injuries and loss of life on both sides are inevitable."[32]

The War Department had more direct experience with the consequences of forced repatriation than USFET did but was equally uncertain as to what course to take. In late 1944, the Army had discovered some 5,000 Soviet nationals among German prisoners of war in camps in the United States.[33] Moscow had promptly charged that its citizens were being illegally imprisoned and deliberately mistreated in the United States. Many of the prisoners, however, insisted that restoring them to Soviet control was equivalent to a death sentence. Mindful of the probable consequences for the men but convinced that the United States should not give refuge to persons who might be guilty of treason to an ally, the JCS had ruled in December

1944 that all prisoners of war in the United States who claimed Soviet citizenship should be returned on request of the Soviet authorities "whether they want to go or not."[34] For a time those who did not claim Soviet citizenship were not affected, but after Yalta an effort was made to send back all who were known to be Soviet citizens.

By June 1945, all prisoners had been repatriated except 154 men who had delayed their departure by protests and appeals. They were being held at Fort Dix, New Jersey. On 29 June, knowing they would soon be put aboard ship, they barricaded themselves in their barracks. Three committed suicide. The others, being driven out of the barracks with tear gas, attacked the guards with mess kit knives and with clubs; nine prisoners and three U.S. soldiers were injured.[35] The Russians were finally put aboard ship for Germany at the end of August, but by then over a hundred more who had concealed their nationality thus far had been identified in prisoner of war camps in the United States.[36] Concerning what to do about these prisoners and about the USFET request for a ruling on forced repatriation in Germany, the SWNCC, which had to make the decision, was divided. McCloy, the chief War Department member, believed "that something ought to be done to make clear that U.S. troops will no longer be used to repatriate by force all Soviet citizens." Other members, how-

---

[32] (1) Hqs, USFET, ACofS G–5, to CofS, sub: Use of Force in Repatriation of Soviet Citizens, 31 Aug 45, and Cable, USFET to CG, Seventh Army, 6 Sep 45, in USFET SGS 383.6/11. (2) Cable, Hqs, USFET, ACofS G–5, to JCS, 4 Sep 45, in USFET SGS 337/2, vol. II.

[33] Memo, ACofS G–1 for Dep CofS, sub: Repatriation of German Prisoners of War of Soviet Nationality, 21 Dec 44, in Army G–1, 383.6, sec. 6.

[34] Memo, ACofS G–1 for Dep CofS, sub: Repatriation of German Prisoners of War of Soviet Nationality, 27 Dec 44, in Army G–1, 383.6, sec. 6.

[35] Radiogram, War Dept, to CG, U.S. Military Mission Moscow, sub: Fort Dix Incident, 11 Jul 45, in Army AG, 091.713 (1).

[36] Memo, G–1 for Gen Handy, 31 Aug 45, and Memo, Actg PMG for ACofS G–1, sub: Prisoners of War of Russian Origin, 11 Oct 45, in Army G–1, 383.6, sec. 6, pt. 2.

ever, felt that the Yalta Agreement compelled forced repatriation.[37]

Still awaiting a decision on 1 October, Eisenhower reported that "for humanitarian reasons and because of danger to the troops" no Soviet citizens had been repatriated by force. "If the decision is made," he added, "to forcibly transfer, there undoubtedly will be casualties and perhaps loss of life among our troops. We do not favor the use of force but prefer to have these people considered non-repatriable and arrange for their peaceable resettlement in other areas."[38] When Davidov, in mid-October, submitted as a test case a demand that K. G. Konopelko, a displaced person who had signed a deposition stating he did not wish to be repatriated, be returned to the Soviet Union under the terms of Yalta, USFET placed Konopelko "under protective and benevolent arrest" and asked the JCS for a decision on him.[39]

Before the JCS decided the question of the Soviet DPs, another completely unanticipated issue arose. General Wood noticed the first sign of it while he was in Prague in September. The Czechs told him that large numbers of DPs were coming into Czechoslovakia from Poland. The Czechs did not want them and did not feed them but neither did they try to keep them out because if they did the DPs "would be killed at the border."[40] That the DPs

themselves did not want to stay in Czechoslovakia became apparent during the succeeding weeks. By November 300 to 400 DPs a day were coming into the U.S. zone and another 150 to 250 a day were entering the U.S. sector in Berlin. Some were Poles who had been repatriated and were coming back, sometimes bringing friends and relatives with them. The great majority were Polish Jews. On 15 November, Third Army had 16,000 Jews registered in its camps and Jewish centers; by the fourth week of December it had 26,000 registered but did not know how many more had come in and not registered. At the rate of influx in November and December, USFET expected the zone's total Jewish population (of all nationalities), which had been about 35,000, to reach 100,000 before the end of winter.[41]

Suddenly the DP problem, which had seemed to be diminishing, was growing in its most troublesome aspect, the category of nonrepatriables. How many would come was impossible to guess, but USFET expected the U.S. reputation "for humanitarian benevolence" to attract large numbers.[42] What made the proportions of the new DP wave most difficult to gauge was that the people in it were not victims of nazism but refugees from the postwar political systems of eastern Europe. A USFET cable informed the War Department that they were "persons who are or may claim to be persecuted because of race, religion, or politics and those seeking less severe economic conditions as well as those desiring a political-economic climate conducive to private enterprise." Accepting them as DPs

[37] Memo for record, ACofS G–1, sub; SWNCC 46/4/D and Draft Report on Same by SWNCC Subcommittee for Europe, 14 Sep 44, in Army G–1, 383.6, sec. 6.

[38] Cable, Hqs, USFET, Eisenhower, to JCS, 1 Oct 45, in USFET SGS 383.6/11.

[39] (1) Memo, Hqs, USFET, Director OMG, for CofS, sub: Repatriation of Soviet Citizen K. G. Konopelko 18 Oct 45, in USFET SGS 383.6/11. (2) Cable, CG, USFET, to the War Dept, 19 Oct 45, in CCS 383.6 (7–4–44), sec. 6.

[40] Memo, US Gp CC, PW & DP Div, for CG, US Gp CC, sub: Report of Negotiations, 14–15 Sep 45, in OMGUS 314.81.

[41] Memo, CG, Third Army, for CG, USFET, sub: Care and Administration of Jewish DPs, 27 Dec 45, and Memo, OMG (Zone) for SGS, USFET, 5 Dec 45, in USFET SGS 383.7/1.

[42] Cable, USFET to War Dept, 14 Dec 45, in USFET SGS 383.7/1.

on the same terms as the victims of nazism, the cable added, threatened to "raise delicate international questions."[43]

The Jews aroused particular concern, because of their large numbers and because existing U.S. policy granted exceptional treatment to Jews. In the wake of the Harrison report, the War Department had appointed Judge Simon H. Rifkind as USFET adviser on Jewish affairs. On his advice and that of U.S. labor union and Jewish Joint Distributing Committee representatives and in response to newspaper and governmental opinion, USFET was providing the Jews with rations and accommodations that were superior to those accorded the other DPs and had begun a training and rehabilitation program for which it was importing textbooks and instructors by air from Palestine. However, what USFET could do for its original Jewish DP contingent, Smith told Hilldring on 22 November, it did not believe it could do for three or four times as many. He explained:

> Six weeks ago . . . our prospects for coping with the Jewish problem seemed very bright. We knew how many indigenous Jews we had. We had, as Rifkind puts it, completed the rescue phase and were embarking on what he called the "domiciliary stage," during which on his recommendation we planned to inaugurate a rather ambitious program of moral and vocational training to equip these people for life in Palestine or elsewhere. . . . This exceeded our directives but because of pressures at home, we thought it ought to be done.
>
> Under the present conditions we are doing the best we can to provide additional shelter and supplies.
>
> In the meantime, you can expect more trouble from the press, since conditions are forcing us back to the rescue phase.[44]

Judge Rifkind, nonetheless, was quite frank about wanting to create a refuge for all European Jews in Germany "to rescue the remnants of a race." He maintained that "Jews would merely be staged in the U.S. zone for movement to Palestine or elsewhere"; but other Jewish representatives, some of whom talked about establishing a permanent Jewish enclave in Bavaria, predicted that the staging period would last three to five years, and Smith doubted whether many Jews except the young would want to go to Palestine at all.[45]

The simplest solution to the problem of the new DP wave—though possibly not practical—was to enforce Military Government Law No. 161, which prohibited civilians from crossing the borders of the U.S. zone without military government permission. In December, USFET proposed to close the border when those who had infiltrated and the Germans expelled from eastern Europe under the Potsdam Agreement raised the zone's population to 16,650,000—or by about a million. But the idea aroused misgivings in Frankfurt and in Washington, as Hilldring indicated when he wrote to Smith:

> In general the attitude is that you are right in your position that the U.S. Army now has no obligation to furnish safe haven to any person who is not the victim of Nazi persecution. However, there is also agreement with you that the U.S. Army should not refuse to offer safe haven to persecutees simply because their persecution has been at the hands of other than Nazi oppressors.[46]

Smith said his chief desire was to get the Army "out of being a nursemaid on a gi-

---

[43] Ibid.

[44] Ltr, Smith to Hilldring, 22 Nov 45, in USFET SGS 383.7/1.

[45] (1) Ibid. (2) Cable, USFET to War Dept, 14 Dec 45, and Ltr, Truscott to Smith, 24 Nov 45, in USFET SGS 383.7/1.

[46] Cable, Hilldring to Smith, 7 Dec 45, in USFET SGS 383.7/1.

gantic scale"; his hope was that the UNRRA organization could be improved "to where it can assume entire responsibility for the DPs." He added, "I am really very much worried. . . . We are going to need help from the War Department."[47] Hilldring agreed to present the matter to the State Department with a request for "a broader policy" and for a civilian agency to take over the DP problem.[48]

The War Department request went to the State Department on 19 December and the answer came back, with what turned out to be dismaying speed, on the 22d in the form of a presidential directive ordering the State Department to establish consulates at or near DP camps and to begin issuing visas for emigration to the United States. The spirit of the directive was humanitarian; its effect in Headquarters, USFET, was just short of devastating. On Christmas day, General McNarney, recently appointed Commanding General, USFET, cabled:[49]

Expect announcement will abruptly halt present repatriation movements. Present holdings 515,000. Prospects are 350,000 will be repatriated by 1 July 1946. If these learn of prospects for going to U.S., it is strongly believed they will not accept repatriation.

Largely as result of unauthorized entry, population of DPs has been increasing about 10,000 per month. Announcement of emigration will greatly increase this.

Recommend announcement be delayed six months.[50]

The War Department reply read, "Presidential directive has been issued 22 December and press announcement made."[51]

The President said he was acting to relieve human misery and to set an example for the other countries that were able to receive DPs. He was limited, however, by the immigration quotas, which fixed the number of people admitted to the United States in one year at 39,000, at a rate of only 10 percent of the quota per month.[52] Although the immigration program was not effective to make a perceptible dent in USFET's DP population, especially since the quotas for the eastern European countries from which most DPs came barely totaled 13,000, neither did it attract the flood of DPs McNarney had feared. During the succeeding months, as USFET continued its repatriation program, some DPs infiltrated across the borders. Between 1 January and 30 June 1946, the population of camps and centers increased from 308,426 to 368,410, but the total of registered DPs, which included those living outside camps, was down slightly to 483,000 on 30 June.[53] The War Department did

---

[47] Ltr, Smith to Hilldring, 22 Nov 45, in USFET SGS 383.7/1.

[48] Cable, Hilldring to Smith, 7 Dec 45, in USFET SGS 383.7/1.

[49] Eisenhower left the theater on 11 November to become Army Chief of Staff, and McNarney assumed command on 26 November.

[50] President's Directive on Emigration from Europe, 22 Dec 45, and Cable, McNarney to WARCOS, 25 Dec 45, in USFET SGS 040.

[51] Cable, War Dept to USFET, 30 Dec 45, in USFET SGS 040.

[52] The Department of State Bulletin, 23 Dec 45, p. 981.

[53] The DP population in the U.S. zone did not change significantly during the next two years. On 30 June 1948, the population was 501,267. After 1 July 1949, when the Displaced Persons Act of 1948 went into effect with expanded quotas for emigration to the United States (and mass emigration to the new state of Israel became possible), the DP population dropped by almost one half in one year and thereafter declined to 183,000 by 1 May 1950, when USFET's successor, the European Command, transferred the responsibility for DPs to the U.S. High Commissioner for Germany. (1) Hqs, USFET, Theater Commander's Weekly Staff Conference No. 28, 2 Jul 45, in Hist Div, Hqs, ETO, 97–USF9–0.5. (2) EUCOM, Office of the Chief Historian, Displaced Persons, p. 118. (3) Fredriksen, The American Military Occupation of Germany, 1945–1953, p. 79f.

GENERAL MCNARNEY

not return again to its proposal for putting the DPs under a civilian agency.

The decision whether or not to forcibly repatriate Soviet citizens had meanwhile rested with Washington from September to December. In late October, after Eisenhower asked for an answer, the response from Washington read, "In view of the delicacy of the general situation it has not been possible yet to reply to the 4 September cable, although it has been the subject of continued consideration at high level."[54]

On 15 November, on demands from Davidov, USFET prohibited the employment of Soviet citizens in German factories or on farms and ordered that Soviet citizens be denied care after 1 December in any but Soviet-administered DP camps. USFET had previously dismissed Soviet DPs from Army employment.[55]

On 20 December, a directive from the SWNCC established the policy on forced repatriation. It instructed USFET to repa-

[54] Cable, AGWAR, Hull, to Smith, 25 Oct 45, and Cable, Eisenhower to JCS, 19 Oct 45, in USFET SGS 383.6/11.

[55] (1) Memo, Hqs, USFET, Director to OMG, for CofS, sub: Release of Soviet Citizens subject to Repatriation, 14 Nov 45, in USFET SGS 383.6/11. (2) USFET, Summary of Decisions, 15 Nov 45, in USFET SGS 016/1., vol. I

triate "without regard to their personal wishes and by force if necessary" persons who were Soviet citizens on 1 September 1939 and were captured in German uniforms, were members of the Soviet Armed Forces on or after 22 June 1941 and were not discharged, or could be demonstrated "in each case with reasonable particularity" to have "voluntarily rendered aid and comfort to the enemy." In all other cases USFET was to make every effort to assure voluntary return to the Soviet Union but was "not authorized to compel involuntary repatriation."[56]

For most of the Soviet DPs—those who had not been German prisoners of war, served in the German forces, or been collaborators—the SWNCC directive ended the threat of forced repatriation. It probably did the same for those whom the Soviet representatives had charged with collaboration, since the directive specifically excluded employment in German industry or agriculture as evidence of collaboration.[57] On USFET instructions, those charged as collaborators were to be held in U.S. custody and given hearings before boards of U.S. officers. If the Soviet charges were not proven the DPs were to be "returned to the original location of apprehension by American troops and resume their previous status."[58] On 31 December,

USFET suspended its earlier order denying Soviet DPs care in other than Soviet-administered camps.[59]

Finally, most of the Soviet citizens and possibly all, forcibly repatriated from Germany by U.S. troops appear to have been men who had been captured in German uniform. On 19 January 1946, a detail of Third Army troops—men and officers far from pleased with their assignment—undertook to put 399 former Soviet soldiers aboard a train at Dachau. The Russians refused to leave their quarters and, after tear gas was used to force them out, 9 were found to have hanged themselves, 2 had stabbed themselves to death, and 20 others had to be hospitalized for self-inflicted wounds. Of the 368 Russians eventually put aboard the train, 11 were found at the last minute not to be Soviet citizens and six escaped en route. In a dismal final scene in the Soviet zone, Russian soldiers threatened to shoot the American guards if they attempted to leave the train. Hoping to avoid another such series of events, Third Army postponed further shipments while it reworked its procedures and awaited the results of appeals from the Russian Orthodox clergy to the President and the Pope.[60]

Third Army resumed forced repatriation on 24 February when its troops put 1,590 Russians captured in German uniform aboard trains at Prisoner or War Enclosure 431 near Plattling, Bavaria. Five of the Russians committed suicide and others attempted it. After that shipment, 1,630 men whom both the Soviet and U.S. authorities

---

[56] Cable, JCS to USFET, 20 Dec 45, in USFET SGS 383.6/5, vol. I.

[57] The SWNCC apparently did not give a separate decision in the Konopelko case, but the Russian and others like him were covered in the directive which also specified that open resistance to repatriation should not be construed as evidence of a person's having given aid and comfort to the enemy. USFET had previously reported that Konopelko had not been a member of the Soviet or German forces. Cable, Smith to Hull, 26 Oct 45, in USFET SGS 383.6/11.

[58] Ltr, Hqs, USFET, to CG, Third Army, sub: Repatriation of Soviet Citizens, 4 Jan 46, in USFET, Hist Div, U–11068/69.

[59] Hqs, USFET, Summary of Decision, 31 Dec 45, in USFET SGS 016/1, vol. I.

[60] (1) Foreign Relations, 1946, vol. V, p. 141f. (2) Hqs, Third Army, AG, to Distribution, sub: Procedure for Repatriation of Russian Nationals, 22 Jan 46, in USFET, Hist Div, U–11068/69. (3) Opns Rpt, Third Army, CofS Sec, 1 Jan–31 Mar, in EUCOM, P-120, 66–98.

considered potentially eligible for forced repatriation remained in custody in the U.S. zone. In April USFET reviewed the cases and reduced the number of Russians it regarded as eligible to 794. Third Army moved out 222 of these men on 13 May. The rest were subsequently judged ineligible and were released.[61]

The Army in Disarray

Three days before he departed to assume his appointment as Army Chief of Staff, Eisenhower had to tell the troops that the conduct of a "relatively small minority" among them could give the U.S. forces "a bad reputation that will take our country a long time to overcome." He cited reckless driving, pcor uniform discipline, and low standards of military and civilian courtesy as the chief shortcomings.[62] Two weeks later, Seventh Army's CIC reported, "The general opinion of the Germans is that American soldiers are men who drink to excess; have no respect for the uniform they wear; are prone to rowdyism and to beat civilians with no regard for human rights; and benefit themselves through the black market."[63] While Eisenhower was no

doubt right that the troops involved were a minority, reports from Seventh Army CIC and other investigations showed the nature of the misconduct to be more serious than he implied. After V–J Day, what appeared to be almost an epidemic of unprovoked attacks on German civilians and robberies by U.S. soldiers had spread across the zone. The Stuttgart police recorded fourteen acts of unprovoked violence against civilians in the last week of October. During one night in *Landkreis* Eschwege in the Western Military District, five drunken soldiers beat a local German official, and another civilian had his jaw broken when he tried to reason with a soldier molesting a woman. In one small town, Boblingen, within five days in November soldiers beat up two civilians, tried to stab another, broke windows, tried to steal dogs, and robbed four civilians of watches and money.[64] The Office of Military Government for Bavaria described the death of a German boy in a hunting accident involving soldiers as "a result of such carelessness as to be almost criminal." In *Landkreis* Burgen, also in Bavaria, three soldiers hunting illegally shot and killed an 18 year-old girl, and in the same *Kreis* the chief of police told investigators that soldiers had emptied several clips of ammunition at him at various times.[65] Nearly all incidents involved liquor or women, often both. The population of vagrant women—which the Army inadvertently increased after November when it released penicillin for treating venereal diseases in German women, thereby shortening for some the "turn around time" from jail or hospital and attracting others who had been deterred by the fear of infection—was often

[61] CMH, General Reference Br, The Exchange With the Soviet Forces of Liberated Personnel—World War II, undated, in CMH file. In April, USFET had apparently used three criteria, the right to bear arms, the right to vote in free elections, and the right to hold public office, as tests of Soviet citizenship and had declared those men who did not possess one or more of the rights not to have been Soviet citizens. A request for a War Department opinion on the legality of the tests brought a negative reply—but not until 7 June 1946. See *Foreign Relations, 1946*, vol. V, pp. 154–56 and 170.

[62] Ltr, Eisenhower to All Unit Commanders, sub: Conduct, 8 Nov 45, in USFET SGS 250.1.

[63] Hqs, Seventh Army, ACofS G–2, Weekly Intelligence Summary, 21 Nov 45, in Seventh Army, Rpt of Opns, Annex No. 2.

[64] *Ibid.*

[65] Hist Rpt, Eastern Military District, 15 Sep–14 Oct 45, in OMGUS 76–3/10.

at the root of soldier attacks on German officials and police. By December, these attacks had grown so alarmingly frequent that Truscott had to issue what the Office of Military Government for Bavaria called "a public plea" for troop co-operation with the U.S.-appointed German officials.[66] Misbehavior was not confined exclusively to the enlisted ranks. In one instance an American officer took an Austrian girl from Linz to Stuttgart, raped her three times, and then transported her to Ulm, where he turned her over to the military police on a charge of having improper papers.[67]

The troop incidents seemed to be associated, on the one hand, with the urge of some soldiers who knew they were soon going to be redeployed and discharged to have a last fling and, on the other hand, with the inexperience and inadequate training of the lowscore men, who were fast becoming the majority in the occupation force. What went unnoticed, or at least unmentioned, was the coincidence of the rise in troop incidents with the hardening of official attitudes toward the Germans that accompained the Patton affair. One of General Truscott's first acts as Commanding General, Third Army, was to order all his subordinate commanders to schedule frequent instruction periods for their units to counteract the tendency of the soldiers, in his view, to lose sight "of the reasons for which we fought the war" and to become "more and more sympathetic toward the German people."[68] While Truscott was only trying to inculcate in the troops a more

disciplined and aloof attitude toward the German people, some soldiers were bound to feel encouraged to ruffianism particularly when they were drunk. Those who had this tendency also had before them the example of the DPs, for whom public sympathy in the United States secured an almost completely free rein from September to December, which did not begin to tighten again until the early months of 1946 when the Army quietly reinstituted controls and put guards back in the camps.

At the year's end trouble arose from another direction. By the time the big redeployment lifts of November and December had reduced the theater strength to 614,000 troops, another 223,000 (enlisted men with 50 points, officers with 70, enlisted WACS with 32, and WAC officers with 37) had become eligible for redeployment and discharge. What this contingent, and the nearly 100,000 who would become eligible after them, were not told—because the information had been classified secret in Washington—was that the freewheeling redeployment was to end on 1 January 1946. The number of troops scheduled to be shipped home for discharge would drop to 47,700 in January (from 303,000 in December and 400,000 in November) and thereafter level off at about 53,500 a month for the next five months. The rates would be somewhat dependent, too, on the inflow of replacements, and as of mid-December, USFET was over 16,000 short on the replacements it had been scheduled to receive in November.[69]

The troops saw no reason why the

[66] (1) *Ibid.* (2) Hist Rpt, Det G–41, Dec 45, in OMGUS 9–1/5.

[67] Hqs, Seventh Army, ACofS G–2, Weekly Intelligence Summary, 24 Oct 45, in Seventh Army, Rpt of Opns, Annex No. 2.

[68] Hqs, Third Army, sub: Letter Directive No. 1, 11 Oct 45, in Third Army, Chief of Staff Section, 66–98 (20).

[69] (1) Hqs USFET, Theater Commander's Weekly Staff Conference No. 1, 18 Dec 45, and No. 2, 2 Jan 46, in Hist Div, Hqs, ETO, 97–USF9–0.5. (2) Memo, Hqs, USFET, Redep Coord Gp, for Dep CofS, sub: Monthly Rpt of Redep Coord Gp, 1 Dec 45, in USFET SGS 322.

monthly redeployment flow could not continue in the hundreds of thousands, and they were given no reason when *Stars and Stripes* announced at the turn of the year that 50-pointers would have at least another three months to serve in the theater. An announcement at the same time that the Army would begin shipping war brides to the United States in January raised a dark suspicion that the women were being given priority over the troops. In Paris, on 7 January, 1,000 50-pointers staged a protest meeting, and two days later 4,000 marched on the USFET headquarters in Frankfurt to take their grievance to McNarney, whom they did not get to see because he was in Berlin attending a Control Council meeting. On the 12th, soldiers in England carried their complaints to Sen. Tom Connally and Sen. Arthur Vandenberg who were then in London. The protests were orderly, and they ended on the 13th when *Stars and Stripes* reported that McNarney had said they "had served their purpose."[70]

These protests, and others that were somewhat less orderly in Manila and other locations in the Pacific, had indeed served their purpose. On 15 January the War Department announced a new demobilization schedule geared to getting all 45-pointers home and discharged by April 1946. To meet the schedule, USFET doubled its shipping quotas for the first four months

of 1946. In response to an appeal from Eisenhower, who said he had not realized how critical the Army's manpower situation was before he left Europe, McNarney had earlier reduced the Occupation Troop Basis to 300,000.[71] By the first week of February it was clear that the 300,000 figure would only be a point on the scale of USFET's declining troop strength, which would sink to 230,000 by 1 September and 200,000 before the year's end.[72]

The replacements coming to Europe were not only unskilled but, in increasing numbers, untrained. In November and December 1945, 95 percent of USFET's requisitions were for men with technical service specialties. Of those who arrived only 13 percent had such qualifications, and not in any high degree. Beginning in January, replacements were shipped after eight weeks of branch immaterial training, which did not attempt to go beyond qualification with the M1 rifle, personal hygiene and sanitation, and "orientation for occupation duty with emphasis on discipline."[73] In the first week of March, the theater inspector general made inspections in Paris, Metz, and several areas of Germany and reported the following:

Discipline is generally poor and at this time is below desirable standards.

Definite responsibility for maintaining discipline where troops of various arms and services are stationed has not been satisfactorily established.

Incident to the shortage of personnel, the majority of replacements are not receiving

---

[70] (1) Hqs, USFET, Theater Commander's Weekly Staff Conference No. 3, 8 Jan 46, No. 4, 15 Jan 46, and No. 5, 22 Jan 46, in Hist Div. Hqs, ETO, 97–USF9–0.5. (2) EUCOM, Office of the Chief Historian, Redeployment, pp. 160–65. For detailed accounts of the demobilization crisis worldwide see John C. Sparrow, *History of Personnel Demobilization in the United States Army* (Washington, 1952), pp. 160–70 and 241–43, or R. Alton Lee, "The Army 'Mutiny' of 1946," *The Journal of American History*, 53:4, Apr 1966, pp. 555–71.

[71] (1) *Ibid.*, p. 165. (2) Hqs, USFET, Theater Commander's Weekly Staff Conference No. 1, 18 Dec 45, in Hist Div, Hqs, ETO, 97–USF–0.5.
[72] Hqs, USFET, to CG's sub: Revision of Theater Logistics Program, 6 Feb 46, in OMGUS 3/35, dec. 320.2.
[73] Hqs, USFET, Theater Commander's Weekly Staff Conference No. 7, 5 Feb 46, in Hist Div, Hqs, ETO, 97–USF–0.5.

additional disciplinary basic training as expected.

Many young officers command important installations and units. Numbers of these have not had sufficient training to carry out their administrative responsibility. Similarly, there are many untrained noncommissioned officers.[74]

At the same time, military government detachments and the Headquarters, U.S. Constabulary, were reporting U.S. troops as the chief source of disturbances in the zone.[75] In the first week of April, when the theater's weekly intelligence summary showed 101 troop incidents in a four-day period, McNarney ordered that all such cases be reported individually to him with the names of the units involved and the specifics of disciplinary actions taken.[76]

[74] Hqs, USFET, Theater Commander's Weekly Staff Conference No. 12, 12 Mar 46, in Hist Div, Hqs, ETO, 97–USF9–0.5.

[75] (1) Rpt, Det B–272, 28 Jun 46, in OMGUS 81–2/10. (2) Hist Rpt, Det G–230, Mar 46, in OMGUS 80–2/10. (3) Hist Rpt, Hqs, U.S. Constabulary, Apr 46, Hist Div, Hqs, ETO, in 97–USF8–0.3.

[76] Hqs, USFET, Theater Commander's Weekly Staff Conference No. 15, 2 Apr 46, and No. 17, 16 Apr 46, in Hist Div, Hqs, ETO, 97–USF9–0.5.

CHAPTER XXIV

Neither an End Nor a Beginning

OMGUS Takes Control

The dismantling of field military government was accomplished in less than two months. The *Kreis* and *Regierungsbezirk* (regional) detachments relinquished most of their functions to German appointees in November and December 1945, and on 1 January 1946, the Offices of Military Government for Bavaria, Wuerttemberg-Baden, and Greater Hesse became independent commands reporting directly to the Office of Military Government (U.S. Zone) and to OMGUS. By then only four functions remained with the Office of Military Government (U.S. Zone) in Frankfurt: legal, public health and welfare, public safety, and civil administration. When the *Land* offices of military government became independent commands, the army-military district commands lost their authority to supervise military government; and in January, Headquarters, Seventh Army, began transferring its personnel and functions to Third Army, which would take command of the U.S. Constabulary and all tactical troops in the zone.[1] (*Chart 3*)

As an OMGUS historian observed later, the German civil government did not break down as had been widely predicted earlier,

but the burden of occupation on the Army was not much lightened either. The civilianization program, which was to have accompanied the transfer of functions, was barely getting off the ground. The offices of military government had established civilian personnel sections, but the job allotments were enmeshed in civil service procedures. Meanwhile, officers eligible for civilian appointments were choosing redeployment when their numbers came up in preference to the uncertainties of the occupation.[2] The detachments had given up most but not all of their functions, and the three out of the four they retained—denazification, property control, and elections (military government courts were the fourth)—were increasing their work loads as redeployment diminished their strengths. Denazification cases under Law No. 8 were at their peak in December and January; property control alone threatened to engulf the military government organization; and the detachments were having to observe the campaigns and screen the candidates and voters in the forthcoming elections.[3]

Whether the Germans were able or willing to assume responsibility for their own affairs remained the big question. One detachment report described the transfer of functions and the elections scheduled for

[1] (1) Hqs, USFET, sub: Responsibility for Military Government in the U.S. Zone, 14 Dec 45, in USFET SGS 014.1/4. (2) Hist Sec, Seventh Army, sub: Commanding General and Staff, 1 Jan–28 Feb 46, in Historical Program Files, Hist Div, USFET.

[2] Hist Rpt, Eastern Military District, 15 Dec 45–14 Jan 46, in OMGUS 76–3/10.
[3] Hqs, USFET, Theater Commander's Weekly Staff Conference No. 1, 18 Dec 45, in Hist Div, Hqs, ETO, 97–USF9–0.5.

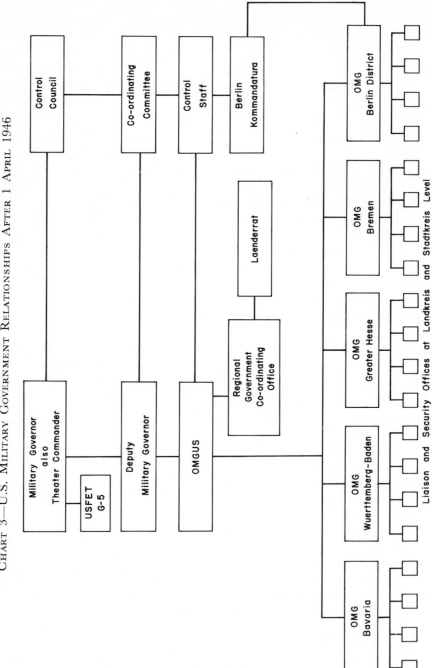

CHART 3—U.S. MILITARY GOVERNMENT RELATIONSHIPS AFTER 1 APRIL 1946

January as constituting for the German people "a bum's rush into what passes for democracy."[4] The Office of Military Government for Wuerttemberg-Baden detected "a glorification of disinterest in politics among large sections of the population."[5] The chief obstacles were what the Germans themselves described as their "burnt finger complex," resulting from their earlier excursions into politics, and the known inability of German parties or officials to influence decisions on the real issues of the time, such as denazification or the economic and political future of the country. In the weeks just before the election, the word "apathy" cropped up in almost every report on the reaction to the campaigns. As the Office of Military Government for Greater Hesse reported:

> The leading posts in the parties are held by former minor political figures who, because of their insignificance, were not accorded by the Nazis the distinction of being exterminated. They have retained the political mannerisms of pre-1933. Negotiations, blocs, and conferences are all being widely indulged in. This continual activity, however, involves only a few with the masses still keeping their distance.[6]

The January elections were for local councils in 10,429 communities with less than 20,000 people. Beforehand, the military government detachments checked the 4,750,000 names on the voting lists for Nazis (and disqualified 326,000) and reviewed the *Fragebogen* of all the candidates for the nearly 70,000 seats on the councils. The Germans went to the polls on the last Sunday in January, and they went in astonishingly large numbers—86 percent of those eligible voted.

In Bavaria, the CSU, with 43 percent of the vote, was the strongest party, and the Social Democrats were a poor second with less than 20 percent. The CDU, with 31 percent of the vote, outstripped the Social Democrats in Wuerttemberg-Baden by a third, while the Social Democrats in Greater Hesse took 40 percent of the vote to the CDU's 30 percent. The Communists and the liberal parties each polled less than 5 percent. Throughout the zone, the CDU–CSU's 37 percent of the vote made them the leading parties. In rural districts they were by far the strongest parties, and their lead would undoubtedly have been greater if all candidates in the small rural communities had announced party affiliations.[7]

The heavy turnout for the January elections was a surprise that OMGUS found "particularly gratifying" because it put local administrations, until then entirely appointed by military government, "on a basis of some popular support and understanding."[8] Whether the vote represented an awakening of interest in democratic self-government, however, was doubtful. The success of the CDU and CSU, in spite of their leniency toward Nazis, seemed vaguely ominous to many military government officers, and the parties' close ties to the Catholic Church suggested that their constituents were voting as they were told from the pulpit and not from inner conviction. The Social Democrats, however, seemed to have attracted a large part of their vote

---

[4] Hist Rpt, Det G–34, Dec 45, in OMGUS 8–2/5.
[5] History of Military Government in *Land* Wuerttemberg-Baden, vol. I, p. 1460.
[6] Hist Rpt, OMG Greater Hesse, Dec 45, in OMGUS 42–3/5.

[7] Military Government of Germany, German Governmental Organization and Civil Administration, Monthly Report No. 7, 20 Feb 46.
[8] JCS 1517/6, Summary of Jan 46 Report of the Military Governor, 16 Apr 46, in CCS 383.21 (2–22–44), sec. 11.

simply as an anti-Catholic protest. Some observers believed the Germans had voted mainly "to convince themselves and their neighbors that the stigma of Nazism had been eradicated not because it was their patriotic duty to elect men who could lead them to democracy."[9] The Office of Military Government for Greater Hesse made the following analysis:

The striking impression that observers received of the elections was the fantastically high percentage of eligible voters participating. Whether it resulted from a lively interest in the issues and in the opportunity to share in the democratic process, whether it was the desire to do what military government expected of them, or whether it was another example of obeying their superiors it is difficult to say. One thing became clear, however . . . the German people had not suddenly shaken off the past and embraced democracy. They had voted, but the political principles were obscure and the faith of the people frail and uncertain.[10]

Similarly, OMGUS itself concluded, "While the voting in the recent elections was gratifying, the fact remains that the average German does not yet recognize the personal responsibilities which go with political freedom."[11] The least optimistic analyses came from Bavaria. From there the regional detachment for Upper Bavaria reported, "In this situation a minority of political opportunists, with little actual popular support, organized a disinterested public into political parties and encouraged them to vote in the first election." Spontaneous political interest, the report con-

cluded, was no more apparent after the election than it had been before.[12]

Alongside politics, denazification held its place as a sore subject. From the beginning Americans had been of two minds: officially they regarded nazism as an unmitigated evil and anyone tainted with it as corrupted beyond redemption; however, more than a few believed that the fine mesh of the Nazi party's net had snared too many Germans for them all to be judged by a single standard. Some actions, such as the use of the 1 May 1937 cutoff date in distinguishing between active and nominal party members, tended to reflect the second point of view. But the dominant trend in the summer and fall of 1945, culminating in Military Government Law No. 8, was toward elevating the idea of permanent taint to the status of doctrine and applying it to broader segments of the population: first to those in public employment, then to businesses with a public aspect, and finally to all private business. For the Germans in all categories who were affected, U.S. policy provided just two possibilities: exclusion from public and private employment above the level of common labor or, if they were important enough to rate automatic arrest, exclusion with a prospect of some punishment yet to be decided.

Denazification had made the Army the warder for dozens of internment camps and made military government the custodian of thousands of Nazi properties, piled up backlogs of *Fragebogen* and appeals cases in detachment offices, and left to military government officers the job of tutoring inexperienced German officials while keeping track of the discharged Nazis. Clay later

---

[9] Hist Rpt, Det D–301, May 46, in OMGUS 79–1/10.

[10] Hist Rpt, OMG Greater Hesse, Jun 46, in OMGUS 42–1/5.

[11] Military Government of Germany, German Governmental Organization and Civil Administration, Monthly Report No. 8, 20 Mar 45.

[12] Monthly Political Activity Rpt, Det 205, 28 Feb 45, in OMGUS 1–2/5.

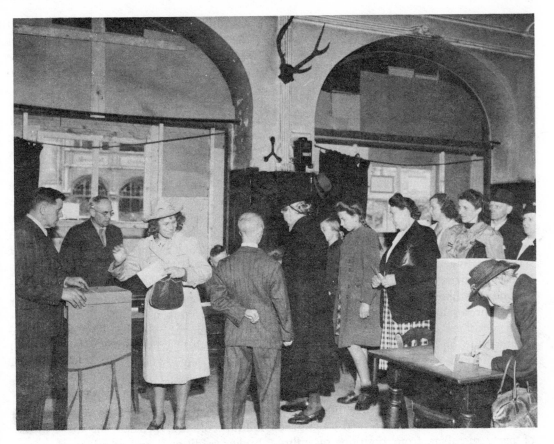

VOTERS CAST THEIR BALLOTS

described the total result as an "administrative problem," which it undeniably was, and more.[13] As has been indicated, trying only the Nazis who might be implicated in criminal organizations could have occupied a battalion of judges for months or even years. As long as Military Government Law No. 8 and the exclusion of Nazis from public and private employment had to be enforced by Americans, military government strength in the field would have to be maintained at levels that even in the fall of 1945 were not feasible; and as the

Schaeffer and Patton incidents had demonstrated, as long as the Americans retained the entire responsibility for denazification, the whole occupation was fused for a political explosion.

In his address to the first meeting of the *Laenderrat* (17 October 1945), Clay hinted that the judging of Nazis would eventually be left to German tribunals. During a session on 4 December, he told the minister presidents that the German people should take denazification into their own hands and directed each of them to have a denazification plan for his *Land*; and after the Minister President of Greater

[13] Clay, *Decision in Germany*, p. 70.

Hesse, Dr. Karl Geiler, recommended that the regulations be uniform in the three *Laender,* the *Laenderrat* appointed a committee to write a statute for the entire zone. Clay's advisers, Lt. Col. Fritz Oppenheimer, Dr. Walter Dorn, and Dr. Karl Loewenstein, assisted the Germans.

From the beginning the German approach differed from the American in two fundamental respects. While the Americans had in the main only distinguished between active and nominal Nazis, the Germans recognized several gradations, particularly within the group the Americans had regarded as active, and eventually settled on five: major offenders, offenders, lesser offenders, followers, and exonerated. Secondly, where the Americans had imposed presumably permanent exclusion from positions of influence in public or business life on all active Nazis, the Germans adopted a scale of sanctions keyed to the offense.[14]

In the Germans' hands the meaning of denazification also changed. Under military government it had meant the removal of party members from positions of influence in the government and private occupations. To the Germans it meant removal of the Nazi stigma from the individual and his reinstatement in society. The early drafts of the German law would have imposed employment restrictions and loss of voting rights on major offenders and lesser restrictions or none at all on followers. The OMGUS advisers, however, although they appear not to have objected to seeing ex-Nazis denazified and restored to social and political equality, insisted that nazism be regarded not merely as a serious lapse in judgment but as a crime and demanded

that the Germans include a schedule of punishments in the law: up to ten years imprisonment for major offenders, five years or less for offenders, fines to 10,000 marks for lesser offenders, and fines to 1,000 marks for followers. The fines, the Americans undoubtedly knew, would be paid in inflated money and hence have small punitive effect, but they would, by forcing a hearing in every case, prevent blanket acquittals.[15] The negotiations on the German law almost broke down in January and February 1946, when the Americans also insisted that it conform with Control Council Directive No. 24 of 12 January 1946. The drafts of the German law had categorized as major offenders only persons who had held relatively significant posts in major Nazi organizations or general officer rank in the military and had been "activists."[16] Control Council Directive No. 24 listed ninety-nine categories of persons who would be classed as major offenders and offenders and recommended very close scrutiny of all career military officers, persons "in the Prussian Junker tradition," and members of university students corps, as well as various others.[17] But the time had not yet come when German officials could stand out against the occupation authority.

On 5 March 1946, in Munich, the minister presidents, without enthusiasm, signed Law No. 104 for Liberation from National

---

[15] Clay later doubted that the attempt to put every party member on trial had been wise. The system became clogged with minor cases, and the serious offenders, who had nothing to gain by seeking a speedy trial, benefited from delays which later ran into months and years. See Constantine FitzGibbon, *Denazification* (New York: W. W. Norton Company, 1969), p. 135.

[16] Fuerstenau, *Entnazifizierung,* pp. 59–61.

[17] Ruhm von Oppen, *Documents on Germany* p. 106.

---

[14] Justus Fuerstenau, *Entnazifizierung* (Berlin: Luchterhand, 1969), pp. 56–58.

Socialism and Militarism. More comprehensive than anything military government had attempted, the law would in some degree affect 13.5 million persons, that is, every resident of the U.S. zone over eighteen years old, all of whom would be required to submit a *Meldebogen,* a shortened form of the military government *Fragebogen.* Those with chargeable associations (eventually 3.6 million) would have to appear before *Spruchkammer,* tribunals of local, non-Nazi citizens somewhat similar to U.S. draft boards. The *Spruchkammer,* after hearing evidence on both sides, would place the defendants in one of the five categories and assess the penalties accordingly. Those who were exonerated or paid fines were considered denazified and recovered their full civil rights.

The Law for Liberation from National Socialism and Militarism, like other earlier important changes in occupation policy, burst as a surprise on both the German population and military government in the field. General Clay has described the decision to turn denazification over to the Germans as "controversial when it was made."[18] He was right. As a first reaction, the regional detachment at Kassel reported, "Greater confusion never existed in the denazification program."[19]

The German man on the street construed the law as a wholesale indictment of the German people and expressed fears that it would provoke unrest, strip the country of its most qualified people, and permanently undermine the economy. The political leaders were caught with a law to which they were committed and, hence, could not ciriticize openly but which they

could not defend either without seeming to subscribe to the collective guilt theory.[20] Some American observers, however, believed the Germans were less apprehensive about the law then they appeared to be. The detachment in *Landkreis* Laufen reported, "The average man is of the opinion that the denazification task was turned over to Germans for the sole purpose of clearing the Nazis. The usual remark when the news of the new German denazification law was released was, 'Thank God. In two or three months I'll have my old job or my business back!' "[21]

Military government opinion on the German law ranged from skeptical approval to outright condemnation. As the Office of Military Government for Wuerttemberg-Baden reported:

The new denazification law, with its provisions for the certification of all German males and females of eighteen years of age and over, and for classification of the population into political categories, bore a revolutionary character. It established a judicial process for the purging of a people and ridding it of the destructive elements which brought disaster upon them in the course of three successive generations. It was obvious that in order to accomplish its purpose, the new law had to become the manifesto of a strong, popular, anti-Nazi movement, much stronger and more popular than had existed heretofore.

But . . . only relatively few groups in the area had evinced the moral courage and historical insight necessary for the carrying of the denazification program to its logical conclusion.[22]

The Office of Military Government for Bavaria dismissed the law as "legislatively

---

[18] Clay, *Decision in Germany,* p. 70.

[19] Hist Rpt, Det E42C, Mar 46, in OMGUS 7–2/5.

[20] History of Military Government *Land* Wuerttemberg-Baden, p. 1445.

[21] Hist Rpt, Det E–281, 30 Jun 46, in OMGUS 77–3/10.

[22] History of Military Government *Land* Wuerttemberg-Baden, p. 1445.

and politically foredoomed to failure." The parties, the Bavarian assessment continued, were aware that the ex-Nazis would comprise a formidable voting bloc and, therefore, would, while giving lip service to denazification, manipulate the law to attract the Nazi votes.[23] The CSU was already refusing to nominate a candidate for the *Land* ministry charged with administering the denazification law and at the same time demanding representation on the appeals boards in full proportion to its electoral strength. The regional detachment for Upper Bavaria added that the law was unenforceable because military government could never do more than spot check the millions of cases and because "incorruptible administrators are impossible to find in Germany today." The regional detachment concluded, "The best thing to do is to wash our hands completely of it and tell the Germans that from now on it is up to them whether they denazify."[24]

While the elections and the Law for Liberation from National Socialism and Militarism touched off squalls of controversy in Germany, one of the chief reasons for their existence—the projected shift to State Department control of the occupation—was having even rougher going in Washington. On 18 December, Secretary of War Patterson talked about the shift with Acting Secretary of State Dean Acheson and Assistant Secretaries of State James Dunn and Donald Russell. Patterson reviewed the War Department's reasons for wanting the transfer, and the State Department representatives proposed that the responsibility remain with the War Department on a

civilianized basis or that it be lodged with the SWNCC or that it be moved to a new agency—"anywhere," Patterson later declared, "but in the State Department."[25] During the next several weeks both Patterson and Eisenhower attempted to convince Secretary of State Byrnes that the State Department should assume control of civil administration in occupied areas. Other solutions, such as setting up a new agency, Patterson argued, would not work because the State Department would still be responsible for policy, and civilian administration under the War Department would not be "forthright civilianization."[26] But on 21 January Eisenhower cabled to McNarney:

My best efforts and those of Sec. War have been devoted to forcing a decision that State Department assume control of administration of military government in Germany on or before 1 June. So far efforts have been completely unavailing. War Department will continue to press . . . however, am without hope that issue will be settled to our satisfaction in the near future.[27]

On 1 April, the Office of Military Government (U.S. Zone) closed in Frankfurt. Headquarters, USFET, was therewith divorced from military government, and control would henceforth be exercised exclusively by OMGUS in Berlin; but the next step, appointment of a civilian high commissioner, was in the distant future. At the end of the month the Secretaries of State, War, and Navy endorsed a memorandum on principles and procedures for administration of occupied areas which reaffirmed

---

[23] Hist Rpt, OMG *Land* Bavaria, 4 May 46, in OMGUS 1–2/5.

[24] Hist Rpt, Det E–205, Apr 46, in OMGUS 1–2/5.

[25] Memo, Secretary of War for Secretary of State, sub: Responsibility for Government of Occupied Enemy Areas, Present Situation, 29 Dec 45, in OPD, ABC 387, sec. 4–F.

[26] *Ibid.*

[27] Cable, ACofS OPD to CG, USFET, 21 Jan 46, in OPD, ABC 387, sec. 4–F.

the division of policy-making and executive responsibilities between the State and War Departments made in August 1945, adding only a somewhat enhanced role for the SWNCC and a Directorate for Occupied Areas to be formed under the SWNCC.[28] In its last paragraph, the memorandum provided for consultation between the War Department and the State Department concerning the appointment of a high commissioner, "In the event that it is decided to reconsider the pattern of American control machinery during the period of War Department responsibility. . . ."

The Road Ahead

Spring came early to Germany in 1946 but brought no renewed hope, either for the people or the nation. On 5 March at Westminster College in Fulton, Missouri, Churchill talked about the iron curtain that had descended across the European continent from the Baltic to the Adriatic. Out of office, he could say what those in office knew but could not yet tell to nations which still expected a better reward for their wartime sacrifices: the world was divided and would likely remain so for years to come. Nowhere was the division clearer than in Germany.

The one substantive step toward putting into effect the Potsdam decision to treat Germany as an economic unit was the level of industry plan. Completed on 26 March 1946, the plan proposed to reduce the German industrial capacity to about 55 percent of the 1938 level and cut the standard of living (in comparison with 1938) by 30 percent.[29] In the U.S. zone, 185 plants had been earmarked for reparations and more were being surveyed, but the real problem, in the view of U.S. authorities, was not to keep Germany down to the contemplated levels but to restore the country's ability to support itself. Since Germany imported food during the best of times, the one way to restore the import flow was to secure sufficient exports to pay for essential imports. In December 1945, OMGUS had submitted a draft agreement, based also on a Potsdam decision, for an export-import program to be operated by the Allied Control Authority for Germany as a whole.[30] After the British had accepted the proposal with some reservations and the French with more, the Russians, in the first week of April 1946, rejected it outright, declaring they would "adhere to the principle of zonal foreign trade and individual responsibilities of the countries for the results of the occupation in their zone."[31] On 3 May, citing the interrelationship of the level of industry plan and the export-import program Clay announced in the Control Council Co-ordinating Committee that, except for two dozen plants already allocated, the United States would halt all dismantling for reparations in its zone "until major overall questions are resolved and we know what area is to compose Germany and

---

[28] The Directorate for Occupied Areas was to have as its director an official of the State Department who had no other duties than policy-making for occupied areas. General Hilldring, who was the director, had been appointed Assistant Secretary of State for Occupied Areas in late February. Maj. Gen. Oliver P. Echols, who had been Assistant Deputy Military Governor in Germany, succeeded Hilldring as Director of the War Department CAD. (1) Department of State, *Foreign Relations of the United States, 1946* (Washington, D.C., 1969), vol. V, pp. 674–77. (2) Department of State, *Bulletin,* 3 Mar 46, p. 369.

[29] JCS 1517/8, Summary of March Report of the Military Governor, U.S. Zone, 5 Jun 46, in OPD, ABC 387, sec. 4–F.

[30] John H. Backer, *Priming the German Economy* (Durham, N.C.: Duke University Press, 1971), p. 108.

[31] *Ibid.,* p. 109.

whether or not that area will be treated as an economic unit."[32] (*Map 3*)

The division was in the open. War rumors, which had never quite died out, again swept across the country. Some Germans seemed to welcome the thought of a war, because they envisioned an East-West clash as a chance for Germany's salvation or, simply, because it would give them an opportunity to say, "I told you so." The more sober minds, however, were painfully aware that Germany could only suffer from any controversy between the Allies, military or otherwise.[33]

In the spring OMGUS launched an export-import program for the U.S. zone and secured orders for $16 million worth of hops, salt, potash, filtration sand, and lumber while simultaneously making commercial import commitments (the first in the zone since the surrender) for vegetable and field seeds. The Economics Division put on a Bavarian export show in Munich in May, and in June sent samples of dolls, toys, chinaware, cameras, and Christmas tree ornaments by air express to the U.S. Commercial Company, a subsidiary of the U.S. Commodity Credit Corporation, for display in New York. In June, also, the Economics Division arranged with the Commodity Credit Corporation to import 50,000 tons of American raw cotton, which was to be paid for by exporting 60 percent of it as finished textiles, leaving 40 percent for the Germany economy. But the program was small and bound to remain so for a long time. The deficit, however, in terms of food

and other items that military government was importing for the benefit of the Germans, was large and growing. Between 1 August 1945 and 30 June 1946, the dollar-based import commitments for Germany amounted to $242,285,000, and the total value of exports actually chargeable against this sum was $7,277,000.[34]

Owing chiefly to increased coal receipts, industrial output in the zone rose measurably during the first quarter of 1946, reaching an estimated 31 percent of the 1936 level. The hold on even this much of a gain was precarious, however, and the obstacles in the path of further progress were formidable. The most important obstacle was the country's lack of a currency. Except for purchases of a small and dwindling selection of rationed items, the Reichsmark had no domestic value and was worthless internationally. With military government sometimes protesting and sometimes promoting, barter had become the norm in business transactions. Nothing moved in trade, not the farmer's potatoes nor the output of factories, except in exchange for some other commodity. The worker found it profitable—and often essential for survival—to spend more time trading on the black market than working on his job, since his salary bought nothing but the daily ration. Clay, in March 1946, appointed Joseph M. Dodge of OMGUS and Gerhard Colm and Raymond Goldsmith, borrowed from Washington, and a staff of economists to devise a currency reform. They had a plan ready in six weeks, but owing to Soviet and French opposition in the Control Council, two years more would pass before Germany had a working currency.[35]

---

[32] (1) *Ibid.,* p. 111. (2) Chronology of OMGUS and Its Predecessor Organizations, 1 Jan–1 Jun 46, in OMGUS 23–3/5, pp. 100 and 119.

[33] Hqs, Seventh Army, ACofS G–2, G–2 Weekly Intelligence Summary No. 36, 22 Mar 46, in Seventh Army, Intelligence Summaries.

---

[34] OMGUS History, pt. I, ch. VIII, pp. 74–77.

[35] Backer, *Priming the German Economy,* p. 91f.

Meanwhile, the zone was supporting a permanent population of half a million DPs, as the Germans being expelled from eastern Europe flooded in. An average of 45,000 of these expelled Germans came each week in May and June totaling 920,000 by the end of June.[36] Only 12 percent could be classified as fully employable; 65 percent needed relief. Contrary to agreements made before the movement to keep families together, the countries expelling Germans were holding back the young, able-bodied men. Of the arrivals, 54 percent were women, 21 percent were children under fourteen years, and only 25 percent men, many of them old or incapacitated.[37]

An additional, significant obstacle to German economic self-sufficiency, in Clay's view, was the occupation force, which had pre-empted a large share of the zone's industrial output—as much as half in the case of building materials such as glass and cement. While the costs were presumably being charged to the Germans, Clay pointed out to McNarney, they were actually being borne by the U.S. taxpayers at the rate of over $200 million a year for relief supplies, and this situation would continue until the German economy could produce enough to pay for imports. In a statement that Colonel Hunt would have thoroughly approved, Clay told McNarney:

Difficulties in discipline, fraternization, disposal of surplus property, guarding of internees, and similar problems, while difficult to solve now, have little if any bearing on history. The bringing of a measure of self-sufficiently to the German people and the institution of self-government under democratic principles, if successful, will stand out in history and perhaps will bring a major contribution to the peace of Europe and the world.[38]

For the average German, however, the most pressing concern in the spring of 1946 was food. The daily ration for the normal consumer in the British zone dropped to 1,042 calories a day in March and in the French zone to 980 calories; the newspapers predicted a cut by as much as 50 percent in the U.S. zone. Grain imports for the zone, which at 100,000 tons a month in the last quarter of 1945 had not been enough to support the 1,550-calorie ration indefinitely, fell below 50,000 tons in February 1946.[39] Germany was feeling the impact not only of its own but of a worldwide food shortage. The war had converted large areas in Asia and the Pacific, which had been self-sufficient and had exported vegetable fats and oils to Europe, into food deficiency areas and had reduced European production by an estimated 25 percent.[40] With almost the whole world waiting in line, the Germans could easily guess that they would not be at the head. On 21 March Brig. Gen. Hugh B. Hester of OMGUS went to Paris to see former President Herbert C. Hoover who was in Europe on the first of his postwar relief missions for President Truman. Hoover said he felt as he had in 1918, that "We will have to feed the Germans"; but he would not go to Germany or make any commitments for it until he had visited the liberated countries. Asked how he would stretch out feeding the Germans, Hoover replied: "General, I would give as much

[36] OMGB, Refugee Section, Annual Report, 9 Jul 46, in OMGUS 65–1/10.

[37] Hist Rpt, OMG Bavaria, 30 Apr 46, in OMGUS 76–3/10.

[38] Memo, Clay for McNarney, 24 Apr 46, in OMGUS 177–2/3.

[39] OMGUS History, pt. I, ch. VIII, p. 68.

[40] OMGUS, Control Office, Hist Br, History of U.S. Military Government in Germany, Econ Div, Food and Agriculture Branch, 1946, in OMGUS 21–3/5.

A 1,275 Calorie Day's Ration, *displayed here as a single meal.*

as I could in April, a little less in May, a little less in June and hope the sunshine and flowers would keep you up through June. And maybe by that time we could do something for you."[41]

Clay had no other choice than to do as Hoover advised. Accordingly, he reduced the ration in the U.S. zone on 1 April to 1,275 calories, which was still about a third more than the indigenous supplies could sustain. In the fourth week of May he had to reduce again to 1,180 calories. To meet

these levels the Army in April and May released from its own stocks over 30,000 tons of cereals, canned goods (corn, peas, and tomatoes), dried skim milk, dehydrated potatoes, and dessert powder.[42] The introduction of corn and corn flour beginning in June into the German diet was taken by many Germans as a form of reprisal, since until then corn had been con-

---

[41] OMGUS, Division Staff Meeting, 23 Mar 46, in OMGUS 178–3/3.

[42] (1) Hqs, USFET, Theater Commander's Weekly Staff Conference Nos. 22 and 23, 21 and 28 May 46, in Hist Div, Hqs, ETO, 97–USF9–0.5. (2) Chronology of OMGUS and Its Predecessor Organizations, 1 Jan–1 Jun 46, in OMGUS 23–3/5, p. 154.

sidered in Germany only suitable as feed for chickens. Many of the released Army supplies were, in fact, low in caloric value. When McNarney talked to Hoover in Frankfurt late in April he pleaded for shipments of wheat, arguing that Germany could not be democratized and would remain politically unstable as long as the people were forced to devote all their thought and effort to the daily search for food.[43] Earlier in the month, after small disturbances had been reported in the British zone, Clay and McNarney had issued a press statement warning that the food crisis might "lead to unrest which may necessitate a larger army of occupation for a longer period of time."[44]

After 83,000 tons of food arrived from the United States in the first three weeks of June and an almost equal amount was en route, Clay raised the ration to 1,330 calories per day on 24 June. Close to half the tonnage, however, was Army surplus food scoured out of depots around the world which, while helping to fill stomachs, could not increase the caloric value of the diet as much as an equal amount of grain would have. The crisis in any case was far from over. In Bavaria the bakers mixed 10 percent raw potatoes into the bread dough, and without continuing imports from the United States, there would be no bread at all in four to six weeks.[45] Short on fertilizer,

machinery, and labor, the zone's agriculture was not likely to produce as good a crop in 1946 as it had a year earlier. To make matters worse, farmers were hoarding thousands of tons of food to sell on the black market, and the unemployed, many of them former white collar workers who feared a loss of social status, were refusing jobs as farm laborers. Meanwhile health checks, such as the one in Mannheim in which 60 percent of the infants showed signs of rickets, revealed increasing evidence of malnutrition among the city populations.[46]

To add to the strains on the unsettled and unhappy country, violence of all kinds, excepting resistance to the occupation authorities, increased in the early half of 1946. Incidents caused by U.S. troops, if no more numerous than they had been in the last months of 1945, were certainly no fewer; they included, as they had earlier, wanton killing, looting, and threats and assaults on German police and civilians. In May, Jewish DPs in big camps at Foehrenwald and Landsberg, Bavaria, rioted against both the Germans and the Americans for no better reason apparently than the unfounded rumors that some Jews had been kidnapped. Attacks by Germans on American soldiers, almost unheard of before, were increasing too, mostly because of fraternization between soldiers and German women. German men resented the women's willingness to consort with U.S. soldiers, the soldiers' affluence, and their own inability to rank even as minor competition for the

---

[43] Hqs, USFET, Weekly Intelligence Summary No. 40, 25 Apr 46, in Hist Div, Hqs, ETO, 97–USF8–0.3.

[44] Hqs, Third Army, Weekly Intelligence Report, 17 Apr 45, in Hist Div, Hqs, ETO, 97–USF8–0.3.

[45] The Army had imported 750,000 tons of food for the U.S. zone and Berlin between V–E Day and 30 June 1946 and released an additional 172,000 tons from Army stocks between 1 February and 30 June 1946. (1) OMGUS, Control Office, Hist Br, History, Food and Agriculture Branch, 8 May 45–30 Jun 46, in OMGUS 440–1/3. (2) Hqs, USFET, Theater Commander's Weekly

Staff Conference No. 28, 2 Jul 46, in Hist Div, Hqs, ETO, 97–USF9–0.5. (3) Hist Rpt, OMG Bavaria, Jun 46, in OMGUS 436–2/3, p. 285.

[46] (1) Wk Rpt, OMG Wuerttemberg-Baden, 12 May 46, in Hist Div, USFET, T–353–1/6. (2) Hqs, Third Army, Weekly Intelligence Report, 17 Apr 46, in Hist Div, Hqs, ETO), 97–USF8–0.3.

Americans. The Negro troops, who were making up an increasing proportion of the occupation force, were particularly resented by German men; and the Negroes, believing they were not getting an equal share of the women, nursed grudges against both the Germans and the white Americans.[47]

Evidence that the *Edelweisspiraten* and other underground clubs were growing and that the zone harbored what was becoming a permanent subculture of vagrant young people revived concern for the German youths. In April, the Munich police picked up over 900 vagrants less than twenty-one years old, nearly a quarter of them girls. The Bavarian Red Cross had 11,000 vagrants listed. It maintained *Wanderhoefe* (homes) for them, but few, especially those in the seventeen to twenty-one age group, stayed more than a few weeks. The director of one *Wanderhof* described the boys as "completely cold and blase, entirely calculating in what they do. They have lost every feeling of relationship with their homeland and home with parents and relatives, even with their mothers. Memories mean nothing to them. Their only interests are food, sleep, money, and girls."[48] One example, certainly not typical but not unique either, was a 12 year-old boy whose father, an SS officer at Mauthausen concentration camp, had committed suicide. The father, according to rumor, had used concentration camp prisoners for rifle practice. The mother was interned at Dachau as a potential war crimes defendant. Placed in a children's

home after having spent most of his life in far from edifying adult company, he adapted quickly and proved to be more clever than the average child; but his counselor observed, "He plays with others and laughs and romps with them but has no close ties with any of the children or the teachers."[49] The young people who had homes and families but lived in bombed-out cities and went to overcrowded, barely functioning schools were not much better off. Boys roved the streets, and girls in their early teens looked for soldier-boyfriends or experimented with amateur prostitution.[50]

In April, McNarney ordered all military government, divisional, and higher headquarters to assign mature officers to check into the youth problem "with a view toward correcting these conditions and increasing proper youth activities that will keep these young people out of trouble. . . . If we fail in this," he added, "we are simply making future trouble for ourselves."[51] During the next month, the *Land* offices of military government organized youth committees and sent youth activity liaison officers to the tactical units. In Bavaria, for a start, Lt. Col. Kenneth E. Van Buskirk, special youth adviser to the Office of Military Government for Bavaria, secured from captured *Wehrmacht* stores 4,000 pairs of skis, 3,000 jackets, 6,000 pairs of ski pants, 70,000 caps, and 40,000 knapsacks. By mid-June, when the youth advisers held a four-day meeting in Munich, *Kreis* youth committees had been organized in every *Kreis* in Wuerttemberg-Baden and Greater Hesse and in more than half of the Ba-

---

[47] (1) Hist Rpt, Hqs, U.S. Constabulary, Apr 46, in Hist Div, Hqs, ETO, 97–USF8–0.3. (2) Cable, CG, USFET, to War Dept, for AG, 1 May 46, in PMGO, classified decimal file, MG Div, Cables. (3) Hist Rpt, Det E–291, 30 Jun 46, in OMGUS 78–3/10.

[48] Hist Rpt, OMG Bavaria, 1–31 May 46, in OMGUS 76–3/10.

[49] *Ibid.*

[50] *Ibid.*

[51] Hqs, USFET, Theater Commander's Weekly Staff Conference No. 15, 2 Apr 46, in Hist Div, Hqs, ETO, 97–USF9–0.5.

varian *Kreise*. By then military government had approved 2,500 youth groups with a total membership over 300,000; and the tactical units were supplying athletic equipment and instructors to teach American games and were releasing or sharing requisitioned gymnasiums, swimming pools, and sports fields.[52]

On 5 May every German in the U.S. zone over eighteen registered under the Law for Liberation from National Socialism and Militarism and filled out the required *Meldebogen*. Hearings were scheduled to begin ten days later, but in most places during the two months the law had been in effect, the military government detachments had not been able to find enough men to staff the tribunals and act as prosecutors. The law required tribunal members to be local residents, known opponents of nazism and militarism, personally beyond reproach, and fair and just. Detachment E–291 in *Landkreis* Wolfratshausen, Bavaria, reported that finding competent prosecutors and judges was impossible; no one, whether anti-Nazi or not, wanted to judge their own friends and the people they had lived with all their lives.[53] People in *Landkreis* Dillingen, Bavaria, were convinced that men who accepted appointments as prosecutors or chairmen of tribunals would have trouble for the rest of their lives, and the local detachment recommended bringing in strangers who "could leave town after it was over."[54] Captain Boring, in *Landkreis* Laufen, drew up a list of twenty-one passive anti-

Nazis. There were not twenty-one active anti-Nazis in the *Kreis*, he said. The prosecutor for Laufen declared outright that he expected to be a ruined man.[55] Detachment G–297 in *Landkreis* Neuburg, Bavaria, said of its candidates: "They made a very poor impression. Some appeared to be semi-literate, others borderline mental cases. The ten most acceptable were selected and approved."[56]

A tribunal at Fuerstenfeldbruck, Bavaria, held the first trial in the U.S. zone on 20 May 1946. Three defendants pleaded guilty to having beaten an anti-Nazi in 1933 and were sentenced to three years at hard labor, confiscation of property, and prohibition from working at anything but ordinary labor for ten years.[57] In the first case tried in Wuerttemberg-Baden, at Heidenheim on 12 June, a former labor front official was found to be an offender and sentenced to imprisonment and loss of property.[58] These two decisions were not enough, however, to lay to rest the doubts about the outcome of denazification in German hands. Detachment E–291 reported on tribunals it had observed, "Verbal evidence by the defense, and usually by Nazis testifying on behalf of another Nazi, is given more weight than documents submitted by the prosecution."[59] The Office of Military Government for Bavaria assessed the German responses as follows:

Those who had clear consciences were hoping the law would wipe out the compara-

---

[52] Hqs, USFET, Theater Commander's Weekly Staff Conferences Nos. 27 and 28, 26 Jun and 2 Jul 46, in Hist Div, Hqs, ETO, 97–USF9–0.5.

[53] Hist Rpt, Det E–291, 30 Jun 45, in OMGUS 78–3/10.

[54] Hist Rpt, OMG Bavaria, 31 Mar 46, in OMGUS 78–3/10.

[55] Hist Rpt, Det E–281, 30 Jun 46, in OMGUS 77–3/10.

[56] Hist Rpt, Det G–297, May 46, in OMGUS 65–2/10.

[57] Hist Rpt, OMG Bavaria, 31 May 46, in OMGUS 76–3/10.

[58] History of Military Government in *Land* Wuerttemberg-Baden, p. 1436.

[59] Hist Rpt, Det E–291, 30 Jun 46, in OMGUS 78–3/10.

tive wealth of the Nazis; those whose consciences were not so clear were sending their wives to bribe the wives of the members of the *Spruchkammer,* or trying to transfer property to persons politically clear, or preparing to move to some other zone where the laws were not so harsh, or just waiting for their fate. While the Nazis were scurrying to avoid trial, members of the *Spruchkammer* seemed just as eager to avoid prosecuting. They either disliked the "toughness" of the law or feared reprisals later. The *Land* political parties were paying lip service. Especially stubborn was the CSU which stood to lose the most by adopting a strong policy.[60]

But, once more, for denazification the time for discussion was past. On 14 June, OMGUS rescinded all existing military government denazification directives; the responsibility passed to the Germans.[61]

On 28 April and 26 May the Germans in the U.S. zone went to the polls to elect *Landkreis* and *Stadtkreis* councils. American reactions ranged from satisfaction in OMGUS with the still high turnouts—72 percent in the *Landkreise* and 83 percent in the *Stadtkreise*—and with the signs that the electorate were not reverting to their pre-Hitler habit of backing splinter parties (only the CDU and CSU and the Social Democrats drew significant percentages), to skepticism of German democracy at the lower military government levels and some apprehension over the heavy vote for the CDU and CSU.[62] Whatever the elections

meant for the future of democracy in Germany, they spelled the end for local military government. The *Landkreis* detachments became liaison and security offices on 1 May, and the *Stadtkreis* detachments were redesignated on 3 June.

Within military government, the withdrawal of the detachments was accompanied by an eleventh-hour drive to civilianize before the end of June. The 194 liaison and security offices, each composed of two officers and two enlisted men, were not affected since they were to remain military personnel for the psychological effect of the uniform. These offices had personnel problems of their own, however: more than a few were in the condition of D–357 in *Landkreis* Neumarkt, Bavaria, which consisted of two officers, neither trained in military government and both several months overdue for redeployment, and two 19-year-old privates, both also untrained.[63] Clay reported at the end of June that the ratio in OMGUS was two civilians to one officer, and he expected to reach similar ratios in the *Land* offices in sixty days.[64] But as of 30 June, the personnel situations in Bavaria and Greater Hesse were probably not much different from that in Wuerttemberg-Baden where only 90 out of a total of 560 workers were civilians.[65] The military government officer was going to be in evidence for a while yet; and in April, the School for Military Government, which

---

[60] Hist Rpt, OMG Bavaria, 31 May 46, in OMGUS 76–3/10.

[61] JCS 1517/11, Summary of June Report of the Military Governor, U.S. Zone, 3 Sep 46, in OPD, ABC 387, sec. 4–H.

[62] In the zonewide tallies, the CDU and CSU received 56 percent of the vote in the *Landkreise* and 37.8 percent in the *Stadtkreise* to the Social Democrats' 29.2 percent and 36.9 percent. In Bavaria, the largest of the *Laender,* the CSU scored 69.4 percent in the *Landkreise* and 43.7 percent in the *Stadtkreise,* and the Social Demo-

crats 22.9 percent and 37.0 percent. Military Government of Germany, German Governmental Organization and Civil Administration, Monthly Report No. 10, 20 May 46.

[63] Monthly Rpt, Det D–357, 1 Jun 46, in OMGUS 79–2/10.

[64] Memo, Clay for Bull, sub: Proposed Reduction of Officer Strength in OMGUS, 28 Jun 46, in OMGUS 177–2/3.

[65] History of Military in *Land* Wuerttemberg-Baden, p. 93.

had graduated its last class at Charlottesville in February and had not trained any officers for Europe since 1944, reopened at Carlisle Barracks, Pennsylvania, to give four-week courses to the estimated 3,000 replacement officers that military government in Germany would need in 1946.[66]

Fully divorced, finally, military government and the tactical commands in the spring of 1946 were again experiencing friction with each other or, at least, what McNarney described as "a definite loss in friendly co-operation." In the field, the friction stemmed, as it had in the past, from the disparity in ranks and in higher echelons, in part, from civilianization. Owing to redeployment, the military government officers in the field were, if anything, even more junior to their counterparts in the tactical commands than they had been in 1945. At the higher levels, Clay complained, "Many times U.S. civilians and military do not look at each other . . ."[67] On the one hand, the tactical commands from USFET on down did not relish being in a support role where they had once been in command. Recognizing this feeling, Clay told the OMGUS divisions they should not "send cables to USFET telling them what to do . . . [but] call for help instead."[68] On the other hand, it did not seem in OMGUS that the tactical commands had correctly assessed their part in the occupation. On this score, Clay wrote to McNarney:

My philosophy . . . envisions the Army of Occupation as having a dual responsibility in Germany. First, to provide such force as necessary to ensure carrying out the objects of the occupation, that is, support of military government. Second, since military government itself is a responsibility of the Army, it is most important that the Army handle this civil responsibility of its own accord with somewhat the same relation between tactical troops and military government as exists at home and in our prewar overseas stations. A civilian high commissioner should not show later a more zealous interest in safeguarding the German economy in the interests of the U.S. budget and in the interest of our object to bring democracy to Germany than does the Army now. If this is a sound philosophy, then your position as theater commander is separate and distinct from your position as Military Governor, and the proper balanced relationships between your staffs are essential.[69]

The balance that needed to be found was between a victorious army living in a conquered nation and an army becoming increasingly concerned for the welfare of its former enemy. In OMGUS opinion the area in which the most serious imbalance existed in the spring of 1946 was that of housing requisitions. The *Land* offices of military government all complained that there was an inverse ratio between the redeployment of troops and the number of rooms occupied by the troops. The Office of Military Government for Wuerttemberg-Baden, for instance, found that while troops had occupied 29,394 rooms in the *Land* in November 1945, the number rose to 42,002 in December and 43,361 in January.[70] However, when Clay expressed surprise that after a reduction from over three

[66] (1) Memo, PMG for CofS, sub: Trained Military Government Replacement Officers, 18 Feb 46, in PMG, MG Div, classified decimal file 352.01. (2) Memo, PMG, Dir, MG Div, for Control Off, sub: Weekly Summary of Important Occurrences, 4 Apr 46, in PMG, MG Div, classified decimal file 319.1.

[67] OMGUS, Division Staff Meeting, 20 Apr 46, in OMGUS 178–3/3.

[68] *Ibid.*

[69] Memo, Clay for McNarney, 29 Apr 46, in OMGUS 177–2/3.

[70] History of Military Government in *Land* Wuerttemberg-Baden, ch. x, sec. v.

million troops to less than half a million, the Army was still requisitioning houses, General Barker, USFET G–1, explained that the troops were now living in smaller groups.[71] The *Land* offices of military government, on checking, also learned that large parts of the increases were belated formal requisitions of houses occupied months before, but they still complained that too many requisitioned buildings were being left vacant or underoccupied. In April, USFET authorized military government to "act as a buffer between the communities and the tactical commanders" and empowered it specifically to prevent houses from being taken from U.S. appointees (which had been a recurring embarrassment to military government) or from Germans who had put much personal effort into repairing their homes.[72]

For the tactical commands the problems in the spring of 1946 and after, as the renewed tension with military government evidenced, were to overcome the shock of redeployment and settle into the status of a permanent occupation force. When Headquarters, Third Army, moved from Munich to Heidelberg on 1 April and became the ground forces command for the U.S. zone, the troop shipments out of the theater still by far exceeded arrivals, and the reinforcements coming in were overwhelmingly recent draftees with only accelerated basic training. Surveys in reinforcement depots in May showed 85 percent of enlisted assignments and 64 percent of officer assignments to the Ordnance and Quartermaster Corps had been made without regard to capabilities.[73] The U.S. Con-

stabulary, projected as an elite force, was having to accept the average spread of reinforcements and had authority only to reject illiterates, men who did not speak English, and outright undesirables.[74] While military government reported improvement in troop conduct and discipline in May, the rate of incidents was still high in proportion to troop strength; and the currency control program was fast becoming a disaster. The modest favorable balances produced by the currency control books in December and January evaporated in February when the troops sent home $10 million more than they received in pay. Thereafter the movement was all downhill as $14 million more went out than came into the theater in March, $17 million each month in April and May, and $18 million in June. The British, in March, went to military scrip, which was not convertible into marks, and the War Department and USFET were considering doing the same in the U.S. zone but were concerned about the effects on commands stationed in other areas and troublesome reactions from the Soviet Union.[75] The clearest symbol of the change from wartime to occupation status was the opening on 1 March in Giessen of the first military community to house military dependents and U.S. civilians, as the directive read, "in a manner comparable to that on U.S. posts in 1937."[76] USFET expected eventually to have 90,000 dependents ac-

[71] OMGUS, Division Staff Meeting, 27 Apr 46, in OMGUS 178–3/3.

[72] OMGUS, Division Staff Meetings, 27 Apr 46, in OMGUS 178–3/3.

[73] Hqs, USFET, Theater Commander's Weekly Staff Conference No. 20, 7 May 46, in Hist Div, Hqs ETO, 97–USF9–0.5.

[74] Snyder, *Constabulary*, p. 64.

[75] Military Payment Certificates, a form of scrip, were introduced in the U.S. zone on 12 September 1946, and the dollar overdrafts ended immediately. EUCOM, Currency Control, pp. 45–66. See also Rundell, *Black Market Money*, pp. 80–91.

[76] Hqs, USFET, Continental Base Section, to Military Community Commanders, 1 Mar 46, in Hist Div, Hqs, ETO, 97–USF8–0.1.

commodated in ninety-seven communities, providing PX's, commissaries, barbershops, beauty parlors, dispensaries, and houses and apartments requisitioned from the Germans. The first special dependents' train arrived from Bremerhaven on 10 May.[77] Between 1 June and 1 July, Third Army entered the final phase of the ground forces reorganization and conversion to the policetype occupation. The U.S. Constabulary became operational in an on-the-job training status because three-fourths of the enlisted men were recent arrivals and the three-division tactical force moved into permanent stations and began training as a tactical and limited strategic reserve.[78]

Army-administered military government would continue in Germany for another three years, the occupation for nine years, and the U.S. military presence for a generation or more; nevertheless, the month of June 1946 marked the crossing of a major divide. Behind lay two world wars and a trail of by then meaningless ambitions and anxieties. The future was far from certain, but one thing was apparent: it would not be anything like what had been expected a year ago or less. The world had changed, Germany had changed, and the rationale of the occupation had changed. The troops who had imposed the Allied will on the conquered country had gone home, as had all but a few of the military government officers and men who had accompanied

them. The Morgenthau Plan was an embarrassing memory. JCS 1067 continued as the statement of U.S. policy, as much as for any other reason, because no one wanted to tackle the job of organizing the jigsaw pieces of subsequent policy and practice into a new directive.[79] The United States was committed to reconstruction, currency reform, and economic reunification in Germany; and to accomplish these goals, Clay would offer, on 20 July 1946 in the Control Council, to enter into agreements with any or all of the other occupying powers. Secretary of State Byrnes would make the same offer publicly in Stuttgart in September. U.S. policy had come full circle. FM 27–5, in its first version, had advocated making friends out of former enemies. JCS 1067 had wanted brought home to the Germans that "Germany's ruthless warfare and fanatical Nazi resistance have destroyed the German economy and made chaos and suffering inevitable."[80] Byrnes, speaking to Germans in Stuttgart, said, "The American people want to help the German people win their way back to an honorable place among the free and peace-loving peoples of the world."[81]

---

[77] (1) Memo, Hqs, USFET, AG, for Distribution, sub: Occupation Planning, 5 Dec 45, in USFET SGS, 322. (2) Annual Rpt, Hqs, Giessen Military Post, Dec 46, in Hist Div, Hqs, ETO, 97–USF8–0.1.

[78] (1) Hqs, Third Army, Operations Plan for Reorganization of U.S. Zone Ground Forces, 15 May 46, Third Army, 66–104. (2) Synder, *Constabulary*, p. 112.

[79] Clay told the War Department that he would rather see JCS 1067 amended than completely rewritten since a complete rewriting would necessitate too many changes in other instructions issued in the theater. He had found JCS 1067 as modified by Potsdam a "workable policy," he said. Cable, OMGUS to War Dept, sub: Modification of JCS 1067, 10 Dec 45, in CCS 383.21 (2–22–44), sec. 10. See also Gimbel, *The American Occupation of Germany*, p. 22.

[80] JCS 1067/6, Directive to the Commander in Chief U.S. Forces of Occupation Regarding the Military Government of Germany, 26 Apr 45, in CCS 383.21 (2–22–44), sec. 7.

[81] Senate Committee on Foreign Relations, *Documents on Germany*, p. 42.

CHAPTER XXV

Conclusion

The categorical imperative for military forces probably should be to conduct each operation so well that it could stand unquestioned as a model for the future. As a practical matter, however, this ideal is seldom achieved, but lessons can be drawn from failures as well as successes. In the study of combat operations this is axiomatic. The course and outcome of a battle are determined by the interaction of judgments made independently on both sides. Occupying and administering enemy territory, on the other hand, has tended consistently to be looked upon as involving primarily unilateral judgments, which therefore should be uniformly correct, given the requisite degree of technical competence. No doubt, President Roosevelt's early determination to turn the work of administering occupied areas over to civilians was strongly motivated by the belief that civilians had more practice in the skills of government and that a successful occupation chiefly required a transfer of these skills. In fact, the assumption could be made that administering occupied enemy territory is less difficult than conducting domestic government. The population does not need to be consulted; the administrator has an army at its back; and the purpose for his being there is simple and direct. The SHAEF Standard Policy and Procedure in 1944 described the Supreme Commander's objective in enemy territory as being "the

military occupation and control of all zones of enemy territory for which he may be responsible."[1] The first objective of military government given in the SHAEF presurrender directive of 9 November 1944 was "Imposition of the will of the Allies upon occupied Germany."[2] The November 1966 *Joint Manual for Civil Affairs* (FM 41–5) describes military government as "the assumption by the military commander of full executive, legislative, and judicial authority over a conquered or otherwise unruly population."[3] FM 41–10 (1966) like its predecessors, defines military government as "The form of administration by which an occupying power exercises executive, legislative, and judicial power over occupied territory."[4] The authority of the occupying power then is apparently complete, requiring mainly the organizations and procedures to exercise it. This study of the Army experience in Germany, how-

---

[1] SHAEF, Standard Policy and Procedure for Combined Civil Affairs Operations in North West Europe, 1 May 44, in Admin Hist Collection, ETOUSA, Nr. 146, G–5 CA.

[2] SHAEF, Office of the CofS, to Hqs, AGps 21, 12, 6, sub: Directive for Military Government of Germany Prior to Defeat or Surrender, 9 Nov 44, in AFHQ G–5, Directives, Military Government of Germany.

[3] Dept of the Army, the Navy, and the Air Force, FM 41–5, *etc., Joint Manual for Civil Affairs,* Nov 66, p. 26.

[4] Hqs, Dept of the Army, FM 41–10, Civil Affairs Operation, Oct 66, p. 2.

ever, has shown that an occupation has residual characteristics of the combat operation and that the occupation is as much the final stage of the war as it is the assumption of the victor's rights and powers.

First and probably most important, an occupation has an objective. In the abstract it may be only to assume executive, legislative, and judicial authority in a defeated nation; but as any actual war is likely to be fought for some more significant purpose than merely to win, so an occupation is likely to be entered into for some reason other than merely to govern. Establishing a valid objective, as the U.S. experience in Germany demonstrated, may not be easy. The combat commander deals with an existing situation, the occupation planner with one that does not yet exist. The combat commander is concerned with an immediate military problem, the occupation planner, working in the political and psychological milieu of the war, with political, economic, social, and military problems of the future. For the U.S. forces in Germany after World War II the principal objective as stated in JCS 1067 was "to prevent Germany from ever again becoming a threat to the peace of the world."[5] This objective, like the President's desire to have the inevitability of "chaos and suffering" brought home to the Germans and introduced into JCS 1067 after the 23 March 1945 conference (see above, p. 213), was set at the height of the war, with an eye more to the past than to the future. JCS 1067 became a directive admirably suited to preventing a repetition of the 1920s and 1930s but inadequate to meet the situation of the late 1940s. This inadequacy,

and not any supposed echo of the Morgenthau Plan, was the document's great defect. The Germans did not have to be shown the consequences of defeat, and after 1945, Germany was not likely again to rank as a major threat to world peace. Consequently, the U.S. authorities in Germany, left without a valid principal objective, were compelled to exploit loopholes, such as the disease and unrest formula, and to improvise.

A pointless or mistaken objective may be less readily recognized in an occupation than in a combat operation. Battle frequently has a way of bringing deficiencies into sharp focus. An occupation is less likely to be subjected to a clear-cut, decisive test. Moreover, a war of sufficient magnitude to result in the large-scale conquest of enemy territory will also probably not be concluded without rancor; and a professionally dispassionate military approach will be hard put to prevail against an aroused public opinion, or even a single fixed opinion, such as that of President Roosevelt in the case of Germany.

In a combat operation, the ability to attain the objective is a major criterion. Despite apparent unrestricted power, the same appears to be true of the objectives in an occupation. In Germany, denazification was probably the chief, and certainly the most energetically pursued, tactical objective of the early occupation period. It was also, as Donnison has concluded regarding the British zone, probably the least satisfactory of all military government undertakings.[6] Before the end of 1945, denazification on the terms originally envisioned had been proven impractical; and in the long run, if less had been attempted,

---

[5] JCS 1067/8, Directive to Commander in Chief of U.S. Forces of Occupation regarding the Military Government of Germany, 26 Apr 45, in OPD, ABC 387, Germany, sec. 4–D.

---

[6] Donnison, *Civil Affairs and Military Government in Northwest Europe*, p. 461.

more might have been accomplished. Of 3,623,112 persons considered chargeable under the Law for Liberation from National Socialism and Militarism, 887,252 were tried before the German *Spruchkammern* by 30 June 1948 with the following results:

tribunals put 2.5 percent of their cases in the first two categories (major offenders), the British zone tribunals 1.3 percent, and the French zone tribunals 0.1 percent.[10] The course of denazification demonstrates how sensitive the objectives of an occupation can be to U.S. public opinion on the

	Charged as	Found as	Maximum Sentence Permitted	Sanctions Imposed
Major Offenders	20,306	1,284	5–10 years	404
Offenders	318,189	18,979	Up to 5 years	7,981
Lesser Offenders	180,263	97,260	1,000 Reichsmark or more fine	75,390
Followers	365,160	445,163	Less than 1,000 Reichsmark fine	463,645
Exonerated	3,334	16,148		
Proceedings Dismissed		298,418		
Total	887,252	887,252		547,420[7]

The *Spruchkammern,* during two years of trials, found 117,523 persons to have been Nazi offenders in some degree—5 out of 6 in the lowest offender category—and imposed sentences or fines of more than 1,000 Reichsmarks on 83,775.[8] Military government, on the other hand, under its standards, had, by 31 May 1946, found 314,000 persons to have been sufficiently active as Nazis to warrant their removal from public employment and important positions in private enterprise.[9] The *Spruchkammern* in the U.S. zone were at least as zealous as their counterparts in the other two western zones. The U.S. zone

one hand, and how vulnerable they can be to resistance by the subjects of the occupation on the other, if they go beyond the limits of the attainable.

Denazification and the reverse of the coin, democratization, also provide the basis for some observations on the role of an occupation force as an instrument of social and political change. Denazification gave the Army the mission of carrying out as radical an experiment in removing a source of international conflict as had been undertaken in modern times. Worthy as denazification was in principle, it was not, as military government was painfully aware, realistically conceived. Conducted as a full-scale social revolution, it imposed dangerous strains on the structure of the occupation without necessarily promising any future returns other than more trouble.

[7] Hqs, Dept of the Army, CAD, Reports and Analysis Br, Civil Affairs and Military Government, Background Summary, 1948, in CMH file H 13–2.3.

[8] By 1949, the *Spruchkammern* in the U.S. zone had heard a total of 950,126 cases. Fuerstenau, *Entnazifizierung,* p. 228.

[9] OMGUS, Econ Div, *A Year of Potsdam,* in CMH file WAR–10, GER–POT.

[10] Fuerstenau, *Entnazifizierung,* pp. 228–30.

The democratization program, however, affords an example of a different sort. By not attempting as much, it accomplished more. Its great virtue was that its form when General Clay put it into effect in the fall of 1945 served practical and useful purposes for both the U.S. authorities and the German people. The preponderant military government opinion at the time would have favored an extended period of tutelage. If this view had prevailed, the outcome might have been the same as with denazification: a train of increasingly expensive and frustrating programs ending in mutual disappointment. Clay made democracy as attainable an objective for the U.S. forces as it was ever likely to be by placing the responsibility for its attainment where it would ultimately have to lie in any case, with the German people.

The military administration of occupied territory, like a combat operation, also requires unity of command. The necessity for clear lines of authority and a single commander on the battlefield is obvious. In an occupation, however, the need is apparently not so obvious. From the outset in the planning for Germany, the War Department had to defend this principle against a strong presidential opinion that civilians were the proper administrators for occupied territory. The issue was in fact never entirely settled, and the principle was in jeopardy throughout the war. Consequently, even though there was no dual command, some of the baneful effects of such a command were felt in the planning for and early occupation of Germany. Certainly, the Supreme Commander's freedom of decision was considerably less in matters pertaining to the occupation than it was in affairs clearly recognized as military. No policy as hopeless as nonfraternization would have been sustained for the better

part of the year nor would any staff entanglements as unseemly and unproductive as those between the SHAEF–USFET G–5 and the U.S. Group Control Council have been allowed to persist if they had affected combat operations.

Aside from the dispute over civilian as opposed to military control, the occupation of Germany exposed a built-in military government proclivity for muddled command channels. World War II produced two distinct and, unfortunately, not entirely compatible modes of military government: the one territorial (AMGOT) with its own chain of command, the other integrated into the tactical commands (Standard Policy and Procedure). The experience in Germany demonstrated that both arrangements were necessary in successive stages of the occupation, and both have continued to have a place in U.S. civil affairs doctrine, as "area support" and "command support" operations.[11] Most likely, both would be used again in future military government situations, and, very likely, the same problems would arise out of their employment. Territorial military government can be readily adapted to political and geographic units of any size from a town or county to a whole country, but it functions best in a separate military government chain of command and does not adjust well to tactical unit boundaries. Integrated military government is best suited to mobile operations, and it preserves unity of command and the integrity of tactical boundaries. Its span of control, however, is limited to the lower governmental levels, and, as the ECAD experiment revealed, it tends to set the military government personnel adrift from their own parent organizations without making them truly

---

[11] FM 41–10, *Civil Affairs Operation*, p. 2–2.

integral parts of the tactical commands. An additional and potentially more serious problem is the apparently natural inclination of military government to want to convert to the territorial form at the earliest possible time and the equally natural tendency of the tactical commands to be slow in relinquishing the prerogatives they have acquired during the period of integrated military government.

Lastly, as Colonel Hunt recommended after World War I, civil affairs–military government is a specialized military function and needs trained personnel. The War Department recognized the need early in World War II and provided the training. In doing so, however, it exposed some concomitant problems which it was not able entirely to solve. Chiefly, these problems were how to sustain the morale of relatively senior specialists during the long period of waiting before they could be employed; how to organize for service in the field a civilian-oriented activity operating within the military framework; and how to sustain an activity that could only be brought into full play after the war had ended and the rest of the Army was going home. Although the same problems could arise again, they were undoubtedly aggravated by the special conditions of World War II. Civil affairs–military government was new. It existed, but it had no established position in the Army. It had to find itself in situations in which neither the commands nor the personnel had adequate precedents from which to make judgments. As a result, ECAD, for instance, was not a table of organization division, and its members, already disgruntled at having been recruited for work they sometimes doubted would ever exist, suspected they were also being deliberately denied promotions and being treated as second class soldiers. Further-

more, having gone through several years of uncertainty, the civil affairs–military government personnel were all too easily caught up in the demobilization fever after V–J Day. Previous errors, however, do not have to be repeated. The World War II experience exists as guidance for the future. In particular, civil affairs–military government did find a place in the Army and did, although the path was not smooth, achieve organizational and doctrinal maturity. However, civil affairs–military government will probably always tend to be somewhat out of phase with the rest of the military structure. The answer appears to be a trained reserve.

Of course, an occupation also differs from a combat operation in various respects and in one in particular: the outcome of a battle will usually—that of an occupation, perhaps, seldom—be clear. In a strict sense, maintenance of law and order sufficient to prevent interference with combat missions during hostilities and unrest or to prevent resistance later on are enough to qualify an occupation as a success, but the judgment of history will demand more. And the Army in Germany accomplished more—more than even the detachment commander believed who summed up the first year, "We gave them enough military government to last a hundred years."[12] Not every Nazi received the full deserts due him in American and some German opinion, but many did. Not all the Germans were converted to democracy, but they were given the opportunity for democracy without any snares or tricks. The tenor of some policy statements was harsh to the point of being vindictive, but the practice was as humane as a defeated enemy had a right

---

[12] Hist Rpt, Det D–309, 24 Jun 46, in OMGUS 80–2/10.

to expect after a long and destructive war. Although many soldiers looted and played the black market, the Army protected and restored the country's art treasures and monuments and imported three-quarters of a billion dollars worth of relief supplies. The DPs were returned to their homes, the concentration camp inmates were cared for, and the numerous services without which a modern society cannot function were put back into operation and kept running. Certainly after 1946 there could be no doubt that civil affairs–military government had proven its value both in and out of combat or that the Army had demonstrated its competence to manage a major occupation in the national interest and the interest of a conquered people.

Note on Sources

The word which best describes the source materials available on the post-World War II occupation of Germany is *awesome*. The combat operations of the war left well-structured, if often extensive, records and after the victory became the subject of interest primarily of two relatively small fraternities, the memoir writers and military historians. The occupation, on the other hand, involved the White House, the War Department, State Department, and Treasury Department, the EAC, the JCS and CCS, SHAEF, USFET, OMGUS, the tactical commands, military government in the field, and a bewildering array of commissions, committees, divisions, and branches. The records are massive. The published *Monthly Reports of the Military Governor, U.S. Zone,* for instance, by themselves make a set the size of a major encyclopedia. Considering the scope of the subject, however, the amount of systematic history written about it is rather surprisingly small. The reason may be that it is considered not sufficiently military to fit into the military history genre and too military to be treated as general history. The dearth in that one respect, however, has been more than made up for by the flood of memoirs, semi-memoirs, commentaries, criticisms, polemics, prognostications, and reportage in book form, in periodicals, both popular and scholarly, and in newspapers. The experience in Germany encompassed many fields of popular and academic interest, and the occupation engaged as participants more professionals in more various disciplines and more persons who felt intense political, social, or moral commitment than, probably, any other undertaking of the war period. To the publications in English, some of which antedate the surrender, must be added the German literature on the occupation which has been growing apace since the mid-1950s.

Consequently, the following note does not in any way aim to be either complete or comprehensive. It lists the official records that the author consulted and the published works he used. Some other works deemed useful for a study of the period have been included.

Primary Sources

Unpublished Documents

The one general comment that can be made about the groups of records pertaining to the occupation is that they defy categorization. Individually and collectively they are an archival smorgasbord. Where information on a specific subject or time period is likely to be found is all but impossible to predict. Within record groups, the decimal system frequently provides only the roughest guidance to the contents of files. Taken as a whole, the records reflect nothing so well as the haphazard evolution of the occupation itself.

Among the Washington-based military agencies and offices the ones principally concerned with the occupation were the Joint Chiefs of Staff (JCS), Combined Chiefs of Staff (CCS), Assistant Secretary of War (ASW), Operations Division of the War Department General Staff (OPD), War Department Civil Affairs Division (CAD), and Provost Marshal General (PMG). The PMG records are the best source for early military government planning, organization, and training. The others cover the later planning and operations in Germany, but the picture they present is not complete without reference to the State Department and European Advisory Commission (EAC) documents and, for crucial months in 1944 and 1945, the *Morgenthau Diary* (see published sources listed below).

The Supreme Headquarters, Allied Expeditionary Force (SHAEF), records are the chief source for in-theater planning, organization, training, and operations to July 1945. The SHAEF G–5 index alone lists 296 decimal numbers relating in some way to the occupation of Germany. Each decimal number represents one or more folders containing as many as several hundred pages of documents apiece. The G–5 Information Branch historical files embrace the whole history of military government and the occupation before and during the SHAEF period. They include information on the agencies in Washington and London; histories and monographs written by G–5 historians; G–5 records of the Army groups, armies, and the European Civil Affairs Division (ECAD); and the army group and army monthly historical reports. The SHAEF G–1, G–2, G–3, and Secretary of the General Staff (SGS) files all contain substantial numbers of folders pertaining to the occupation. The G–1 and SGS files, for instance, are the prime sources for information on nonfraternization.

The European Theater, U.S. Army (ETOUSA), records, while not nearly as voluminous as those of SHAEF, have some valuable items on military government in the Historical Division files and in the Administrative History Collection and on U.S.-conducted war crimes investigations and trials in the Theater Judge Advocate files. The most pertinent Sixth and Twelfth Army Group documents appear to have been incorporated into the SHAEF records. The First, Third, Seventh, Ninth, and Fifteenth Army G–5 files contain reports on military government operations in the field not to be found elsewhere, as do also the V, XII, XIII, XV, and XXIII Corps G–5 files. The XV Corps records also include a headquarters diary for the period 8 October to 10 December 1945 that appears to be a mislabeled Third Army diary. The USFET General Board in its investigation of the conduct of the war made several studies having to do with military government and the occupation in general.

For the period after July 1945, the main collections are those of the U.S. Forces in the European Theater (USFET) and the Office of Military Government (U.S.) (OMGUS). The USFET SGS file is possibly the best single source for the period before mid-1946. In addition to important post-July 1945 records, it contains significant 1944 and 1945 documents taken over from the SHAEF files. The OMGUS collection, which reportedly filled over 1,400 footlockers when it was shipped to the United States, is overwhelming in bulk and difficult to research. It has no indexes, and the shipping lists often convey only the vaguest impressions of the actual contents of the folders. Furthermore, in spite of its bulk it is limited as a source on policy- and decision-making. Nevertheless, it contains an enormous quantity of information, principally in the form of OMGUS divisional histories and monthly and annual detachment reports.

Published Documents

Long-standing gaps in the documentation of U.S. planning and policy development for the occupation were filled in the late 1960s when the State Department published the 1944–1946 volumes of the *Foreign Relations of the United States* series and the U.S. Senate Committee on the Judiciary, Subcommittee to Investigate the Administration of the Internal Security Act and Other Internal Security Laws, put into print the *Morgenthau Diary (Germany)* (Washington: Government Printing Office, 1967). The *Morgenthau Diary* is not a diary in the conventional sense but a massive collection of minutes, transcripts, notes, and documents. The specific volumes in the *Foreign Relations* series referred to above are *1944, Volume I, General* (Washington: Government Printing Office, 1966); *1945, Volume III, European Advisory Commission; Austria; Germany* (Washington: Government Printing Office, 1968); *1945, Volume V, Europe* (Washington: Government Printing Office, 1967); and *1946, Volume V, The British Commonwealth; Western and Central Europe* (Washington: Government Printing Office, 1969). Also essential to the history of the planning for the postwar treatment of Germany are the *Foreign Relations* series volumes *Conferences at Washington, 1941–1942 and Casablanca, 1943* (Washington: Government Printing Office, 1968); *Conferences at Washington and Quebec, 1943* (Washington: Government Printing Office, 1970); *Conferences at Cairo and Tehran, 1943* (Washington: Government Printing Office, 1961); *Conferences at Malta and Yalta, 1945* (Washington: Government Printing Office, 1955); *The Conference at Quebec, 1944* (Washington: Government Printing Office, 1972); and *The Conference of Berlin* (Washington: Government Printing Office, 1960).

The following are additional volumes of documents pertinent to the occupation:

Pollock, James K., *et al.*, eds. *Germany Under Occupation*. Ann Arbor: G. Wahr Publishing Co., 1949.

Ruhm von Oppen, Beate. *Documents on Germany Under Occupation, 1945–1954.* New York: Oxford University Press, 1955.

Secretary of State for Foreign Affairs. *Selected Documents on Germany and the Question of Berlin, 1944–1961.* London: H. M. Stationery Office, 1961.

Taylor, Telford. *Final Report to the Secretary of the Army on the Nurenberg War Crimes Trials Under Control Council Law No. 10.* Washington: Government Printing Office, 1949.

U.S. Senate, Committee on Foreign Relations. *Documents on Germany 1944–1959.* Washington: Government Printing Office, 1959.

U.S. Senate, Committee on Foreign Relations. *Documents on Germany, 1944–1970.* Washington Printing Office, 1971.

Von der Gablentz, O. M., ed. *Documents on the Status of Berlin, 1944–1959.* Munich: R. Oldenbourg Verlag, 1959.

Von der Gablentz, O. M., ed. *Dokumente zur Berlin–Frage, 1944–1966.* (Munich: R. Oldenbourg Verlag, 1967..

Secondary Sources

U.S. Official Histories

A number of volumes in the U.S. ARMY IN WORLD WAR II series bear directly on the occupation or on matters related to it. Harry L. Coles and Albert K. Weinberg, *Civil Affairs: Soldiers Become Governors* (Washington: Government Printing Office, 1964), a compilation of documents, is at once a major source on early military government organization and a history of civil affairs–military government operations in Europe outside of Germany. Charles B. MacDonald, *The Last Offensive* (Washington: Government Printing Office, 1973), covers the military operations in Germany in 1945. Other volumes in the series that bear on the occupation are the following:

Cline, Ray S. *Washington Command Post: The Operations Division*. Washington: Government Printing Office, 1951.

Coakley, Robert W. and Richard M. Leighton. *Global Logistics and Strategy, 1943–1945*. Washington: Government Printing Office, 1968.

Cole, Hugh M. *The Ardennes: The Battle of the Bulge*. Washington: Government Printing Office, 1965.

MacDonald, Charles B. *The Siegfried Line Campaign*. Washington: Government Printing Office, 1963.

Matloff, Maurice. *Strategic Planning for Coalition Warfare, 1943–1944*. Washington: Government Printing Office, 1959.

Pogue, Forrest C. *The Supreme Command*. Washington: Government Printing Office, 1954.

The organization and activities of the occupation forces are described in Oliver J. Frederiksen, *The American Military Occupation of Germany, 1945–1953* (Karlsruhe: Historical Division, Hqs., USAREUR, 1953). The planning for the postwar treatment of Germany is compactly presented in Harley A. Notter, *Postwar Foreign Policy Preparation* (Washington: Government Printing Office, 1949). While not an official publication, William M. Franklin, "Zonal Boundaries and Access to Berlin," *World Politics*, 16:1, October 1963, written by the Director of the State Department Historical Office, is an excellent summary of the State Department view of the subject.

Manuscripts

Manuscript histories are scattered throughout the records, particularly those of SHAEF, ETOUSA, and OMGUS. The *Land* detachment histories of the first year of the occupation, in the OMGUS files, are complete, detailed works. The others, valuable as they often are, are for the most part fragments. A notable exception is James L. Snyder, "The Establishment of the U.S. Constabulary," in the Historical Division, ETOUSA records (apparently misfiled), which is, very likely, as authoritative an account of the subject as can ever be written.

Among the manuscripts held by the Center of Military History are thirty-eight monographs in the USFET–EUCOM (European Command) Occupation in Europe series. Written in Germany in the 1940s by Army historians, they range in subject matter from the planning for the occupation to PX operations. The Occupation Forces in Europe series also includes a set of multivolume annual histories. A most useful work is "The History of the Civil Affairs Division, War Department Special Staff, World War II to March 1946," written in the late 1940s from the division's files by CAD historians. Book I and Book VI, Edwin J Hayward, "Overall Civil Affairs History," and Richard M. Welling "Germany," are essential to the study of the occupation. Additional pertinent manuscripts in the CMH files are Edgar L. Erickson, "An Introduction to Military Government and Civil Affairs in World War II," and R. A. Winnacker, "The Office of the Secretary of War Under Henry L. Stimson."

British Official Histories

S. F. V. Donnison, *Civil Affairs and Military Government Central Organization and Planning* (London: H. M. Stationery Office, 1966) and *Civil Affairs and Military Government North-West Europe, 1944–1946* (London: H. M. Stationery Office, 1961), in the United Kingdom History of the Second World War military series, deal from the British point of view with the same time period and many of the same events that the author has covered in the present volume. The *Grand Strategy* volumes in the United Kingdom series and C. R. S. Harris, *Allied Military Administration of Italy, 1943–1945* (London: H. M. Stationery Office, 1957), provide valuable collateral information.

Memoirs and Other Works

The World War II memoirs of nearly every high-level U.S. or British military and political figure address themselves at some point to the question of postwar Germany. Those that touch most closely on the subject matter and time span of this volume are Henry L. Stimson and Mc-George Bundy, *On Active Service in Peace and War* (New York: Harper and Brothers, 1948); William, Lord Strang, *Home and Abroad* (London: Andre Deutsch, 1956); Cordell Hull, *The Memoirs of Cordell Hull*, 2 vols. (New York: The Macmillan Company, 1948); Sir Frederick E. Morgan, *Overture to OVERLORD* (London: Hodder, 1950); and Harry S. Truman, *Memoirs, Year of Decisions* (Garden City: Doubleday and Company, Inc., 1955). Lucius D. Clay, *Decision in Germany* (Garden City: Doubleday and Company, Inc., 1950) and Robert D. Murphy,

Diplomat Among Warriors (Garden City: Doubleday and Company, Inc., 1964) are especially notable because of General Clay's and Ambassador Murphy's positions in the occupation.

Among the works concerned specifically with the occupation it is frequently difficult to distinguish between types. Frank L. Howley, *Berlin Command* (New York: G. P. Putnam's Sons, 1950) and Saul Padover, *Experiment in Germany* (New York: Duell, Sloan and Pearce, 1946) are clearly memoirs. John J. Maginnis, *Military Government Journal, Normandy to Berlin* (Amherst: University of Massachusetts Press, 1971) is an abridgment of a diary General Maginnis kept as a lieutenant colonel in World War II military government. On the other hand, B. U. Ratchford and W. D. Ross, *Berlin Reparations Assignment* (Chapel Hill: University of North Carolina Press, 1947) and John H. Backer, *Priming the German Economy* (Durham: Duke University Press, 1971) are books in which the author's personal experience is reinforced by research. Harold Zink, *American Military Government in Germany* (New York: The Macmillan Company, 1947) is a history drawn from and colored by the personal experience of a professional historian who was a SHAEF G–5 and OMGUS historian.

Philip E. Moseley's articles, "Dismemberment of Germany, The Allied Negotiations from Yalta to Potsdam," *Foreign Affairs*, 28:3, April 1950, and "The Occupation of Germany, New Light on How the Zones were Drawn," *Foreign Affairs*, 28:4, July 1950, present the judgments of an eminent historian drawn from his experience as Chief of the State Department Division of Territorial Studies and as Ambassador Winant's political adviser in the EAC. Walter L. Dorn relied both on his skill as a professional historian and on extensive personal knowledge acquired through service in the upper levels of military government in writing "The Debate Over American Occupation Policy in Germany in 1944–1945," *Political Science Quarterly,* 72:4, December 1972.

Two recently published histories of the occupation are John Gimbel, *The American Occupation of Germany* (Stanford: Stanford University Press, 1968) and Franklin M. Davis, *Come as Conqueror: The United States Army's Occupation of Germany, 1945–1949* (New York: The Macmillan Company, 1967). Gimbel's thoroughly researched study is concerned primarily with policy and policy development. In an earlier book, *A German Community under American Occupation, Marburg, 1945–1952* (Stanford: Stanford University Press, 1961), he described the effects of the occupation at the local level. *Come as Conqueror,* its author a former Army officer, is a popular account combining research and reminiscence. Some earlier works are Carl J. Friedrich, ed., *American Experiences in Military Government in World War II* (New York: Rinehart and Company, Inc., 1948), which gives the views of scholars who were also closely involved with the problems of military government and occupation; Eugene Davidson, *The Death and Life of Germany* (New York: Alfred A. Knopf, 1959); Hajo Holborn, *American Military Government* (Washington: Infantry Journal Press, 1947), which is a study by a distinguished historian who had first-hand experience with nazism and with the occupation; Edward H. Litchfield, ed., *Governing Postwar Germany* (Ithaca: Cornell University Press, 1953); Arthur Settel, ed., *This is Germany* (New York: William Sloane Associates, Inc., 1950); and John

L. Snell, *Wartime Origins of the East-West Dilemma Over Germany* (New Orleans: Hauser Press, 1959). Walter Rundell, Jr., *Black Market Money* (Baton Rouge: Louisiana State University Press, 1964) and Constantine Fitz-Gibbon, *Denazification* (New York: W. W. Norton Company, 1969) treat in detail two aspects of the occupation that are also principal concerns of this volume. Henry Morgenthau, Jr., *Germany is Our Problem* (New York: Harper & Brothers, 1945) and John Morton Blum, *From the Morgenthau Diaries: Years of War* (Boston: Houghton Mifflin Company, 1967) shed light on the pre-surrender planning for the occupation.

Among the many Germans who have published memoirs dealing in some way with the occupation, the most prominent is Konrad Adenauer, whose *Erinnerungen,* 4 vols. (Stuttgart: Deutsche Verlags-Anstalt, 1965–1968), span the postwar period to 1963. Aside from the memoirs, the publications in German fall into three categories: histories, polemics, and—surprisingly—nostalgia. The histories, except for general works covering the whole postwar period, such as, Gerhart Binder, *Deutschland Seit 1945* (Stuttgart: Seewald Verlag, 1969), for the most part are intensively researched monographs. Examples are Karl-Ernst Bungenstab, *Umerziehung zur Demokratie? Re-education-Politik im Bildungswesen der U.S.-Zone, 1945–1949* (Duesseldorf: Bertelsmann Universitaetsverlag, 1970) and Justus Fuerstenau, *Entnazifizierung* (Neuwied: Luchterhand Verlag, 1969). Some of the works in the first category are also at least partial candidates for inclusion in the second. Otherwise, the second category is small, but it does include probably the most widely read book on the occupation published in Germany, Caspar Schrenck-Notzing, *Charak-*

terwaesche (Stuttgart: Seewald Verlag, 1965). Schrenck-Notzing freely interpreted a wide variety of secondary sources to attempt to demonstrate that the Roosevelt New Deal, having abandoned its liberal principles before the war began and turned to raw power politics, used psychoanalytic methods to "character wash" the Germans. The literature of nostalgia, by describing "how bad it was" seems to attempt to provide the Germans with a vicarious escape from the sameness of prosperity. Examples of the form are Ingeborg Drewitz, ed., *Staedte 1945* (Duesseldorf: Eugen Dietrichs Verlag, 1970); Madlen Lorei and Richard Kirn, *Frankfurt und die drei wilden Jahre* (Frankfurt a. M.: Verlag Frankfurter Buecher, 1968); and Bernd Ruland, *Geld Wie Heu und nichts zu fressen* (Bayreuth: Hestia-Verlag, 1968).

Glossary

ACLS	American Council of Learned Societies
ACofS	Assistant Chief of Staff
AMGOT	Allied Military Government (used only in Italy)
ASHCAN	Detention center for important German war crimes suspects
AT (E) Committee	Administration of Territories Committee (Europe)
Buergermeister	Mayor
CA	Civil affairs
CAD	Civil Affairs Division
CAO	Civil Affairs Officer
CATP	Civil Affairs Training Program
CCAC	Combined Civil Affairs Committee
CCAC (L)	Combined Civil Affairs Committee (London)
CCMS	Control Commission (Military Section)
CCS	Combined Chiefs of Staff
CDPX	Combined Displaced Persons Executive
CDU	Christian Democratic Union
CIC	Counterintelligence Corps
CMH	Center of Military History
COSSAC	Chief of Staff to the Supreme Allied Commander (designate)
CROWCASS	Central Registry of War Criminals and Security Suspects
CSU	Christian Social Union
DANA	*Deutsche Allgemeine Nachrichten Agentur* (German General News Agency)
DCCAO	Deputy Chief Civil Affairs Officer
DISCC	District Information Services Control Command
DP	Displaced person
DPX	Displaced Persons Executive
DUSTBIN	Detention and interrogation center for German scientific and technical personnel
EAC	European Advisory Commission
ECAD	European Civil Affairs Division
ECAR	European Civil Affairs Regiment
ECLIPSE	November 1944 posthostilities plan for Germany
Edelweisspiraten	German adolescent gangs of the Nazi and occupation periods
ETO	European Theater of Operations
ETOUSA	European Theater of Operations, U.S. Army
FEA	Foreign Economics Administration
FIAT	Field Information Agency Technical
Fragebogen	Questionnaire used by military government to determine Nazi and militarist associations of Germans

G–1	Personnel section of a divisional or high staff
G–2	Intelligence section
G–3	Operations section
G–4	Supply section
G–5	Civil affairs–military government section
Gauleiter	Regional leader of the Nazi party
Gemeinde	Municipality
Gestapo	*Geheimestaatspolizei* (secret political police)
GOLDCUP	SHAEF plan for assuming control of German governmental agencies
HUSKY	Allied Invasion of Sicily, July 1943
ICD	Information Control Division, USFET
IPCOG	Informal Policy Committee on Germany
JAG	Judge Advocate General
JCS	Joint Chiefs of Staff
Land	German state
Laenderrat	Council of Minister Presidents
Landkreis	Rural administrative area similar to U.S. county
Landrat	Chief administrative officer of a *Landkreis*
Meldebogen	Questionnaire used under the Law for Liberation from Nazism and Militarism to determine Nazi and militarist associations of Germans
MFA&A	Monuments, Fine Arts, and Archives
MG	Military government
MGO	Military Government Officer
MMLA	*Mission Militaire de Liaison Administrative* (French organization concerned mainly with DP care)
Oberbuergermeister	Chief mayor
OCTAGON	U.S.-British conference at Quebec, September 1944
OMG	Office of Military Government
OMGUS	Office of Military Government (U.S.)
Ortsgruppenleiter	Local Nazi party group leader
OSS	Office of Strategic Services
OVERCAST	Program to move German scientific and technical specialists to the United States
OVERLORD	Invasion of northwest Europe, June 1944
OWI	Office of War Information
PAPERCLIP	See OVERCAST
PMG	Provost Marshal General
RAMP	Recovered Allied military personnel (used to designate freed Allied prisoners of war)
RANKIN	Plans for return to the Continent in the event of a German withdrawal or collapse
RANKIN C	Plan for return to the Continent in the event of a German collapse
Regierungsbezirk	District

Reichsbahn	The German railroads
ROUNDHAMMER	Variant of ROUNDUP
ROUNDUP	Plan for a cross-Channel operation in 1943
SA	*Sturmabteilung* (paramilitary organization of the Nazi party)
SCAEF	Supreme Commander, Allied Expeditionary Force
SHAEF	Supreme Headquarters, Allied Expeditionary Force
SLOE	Special list of equipment
Spruchkammer	German denazification tribunals established under the Law for Liberation from Nazism and Militarism
SS	*Schutzstaffel* (the elite military and police organization of the Nazi party)
Stadtkreis	The area within the city limits of a city or town
SWNCC	State-War-Navy Co-ordinating Committee
TALISMAN	August 1944 posthostilities plan for Germany
TALLYHO	USFET check and search operation, July 1945
T/O	Table of organization
TORCH	Allied invasion of North Africa, November 1942
TRIDENT	U.S.-British conference in Washington, May 1943
UNRRA	United Nations Relief and Rehabilitation Administration
USFET	U.S. Forces in the European Theater
USO	United Services Organizations
Volkssturm	German militia composed of men too young, too old, or physically unfit for regular military service
WAC	Women's Army Corps
Wac	A member of the Women's Army Corps
Wehrmacht	German Armed Forces
Werwolf	Nazi-sponsored German guerrilla and resistance movement
WSC	Working Security Committee

Index

U.S. GOVERNMENT PRINTING OFFICE: 1975 O—560-002

DATE DUE